CONCLUDING UNSCIENTIFIC POSTSCRIPT TO *PHILOSOPHICAL FRAGMENTS*

VOLUME I

KIERKEGAARD'S WRITINGS, XII.1

CONCLUDING UNSCIENTIFIC POSTSCRIPT TO *PHILOSOPHICAL FRAGMENTS*

by Søren Kierkegaard

VOLUME I: TEXT

Edited and Translated
with Introduction and Notes by

Howard V. Hong and
Edna H. Hong

PRINCETON UNIVERSITY PRESS
PRINCETON, NEW JERSEY

Published by Princeton University Press,
41 William Street, Princeton, New Jersey 08540
In the United Kingdom: Princeton University Press, Chichester, West Sussex

Library of Congress Cataloging-in-Publication Data

Kierkegaard, Søren, 1813-1855.
[Afsluttende uvidenskabelig efterskrift. English]
Concluding unscientific postscript to Philosophical fragments / by Søren Kierkegaard; edited and translated with introduction and notes by Howard V. Hong and Edna H. Hong.
p. cm.—(Kierkegaard's writings ; 12)
Translation of: Afsluttende uvidenskabelig efterskrift.
Includes index.

ISBN 0-691-07395-3 (v. 1 : alk. paper)—ISBN 0-691-02081-7 (pbk : v. 1)—
ISBN 0-691-07395-3 (v. 2 ; alk paper)—ISBN 0-691-02081-7 (pbk. :v. 2)
1. Christianity—Philosophy. 2. Apologetics—19th century.
I. Hong, Howard Vincent, 1912- . II. Hong, Edna Hatlestad, 1913- . III. Title.
IV. Series: Kierkegaard, Søren, 1813-1855. Works.
English. 1978 ; 12.
B4373.A472E5 1992
201—dc20 91-4093

Preparation of this volume has been made possible in part by a grant from the Division of Research Programs of the National Endowment for the Humanities, an independent federal agency

Princeton University Press books are printed on acid-free paper and meet the guidelines for permanence and durability of the Committee on Production Guidelines for Book Longevity of the Council on Library Resources

Designed by Frank Mahood

Printed in the United States of America

10

ISBN-13: 978-0-691-02081-5 (pbk.)

CONTENTS

CONCLUDING UNSCIENTIFIC POSTSCRIPT TO *PHILOSOPHICAL FRAGMENTS*

A MIMICAL-PATHETICAL-DIALECTICAL COMPILATION
AN EXISTENTIAL CONTRIBUTION

by

JOHANNES CLIMACUS

Edited by

S. Kierkegaard

'Αλλὰ δή γ', ὦ Σώκρατες, τί οἴει ταῦτ' εἶναι ξυνάπαντα; κνίσματά τοί ἐστι καὶ περιτμήματα τῶν λόγων, ὅπερ ἄρτι ἔλεγον, κατὰ βραχὺ διῃρημένα
[But I must ask you, Socrates, what do you suppose is the upshot of all this? As I said a little while ago, it is the scrapings and shavings of argument, cut up into little bits].

Greater Hippias, 304 a

PREFACE VII v

Rarely, perhaps, has a literary undertaking been so favored by fate in accord with the author's wishes as has my *Philosophical Fragments*. Doubtful and reticent as I am with regard to every private opinion and self-appraisal, I do without any doubt dare to say truthfully one thing concerning the fate of the little pamphlet:[1] it has aroused no sensation, none whatever. Undisturbed and in accordance with the motto ("Better well hanged than ill wed"[2]), the hanged, indeed, the well-hanged, author has remained hanging. No one—not even in sport or jest—has asked him for whom he did hang. But that was as desired: better well hanged than by a hapless marriage to be brought into systematic in-law relationship with the whole world. Relying on the nature of the pamphlet, I was hoping this would happen, but in view of the bustling ferment[3] of the age, in view of the incessant forebodings of prophecy and vision and speculative thought, I feared to see my wish frustrated by some mistake. Even if one is a very insignificant traveler, it is always hazardous to arrive in a town at a time when everyone is most excitedly and yet most variously expectant—some with cannons mounted and fuses lit, with fireworks and illuminated banners in readiness; some with the
town hall festively decorated, the reception committee all VII vi
dressed up, speeches ready; some with the dipped pen of systematic urgency and the dictation notebook wide open in anticipation of the arrival of the promised one incognito[4]—a mistake is always possible. Literary mistakes of that kind belong to the order of the day.

Fate be praised, therefore, that it did not happen. Without any commotion whatever, without the shedding of blood and ink, the pamphlet has remained unnoticed—it has not been reviewed, not mentioned, anywhere; no literary clangor about it has increased the ferment; no scholarly outcry has led the expectant host astray; no shouting about it from the outpost has brought the citizenry of the reading world to their feet.[5] Just as the undertaking itself was devoid of all witchcraft, so also has fate exempted it from every false alarm.[6] The author *qua* author is thereby also in the fortunate position of owing no one anything. I am referring to critics, reviewers, intermediaries, appraisers, etc., who in the literary world are just like the tailors, who in civil life "create the man"—they set the fashion for the author, the point of view for the reader. With their help and art, a book amounts to something. But then it is with these benefactors as, according to Baggesen, with the tailors: "In turn they slay people with bills for the creation."[7] One comes to owe them everything, yet without even being able to pay off this debt with a new book, because the importance of the new book, if it comes to have any, will in turn be due to the art and help of these benefactors.

Encouraged by this favor of fate, I now intend to proceed. Without being hampered by anything or any hasty connection with the demands of the times, solely following my inner
VII promptings, I continue, as it were, to knead my thoughts un-
vii til, to my notion, the dough is good. Somewhere Aristotle states that people in his day set up the ludicrous rule for the narrative that it must move fast, and, he continues, "Here the answer applies that was given to the one kneading dough when he asked whether he was to make the dough stiff or soft: 'What, isn't it possible to make the dough just right?' "[8] The only thing I fear is a sensation, especially the approving variety. Although the age is open-minded, liberal, and speculative, although the sacred demands of individual rights advocated by many a cherished spokesman are greeted with acclamation, it nevertheless seems to me that the case in point is not comprehended dialectically enough, for otherwise the efforts of the chosen ones would scarcely be rewarded with noisy jubilation, a triple hip-hip-hurrah at midnight, torchlight processions, and other disturbing interventions in individual rights. It seems fair that in things permissible everyone should be allowed to do what he pleases. An intervention is accomplished only when what one person does will place another under obligation to do something. Any expression of

displeasure is permissible, because it does not intervene with an obligation in another person's life. If the crowd thus presents a man with a *pereat* [let him die], there is no intervention whatever in his freedom. He is not summoned to do something; nothing is demanded of him. He can lounge undisturbed in his living room, smoke his cigar, busy himself with his thoughts, jest with his beloved, make himself comfortable in his robe, sleep soundly—indeed, he may even absent himself, because his personal presence is not in the least required. But a torchlight procession is a different matter; if the celebrity is absent, he must come home at once; if he has just lit up a fragrant cigar, he must put it down at once; if he has gone to bed, he must get up at once, scarcely has time to put on his trousers, and must then dash out bareheaded under the open sky to give a speech. What applies to prominent individualities[9] in regard to such manifestations of the populace en VII viii
masse also applies in the same way to us humbler folk on a smaller scale. A literary attack, for example, is not an intervention in an author's personal freedom; why should not everyone be allowed to express his opinion, and of course the one attacked can calmly tend to his work, stuff his pipe, leave the attack unread, etc. Approval, however, is more dubious. A critical review that ushers [*vise*] one to a place outside the realm of literature is not an intervention, but a critical review that assigns [*anvise*] him a place inside is indeed alarming. A passerby who laughs at you does not obligate you to do anything at all;[10] on the contrary, he rather becomes indebted to you, because you have given him an occasion to laugh. Each one minds his own business without any disturbing or obligating reciprocity. A passerby who looks at you defiantly, suggesting with his stare that he finds you unworthy of a tip of the hat, does not obligate you to do anything; on the contrary, he exempts you from doing something, from the inconvenience of raising your hat. An admirer, however, is not so easily dismissed. His tender affability quickly turns into so much liability for the poor admired person who, before he knows it, has taxes and duties imposed on him for life, even if he should happen to be the most independent of all. If an au-

thor borrows an idea from another author without crediting him, if he misuses what he has borrowed, he does not intervene in the individual rights of the other person. But if he names his author, perhaps even with admiration, as the one to whom he is indebted—for what was misused—then he is exceedingly bothersome. Therefore, dialectically understood, the negative is not an intervention, but only the positive. How strange! Just as that freedom-loving nation of North Americans has invented the most cruel punishment, silence,[11] so a liberal and open-minded age has invented the most illiberal chicaneries—torchlight processions at night, acclamation three times a day, a triple hip-hip-hurrah for the great ones, and similar lesser chicaneries for humble folk. The principle of sociality[12] is precisely illiberal.

VII What is offered here is again a pamphlet *proprio marte, pro-*
ix *prio stipendio, propriis auspiciis* [by one's own hand, at one's own expense, on one's own behalf].[13] The author is proprietor insofar as he is private owner of whatever little fragment he does own, but otherwise he is as far from having bond servants as from being one himself. His hope is that fate will again favor this little undertaking and above all ward off the tragic-comic eventuality that some seer in deep earnestness or a rogue in jest will proceed to make the present age fancy that it is something and then run away and leave the author stuck with it like the pawned farm boy.[14]

J. C.

INTRODUCTION[15] VII 1

You will perhaps recall, my dear reader, that there was a remark at the end of *Philosophical Fragments* (p. 162[16]), something that might look like the promise of a sequel. Regarded as a promise [*Løfte*], that remark ("if I ever do write a second section") was certainly as casual as possible, as far as possible from a solemn pledge [*Tro-Lovelse*]. Therefore I have not felt bound by that promise, even though from the beginning it was my intent to fulfill it and the prerequisites were already on hand concurrently with the promise. Accordingly, the promise could very well have been made with great formality, *in optima forma* [in the best form], but it would have been inconsistent to publish a pamphlet so constituted that it was not able, and did not want, to cause a sensation and then in it to make a formal promise that, if nothing else, is bound to cause a sensation and certainly would have caused an enormous sensation. You know how these things happen. An author publishes a very sizable book; it has been out scarcely a week when by chance he falls into conversation with a reader who, in a glow of longing, courteously and congenially asks if he will not write a new book soon. The author is enthralled—to have a reader who so quickly works his way through a big book and, despite the labor, retains a keen desire. Alas, the poor deceived author! In the course of the conversation, that sympathetically interested reader of the book, who so ardently looks forward to the new book, admits, yes, he admits that he has not even read it and probably never will find the time to do so, but at a social gathering he had attended he had heard VII 2
mention of a new book by the same author, and to make certain of this matter is of extraordinary concern to him.

An author publishes a book and thinks as follows: Now I have a month's respite before the esteemed critics get it read. What happens? Three days later, a book notice appears, a hastily concocted outcry that ends with a promise of a review.

This outcry creates an enormous sensation. Little by little, the book is forgotten; the review never appears. Two years later, there is mention of that book in some group, and a well-informed person recalls it to the recollection of the forgetful by saying: That, of course, was the book that was reviewed by F. F. Thus a promise satisfies the demands of the times. First, it causes an enormous sensation, and two years later the person making the promise still enjoys the honor of having fulfilled it. The promise is of interest, but if the promiser were to fulfill it, he would merely harm himself, because fulfilling it is of no interest.

As far as my promise is concerned, its casual form was not in the least accidental, because the promise, essentially understood, was no promise, inasmuch as it had been fulfilled in the pamphlet itself. If an issue is divided into an easier part and a more difficult one, the author making the promise ought to proceed by beginning with the easier part and promise the more difficult part as a sequel. Such a promise is in earnest and in every respect worthy of acceptance. But it is much more frivolous of him to complete the more difficult part and then to promise a sequel, especially the sort of sequel that any attentive reader of the first part, provided he has the requisite education, can easily write on his own—if he should find it worth the trouble.

So it is with *Philosophical Fragments:* the sequel, as mentioned, was only supposed to clothe the issue in historical costume. The issue was the difficulty, that is, if there is anything difficult at all in the whole matter; the historical costume is easy enough. Without wanting to affront anyone, I am of the opinion that not every young graduate in theology would have been capable of presenting the issue with even the same dialectical rhythm with which it is done in the pamphlet. I am also of the opinion that not every young graduate in theology, after reading the pamphlet, would be able to set it aside and then on his own to present the issue with just the same dialectical clarity with which it is elucidated in the pamphlet. With regard to the sequel, however, I remain convinced, yet without knowing whether this conviction would flatter anyone,

that every young graduate in theology will be capable of writing it—provided he is capable of imitating the intrepid dialec- VII
tical positions and movements. 3

This was the nature of the promise regarding the sequel. It is therefore quite in order that it be fulfilled in a postscript,[17] and the author can scarcely be accused of the feminine practice of saying the most important thing in a postscript, that is, if the whole matter is of any importance at all. In essence, there is no sequel. In another sense, the sequel could become endless in proportion to the learnedness and erudition of the one who clothed the issue in historical dress. Honor be to learning and knowledge; praised be the one who masters the material with the certainty of knowledge, with the reliability of autopsy.[18] But the dialectical is nevertheless the vital power in the issue. If the issue is not dialectically clear, if, on the other hand, rare learning and great acumen are expended on particulars—the issue becomes only more and more difficult for the dialectically interested person.

There is no denying that, in terms of thorough erudition, critical acumen, and organizational skill, much superb work has been accomplished in regard to that issue by men for whom the present author has a deep veneration and whose guidance in those student days he had wished himself capable of following with greater talent than he possesses, until, with mixed feelings of admiration for the experts and of despondency in his abandoned, doubting distress, he thought he had discovered that, despite those excellent efforts, the issue was not being advanced but suppressed. Thus, if naked dialectical deliberation shows that there is *no approximation*, that *wanting to quantify oneself into faith* along this path is a misunderstanding, a *delusion*, that wanting to concern oneself with such deliberations is a *temptation* for the *believer*, a temptation that he, keeping himself in the passion of faith, must resist with all his strength, lest it end with his succeeding (note well, through yielding to a temptation [*Anfægtelse*[19]], consequently through the greatest calamity) in changing faith into something else, into another kind of certainty, in substituting probabilities and guarantees, which were specifically rejected when he, himself

beginning, made the qualitative transition of the leap from unbeliever to believer—if this is so, then everyone who, not entirely unfamiliar with learned scientificity and not bereft of willingness to learn, has understood it this way must also have felt his hard-pressed position when he in admiration learned to think meanly of his own insignificance in the face of those distinguished by learning and acumen and deserved renown, so that, seeking the fault in himself, he time and again returned to them, and when in despondency he had to admit that he himself was in the right. Dialectical intrepidity is not
VII 4 easily acquired, and the feeling of one's abandonment (although one believes oneself to be in the right), admiration's taking leave of those reliable teachers, is its *discrimen* [distinctive mark].

What is written in the form of an introduction is related to the dialectical in a way comparable to the relation of an orator to the dialectician. The orator requires permission to speak, to expatiate in a coherent address; the other indeed desires it, since he hopes to learn from him. But the orator has rare gifts, is well acquainted with human passions, has the power of imagination to depict, and has terror at his disposal for the moment of decision. So he speaks, he carries away, and the listener loses himself in the depiction. Admiration for the distinguished speaker makes him surrender with feminine abandon; he feels his heart pounding; his whole soul is moved. Now the orator concentrates all earnestness and terror in his demeanor; he commands every objection to be silent. He carries his case to the throne of the Omniscient One. He asks if anyone in all honesty before God dares to deny what only the most ignorant, the most pitifully perplexed, would dare to deny. Gently moved, he adds the exhortation not to yield to such doubts; the only terrible thing is to fall into the temptation of doing so. He revives the troubled one, wrests him out of the terror as a mother her child, who feels reassured by the most affectionate caresses—and the poor dialectician goes home dejected. He discerns very well that the issue was not even presented, much less solved, but he does not yet have the strength to stand victorious against the force of eloquence.

Here he understands with the unhappy love of admiration that there must be a prodigious legitimacy in eloquence also.

When the dialectician has eventually freed himself from the orator's domination, the systematician enters and declares with the emphasis of speculative thought: Not until the end of it all will everything become clear. Here it is a matter of persevering for a long time before there can be any question of raising a dialectical doubt. The dialectician is indeed amazed to hear the same systematician say that the system is not yet completed. Oh yes, in the end everything will become clear, but the end is not here yet. The dialectician, however, has not yet achieved dialectical intrepidity; otherwise this intrepidity would soon teach him to smile ironically at a proposition in which the thimblerigger has to such a degree assured himself of subterfuges, for it is indeed ludicrous to treat everything as completed and then to say at the end [*Slutning*] that the conclusion [*Slutning*] is lacking. In other words, if the conclusion is lacking at the end, it is also lacking at the beginning. This should therefore have been said at the beginning. But if the VII
conclusion is lacking at the beginning, this means that there is 5
no system. A house can indeed be finished even though a bell pull is lacking, but in a scholarly construction the lack of a conclusion has retroactive power to make the beginning doubtful and hypothetical, that is, unsystematic.

So it is with dialectical intrepidity. But our dialectician has not yet acquired it. Consequently, with youthful decorum he abstains from every conclusion regarding the lack of a conclusion—and full of hope he begins his work. So he reads, and he is amazed. Admiration holds him captive; he submits himself to a superior power. He reads and reads and understands something, but above all he sets his hope on the clarifying reflection of the conclusion upon the whole. He finishes the book but has not found the issue presented. And yet the young dialectician puts the entire awesome trust of youth in the renowned person; yes, like a maiden who has only one wish, to be loved by that someone, so he wishes only one thing—to become a thinker. Alas, the renowned person has it in his power to decide his fate, because the youth, if he fails to understand him, is rejected and has suffered shipwreck on his one and only wish. Therefore, he does not yet dare to entrust himself to anyone and to initiate anyone into his misfortune, into the disgrace of his not understanding the renowned one. So he makes a fresh start. He translates all the more important passages into his mother tongue in order to be sure that he understands them and has not overlooked anything and thereby possibly something about the issue (for he simply cannot understand that this is nowhere to be found). Much of this he memorizes; he sketches the train of thought; he takes it along wherever he goes, occupying himself with it. He tears the notes to pieces and takes notes again. What will a person not do for the sake of his one and only wish! Then he comes to the end of the book a second time but no closer to the issue. He then buys a new copy of the same book, lest he be bothered by discouraging recollections, and journeys to a far country so as to be able to begin with renewed energy. And then what? Then he persists in this way until he finally learns dialectical intrepidity. And then what? Then he learns to render unto Caesar what is Caesar's[20]—his admiration unto the renowned person—but he also learns to hold fast to his issue despite all celebrities.

The scholarly introduction distracts by its very erudition, and it looks as if the issue had been formulated the moment the learned research had reached its peak, that is, as if learned and critical striving toward perfection were identical with
VII striving toward the issue. The rhetorical address distracts by
6 intimidating the dialectician. The systematic process promises everything and keeps nothing at all. In none of these three ways does the issue emerge, especially not in the systematic process. The system presupposes faith as given[21] (a system that has no presuppositions![22]). Next, it presupposes that faith should be interested in understanding itself in a way different from remaining in the passion of faith, which is a presupposition (a presupposition for a system that has no presuppositions!) and a presupposition insulting to faith, a presupposition that shows precisely that faith has never been the given. The presupposition of the system—that faith is the given—

dissolves into a make-believe in which the system has made itself fancy that it knew what faith is.

The issue presented in that pamphlet, yet without the pretense of having solved it, since the pamphlet wanted only to present it, reads as follows: *Can a historical point of departure be given for an eternal consciousness; how can such a point of departure be of more than historical interest; can an eternal happiness be built on historical knowledge?* (see the title page). In the pamphlet itself (p. 162[23]), the following passage is found: "As is well known, Christianity is the only historical phenomenon that despite the historical—indeed, precisely by means of the historical—has wanted to be the single individual's point of departure for his eternal consciousness, has wanted to interest him otherwise than merely historically, has wanted to base his happiness on his relation to something historical." Thus, in historical costume, the issue in question is Christianity. Accordingly, the issue pertains to Christianity. In treatise form, the issue could be formulated less problematically this way: the apologetical presuppositions of faith, approximational transitions and overtures to faith, the quantifying introduction to the decision of faith. What would then be treated would be numerous considerations that are discussed or have been discussed by theologians in introductory disciplines, in the introduction to dogmatics and in apologetics.

In order, however, to avoid confusion, it should immediately be borne in mind that the issue is not about the truth of Christianity but about the individual's relation to Christianity, consequently not about the indifferent individual's systematic eagerness to arrange the truths of Christianity in paragraphs but rather about the concern of the infinitely interested individual with regard to his own relation to such a doc- VII
trine. 7 To state it as simply as possible (using myself in an imaginatively constructing way [*experimenterende*[24]]): "I, Johannes Climacus, born and bred in this city and now thirty years old, an ordinary human being like most folk, assume that a highest good, called an eternal happiness, awaits me just as it awaits a housemaid and a professor. I have heard that Christianity is one's prerequisite for this good. I now ask how

I may enter into relation to this doctrine." "What matchless audacity," I hear a thinker say, "what horrendous vanity, to presume to attach such importance to one's own little self in this world-historically concerned, this theocentric, this speculatively significant nineteenth century." I shudder; if I had not hardened myself against various terrors, I would probably stick my tail between my legs. But in that respect I find myself free of all guilt, because it is not I who of my own accord have become so audacious; it is Christianity itself that compels me. It attaches an entirely different sort of importance to my own little self and to every ever-so-little self, since it wants to make him eternally happy, if he is fortunate enough to enter into it. That is, without having comprehended Christianity—since I am merely presenting the question—I have at least understood this much, that it wants to make the single individual eternally happy and that precisely within this single individual it presupposes this infinite interest in his own happiness as *conditio sine qua non* [the indispensable condition], an interest with which he hates father and mother[25] and thus probably also makes light of systems and world-historical surveys.

Although an outsider, I have at least understood this much, that the only unforgivable high treason against Christianity is the single individual's taking his relation to it for granted. However modest it may seem to be included as part of the bargain in this way, Christianity specifically regards it as effrontery. I must therefore most respectfully refuse all theocentric helpers and the assistance of helpers' helpers to help me into Christianity in that way. So I prefer to remain where I am, with my infinite interest, with the issue, with the possibility. In other words, it is not impossible that the individual who is infinitely interested in his own eternal happiness can some day become eternally happy; on the other hand, it is cer-
VII 8 tainly impossible that the person who has lost a sense for it (and such a sense can scarcely be anything but an *infinite* concern) can become eternally happy. Indeed, once lost, it is perhaps impossible to regain it. The five foolish maidens[26] had indeed lost the infinite passion of expectancy.[27] So the lamp went out. Then a cry arose that the bridegroom was coming.

Then they rushed to the dealer and bought new oil and wanted to start afresh and let everything be forgotten. And, of course, everything was indeed forgotten. The door was shut and they were shut out, and when they knocked at the door, the bridegroom said to them: I do not know you. This was not just a quip by the bridegroom but a truth, for in a spiritual sense they had become unrecognizable through having lost the infinite passion.

The objective issue, then, would be about the truth of Christianity. The subjective issue is about the individual's relation to Christianity. Simply stated: How can I, Johannes Climacus, share in the happiness that Christianity promises? The issue pertains to me alone, partly because, if properly presented, it will pertain to everyone in the same way, and partly because all the others do have faith already as something given, as a trifle they do not consider very valuable, or as a trifle amounting to something only when decked out with a few demonstrations. So the presentation of the issue is not some sort of immodesty on my part, but merely a kind of lunacy.

In order to make my issue as clear as possible, I shall first present the objective issue and show how that is treated. The historical will thereby receive its due. Next, I shall present the subjective issue. That is really more than the promised sequel as a clothing in historical costume, since this costume is provided merely by mentioning the word "Christianity." [28]The first part is the promised sequel; the second part is a renewed attempt in the same vein as the pamphlet, a new approach to the issue of *Fragments*.

Part One

THE OBJECTIVE ISSUE OF THE TRUTH OF CHRISTIANITY

[1]OBJECTIVELY viewed, Christianity is a *res in facto posita* VII
[given fact], the truth of which is asked about in a purely ob- 11
jective way because the modest subject is much too objective not to leave himself out or *ohne weiter res* [without further ado] to include himself as someone who has faith as a matter of course. Thus, objectively understood, truth can signify: (1) historical truth, (2) philosophical truth. Viewed as historical truth, the truth must be established by a critical consideration of the various reports etc., in short, in the same way as historical truth is ordinarily established. In the case of philosophical truth, the inquiry turns on the relation of a doctrine, historically given and verified, to the eternal truth.

The inquiring, speculating, knowing subject accordingly asks about the truth but not about the subjective truth, the truth of appropriation.[2] Accordingly, the inquiring subject is indeed interested but is not infinitely, personally, impassionedly interested in his relation to this truth concerning his own eternal happiness. Far be it from the objective subject to be so immodest, so vain.

Now, the inquiring subject must be in one of two situations: either he must in faith be convinced of the truth of Christianity and his own relation to it, in which case all the rest cannot possibly be of infinite interest, since faith is precisely the infinite interest in Christianity and any other interest VII
easily becomes a temptation;[3] or he is not in a relationship of 12
faith but is objectively in a relationship of observation and as such is not infinitely interested in deciding the question.

This is merely to call attention in advance to what will be expounded in Part Two[4]—namely, that along this line the issue never emerges decisively, that is, does not emerge inasmuch as the issue is rooted specifically in decision. Let the scientific researcher labor with restless zeal, let him even shorten his life in the enthusiastic service of science and scholarship; let the speculative thinker spare neither time nor effort—they are nevertheless not infinitely, personally, impassionedly interested. On the contrary, they do not want to be. Their observations will be objective, disinterested. With regard to the subject's relation to known truth, it is assumed that if only the objective truth has been obtained, appropriation is an easy matter; it is automatically included as part of the bargain, and *am Ende* [in the end] the individual is a matter of indifference. Precisely this is the basis of the scholar's elevated calm and the parroter's comical thoughtlessness.

Chapter I[5]

The Historical Point of View[6]

If Christianity is viewed as a historical document, the important thing is to obtain a completely reliable report of what the Christian doctrine really is. If the inquiring subject were infinitely interested in his relation to this truth, he would here despair at once, because nothing is easier to perceive than this, that with regard to the historical the greatest certainty is only an *approximation*, and an approximation is too little to build his happiness on and is so unlike an eternal happiness that no result can ensue. Since, however, the inquiring subject is merely historically interested (whether he as a believer is also infinitely interested in the truth of Christianity, whereby his entire striving could easily involve him in various contradictions, or whether he stands on the outside, yet without any impassionedly negative decision as an unbeliever), he takes the work in hand, the enormous studies, to which he himself
makes new contributions until his seventieth year. A fortnight VII
before his death, to be exact, he is looking forward to a new 13
publication that will shed light upon an entire aspect of the discussion. Such an objective state of mind is an epigram[7] (unless its opposite is an epigram on it) on the restlessness of the infinitely interested subject, who must indeed have an answer to such a question, which pertains to the decision about his eternal happiness, and who in any case would not at any price dare to forego his infinite interest until the very last moment.

When the truth of Christianity is asked about historically, or what is and what is not Christian truth, Holy Scripture immediately presents itself as a crucial document. Therefore, the historical point of view focuses first on the Bible.

§ 1. *Holy Scripture*

Here the important thing for the research scholar is to secure for himself the greatest possible reliability; for me, however, it is not a matter of exhibiting any knowledge or of showing that I have none. For my deliberation, it is more important that it be understood and borne in mind that even with the most stupendous learning and perseverance, and even if the heads of all the critics were mounted on a single neck,[8] one would never arrive at anything more than an approximation, and that there is an essential misrelation between that and a personal, infinite interestedness in one's own eternal happiness.*

VII If Scripture is viewed as the secure stronghold that decides
14 what is Christian and what is not, the important thing is to secure Scripture historically-critically.**

Here the canonicity of particular books is dealt with, their authenticity and integrity, the author's axiopisty,[10] and a dog-

* In emphasizing this contradiction, the pamphlet *Philosophical Fragments* stressed or set forth the issue: Christianity is something historical (in relation to which the highest knowledge is only an approximation, the most masterly historical deliberation only the most masterly "as-good-as," "almost"), and yet *qua* historical and precisely by means of the historical, it proposes to have decisive significance for a person's eternal happiness.[9] It follows as a matter of course that the humble achievement of the pamphlet was always only to present the issue, to extricate it from all prattling and speculative attempts at explanation, which indeed explain that the explainer does not know at all what the question is.

** The dialectical still cannot be excluded. It may be that one generation, or perhaps two, can pass its years in the presumption of having found a stockade that is the end of the world and of dialectics. It is of no use. Thus for a long time it was deemed possible to exclude dialectics from faith by saying that its conviction was upheld by virtue of authority. Then if someone wanted to question the believer, that is, to speak dialectically with him, with a certain *unbefangen* [uninhibited] frankness he would turn the matter this way: I am not able and should not be able to account for it, because I rest in a confidence in others, in the authority of the saints, etc. This is an illusion, because dialectics merely turns and asks, that is, speaks dialectically with him about what authority is then and why he now regards these as authorities. Consequently it speaks dialectically with him not about *the faith* he has *out of confidence in them* but about *the faith* he has *in them*.

matic guarantee is posited: inspiration.[11]* When one thinks of the work of the English on the tunnel,[12] the enormous expenditure of energy, and how a minor accident can interrupt the entire project for a long time—one has an appropriate notion of this entire critical enterprise. What time, what diligence, what superb abilities, what exceptional knowledge have been requisitioned from generation to generation for the sake of this marvel. And nevertheless a little dialectical doubt
suddenly touching the presuppositions here can disturb the VII
entire project for a long time, disturb the subterranean way to 15
Christianity that one has wanted to construct objectively and scientifically instead of permitting the issue to arise as it is—subjective.

One occasionally hears uneducated or half-educated individuals or pompous geniuses scoff at critical work with ancient writings. They belittle the learned researcher's scrupulousness about the most insignificant detail, which is precisely to his credit, that scientifically he does not consider anything to be insignificant. No, philological scholarship is wholly legitimate, and the present author certainly has respect, second to none, for that which scholarship consecrates. On the other hand, one gets no unalloyed impression of critical theological scholarship. Its entire effort suffers from a certain conscious or unconscious duplexity. It always looks as if something for faith, something pertaining to faith, should suddenly result from this criticism. Therein lies the dubiousness. When, for example, a philologist publishes a book by Cicero[13] and does it with great acumen, with scholarly apparatus in noble obedience to the supremacy of the mind; when his ingenuity and

* The misrelation between inspiration and critical research is like that between eternal happiness and critical deliberations, because inspiration is an object only of faith. Or are people so critically zealous because the books are inspired? Consequently, the believer who believes that the books are inspired is not cognizant of which books he believes to be inspired. Or does inspiration ensue as a result of the critique, so that when it has done its job it has also demonstrated that the books are inspired? In that case, one will never come to accept inspiration, because the critical work is at its *maximum* only an approximation.

his intimate knowledge of antiquity, obtained by indefatigable diligence, help his ferreting sensibility to remove difficulties, to prepare the way for the process of thought amid a confusion of variant readings, etc.—then it is safe to abandon oneself to admiration, for when he has completed his work, nothing follows from it except the admirable feat that through his skill and competence an ancient text has been made available in the most reliable form. But it in no way follows that I am now supposed to build my eternal happiness on this book, because I certainly admit that with regard to my eternal happiness his amazing acumen is too little for me; I certainly admit that my admiration for him would be downcast rather than cheerful if I thought he had something like that *in mente* [in mind].[14] But that is precisely what critical theological scholarship does; when finished—and until then it holds us *in suspenso*, but with this very prospect in mind—it concludes: ergo, now you can build your eternal happiness on these writings.

Anyone who as a believer posits inspiration must consistently regard every critical deliberation—whether for or against—as something dubious, a kind of temptation. And anyone who, without having faith, ventures out into critical deliberations cannot possibly want to have inspiration result from them. To whom, then, is it all really of interest?

VII 16 But the contradiction goes unnoticed because the matter is treated purely objectively. Indeed, it is not even there when the research scholar himself forgets what he has up his sleeve, except insofar as he once in a while uses it lyrically to encourage himself in the work or lyrically polemicizes with the aid of eloquence. Have an individual appear; have him with infinite, personal interest impassionedly want to attach his eternal happiness to this result, to the expected result—he will easily see that there is no result and none to expect, and the contradiction will bring him to despair. Luther's rejection of the Letter of James[15] is alone enough to bring him to despair. In relation to an eternal happiness and an impassioned, infinite interest in this (the former can be only in the latter), an iota is of importance, of infinite importance; or conversely: despair over the contradiction will teach him precisely that it is of no avail to press forward along this road.

And yet that is how things have gone on. One generation after the other has died; new difficulties have arisen, have been conquered, and new difficulties have arisen. As an inheritance from generation to generation, the illusion has persisted that the method is the correct one, but the learned research scholars have not yet succeeded etc. All seem to feel comfortable; they all become more and more objective. The subject's personal, infinite, impassioned interestedness (which is the possibility of faith and then faith, the form of eternal happiness and then eternal happiness) fades away more and more because the decision is postponed, and is postponed as a direct result of the results of the learned research scholar. That is to say, the issue does not arise at all. One has become too objective to have an eternal happiness, because this happiness inheres precisely in the infinite, personal, impassioned interestedness, and it is precisely this that one relinquishes in order to become objective, precisely this that one lets oneself be tricked out of by objectivity. With the aid of the clergy, who occasionally display some scholarship, the congregation learns about it. The communion of believers finally becomes an honorific title, since the congregation becomes objective merely by looking at the clergy and then looks forward to an enormous result etc. Then an enemy dashes forth against Christianity. Dialectically he is just as equipped as the research scholars and the bungling congregation. He attacks a book in the Bible, a group of books. Instantly the learned emergency choir[16] rushes in etc. etc.

Wessel has said that he stays out of jostling crowds.[17] Like- VII
wise, it is not suitable for a pamphlet writer to come lickety- 17
split with his respectful supplication on behalf of a few dialectical deliberations. He would be just like a dog in a bowling alley. Likewise, it is not suitable for a stark-naked dialectician to enter into a scholarly dispute in which, despite all the talent and learning *pro et contra*, it is nevertheless, in the last resort, not dialectically decided what the dispute is about. If it is a purely philological controversy, then let learning and talent be

honored with admiration, as they deserve to be, but then it has no bearing on faith. If the disputants have something up their sleeves, let us get it out in order to think it through in all dialectical equanimity. Whoever defends the Bible with regard to faith must certainly have made clear to himself whether all his work, if it succeeded according to the highest expectations, would result in something in that respect, lest he become stuck in the parenthesis of his labor and, amid the difficulties of scholarship, forget the decisive dialectical *claudatur* [let it be closed]. Whoever attacks must likewise have reckoned whether the attack, if it succeeded on the largest possible scale, would result in something other than the philological result, or at most in a victory by contending *e concessis*,[18] in which, please note, one can lose everything in a different way, that is, if the mutual agreement is illusory.

In order to do justice to the dialectical and, undisturbed, just think the thoughts, let us assume first the one and then the other.

I assume, then, that with regard to the Bible there has been a successful demonstration of whatever any theological scholar in his happiest moment could ever have wished to demonstrate about the Bible. These books, no others, belong to the canon; they are authentic, are complete; their authors are trustworthy—one may say that it is as if every letter was inspired[19] (more cannot be said, because inspiration is indeed an object of faith, is qualitatively dialectical, not attainable by means of quantification). [20]Furthermore, there is not a trace of contradiction in the sacred books. Let us be circumspect in our hypothesis. If only as much as a single word is rumored about such a thing, the parenthesis appears again and the philological-critical busy trifling will promptly lead one astray. On the whole, what is needed here to make the issue easy and simple
VII is merely a dietetic precaution, a renunciation of every learned
18 intermediate clause, which one, two, three could develop into a hundred-year-old parenthesis. Perhaps this is not so easy, and just as a person walks in danger wherever he walks,[21] so the dialectical development walks in danger everywhere, walks in danger of slipping into a parenthesis. It is the same

with both great and small, and what generally makes debates boring listening for a third party is that in the second round the debate has already entered a parenthesis and now with growing intensity proceeds in the wrong direction away from the real topic. Accordingly, a fencing trick is used to tempt the opponent a little in order to find out whether one is encountering a dialectical parade horse or one that runs riot in parentheses, that goes giddap and gallop as soon as it is a matter of the parenthetical. How many an entire human life has passed in this way, so that from early youth it has moved incessantly in parentheses!

But here I shall break off these moralizing observations aimed at the common good, whereby I intended to compensate for my lack of historical-critical competence. Thus everything is assumed to be in order with regard to the Holy Scriptures—what then? Has the person who did not believe come a single step closer to faith? No, not a single step. Faith does not result from straightforward scholarly deliberation, nor does it come directly; on the contrary, in this objectivity one loses that infinite, personal, impassioned interestedness, which is the condition of faith, the *ubique et nusquam* [everywhere and nowhere] in which faith can come into existence.

Has the person who did believe gained anything with regard to the power and strength of faith? No, not in the least; in this prolix knowledge, in this certainty that lurks at faith's door and craves for it,[22] he is rather in such a precarious position that much effort, much fear and trembling will be needed lest he fall into temptation and confuse knowledge with faith. Whereas up to now faith has had a beneficial taskmaster in uncertainty,[23] it would have its worst enemy in this certainty. That is, if passion is taken away, faith no longer exists, and certainty and passion do not hitch up as a team. Let an analogy illustrate this. Whoever believes that there is a God and also a providence has an easier time (in preserving the faith), an easier time in definitely gaining the faith (and not an illusion) in an imperfect world, where passion is kept vigilant, than in an absolutely perfect world. In such a world, faith is indeed in- VII 19 conceivable. Therefore it is also taught that faith is abolished in eternity.[24]

How fortunate, then, that this wishful hypothesis, this most noble desire of critical theology, is an impossibility, because even its most consummate fulfillment would still remain an approximation. And in turn how fortunate for the scholars that the fault is by no means theirs! If all the angels united, they would still be able to produce only an approximation, because in historical knowledge an approximation is the only certainty—but also too little on which to build an eternal happiness.

So I assume the opposite, that the enemies have succeeded in demonstrating what they desire regarding the Scriptures, with a certainty surpassing the most vehement desire of the most spiteful enemy—what then? Has the enemy thereby abolished Christianity? Not at all. Has he harmed the believer? Not at all, not in the least. Has he won the right to exempt himself from the responsibility for not being a believer? Not at all. That is, because these books are not by these authors, are not authentic, are not *integri* [complete], are not inspired (this cannot be disproved, since it is an object of faith), it does not follow that these authors have not existed and, above all, that Christ has not existed. To that extent, the believer is still equally free to accept it, equally free, please note, because if he accepted it by virtue of a demonstration, he would be on the verge of abandoning the faith. If matters ever go that far, the believer will always have some guilt if he himself has invited it and started with giving victory into the hands of disbelief by himself wanting to demonstrate.

Here lies the difficulty, and I am again led back to learned theology. For whose sake is the demonstration conducted? Faith does not need it, indeed, must even consider it its enemy. When faith, however, begins to feel ashamed of itself, when, like a young woman in love who is not satisfied with loving but subtly feels ashamed of the beloved and consequently must have it substantiated that he is something exceptional, that is, when faith begins to lose passion, that is, when faith begins to cease to be faith, then the demonstration is made

necessary in order to enjoy general esteem from unbelief. [25]Alas, and let us not mention what on this point is perpetrated by a confusion of categories in the rhetorical stupidities of ecclesiastical speakers. Faith taken in vain[26] (a modern substitute—how can they believe who receive glory from one an- VII
other, John 5:44) will not and cannot, of course, bear the 20
martyrdom of faith, and in our day an address informed by real faith is perhaps the address most rarely heard in all Europe. Speculative thought has understood everything, everything, everything! The ecclesiastical speaker still exercises some restraint; he admits that he has not yet understood everything; he admits that he is striving (poor fellow, that is a confusion of categories!). "If there is anyone who has understood everything," he says, "then I admit (alas, he is sheepish and is not aware that he should use irony toward the others) that I have not understood it and cannot demonstrate everything, and we lesser ones (alas, he senses his lowliness in the wrong place) must be content with faith." (Poor, misunderstood, supreme passion: faith—that you have to be content with such a defender; poor preacher-fellow, that you do not know what the question is! Poor intellectual pauper Per Eriksen,[27] who cannot quite make it in scholarship and science but who has faith, because that he has, the faith that turned fishermen into apostles, the faith that can move mountains[28]—if one has it!)

When the matter is treated objectively, the subject cannot impassionedly relate himself to the decision, can least of all be impassionedly, infinitely interested. To be infinitely interested in relation to that which at its maximum always remains only an approximation is a self-contradiction and thus is comical. If passion is posited nevertheless, zealotism[29] ensues. Every iota is of infinite value for the infinitely interested passion.* The fault inheres not in the infinitely interested passion but in this, that its object has become an approximation-object.

* The objective point of view is hereby also reduced *in absurdum*, and subjectivity is posited. If we were to ask why the smallest iota is of infinite importance, the answer would have to be: because the subject is infinitely interested. Consequently, the subject's infinite interestedness is what tips the scale.

The objective view, however, continues from generation to generation precisely because the individuals (the observers) become more and more objective, less and less infinitely, passionately interested. On the assumption that one would in this way continue to demonstrate and to seek a demonstration of
VII the truth of Christianity, something remarkable would finally
21 emerge, that just as one was finished with the demonstration of its truth, it would have ceased to exist as something present; it would have become something historical to such a degree that it would be something past, whose truth, that is, whose historical truth, had now been brought to the point of reliability. In this way the concerned prophecy of Luke 18:8 could be fulfilled: Nevertheless, when the Son of man comes, will he find faith on earth?

The more objective the observer becomes, the less he builds an eternal happiness, that is, his eternal happiness, on his relation to his observation, because an eternal happiness is a question only for the impassioned, infinitely interested subjectivity. The observer (whether he is an inquiring [*forskende*] scholar or a dabbling [*fuskende*] member of the congregation) now understands himself objectively in the following valedictory at the boundary of life: when I was young, such and such books were in doubt. Their authenticity has now been demonstrated, but then in turn doubt has arisen lately about some books never previously held in doubt. But I am sure that a scholar will come along etc.

With applauded heroism, the modest objective subject keeps himself aloof; he is at your service and willing to accept the truth as soon as it has been obtained. Yet the goal to which he aspires is a distant one (undeniably so, since an approximation can continue as long as it pleases)—and while the grass grows, the observer dies,[30] calm, for he was objective. O objectivity, you are not praised for nothing. You are capable of everything; not even the firmest believer has been so certain of his eternal happiness, and above all so sure of not losing it, as the objective subject has been! It must then be that this objectivity and this modesty were out of place, were un-Christian. Then it certainly would be dubious to enter the truth of Christianity in this manner. Christianity is spirit; spirit is inwardness; inwardness is subjectivity;[31] subjectivity is essentially passion, and at its maximum an infinite, personally interested passion for one's eternal happiness.

As soon as subjectivity is taken away, and passion from subjectivity, and infinite interest from passion, there is no decision whatever, whether on this issue or any other. All decision, all essential decision, is rooted in subjectivity. At no point does an observer (and that is what the objective subject is) have an infinite need for a decision, and at no point does he see it. This is the *falsum* [falsehood] of objectivity and the meaning of mediation[32] as a passing through in the continuous
process in which nothing abides and in which nothing is infi- VII 22
nitely decided either, because the movement turns back on itself and turns back again, and the movement itself is a chimera, and speculative thought is always wise afterward.*[33]

* This must also be the way to understand the skepticism of Hegelian philosophy, much promoted for its positivity. According to Hegel, the truth is the continuous world-historical process.[34] Each generation, each stage of this process, is legitimated and yet is only an element in the truth. Short of resorting to a bit of charlatanry, which helps by assuming that the generation in which Hegel lived or the one after him is *imprimatur*,[35] that this generation is the last and world history is past, we are all implicated in skepticism. The passionate question of truth does not even come up, because philosophy has first tricked the individuals into becoming objective. The positive Hegelian truth is just as deceptive as happiness was in paganism. Not until afterward does one come to know whether or not one has been happy,[36] and thus the next generation comes to know what truth was in the preceding generation. The great secret of the system (yet this remains *unter uns* [between us] just like the secret among the Hegelians) is close to Protagoras's sophism "Everything is relative,"[37] except that here everything is relative in the continuous progress. But no living soul is served by that, and if he happens to be familiar with an anecdote by Plutarch (in *Moralia*[38]) about the Lacedaimonian Eudamidas, he will certainly come to think of it. When Eudamidas in the academy saw the senescent Xenocrates seeking the truth together with his followers, he asked: Who is this old man? And when the reply was given that he was a wise man, one of those seeking after virtue, he exclaimed, "When, then, will he use it?" Presumably, this continuous progress has also given rise to the misunderstanding that it takes a devil of a fellow in speculative thought to free himself from Hegelianism. Far from it; only sound common sense is needed, a pithy sense of the comic, a little Greek ataraxia. Apart from logic, and also

Objectively understood, there are more than enough results
VII 23 everywhere, but no decisive result anywhere. This is quite in order, precisely because decision is rooted in subjectivity, essentially in passion, and *maxime* [maximally] in the infinitely interested, personal passion for one's eternal happiness.

§ 2. *The Church*

The protection against the encroachment of dialectics that the Catholic Church enjoys in the visible presence of the pope will
VII 24 be omitted from the discussion.* But also within Protestant-

---

somewhat in logic because of an ambiguous light that Hegel has not excluded, Hegel and Hegelianism are a venture in the comic. By now, the late Hegel has presumably met his master in the deceased Socrates, who undoubtedly has something to laugh about, that is, if Hegel has remained unchanged. Yes,
VII 23 there Socrates has found a man worth talking with and especially worth asking (something Socrates intended to do with all the dead[39]) in Socratic fashion whether or not he knows something. Socrates must have changed considerably if he would be even remotely impressed if Hegel were to begin to reel off paragraphs and promise that everything would become clear at the end. —Perhaps this note is an appropriate place for something I have to complain about. In *Paul Møllers Levnet*[40] there is only a single reference that conveys any idea of how he in his last years viewed Hegel. In this restraint, the distinguished editor has presumably permitted himself to be guided by partiality and reverence for the deceased, by an uneasy regard for what certain people would say, what a speculative and almost Hegelian public might judge. Nevertheless, precisely when he thought he was acting out of partiality for the deceased, the editor perhaps damaged the impression of him. It is more noteworthy than many an aphorism included in the printed collection, and just as noteworthy as many a youthful episode preserved by the careful and tasteful biographer in his lovely and noble presentation, that P. M., when everything here at home was Hegelian, judged quite differently, that for some time he first spoke of Hegel almost with indignation, until his wholesome, humorous nature made him smile, especially at Hegelianism, or, to recall P. M. even more clearly, made him laugh at it heartily. Who has been enamored of P. M. and forgotten his humor; who has admired him and forgotten his wholesomeness; who has known him and forgotten his laughter, which did one good even when it was not entirely clear what he was laughing at, because his absentmindedness occasionally left one perplexed.

* On the whole, the infinite reflection in which the subjective individual is first able to become concerned about his eternal happiness is immediately recognizable by one thing, that it is everywhere accompanied by the dialectical.

ism, after the Bible has been abandoned as a secure stronghold, there has been recourse to the Church. Although attacks are still being made on the Bible, although learned theologians defend it linguistically and critically, this entire procedure is now partly antiquated; and above all, precisely because one becomes more and more objective, one does not have in mind the crucial conclusions with regard to faith. Letter-zealotry, which did have passion, has vanished. Its merit was that it had passion. In another sense, it was comic. And just as the age of chivalry actually concluded with Don Quixote[42] (the comic conception is always the concluding one), a poet, by comically eternalizing such an unfortunate servant of the letter in his tragic-comic romanticism,[43] could still make it plain that literalist theology is something of the past. Wherever there is passion, there is also romanticism, and the one who has flexibility and a sense of passion and has not learned by rote what poetry is will see in such a figure a beautiful infatuation, just as when a loving maiden embroiders an artistic border for the Gospel in which she reads of the joyousness of her erotic love, or just as when a loving maiden counts the written characters in the letter he has written to her—but then he would also see the comic.

Such a figure would undoubtedly become a laughingstock. With what right one would laugh is another question, because the fact that the whole age has become devoid of passion does not entitle it to laugh. The ludicrous aspect of the zealot was

---

Whether it is a word, a sentence, a book, a man, a society, whatever it is, as soon as it is supposed to be a boundary, so that the boundary itself is not dialectical, it is superstition and narrow-mindedness. In a human being there is always a desire, at once comfortable and concerned, to have something really firm and fixed that can exclude the dialectical, but this is cowardliness and fraudulence toward the divine. Even the most certain of all, a revelation, *eo ipso* [precisely thereby] becomes dialectical when I am to appropriate it; even the most fixed of all, an infinite negative resolution, which is the individuality's infinite form of God's being within him, promptly becomes dialectical. As soon as I take away the dialectical, I am superstitious and defraud God of the moment's strenuous acquisition of what was once acquired. It is, however, far more comfortable to be objective and superstitious, boasting about it and proclaiming thoughtlessness.[41]

VII 25 that his infinite passion thrust itself upon a wrong object (an approximation-object), but the good aspect of him was that he did have passion.

Turning the matter so as to relinquish the Bible and resort to the Church is indeed a Danish idea. Nevertheless, I cannot in the name of compatriotism either rejoice personally over this "matchless discovery"[44] (which is the official designation of this idea among the ingenious persons concerned: the originator and Messrs. Admirers) or find it desirable for the government to order a *Te Deum* [We praise thee, O God] from the entire population in pious thanksgiving for the "matchless discovery." It is better and, at least for me, indescribably easy to let Grundtvig keep what is his: the matchless discovery. To be sure, at one time it was rumored, especially when a similar little movement had started in Germany with Delbrück[45] and others, that Grundtvig actually owed the idea to Lessing,[46] yet without owing him the matchlessness of it. Then it would be Grundtvig's merit to have transformed a little Socratic moot point, problematically formulated with ingenious sagacity and rare skeptical craftsmanship and superb dialectic, into an eternal, matchless, world-historical, absolute, heaven-reaching, sunlit truth. But even assuming that there was a connection on Grundtvig's part, which I do not assume at all, since the matchless discovery in its matchless absoluteness bears the unmistakable imprint of Grundtvigian originality, it would nevertheless be an injustice to say it was a borrowing from Lessing, since in everything Grundtvigian there is nothing whatever that calls Lessing to mind or that the grand master of the understanding could, without matchless resignation, claim as his property. If it had at least been said that the sagacious, dialectical Magister Lindberg,[47] the gifted attorney general and guardian of the matchless discovery, was possibly indebted to Lessing, that would be something. In any case, the discovery is much indebted to Lindberg's talent, inasmuch as through him it [48]was given form and was forced into a dialectical stance, became less hiatic, less matchless—and more accessible to sound common sense.[49]

VII 26 Grundtvig had correctly perceived that the Bible could not possibly withstand the invading doubt, but he did not perceive that the reason for this was that the attack and the defense were both rooted in a method of approximation, which in its perpetually continued striving is not dialectically adequate for an infinite decision on which an eternal happiness is built. Since he was not dialectically aware of this, it must have been a stroke of sheer luck that he actually went outside the presuppositions within which the Bible theory has its great merit, its venerable scholarly significance. But a stroke of luck is inconceivable in relation to the dialectical. As far as that goes, it was more probable that with his theory of the Church he would eventually remain within the same presuppositions. Abusive language against the Bible, with which he at one time really offended the older Lutherans, abusive language and dictates instead of thoughts, can of course satisfy only devotees, and then of course to an extraordinary extent. When thought is lacking in the boisterous talk, everyone else will readily perceive that thoughtlessness has a fling in the looseness of the expression.

Just as previously the Bible was supposed to decide objectively what is the essentially Christian and what is not, now the Church was supposed to be the secure objective stronghold. More specifically, it is the Living Word[50] in the Church, the Creed, and the Word with the sacraments.

It is now clear for the first time that the issue is to be treated objectively. The modest, immediate, totally unreflective subject remains naively convinced that if only the objective truth stands firm, the subject will be ready and willing to slip it on. Here we instantly witness the youthfulness (the elderly Grundtvig also prides himself on this) that has no inkling of that subtle little Socratic secret: that the relation of the subject is precisely the knotty difficulty. If truth is spirit, then truth is inward deepening and is not an immediate and utterly uninhibited relation of an immediate *Geist* [spirit, mind] to a sum total of propositions, even though this relation is confusingly given the name of the most decisive expression of subjectivity: faith. The direction of unreflectiveness is always oriented out-

ward, thereunto, toward, in striving to reach its goal, toward the objective. The Socratic secret—which, unless Christianity is to be an infinite retrogression, can be infinitized in Christianity only by an even deeper inwardness—is that the move-
VII ment is inward, that the truth is the subject's transformation
27 within himself. The genius who foretells a matchless future for Greece[51] is simply not familiar with Greek culture. A study of Greek skepticism[52] is much to be recommended. There one learns thoroughly what will always require time and practice and discipline to understand (a narrow way for careless speech!), that sensate certainty, to say nothing of historical certainty, is uncertainty, is only an approximation, and that the positive and an immediate relation to it are the negative.

The first dialectical difficulty with the Bible is that it is a historical document, that as soon as it is made the stronghold an introductory approximation commences, and the subject is diverted into a parenthesis, the conclusion of which one awaits for all eternity. The New Testament is something of the past and is thus historical in a stricter sense. This is the beguiling aspect that prevents making the issue subjective and treats it objectively, whereby it never comes into existence at all. —*Philosophical Fragments* focuses on this difficulty in chapters IV and V by canceling the difference between the contemporary follower and the latest follower, who are presumed to be separated by 1800 years. This is of importance lest the issue (the contradiction that the god[53] has existed in human form) be confused with the history of the issue, that is, with the *summa summarum* [sum total] of 1800 years of opinions etc.

Imaginatively constructing in this way, *Fragments* emphasized the issue. The difficulty with the New Testament as something past now seems to be canceled by the Church, which is indeed something present.

On this point Grundtvig's theory has merit. It has been developed, particularly by Lindberg, with skilled, juridical keen-

ness, that the Church eliminates all the proving and demonstrating that was required in connection with the Bible, since that is something past, whereas the Church is something present. To demand from it a demonstration that it exists [*er til*], says Lindberg correctly, is nonsense, like demanding from a
living person a demonstration that he exists.* Lindberg is en- VII
tirely right in this matter and has the merit of the imperturb- 28
ability and clarifying assurance with which he sticks to a point.

Thus the Church exists [*er til*]; from the Church (as present to, as contemporary with the inquirer, whereby the issue is endowed with the equality of contemporaneity[55]), it is possible to learn what is essentially Christian, since that is indeed what the Church professes.

Correct. But not even Lindberg has been able to restrict the matter to this point (and I much prefer to face a dialectician and leave the matchless to Grundtvig). That is, after it has been said about the Church that it exists and that one can learn from it what the essentially Christian is, it is in turn asserted that this Church, the present Church, is the apostolic Church, that it is the same Church that has persisted for eighteen centuries. Consequently, the predicate "Christian" is more than a predicate of the present Church; predicated of the present Church, it designates pastness, consequently a historicity in quite the same sense as that of the Bible. Now all merit has amounted to nothing. The only historicity superior to proof is contemporary existence; every qualification of pastness requires demonstration. Thus, if someone says to a man: Demonstrate that you exist, the latter will quite properly reply: That is nonsense. If, on the other hand, he says: I, who now exist, existed essentially as the same person more than four hundred years ago, the former would properly respond: Here

* More precisely defined, dialectically-metaphysically, this is because existence [*Tilværelse*] is a higher concept than all demonstration on its behalf, and it is therefore foolishness to demand a demonstration, whereas it is, inversely, a leap to draw an inference from essence [*Væsen*] to existence.[54]

a demonstration is needed. It is indeed peculiar that this has gone unnoticed by such a seasoned dialectician as Lindberg, who is so very capable of pushing a point to its logical conclusion.

As soon as continuity is advanced with the aid of the Living Word, the issue has been brought to the very same point where it was in the Bible theory. Objections are like the nisse:[56] a man moves his residence—the nisse moves with him. At times this is deceptive for a moment. By suddenly changing the plan of operation, if one is also so fortunate that no one attacks the new line of defense, a genius like Grundtvig can easily be made blissfully happy in the opinion that now everything is fine with the aid of his matchless discovery. But let the Church theory bear the brunt just as the Bible had to do, let all objections try to kill it, what then? Then, quite consistently, an introductory scholarly discipline again becomes necessary (any other procedure would demolish the Church theory itself and translate the issue into the realm of subjectivity, where it most certainly belongs, but this is not assumed
VII by the objective Grundtvig). This scholarly discipline is to
29 demonstrate the originality of the Creed, its synonymity everywhere and at every moment through eighteen centuries (where the critical task would encounter difficulties completely unknown to the Bible theory),* and then there will be ferreting around in old books. The Living Word does not help, and, of course, neither will it help to point this out to Grundtvig. Therefore, this is done not in any sort of hope, [57]but rather in wanhope. The Living Word proclaims the Church's existence [*Tilværelse*]. Correct, even Satan himself cannot deprive anyone of that, but the Living Word does not proclaim that the Church has existed for eighteen centuries,

* As a precaution, I must here repeat the dialectic. It is not inconceivable that someone with enough imagination to become really aware of the prolixity of these difficulties would say: No, then the Bible works better. Yet we must not absentmindedly forget that this more or less, this better or not better, lies within the essential imperfection of an approximation that is incommensurate with the decision of an eternal happiness.

that it is essentially the same, that it has existed completely unchanged, etc.; even a dialectical novice can perceive this. The Living Word as a manifestation of existence corresponds to the immediate undemonstrable existence [*Tilvær*] of what is contemporaneously present, but as little as pastness is demonstrable (that is, it is superior to demonstration), so little does the Living Word correspond to it, inasmuch as the added predicate indicates only an immediate presence. A Grundtvigian anathema upon those who might not understand the beatific or decisive power of the Living Word with regard to the category of the historical past (a Living Word by those who have departed) demonstrates neither that Grundtvig is thinking nor that the opponent is not thinking.

Magister Lindberg, who has too good a head to be content with sounding the alarm year after year, is himself the very one who has given the matter this turn. Once when a dispute arose about whether it is more correct to say "I believe in a Christian Church" or "I believe that there is a Christian Church," he himself had recourse to old books in order to demonstrate when the faulty variant had appeared.[58] There is, of course, nothing else to be done, unless a new renunciation is added to the Christian creed, namely, the renunciation of all
sound thinking with regard to the matchless discovery and the VII
abracadabra of the Living Word.* 30

Along this path the approximation process commences again. The parenthesis is posited, and no one can say when it will end, for this is and remains merely an approximating, and this approximating has the curious quality of being able to continue as long as it pleases.

Accordingly, the Church theory, compared with the Bible theory, had the merit of eliminating the later-historical and

* On the other hand, anyone whose imagination is not completely inflexible, if he happens to recall that dispute,[59] will certainly not deny that Lindberg's approach was a vivid reminder of the learned efforts of a concerned biblical exegesis. I have never been able to detect anything sophistical in Lindberg's procedure, provided, as is reasonable and just, that one does not, inspired, presume to judge the heart, a judgment with which Lindberg has always been pestered.[60]

turning the historical into the present. But this merit promptly disappears as soon as the more specific qualifications enter the picture.

Whatever else has occasionally been said about the superiority of the Creed to the Bible as a safeguard against attack is rather obscure. That the Bible is a large book and the Creed a few lines is an illusory consolation and holds true only for people who fail to discover that copiousness of thought is not always proportionate to copiousness of words. Indeed, the attackers merely need to shift the attack, that is, to direct it against the Creed, and then everything will again be in full swing. If the attackers, in order to deny the personality of the Holy Spirit, can try their hand at New Testament exegesis, they can just as well adhere to the distinction expounded by Lindberg—whether the Creed should read "the holy spirit [*den hellige Aand*]," or "the Holy-Spirit [*den Hellig-Aand*]."[61] This is merely an example, for with regard to historical issues it is of course impossible to reach an objective decision of such a nature that no doubt would be able to insinuate itself. This also indicates that the issue is to be formulated subjectively
VII 31 and that it is indeed a misunderstanding to want to assure oneself objectively and thereby avoid the risk in which passion chooses and in which passion continues upholding its choice. It would also be a gross injustice if any later generation would safely, that is, objectively, be able to insinuate itself into Christianity and thus partake of what an earlier generation had purchased in the utmost danger of subjectivity and had spent a lifetime acquiring in this very danger.

If someone says that a briefer statement is easier to hold fast and harder to attack, he suppresses something, namely, how many thoughts are contained in the brief statement. Accordingly, someone else could with equal right say (when, as *in casu* [in this case], both are by the same, here the apostles) that a more copious elaboration is clearer and thus easier to hold fast and harder to attack. But everything said in this vein, *pro et contra*, is again only approximation-skepticism.

The Church theory has been sufficiently lauded as objective, a word that in our age has become a way of making honorable amends by which thinkers and prophets believe they are telling one another something of great importance. It is just too bad that where one should be objective, in strict scholarship, objectivity is rare, because a savant equipped with expert autopsy is a great rarity. In relation to Christianity, however, objectivity is an extremely unfortunate category, and the one who has objective Christianity and nothing else is *eo ipso* [precisely thereby] a pagan, because Christianity is precisely a matter of spirit and of subjectivity and of inwardness.

Now, I shall not deny that the Church theory is objective but rather point it out in the following way. When an individual infinitely, impassionedly interested in his own eternal happiness is placed in relation to the Church theory in such a way that he intends to base his eternal happiness on it, he becomes comic. He becomes comic not because he is infinitely, impassionedly interested—this is indeed the good thing about him—but he becomes comic because the objectivity is incongruous with his interest. If the historical aspect of the Creed (that it is from the apostles etc.) is to be decisive, then every iota must be infinitely insisted upon, and since this can be attained only *approximando* [by approximation], the individual finds himself in the contradiction of tying, that is, wanting to tie his eternal happiness to it and not being able to do so because the approximation is never finished. From this it follows in turn that he will not manage in all eternity to tie his eternal happiness to it but will tie it to a less passionate something. If VII 32
agreement could be reached on using the Creed instead of the Scriptures, phenomena would arise entirely analogous to the zealotry of a concerned biblical exegesis. The individual is tragic because of his passion and comic because of staking it on an approximation.

If someone wants to emphasize the Sacrament of Baptism and base his eternal happiness on having been baptized, he again becomes comic, not because the infinitely interested passion is comic (far from it, precisely this is venerable), but because the object is only an approximation-object. We all live assured in the conviction of being baptized, but if Baptism is to be decisive, infinitely decisive for my eternal happiness, then I—and consequently everyone who has not been made objectively blessed and has not dismissed passion as child's play (and such a person indeed has no eternal happiness for which to seek a basis; so he can easily base it on little)—then I must ask for certainty. Alas, the trouble is that in relation to a historical fact I can obtain only an approximation. My father has said so; it says so in the parish register; I have a certificate,* and so forth. Yes, I am assured. But let a person have passion enough to grasp the meaning of his own eternal happiness, and then let him try to tie it to his having been baptized—he will despair. Along this path, the Church theory would have to lead directly to the Baptist movement or else to a repetition of Baptism and also of Holy Communion in order to be sure of its case,[62] that is, provided the Church theory has had any influence at all and everything has not become very objective.[63]

Just because Grundtvig as poet is tossed about and moved in immediate passion, which is the magnificent thing about him, he feels a need, and in an immediate sense feels it deeply, for something firm with which the dialectical can be held at bay. But such a need is simply a need for a superstitious fixed point, because, as mentioned above, every boundary that wants to exclude the dialectical is *eo ipso* superstition. Just because Grundtvig is moved in immediate passion, he is not unfamiliar with temptations. With regard to these, a shortcut is now taken by obtaining something magical to hold on to, and then there will be plenty of time for being world-historically concerned. But this is precisely where the contradiction lies: to rely on something magical in relation to oneself and then to be busy with all of world history. When the temptation takes
VII hold dialectically, when the victory also is continually con-
33 strued dialectically, a human being will have enough to do with himself. Of course, then there will be no opportunity to make all humankind happy with matchless visions.

On this question of one's eternal happiness, I shall not un-

* God knows whether Pastor Grundtvig assumes that there is also a Living Word that demonstrates that one is actually baptized.

dertake to decide whether in other respects it is not un-Christian to find repose in the certainty that one is baptized, just as the Jews appealed to circumcision and to their being Abraham's children[64] as a decisive demonstration of the God-relationship, that is, to find repose not in a spiritual relationship with God in freedom (and then we are indeed in the theory of subjectivity, where the authentic religious categories belong, where each person is supposed only to save himself and has his hands full with that, because the saving continually becomes more difficult—more intensive in inwardness—the more important the individuality is, and where playing the world-historical genius and fraternizing world-historically as an *extraordinarius* with God is much like flippancy in relation to the moral life) but in an external event, that is, to hold the temptation away by means of this magical Baptism* and not to want to permeate it with faith. Here as everywhere I have no opinion of my own but, imaginatively constructing, simply present the issue.

As far as the Bible theory is concerned, the present author, even if he became more and more convinced of the dialectical
distortion concealed in it, nevertheless cannot but remember VII
with gratitude and admiration the splendid accomplishments 34
within the presupposition, remember those writings invested with rare learnedness and thoroughness, remember the salu-

* When it is said that the safeguard against all temptation in thinking about Baptism is that in it God does something with us, it is of course only an illusion that intends to hold the dialectical away by means of such a qualification, because the dialectical promptly returns with the inward deepening of this thought, with the appropriation. Each and every genius, even the greatest who has ever lived, is to use all of his strength exclusively on this, on inward deepening within himself. But people wish to be free from temptation once and for all, and therefore faith does not attend to God in the moment of temptation but faith becomes *faith in* one's actually having been baptized. If much masquerading were not concealed here, there would long since have emerged psychologically noteworthy cases of concern about getting to know for certain that one is actually baptized. If a mere ten thousand rix-dollars were at stake, the matter would scarcely be permitted to stand with the sort of certainty we now all have in our having been baptized.

tary impression of the entire effort that is embodied in a literature of whose total range the present author in no way claims to have any special scholarly knowledge. As far as Grundtvig's theory is concerned, the author does not exactly feel any pain in the moment of parting, nor does he exactly feel abandoned at the thought of being in disagreement with this thinker. No one wishing to know definitely where he stands could possibly wish to have Grundtvig for an ally, especially a person who does not wish to stand where there is commotion, especially when the commotion is the only more specific definition of where he stands. As for Magister Lindberg, he is such a richly knowledgeable man and such a seasoned dialectician that as an ally he is always a great gain and as a foe always makes the battle difficult for one—yet also enjoyable, because he is a skilled fencer[65] who hits home but does not slay absolutely, so that the survivor readily convinces himself that it was not he who has been slain but rather some enormous absoluteness. It has always seemed to me an injustice to Lindberg that while Pastor Grundtvig receives a certain amount per annum in offerings of admiration and incidental income from the worshiping party membership, Lindberg, on the other hand, has had to stand in the shade. And yet it is in truth something, and something that can with truth be said of Lindberg, that he has a good head on his shoulders; however, what in truth all this is that is said about Grundtvig is highly dubious, that he is a seer, bard, skald, prophet, with an almost matchless outlook upon world history and with one eye for the profound.[66]

§ 3. *The Evidence of the Centuries for the Truth of Christianity*

The issue is raised objectively; the solid, sensible subject thinks this way: "Just let there be clarity and certainty about the truth of Christianity and I will surely be man enough to accept it; that will follow as a matter of course." The trouble, however, is that in its paradoxical form* the truth of Christi-

* On this, see *Fragments*.[67]

anity has something in common with the nettle: the solid, sen- VII
sible subject only stings himself when he wants to grasp it 35
summarily this way, or rather (since it is a spiritual relationship, the stinging can be understood only in a figurative sense) he does not grasp it at all; he grasps its objective truth so objectively that he himself remains outside.

This argument cannot be treated in a genuinely dialectical way, because with the very first word[68] it changes into a hypothesis. And a hypothesis may become more probable by lasting three thousand years, but it does not on that account ever become an eternal truth that can be decisive for a person's eternal happiness. Has not Mohammedanism survived for twelve hundred years? The reliability of the eighteen centuries, the fact that Christianity has permeated all relations of life, reshaped the world, etc., this reliability is just an illusion by which the resolving and choosing subject is trapped and he enters the perdition of the parenthesis. In relation to an eternal truth that is supposed to be decisive for an eternal happiness, eighteen centuries have no greater demonstrative weight than a single day. On the contrary, eighteen hundred years and everything, everything that can be told and said and repeated in that regard, have a diversionary power that is extremely distracting. Every human being is by nature designed to become a thinker (all honor and praise to the God who created man in his image![69]). God is not to be faulted if habit and routine and lack of passion and affectation and chatter with neighbors right and left gradually corrupt most people, so that they become thoughtless—and build their eternal happiness on one thing and another and a third something—and do not notice the secret that their talk about their eternal happiness is an affectation because it is devoid of passion, and therefore it might as well be built on matchstick arguments.

The argument can, therefore, be treated only rhetorically.* True eloquence is certainly a rarity now; true eloquence would

* Perhaps most aptly with a humorous twist, as when Jean Paul says that if all demonstrations of the truth of Christianity were abandoned or disproved, one demonstration would nevertheless remain, namely, that it has survived for eighteen hundred years.[70]

undoubtedly think twice before using it—perhaps that is why the argument is heard so often. At best, then, the argument does not seek to proceed dialectically (only dabblers begin that way and only later seize upon the rhetorical); it seeks to impress. The speaker isolates the observing or the doubting sub-
VII ject from all association with others and confronts the poor
36 sinner with countless generations and millions upon millions
upon millions. Then he says to him: Do you now dare to be brazen enough to deny the truth? Do you dare, do you dare to imagine that you possess the truth and that for eighteen centuries those countless generations and millions upon millions upon millions have lived on and on in error? Do you dare, you miserable solitary fellow, do you dare to want, as it were, to plunge [*styrte*] all those millions upon millions upon millions, indeed all humankind, into perdition? See, they rise from their graves. See, they parade, as it were, past my thought, generation after generation of all those believers who found repose in the truth of Christianity, and their looks judge you, you brazen rebel, until the separation of judgment day keeps you from seeing them, because you were found wanting[71] and were shut out in the darkness, far from that eternal happiness, etc. Yet behind this enormous barrage (of millions upon millions upon millions), the cowardly speaker trembles at times when using the argument because he suspects that there is a contradiction in his entire approach.

But he does the sinner no harm. Such a rhetorical shower bath [*Styrtebad*] from an altitude of eighteen centuries is very bracing. The speaker is beneficial, although not in exactly the way he thinks; he is beneficial by singling out the subject over against all other people—alas, that is a great service, because only a few are capable of doing that by themselves, and yet testing in this position is an absolute condition for entering Christianity. The eighteen centuries are indeed supposed to instill terror. As a demonstration *pro*, they = 0 for the individual subject in the moment of decision, but as a terror *contra*, they are superb. The question is only whether the rhetorician will succeed in bringing the sinner in under the shower bath; that is, he does him an injustice inasmuch as the sinner by no means affirms or denies the truth of Christianity but simply and solely ponders his own relation to it. Just as the Icelander in the story told the king, "That is too much, Your Reverence,"[72] so the sinner could say, "That is too much, Right Reverend; what is the use of these millions and millions upon millions? A person gets so mixed up in his head that he does not know right from left." As noted above, it is Christianity itself that attaches an enormous importance to the individual subject; it wants to be involved with him, him alone, and thus with each one individually. It is in a way an un-Christian use of eighteen centuries to intend with them to entice the single individual into Christianity or to frighten him into it: he still does not enter into it. And if he does enter into it, he does so whether he has eighteen centuries for him or against him.

What has been intimated here has been emphasized in *Frag-* VII
ments frequently enough, namely, that there is no direct and 37
immediate transition to Christianity, and that therefore all those who in that way want to give a rhetorical push in order to bring one into Christianity or even help one into it by a thrashing—they are all deceivers—no, they know not what they do.[73]

Chapter II[74]

The Speculative Point of View

The speculative point of view conceives of Christianity as a historical phenomenon; the question of its truth therefore becomes a matter of permeating it with thought in such a way that finally Christianity itself is the eternal thought.

Now, the speculating point of view has the good quality of having no presuppositions.[75] It proceeds from nothing, assumes nothing as given, does not begin "*bittweise* [beggingly, by begging the presuppositions]."[76] So here we can be sure of avoiding the sort of presuppositions encountered earlier.

Yet one thing is assumed: Christianity as given. It is assumed that we are all Christians. Alas, alas, alas, speculative thought is much too courteous. Yes, how strange the course of the world is! At one time it was perilous to profess being a Christian; now it is precarious to doubt that one is, especially if this doubt does not mean that one storms forth to have Christianity abolished, for that would really be something! No, if someone were to say, plainly and simply, that he was concerned about himself, that it was not quite right for him to call himself a Christian, he would not be persecuted or executed, but people would give him an angry look and say, "It
VII 38 is really boring of this fellow to make so much ado about nothing; why can't he be like the rest of us, who are all Christians. He is just like F. F., who does not want to wear a hat, as the rest of us do, but has to be eccentric." If he were married, his wife would tell him, "Hubby, darling, where did you ever pick up such a notion? How can you not be a Christian? You are Danish, aren't you? Doesn't the geography book say that the predominant religion in Denmark is Lutheran-Christian? You aren't a Jew, are you, or a Mohammedan? What else would you be, then? It is a thousand years since paganism was

superseded; so I know you aren't a pagan. Don't you tend to your work in the office as a good civil servant; aren't you a good subject in a Christian nation, in a Lutheran-Christian state? So of course you are a Christian."

Lo, we have become so objective that even the wife of a civil servant argues from the whole, from the state, from the idea of society, from geographic scientificity to the single individual. It follows so automatically that the single individual is Christian, has faith, etc. that it is flippant to make so much ado about it, or certainly capricious. Since it is always unpleasant to have to admit the lack of something that everybody is assumed to possess as a matter of course, something that rightfully takes on a significance of sorts only when somebody is foolish enough to betray his flaw, [77]no wonder, then, that nobody admits it. When it is a matter of something that presupposes proficiency and the like, it is easier to make an admission. But the less significant the object, that is, less significant because everyone possesses it, the more embarrassing is the admission. And this is really the modern category pertaining to a concern about not being a Christian: it is embarrassing. —Ergo, it is a given that we are all Christians.

But perhaps speculative thought says, "These are popular and commonplace observations such as are made by normal-school graduates and popularizing philosophers. Speculative thought has nothing to do with them." Oh, how horrible to be shut out from the superior wisdom of speculative thought! And yet it seems a bit peculiar to me that there is continual talk about speculation and speculation as if this were a man or as if a man were speculation. Speculation does everything—it doubts everything etc. The speculative thinker, on the other hand, has become too objective to talk about himself. Therefore he does not say that he doubts everything but that speculation does it and that he says this of speculation—he says no more, as in a case of private proceedings. Now, should we not agree to be human beings![78] As is well known, Socrates states VII
that when we assume flute-playing, we must also assume a 39
flutist,[79] and consequently if we assume speculative thought, we also have to assume a speculative thinker or several specu-

lative thinkers. "Therefore, my precious human being, most honorable Mr. Speculative Thinker, you at least I venture to approach in subjective address: O my friend! How do you view Christianity, that is, are you a Christian or are you not? The question is not whether you are going further[80] but whether you are a Christian, unless going further in a speculative thinker's relation to Christianity means ceasing to be what one was, a true feat *à la* Münchhausen,[81] a feat that perhaps is possible for speculative thought, for I do not comprehend this enormous power, but certainly is impossible for the speculative thinker *qua* human being."

The speculative thinker (that is, if he is not just as objective as the wife of that civil servant) thus wants to look at Christianity. It is a matter of indifference to him whether or not anyone accepts it; that sort of concern is left to normal-school graduates and lay people—and then, of course, also to the actual Christians, to whom it is by no means a matter of indifference whether or not they are Christians. He now looks at Christianity in order to permeate it with his speculative thought, yes, his genuine speculative thought. What if this entire undertaking were a chimera, what if it could not be done; what if Christianity is indeed subjectivity, is inward deepening, that is, what if only two kinds of people can know something about it: those who are impassionedly, infinitely interested in their eternal happiness and in faith build this happiness on their faith-bound relation to it, and those who with the opposite passion (yet with passion) reject it—the happy and the unhappy lovers? Consequently, what if objective indifference cannot come to know anything whatever? Like is understood only by like, and the old sentence, *quicquid cognoscitur per modum cognoscentis cognoscitur* [whatever is known is known in the mode of the knower],[82] must indeed be amplified in such a way that there is also a mode in which the knower knows nothing whatever or that his knowing amounts to a delusion. With reference to a kind of observation in which it is of importance that the observer be in a definite state, it holds true that when he is not in that state he does not know anything whatever. Now, he can deceive one by saying that he is in that state although he is not, but if it turns out so fortunately that he himself declares that he is not in the requisite state, he deceives no one.

If Christianity is essentially something objective, it be- VII 40
hooves the observer to be objective. But if Christianity is essentially subjectivity, it is a mistake if the observer is objective. In all knowing in which it holds true that the object of cognition is the inwardness of the subjective individual himself, it holds true that the knower must be in that state. But the expression for the utmost exertion of subjectivity is the infinitely passionate interest in its eternal happiness. Even with regard to earthly erotic love it holds true that the observer must indeed be in the inwardness of erotic love [*Elskov*]. But here the interest is not so great, because all erotic love is rooted in illusion, and that is why it has a kind of objective side, which means that speaking of an experience at second hand is still possible. If, however, erotic love is permeated by a God-relationship, then the imperfect illusion, the remaining semblance of objectivity, fades away, and it now holds true that whoever is not in this state gains nothing by all his observing. With the infinite, passionate interest in his eternal happiness, the subjective individual is at the extreme point of his exertion, at the extreme point, not where there is no object (an imperfect and undialectical distinction) but where God is negatively present in the subjectivity that with this interest is the form of the eternal happiness.

The speculative thinker looks at Christianity as a historical phenomenon. But suppose Christianity is not that at all. "What obtuseness," I hear someone say, "what matchless pursuit of originality to say that sort of thing, especially in these times when speculative thought has grasped the necessity of the historical."[83] Yes, what is speculative thought not capable of comprehending! If a speculative thinker were to say that he had comprehended the necessity of a historical phenomenon, I would indeed bid him to occupy himself for a moment with the misgivings set forth in all simplicity in the Interlude between chapters IV and V of *Fragments*. Thus, for the time being, reference is made to that little section. I shall always be willing to make it the basis of further dialectical development when I have the good fortune of dealing with a speculative thinker, with a human being, because I dare not become involved with speculative thought.

And now this matchless pursuit of originality! Let us take an analogy. Take a married couple. See, their marriage clearly leaves its mark in the external world; it constitutes a phenomenon in existence (on a smaller scale, just as Christianity world-historically has left its mark on all of life). But their married love is not a historical phenomenon; the phenomenal is the insignificant, has significance to the marriage partners only through their love, but looked at in any other way (that is, objectively), the phenomenal is a deception. So it is with
VII 41 Christianity. Is that so original? Compared with the Hegelian notion that the outer is the inner and the inner the outer,[84] it certainly is extremely original. But it would be even more original if the Hegelian axiom were not only admired by the present age but also had retroactive power to abolish, backward historically, the distinction between the visible and the invisible Church.[85] The invisible Church is not a historical phenomenon; as such it cannot be observed objectively at all, because it is only in subjectivity. Alas, my originality seems only mediocre. Despite all pursuit of it, of which I am nevertheless not aware, I say only what every schoolchild knows, even though he does not know how to enunciate it as clearly, something that the schoolchild indeed has in common with the great speculative thinkers, only that the schoolchild is still too immature, and the speculative thinker too overmature.

There is no denying that the speculative point of view is objective. On the contrary, in order to indicate this even further, I shall again repeat my attempt to place in relation to it a subjective individual impassionedly, infinitely concerned for his eternal happiness, whereupon it will indeed become apparent that the speculative point of view is objective, inasmuch as the subjective individual becomes comic. He is not comic because he is infinitely interested (on the contrary, everyone is comic who is not infinitely, impassionedly interested and yet wants to make people think that he is interested in his eternal happiness). No, the comic is rooted in the misrelation of the objective.

If the speculative thinker is also a believer (which is also claimed), he must long since have perceived that speculative thought can never have the same meaning for him as faith. Precisely as a believer he is indeed infinitely interested in his own eternal happiness and in faith is assured of it (*N.B.* the way a believing person can be assured, that is, not once for all but, with infinite, personal, passionate interest, by daily acquiring the certain[86] spirit of faith), and he does not build an eternal happiness on his speculative thought. Instead, he handles speculative thought with suspicion, lest it trick him out of the certitude of faith (which at every moment has within itself the infinite dialectic of uncertainty) into indifferent objective knowledge. Simply understood, dialectically, that is how the matter stands. Therefore, if he says that he builds his eternal happiness on speculative thought, he contradicts himself comically, because speculative thought, in its objectivity, is indeed totally indifferent to his and my and your eternal
happiness, whereas an eternal happiness is specifically rooted VII
in the subjective individual's diminishing self-esteem acquired 42
through the utmost exertion. Furthermore, he is lying with regard to posing as a believer.

Or the speculative thinker is not a believer. The speculator, of course, is not comic, for he does not at all ask about his eternal happiness. The comic first emerges when the impassioned, infinitely interested subjective individual wants to relate his happiness to speculative thought. But the speculative thinker does not raise the issue we are discussing, because as a speculative thinker he becomes precisely too objective to concern himself with his eternal happiness. But I should add a word here, in case anyone misunderstands a number of my remarks, in order to make clear that he is the one who wants to misunderstand me, whereas I am not at fault. Honor be to speculative thought, praised be everyone who is truly occupied with it. To deny the value of speculative thought (even though one could wish to have the money-changers in the temple courtyard[87] etc. chased away as desecraters) would, in

my eyes, be to prostitute oneself and would be especially foolish for one whose life in large part and at its humble best is devoted to its service, and especially foolish for one who admires the Greeks. After all, he must know that Aristotle, when discussing what happiness is, lodges the highest happiness in thinking, mindful of the eternal gods' blissful pastime of thinking.[88] Furthermore, he must have both a conception of and a respect for the dauntless enthusiasm of the scholar, his perseverance in the service of the idea. But for the speculating thinker the question of his personal eternal happiness cannot come up at all, precisely because his task consists in going away from himself more and more and becoming objective and in that way disappearing from himself and becoming the gazing power of speculative thought. I am well acquainted with all this. But note that the blessed gods, those grand prototypes for the speculative thinker, were not in the least concerned about their eternal happiness. Therefore, the issue never arose in paganism. But to deal with Christianity in the same way leads only to confusion. Since a human being is a synthesis of the temporal and the eternal,[89] the speculative happiness that a speculator can enjoy will be an illusion, because he wants to be exclusively eternal within time. Therein lies the speculator's untruth. Higher, therefore, than that happiness is the impassioned, infinite interest in one's personal
VII 43 eternal happiness. It is higher precisely because it is truer, because it definitely expresses the synthesis.

Understood in this way (and in a certain sense it would not even need to be explained whether the infinite interest in one's eternal happiness is something higher, since the main consideration is simply that this is what is being asked about), the comic readily becomes manifest in the contradiction. The subjective individual is impassionedly, infinitely interested in his eternal happiness and is now supposed to be helped by speculative thought, that is, by his own speculating. But in order to speculate, he must take the very opposite path, must abandon and lose himself in objectivity, disappear from himself. This incongruity will completely prevent him from beginning and will pass comic judgment on every affirmation that he has gained something in taking this path. This is, from the opposite side, identical with what was said previously about the observer's relation to Christianity. Christianity cannot be observed objectively, precisely because it wants to lead the subject to the ultimate point of his subjectivity, and when the subject is thus properly positioned, he cannot tie his eternal happiness to speculative thought. By means of a metaphor, I shall try to illustrate the contradiction between the impassioned, infinitely interested subject and speculative thought, if it is supposed to help him. In sawing wood, one should not press down too hard on the saw; the lighter the touch of the sawer, the better the saw functions. If one presses down on the saw with all one's might, one will never manage to saw at all. Similarly, the speculative thinker should make himself objectively light, but whoever is impassionedly, infinitely interested in his eternal happiness makes himself as subjectively heavy as possible. Precisely thereby he makes it impossible for himself to speculate. Now, if Christianity requires this infinite interest in the individual subject (which is assumed, since the issue revolves around it), it is easy to see that in speculative thought he cannot possibly find what he is seeking. —This can also be expressed as follows: speculative thought does not permit the issue to arise at all, and thus all of its response is only a mystification.[90]

Part Two

THE SUBJECTIVE ISSUE, THE SUBJECTIVE INDIVIDUAL'S RELATION TO THE TRUTH OF CHRISTIANITY, OR BECOMING A CHRISTIAN

SECTION I

SOMETHING ABOUT LESSING

[1]Chapter I VII 47

An Expression of Gratitude to Lessing[2]

If a poor private thinker, a speculative capricemonger, who, like an indigent lodger, occupied an attic room at the top of a huge building, sat there in his little cubbyhole, held captive in what seemed to him difficult thoughts; if he had a premonitory suspicion that there must be a flaw somewhere or other in the foundations, without discovering more precisely so as to be able to understand how or where; if he, whenever he looked out from his attic window, observed with a shudder the redoubled and rushed efforts to beautify and expand the building, so that after he had seen and shuddered he would lapse into lethargy and feel like a spider that in its hidden corner leads a miserable life since the last housecleaning, anxiously sensing all the while that a storm is brewing; if he, every time he expressed his doubts to someone, found that his manner of speech, because of its deviation from the prevailing fashion of thought, was viewed as the shabby and eccentric dress of a decayed character—if, as I say, such a private thinker and speculative capricemonger suddenly made the acquaintance of a man whose fame was not exactly an outright guarantee to him for the correctness of his thoughts (because the poor lodger was not so objective that he automatically could draw an inference in reverse from fame to truth) but whose VII 48
fame was nevertheless a smile of fortune to the abandoned one, who found some of those difficult thoughts touched upon by the famous person—ah, what joy, what celebration in the little garret room when that poor lodger consoled himself with the glorious memory of the famous one, while his preoccupation with thought gained bold confidence, and the difficulty assumed shape, and hope was born, the hope of understanding himself, that is, first of understanding the diffi-

culty and then perhaps even of surmounting it! What Per Degn improperly wants to have incorporated into the order of ecclesiastical advancement—first the parish clerk [*Degn*][3] . . . . . —holds true with regard to understanding the difficulty: first understand the difficulty, and then one can always proceed to explain it—if one is able.

Now, then, in jest and in earnest: Pardon, renowned Lessing, this expression of rapturous gratitude, pardon its jesting form! The expression is certainly kept at a proper distance, is not at all obtrusive; devoid of world-historical bellowing and systematic coerciveness, it is purely personal. If it is untrue, the reason is that it is much too rapturous, for which, however, the jest makes amends. Besides, this jest has a deeper basis [4]in the inverted relationship of the person who, imaginatively constructing, raises doubts without explaining why he does it, and of one who, imaginatively constructing, seeks to show forth the religious in its supranatural magnitude without explaining why he does it.

The expression of gratitude does not pertain to what is generally and, as I assume, also rightly admired about Lessing. I do not consider myself justified in admiring in that way. My expression does not pertain to Lessing in the capacity of a savant, or to what appeals to me as an ingenious myth, that he was a librarian,[5] or to what appeals to me as an epigram, that he was the soul in a library, that with an almost ubiquitous autopsy he possessed an enormous body of knowledge, a gigantic apparatus ruled by the insight of thought, obedient to the intimations of the spirit, engaged in the service of the idea. It pertains not to Lessing as poet, not to his mastery in constructing the dramatic line, not to his psychological authority in poetically making something manifest, not to his as yet unsurpassed dramaturgical lines, which, although laden with thought, with the easy flow of conversation move along freely and without constraint in the intertwining of the dialogue. It pertains not to Lessing as an esthetician, not to that line of demarcation decisive in a way quite different from that of a pope[6] that on his order was drawn between poetry and the
VII 49 visual arts,[7] or to that wealth of esthetic observations that con-

tinue to suffice even in our own age. It pertains not to Lessing as a sage, not to that ingenious wisdom that was his and that modestly concealed itself in the lowly garb of the fable.[8]

No, it pertains to something in which the knotty difficulty is precisely that one cannot come to admire him directly or by one's admiration enter into an immediate relation to him, for his merit consists precisely in having prevented this: he closed himself off in the isolation of subjectivity, did not allow himself to be tricked into becoming world-historical or systematic with regard to the religious, but he understood, and knew how to maintain, that the religious pertained to Lessing and Lessing alone, just as it pertains to every human being in the same way, understood that he had infinitely to do with God, but nothing, nothing to do directly with any human being. See, this is the object of my expression, the object of my gratitude—now, if only it is certain that this is how it is with Lessing—if. And if it were certain, Lessing would justifiably be able to say: There is nothing to thank me for. If only it is certain! Yes, I would burst upon him in vain with the persuasion of my admiration, would plead, threaten, defy in vain. He has indeed grasped that Archimedean point[9] of religiousness, by which one is not exactly able to move the whole world, but for the discovery of which a world-force is needed when one has Lessing's presuppositions. If only it is so!

But now his result! Has he accepted Christianity, has he rejected it, has he defended it, has he attacked it?—so that I, too, may accept the same opinion with confidence in him who at any given moment had poetic imagination enough to become contemporary with the event that occurred 1812 years ago now, and in so primitive[10] a way that every historical illusion, every objectively inverted fallacy, was prevented. All right, then, catch Lessing on that point. No, he also had enough skeptical ataraxia[11] and religious sense to discern the category of the religious. If anyone wants to deny this, I shall demand that a vote be taken on it. But now to his result! Wonderful Lessing! He has none, none at all; there is not the slightest trace of any result. Truly, no father confessor who received a secret to be kept, no maiden who had pledged herself and her love to silence and became immortal by keeping her pledge, no one who took every piece of information with him into the grave—no one could act more carefully than Lessing in the more difficult task: also to speak. Not even Satan himself is able, as a third party, to say anything with definiteness as a third party.[12] God, however, can never become a third party when he is a part of the religious; this is precisely the secret of the religious.

VII 50 The world has perhaps always had a lack of what could be called authentic individualities, decisive subjectivities, those artistically permeated with reflection, the independent thinkers who differ from the bellowers and the didacticizers. The more objective the world and individual subjectivities become, the more difficult it becomes with the religious categories, which are precisely in the sphere of subjectivity. That is why it is almost an irreligious exaggeration to want to be world-historical, scholarly-scientific, and objective with regard to the religious. But I have not summoned Lessing in order to have someone to appeal to, because even wanting to be only subjective enough to appeal to another subjectivity is already an attempt to become objective, is a first step toward getting the majority vote on one's side and one's God-relationship transformed into a speculative enterprise on the basis of probability and partnership and fellow shareholders.

But with regard to actually becoming subjective, it is again a matter of what reflective presuppositions the subject has to penetrate, what ballast of objectivity he must dispose of, and what infinite conception he has of the significance of this turning, its responsibility and its *discrimen* [distinctive mark]. Even though this way of looking at the matter implies a requirement that drastically reduces the number of individualities among whom a choice could be made, even though Lessing, it seems to me, is the only one, I do not put him forward in order to appeal to him (ah, if only one dared to do that, if only one dared to establish an immediate relation to him, one would surely be helped!). It also occurs to me that it would be rather dubious, because with such an appeal I would also have contradicted myself and canceled everything. If the subjective

individual himself has not worked himself through and out of his objectivity, all appeal to another individuality will be only a misunderstanding. And if the subjective individual has done that, he will certainly know his own course and the dialectical presuppositions in and according to which he has his religious existence. The course of development of the religious subject has the peculiar quality that the pathway comes into existence for the single individual and closes up behind him. And why should the Deity not know how to maintain his price! Wherever there is anything extraordinary or valuable to be seen, there is sure to be a jostling crowd, but the owner carefully arranges things so that only one at a time is allowed to come in. The jostling crowd, the mass, the mob, the world-histor- VII 51
ical tumult remains outside. And the Deity certainly does possess what is the most precious of all, but also knows how to safeguard himself in a way entirely different from all earthly supervision, knows in an entirely different way how to prevent anyone from slipping in world-historically, objectively, and scholarly-scientifically by utilizing the jostling crowd.

The one who comprehends this will presumably also express the same thing in his conduct, although the same conduct can in one person be brazenness and in another religious courage, but there is no objective way of distinguishing. Now, whether Lessing has accomplished this great thing, whether, humbling himself under the divine and loving the human, he has come to the assistance of the Deity by expressing his God-relationship in his relation to others in such a way that the meaningless situation would not develop that he would indeed have his own God-relationship, whereas some other person would have his God-relationship only through him—who knows this definitely? If I knew this definitely, I could appeal to him, and if I could appeal to him and do this legitimately, Lessing surely would not have accomplished it.

Lessing belongs, of course, to the distant past, a receding little station on the systematic world-historical railroad. To resort to him is to pass judgment upon oneself and to justify every contemporary in the objective opinion that one is incapable of keeping up with the age that travels by railroad—and therefore the whole trick is to jump into a passenger car, the first the best, and leave things to the world-historical. To recall Lessing is an act of desperation, because then it certainly is all over for a person; one is far, far behind if Lessing has already said something about what one wants to say—unless either what Lessing said was true (in which case it would be precarious to steer away from it at railway speed) or one had not taken the time to understand Lessing, who ingeniously always knew how to keep himself and his dialectical knowledge, and his subjectivity within it, from any quick transfer to the bearer. But lo and behold, when a person has armed himself against all this humiliation and temptation, the worst still remains: suppose that Lessing deceived him. No, he was indeed an egotist, that Lessing! With regard to the religious, he always kept something to himself, something that he certainly did say but in a crafty way, something that could not be reeled off by tutors, something that continually remained the same while it continually changed form, something that was not distributed stereotyped for entry in a systematic formula book, but something that a gymnastic dialectician produces VII and alters and produces, the same and yet not the same.

52 It was downright odious of Lessing continually to change the lettering in connection with the dialectical, just the way a mathematician does and thereby confuses a learner who does not keep his eye mathematically on the demonstration but is satisfied with a fleeting acquaintance that goes by the letters. It was shameful of Lessing to embarrass those who were so exceedingly willing to swear *in verba magistri* [to the master's words],[13] so that with him they were never able to enter the only relation natural to them: the oath-taking relation. It was shameful of him not to state directly, "I am attacking Christianity," so that the swearers could say, "We swear." It was shameful of him not to state directly, "I will defend Christianity," so that the swearers could say, "We swear." It was a misuse of his dialectical skill that he must necessarily occasion them to swear falsely (since they necessarily had to swear), both when they swore that what he said now was the same as what he had said before because the form and clothing were

the same, and also when they swore that what he said now was not the same because the form and the clothing had changed—much like the traveler who under oath had identified an innocent person as the robber because he merely recognized the robber's wig and did not recognize his robber and therefore should have prudently confined himself to swearing that he recognized the wig. No, Lessing was not an earnest man. His entire presentation is devoid of earnestness and devoid of that genuine trustworthiness that is sufficient for those others who think afterward [*tænke bagefter*], yet without thoughtfulness [*Eftertanke*].

And now his style! This polemical tone, which at every moment has plenty of time for a joke, even in a period of ferment. According to an old newspaper I found, the age then (just as now) was supposed to have been a period of ferment the likes of which the world had never seen. This stylistic nonchalance that works out a simile down to the minutest detail, as if the presentation itself had a value, as if peace and quiet prevailed, although the printer's devil and world history, indeed, all of humankind, were waiting for him to finish. This scholarly idleness that does not subscribe to the paragraphic norm. This mixture of jest and earnestness that makes it impossible for a third person to know definitely which is which—unless the third person knows it by himself. This craftiness that now and then perhaps even places a false stress on the indifferent, so that the expert may precisely in this way best grasp what is VII 53 dialectically decisive and the heretics may obtain nothing to gossip about.[14] This mode of presentation, so integral to his individuality, that briskly and refreshingly blazes its own trail and does not expire in a mosaic of slogans and authorized clichés and current locutions that with quotation marks betray to one that the writer is keeping up with the times, whereas Lessing confides to one *sub rosa* [privately] that he is keeping up with the thought. This nimbleness in teasingly employing his own *I*, almost like Socrates, in declining partnership or, more accurately, guarding himself against it in relation to that truth in which the cardinal point is precisely to be left alone with it, without wishing to have others with him for the sake of the triumph, since none is to win here, unless it is infinitude's jest of being nothing before God, without wishing to have people around one amid the perils of solitary thinking, since this is indeed the way.

All of this, is it earnestness? Is it earnestness that he conducts himself in the same way toward everyone, although differently in form? Is it earnestness that he not only dodges the obtuse attempts of the fanatics to enlist him in positive sociality and chaffs their foolish presumptuousness when they want to exclude him, but he is immune even to the enthusiastic eloquence of the noble Jacobi,[15] and he is untouched by the amiable, guileless concern of a Lavater for his soul?[16] Is this the outcome of an earnest man's life, that his parting words
VII 54 are just as enigmatic as all the rest,* that the noble Jacobi does not even dare to vouch for the salvation[19] of Lessing's soul, about which Jacobi was earnest enough to be concerned—almost as much as about his own? Is this earnestness? Well, let those decide who are so earnest that they do not even understand jest. Presumably they are competent judges nevertheless, that is, unless it would be impossible to understand earnestness if one does not understand jest, something (according to Plutarch's *Moralia*) that the earnest Roman Cato Uticencis

* Similarly Hegel also is supposed to have died with the words that no one understood him except one person, who misunderstood him,[17] and if Hegel has done the same thing, it perhaps could serve Lessing for good. But alas, there was quite a difference. In the first place, Hegel's statement has the flaw that it is a direct statement and thus is totally inadequate for such a misunderstanding, and this sufficiently shows that Hegel did not exist artistically in the illusiveness of double-reflection. Next, it has the flaw that Hegel's communication in the seventeen whole volumes[18] is direct communication, so that if he has not found anyone who has understood him, it is all the worse for Hegel. It would be a different matter with Socrates, for instance, who artistically arranged his entire mode of communication so as to be misunderstood. Regarded as a dramatic utterance at the moment of death, Hegel's statement is best regarded as delirium, as thoughtlessness on the part of one who, now in death, wants to take paths he had never taken in life. If Hegel as a thinker is one of a kind, then there is indeed no one with whom he can be compared,
VII 54 and if there should nevertheless be someone with whom he could be compared, so much is certain, that he would have absolutely nothing in common with Socrates.

is supposed to have pointed out long ago by pointing to the dialectical reciprocity between jest and earnestness.[20] But then if Lessing is not an earnest man, what hope is there for the person who relinquishes so very much, the world-historical and contemporary systematics, in order to have recourse to him?

That is how difficult it is to approach Lessing with regard to the religious. If I were to present a few thoughts and then by rote ascribe them directly to him, if I were to clasp him affably in admiration's embrace as the one to whom I owed everything, he perhaps would withdraw with a smile and leave me in the lurch, an object of laughter. If I wanted to conceal his name and step forth bellowing, happy about my matchless discovery, previously made by no man, then that [21]πολύμητις 'Οδυσσεύς [Odysseus of many wiles],[22] if I imagined him present, would approach me with an ambiguously admiring expression on his face, would pat me on the shoulder and say: *Darin haben Sie Recht, wenn ich das gewuszt hätte* [You are right in that, if only I had known it]. And then I, if no one else, would understand that he had the better of me.

[23]Chapter II

Possible and Actual Theses by Lessing

Without daring, then, to appeal to Lessing, without daring definitely to refer to him as my guarantor, without putting VII 55 anyone under obligation to want, because of Lessing's renown, most dutifully to understand or to claim to have understood something that brings the one who understands into a dubious relation to my lack of renown, which certainly is just as repelling as Lessing's renown is compelling—I now intend to present something that I shall, what the deuce, ascribe to Lessing, without being certain that he would acknowledge it, something that I in teasing exuberance could easily be tempted to want to foist upon him as something he said, although not directly, something for which in a different sense I in admiration could enthusiastically wish to dare to thank him, something that in turn I ascribe to him with proud restraint and self-esteem, just out of generosity, and then again something that I fear will offend or bother him by linking his name to it. One rarely finds an author who is such pleasant company as Lessing. And why is that? I think it is because he is so sure of himself. All this banal and easy association of someone exceptional with someone less exceptional—one is a genius, a master, the other an apprentice, a messenger, a day laborer, etc.—is prevented here. If I wanted to be Lessing's follower by hook or by crook, I could not; he has prevented it. Just as he himself is free, so, I think, he wants to make everyone free in relation to him, declining the exhalations and impudence of the apprentice, fearful of being made a laughingstock by the tutors: a parroting echo's routine reproduction of what has been said.

1. [24]*The subjective existing thinker is aware of the dialectic of communication.* Whereas objective thinking is indifferent to the

thinking subject and his existence, the subjective thinker as existing is essentially interested in his own thinking, is existing in it. Therefore, his thinking has another kind of reflection, specifically, that of inwardness, of possession, whereby it belongs to the subject and to no one else. Whereas objective thinking invests everything in the result and assists all humankind to cheat by copying and reeling off the results and answers, subjective thinking invests everything in the process of becoming and omits the result, partly because this belongs to him, since he possesses the way, partly because he as existing is continually in the process of becoming, as is every human being who has not permitted himself to be tricked into becoming objective, into inhumanly becoming speculative thought.

The reflection of inwardness is the subjective thinker's dou- VII
ble-reflection. In thinking, he thinks the universal, but, as ex- 56
isting in this thinking, as acquiring this in his inwardness, he
becomes more and more subjectively isolated.

The difference between subjective and objective thinking must also manifest itself in the form of communication.* This

[25]* Double-reflection is already implicit in the idea of communication itself: that the subjective individual (who by inwardness wants to express the life of the eternal, in which all sociality and all companionship are inconceivable because the existence-category, movement, is inconceivable here, and hence essential communication is also inconceivable because everyone must be assumed to possess everything essentially), existing in the isolation of inwardness, wants to communicate himself, consequently that he simultaneously wants to keep his thinking in the inwardness of his subjective existence and yet wants to communicate himself. It is not possible (except for thoughtlessness, for which all things are indeed possible) for this contradiction to become manifest in a direct form. —It is not so difficult, however, to understand that a subject existing in this way may want to communicate himself. A person in love, for instance, to whom his erotic love is his very inwardness, may well want to communicate himself, but not directly, just because the inwardness of erotic love is the main thing for him. Essentially occupied with continually acquiring the inwardness of erotic love, he has no result and is never finished, but he may nevertheless want to communicate; yet for that very reason he can never use a direct form, since that presupposes results and completion. So it is also in a God-relationship. Just because he himself is continually in the process of becoming in an inward direction, that is, in inward-

means that the subjective thinker must promptly become aware that the form of communication must artistically possess just as much reflection as he himself, existing in his thinking, possesses. Artistically, please note, for the secret does not consist in his enunciating the double-reflection directly, since such an enunciation is a direct contradiction.

VII 57 Ordinary communication between one human being and another is entirely immediate, because people ordinarily exist in immediacy. When one person states something and another acknowledges the same thing verbatim, they are assumed to be in agreement and to have understood each other. Yet because the one making the statement is unaware of the duplexity [*Dobbelthed*] of thought-existence, he is also unable to be aware of the double-reflection of communication. Therefore, he has no intimation that this kind of agreement can be the greatest misunderstanding and naturally has no intimation that, just as the subjective existing thinker has set himself free by the duplexity, so the secret of communication specifically hinges on setting the other free, and for that very reason he must not communicate himself directly; indeed, it is even irreligious to do so. This latter applies in proportion to the essentiality of the subjective and consequently applies first and foremost within the religious domain, that is, if the communicator is not God himself or does not presume to appeal to the miraculous authority of an apostle but is just a human being and also cares to have meaning in what he says and what he does.

Therefore, the subjective religious thinker, who has com-

---

ness, he can never communicate himself directly, since the movement is here the very opposite. Direct communication requires certainty, but certainty is impossible for a person in the process of becoming, and it is indeed a deception. Thus, to employ an erotic relationship, if a maiden in love yearns for the wedding day because this would give her assured certainty, if she wanted to make herself comfortable in legal security as a spouse, if she preferred marital yawning to maidenly yearning, then the man would rightfully deplore her unfaithfulness, although she indeed did not love anyone else, because she would have lost the idea and actually did not love him. And this, after all, is the essential unfaithfulness in an erotic relationship; the incidental unfaithfulness is to love someone else.

prehended the duplexity of existence in order to be such a thinker, readily perceives that direct communication is a fraud toward God (which possibly defrauds him of the worship of another person in truth[26]), a fraud toward himself (as if he had ceased to be an existing person), a fraud toward another human being (who possibly attains only a relative God-relationship), a fraud that brings him into contradiction with his entire thought. In turn, to enunciate this directly would again be a contradiction, because the form would then become direct despite the entire double-reflection of what is said. To require of a thinker that he contradict his entire thought and his world-view by the form he gives his communication, to console him by saying that in this way he will be beneficial, to let him remain convinced that nobody cares about it, indeed, that nobody notices it in these objective times, since such extreme conclusions are merely tomfoolery, which every systematic day laborer regards as nothing—well, that is good advice, and also quite cheap. Suppose it was the life-view of a religiously existing subject that one may not have followers, that this would be treason to both God and men; suppose he were a bit obtuse (for if it takes a bit more than honesty to do well in this world, obtuseness is always required in order to be truly successful and to be truly understood by many) and announced this directly with unction and pathos—what then? Well, then he would be understood and soon ten would apply who, just for a free shave each week, would offer their services in proclaiming this doctrine; that is, in further substantiation of the VII
truth of his doctrine, he would have been so very fortunate as 58
to gain followers who accepted and spread this doctrine about having no follower.

Objective thinking is completely indifferent to subjectivity and thereby to inwardness and appropriation; its communication is therefore direct. It is obvious that it does not therefore have to be easy. But it is direct; it does not have the illusiveness and the art of double-reflection. It does not have that God-fearing and humane solicitude of subjective thinking in communicating itself; it can be understood directly; it can be reeled off. Objective thinking is therefore aware only of itself and is therefore no communication,* at least no artistic communication, inasmuch as it would always be required to think of the receiver and to pay attention to the form of the communication in relation to the receiver's misunderstanding. Objective thinking** is, like most people, so fervently kind and communicative; it communicates right away and at most resorts to assurances about its truth, to recommendations and promises about how all people someday will accept this truth—so sure is it. Or perhaps rather so unsure, because the assurances and the recommendations and the promises, which are indeed for the sake of those others who are supposed to accept this truth, might also be for the sake of the teacher, who needs the security and dependability of a majority vote. If his contemporaries deny him this, he will draw on posterity—so sure is he. This security has something in common with the independence that, independent of the world, needs the world as witness to one's independence so as to be certain of being independent.

The form of a communication is something different from the expression of a communication. When a thought has gained its proper expression in the word, which is attained
VII through the first reflection, there comes the second reflection,
59 which bears upon the intrinsic relation of the communication to the communicator and renders the existing communicator's own relation to the idea. Let us once again cite a few examples. We do have plenty of time, because what I write is

* That is how it always goes with the negative; wherever it is unconsciously present, it transmutes the positive into the negative. In this case, it transmutes communication into an illusion, because no thought is given to the negative in the communication, but the communication is thought of purely and simply as positive. In the deception of double-reflection, consideration is given to the negativity of the communication, and therefore this communication, which seems to be nothing compared with that other mode of communication, is indeed communication.

** It is always to be borne in mind that I am speaking of the religious, in which objective thinking, if it is supposed to be supreme, is downright irreligiousness. But wherever objective thinking is within its rights, its direct communication is also in order, precisely because it is not supposed to deal with subjectivity.

not the awaited final paragraph that will complete the system. Suppose,* then, that someone wanted to communicate the following conviction: truth is inwardness; objectively there is no truth, but the appropriation is the truth. Suppose he had enough zeal and enthusiasm to get it said, because when people heard it they would be saved. Suppose he said it on every occasion and moved not only those who sweat easily but also the tough people—what then? Then there would certainly be some laborers who had been standing idle in the marketplace and only upon hearing this call would go forth to work in the vineyard[27]—to proclaim this teaching to all people. And what then? Then he would have contradicted himself even more, just as he had from the beginning, because the zeal and enthusiasm for getting it said and getting it heard were already a misunderstanding. The main point was indeed to become understood, and the inwardness of the understanding would indeed be that the single individual would understand this by himself. Now he had even gone so far as to obtain barkers, and a barker of inwardness is a creature worth seeing.

Actually to communicate such a conviction would require art and self-control: enough self-control to comprehend inwardly that the God-relationship of the individual human being is the main point, that the meddling busyness of a third person is a lack of inwardness and a superfluity of amiable obtuseness, and enough art to vary inexhaustibly, just as inwardness is inexhaustible, the doubly reflected form of the communication. The more art, the more inwardness—yes, if he had considerable art, it would even be quite possible for him to say that he was using it with the assurance of being able the next moment to ensure the inwardness of the communication, because he was infinitely concerned to preserve his own in-

* I say only "suppose," and in this form I have permission to present what is most certain and most unreasonable, for even the most certain is not posited as the most certain but is posited as what is assumed for the purpose of shedding light on the matter; and even the most unreasonable is not posited essentially but only provisionally, for the purpose of illustrating the relation of ground and consequent.

wardness, a concern that saves the concerned person from all positive chattiness.

Suppose someone wanted to communicate that the truth is not the truth but that the way is the truth, that is, that the truth is only in the becoming, in the process of appropriation, that consequently there is no result. Suppose he were a humanitar-
VII 60 ian who necessarily had to publicize this to all people. Suppose he took the splendid shortcut of communicating this in direct form in *Adresseavisen*,[28] by which means he gained masses of supporters, whereas the artistic way, despite his utmost efforts, would leave undecided whether or not he had helped anyone—what then? Well, then his assertion would indeed turn out to be a result.

Suppose someone wanted to communicate that all receiving is a producing. Suppose he repeated it so frequently that this thesis even came to be used as copy in teaching penmanship—then he would certainly have gotten his thesis confirmed.

Suppose someone wanted to communicate the conviction that a person's God-relationship is a secret. Suppose he was a very congenial kind of man who was so fond of other people that he simply had to come out with it. Suppose he nevertheless still had enough understanding to sense a bit of the contradiction in communicating this directly and consequently he communicated it under a pledge of secrecy—[29]what then? Then either he must assume that the pupil was wiser than the teacher, that the pupil was actually able to keep silent, something the teacher was unable to do (a superb satire on being a teacher!), or he must become so blissful in gibberish that he completely failed to discover the contradiction. It is a curious thing about these congenial people; it is so touching that they have to come out with it—and it is so vain of them to believe that some other human being needs one's assistance in his God-relationship, as if God were not able to help himself and the person involved. But it is a bit strenuous: in existing to hold on to the thought that one is nothing before God, that all personal effort is only a jest. It is a bit chastening to respect every human being so that one does not dare to meddle directly in his God-relationship, partly because one ought to have enough in dealing with one's own, partly because God is no friend of impertinence.

Wherever the subjective is of importance in knowledge and appropriation is therefore the main point, communication is a work of art; it is doubly reflected, and its first form is the subtlety that the subjective individuals must be held devoutly apart from one another and must not run coagulatingly together in objectivity. This is objectivity's word of farewell to subjectivity.

Ordinary communication, objective thinking, has no secrets; only doubly reflected subjective thinking has secrets; that is, all its essential content is essentially a secret, because it cannot be communicated directly. This is the significance of the secrecy. That this knowledge cannot be stated directly, because the essential in this knowledge is the appropriation itself, means that it remains a secret for everyone who is not through himself doubly reflected in the same way, but that VII
this is the essential form of truth means that this cannot be said 61
in any other way.* Therefore, when someone is set on communicating this directly, he is obtuse; and when someone else is set on demanding this of him, he also is obtuse. Faced with such an illusive, artistic communication, ordinary human obtuseness will cry: It is egotism. So, when obtuseness prevails and communication becomes direct, obtuseness will have won so much that the communicator will have become just as obtuse.

It is possible to distinguish between an essential secret and an accidental one. For example, what has been said in a privy council is an accidental secret as long as it is not publicly

* If in our age there lived a person who, subjectively developed, was aware of the art of communication, he would experience the most glorious buffoonery and farce. He would be turned out of doors as one who is incapable of being objective, until at long last a good-natured objective chap, a systematic devil of a fellow, would most likely have mercy upon him and help him halfway into the paragraphs. What was once regarded as an impossibility—namely, to paint a picture of Mars in the armor that makes him invisible[30]—would now succeed extremely well; in fact, what is even more curious, it would now succeed halfway.

known, because the statement itself can be understood directly as soon as it is made public. That no one knows what will happen in a year is an accidental secret, because when it has happened it can be understood directly. On the other hand, when Socrates, on account of his daimon,[31] isolated himself from any and every relation and, for instance, *posito* [as a supposition] presumed that everyone had to do it in that way, such a life-view would essentially become a secret or an essential secret, because it could not be communicated directly; at most he was capable of artistically, maieutically helping another person negatively to the same view. Everything subjective, which on account of its dialectical inwardness evades the direct form of expression, is an essential secret.

In its inexhaustible artistry, such a form of communication corresponds to and renders the existing subject's own relation to the idea. In order to make this clear in the form of an imag-
VII inary construction, without determining whether someone
62 actually existing has himself been conscious of this or not, i.e., has existed in this way or not, I will characterize the existence-relation.

2. [32]*In his existence-relation to the truth,* [33]*the existing subjective thinker is just as negative as positive, has just as much of the comic as he essentially has of pathos, and is continually in a process of becoming, that is, striving.* Since the existing subject is existing (and that is the lot of every human being, except the objective ones, who have pure being to be in), he is indeed in the process of becoming. Just as his communication must in form essentially conform to his own existence, so his thought must correspond to the form of existence. Through Hegel, everyone is now familiar with the dialectic of becoming.[34] That which in the process of becoming is the alternation between being and non-being (a category that is nevertheless somewhat unclear, inasmuch as being is itself also the continuity in the alternation) is later the negative and the positive.[35]

In our time, we often enough hear talk about the negative and about negative thinkers, and in that connection often enough hear the preaching of the positive ones and their pray-

ers offering thanks to God and Hegel that they are not like those negative ones[36] but have become positive. In the domain of thinking, the positive can be classed in the following categories: sensate certainty, historical knowledge, speculative result. But this positive is precisely the untrue. Sensate certainty is a delusion (see Greek skepticism and the entire presentation in modern philosophy, from which a great deal can be learned[37]); historical knowledge is an illusion (since it is approximation-knowledge); and the speculative result is a phantom. That is, all of this positive fails to express the state of the knowing subject in existence; hence it pertains to a fictive objective subject, and to mistake oneself for such a subject is to be fooled and to remain fooled. Every subject is an existing subject, and therefore this must be essentially expressed in all of his knowing and must be expressed by keeping his knowing from an illusory termination in sensate certainty, in historical knowledge, in illusory results. In historical knowledge, he comes to know much about the world, nothing about himself; he is continually moving in the sphere of approximation- VII 63
knowledge, while with his presumed positivity he fancies himself to have a certainty that can be had only in infinitude, in which, however, he cannot be as an existing person but at which he is continually arriving. Nothing historical can become infinitely certain to me except this: that I exist [38](which in turn cannot become infinitely certain to any other individual, who in turn is only in the same way infinitely cognizant of his own existence), which is not something historical. The speculative result is an illusion insofar as the existing subject, thinking, wants to abstract from his existing and wants to be *sub specie aeterni* [under the aspect of eternity].[39]

The negative thinkers therefore always have the advantage that they have something positive, namely this, that they are aware of the negative; the positive thinkers have nothing whatever, for they are deluded. Precisely because the negative is present in existence [*Tilværelse*] and present everywhere (because being there, existence [*Existents*],[40] is continually in the process of becoming), the only deliverance from it is to become continually aware of it. By being positively secured, the subject is indeed fooled.

The negativity that is in existence, or rather the negativity of the existing subject (which his thinking must render essentially in an adequate form), is grounded in the subject's synthesis, in his being an existing infinite spirit. The infinite and the eternal are the only certainty, but since it is in the subject, it is in existence [*Tilværelse*], and the first expression for it is its illusiveness and the prodigious contradiction that the eternal becomes, that it comes into existence [*blive til*].[41]

It is therefore important for the thinking of the existing subject to have a form in which he is able to render this. If he says this in direct utterance, he says something untrue, because in direct utterance the illusiveness is left out, and consequently the form of the communication interferes, just as when the tongue of an epileptic utters the wrong word, although the speaker may not notice it as clearly as the epileptic. Let us consider an example. The existing subject is eternal, but as existing he is temporal. Now, the illusiveness of the infinite is that the possibility of death is present at every moment. All positive dependability is thus made suspect. If I am not conscious of this at every moment, my positive trust in life is mere childishness, although it has become speculative, stately and superior in systematic cothurni; but if I do become conscious of this, then the thought of the infinite is so infinite that it seems
VII 64 to transform my existence into a vanishing nothing. How, then, does the existing subject render this thought-existence of his? Everyone knows that this is how it is to exist, but the positive ones know it positively, that is, they do not know it at all—but then they are, of course, so very busy with all of world history. Once a year on a solemn occasion, this thought grips them, and they now announce in the form of assurances that this is how it is. But that they observe it only once on a solemn occasion sufficiently betrays that they are very positive, and that they say it with the dependability of assurances shows that even while stating it they do not know what they are saying; hence they are also able to forget it a moment later.

In connection with negative thoughts of the kind men-

tioned, an illusive form is the only adequate one, because direct communication implies the dependability of continuity, whereas the illusiveness of existence, when I grasp it, isolates me. Whoever is aware of this, whoever, content with being human, has enough strength and leisure not to want to be deceived in order to receive permission to *sprechen* [talk] about all of world history, admired by the like-minded but mocked by existence—he will avoid direct utterance. As is known, Socrates was a loafer who cared for neither world history nor astronomy (he gave it up, according to Diogenes,[42] and when he later stood still and gazed into space,[43] I cannot simply assume, yet without otherwise deciding what he was doing, that he was stargazing). But he had plenty of time and enough eccentricity to be concerned about the merely *human*, a concern that, strangely enough, is considered an eccentricity among *human beings*, whereas it is not at all eccentric to be busy with world history, astronomy, and other such matters. In a superb article in *Fyenske Tidsskrift*,[44] I see that Socrates is supposed to have been somewhat ironic. It is really high time that this be said, and I am now in the position of daring to appeal to that article when I assume something similar. When Socrates specifically wants to emphasize the infinite, one of the forms his irony takes is that he initially speaks like a madman. Just as existence is sly, so also is his speech, perhaps (I
say "perhaps," since I am not nearly as wise a man as that pos- VII
itive writer[45] in *Fyenske Tidsskrift*) so as to prevent gaining a 65
moved and believing listener who would positively appropriate the statement about the negativity of existence. For Socrates, this initial madness may also have meant that while conversing with people he also conferred privately with the idea in what was being said. No one who can speak only directly will be able to understand this; nor is it any use telling a person this once and for all, since the secret is precisely that it must always be present everywhere in the thought and in its rendition, just as it is everywhere present in existence. To that extent, it is exactly right not to be understood, for one is thereby protected against misunderstanding. Thus when Socrates says somewhere[46] that it is remarkable that the skipper, after trans-

porting passengers from Greece to Italy, upon arrival walks calmly back and forth on the beach and collects his pay as if he had done something good, although he cannot know whether he has benefited the passengers or whether it might not have been better for them to lose their lives at sea—then he does speak much like a madman.* Perhaps some of those present actually considered him lunatic (for, according to Plato and Alcibiades,[47] there was a broad consensus that he was at least a bit odd, ἄτοπος); perhaps someone else thought that it was a droll way of talking, perhaps. At the same time, however, Socrates perhaps kept a little tryst with his idea, with ignorance. If he did grasp the infinite in the form of ignorance, he had to have this with him everywhere. An assistant professor does not bother with that sort of thing. He does it with pathos once a year in paragraph 14, and he does well in not doing otherwise, that is, if he has a wife and children and prospects for a good livelihood—but no understanding to lose.

[48]The subjective existing thinker who has the infinite in his soul has it always, and therefore his form is continually negative. When this is the case, when he, actually existing, renders
VII the form of existence [*Tilværelse*] in his own existence [*Exist-*
66 *ents*], he, existing, is continually just as negative as positive, for his positivity consists in the continued inward deepening in which he is cognizant of the negative. Among the so-called negative thinkers, however, there are a few who, after gaining an inkling of the negative, succumb to the positive and go roaring out into the world in order to recommend, urge, and offer their beatifying negative wisdom for sale—and one can surely hawk a result just as one hawks Holstein herring etc. These hawkers are scarcely more sagacious than the positive thinkers, but it is rather inconsistent of the positive thinkers to become angry with them, for they are essentially positive. The hawkers are not existing thinkers. Perhaps they were so

* If someone now living were to speak this way, everyone would undoubtedly perceive that he was lunatic, but the positive ones know, and they know with positive definiteness, that Socrates was a wise man. That is supposed to be quite definite—ergo.

once, until they found a result; from that moment they no longer exist as thinkers but as hawkers and auctioneers.

But the genuine subjective existing thinker is always just as negative as he is positive and vice versa: he is always that as long as he exists, not once and for all in a chimerical mediation. And his communication corresponds to this, lest by being overly communicative he meaninglessly transform a learner's existence into something other than what human existence is on the whole. He is cognizant of the negativity of the infinite in existence [*Tilværelse*]; he always keeps open the wound of negativity, which at times is a saving factor (the others let the wound close and become positive—deceived); in his communication, he expresses the same thing. He is, therefore, never a teacher, but a learner, and if he is continually just as negative as positive, he is continually striving.

In this way, such a subjective thinker does indeed miss something; he does not derive positive, cozy joy from life. For most people, life changes when they have come to a certain point in their searching. They marry, they enter occupations, in consequence of which they must out of decency finish something, must have results (because shame before people bids them to have results; what modesty before the god [*Guden*] might bid is given far less thought). So they believe that they themselves actually have arrived, or they must believe it out of custom and habit, or else they sigh and complain of the many things that keep them from striving (what an insult to the god, if the sigh sought him; what an insult to the god, if this sigh is simply a matter of custom and habit; what a contradiction to sigh over one's inability to pursue the higher because one is grasping for the lower, instead of refraining from sighing and refraining from grasping for the VII 67
lower!). So off and on they also engage in a little striving, but the last is merely a skimpy marginal note to a text finished long ago. In this way, one is exempted from becoming aware, in action [*exequerende*], of the strenuous difficulties contained in the simplest statement about existing *qua* human being, whereas in the capacity of a positive thinker, one knows all about world history and our Lord's most private thoughts.

One who is existing is continually in the process of becoming; the actually existing subjective thinker, thinking, continually reproduces this in his existence and invests all his thinking in becoming. This is similar to having style. Only he really has style who is never finished with something but "stirs the waters of language"[49] whenever he begins, so that to him the most ordinary expression comes into existence with newborn originality.

To be continually in the process of becoming in this way is the illusiveness of the infinite in existence. It could bring a sensate person to despair, for one continually feels an urge to have something finished, but this urge is of evil and must be renounced. The perpetual process of becoming is the uncertainty of earthly life, in which everything is uncertain. Every human being knows this and says so once in a while, especially on a solemn occasion and not without sweat and tears, says it directly and moves himself and others—and shows in action what he has already shown in the form of his utterance, that he does not understand what he himself is saying!*

VII 68 Lucian has Charon tell the following story in the underworld. A man in the upper world stood conversing with one of his friends and, promising him a rare dish, invited him to dinner at his home. The friend thanked him for the invitation. Then the man said: But now be sure to come. Definitely, answered the invited friend. Then they parted, and a roof tile fell down and killed the one invited. Isn't that something to die laughing over, adds Charon.[50] Suppose the invited guest had

* The thoroughly educated and developed individuality is known by how dialectical the thinking is in which he has his daily life. To have his daily life in the decisive dialectic of the infinite and yet to go on living—that is the art. Most people have comfortable categories for daily use and the categories of the infinite only on solemn occasions, that is, they never have them. But to have the dialectic of the infinite for daily use and to exist in it is, of course, the greatest strenuousness, and in turn the greatest strenuousness is needed lest the practice, instead of exercising a person in existing, deceptively trick him out of it. —It is well known that a cannonade makes a person unable to hear, but it is also well known that by persevering one can hear every word just as when all is quiet. And that is the way it is with a spiritual existence intensified by reflection.

been an orator who a moment earlier had moved himself and others by speaking about—the uncertainty of everything! That is how people speak: one moment they know everything, and at the very same moment they do not. And that is why it is considered foolish and eccentric to bother with it and with the difficulties, because everyone knows it. In other words, it is glorious to be concerned about what not everyone knows, about differential knowledge, but it is wasted effort to bother with what everyone knows—in regard to which the difference is the tomfoolery of how one knows it—because no one can thereby become important. Suppose the invited guest had answered on the basis of the uncertainty—what then? Then his response would not have been unlike that of a madman, although it would still not be noticed by many, since it can indeed be said so illusively that only the one who is himself conversant with such thoughts will discover it. Nor will such a person consider it madness, which it is not, for while the statement in jest perhaps weaves its way drolly into the rest of the conversation, the speaker may privately have a tryst with the god, who is present just as soon as the uncertainty of everything is thought infinitely. Therefore, the one who actually has an eye for the god can see him everywhere; whereas he who sees him only on extraordinary occasions actually does not see him at all but is superstitiously deluded by seeing a phantom.

That the subjective existing thinker is just as positive as negative can also be expressed by saying that he has just as much of the comic as of pathos. According to the way people exist ordinarily, pathos and the comic are apportioned in such a way that one has the one, another the other, one a little more of the one, another a little less. But for the person existing in double-reflection, the proportion is this: just as much of pathos, just as much of the comic. The proportion provides an interdependent safeguard. The pathos that is not safeguarded by the comic is an illusion; the comic that is not safeguarded by pathos is immaturity. Only he who himself produces this will understand it, otherwise not. What Socrates said about the passage across the water sounds simply like a jest, and yet it

was the highest earnestness. If it were meant solely as a jest,
VII perhaps many would go along with it; if it were meant solely
69 in earnest, surely many of those who sweat easily would be agitated. But suppose Socrates did not understand it this way at all. It would sound like jesting if a person in receiving an invitation replied: I will come, definitely, believe me, except in case a roof tile falls down and kills me, because then I cannot come. And yet this may also be the highest earnestness, and the speaker, while jesting with someone, may be in the presence of the god.

Suppose there was a maiden who expected her beloved to come with the ship Socrates mentioned. Suppose she rushed to the harbor, met Socrates, and with all her amorous passion inquired about her beloved. Suppose that old teaser Socrates, instead of answering her, were to say: Well, yes, certainly the skipper is walking smugly back and forth and is stroking the money in his pocket, although he cannot know for sure if it would not have been better for the passengers to perish at sea—what then? If she were a smart little miss, she would perceive that Socrates had in a way said that her beloved had arrived, and if that were certain—what then? Why, then she would laugh at Socrates, for she was not so frantic that she would not know definitely how splendid it was that her beloved had arrived. Now, of course, such a little miss was in the mood only for a tryst with her beloved in erotic embraces on the safe shore, but she was not sufficiently developed for a Socratic tryst with the god in the idea on the boundless sea of uncertainty.

But suppose the smart little miss had been confirmed—what then? Then, of course, she would have known the very same thing as Socrates—the only difference would be how it was known. And yet Socrates presumably has concentrated his whole life in this difference. Even in his seventieth year, he was not finished with his striving to practice ever more inwardly what every sixteen-year-old girl knows. For he was not like the one who knows Hebrew and consequently can say to the young girl: You do not know that, and it takes a long time to learn. He was not like the one who can carve in stone,

something the young girl would readily understand she could not do and would understand how to admire. No, he knew no more than she. No wonder, then, that he was so indifferent about dying, because presumably the poor fellow had himself perceived that his life had been wasted and that it was now too late to start afresh in order to learn what only the experts know. No wonder, then, that he raised no fuss at all about his death, as if in him the state would lose something irreplaceable. Alas, he may well have thought something like this: If only I had been a professor of Hebrew, if only I had been a sculptor or a solo dancer—not to mention a world-historical, bliss-bestowing genius—how could the state ever have re- VII
covered from the loss of me, and how could its inhabitants 70
ever come to know what I could tell them! But there will be no question about me, for what I know everyone knows. What a jester [*Spøgefugl*] this Socrates was, to jest [*spøge*] this way with Hebrew, the art of sculpture, ballet, and world-historical bliss-making, and then in turn to care so much about the god that, although practicing lifelong without interruption (indeed, as a solo dancer to the honor of the god), he looked ahead with doubt about whether he would be able to pass the god's examination—what would that be?

The relative difference between the comic and the tragic within immediacy vanishes in double-reflection, where the difference becomes infinite and identity is thereby posited. Religiously, the comic expression of worship is therefore just as devout as its pathos-filled expression. What lies at the root of both the comic and the pathos-filled is the misrelation, the contradiction between the infinite and the finite, the eternal and the becoming. A pathos that excludes the comic is therefore a misunderstanding, is not pathos at all. The subjectively existing thinker is therefore just as bifrontal[51] as the existence-situation itself. The interpretation of the misrelation, viewed with the idea ahead, is pathos; the interpretation of the misrelation, viewed with the idea behind, is the comic. When the subjective existing thinker turns his face toward the idea, his interpretation of the misrelation is pathos-filled; when he turns his back to the idea, allowing it to shine from behind into the same misrelation, his interpretation is comic. Thus it is the infinite pathos of religiousness to say *Du*[52] to God; it is infinitely comic when I turn my back and now within the finite look at that which from behind falls into the finite. If I have not exhausted the comic in its entirety, I do not have the pathos of the infinite; if I have the pathos of the infinite, I immediately have the comic also.

VII Praying is thus the highest pathos of the infinite,* and yet it
71 is comic,** precisely because in its inwardness praying is incommensurate with every external expression, especially if one complies with what the Bible says about anointing one's head and washing one's face when fasting.[55] Here the comic is present in two ways. An improper mode of the comic would emerge if, for instance, a Herculean man stepped forth

* The Socratic gazing is also an expression of the highest pathos and therefore also just as comic. Let us try it out. Socrates is standing and gazing into space; then two passers-by come along and the one says to the other: What is that man doing? The other replies: Nothing. Let us suppose that one of them
VII has a little more of an idea of inwardness. He describes Socrates' action as a
71 religious expression and says: He is absorbed in the divine; he is praying. Let us concentrate on the latter expression, "He is praying." But is he using words, perhaps ever so many words? No, Socrates understood his God-relationship in such a way that he did not dare to say anything at all for fear of talking a lot of nonsense and for fear of having a wrong desire fulfilled. Instances of the latter are said to have occurred, for example, when the oracle prophesied to a man that all his sons would become distinguished, and the troubled father went on to ask: And then will they all probably die a miserable death? The oracle replied: This, too, you shall see fulfilled.[53] Here the oracle is consistent enough to assume that the person who consults it is a supplicant, and therefore it consistently uses the word "fulfilled," which is grievous irony for the person involved. Consequently, Socrates does nothing whatever; he does not even in his inner being converse with the god—and yet he does the highest of all. Socrates himself presumably had perceived this and also knew how to emphasize it in a teasing manner. Magister Kierkegaard, on the other hand, has scarcely understood this, as can be inferred from his dissertation. Citing the dialogue *Alcibiades secundus*, he mentions Socrates' negative relation to prayer, but, as might be expected of a positive graduate in theology in our day, he cannot refrain from informing Socrates (in a footnote) that this negativity is true only to a certain degree.[54]

** Here I am not referring to what is accidentally comic, as when a man in prayer holds his hat before his eyes without noticing that the crown is missing, and someone accidentally happens to see him face-to-face.

while praying and, in order to indicate the inwardness of prayer, twisted and turned in forceful poses that would be instructive, especially if the speaker had bare arms, to an artist studying arm muscles. The inwardness and the unutterable sighs of prayer[56] are incommensurate with the muscular. The truly comic is that the infinite can be at work in a human being, and no one, no one discovers it by looking at him. With regard to the perpetual process of becoming, the comic and the pathos-filled are concurrently present in the repetition of prayer; yet its infinitude in inwardness seems to make a repe- VII
tition impossible, and therefore the repetition itself is some- 72
thing to smile at and also to mourn over.

Just as the subjective existing thinker himself exists this way, so also does his presentation render it, and therefore no one can appropriate his pathos as a matter of course. Like the comic parts in a romantic drama, the comic winds its way through Lessing's presentation at times perhaps in the wrong place, perhaps, perhaps not; I cannot say for sure. Hauptpastor Götze[57] is a highly *ergötzlich* [amusing] figure whom Lessing has comically preserved for immortality by making him inseparable from his presentation. It is, of course, disturbing not to be able to abandon oneself to Lessing with the same confidence as to the presentation of those who with genuine speculative earnestness make everything out of one thing and thus have everything finished.

That the existing subjective thinker is continually striving does not mean, however, that in a finite sense he has a goal toward which he is striving, where he would be finished when he reached it. No, he is striving infinitely, is continually in the process of becoming, something that is safeguarded by his being just as negative as positive and by his having just as much of the essentially comic as of the essentially pathos-filled, and that has its basis in the circumstance that he is existing and renders this in his thinking. The process of becoming is the thinker's very existence, from which he can indeed thoughtlessly abstract and become objective. How far the subjective thinker might be along that road, whether a long way or a short, makes no essential difference (it is, after all, just a finitely relative comparison); as long as he is existing, he is in the process of becoming.

Existence itself, existing, is a striving and is just as pathos-filled as it is comic: pathos-filled because the striving is infinite, that is, directed toward the infinite, is a process of infinitizing, which is the highest pathos; comic because the striving is a self-contradiction. From a pathos-filled perspective, one second has infinite value; from a comic perspective, ten thousand years are but a prank, like a yesterday, and yet the time the existing individual is in does consist of such parts. When ten thousand years are simply and directly declared to be a prank, many a fool will go along and find it to be wisdom but forget the other, that a second has infinite value. When a second is said to have infinite value, someone or other will be startled and better understand that ten thousand years have in-
VII 73 finite value. And yet the one is just as difficult to understand as the other if only one takes time to understand what is to be understood, or if in another way one is seized so infinitely by the thought of having no time to waste, not one second, that a second acquires infinite value.

This nature of existence calls to mind the Greek conception of Eros as found in the *Symposium*[58] and which Plutarch correctly explains in his work on Isis and Osiris (§ 57).[59] The parallel with Isis, Osiris, and Typhon does not concern me, but when Plutarch calls to mind that Hesiod assumed Chaos, Earth, Tartarus, and Eros to be primordial entities,[60] it is very correct in this connection to recall Plato. Here erotic love manifestly means existence or that by which life is in everything, the life that is a synthesis of the infinite and the finite. According to Plato, Poverty and Plenty begot Eros, whose nature is made up of both. But what is existence? It is that child who is begotten by the infinite and the finite, the eternal and the temporal, and is therefore continually striving. [61]This was Socrates' view—therefore love is continually striving, that is, the thinking subject is existing. Only the systematicians and the objectivists have ceased to be human beings and have become speculative thought, which dwells in pure being. Of course, the Socratic is not to be understood finitely as a continued and perpetually continued striving toward a goal without reaching it. No, but however much the subject has the infinite within himself, by existing he is in the process of becoming.

The thinker who in all his thinking can forget to think conjointly that he is existing does not explain existence; he makes an attempt to cease to be a human being, to become a book or an objective something that only a Münchhausen can become. That objective thinking has its reality [*Realitet*[62]] is not denied, but in relation to all thinking in which precisely subjectivity must be accentuated it is a misunderstanding. Even if a man his whole life through occupies himself exclusively with logic, he still does not become logic; he himself therefore exists in other categories. Now, if he finds that this is not worth thinking about, then let him have his way. It will scarcely be a pleasure for him to learn that existence mocks the one who keeps on wanting to become purely objective.

3. The subject to be discussed here and in the next segment VII 74 can be traced more definitely to Lessing, insofar as the statement can be cited directly, yet again not with any direct definiteness, since Lessing is not didactic but subjectively evasive, without wanting to obligate anyone to accept it for his sake and without wanting to help anyone attain direct continuity with the originator. Perhaps Lessing himself understood that such things cannot be expounded directly; at least his procedure can be explained this way, and perhaps the explanation is correct, perhaps.

Lessing has said (S.W., *V, p. 80*[63]) *that contingent*[64] *historical truths can never become a demonstration of eternal truths of reason, also (p. 83*[65]*) that the transition whereby one will build an eternal truth on historical reports is a leap.*[66] I shall now scrutinize these two assertions in some detail and correlate them with the issue of *Fragments*: Can an eternal happiness be built on historical knowledge?[67] But first I wish to make room for an observation that may serve to show how deceptive human thinking is, which is just like the pupil's reading—"He pretends to be reading and isn't reading at all."[68] When two thoughts are in-

separably related to each other so that if a person can think the one he can *eo ipso* [precisely thereby] think the other, then it not uncommonly happens that from mouth to mouth, from generation to generation, a public opinion passes that makes it easy to think the one thought, whereas an opposite public opinion makes it difficult to think the other thought, even establishes the practice of skepticism with regard to it. And yet the true dialectical relation is that whoever can think the one *eo ipso* can think the other, indeed, has *eo ipso* thought the other—if he has thought the one. Here I have in mind the quasi-dogma of eternal punishment.[69] The issue enunciated in *Fragments* is this: How can something historical be decisive for an eternal happiness? When "decisive" is predicated, it is *eo ipso* said that when eternal happiness is decided, eternal unhappiness is also decided, whether as posited or excluded. The
VII 75 first is supposed to be easy to understand; every systematician has thought so, every believer, and we are indeed all believers. It is as easy as pie to find a historical point of departure for one's eternal happiness and to think it. Amid this security and reliability, the question will occasionally arise with regard to an eternal unhappiness decided by a historical point of departure in time—see, that is a difficult question! It is impossible to make up one's mind about which to accept, and one agrees to let it stand as something that can be used occasionally in a popular address but is undecided. Alas, alas, alas, and so it is indeed decided; nothing is easier—if the first has been decided. [70]Wondrous human thoughtfulness—who can gaze into your thoughtful eyes without quiet elevation! Here, then, is the result of the continued thoughtfulness: the one thought is understood; the other is left in abeyance, that is, cannot be understood. And yet, this one and that other are, well, I am almost embarrassed to say it, they are one and the same.*

If time and a relation to a historical phenomenon within time can be decisive for an eternal happiness, they are *eo ipso*

* As far as that goes, *Fragments* could just as well have advanced the opposite and made this the issue: How can something historical be decisive for an eternal unhappiness? In that case, human thoughtfulness would certainly have found it something to ask about, since it could not even be answered.

that for the decision of an eternal unhappiness. Human thoughtfulness proceeds otherwise. That is, an eternal happiness is an eternal presupposition from behind, within immanence, for every individual. As eternal, the individual is above time and therefore always has his eternal happiness behind him; that is to say, only an eternal happiness can be thought; an eternal unhappiness cannot be thought at all. Philosophically understood, this is quite in order. Now Christianity enters and posits the disjunction: either an eternal happiness or an eternal unhappiness, and a decision within time. So what does human thoughtfulness do? It does not do what *Fragments* does; it does not become aware that this is a difficult question and that the summons to think it is the most difficult proposal that can be made. Consequently, it does not do what can be done in the first place; it does not even raise the issue. No, it lies a little and then things go easily enough. It takes the first part of the disjunction (either an eternal happiness) and by it understands immanental thought, which specifically excludes the disjunction, and then it has thought the whole thing, until
it declares bankruptcy with regard to the second part of the VII
disjunction and explains that it cannot think it, which 76
amounts to contradicting itself and denouncing itself as that which has not thought the first part. The basis of the paradox of Christianity is that it continually uses time and the historical in relation to the eternal. All thinking lies in immanence, and then what does human thoughtfulness do? It thinks immanence, pretends that this is the first half of the disjunction, and so it has thought Christianity.*

Now to Lessing. The passage is found in the little essay "*Über den Beweis des Geistes und der Kraft; an den Herrn Director Schumann*."[71] Lessing opposes what I would call quantifying oneself into a qualitative decision; he contests the direct transition from historical reliability to a decision on an eternal

* The demonstrations with which a devout orthodoxy has sought to safeguard that dogma of eternal punishment must be considered a misunderstanding. Yet its approach is by no means of the same character as that of speculative thought, for inasmuch as it is actually rooted in the disjunction, every demonstration is a superfluity.

happiness. He does not deny (for he is quick to make concessions so that the categories can become clear) that what is said in the Scriptures about miracles and prophecies is just as reliable as other historical reports, in fact, is as reliable as historical reports in general can be. *Aber nun, wenn sie* ***nur*** *eben so zuverlässig sind, warum macht man sie bei dem Gebrauche auf einmal unendlich zuverlässiger* [But now, if they are *only* as reliable as this, why are they treated as if they were infinitely more reliable]? (p. 79)—precisely because one wants to base on them the acceptance of a doctrine that is the condition for an eternal happiness, that is, to base an eternal happiness on them. Like everyone else, Lessing is willing to believe that an Alexander who subjugated all of Asia did live once, *aber wer wollte auf diesen Glauben hin irgend etwas von groszem und dauerhaftem Belange, dessen Verlust nicht zu ersetzen wäre, wagen* [but who, on the basis of this belief, would risk anything of great, permanent worth, the loss of which would be irreparable]? (p. 81).

It is the transition, the direct transition from historical reliability to an eternal decision, that Lessing continually contests. Therefore he takes the position of making a distinction between reports of miracles and prophecies—and contemporaneity with these. (*Fragments* has been attentive to this dis-
VII tinction by poetically constructing so as to bring out contem-
77 poraneity and in this way to exclude what has been called the
later-historical.[72]) Nothing follows from the reports, that is, from their admitted reliability, says Lessing, but, he adds, he would have been helped if he had been contemporary with the miracles and the prophecies.* Well informed, as Lessing always is, he therefore protests against a half-deceptive quotation from Origen[75] that has been cited to make this demonstration of the truth of Christianity stand out in relief. He protests by adding Origen's closing statement, from which it is seen that Origen assumes that miracles occurred even in his

* Perhaps a reader will here recall what was presented in *Fragments* on the impossibility of becoming contemporary (in an immediate sense) with a paradox,[73] also on the point that the distinction between the contemporary and the later follower is a vanishing factor.[74]

own day and that he assigns demonstrative power to these miracles, with which he was indeed contemporary, as well as to those he read about.

Since Lessing has taken such a position with regard to a given explanation, he has no opportunity to raise the dialectical issue of whether contemporaneity would be of some help, whether it could be more than an *occasion*, which the historical report can also be. Lessing seems to assume the opposite, but perhaps this semblance is produced in order *e concessis* [on the basis of the opponent's premises] to give his swordplay greater dialectical clarity vis-à-vis a particular individual. *Fragments*, however, attempted to show that contemporaneity does not help at all, because there is in all eternity no direct transition, which also would indeed have been an unbounded injustice toward all those who come later, an injustice and a distinction that would be much worse than that between Jew and Greek, circumcised and uncircumcised, which Christianity has canceled.[76]

Lessing has himself consolidated his issue in the following words, which he has in boldface: ***zufällige Geschichtswahrheiten können der Beweis von nothwendigen Vernunftwahrheiten nie werden*** [contingent truths of history can never become the demonstration of necessary truths of reason].*[77] What jolts here is the predicate *zufällige* [contingent]. This is VII 78
misleading; it might seem to lead to the absolute distinction between essential and contingent historical truths, a distinction that is nevertheless only a subdivision. If, despite the identity of the higher predicate ("historical"), an absolute distinction is made here, it might seem to follow that a direct transition could be formed in relation to essential historical truths. I could now lose my temper and say: It is impossible that Lessing could be so inconsistent; ergo—and my temper would probably convince many. I shall, however, restrict myself to a courteous "perhaps," which assumes that Lessing has

* In this presentation of the matter, it is evident that *Fragments* really opposes Lessing, insofar as he has stipulated the advantage of contemporaneity, in the negation of which lies the real dialectical issue, and thereby the solution of Lessing's issue gains a different significance.

concealed everything in the predicate "contingent" but has said something only in part, so that "contingent" is not a relatively distinguishing predicate or a distributive predicate but a generic predicate: "historical truths," which as such are contingent. If not, there lies here the entire misunderstanding that recurs time and again in modern philosophy: to make the eternal historical as a matter of course and to assume an ability to comprehend the necessity of the historical.*[78] Everything that becomes historical is contingent, inasmuch as precisely by coming into existence, by becoming historical, it has its element of contingency, inasmuch as contingency is precisely the one factor in all coming into existence. —And therein lies again the incommensurability between a historical truth and an eternal decision.

[80]Understood in this way, the transition whereby something historical and the relation to this becomes decisive for an eternal happiness is a μετάβασις εἰς ἄλλο γένος [shifting from one genus to another][81] (Lessing even says that if it is not that, then I do not know what Aristotle has understood by it, p. 82[82]), a leap for both the contemporary and the one who comes later. It is a leap, and this is the word that Lessing has employed within the accidental limitation that is characterized
VII 79 by an illusory distinction between contemporaneity and noncontemporaneity. His words read as follows: *Das, das ist der garstige breite Graben, über den ich nicht kommen kann, so oft und ernstlich ich auch den Sprung versucht habe* [That, that is the ugly broad ditch that I cannot cross, however often and however earnestly I have tried to make the leap] (p. 83).[83] Perhaps that word "leap" is only a stylistic turn.[84] Perhaps that is why the metaphor is expanded for the imagination by adding the predicate *breit* [broad], as if even the smallest leap did not possess the quality of making the ditch infinitely broad, as if it would

* Perhaps the reader will recall what was emphasized in *Fragments* regarding this systematic topsy-turvy feat, that nothing comes into existence by way of necessity (because coming into existence and necessity contradict each other), and far less does something become necessary by having come into existence, since only the necessary cannot become, because it is always presupposed to be.[79]

not be equally difficult for the one who *cannot* leap *at all*, whether the ditch is broad or narrow, as if it were not the dialectically passionate loathing of a leap that makes the ditch infinitely broad, just as Lady Macbeth's passion makes the blood spot so immensely large that the ocean cannot wash it away.[85] Perhaps it is also cunning on Lessing's part to employ the word *ernstlich* [earnestly], because with regard to what it means to leap, especially when the metaphor is developed for the imagination, earnestness is droll enough, inasmuch as it stands in no relation, or in a comic relation, to the leap, since it is not the breadth of the ditch in an external sense that prevents it but the dialectical passion in an internal sense that makes the ditch infinitely broad. To have been very close to doing something already has its comic aspect, but to have been very close to making the leap is nothing whatever, precisely because the leap is the category of decision. And now in utmost earnestness to have wanted to make the leap—yes, that Lessing is indeed a rogue, for surely he has, if anything, with the utmost earnestness made the ditch broad—is that not just like making fun of people! Yet, as is well known, with regard to the leap it is also possible to make fun of people in a more popular manner: one closes one's eyes, grabs oneself by the neck *à la* Münchhausen, and then—then one stands on the other side, on that other side of sound common sense in the promised land of the system.

Furthermore, the term "leap" is linked to Lessing's name also in another way. On the whole, it is rare that any thinker of the modern period calls to mind the beautiful Greek way of philosophizing by ingeniously concentrating himself and his thought-existence in a single brief felicitous statement regarding a certain relation, but Lessing reminds us vividly of the Greeks. His knowledge is not a learned jumble or a ditto ditto genuinely speculative mediation of what every Tom, Dick, and Harry, geniuses, and assistant professors have thought
and written. His merit does not consist in stringing all this VII
splendor on the thread of the historicizing method; no, briefly 80
and simply, he has something of his own. Just as one can cite the watchword of many a Greek thinker instead of naming his

name, so Lessing has also left a last word. It is commonly known that Lessing's "last word" provided the occasion for some scribbling at that time. The enthusiastic and noble Jacobi, who often and with such amiable sympathy speaks of the need of being understood by other thinkers, of the desirability of being in agreement with others, was the father confessor to whom the preservation of Lessing's last word was assigned.[86] It was, of course, difficult to be father confessor to an ironist like Lessing, and Jacobi has had to endure much, undeservedly, inasmuch as he has been unjustly attacked; deservedly, inasmuch as Lessing had certainly not sent for him in the role of father confessor, even less had asked him to publicize the conversation, and least of all to put the accent of pathos in the wrong place.

There is something highly poetic in the entire situation: two pronounced individualities such as Lessing and Jacobi conversing with each other. The inexhaustible spokesman of enthusiasm as observer and the wily Lessing as catechumen. So Jacobi proceeds to examine how matters really stand with Lessing. What happens? Appalled, he discovers that basically Lessing is most certainly a Spinozist.[87] The enthusiast ventures the utmost and proposes to him the one and only saving *salto mortale* [somersault].

Here I must pause for a moment. It might seem, after all, that Jacobi is the originator of the leap.[88] Yet it must be noted, first of all, that Jacobi is really not clear about where the leap essentially belongs. If anything, his *salto mortale* is only a subjectivizing act in comparison with Spinoza's objectivity; it is not a transition from the eternal to the historical. Next, he is not dialectically clear about the leap, that this cannot be expounded or communicated directly, precisely because the leap is an act of isolation, since it is left to the single individual to decide whether he will by virtue of the absurd[89] accept in faith that which indeed cannot be thought. With the aid of eloquence, Jacobi wants to help one to make the leap. But this is a contradiction, and all direct incitement is simply an obstacle to actually doing it, which must not be confused with assurances about wanting to have done it. Suppose that Jacobi him-

self has made the leap; suppose that with the aid of eloquence he manages to persuade a learner to want to do it. Then the
learner has a direct relation to Jacobi and consequently does VII
not himself come to make the leap. The direct relation be- 81
tween one human being and another is naturally much easier and gratifies one's sympathies and one's own need much more quickly and ostensibly more reliably. It is understood directly, and there is no need of that dialectic of the infinite to keep oneself infinitely resigned and infinitely enthusiastic in the sympathy of the infinite, whose secret is the renunciation of the fancy that in his God-relationship one human being is not the equal of another, which makes the presumed teacher a learner who attends to himself and makes all teaching a divine jest, because every human being is essentially taught solely by God.

Now, in relation to Lessing, Jacobi only desires companionship in making the leap; his eloquence is that of one enamored of Lessing, and that is why it is so important to him to have Lessing with him. [90]The dialectical dubiousness of this is promptly noted. The eloquent person, the one who is eternally convinced, feels in himself the strength and the power to win others to his conviction, that is, he is uncertain enough to need the sanction of others in his enthusiastic conviction. On the whole, the enthusiast who in relation to every human being is incapable of expressing his enthusiasm in contrasting form is not the stronger but the weaker and has only a woman's strength, which is in frailty.[91] Jacobi did not understand how to discipline himself artistically so as to be satisfied with expressing the idea existentially. The constraint of isolation, which is specifically posited in the leap, cannot constrain Jacobi. He has to divulge something. He is always bubbling over in the eloquence that in pithiness and substance and lyrical seething ranks at times with Shakespeare but nevertheless seeks to help others in a direct relation to the orator or, as *in casu* [in this case], seeks to win for him the consolation that Lessing is in agreement with him.

Let us proceed. Consequently, when Jacobi to his *horreur* discovers that Lessing is actually a Spinozist, he speaks out of his total conviction. He wants to sweep Lessing off his feet. Lessing replies, "*Gut, sehr gut! Ich kann das alles auch gebrauchen; aber ich kann nicht dasselbe damit machen. Überhaupt gefällt Ihr* Salto mortale *mir nicht übel, und ich begreife wie ein Mann* VII 82 *von Kopf auf diese Art Kopf-unten machen kann, um von der Stelle zu kommen; nehmen Sie mich mit, wenn es angeht* [Good, very good! I can indeed make use of all that; but I cannot do the same thing with it. On the whole, I quite like your *salto mortale*, and I see how a man with a good head can lower his head in a somersault in this way in order to get moving; take me along, if at all possible]."* Here Lessing's irony is superbly apparent; he presumably knows that when someone is to leap, he must certainly do it alone and also be alone in properly understanding that it is an impossibility. His urbanity and his partiality for Jacobi are truly admirable, also his conversational artistry in courteously stating, "*nehmen Sie mich mit—wenn es angeht* [take me along—if at all possible]." And Jacobi proceeds, saying, "*Wenn Sie nur auf die elastische Stelle treten wollen, die mich fortschwingt, so geht es von selbst* [If you will just step on the elastic spot that catapults me, it will come by itself]." That, incidentally, is rather well said, but there is the incorrectness that he wants to make the leap into something objective and the leaping into something analogous to, for example, finding the Archimedean point.[92] The good thing about the reply is that he does not want to have a direct relationship, a direct companionship, in the leap.

Then Lessing's *last* words follow, "*Auch dazu gehört schon ein Sprung, den ich meinen alten Beinen und meinem schweren Kopfe nicht mehr zumuthen darf* [That also takes a leap, which I may no longer expect from my old legs and my heavy head]." Here Lessing is ironic by means of the dialectical, whereas the last turn of phrase has a thoroughly Socratic coloring—[93]speaking of food and drink, doctors, pack asses, and the like,[94] *item* [also] of his old legs and heavy head.[95] Although, as frequently noted, the leap is the decision, Jacobi nevertheless wants to fashion a little transition to it. He, the eloquent speaker, wants

* See Fr. H. Jacobi, *Werke*, IV[1], p. 74.

to entice Lessing. "It does not amount to much," he says, "it is not such a difficult matter. Just step on this elastic spot—then the leap will come by itself." This is a very good example of the pious fraud of eloquence; it is as if someone were to recommend execution by guillotine and say, "This whole business is an easy matter. You just lie down on a board, a string is pulled, then the ax falls down—and you have been executed." But suppose now that being executed is what one does not want, and it is the same with making the leap. When someone is averse to the leap [*Spring*], so averse that this passion makes "the ditch infinitely broad," the most ingeniously contrived springboard [*Springemaskine*] will not help one at all. Lessing perceives very well that the leap, as decisive, is qualitatively dialectical and permits no approximating transition. His reply is therefore a jest. It is far from being dogmatic; it is dialectically altogether correct, is personally evasive, and instead of precipitously devising mediation, he makes use of his old legs and his heavy head. And it goes without saying that whoever has young legs and a light head can easily leap. VII 83

The psychological contrast between Lessing and Jacobi is rounded off in this way. Lessing reposes in himself and feels no need of companionship; therefore he parries ironically and slips away from Jacobi on his old legs—which are unfit for leaping. He does not attempt to convince Jacobi that there is no such thing as the leap.* But Jacobi, despite all his enthusiasm for others, is self-seeking. That he by all means wants to convince Lessing is precisely his need; that he obtrudes upon [*trænge paa*] Lessing so vehemently shows that he has a need for [*trænge til*] Lessing—to play with prepositions, something that Jacobi so greatly relished.[96]

From what was discussed by Jacobi and Mendelssohn, with Emilie (Reimarus)[97] as intermediary, regarding Jacobi's relation to Lessing, one gains a general picture of how inexhaust-

* It was fortunate for Lessing that he did not live in the nineteenth century, which is just as earnest as it is genuinely speculative-dogmatic. He would perhaps have lived to see that some very earnest gentleman with no sense of jest at all would earnestly petition that Lessing should attend confirmation classes again in order to learn earnestness.

ible Lessing was in jesting dialectically (with Greek elation) with Jacobi, whom he otherwise esteemed so highly. According to Jacobi, Lessing once said *mit halbem Lächeln: Er selbst wäre vielleicht das höchste Wesen, und gegenwärtig in dem Zustande der äussersten Contraction* [with half a smile: He himself was perhaps the highest being and currently in a condition of extreme contraction].*[98] No wonder, then, that Lessing was de-
VII 84 clared to be a pantheist. And yet the jest is so explicit (but the remark itself need not therefore be merely jest) and is especially superb in a later reference to the same remark. When he and Jacobi were together at Gleim's place[101] and it started to rain during the meal—something Gleim deplored, since they had planned to walk out into the garden after dinner—Lessing said to Jacobi (presumably again *mit halbem Lächeln*): *Jacobi, Sie wissen, das thue ich vielleicht* [You know, Jacobi, I just might do that].[102]

Incidentally, Mendelssohn, who also happens to have commented on these matters, has quite correctly indicated the lyrical culmination of thinking in the leap. That is, in lyrically seeking to surpass itself, thinking** wills to discover the paradoxical. This presentiment is a unity of jest and earnestness, and all Christian categories are situated at this point. Apart from this point, any and every dogmatic qualification is a *philosophem* [philosophical dictum] that has arisen in the heart of humankind[104] and is to be thought immanently. The last thing

* This confusion is not very easily solved dialectically. In *Fragments*,[99] I have reminded the reader of how it arises and how Socrates' self-knowledge ran aground on the oddity that he did not know for sure whether he was a human being or a more composite creature than Typhon.[100]

** I am, of course, speaking only of thinking as it is in the subjective existing thinker; I have never been able to understand how a human being could become speculative thought, objective speculative thought and pure being. That is, a human being can become many things in the world. As it says in the rhyme, he can become "*Edelmann, Bettelmann, Doctor, Pastor, Schuster, Schneider* [nobleman, beggar, doctor, pastor, shoemaker, tailor] . . . . . ."[103] Thus far I can understand the Germans. He can also become a thinker or a dunderhead, but to become speculative thought is the most incomprehensible of all miracles.

human thought can will is to will beyond itself in the paradoxical. And Christianity is indeed the paradoxical.

Mendelssohn says, "*Zweifeln, ob es nicht etwas giebt, das nicht nur alle Begriffe übersteigt, sondern völlig auszer dem Begriffe liegt, dieses nenne ich einen Sprung über sich selbst hinaus* [To doubt whether there is not something that not only surpasses all concepts but also lies completely beyond the concept, that I call a leap beyond oneself]." Mendelssohn, of course, wants none of it and does not know how to treat it in jest or in earnest.*

This is almost all that can be said about Lessing's relation to the leap. In itself it is not very much, and it is just not dialectically clear what he wanted to make of it; indeed, it is not VII
even clear whether the passage from his own writings may be 85
but a pathos-filled stylistic turn and in his conversation with Jacobi only a Socratic jest, or whether these two contrasts proceed from and are sustained by one and the same categorical thought of the leap. The little that can be found in Lessing has had its importance for me. Before getting a chance to read that volume by Lessing, I had read *Fear and Trembling* by Johannes de Silentio.[105] In that book I had perceived how the leap, according to the author, as the decision κατ' ἐξοχήν [par excellence] becomes specifically decisive for what is Christian and for every dogmatic category.[106] [107]This can be achieved neither through Schelling's intellectual intuition[108] nor through what Hegel, flouting Schelling's idea, wants to put in its place, the method, because the leap is the most decisive protest against the inverse operation of the method.[109] All Christianity is rooted in the paradox, according to *Fear and Trembling*—yes, it is rooted in fear and trembling (which are specifically the desperate categories of Christianity and the leap)—whether one accepts it (that is, is a believer) or rejects it (for the very reason that it is the paradox). Through a subsequent reading of Lessing, the matter certainly did not become clearer, because what L. says is so very little, but to me it was nevertheless an encouragement to see that he was aware of it. It is just too bad that he did not care to pursue this thought himself.

* See Fr. H. Jacobi, *Werke*, IV[1], p. 110.

But then he was not encumbered with "mediation" either, the divine and idolized mediation that works and has worked miracles and has turned human beings into speculative thought and has bewitched Christianity. All honor to mediation! No doubt it can help a person in yet another way, as it presumably helped the author of *Fear and Trembling* to seek the leap as a desperate [110]way out, just as Christianity was a desperate way out when it entered the world and will continue to be that for everyone who actually accepts it. It may very well happen that a fiery and mettlesome steed loses its wind and proud bearing when it is turned into a rental horse and is ridden by every dabbler—but sloth is never victorious in the world of the spirit; it always loses and stays outside. Whether or not Johannes de Silentio became aware of the leap by reading Lessing, I leave undecided.

VII 86 4. Lessing has said: *Wenn Gott in seiner Rechten alle Wahrheit, und in seiner Linken den einzigen immer regen Trieb nach Wahrheit, obschon mit dem Zusatze, mich immer und ewig zu irren, verschlossen hielte, und spräche zu mir: wähle! Ich fiele ihm mit Demuth in seine Linke, und sagte: Vater, gieb! die reine Wahrheit ist ja doch nur für dich allein [If God held all truth enclosed in his right hand, and in his left hand the one and only ever-striving drive for truth, even with the corollary of erring forever and ever, and if he were to say to me: Choose!—I would humbly fall down to him at his left hand and say: Father, give! Pure truth is indeed only for you alone]!* (See Lessing's *S.W.*, V, p. 100.)[111] When Lessing said these words, the system was presumably not finished; alas, and now he is dead! If he were living now, now when the system has been completed for the most part or is at least in the works and will be finished by next Sunday, believe me, Lessing would have clutched it with both hands. He would not have had the time and the propriety and the elation to play in jest, as it were, odds and evens with God and to choose in earnest the left hand. But the system also has more to offer than what God has in both his hands; even at this very moment it has more, not to mention next Sunday, when it will definitely be finished.

The words are found in a little essay ("*Eine Duplik,*" 1778) occasioned by a devout man's defense of the story of the Resurrection[112] against an attack made upon it in the fragments published by Lessing.[113] It is generally known that people could not make out L.'s intention in publishing these fragments. Not even the worthy, learned Hauptpastor Götze could say for sure which passage in the Apocalypse applied to, indeed, was fulfilled in Lessing. To that extent, Lessing has in an odd way compelled people, in their relation to him, to accept his principle. Although results and accomplishments were otherwise plentiful in those days, no one was equal to putting an end to Lessing and having him world-historically butchered, salted, and packed in a paragraph. He was and remained an enigma. If someone now wants to call him forth again—he will get no further with him.

But first an assurance here regarding my own lowly person. I am as willing as anyone to fall down in worship before the system if I could only catch a glimpse of it. So far I have not succeeded, and although I do have young legs, I am almost worn out by running from Herod to Pilate.[114] A few times I have been very close to worshiping, but behold, at the very moment I had already spread my handkerchief on the ground, so as to avoid dirtying my trousers by kneeling, when I for the last time very innocently said to one of the initiates, "Now, tell me honestly, is it indeed completely finished, because if VII 87
that is the case, I will prostrate myself, even if I should ruin a pair of trousers" (on account of the heavy traffic to and from the system, the road was rather muddy)—I would invariably receive the answer, "No, it is not entirely finished yet." And so the system and the kneeling were postponed once again.

System and conclusiveness are just about one and the same, so that if the system is not finished, there is not any system. Elsewhere I have already pointed out that a system that is not entirely finished is a hypothesis, whereas a half-finished system is nonsense. If someone were to declare that this is mere word-splitting, that on the contrary the systematicians themselves say that the system is not finished, I would merely ask: Why do they call it a system? Why speak with a forked tongue at all? When they recite their compendia, they do not mention that anything is missing. Consequently, they induce the less knowledgeable to assume that everything is finished, unless they are writing for readers more knowledgeable than they are themselves, which presumably would strike the systematicians as unthinkable. But if the building is touched, the builder steps forth. He is an exceedingly pleasant man, polite and kind to the visitor. He says: Yes, indeed, we are still involved in building; the system is not entirely finished yet. Did he not, then, know that before; did he not know it when he had his bliss-bestowing invitation issued to everyone? But if he knew it, why did he not say so himself, that is, why did he not abstain from calling the produced fragment a system? For here it is again: a fragment of a system is nonsense.

On the other hand, a continued striving for a system is indeed a striving, and a striving, yes, a continued striving, is indeed what Lessing is talking about. But certainly not a striving for nothing! On the contrary, Lessing speaks of a striving for truth; and he uses a peculiar phrase regarding this urge for truth: *den einzigen immer regen Trieb* [the one and only ever-striving drive]. This word *einzig* [one and only] can scarcely be understood as meaning anything other than the infinite in the same sense as it is higher to have one thought, one only, than to have many thoughts. So these two, Lessing and the systematician, both speak of a continued striving—the only difference is that Lessing is obtuse or truthful enough to call it a continued striving, the systematician sagacious or untruthful enough to call it the system. How would this difference be judged in another context? When commission agent
VII Behrend[115] had lost a silk umbrella, he advertised for a cotton
88 umbrella, because he thought this way: If I say that it is a silk umbrella, the finder will be more easily tempted to keep it. Perhaps the systematician thinks this way: If on the title page or in the newspaper I call my production a continued striving for the truth, alas, who will buy it or admire me; but if I call it the system, the absolute system, everyone will buy the system—if only the difficulty did not remain that what the systematician is selling is not the system.

Let us then proceed, but let us not make sport of each other. I, Johannes Climacus, am neither more nor less than a human being; and I assume that the one with whom I have the honor of conversing is also a human being. If he wants to be speculative thought, pure speculative thought, I must give up conversing with him, because at that moment he becomes invisible to me and to the weak mortal eye of a human being.

Consequently, *(a) a logical system can be given; (b) but a system of existence [Tilværelsens System] cannot be given.*

a.

α. If, however, a logical system is to be constructed, special care must be taken not to incorporate anything that is subject to the dialectic of existence, accordingly, anything that is [*er*] solely by existing [*være til*] or by having existed [*have været til*], not something that is [*er*] simply by being [*være*]. It follows quite simply that Hegel's matchless and matchlessly admired invention—the importation of movement into logic[116] (not to mention that in every other passage one misses even his own attempt to make one believe that it is there)—simply confuses logic.* It is indeed curious to make movement the basis in a VII 89

* The light-mindedness with which systematicians admit that Hegel has perhaps not been successful everywhere in importing movement into logic, much like the grocer who thinks that a few raisins do not matter when the purchase is large—this farcical docility is, of course, contempt for Hegel that not even his most vehement attacker has allowed himself. There have certainly been logical attempts prior to Hegel, but his method is everything.[117] For him and for everyone who has intelligence enough to comprehend what it means to will something great, the absence of it at this or that point cannot be a trivial matter, as when a grocer and a customer bicker about whether there is a little underweight or overweight. Hegel himself has staked his whole reputation on the point of the method. But a method possesses the peculiar VII 89
quality that, viewed abstractly, it is nothing at all; it is a method precisely in the process of being carried out; in being carried out it is a method, and where it is not carried out, it is not a method, and if there is no other method, there is no method at all. To turn Hegel into a rattlebrain must be reserved for his admirers; an attacker will always know how to honor him for having willed something great and having failed to achieve it.

sphere in which movement is inconceivable or to have movement explain logic, whereas logic cannot explain movement.

On this point, however, I am very happy to be able to refer to a man who thinks soundly and fortunately is educated by the Greeks (rare qualities in our age!); a man who has known how to extricate himself and his thought from every trailing, groveling relation to Hegel, from whose fame everyone usually seeks to profit, if in no other way, then by going further, that is, by having absorbed Hegel; a man who has preferred to be content with Aristotle and with himself—I mean Trendlenburg (*Logische Untersuchungen*).[118] One of his merits is that he comprehended movement as the inexplicable presupposition, as the common denominator in which being and thinking are united, and as their continued reciprocity. I cannot attempt here to show the relation of his conception to the Greeks, to Aristotelian thought, or to what, oddly enough, although in a popular sense only, bears a certain resemblance to his presentation: a small section in Plutarch's work on Isis and Osiris.[119] It is by no means my view that Hegelian philosophy has not had a salutary influence on Trendlenburg, but it is fortunate that he has perceived that wanting to improve Hegel's structure, to go further etc., will not do (a mendacious approach by which many a botcher in our age arrogates Hegel's celebrity to himself and mendicantly fraternizes with him); on the other hand, it is fortunate that Trendlenburg, sober like a Greek thinker, without promising everything and without claiming to beatify all humankind, does indeed accomplish much and beatifies whoever would need his guidance in learning about the Greeks.

VII 90 In a logical system, nothing may be incorporated that has a relation to existence, that is not indifferent to existence. The infinite advantage that the logical, by being the objective, possesses over all other thinking is in turn, subjectively viewed, restricted by its being a hypothesis, simply because it is indifferent to existence understood as actuality. This duplexity distinguishes the logical from the mathematical, which has no relation whatever toward or from existence [*Tilværelse*] but has only objectivity—not objectivity and the hypothetical as unity and contradiction in which it is negatively related to existence [*Existents*].

The logical system must not be a mystification, a ventriloquism, in which the content of existence [*Tilværelse*] emerges cunningly and surreptitiously, where logical thought is startled and finds what the Herr Professor or the licentiate has had up his sleeve. Judging between the two can be done more sharply by answering the question: [120]In what sense is a category an abbreviation of existence, whether logical thinking is abstract after existence or abstract without any relation to existence. I would like to treat this question a little more extensively elsewhere, and even if it is not adequately answered, it is always something to have inquired about it in this way.

β. The dialectic of the beginning must be clarified. The almost amusing thing about it, that the beginning is and then in turn is not,[121] because it is the beginning—this true dialectical remark has long enough been like a game that has been played in Hegelian society.

The system, so it is said, begins with the immediate;[122] some, failing to be dialectical, are even oratorical enough to speak of the most immediate of all, although the comparative reflection contained here might indeed become dangerous for the beginning.* The system begins with the immediate and VII 91
therefore without presuppositions and therefore absolutely, that is, the beginning of the system is the absolute beginning. This is entirely correct and has indeed also been adequately admired. But why, then, before the system is begun, has that other equally important, definitely equally important, question not been clarified and its clear implications honored: *How does the system begin with the immediate, that is, does it begin with*

* To show how would become too prolix here. Frequently it is not worth the trouble either, because, after a person has laboriously advanced an objection sharply, from a philosopher's rejoinder he discovers that his misunderstanding was not that he could not understand the idolized philosophy but rather that he had allowed himself to be persuaded to believe that the whole thing was supposed to be something—and not flabby thinking concealed by the most overbearing expressions.

it immediately? The answer to this must certainly be an unconditional no. If the system is assumed to be after existence (whereby a confusion with a system of existence is created), the system does indeed come afterward and consequently does not begin immediately with the immediate with which existence began, even though in another sense existence did not begin with it, because the immediate never is but is annulled when it is. The beginning of the system that begins with the immediate *is then itself achieved through reflection*.

Here is the difficulty, for if one does not let go of this one thought, deceptively or thoughtlessly or in breathless haste to have the system finished, this thought in all its simplicity is capable of deciding that there can be no system of existence and that a logical system must not boast of an absolute beginning, because such a beginning is just like pure being, a pure chimera.

In other words, if a beginning cannot be made immediately with the immediate (which would then be conceived as a fortuitous event or a miracle, that is, which would mean not to think), but this beginning must be achieved through reflection, then the question arises very simply (alas, if only I am not put in the doghouse on account of my simplicity, because everyone can understand my question—and consequently must feel ashamed of the questioner's popular knowledge): How do I bring to a halt the reflection set in motion in order to reach that beginning? Reflection has the notable quality of being infinite. But being infinite must in any case mean that it cannot stop of its own accord, because in stopping itself it indeed uses itself and can be stopped only in the same way as a sickness is cured if it is itself allowed to prescribe the remedy, that is, the sickness is promoted. Perhaps this infinity of reflection is the bad or spurious infinity.[123] In that case, we are indeed almost finished, since the spurious infinity is reputedly something despicable that one must give up, the sooner the better. In that connection, may I not ask a question: How is it that Hegel and all Hegelians, who are generally supposed to
VII be dialecticians, at this point become angry, yes, as angry as
92 Germans? Or is "spurious" a dialectical qualification? From

where does such a predicate enter logic? How do scorn and contempt and ways of frightening find a place as legitimate means of movement within logic, so that the absolute beginning is assumed by the individual because he is afraid of what his neighbors on all sides will think of him if he does not do it? Is not "spurious" an ethical category?*

What do I mean by speaking of the spurious infinity? I am charging the individual in question with not willing to stop the infinity of reflection. Am I requiring something of him, then? But on the other hand, in a genuinely speculative way, I assume that reflection stops of its own accord. Why, then, do I require something of him? And what do I require of him? I require a resolution. And in that I am right, for only in that way can reflection be stopped. But, on the other hand, it is never right for a philosopher to make sport of people and at one moment have reflection stop of its own accord in the absolute beginning and at the next moment taunt someone who has only one flaw, that he is obtuse enough to believe the first, taunt him so as to help him in this fashion to the absolute beginning, which then occurs in two ways. But if a resolution is required, presuppositionlessness is abandoned. The beginning can occur only when reflection is stopped, and reflection can be stopped only by something else, and this something else is something altogether different from the logical, since it is a resolution. Only when the beginning, at which point reflection comes to a halt, is a breakthrough, so that the absolute beginning itself breaks forth through the endlessly perpetuated reflection—only then is the beginning presuppositionless. But if it is a break whereby reflection is broken off in order that the beginning can emerge, then this beginning is not absolute, since it has occurred by a μετάβασις εἰς ἄλλο γένος [shifting from one genus to another].

When a beginning with the immediate is achieved by reflec- VII 93

* And if it is not that, it is in any case an esthetic category, as when Plutarch states that some have assumed one world because they feared that otherwise the result would be an unlimited and embarrassing infinity of worlds (εὐθὺς ἀορίστου καὶ χαλεπῆς ἀπειρίας ὑπολαμβανούσης. *De defectu oraculorum*, XXII[124]).

tion, the immediate must mean something different from what it usually does. Hegelian logicians have correctly discerned this, and therefore they define the immediate, with which logic begins, as follows: the most abstract remainder after an exhaustive abstraction.[125] There is no objection to this definition, but it is certainly objectionable that they do not respect what they themselves are saying, inasmuch as this definition indirectly states that there is no absolute beginning. "How is that?" I hear someone say. "When one has abstracted from everything, is there not then, etc.?" Indeed, *when* one has abstracted from everything. Let us be human beings.[126] Like the act of reflection, this act of abstraction is infinite; so how do I bring it to a halt—and it is indeed first when . . . . . that . . . . . .[127] Let us even venture an imaginary construction in thought.[128] Let that act of infinite abstraction be *in actu* [in actuality]; the beginning is not an act of abstraction but comes afterward. But then with what do I begin, now that there has been an abstraction from everything? Alas, at this point a Hegelian, deeply moved, perhaps would collapse on my chest and blissfully stammer: With nothing. And this is precisely what the system declares—that it begins with nothing.[129] But I must pose my second question: How do I begin with this nothing? If, namely, the act of infinite abstraction is not the kind of trick of which two can very well be done at the same time, if, on the contrary, it is the most strenuous work that can be done—what then? Then all my strength will go into maintaining it. If I do not use all my strength, I do not abstract from everything. If, then, on this presupposition I make a beginning, I do not begin with nothing, simply because at the moment of beginning I did not abstract from everything. This means that if it is possible for a human being, thinking, to abstract from everything, it is impossible for him to do more, since this act, provided that it does not surpass human strength altogether, in any case completely exhausts it. To become tired of the act of abstraction and thus to manage to begin is only an explanation befitting grocers, who are not particular about a little irregularity.

The expression "to begin with nothing," even apart from

its relation to the infinite act of abstraction, is itself deceptive. That is, to begin with nothing is neither more nor less than a new paraphrasing of the very dialectic of beginning. The beginning is and in turn is not, simply because it is the beginning, VII 94 something that can also be expressed in this way: the beginning begins with nothing. It is merely a new expression, not a single step ahead. In the one instance, I only think a beginning *in abstracto*; in the other instance, I think the relation of the equally abstract beginning to a something with which a beginning is made. Now it is quite properly manifest that this something, indeed, the only something that corresponds to such a beginning, is nothing. But this is merely a tautological paraphrasing of the second thesis: the beginning is not. "The beginning is not" and "the beginning begins with nothing" are altogether identical theses, and I do not move from the spot.

What if, rather than speaking or dreaming of an absolute beginning, we speak of a leap?[130] To want to be satisfied with a "mostly," an "as good as," a "one can almost say that," an "if you sleep on it until tomorrow, you may well say that" merely shows that one is related to Trop, who little by little went so far as to assume that having almost taken the bar examination was the same as having taken it.[131] Everyone laughs at this, but when one chatters speculatively in the same manner in the realm of truth, in the shrine of science and scholarship, then it is good philosophy—genuine speculative philosophy. Lessing was no speculative philosopher; therefore he assumed the opposite, that an infinitely little distance makes the ditch infinitely broad, because the leap itself makes the ditch that broad.

It is very odd—the Hegelians, who in logic know that reflection is stopped by itself and that doubting everything flips over into its opposite by itself[132] (a true sailor's yarn, that is, truly a sailor's yarn), know for daily use, however, when they are pleasant people, when they are like the rest of us (only more learned and gifted etc., something I shall always be willing to admit)—they know that reflection can be stopped only by a leap. Let us dwell on this point for a moment. If the in-

dividual does not stop reflection, he will be infinitized in reflection, that is, no decision is made.* By thus going astray in reflection, the individual really becomes objective; more and more he loses the decision of subjectivity and the return into
VII himself. Yet it is assumed that reflection can stop itself objec-
95 tively, whereas it is just the other way around; reflection cannot be stopped objectively, and when it is stopped subjectively, it does not stop of its own accord, but it is the subject who stops it.

For example, as soon as Rötscher (who in his book on Aristophanes does indeed understand the necessity of transition in the world-historical development,[133] and who in the realm of logic must have understood the passage of reflection through itself to the absolute beginning) sets himself the task of interpreting Hamlet, he knows that reflection is stopped only by a resolution.[134] He does not assume (shall I say "oddly enough"?), oddly enough, he does not assume that Hamlet finally arrived at the absolute beginning by continuing to reflect; but in logic he assumes (shall I say "oddly enough"?), oddly enough, there he most likely assumes that the passage of reflection through itself comes to a halt at the absolute beginning. This I do not understand, and it pains me not to understand it, because I have admiration for Rötscher's talent, for his classical education, for his esthetically sensitive and yet primitive[135] conception of psychological phenomena.

What has been said here about a beginning in logic (that the same thing shows that there is no system of existence will be pursued in detail in *b*) is very plain and simple. I am almost embarrassed to say it or embarrassed to have to say it, embarrassed because of my situation—that a poor pamphlet writer, who would rather be worshiping on his knees before the system, should be constrained to say such a thing. What has been said could be stated in yet another way whereby it would perhaps make an impression on someone or other because the

* Perhaps the reader will recall that when the issue becomes objective, there is no question of an eternal happiness, because this lies precisely in subjectivity and in decision.

presentation would recall more specifically the scholarly disputes in the past.[136] It would then become a question of the importance of the Hegelian phenomenology for the system,[137] whether it is an introduction, whether it remains outside, and if it is an introduction, whether it is in turn incorporated in the
system; further, whether Hegel may not even have the amaz- VII
ing merit of having written not only the system but two or 96
even three systems, which always takes a matchless systematic head, and which nevertheless seems to be the case, since the system is completed more than once etc. Actually, all this has been said often enough, but frequently it has also been said in a confusing way. A large book[138] has been written about it. First everything is said that Hegel has said, and thereafter consideration is given to this or that later addition, all of which merely diverts attention and shrouds in distracting prolixity what can be stated very briefly.

γ. In order to shed light on logic, it might be desirable to become oriented psychologically in the state of mind of someone who thinks the logical—what kind of dying to oneself is required for that purpose, and to what extent the imagination plays a part in it. The following is again another meager and very simple comment, but it may be quite true and not at all superfluous: a philosopher has gradually come to be such a marvelous creature that not even the most prodigal imagination has invented anything quite so fabulous. How, if at all, is the empirical *I* related to the pure *I-I*?[139] Whoever wants to be a philosopher will certainly also want to be somewhat informed on this point and above all not want to become a ludicrous creature by being transmogrified—*eins, zwei, drei, kokolorum* [one, two, three, hocus pocus]—into speculative thought. If the person occupied with logical thought is also human enough not to forget that he is an existing individual, even if he has finished the system, the fantasticality and the charlatanry will gradually vanish. And even though it takes an eminently logical head to recast Hegel's logic, only sound common sense is needed for the person who at one time enthusiastically believed in the great thing Hegel claimed to have

done and who demonstrated his enthusiasm by believing [*tro*] it, and his enthusiasm for Hegel by crediting [*tiltro*] him with it—and it takes only sound common sense to perceive that in many places Hegel behaved irresponsibly—not toward grocers, who believe only half of what a person says anyway, but toward enthusiastic youths who believed him. Even if such a young person was not exceptionally and splendidly endowed, yet when he has had the enthusiasm to believe the highest, as attributed to Hegel, when he has had the enthusiasm to despair over himself in a dubious moment in order not to abandon Hegel—when such a young person comes to himself again, he has a right to demand the nemesis of having laughter consume in Hegel what laughter may legitimately claim as its
VII own. And such a young person has indeed vindicated Hegel
97 in a way much different from that of many an adherent who
in deceptive asides would now make Hegel everything, now a trifle.

b.

A system of existence [*Tilværelsens System*] cannot be given. Is there, then, not such a system? That is not at all the case. Neither is this implied in what has been said. Existence itself is a system—for God, but it cannot be a system for any existing [*existerende*] spirit. System and conclusiveness correspond to each other, but existence is the very opposite. Abstractly viewed, system and existence cannot be thought conjointly, because in order to think existence, systematic thought must think it as annulled and consequently not as existing. Existence is the spacing that holds apart; the systematic is the conclusiveness that combines.

Actually there now develops a deception, an illusion, which *Fragments* has attempted to point out.[140] I must now refer to this work, namely, to the question of whether the past is more necessary than the future.[141] That is, when an existence is a thing of the past, it is indeed finished, it is indeed concluded, and to that extent it is turned over to the systematic view. Quite so—but for whom? Whoever is himself existing cannot

gain this conclusiveness outside existence, a conclusiveness that corresponds to the eternity into which the past has entered. Even if a good-natured thinker is so absentminded as to forget that he himself is existing, speculative thought and absentmindedness are still not quite the same thing. On the contrary, that he himself is existing implies the claim of existence upon him and that his existence, yes, if he is a great individual, that his existence at the present time may, as past, in turn have the validity of conclusiveness for a systematic thinker. But who, then, is this systematic thinker? Well, it is he who himself is outside existence and yet in existence, who in his eternity is forever concluded and yet includes existence within himself—it is God. So why the deception! Just because the world has lasted now for six thousand years,[142] does existence therefore not have the very same claim upon the existing individual that it has always had, which is not that he in make- VII
believe should be a contemplating spirit but that he in actuality 98
should be an existing spirit. All understanding comes afterward.[143] Whereas an individual existing now undeniably comes afterward in relation to the six thousand years that preceded, the curiously ironic consequence would emerge—if we assumed that he came to understand them systematically—that he would not come to understand himself as an existing being, because he himself would acquire no existence, because he himself would have nothing that should be understood afterward. It follows that such a thinker must be either the good Lord or a fantastical *quodlibet* [anything].[144] Certainly everyone will perceive the immorality in this, and certainly everyone will also perceive that what another author has observed regarding the Hegelian system is entirely in order: that through Hegel a system, the absolute system, was brought to completion—without having an ethics.[145] By all means, let us smile at the ethical-religious fantasies of the Middle Ages in asceticism and the like, but above all let us not forget that the speculative, farcical exaggeration of becoming an *I-I*—and then *qua* human being often such a philistine that no enthusiast would have cared to lead such a life—is equally ludicrous.

So let us ask very simply, as a Greek youth would ask his master (and if the lofty wisdom can explain everything else but cannot answer a simple question, one surely sees that the world is out of joint), about the impossibility of a system of existence: Who is supposed to write or finish such a system? Surely a human being, unless we are to resume the peculiar talk about a human being's becoming speculative thought, a subject-object. Consequently, a human being—and surely a living, that is, an existing, human being. Or if the speculative thought that produces the system is the joint effort of these various thinkers, in what final conclusion does this fellowship combine? How does it come to light? Surely through a human being? And how, in turn, do the individual thinkers relate themselves to this effort; what are the middle terms between the particular and the world-historical; and in turn what sort of being is the one who is stringing it all on the systematic thread? Is he a human being or is he speculative thought? But if he is a human being, then he is indeed existing. Now, all in
VII 99 all, there are two ways for an existing individual: either he can do everything to forget that he is existing and thereby manage to become comic (the comic contradiction of wanting to be what one is not, for example, that a human being wants to be a bird is no more comic than the contradiction of not wanting to be what one is, as *in casu* [in this case] an existing individual, just as in the use of language it is comic when someone forgets his name, which signifies not so much forgetting his name as the singularity of his nature), because existence possesses the remarkable quality that an existing person exists whether he wants to or not; or he can direct all his attention to his existing. It is from this side that an objection must first be made to modern speculative thought, that it has not a false presupposition but a comic presupposition, occasioned by its having forgotten in a kind of world-historical absentmindedness what it means to be a human being, not what it means to be human in general, for even speculators might be swayed to consider that sort of thing, but what it means that we, you and I and he, are human beings, each one on his own.

The existing individual who directs all his attention to the actuality that *he* is existing will approvingly look upon those words of Lessing about a continued striving as a beautiful saying, not as something that gained its author immortal fame, because the saying is so very simple, but as something every attentive person must certify. The existing individual who forgets that he is existing will become more and more absentminded, and just as people occasionally set down the fruits of their *otium* [leisure] in books, so we may expect the expected existential system as the fruit of his absentmindedness—well, not all of us, but only those who are as absentminded as he is. Whereas the Hegelian system in absentmindedness goes ahead and becomes a system of existence, and what is more, is finished—without having an ethics (the very home of existence), that other simpler philosophy, presented by an existing individual for existing individuals, is especially intent upon advancing the ethical.

As soon as it is remembered that philosophizing is not speaking fantastically to fantastical beings but speaking to existing individuals, consequently that a decision about whether a continued striving is somewhat inferior to systematic conclusiveness is not to be made fantastically *in abstracto*, but that the question is what existing beings have to be satisfied with insofar as they are existing—then the continued striving will be unique in not involving illusion. Even if a person has
achieved the highest, the repetition by which he must indeed VII
fill out his existence, if he is not to go backward (or become a 100
fantastical being), will again be a continued striving, because here in turn the conclusiveness is moved ahead and postponed. This is just like the Platonic conception of love; it is a want, and not only does that person feel a want who craves something he does not have but also that person who desires the continued possession of what he has.[146] In the system and in the fifth act of the drama, one has a positive conclusiveness speculatively-fantastically and esthetically-fantastically, but such a conclusiveness is only for fantastical beings.

The continued striving is the expression of the existing subject's ethical life-view. The continued striving must therefore not be understood metaphysically, but neither is there any individual who exists metaphysically. Thus through a misunderstanding a contrast could be drawn between systematic conclusiveness and the continued striving for truth. One might then be able, and perhaps has even tried, to bear in mind the Greek notion of continually wanting to be a learner.[147] But that is only a misunderstanding in this sphere. On the contrary, ethically understood, the continued striving is the consciousness of being an existing individual, and the continued learning the expression of the perpetual actualization, which at no moment is finished as long as the subject is existing; the subject is aware of this and is therefore not deluded. But Greek philosophy had a continual relation to ethics. That was why continually wanting to be a learner was not regarded as a great discovery or the inspired undertaking of an exceptional individual, since it was neither more nor less than the understanding that one is existing and that to be conscious of this is no merit but to forget it is thoughtlessness.

So-called pantheistic systems have frequently been cited and attacked by saying that they cancel freedom and the distinction between good and evil. This is perhaps expressed just as definitely by saying that every such system fantastically volatilizes the concept *existence*. But this should be said not only of pantheistic systems, for it would have been better to show that
VII every system must be pantheistic simply because of the con-
101 clusiveness. Existence must be annulled in the eternal before the system concludes itself. No existing remainder may be left behind, not even such a tiny little dingle-dangle as the existing Herr Professor who is writing the system. [148]But the issue is not presented this way. No, the pantheistic systems are contested, partly with tumultuous aphorisms that again and again promise a new system, partly with a compilation that is supposed to be a system and has a separate paragraph in which it is declared that emphasis is placed on the concepts "existence" and "actuality." That such a paragraph mocks the entire system, that instead of being a paragraph in the system it is an absolute protest against the system, is of no consequence to

busy systematic triflers.[149] If the concept of existence is actually to be emphasized, this cannot be stated directly in a paragraph in a system, and all direct oaths and "the devil take me" only make the didacticizing upside-downness even more ludicrous. That existence is actually emphasized must be expressed in an essential form, and in relation to the illusiveness of existence this is an indirect form—that there is no system. Yet this must not in turn become a reassuring standardized formula, because the indirect expression will always be regenerated in the form. In committee deliberations, it is quite all right to include a dissenting vote, but a system that has a dissenting vote as a paragraph within it is a queer monstrosity. No wonder, then, that the system survives. It proudly ignores objections; and if it comes across a particular objection that appears to draw a little attention, the systematic entrepreneurs proceed to have a copyist make a copy of the objection, which is thereupon recorded in the system, and with the bookbinding the system is finished.

The systematic idea is subject-object, is the unity of thinking and being; existence, on the other hand, is precisely the separation. From this it by no means follows that existence is thoughtless, but existence has spaced and does space subject from object, thought from being. Objectively understood, thinking is pure thinking, which just as abstractly-objectively corresponds to its object, which in turn is therefore itself, and truth is the correspondence of thinking with itself. This objective thinking has no relation to the existing subjectivity, and while the difficult question always remains—namely, how the existing subject gains entrance into this objectivity in which subjectivity is pure abstract subjectivity (which again is an objective qualification and does not signify any existing human being)—it is certain that the existing subjectivity evaporates VII 102
more and more. And finally, if it is possible that a human being can become such a thing and that all this is not something of which he at best can become cognizant through imagination, this existing subjectivity becomes a pure abstract co-knowledge [*Medviden*] in and knowledge of this pure relation between thinking and being, this pure identity, indeed this tau-

tology, because here being does not mean that the thinking person is, but basically only that he is a thinker.

The existing subject, however, is existing, and so indeed is every human being. Yet let us not do the wrong of calling the objective tendency impious, pantheistic self-worship but rather view it as a venture in the comic, because the idea that from now on to the end of the world nothing should be said except what would suggest a further improvement in a nearly finished system is simply a systematic consequence for systematizers.[150]

By beginning straightway with ethical categories against the objective tendency, one does wrong and fails to hit the mark, because one has nothing in common with the attacked. But by remaining within the metaphysical, one can employ the comic, which also is in the metaphysical sphere, in order to overtake such a transfigured professor. If a dancer could leap very high, we would admire him, but if he wanted to give the impression that he could fly—even though he could leap higher than any dancer had ever leapt before—let laughter overtake him. Leaping means to belong essentially to the earth and to respect the law of gravity so that the leap is merely the momentary, but flying means to be set free from telluric conditions, something that is reserved exclusively for winged creatures, perhaps also for inhabitants of the moon, perhaps—and perhaps that is also where the system will at long last find its true readers. To be a human being has been abolished, and every speculative thinker confuses himself with humankind, whereby he becomes something infinitely great and nothing at all. In absentmindedness, he confuses himself with humankind, just as the opposition press uses "we" and the skippers say "the devil take me." But having cursed for a long time, one finally returns to the direct statement, because all swearing cancels itself; and when one has learned that every urchin can say "we," one learns that it nevertheless means a little more to be *one*; and when one sees that every cellar dweller[151] can play the game of being humankind, one finally perceives
VII that to be simply and solely a human being means something
103 more than playing party games this way. And one thing

more—when a cellar dweller plays this game, everyone thinks it ludicrous; and yet it is just as ludicrous when the greatest human being does it. And in that regard one may laugh at him and, as is fitting, still have respect for his abilities, his learning, etc.[152]

SECTION II[153]

THE SUBJECTIVE ISSUE, OR HOW SUBJECTIVITY MUST BE CONSTITUTED IN ORDER THAT THE ISSUE CAN BE MANIFEST TO IT

Chapter I[154] VII 104

Becoming Subjective

What ethics would have to judge if becoming subjective were not the highest task assigned to a human being; what must be disregarded in a closer understanding of this task; examples of thinking oriented to becoming subjective

Objectively, one continually speaks only about the case in point; subjectively, one speaks about the subject and subjectivity—and see, the subjectivity itself is the case in point. It must continually be insisted upon that the subjective issue is not something about the case in point but is the subjectivity itself. In other words, since the issue is the decision and all decision, as shown previously, is rooted in subjectivity, it is important that objectively there be no trace whatever of any case in point, because at that very moment the subjective individual wants to evade some of the pain and crisis of decision, that is, wants to make the issue somewhat objective. If the introductory intellectual discipline is waiting for one more book before the matter is submitted to judgment, if the system lacks one more paragraph, if the speaker holds one more argument in reserve—then the decision is postponed. Thus there is not a question of the truth of Christianity here in the sense that if this was decided the subjective individual would then be ready and willing to accept it. No, the question is VII 105
about the subject's acceptance of it. And here it must be regarded as perdition's illusion (which has remained ignorant of the fact that the decision is rooted in subjectivity) or as an equivocation of illusiveness (which shoves off the decision by objective treatment in which there is no decision in all eternity) to assume that this transition from something objective

to a subjective acceptance follows directly of its own accord, since precisely this is the decisive point and an objective acceptance (*sit venia verbo* [pardon the expression]) is paganism or thoughtlessness.

Christianity wants to give the single individual an eternal happiness, a good that is not distributed in bulk but only to one, and to one at a time. Even though Christianity assumes that subjectivity, as the possibility of appropriation, is the possibility of receiving this good, it nevertheless does not assume that as a matter of course the subjectivity is all set, as a matter of course has even an actual idea of the significance of this good. This development or remaking of the subjectivity, its infinite concentration in itself under a conception of the infinite's highest good, an eternal happiness, is the developed possibility of the subjectivity's first possibility. Christianity, therefore, protests against all objectivity; it wants the subject to be infinitely concerned about himself. What it asks about is the subjectivity; the truth of Christianity, if it is at all, is only in this; objectively, it is not at all. And even if it is only in one single subject, then it is only in him, and there is greater Christian joy in heaven over this one[155] than over world history and the system, which as objective powers are incommensurate with the essentially Christian.

[156]It is generally thought that to be subjective is no art. Well, of course, every human being is something of a subject. But now to become what one is as a matter of course—who would waste his time on that? That would indeed be the most dispensable of all tasks in life. Quite so. But that is why it is already so very difficult, indeed, the most difficult of all, because every human being has a strong natural desire and drive to become something else and more. That is how it is with all apparently insignificant tasks: just this apparent insignificance makes them infinitely difficult, because the task does not
VII clearly beckon and thus lend support to the aspirer, but works
106 against him so that it takes an infinite effort just to discover the task, that is, that this is the task, a drudgery from which one is otherwise exempted. To think about the simple, something that the simple person also knows, is extremely deter-

ring, for even through the most extreme effort the difference itself by no means becomes obvious to the sensate person. No, then the grandiose is glorious in a quite different way.

[157]When one ignores this little Socratically jesting and Christianly infinitely concerned distinction between being a so-called subject of sorts and being a subject or becoming one and being what one is by having become that—then the admired wisdom turns out to be that the subject's task is to strip away more and more of his subjectivity and become more and more objective. From this it is easy to see what this guidance understands by being a so-called subject of sorts, that it thereby quite correctly understands the accidental, the angular, the selfish, the eccentric, etc., of which every human being can have plenty. Christianity does not deny, either, that such things are to be discarded; it has never been a friend of impudent antics. But the difference is simply that science and scholarship want to teach that becoming objective is the way, whereas Christianity teaches that the way is to become subjective, that is, truly to become a subject. Lest this seem to be a verbal dispute, let it be said that Christianity explicitly wants to intensify passion to its highest, but passion is subjectivity, and objectively it does not exist at all.

[158]In an odd indirect and satirical way, it is often enough enjoined—although people do not take the lesson to heart—that the guidance of science and scholarship is misguidance. Although we are all so-called subjects of sorts and work at becoming objective, something in which many people have considerable brutish success, poetry walks about in troubled concern and seeks its object. Although we are all subjects, poetry must be satisfied with a very sparse selection of subjects that it can use; and yet poetry definitely must have subjective individuals. So why does it not take from among our honored selves the very first one to come along? Alas, no, he will not do, and if he does not want to do anything but become objective, then he will never do. This does seem to suggest that to be a subject is something distinctive. Why have only a few become immortal as inspired lovers, a few as noble heroes, etc., if everyone in every generation was that as a matter of

course by being a subject as a matter of course? But to be a lover, a hero, etc. is reserved specifically for subjectivity, be-
VII 107 cause objectively one does not become that.

And now the clergy! Why is there a certain core of pious men and women to whose venerable remembrance the discourse always returns? Why does the pastor not take from among our honored selves the first one to come along and make that person the prototype—for we are all so-called subjects of sorts. And yet piety is rooted precisely in subjectivity; one does not become pious objectively.

Behold, erotic love is a qualification of subjectivity, and yet lovers are very rare. Indeed, we do say (in about the same way people talk about being a subject of sorts): There went a couple of lovers, there is another couple, last Sunday banns were read for sixteen couples, a couple of lovers living in Stormgade[159] cannot get along—but when poetry transfigures erotic love in its celebratory conception of it, the name lauded sometimes takes us back several centuries, whereas daily life puts us in about the same humor as funeral orations usually do—since, of course, a hero is buried every moment. Is this just chicanery on the part of poetry, which is ordinarily a friendly power, a comforter by elevating us in the contemplation of the distinguished—distinguished by what? Well, by subjectivity. So, then, there is something distinctive in being a subjective individual.

Behold, faith is indeed the highest passion of subjectivity. But just pay attention to what the clergy say about how rarely it is found in the community of believers (this phrase, "the community of believers," is used in about the same sense as when people speak of what is called a subject of sorts). Stop right there; do not be so ironic as to inquire further about how rarely faith is perhaps found among the clergy! Is this merely a sly strategy on the part of the clergy, who have dedicated themselves to caring for our souls by enrapturing us in devotional services, whereas the longing of the soul yearns for those transfigured ones—which transfigured ones? Well, those who had faith. But faith is indeed rooted in subjectivity—so, then, there is something distinctive in being a subjective individual.

The objective orientation (which wants to turn everyone into an observer [*Betragter*][160] and at its maximum into such an observer that, almost like a ghost, he is easily confused with the prodigious spirit of ages past) naturally wants to hear nothing and know nothing except that which stands in relation to itself. [161]If within the given presupposition a person is fortunate enough to be able to be of service with some information regarding a perhaps previously unknown tribe that now, aided by a flag, will join the paragraph parade, if within the given presupposition he is competent to assign China a place other than the one it has hitherto occupied in the system- VII 108
atic procession,[162] then he is welcome. Anything else is normal-school rigmarole, inasmuch as it is supposed to be certain that the objective trend toward becoming an observer is in modern linguistic usage the *ethical* answer to the question of what I am to do ethically. (To be an observer, that is the ethical! That a person ought to be an observer is the *ethical* answer—otherwise one is compelled to assume that there is no question whatever about the ethical and hence no answer either.) And it is supposed to be certain that world history is the task assigned to our observing nineteenth century—the objective orientation is the way and the truth.[163]

Let us, however, very simply review for ourselves a little moot point of subjectivity regarding the objective orientation. Just as *Fragments* called attention to a little introductory observation[164] before proceeding to point out the idea's world-historical process *in concreto*—what it means that the idea becomes historical—so I, too, shall now pause with a few introductory observations regarding the objective orientation: *what ethics would have to judge if becoming a subjective individual were not the highest task assigned to every human being.* What must it judge? Well, it must, of course, be driven to despair, but what does the system care about that? It is indeed consistent enough not to allow ethics to enter into the system.

The world-historical idea increasingly concentrates everything systematically.[165] What a Sophist once said, that he

could carry the whole world in a nutshell,[166] now seems to be accomplished in modern surveys of world history: they are becoming more and more compendious. It is not my intention to point out the comic in this. However, through various thoughts leading to the same goal, I shall attempt to clarify what ethics and the ethical object to in this entire order of things. In our day, it is not a matter of a particular scholar's or thinker's occupying himself with world history; no, the whole age is clamoring for world history. Yet ethics and the ethical, by being the essential stronghold of individual existence, have an irrefutable claim upon every existing individual, an irrefutable claim of such a nature that whatever a person achieves in the world, even the most amazing thing, is nevertheless dubious if he himself has not been ethically clear when he chose and has not made his choice ethically clear to
VII himself. The ethical quality is jealous of itself and spurns the
109 most amazing quantity.

Therefore ethics looks with a suspicious eye at all world-historical knowledge, because this easily becomes a trap, a demoralizing esthetic diversion for the knowing subject, because the distinction between what does and does not become world-historical is quantitative-dialectical. That is also why the absolute ethical distinction between good and evil is world-historically-esthetically neutralized in the esthetic-metaphysical category of "the great," "the momentous," to which the bad and the good have equal access. In the world-historical, an essential role is played by factors of another kind, different from the ethical-dialectical: namely, the accidental, circumstances, that play of forces in which the reshaping totality of historical life absorbs the individual's action in order to transform it into something different that does not directly belong to him. Neither by willing the good to the utmost of his ability nor by willing evil with diabolical callousness is a person assured of becoming world-historical; even in the case of misfortune, it holds true that it takes luck to become world-historical. How, then, does an individual become world-historical? Ethically viewed, he becomes world-historical by accident. But ethics also considers unethical the transition whereby a person abandons the ethical quality in order to try his hand, cravingly, wishfully, etc., at the quantifying other.

An age and a person can be immoral [*usædelig*] in various ways, but it is also immoral or at least a temptation to consort too much with world history, a temptation that can easily lead a person to want also to be world-historical when the time comes that he himself is going to act. By continually being occupied as an observer of the accidental, that *accessorium* [addition] by which world-historical figures become world-historical, a person is easily misled into confusing this *accessorium* with the ethical and easily misled, unhealthily, flirtingly, and cowardly, to being concerned about the accidental, instead, himself existing, of being infinitely concerned about the ethical. Perhaps the reason our age is dissatisfied when it is going to act is that it has been coddled by observing. That is perhaps why there are so many fruitless attempts to become something more than one is by lumping together socially in the hope of impressing the spirit of history numerically. Spoiled by constant association with world history, people want the momentous and only that, are concerned only with the accidental, the world-historical outcome, instead of being concerned with the essential, the innermost, freedom, the ethical.

In other words, continual association with the world-his- VII
torical makes a person incompetent to act. True ethical enthu- 110
siasm consists in willing to the utmost of one's capability, but also, uplifted in divine jest, in never thinking whether or not one thereby achieves something. As soon as the will begins to cast a covetous eye on the outcome, the individual begins to become immoral—the energy of the will becomes torpid, or it develops abnormally into an unhealthy, unethical, mercenary hankering that, even if it achieves something great, does not achieve it ethically—the individual demands something other than the ethical itself. A truly great ethical individuality would consummate his life as follows: he would develop himself to the utmost of his capability; in the process he perhaps would produce a great effect in the external world, but this would not occupy him at all, because he would know that the external is not in his power and therefore means nothing either

pro or *contra.* He would remain in ignorance about it, lest he be delayed by the external and fall into its temptation, because that which a logician fears most, an erroneous inference, a μετάβασις εἰς ἄλλο γένος [shifting from one genus to another], the ethicist equally fears drawing a conclusion or making a transition from the ethical to something other than the ethical. He would, then, remain in ignorance about it through a resolution of the will, and even in death he would *will* not to know that his life had had any significance other than that of having ethically prepared the development of his soul. Then if the power governing all things would want to dispose circumstances so that he became a world-historical figure—well, that is something he would first inquire about jestingly in eternity, for not until then is there time for the light-minded questions of carelessness.

In other words, if a person cannot by his own efforts, in freedom, by willing the good, become a world-historical figure—which is impossible precisely because it is only possible, that is, perhaps possible, that is, dependent on something else—then it is unethical to be concerned about it. And when, instead of renouncing this concern and tearing himself loose from its temptation, a person prinks it up with the pious appearance of benefiting others, he is immoral and wants sneakily to insinuate into his account with God the thought that God nevertheless does need him just a little bit. But this is obtuseness, for God needs no human being. How highly embarrassing to be Creator if it turned out that God came to need the creature. On the contrary, God can require everything of every human being, everything and for nothing, since every human being is an unworthy servant,[167] and the ethically inspired person is different from others only in knowing this and in hating and loathing all deception.

When a headstrong person is battling with his contemporaries and endures it all but also shouts, "Posterity, history
VII will surely make manifest that I spoke the truth," then people
111 believe that he is inspired. Alas, no, he is just a bit smarter than
the utterly obtuse people. He does not choose money and the prettiest girl or the like; he chooses world-historical impor-

tance—yes, he knows very well what he is choosing. But in relation to God and the ethical, he is a deceitful lover; he is also one of those for whom Judas became a guide (Acts 1:16)—he, too, is selling his relationship with God, though not for money. And although he perhaps reforms an entire age through his zeal and teaching, he confounds existence *pro virili* [to the very extent of his powers], because his own form of existence is not adequate to his teaching, because by excepting himself he establishes a teleology that renders existence meaningless.

A king or a philosopher can perhaps be served in a finite sense by a sagacious, talented fellow who safeguards the king's power and upholds the philosopher's teaching and binds everyone in submission to the king and the philosopher, although he himself is neither a good subordinate nor a true adherent. But in relation to God this is rather obtuse. The deceitful lover who does not want to be faithful as lover, but only as world-historical entrepreneur, will not be faithful to the utmost. He does not want to understand that there is nothing between him and God but the ethical; he does not want to understand that he ought to be made enthusiastic by it; he does not want to understand that God, without doing any injustice and without denying his nature, which is love, could create a human being endowed with capacities unmatched by all others, place him in a remote spot, and say to him, "Now go and live the human life through with a strenuousness unmatched by all others; work so that one-half would be sufficient to transform an age, but you and I are alone in this. All your effort will have no importance whatever for any other human being, and yet you shall, do you understand, you shall will the ethical, and you shall, do you understand, you shall be enthusiastic, because this is the highest."

The deceitful lover does not understand this. Even less does he understand the next thing, when a truly enthusiastic ethical individuality, moved in earnestness, elevated in the holy jest of divine madness,[168] says, "Let me be as if created for the sake of a whim; this is the jest. Yet I shall with utmost strenuousness will the ethical; this is the earnestness. I want nothing

else, nothing. O insignificant importance, O jesting earnest-
VII 112 ness, O blessed fear and trembling! How blessed to be able to fulfill God's requirements while smiling at the demands of the times. How blessed to despair over not being able to do it as long as one does not let go of God!" Only such an individuality is ethical, but he has also comprehended that the world-historical is a composite that is not directly dialectical for the ethical.

The longer life goes on and the longer the existing person through his action is woven into existence, the more difficult it is to separate the ethical from the external, and the easier it seems to corroborate the metaphysical tenet that the outer is the inner, the inner the outer, the one wholly commensurate with the other.[169] This is precisely the temptation, and the ethical becomes more difficult day by day, because it consists in infinity's true hypertension, which is the beginning, where it therefore is most clearly manifest.

Let us imagine an individual who stands at the beginning of life. He now resolves, for example, to spend his whole life pursuing the truth and actualizing known truth. So in the moment of resolution he rejects everything, everything, including, of course, world-historical importance. But now, what if momentous importance comes to him little by little as the fruit of his labor? Well, if it comes as the fruit of his labor—but it never does that. If it comes, then it is Governance who adds it to his ethical striving in itself, and consequently it is not the fruit of his labor. It is a *pro* that must be regarded as a temptation just as much as any *contra*. It is the most dangerous of all temptations, and many a glorious beginning in the hypertension of the infinite has grown slack in what for the fallen one became a soft, effeminate embrace.

But back to the beginning. With the true ethical hypertension of the infinite, he rejects everything. In fables and fairy tales there is a lamp called the wonderful lamp; when it is rubbed, the spirit appears.[170] Jest! But freedom, that is the wonderful lamp. When a person rubs it with ethical passion, God comes into existence for him. And look, the spirit of the lamp is a servant (so wish for it, you whose spirit is a wish),

but the person who rubs the wonderful lamp of freedom becomes a servant—the spirit is the Lord. This is the beginning. Let us now see if it will do to add something else to the ethical. So the resolving person says: I will—but I also want to have world-historical importance—*aber* [but]. So there is an *aber*— VII
and the spirit vanishes again, because the rubbing has not been 113
done properly, and the beginning does not occur. But if it has occurred or has been done properly, every subsequent *aber* must again be renounced, even if existence in the most flattering and inveigling way did everything to force it upon one.

Or the resolved person says: I will this, but I also will that my efforts shall benefit other people, because, just between us, I am such a good person that I want to benefit, if possible, all of humankind. Even if the spirit did appear when the rubbing is done this way, I think it would rise up in wrath and say: "Obtuse fellow, do I not exist, I, the Almighty, and even if human beings—all of whom I created and counted, I, who count the hairs on a person's head[171]—were as countless as the sands of the sea,[172] am I still not able to help everyone just as I am helping you? You presumptuous fellow! Can you demand anything? But I can demand everything. Do you have anything of which you could give me some? Or when doing your utmost, are you not simply returning my property to me, and perhaps in rather poor condition?"

So here the beginner stands—the slightest trace of an *aber*, then the beginning miscarries. But if it is this way at the beginning, the continuation must fully correspond to it. If that beginner began well, if he also achieved something amazing, if all his contemporaries were much indebted to him and thanked him, then it is indeed important for him to understand in jest what jest is. The earnestness is his own inner life; the jest is that it pleases God to attach this importance to his striving, to the striving of one who is only an unworthy servant. When a mirage in its absolute transforming power picks up a person and shows him in preternatural magnitude to the astonished observer: is it that person's merit? Likewise, when Governance arranges things so that a person's inner striving is reflected magically in the shadow play of world history: is that his merit? I should think that the true ethicist to whom this happened, if he were to speak of it, would waggishly recall a certain Don Quixote. He would say that just as that knight, perhaps as payment for wanting to be world-historical, was persecuted by a nisse, who spoiled everything for him, so he also had to have a nisse who played his game with him in reverse—for only obtuse schoolmasters and just as obtuse geniuses make the mistake of believing that it is they themselves [who do it] and forget themselves over their great consequence in world history.

Whoever cannot perceive this is obtuse; and with the power I have in the comic at this moment I intend to make ridiculous VII 114 whoever ventures to raise an objection. I say no more, for it perhaps could please Governance to take this power away from me even today and to give it to someone else just to test me. It perhaps could please Governance to let me do the work and then to give the gratitude of my contemporaries to a barber's apprentice, as if it were he who had done it. This I cannot know; I know only that I must stick to the ethical and demand nothing, nothing whatever, but be inspired only by my ethical relationship with God, which may very well endure, indeed, could become even more inward if he took away from me a gift such as that. Therefore it perhaps would be more sagacious not to say anything in advance, lest people mock me even more if I fail. But the ethical never asks about sagacity; it requires merely enough understanding to discover the danger—in order then to enter into it boldly, which seems very obtuse indeed. O singular power that resides in the ethical! If a king were to say to his enemies: Do as I command; if not, tremble before my scepter, which will remain as a terror over you—unless it should please Governance to take my throne away from me this very day and make a swineherd my successor! Why do we so seldom hear this "if," this "unless," this last part of the speech, which is the ethical truth? It is indeed truth—and the art is only this, to be enthusiastic, or as another author has said: to be happy out on 70,000 fathoms of water.[173] And the person who, himself existing, has understood life in this way will not be mistaken about world history, which in the foggy vision of speculative thought only runs together into something quite different, about which the speculative thinker becomes profoundly wise afterward.

Admittedly it is said that *die Weltgeschichte ist das Weltgericht* [world history is world judgment],[174] and the word "judgment" seems to make the claim that the statement contains an ethical view of life. Perhaps it is this way for God, because in his eternal co-knowledge he possesses the medium that is the commensurability of the outer and the inner. But the human mind cannot see world history in this way, even if one disregards difficulties and objections that I do not wish to dwell upon in detail here, lest attention be drawn away from the ethical, but merely point out and touch upon as concessively as possible in order not to turn interest to them.

α. *We must disregard*, as already suggested, *the idea that access to* VII
becoming world-historical is quantitatively dialectical, so that what 115
has become world-historical has gone through this dialectic. That there is no such distinction for the omniscient God cannot console a finite mind, because, well, I dare not say aloud what I mean; that would not do in the world-historical nineteenth century. But I probably dare to whisper it in the ear of the systematician: There is a difference between King Solomon and Jørgen Hattemager[175]—but do not breathe a word about this to anyone else. For God the conception of the world-historical is infused by and with his co-knowledge of the innermost secret in the conscience of the greatest and of the lowliest human being. If a human being wants to take this position, he is a fool; but if he does not want this, he will have to be satisfied with a survey that looks for salient points, and that is precisely why it is quantity that tips the scale. That the ethical is present in world history, just as it is present wherever God is, is therefore not denied, but rather that a finite spirit can in truth see it; wanting to see it there is a presumptuous and risky undertaking that can easily end with the observer's losing the ethical in himself.

[176]In order to study the ethical, every human being is assigned to himself. In that regard, he himself is more than

enough for himself; indeed, he is the only place where *he* can with certainty study it. Even another person with whom he is living can become intelligible to him only through the external, and inasmuch as that is so, the conception is already involved in dubiousness. But the more complicated the externality is in which the ethical internality is to reflect itself, the more difficult the observing becomes, until finally it goes astray in something quite different, in the esthetic. Therefore, the conception of world history easily becomes a half-poetic astonishment instead of an ethical consideration. The more important the parties are, the more difficult it becomes to disentangle the matter, even for a judge. And yet the judge is not to pronounce an ethical judgment, but only a civil judgment, where guilt and merit are made dialectical by a quantifying regard for the major or minor circumstances and an incidental regard for the outcome. This possible confusion gains far more latitude in the world-historical point of view, where it often seems that good and evil are quantitatively dialectical and that there is a certain magnitude of crime and cunning linked to millions and the nation, where the ethical becomes as shy as a sparrow in a dance of cranes.[177]

VII 116 But looking again and again at this incessant quantifying is harmful to the observer, who easily loses the chaste purity of the ethical, which in its holiness infinitely scorns all quantifying, which is the lust of the eye of the sensate person and the fig leaf of the sophistical.

The ethical as the absolute is infinitely valid in itself and does not need embellishment in order to look better. But the world-historical is just such a dubious embellishment (when it is not the eye of an omniscient one but the eye of a human being that is to see through it), and in world history, the ethical, just like nature, according to the poet, serves *knechtisch dem Gesetz der Schwere* [the law of gravity slavishly],[178] since the differential of quantity is also a law of gravity. The more the ethical can be simplified, the better one sees it. Thus it is not the case, as is deceitfully imagined, that the ethical is seen better in world history, where everything involves millions, than in a person's own poor life. On the contrary, it is just the

opposite; he sees it better in his own life simply because he makes no mistake about substance and mass. The ethical is inwardness, and the smaller the range in which one sees it, if one does see it in its infinity, the better one sees it; whereas the person who thinks he must have world-historical embellishments in order thereby to see it better shows in doing so that he is ethically immature. The person who does not comprehend the infinite validity of the ethical, even if it pertained to him alone in the whole world, does not really comprehend the ethical; that it pertains to all human beings is in a certain sense none of his business, except as a shadow that accompanies the ethical clarity in which he lives. Comprehension of the ethical is like doing arithmetic: one learns to calculate best by calculating with abstract numbers; if one begins with denominate numbers, the interest easily comes to revolve around something else. World-historical calculation is done with denominate quantities and enormously huge quantities, which by their multiplicity in multiple ways stimulate multiplicity in the observer. But the sensate person has a great predilection for this quantifying, and therefore, to recall once again the simile and its dissimilitude, here it is not at all the beginner who calculates with abstract numbers, since, on the contrary, it is a sign of true ethical maturity to renounce what one hankers for perhaps quite early and quite naturally: to calculate
with world-historical quantities. Just as a noble Greek (Em- VII
pedocles—Plutarch) has said that one should fast with re- 117
gard to evil (νηστεύειν κακότητος),[179] so the true ethical conception of the ethical has to be sober and fasting; the point is that one is not to desire to go world-historically to the banquet and become intoxicated on the amazing. But, ethically understood, this abstinence is in turn the most divine enjoyment and eternity's fortifying refreshment. World-historically, however, an individual is easily tempted to assume that if he is an insignificant person, his making a mistake has no infinite significance; and if he is a very great person, the magnitude of his situation can turn the slip into something good.

But even if the observing individual is not demoralized in this way, if the ethical is nevertheless confused with the world-historical so that it essentially becomes something else by pertaining to millions rather than by pertaining to one, another confusion readily occurs, namely, that the ethical is supposed to find its concretion first in the world-historical, and only then in this concretion is it a task for the living. In this way the ethical does not become the original, the most original, element in every human being but rather an abstraction from the world-historical experience. One observes world history, and, lo and behold, every age has its moral substance; one becomes objectively haughty and, although existing, one does not want to be satisfied with the so-called subjective ethical—no, the present generation, already in its own lifetime, wants to discover its world-historical moral idea and to act on that basis. Alas, "what the German will not do for money"[180]—and what will the Dane not do afterward, once the German has done it!

With regard to the past, it is easy to have the illusion that forgets, and in part cannot know, what belongs to the individual and what belongs to that objective order of things that is the spirit of world history. But with regard to the present generation and every single individual, to let the ethical become something whose discovery requires a prophet with a world-historical eye on world history[181]—that is a rare, ingeniously comic invention. O fortunate nineteenth century! If no such
VII prophet arises, we can all call it a day, for then no one knows
118 what the ethical is. It is indeed odd enough that the ethical is in such low esteem that instruction in it is preferably left to normal-school graduates and parish clerks; it would indeed be ludicrous if someone were to say that the ethical has not yet been discovered but is still to be discovered. And yet, it would not be insane if he meant that it was to be discovered by the individual's becoming immersed in himself and in his relationship with God. But that it takes a prophet, not a judge, no, but a seer, a world-historical brawler, who, aided by one deep and one blue eye, aided by familiarity with world history, perhaps aided also by coffee grounds and fortune-telling cards, believes he discovers[182] the ethical, that is, what the times demand (for this is the modern slogan of the demoralizing ethics)—now that is confusion-producing in two ways,

something for which a person who likes to laugh must always feel indebted to the wise men! How ludicrous that something like this is supposed to be the ethical! How ludicrous that a seer is supposed to discover it by looking at world history, where it is so difficult to see.

Finally, how ludicrous that the incessant association with world history has given birth to this conclusion. What the most obtuse person, confirmed in a house of correction,[183] is able to understand is improved by cathedral wisdom and made into that genuine speculative profundity. Alas, while the speculating, honorable Herr Professor is explaining all existence, he has in sheer absentmindedness forgotten what he himself is called, namely, that he is a human being, a human being pure and simple, and not a fantastical three-eighths of a paragraph. He concludes the system; he announces in a concluding paragraph that he will discover the ethical—which this generation, including him and me, is supposed to actualize—for it has not yet been discovered! But what? The ethical or the demand of the times? Alas, the ethical is an ancient discovery; on the other hand, I can well believe that what the times demand has not yet been discovered, despite the many satisfying and highly respectable, yet always only promissory, ventures in rigmarole.

Now, if someone says that this is a pettifogging overstatement, that those who are occupied with world history gladly allow normal-school graduates and parish clerks to lecture on popular ethics and do not mind that the lower classes in particular seek to live according to it, but that the world-historical interest designates only something superior, the much greater tasks—then this answer adequately shows that it was no pettifogging overstatement. If the other is something superior, then let us get started, the sooner the better, [184]but the trouble is that most likely it has not yet been discovered. As for the much greater tasks, let us talk quite simply about them, as neighbor speaks with neighbor in the evening twi- VII
119 light. The general statement that the task is much greater is still not sufficient; to a reasonable person this statement would be encouraging only if it also became clear that the yield for

the individual participants would be greater. When, for example, out in the country, where peace is at home in the shade of the leafy roof, when, according to the beloved king's devout wish,[185] the little family places a chicken on the table, and there is plenty for the few—is this not a bounteous meal compared with that great repast where, it is true, an ox was served, but where the partakers were so numerous that there was hardly a taste for each one? Or when someone who usually loves silence secretly finds the enigmatic way to the solitariness of a forlorn person and here finds the time and occasion to say the brief word that is indescribably refreshing—does not such a speaker produce just as great an effect, or rather, an infinitely greater effect than the admired one who is rewarded with a triple hip-hip-hurrah? And why? Because he uses the slogan the crowd likes to hear, consequently not because he spoke wisely, for what he said could not be heard clearly on account of the noise, but because he used a line that any blockhead can say, consequently because he was not a speaker but a bellows pumper.

The speculative absentmindedness may be psychologically explained only by the constant association with world history, with the past. Instead of really being aware of himself as one who is living in the present and has the future before him, in order thus to come to the point of being psychologically able to reproduce the individual element, which is only one factor among others in world history, the speculative thinker mingles everything and wants to anticipate his own pastness—in order then to act, although it seems fairly easy to understand that if a person has first become something past, then he has acted.

Only by paying sharp attention to myself can I come to realize how a historical individuality acted when he was living, and I understand him only when I keep him alive in my understanding and do not, as children do, break up the clock in order to understand the life in it, and do not, as speculative thought does, change him into something totally different in
VII order to understand him. But what it is to live I cannot learn
120 from him as someone dead and gone. I must experience that

by myself, and therefore I must understand myself, not the reverse: after first having world-historically misunderstood him now go further and allow this misunderstanding to help me misunderstand myself, as if I, too, were dead and gone. When he was alive, the world-historical individuality probably helped himself with the subjective ethics, and then Governance added world-historical importance, if he obtained
any.* A certain class of people has correctly discerned this, al- VII
though ordinarily they are far from finding the truth, since 121
they go to the opposite extreme. These are the mockers and the unbelievers who think that all world history revolves around sheer trifles, around "a glass of water."[190] At the op-

* Surely Socrates stands out as one of the most distinguished and important of world-historical figures. How was it with him? Well, let the system grasp his necessity afterward, the necessity of his coming into existence and of his mother's being a midwife, the necessity of his father's being ordered by an oracle to allow the child to tend to himself and never to compel him[186] (what a curious life when it is regarded as a task for a necessary method), the necessity of his being married, specifically to Xanthippe, of his being condemned to death by a majority of only three votes[187]—for here everything is necessary, and it is good that the system deals only with the dead; it must be unbearable for a living person to be understood in this way. But now let us also see, less systematically and more simply, how he acted when he was living, when he walked around in the marketplace and mockingly goaded the Sophists, when he was a human being and even in perhaps the most ludicrous situation preserved about him (see *Antoninus philosophus—ad se ipsum*, XI, 28[188])—in which he, because Xanthippe had put on his clothes and gone out, had to throw a hide around himself and to the great amusement of his friends appeared in the marketplace dressed like that—nevertheless he still remained a human being and even in his hide was not nearly as ludicrous as he later became in the system, where he shows up fantastically wrapped in the rich systematic drapery of a paragraph. Did Socrates talk about what the times demanded, did he understand the ethical as something that a prophet with a world-historical gaze was supposed to discover or had discovered, or as something to be decided by voting? No, he was occupied solely with himself, did not even know how to count to five when it was a matter of counting votes (see Xenophon[189]), was unfit to be included when it was a matter of a commission involving several people, not to mention a commission involving a world-
historical mob. He minded his own business—and then Governance comes VII
and adds a world-historical significance to his ironic self-satisfaction. It is too 121
bad that now, two thousand years later, nothing at all has been heard from him; only the god knows what he thinks of the system.

posite extreme is speculative thought, which wants to turn the exanimated historical individuality into a metaphysical qualification, a kind of categorical designation for the relation between cause and effect immanently understood. Both are wrong. The mocker commits a wrong against the human being; speculative thought commits a wrong against God. World-historically, the individual subject certainly is a trifle, but the world-historical is, after all, an addendum; ethically, the individual subject is infinitely important.

Take any human passion and have it be related to the ethical in the individual; ethically viewed, this will have great significance; world-historically, perhaps none at all or perhaps very great significance, for the world-historical, viewed ethically, enters by way of a "perhaps." Whereas that relation between passion and the ethical occupies the existing individual to the utmost (it is this that the mocker calls nothing and speculative thought speculatively ignores with the help of immanence), world-historical Governance perhaps shapes a reflecting context for this individual, whereby his life-situation acquires widespread world-historical importance. He does not have it, but Governance adds it to him. The mocker laughs and says: Look, all this revolved around injured pride—that is, around nothing. But this is untrue, because the relation of injured pride to the ethical is not, ethically viewed, a matter of indifference, is not a nothing; and the world-historical is something entirely different that does not directly follow from that relation. For speculative thought, everything runs together into one. It has vanquished mockery and disbelief, not by rescuing the ethical from the world-historical but by getting bag and baggage brought together *durcheinander* [in confusion] in a declaiming immanence-theory. But mockery avenges itself;
VII it is so far from being locked out that one would rather think
122 that speculative thought had locked itself in with it—so ludicrous has it become. Absentmindedness avenges itself when in ethics speculative thought wants a living individual to act on the basis of an immanence-theory, that is, to act by not acting, because immanence is only for the observing view-

point, essentially and in truth only for God, only in make-believe for honored professors and their families and friends.

But if it is so risky to become involved with world-historical observation, perhaps the objection is due to cowardliness and sloth, which are indeed always ready to delay the enthusiasts, in this case the high flying of the world-historicals, who certainly know how risky it is but for that reason also venture. Not at all! If anything in the world can teach a human being to venture, it is ethics, which teaches to venture everything for nothing, to venture everything—also to renounce world-historical flattery—in order to become nothing. No, the objection is high-minded precisely because it is ethical; it says that the ethical is absolutely and for all eternity the highest and that not every bold venture is half-won, for there is also a bold venture in which much is lost. Furthermore, a bold venture is not a high-flown phrase, not an exclamatory outburst, but arduous work; a bold venture, no matter how rash, is not a tumultuous proclamation but a quiet dedication that receives nothing in advance but stakes everything. Therefore venture, says the ethical, dare to renounce everything, including also that highly ranked yet delusive association with world-historical observation; dare to become nothing at all, to become a single individual from whom God ethically requires everything, but without daring for all that to cease being enthusiastic—see, that is the venturesome deed! But then your gain is also that God in all eternity cannot get rid of you, for your eternal consciousness is only in the ethical—see, that is the reward! World-historically, to be a single individual is nothing at all, infinitely nothing—and yet this is a human being's only true and highest significance, and thus higher than any other significance, which is a phantom, not, to be sure, in itself, but always a phantom if it is supposed to be the highest.

β. *We must disregard the idea that the world-historical view as a cognitive act is an approximation,* subject to the same dialectic as* VII 123

* Even if one must concede Hegel everything, there is still one preliminary question he has not answered: What on the whole does it mean that world-

every dispute between idea and experience, which at every moment will prevent the beginning and, once begun, at every moment threatens a revolt against the beginning. The world-historical material is endless, and consequently the limit must in one way or another be arbitrary. Although the world-historical is something past, as material for cognitive observation it is incomplete; it continually comes into existence through ever-new observation and research, which discover more and more or make rectifying discoveries. Just as the number of discoveries in the natural sciences is augmented by sharpening the instruments, so also in the world-historical when the critical quality of the observation is sharpened.

Would that I could display scholarship at this point! Would that I could show how the authorized and yet *valore intrinseco* [according to its intrinsic worth] rather dubious Hegelian ordering of the world-historical process depends upon arbitrariness and leaps, how China ought to be assigned another
VII 124 place* and a new paragraph be inserted for a recently discovered tribe in Monomotapa;[193] would that I could show how

---

VII 123 historical observation is an approximation? It is true that he has made light of Schelling's intellectual intuition[191] (Schelling's expression for the beginning). He himself has said, and it has often been repeated, that his merit is the method, but he has never said how the method is related to the intellectual intuition, whether or not a *leap* is again required here. As for the method and the beginning of the method, what is continually said is only that one must start on it and with it. But if a beginning such as that is not to be only a fancy, reflection must have preceded, and the preliminary question is rooted precisely in this reflection.

* That is, it has not yet become world-historically clear where China is to be placed in the world-historical process,[192] in which every assistant professor since the day before yesterday clearly and definitely finds plenty of room. In other words, all assistant professors are included, and as soon as the method reaches our day, it will go like a prairie fire, and we shall all find a place. The method admits only one Chinese, but not a single German assistant professor is excluded, especially no Prussian, because whoever has the cross blesses himself first. But then the system is not entirely finished yet; perhaps it ex-
VII 124 pects to be able systematically, one, two, three, to make capital of the arduous work of a genuine scholar by having a few extra Chinese placed at its disposal. Then it will be all right; now it certainly looks a little embarrassing to have only one Chinese when there are so many Germans.

the Hegelian method looks almost like a prank when it is used on a minor detail—then perhaps I could satisfy some reader. That is, the interest in ordering the world-historical would remain essential, but what I said about Monomotapa would be impressive, just as Jeronimus is impressed by what the schoolmaster in *Julestuen* says about the phoenix bird native to Arabia.[194] But wanting to regard the entire world-historical interest—that is, when it does not lovingly seek with philological scholarship to interpret disinterestedly a particular detail of world history for the sake of knowledge and cognition as such, but seeks speculatively to be of assistance in confusing the ethical task for the single individual with the world-historical task for the human race, and even more when this interest seeks to be everyone's business—wanting to regard this as an immoral and neurotic curiosity would certainly be abhorrent ethical narrow-mindedness.

[195]Only a very dense person or someone who slyly wants to avoid feeling that the cap fits him could at this point think that I am a vandal who wants to trespass upon the sacred field of science and scholarship and let the cattle loose, that I am a vagabond who at the head of newspaper readers and voting vagrants wants to stir up a rabble-revolt and despoil the peaceful scholar of his joyous gift, his possession legally acquired through submissive labor. Indeed, there are many, many, who possess more than I do in the world of the mind, but there is no one who more proudly and with more gratitude to the god believes that in the world of the mind there is eternal security of property, that the street-corner loafers do remain outside. But when a generation *en masse* wants to dabble world-historically, when, demoralized by this dabbling just as by playing the lottery, it rejects the highest, when speculative thought does not want to be disinterested but causes double confusion, first by skipping the ethical and then by advancing something world-historical as the ethical task for individuals—then scholarship itself would prefer that something be said about it. No, praised be scholarship, praised be everyone who chases
the cattle away from its sanctuary.[196] The ethical is and re- VII
mains the highest task assigned to every human being. It may 125

also be required of a devotee of scholarship that he understand himself ethically before he dedicates himself to his intellectual discipline, that he continue to understand himself ethically in all his labor, because the ethical is the eternal drawing of breath and in the midst of solitude the reconciling fellowship with every human being. But then not a word more, except admiration for those who distinguish themselves and enthusiastic cheers for those who are striving. The quiet scholar does not disturb life; he is erotically preoccupied in his noble pursuit. If, however, a noisy scholar wants to force his way into the existence-spheres and to confuse what is there the life-principle of the whole, the ethical, then as a scholar he is no faithful lover, then scholarship hands him over for comic treatment.

Only a dense person could think that the objection, which recalls that the world-historical view is an approximation, had its source in a cowardliness and lethargy that shrink from the overwhelming work. If the direction toward this goal is indeed the highest and the fear is only of the prodigious work, then the objection is not worthy of attention. But the objection is ethical; therefore it is high-minded, and therefore it does not in all its humility fall short of its goal and aim, which is the very highest. The objection says: The ethical is the only certainty, to concentrate upon this the only knowledge that does not change into a hypothesis at the last moment, to be in it the only secure knowledge, where the knowledge is secured by something else.

To want to be involved ethically with world history is an ethical misunderstanding of which true scholarship is never guilty. But although there is a low opinion of the ethical everywhere, what does life teach? Just as the lovers were few, just as the believers were few, so the true ethical individualities are probably also few. Falstaff says somewhere that he once had an honest face, but the year and the date of it are obliterated.[197] This "once" can be said in countless different ways, all according to the nature of the obliteration, but this "once" is still a decisive word. Perhaps the poet wants to teach us what a rarity it is that an individuality exists upon whom the Dei-

ty's eternal stamp, which expresses itself in the ethical, stands out purely, clearly, and distinctly as it once did, an individuality for whom time does not interpose like an eternity be- VII
tween him and that recollected eternal impression, but for 126
whom even the longest life, compared with the powerful presence of that eternity, is only a yesterday, an individuality (let us not speak esthetically as if the ethical were a fortunate quality of genius) who day after day struggles backward in order to gain the originality that was his eternal source! How rare, perhaps, is an individuality for whom the ethical preserves that holy chasteness that is infinitely impervious to every, even the most remote, alien qualification, an individual who preserves it—but no (let us speak ethically)—who gains it, who in life gains the virginal purity of the ethical passion, compared with which a child's purity is but an endearing jest! Esthetically, a human being has an originality, a wealth of which he may even afford to lose a little in life, but ethically, he has possessed it—if he gains nothing, all is lost.

If anyone says that this is only an exercise in elocution, that I have only a bit of irony, a bit of pathos, a bit of dialectic with which to work, I shall answer: What else should the person have who wants to present the ethical? Should he perhaps have managed to put it objectively in paragraphs and *geläufigt*[198] [glibly] by rote, and thus contradict himself by the form? I believe that if the ethical is *quod erat demonstrandum* [that which was to be demonstrated], then irony, pathos, and dialectic are *quod desideratur* [that which is wanted]. Yet I do not at all think that I have exhausted the ethical by my scribblings, because it is infinite.[199] But it is all the more to be wondered over that the ethical is considered so insignificant that the certain is given away in return for the uncertain, the most certain of all is given away in return for the various beckoning tasks of approximation. Let world history be a mirror, let the observer sit and look at himself in the mirror, but let us not forget the dog that also looked at itself in the mirror—and lost what it had.[200] The ethical is also a mirror, and the person who looks at himself in it certainly loses something, and the more he looks at himself in it, the more he loses—that is, all the uncertain in order to gain the certain. Only in the ethical is there immortality and eternal life; understood otherwise, world history is perhaps a play, a show, which perhaps goes on and on, but the observer dies, and his observing was perhaps a very important—pastime.

γ. Now, if this is disregarded and the admission is made that one is not to give up the world-historical because association
VII with it is risky or because one cowardly fears the toil and dif-
127 ficulty of approximation, let us then consider world history—not, however, *in concreto*, in order not to become verbose, which even the person who knows only Kofod's history[201] can easily become, but *in abstracto*—let us ponder: *what there is to see in the world-historical*.

If the world-historical is to amount to something and not be an utterly vague category in which, despite the great amount one comes to know about China and Monomotapa, the boundary between the individual and the world-historical nevertheless ultimately remains undecided (while the confusion arises again and again that a king is included because he is a king, and a hermit because in his isolation he is an important individuality), whether there is any boundary (or whether it speculatively runs together so that all are included and world history is the history of individuals), whether the boundary is accidental (relative merely to what one knows now), whether the boundary perhaps is dialectically arbitrary, relative only to what the honored systematizing professor has read most recently or must include because of his literary in-law affinities[202]—consequently, if the world-historical is to amount to something, it must be the history of the human race. Here is an issue that, in my opinion, is one of the most difficult: how and to what extent does the human race result from individuals, and what is the relation of the individuals to the human race? I shall not attempt to answer that question, and the attempt might fail anyway, but I shall instead entertain myself by bearing in mind that the survey of world history has for the most part been completed, or is at least in full swing, without having removed this difficulty.

If world history is the history of the human race, it follows automatically that I do not come to see the ethical in it. What I do come to see must correspond to the abstraction that the human race is, must be something just as abstract. The ethical, on the other hand, is predicated on individuality and to such a degree that each individual actually and essentially comprehends the ethical only in himself, because it is his co-knowledge with God. In other words, although in a certain sense the ethical is infinitely abstract, in another sense it is infinitely concrete, indeed, the most concrete of all, because it is dialectical for every human being as this individual human being.

Thus the observer sees world history in purely metaphysical categories, and he sees it speculatively as the immanence of cause and effect, ground and consequent. Whether he is able VII
to discern a τέλος [end, goal] for the whole human race, I do 128
not decide, but that τέλος is not the ethical τέλος, which is for individuals, but is a metaphysical τέλος. Insofar as the individuals participate in the history of the human race by their deeds, the observer does not see these deeds as traced back to the individuals and to the ethical but sees them as traced away from the individuals and to the totality. Ethically, what makes the deed the individual's own is the intention, but this is precisely what is not included in world history, for here it is the world-historical intention that matters. World-historically, I see the effect; ethically, I see the intention. But when I ethically see the intention and understand the ethical, I also see that every effect is infinitely indifferent, that what the effect was is a matter of indifference, but then of course I do not see the world-historical.

Insofar as the categories of cause and effect sometimes also take on a kind of semblance of guilt and punishment, this is only because the observer does not relate himself world-historically, is not able completely to strip away the ethical that is in him. But this is no merit whatever in relation to the world-historical, and the observer who is aware of it ought to stop his observing precisely at this moment in order to make clear to himself whether it was not the ethical that he should first and last develop to its maximum within himself, instead of wanting to aid world history with a little of it. World-historically, one does not see the individual's guilt such as it is only in the intention, but one sees the external deed consumed by the totality and in this totality sees it bringing upon itself the consequence of the deed. Therefore he sees something that ethically is altogether confusing and nonsensical, sees the well-intentioned deed bring down upon itself the same consequence as the ill-intentioned deed—the best of kings and a tyrant occasion the same calamity. Or more correctly, he does not see even this, for this is an ethical reminiscence. No, he sees something that ethically is an offense, namely, that world-historically he must ultimately disregard the true distinction between good and evil, since this is only in the individual, and in each individual actually only in his relationship with God.

Viewed world-historically, a thesis becomes untrue that viewed ethically is true and is the vital force in the ethical, namely, that every existing individuality has a possibility-relationship with God. This is of no concern world-historically, because everything is understood afterward, and thus it is for-
VII gotten that the dead also were once alive. Therefore God does
129 not play the role of the Lord in the world-historical process as
it is seen by human beings. Just as one does not see the ethical in it, so also one does not see God, because if he is not seen in the role of Lord, one does not see him. In the ethical he does play this role in that possibility-relationship, and the ethical is for the existing, for the living, and God is the God of the living.[203] In the world-historical process, the dead are not called to life but only to a fantastical-objective life, and in a fantastical sense God is the moving spirit in a process. In the world-historical process, God is metaphysically laced in a half-metaphysical, half-esthetic-dramatic, conventional corset, which is immanence. What a devil of a thing to be God in that way. A dramatic critic enjoins the poet to be so good as to use the characters he has listed on the playbill and to bring out of them everything that is in them. For example, if there are young women, they must be married before the play is over—otherwise it is wrong. In relation to the past, it seems quite in order

that God has used such and such individualities, but when they lived, how many were rejected at the time? And those who were used, how often were they, ethically humbled, obliged to understand that before God no immanence-privilege is valid and God is not bothered with theatrical conventions? They were obliged to understand something, in the understanding of which our enthusiastic ethicist, whom we have introduced as speaking, found his enthusiasm—that God does not need them. We do not thereby say that God should contradict himself, create and then not want to use. No, ethically there will be enough for each one to do, and that possibility-relationship, which is the enthusiasm of the ethical in joy over God, is God's freedom, which, if properly understood, will not in all eternity, neither before nor afterward, become immanence.

World-historical immanence is always confusing for the ethical, and yet the world-historical view is rooted precisely in immanence. If an individual sees something ethical, it is the ethical in himself, and a reflection of this induces him to see what he nevertheless does not see. On the other hand, by this he is or has been ethically prompted to make himself clear to himself. In other words, it would be incorrect to conclude that the more developed a person is ethically, the more he will see the ethical in world history; no, the very opposite is the case: the more developed he is ethically, the less he will concern himself with the world-historical.

Permit me by way of metaphor to call to mind more graphically the difference between the ethical and the world-historical, the difference between the ethical relation of the individual to God and the relation of the world-historical to God. A
king sometimes has a royal theater solely for himself, but this VII
difference, which excludes the ordinary citizens, is accidental. 130
Not so when we speak of God and the royal theater he has for himself. Accordingly, the individual's ethical development is the little private theater where God certainly is the spectator,[204] but where on occasion the individual also is himself a spectator, although essentially he is supposed to be an actor, not, however, one who deceives but one who discloses, just

as all ethical development consists in becoming disclosed before God. But to God, world history is the royal stage where he, not accidentally but essentially, is the only spectator, because he is the only one who *can* be that. Admission to this theater is not open to any existing spirit. If he fancies himself a spectator there, he is simply forgetting that he himself is supposed to be the actor in that little theater and is to leave it to that royal spectator and poet how he wants to use him in that royal drama, *Drama Dramatum* [The Drama of Dramas].

This applies to the living, and only they can be told how they ought to live; and only by understanding this for oneself can one be led to reconstruct a dead person's life, if it must be done at all and if there is time for it. But it is indeed upside-down, instead of learning by living one's own life, to have the dead live again, then to go on wanting to learn from the dead, whom one regards as never having lived, how one ought—indeed, it is unbelievable how upside-down it is—to live—if one is already dead.

δ. If becoming subjective were not the task, that is, the highest task assigned to every human being, a task that can indeed be sufficient for even the longest life, since it has the singular quality that it is not over until life is over—if this were not the case with becoming subjective, then a difficulty would remain that must, it seems to me, so press down like a leaden weight upon every human being's troubled conscience that he would wish himself dead today rather than tomorrow. This objection is not mentioned in our objective and yet liberal age, which is much too busy with the system and with forms to bother about human life. The objection is this: *If one posits only the development of the generation or the race or at least posits it as the highest, how does one explain the divine squandering that uses the*
VII *endless host of individuals of one generation after the other in order to*
131 *set the world-historical development in motion?* The world-historical drama proceeds extremely slowly. Why does God not make haste if that is all he wants? What undramatic forbearance or, more correctly, what a prosaic and boring spinning-out process! And if that is all he wants, how horrible, tyran-

nically to squander myriads of human lives. But what does the observer care about that? The observer world-historically catches a glimpse of the play of colors in the generations, just like a shoal of herring in the sea—the individual herring is not worth much. The observer stares numbly into the immense forest of the generations, and like someone who cannot see the forest for the trees, he sees only the forest, not a single tree. He hangs up curtains systematically and uses people and nations for that purpose—individual human beings are nothing to him; even eternity itself is draped with systematic surveys and ethical meaninglessness. Poetry squanders poetically, but, far from fasting itself, it does not dare to presuppose the divine frugality of the infinite that ethically-psychologically does not need many human beings but needs the idea all the more. No wonder, then, that one even admires the observer when he is noble, heroic, or, perhaps more correctly, absent-minded enough to forget that he, too, is a human being, an existing individual human being! By steadily staring into that world-historical drama, he dies and departs; nothing of him remains, or he himself remains like a ticket the usher holds in his hand as a sign that now the spectator has gone.

If, however, becoming subjective is the highest task assigned to a human being, then everything turns out beautifully. From this it first follows that he no longer has anything to do with world history but in that respect leaves everything to the royal poet. Second, there is no squandering, for even though individuals are as innumerable as the sands of the sea,[205] the task of becoming subjective is indeed assigned to every person. Finally, this does not deny the reality [*Realitet*] of the world-historical development, which, reserved for God and eternity, has both its time and its place.

ε. First, then, the ethical, to become subjective, then the world-historical. Surely even the most objective person is basically in secret agreement with what has been stated here, that first of all the wise person ought to understand the same thing that the simple person understands and ought to feel bound to the same thing that binds the simple person—and that only

then should he pass on to the world-historical. First, then, the simple. But of course this is so easy for the wise person to understand (why else is he called wise?) that understanding it is merely a matter of a moment, and at the very same moment
VII 132 he is in full swing with the world-historical. And so it presumably goes with my simple comments—he has understood them instantly and at the very same moment is far beyond.

If only, even for a moment, I might engage the wise person in conversation, because I would gladly be the simple one who stops him with the following simple observation: *Is it not precisely the simple that is most difficult for the wise man to understand?* The simple person understands the simple directly, but when the wise person is to understand it, it becomes infinitely difficult. Is it an insult to the wise person to attach such importance to him that the simplest becomes the most difficult just because he is the one who is supposed to deal with it? Not at all. When a maidservant marries a manservant, everything proceeds quietly, but when a king marries a princess, it becomes an event. In saying this, does one have a low opinion of the king? When the child babbles away, his babbling is perhaps quite simple, and when the wise person says exactly the same thing, it has perhaps become the most ingenious of all. The wise person relates himself to the simple in this way. When he enthusiastically honors this as the highest, it honors him in turn, for it is as if it became something else through him, although it still remains the same. The more the wise person thinks about the simple (that there can be any question of a longer preoccupation with it already shows that it is not so easy after all), the more difficult it becomes for him. Yet he feels gripped by a deep humanness that reconciles him with all of life: that the difference between the wise person and the simplest person is this little evanescent difference *that the simple person knows the essential* and the wise person little by little *comes to know* that he knows it or *comes to know* that he does not know it, but what they know is the same. Little by little—and then also the wise person's life comes to an end—so when was there time for the world-historical interest?

But the ethical is not only a knowing; it is also a doing that is related to a knowing, and a doing of such a nature that the repetition of it can at times and in more ways than one become more difficult than the first doing. Once again a new delay—if one must of necessity proceed to the world-historical.

At this point, however, I owe it to everyone who insists on proceeding to the world-historical to admit something about myself, something regrettable, something that perhaps is to blame for my catching sight of tasks that are sufficient for a whole human life, whereas others may be able to be done with them before this sentence is finished. Most people are by nature such good people; first they are good children, then good young people, then good husbands and wives. This, of VII
course, is something quite different. As soon as one has come 133
so far that one's wife and all of one's sisters-in-law say *en masse*: He is, God knows, an unusually good man—well, then one can no doubt find time to attend to world history. Unfortunately this is not the case with me. Alas, it is only too well known to the few who know me and, I admit, to myself also, that I am a corrupt and corruptible man. It is all too true. Whereas all the good people are promptly all set to attend to the future of world history, I am obliged many a time to sit at home and mourn over myself. Although my father is dead and I no longer attend school, although I have not been turned over to the public authorities for correction, I have nevertheless seen the necessity of attending a little to myself, even though I would undeniably much prefer to go to Frederiksberg[206] and deal with world history. But then, of course, I have no wife to tell me that God knows I am a good man; I am obliged to grapple alone with myself. The only one who consoles me is Socrates. He is supposed to have discovered within himself, so it is said, a disposition to all evil; it may even have been this discovery that prompted him to give up the study of astronomy, which the times now demand.[207] I willingly admit how little I resemble Socrates otherwise. Very likely his ethical knowledge helped him to make that discovery. Such is not the case with me; in strong passions and the like, I have material enough, and therefore pain enough in forming something good out of it with the aid of reason.*

* With these words I wish to call to mind Plutarch's splendid definition of

Let us, then, lest we be disturbed by thinking about me, stick to Socrates, to whom *Fragments* also had recourse. By means of his ethical knowledge, he discovered that he had a disposition to all evil. Now it is no longer so easy—one, two, three—to arrive at the world-historical. On the contrary, the way of the ethical becomes exceedingly long, because it begins
VII 134 with making this discovery first of all. The more profoundly one makes it, the more one has to do; the more profoundly one makes it, the more ethical one becomes; the more ethical one becomes, the less time there is for the world-historical.

That the simple can be so protracted is indeed very strange. Let us take an example from the religious sphere (to which the ethical lies so close that they continually communicate with each other). To pray is, of course, a very simple matter; one would think it to be as easy as buttoning one's trousers, and if nothing else stood in the way, one could promptly tackle the world-historical. And yet how difficult! Intellectually, I must have an altogether clear conception of God, of myself, and of my relationship with him, and of the dialectic of the relationship of prayer—lest I confuse God with something else so that I do not pray to God, and lest I confuse myself with something else so that I do not pray—so that in the relationship of prayer I maintain the distinction and the relationship. Reasonable married people confess that they need months and years of daily life together in order to learn to know each other, and yet God is much more difficult to know. God is not something external, as is a wife, whom I can ask whether she is now satisfied with me. If in my relationship with God I regard what I am doing as good and do not keep watch over myself with the infinite's mistrust of me, then it is just as if God, too, were content with me, because God is not something external, but is the infinite itself, is not something external that quarrels with me when I do wrong but the infinite itself that does not need scolding words, but whose vengeance is terri-

---

virtue: "Ethical virtue has the passions for its material, reason for its form." See his little book on ethical virtues.[208]

ble—the vengeance that God does not exist for me at all, even though I pray.

To pray is also an action. Ah, in this regard, Luther was indeed a tried and tested man, and he is supposed to have said that never in his life had he even once prayed so fervently that, while praying, some disturbing thought did not intrude.[209] So one could almost think that to pray is just as difficult as to play the role of Hamlet, of which the greatest actor is supposed to have said that only once had he been close to playing it well;[210] nevertheless he would devote all his ability and his entire life to the continued study of this role. Should not praying be almost as important and significant?

But then to become subjective is a very praiseworthy task, VII
a *quantum satis* [sufficient amount] for a human life. Although 135
I have the sorry necessity of having to hurry, like Lot's wife,[211] even the best of persons will have plenty to do. If in this regard I should in any way be able to serve an individual among my contemporaries, my service would include a reference to the parable of the trees that wanted the cedar tree for king in order to rest in its shade. In like manner, our age wants to have a systematic Christmas tree raised in order to rest and take time off, but the trees had to be content with a bramble bush. If I, not in the capacity of king but as a lowly servant, were to compare myself with this bush,[212] I would say: I am as unfruitful as it is; there is not much shade, and the thorns are sharp.

Consequently, to become subjective should be the highest task assigned to every human being, just as the highest reward, an eternal happiness, exists only for the subjective person or, more correctly, comes into existence for the one who becomes subjective. Moreover, becoming subjective should give a person plenty to do as long as he lives; thus it should not happen to the zealous person but only to the busy trifler that he will be finished with life before life is finished with him. And he should not be entitled to ignore life but should instead be obliged to understand that he very likely had not comprehended life's task correctly, since it otherwise would follow as a matter of course that the task of life would last as long as life lasts, that is, the task of living.[213] Consequently, if the individual comprehends that to become subjective is his highest task, then, in the carrying out of that task, issues should become manifest to him that in turn could suffice for the subjective thinker fully as well as the objective issues that the objective thinker has at hand suffice for him, this person who goes further and further, who, scorning repetition's ever-deepening absorption in the one thought, never repeats himself but astounds the age first by being a systematician, then a world historian, then an astronomer, veterinarian, waterworks inspector, geographer, etc.

Amazing! But why should it not be sufficient when one, from the Socratic wisdom that discovers one's own disposition to all evil before one begins with being finished as a good
VII person, learns to make a similar discovery: that to finish too
136 quickly is the greatest danger of all. This is a very upbuilding observation that has an extraordinary capacity to stretch out the task, even to the point of going a long way. Let us consider the oddity that with speed and haste, which are ordinarily praised and commended, there is one instance in which the praise is inversely related to the speed. Generally, speed is lauded and in some instances is regarded as neutral, but in this instance it is even reprehensible. When in a written examination young people are given four hours to write the paper, it makes no difference whether the individual finishes ahead of time or uses the whole time. Here, then, the task is one thing and time something else. But when time itself is the task, it is a defect to finish ahead of time. Suppose a person is given the task of entertaining himself for one day and by noon is already finished with the entertainment—then his speed would indeed be of no merit. So it is also when life is the task. To be finished with life before life is finished with one is not to finish the task at all.

That is how the matter stands. Believe me, I, too, am one of those who have power, even though I do say so myself, although ordinarily I would be ranked with normal-school graduates and village parish clerks. I am one of those who have power; yet my power is not that of a ruler or a conqueror, for the only power I have is the power to restrain. My power, however, is not extensive, for I have power only over myself, and I do not have even that if I do not exercise restraint every moment. I do not have time to try to exercise restraint directly upon the age in which I live, and furthermore I think that trying to restrain the age directly is as futile as for a passenger on a train to try to stop it by clutching the seat ahead of him—he identifies himself directly with the age and yet he wants to restrain it. No, the only thing to do is to get off the train and restrain oneself.

If one gets off the train (and especially in our day, when one is keeping up with the age, one is continually *auf der Eisenbahn* [on the railway][214]) and never forgets that the task is to exercise restraint, since the temptation is to finish too quickly, then nothing is more certain than that the task is enough for a lifetime. Then the defect cannot possibly be in the task, because the task is precisely that the task will be enough. To be considered a normal-school graduate and a straggler is a good sign, because normal-school graduates and stragglers are considered slow-witted.[215]

Here are a few examples that in all brevity show how the VII
simplest issue is changed by restraint into the most difficult. 137
Thus there is no reason for hastily choosing astronomy, veterinary science, and the like if one has not understood the simple. Here brevity cannot be a hindrance, for the issues are not finished.

For example, *what it means to die.* On that topic I know what people ordinarily know: that if I swallow a dose [216]of sulfuric acid I will die, likewise by drowning myself or sleeping in coal gas etc. I know that Napoleon always carried poison with him, that Shakespeare's Juliet took it;[217] that the Stoics regarded suicide as a courageous act and others regard it as cowardice, that one can die from such a ludicrous trifle that the most solemn person cannot help laughing at death, that one can avoid certain death, etc. I know that the tragic hero dies in the fifth act and that death here gains infinite reality [*Realitet*] in pathos but has no such pathos when an alehouse keeper dies. I know that the poet interprets death in a variety of moods to the point of verging on the comic; I pledge myself to produce in prose the same variety of effects in mood. Moreover, I know what the clergy usually say; I know the stock themes dealt with at funerals. If there is no other hindrance to moving on to world history, then I am ready; I need only buy some black cloth for a clerical gown, and then I shall deliver funeral orations as well as any ordinary clergyman. I readily admit that those with velvet panels[218] do it more elegantly, but this difference is not any more essential than the difference between a five- and a ten-rix-dollar hearse.

However, despite this almost extraordinary knowledge or proficiency of knowledge, I am by no means able to regard death as something I have understood. So before I move on to world history, about which I still must always say: God knows if it actually does concern you; I think it would be better to consider this, lest existence mock me for having become so erudite that I had forgotten to understand what will happen to me and every human being sometime—sometime, but what am I saying! Suppose death were insidious enough to come tomorrow! Just this uncertainty, if it is to be understood and held firm by an existing person and consequently be thought
VII into everything precisely because it is uncertainty, even into
138 my beginning with world history, so that I make it clear to myself whether I am beginning something worth beginning if death should come tomorrow—this uncertainty already gives rise to unbelievable difficulties, of which not even the orator is aware. Thus he presumes to think of the uncertainty of death and yet forgets to think the uncertainty into what he is saying about uncertainty when he, moved, speaks harrowingly about the uncertainty of death and ends by urging a purpose for the whole of life. Consequently, he ends by having essentially forgotten the uncertainty of death, since otherwise his enthusiastic purpose for the whole of life must have been made dialectical in relation to the uncertainty of death. To think this uncertainty once and for all, or once a year at matins on New Year's morning, is nonsense, of course, and is not to think it at all. If the one who thinks it in this way also explains world history, what he says about world history can perhaps be splendid, but what he says about death is obtuse. If death

is always uncertain, if I am mortal, then this means that this uncertainty cannot possibly be understood in general if I am not also such a human being in general. But this I am not. That is something only absentminded people are, for example, Soldin, the bookseller.[219] And even if I am that at my beginning, the life-task is indeed to become subjective, and to the same degree the uncertainty becomes more and more dialectically penetrating in relation to my personality. Therefore it becomes more and more important to me to think it into every moment of my life, because, since its uncertainty is at every moment, this uncertainty is vanquished only by my vanquishing it every moment.

If, however, the uncertainty of death is something in general, then my dying is also something in general. Perhaps dying is also something in general for systematicians, for absentminded people. For the late bookseller Soldin, dying is said to have been something in general—"When he was going to get up in the morning, he was not aware that he was dead." But for me, *my* dying is by no means something in general; for others, my dying is some such thing. Nor am *I* for myself some such thing in general; perhaps for others I am some such thing in general. But if the task is to become subjective, then every subject becomes *for himself* exactly the opposite of some such thing in general. I think it is embarrassing to be so much for world history and then at home with oneself to be for one- VII 139
self some such thing in general. It is already embarrassing enough when a man who is so extraordinarily important in the people's assembly comes home to his wife and for her is only some such thing in general, or to be a world-historical Diedrich Menschenschreck[220] and then at home to be—well, I prefer not to say more. But it is even more embarrassing to be on such bad terms with oneself and even worse to remain ignorant of it.

The exalted devotee of world history can nevertheless not deny me an answer to the question of what it means to die, and the moment he answers, the dialectic begins. Let him give whatever reason he wishes for not dwelling further on such thoughts; it will not help, because the reason will in turn be made dialectical in order to see what it essentially is. Then I would have to ask whether it is at all possible to have an idea of death, whether death can be anticipated and *anticipando* [by being anticipated] be experienced in an idea, or whether it is only when it actually is. And since its actual being is a non-being, [I would have to ask] whether it therefore is only when it is not, in other words, whether the ideality can ideally vanquish death by thinking it, or whether materiality conquers in death, so that a human being dies like a dog, whereas death can be annulled only by the dying person's idea of death at the moment of death.

That difficulty can also be expressed in this way: is it so that the living person cannot approach death at all, since he, experimenting, cannot come close enough without comically becoming a victim of his own experiment, and since he, as experiencing, cannot exercise any restraint but learns nothing from the experience, since he cannot pull himself back out of the experience and have the benefit of it later but remains stuck in the experience? Now, if the answer is that death cannot be drawn up into an idea, the matter is by no means settled. A negative answer, a no, must be defined dialectically just as fully as a positive answer, and only a child and a simple person are satisfied with: *das weisz man nicht* [one does not know that]. The thinking person wants to know more, not positively of course, about that which according to the assumption can be answered only negatively, but he does want to have it made dialectically clear that the answer must be no, and this dialectical clarification places this negative answer in relation to all other existence-issues, and thus there will be difficulties enough.

If the answer is yes, then there is the question about what
VII death is and what it is for the living person, how the idea of it
140 must change a person's whole life if he, in order to think its
uncertainty, must think it every moment in order thereby to
prepare himself for it. Then there is the question about what
it means to prepare oneself for it, since here again a distinction
is made between its actual coming and the idea of it (a distinction that seems to make all my preparation something mean-

ingless if that which actually comes is not the same as that for which I have prepared myself, and if it is the same, the preparation, if consummate, is death itself), and since it can indeed come at the very moment I am beginning the preparation. And then there is the question of an ethical expression for the meaning of death, a religious expression for vanquishing it. An unraveling word is required to explain its riddle and a binding word by which the living person protects himself against the unremitting idea, for we certainly dare not openly recommend thoughtlessness and forgetfulness as the wisdom of life.

Moreover, for the subject it is an act to think his death. For a human being in general, an absentminded man like Soldin, the bookseller, or a systematician, to think death in general certainly is not an act; it is merely some such thing in general, and basically it is not easy to say what a some such thing is. But if the task is to become subjective, then for the individual subject to think death is not at all some such thing in general but is an act, because the development of subjectivity consists precisely in this, that he, acting, works through himself in his thinking about his own existence, consequently that he actually thinks what is thought by actualizing it, consequently that he does not think for a moment: Now, you must keep watch every moment—but that he keeps watch every moment. Here everything becomes more and more subjective, which is natural when it is a matter of beginning to develop the subjectivity.

Moreover, it seems that communication between one human being and another is given over to lies and deception if one is so inclined, for a person need only say, "I have done it," and we can go no further. Well, what then? What if he had not done it nevertheless? Indeed, what is that to me—it is all the worse for him. When it is a matter of something objective, we can exercise better control. For example, if someone were to say that Frederik VI is emperor of China, we would call it a lie. But if someone speaks of death, of how he has been thinking it and has thought, for example, its uncertainty, it still does not follow that he has done it. Certainly! Yet there is a

more subtle way to find out whether he is lying. Just let him talk. If he is a deceiver, he will contradict himself precisely when he is giving the most solemn assurances. The contradic-
VII tion will not be direct; no, it will be that the statement itself
141 does not contain in itself the consciousness of that which the statement directly declares. Objectively understood, the statement itself can be direct; the man has merely the defect that he recites by rote.* That he also perspires and pounds the table does not demonstrate that he is not reciting by rote but merely demonstrates either that he is very obtuse or that he himself is also secretly conscious of reciting by rote. In other words, it is very obtuse to think that reciting by rote would excite someone, since excitement is internal and reciting by rote is something external, equivalent to making water, and wanting to hide one's lack of inwardness by pounding the table is at best a mediocre deception.

See, when dying is to be placed in relation to the subject's whole life in this way, I am, even if my life were at stake, very far indeed from having comprehended death, and even less have I existentially carried out my task. And yet I have thought again and again, have sought guidance in books—and found none.**

* Just pay attention to the reduplicated presence of the stated thought in every word, in every intermediate clause, in the digression, in the unguarded moment of simile and comparison, if one wants to take the trouble of checking whether a person is lying—if one then scrupulously keeps watch over oneself. The ability to keep watch in this way is gained by restraining oneself; then one gains it purely gratis and ordinarily does not care to make particular use of it.

** Although it has been said frequently, I wish to repeat it again here: What is developed here by no means pertains to the simple folk, whom the god will preserve in their lovable simplicity (although they sense the pressure of life in another way), the simplicity that feels no great need for any other kind of understanding, or, insofar as it is felt, humbly becomes a sigh over the misery of this life, while this sigh humbly finds comfort in the thought that life's happiness does not consist in being a person of knowledge. On the other hand, it does pertain to the person who considers himself to have the ability and the opportunity for deeper inquiry, and it pertains to him in such a way that he does not thoughtlessly settle down to world history but first of all calls to mind that being an existing human being is such a strenuous and yet natural

For example, *what it means to be immortal.* On that topic, I know what people ordinarily know. I know that some accept immortality, that others say they do not. Whether they actually accept it, I do not know. That is why it does not occur to me to want to contend with them, for such a procedure is so dialectically difficult that it would take ages for me to become VII
dialectically clear about whether such contention has any real- 142
ity [*Realitet*]; whether the dialectic of communication, if understood, would sanction such conduct or transform it into shadowboxing; whether the consciousness of immortality is an instructional topic that can be taught and how the instruction must be dialectically qualified in relation to the learner's qualifications; whether these are not so essential that the instruction becomes an illusion if one is not promptly aware of this and in that case changes the instruction into noninstruction. Furthermore, I know that some have found immortality in Hegel; others have not.[221] I know that I have not found it in the system, since it is unreasonable to look for it there anyway, because in a fantastical sense all systematic thinking is *sub specie aeterni* [under the aspect of eternity] and to that extent immortality is there as eternity. But this immortality is not at all the one inquired about, since the question is about the immortality of a mortal, and that question is not answered by showing that the eternal is immortal, because the eternal is, after all, not the mortal, and the immortality of the eternal is a tautology and a misuse of words. I have read Professor Heiberg's *Sjæl efter Døden* [Soul after Death][222]—indeed, I have read it with Dean Tryde's commentary.[223] I wish I had not done so, because a poetic work gives esthetic delight and does not require the ultimate dialectical exactitude commensurate with a learner who wants to organize his life according to such guidance. If a commentator forces me to look for something of that kind in the poem, he has not benefited the poem. From the commentator I perhaps could hope to learn what I did not learn by reading the commentary—if Dean Tryde, in cate-

task for every human being that one naturally chooses it first and in this strenuous effort most likely finds enough for a lifetime.

chizing, would have mercy on me and show how just one life-view is constructed upon the profundity he has achieved in his paraphrases. All honor to Dean Tryde! Just from this little piece of his it would certainly be possible to construct various life-views extractively—but I cannot make *one* out of it. Alas, that is just the trouble; one is what I need, not more, since I am not a pundit. Moreover, I know that the late Professor Poul Møller, who certainly was familiar with the newest phi-
VII 143 losophy, did not until late in life become really aware of the infinite difficulty of the question of immortality when it is made simple, when the question is not about a new demonstration and about the opinions, strung on a thread, of Tom, Dick, and Harry or about the best way of stringing opinions on a thread. I also know that in a treatise[224] he tried to give an account and that this monograph clearly reflects his aversion to modern speculative thought.

The difficulty in the question arises precisely when it is made simple, not in the way a well-trained assistant professor inquires about the immortality of human beings, abstractly understood as humankind in general, and thus about the immortality of human beings in general, fantastically understood as the race, and thus about the immortality of the human race. A well-trained assistant professor like that inquires and in turn answers in the way well-trained readers assume the answer must be given. A poor, untrained reader is only made to look the fool by such deliberations, just like an auditor at an oral examination for which questions and answers have been prearranged, or like someone visiting a family whose members speak a private language and use the words of the mother tongue but understand something different by them. The consequence is that the answer is usually very easy, because the question has already been changed. One cannot for that reason deny that they answer the question but can indeed rightfully insist that the question is not what it seems to be. When in an oral examination on the history of Denmark, the teacher, aware that the pupil does not know anything about it, promptly turns the examination in another direction, for example, by asking about the relation of another country to

Denmark and then asking about the history of that other country, can it then be said that the examination was on the history of Denmark? When schoolchildren write a word in their books and add, "See also p. 101," and on p. 101, "See p. 216," and on p. 216, "See p. 314," and then finally, "April fool," can it rightfully be said that one derives benefit from this guidance—in being made a fool?

A book propounds the question of the immortality of the soul;[225] the contents of the book are, of course, the answer. But the contents of the book, as the reader convinces himself by reading it through, consist of all the wisest and best men's opinions, strung on a thread, concerning immortality. Consequently immortality is the opinions of all the wisest and best men concerning immortality. O thou great Chinese god! Is this immortality? Is, then, the question about immortality a learned question? Honor be to learning! Honor be to the one who can learnedly treat the learned question of immortality! But essentially the question of immortality is not a learned VII 144
question; it is a question belonging to inwardness, which the subject by becoming subjective must ask himself.

Objectively the question cannot be answered at all, because objectively the question of immortality cannot be asked, since immortality is precisely the intensification and highest development of the developed subjectivity. Not until one rightly wills to become subjective can the question rightly arise—how, then, could it be answered objectively?

Socially the question cannot be answered at all, because socially it cannot be enunciated, since only the subject who wills to become subjective can grasp the question and rightly ask: Do *I* become immortal or am *I* immortal? See, people can very well join together in various things. For example, several families can join together for a box at the theater, and three single gentlemen can join together for a riding horse so that each one rides every third day. But this is not the way it is with immortality; the consciousness of my immortality belongs simply and solely to me. The very moment I am conscious of my immortality, I am completely subjective, and I cannot become immortal in partnership in rotation with two other single gentlemen. Subscription collectors who produce long subscription lists of men and women who feel a need in general to become immortal receive no benefit for their trouble, because immortality is a good that cannot be obtained by bullying one's way with a long list of signatures.

Immortality cannot be demonstrated systematically, either. The defect is not in the demonstrations but in the refusal to understand that, viewed systematically, the whole question is nonsense; thus, instead of seeking further demonstrations, one should rather seek to become a little subjective. Immortality is the subjective individual's most passionate interest; the demonstration lies precisely in the interest. When one, systematically quite consistent, objectively abstracts from it systematically, God only knows what immortality is then, or just what it means to want to demonstrate it, or just what kind of fixation it is to bother about it further. If one could systematically get immortality hung up like Gessler's hat,[226] before which we all in passing would take off our hats—that is not being immortal or being conscious of immortality. The astounding labor of the system in demonstrating immortality is wasted effort and a ridiculous contradiction—to want to answer systematically a question that has the remarkable quality that it cannot be raised systematically. It is like wanting to
VII paint Mars in the armor that makes him invisible. The point
145 is the invisibility, and with immortality the point is the subjectivity and the subjective individual's subjective development.

In all simplicity, then, the existing subject asks not about immortality in general, because a phantom such as that does not exist at all, but about his immortality. He asks about his immortality, about what it means to become immortal, whether he can do anything in order to become immortal or whether he becomes that automatically, or whether he is immortal but can become that. In the first case, he asks what meaning it may have, if any, that he has let some time pass by unused, whether there are perhaps a greater and a lesser immortality. In the second case, the question is asked: What meaning may it have for his entire human existence that the

highest in life turns out to be like a prank, so that the passion of freedom within him is assigned only the lower tasks but has nothing to do with the highest, not even negatively, since a negative action in relation to the highest would in turn certainly be the most strenuous action—that is, after enthusiastically willing to do everything to the utmost of one's ability, then to learn that the highest is at every moment only to keep oneself receptive toward that for the acquiring of which one would so very willingly want to do something? The question is asked: How does he conduct himself in speaking about his immortality; how can he simultaneously speak from the standpoint of the infinite and of the finite and think the two together in the one moment, so that he does not say one thing now and then something else? The question is asked: How are language and all communication related to this when it is a matter of being consistent in every single word, lest the casual little adjective or the garrulous intermediate clause break in disruptively and mock the whole thing; where is the place, as it were, the place for speaking about immortality, since he surely knows how many pulpits there are in Copenhagen and that there are two chairs of philosophy—but where is the place that is the unity of the infinite and the finite, where he, who is simultaneously infinite and finite, can speak simultaneously of his infinitude and his finitude, and whether it is indeed possible to find this dialectically difficult place, which is nevertheless requisite? The question is asked: How does he, existing, hold on to his consciousness of immortality, lest the metaphysical conception of immortality go and confuse the ethical conception to the point of its becoming an illusion, because ethically everything culminates in immortality, without which the ethical is merely custom and habit, and metaphysically immortality swallows existence, indeed, the seventy years of existence, as if they were nothing, and yet ethically this nothing is supposed to be infinitely important? The question is asked: How does immortality transform his life; in VII
what sense must he have the consciousness of immortality 146
present in him at all times, or whether it is perhaps sufficient to think this through once and for all? If that is indeed the

answer, the question is whether the answer shows that the issue has not even been raised, since a once-and-for-all consciousness of immortality would be equivalent to being a subject of sorts and in general, whereby the question about immortality is fantastically made ridiculous, just as the opposite is ridiculous, that is, when people who have fantastically dabbled in everything, have been everything possible, one day in concern ask the pastor whether they will actually remain the same in the beyond—after they have not been able in this life to endure being the same for a fortnight and therefore have gone through all kinds of transmutations. Immortality would admittedly be a peculiar metamorphosis if it could transmute an inhuman centipede such as that into the eternal identity with itself, which "to be the same" means.

He asks whether it is now definite that he is immortal, what kind of definiteness this immortality has, whether this definiteness, if he lets it stand as definite once and for all (using his life to take care of his fields, to take a wife, to arrange world history), is not indeed indefiniteness, so that despite all the definiteness he has progressed no further, because the issue has not even been grasped. But since he has not used his life to become subjective, his subjectivity has become some indefinite something in general, and that is why that abstract definiteness has become indefiniteness. If he uses his life to become subjective, he asks whether the definiteness, by having to be present to him at every moment, is not made dialectically difficult by the incessant self-relating to the alternation, which existence is, so that it becomes indefiniteness. He asks, if this (that the definiteness becomes indefiniteness) is the highest attainable by him, whether it is not then better to abandon the whole thing or whether he should stake all his passion on the indefiniteness and infinitely passionately relate himself to the indefiniteness of the definiteness, and whether this would be the only possible way for him to become cognizant of his immortality as long as he is existing, because as an existing being he is wondrously constituted, so that the definiteness of immortality can be possessed in definiteness only by the eternal, but its definiteness can be possessed by the existing person only in indefiniteness.

To ask about his immortality is indeed also an act for the existing subject who asks the question, which it certainly is not for absentminded people who once in a while in an altogether general way ask about what it means to be immortal, as if being immortal were something a person is once in a VII
while and the one asking the question were such a something 147
in general. Consequently, he asks how he, existing, is to conduct himself in expressing his immortality, whether he actually does express it, and for the time being he is content with this task, which can easily be sufficient for a person's lifetime, since it is to be sufficient for an eternity. And then? Well, when he is finished, the turn comes for world history. Nowadays the very opposite is indeed the case; nowadays one attends to world history first, with the amusing result, as another author has pointed out, that while immortality in general is proved and proved, faith in immortality declines more and more.[227]

For example, what does it mean that I should thank God for the good that he gives me?[228] The pastor says I am to do this; we all know that, and if we just attend to that, then for those who do not have to be content with the lowly lifework of simple people there will be time for attending to world history. In order to make everything as easy as possible, I shall not even object that it nevertheless does perhaps take some time. No, to indulge the pastor, I assume that I am even exceedingly willing to do it, so that I do not even need to calculate the time I use between being disinclined to do it, as the pastor assumes, and becoming inclined through the pastor's admonition. Consequently, I am assuming that I am exceedingly eager to thank God; more than this I do not say. I do not say that it is actually the case, that I know it definitely, because in relation to God I always speak indefinitely about myself, since he is the only one who definitely knows about my relationship with him. This circumspection in expressing oneself about one's relationship with God already contains a multiplicity of dialectical qualifications, and without it one probably will be like many world-historical people who contradict themselves in every third line when they speak about what is simple.

So I am to thank God, says the pastor, and for what? For the good that he gives me. Excellent! But for what good? Presumably for the good that I can discern is a good. Stop! If I thank God for the good I can discern to be a good, I am making a fool of God, because then my relationship with God means that I am transforming God in likeness to me instead of my being transformed in likeness to him. I thank him for the VII good that I know is a good, but what I know is the finite, and 148 consequently I go ahead and thank God for complying with my notion. And yet, in my relationship with God, I am specifically supposed to learn that I know nothing definitely, consequently not whether this is a good, either—and yet I am to thank him for the good I know is a good, something I nevertheless may not know. What then? Shall I omit giving thanks to him when that which happens to me is a good according to my poor finite understanding, something I perhaps have ardently wished for and which, now that I have received it, makes me feel so overwhelmed that I must of necessity thank God? Not quite that, but I am to bear in mind that my having wished it so ardently is no merit and becomes no merit through receiving what I wished. Consequently, with my giving thanks I am to include an apology so as to be sure that it is God with whom I have the honor of speaking and not my friend and comrade [*Dusbroder*[229]] Councilor Andersen. I must shamefacedly admit that it looks so good to me that I must pray for forgiveness for giving thanks for it, because I cannot help it. Consequently, I must pray for forgiveness for giving thanks. That is not what the pastor said. So either the pastor must want to make a fool of me or he does not know what he himself is saying—if only this pastor is not also concerned with the world-historical. In my relationship with God, I must learn simply to give up my finite understanding, and with it the drawing of distinctions that is natural to me, in order always to be able in divine madness to give thanks.

Always to give thanks—is this something in general, a once-and-for-all kind of thing? Does "always to thank God" mean that once a year, on the second Sunday in Lent at vespers,[230] I bear in mind that I am always to thank God, and perhaps do not even do that, for if I should happen to be in a strange mood that Sunday, I do not understand it even on that day. Consequently, thanking God, this simple matter, suddenly assigns me one of the most strenuous tasks, one that will be sufficient for my entire life. So it may take a little time before I achieve this, and if I did achieve it, what is that something higher I should reach for in order to let go of this?

Thus, while his friend, while his beloved, troubled and almost despairing, look at him and say: Unhappy man, what you must suffer—the God-fearing person must have the courage to say and express in action what he says: Dear ones, you are mistaken; what is happening to me is a good. I feel dis- VII 149 posed to thank God, if only my thanksgiving might please him. And until that point is reached, I shall, when thanking God for the good the pastor speaks about, do it shamefacedly.

The difficulty that here and at every point in the relationship with God (accordingly at innumerable points) manifests itself as the thoroughfare to the true infinitizing in God, the difficulty of always giving thanks, whereas the pastor's discourse was inauthentic elegance—this difficulty I could didactically express in this way. What the simple religious person does directly, the simple religiously aware person does only through humor (the humorous would consist, upon closer scrutiny, in my still having to make an apology for doing what the lowly court commands and commends as the highest), yet not in the sense that his religiousness is humor, but that humor is the boundary from which he defines his religiousness if he is going to declare it, the boundary that distinguishes between him and the immediate. It is a transit point that is already difficult enough to reach, but the true religious infinitizing has in turn forgotten this. It is not, however, my intention to didacticize, lest I myself become accustomed to reciting by rote or prompt anyone to do it.

For example, what does it mean to marry? What I know about this is what people ordinarily know. I have access to the garden where the amorist gathers bouquets of flowers—mine will

be as fragrant as most of the others'. I know where the storeroom is from which pastors obtain their discourses. If there is no other hindrance to becoming world-historical, well, then, let us begin. But—and still a "but"—but what is the midpoint that marriage expresses between the spiritual and the psychosomatic? In what way is it not an impediment? How is it, spiritually understood, a blessing (since what it is erotically is indeed an answer to only one part of the question)? How does it ethically become a task *in concreto* at the same time as the erotic everywhere declares the wonder? How is it that, as the perfection of existence, it is not exactly altogether perfect and gives a satisfaction (apart from the extent to which financial worries and the like cause disturbance, which must be excluded from the account here) that seriously intimates that the spirit within me is obscured and does not clearly grasp the contradiction, which indeed it is, that an immortal spirit has become an existing being. In other words, the question arises whether marital bliss might not be dubious, although an unhappy marriage is hardly to be commended, and its suffering is in no way identical with the suffering of the spirit, which in existence is
VII 150 the sure sign that I am existing *qua* spirit. The question arises whether paganism is not still haunting marriage and whether the theological paragraphs on marriage, together with the clergymen's highly esteemed embellishments (whether priced at one or two hundred rix-dollars), are not a jumbled diversity of knowledge that sometimes does not detect the difficulty inherent in the erotic, sometimes does not dare to say it, sometimes does not detect the difficulty in the religious, sometimes does not dare to say it.

Indeed, if a maidservant would wish to have me pay the musicians when she marries a manservant, I shall gladly do so if I can afford it; and if I have the time, I shall gladly dance with her on the wedding day, rejoicing with those who rejoice[231]—she most likely feels no need for a deeper understanding. That I would be superior to her because I feel this need is nonsense and is far removed from my laborious train of thought. Even if I were to find what I was seeking, I would perhaps not be half as good. But I feel this need to know what I am doing, a need that at the peak of its triumph is rewarded with that foolish little difference between the simple person's and the wise person's knowledge of the simple thing—that the simple person knows it, and the wise person knows that he knows it or knows that he does not know it. Yes, everyone who simply and honestly can say that he feels no need for this understanding—he is indeed without blame. Woe to the person who disturbs him, who will not leave up to the god [*Guden*] what he requires of each one individually. Yes, the person who, humble and cheerful in his happiness, in genuine modesty holds the opinion that the human race certainly does not begin with him but believes that he is trustingly following the *impressa vestigia* [footprints][232] of the human race because erotic love impels him to believe that he, "humble before God [*Gud*], submissive to the royal majesty of love,"[233] does not credit himself with having understood what is, in contentment with little, his earthly bliss—yes, he is indeed worthy of honor; and woe to the person who risks trying to pull the dangers and horrors of intellectual warfare down upon his blessed security in the enclosure of marriage.

But when there is bombast everywhere, when people want to bamboozle God world-historically and systematically, when even the pastors quickly turn their clerical robes inside out so that they might almost look like professors' gowns,[234] when the immediate is everywhere said to be annulled—the god does not resent it if one asks these lofty sages what they know about this simple matter. I have read what the judge has written on marriage in *Either/Or* and *Stages on Life's Way*;[235] I
have read it carefully. It has not surprised me to learn that VII
many who are in full swing with world history and the future 151
of humankind have taken exception to a rejoinder that first makes the matter as difficult as it is before it attempts an explanation. I do not blame the judge for this, nor for his enthusiastic zeal for marriage, but nevertheless I do think that the judge, provided I can get hold of him, if I whisper a little secret in his ear, will admit that difficulties remain.

We shall stop with these few examples. Examples I have aplenty; I can keep on as long as need be; I have enough for a lifetime and therefore do not need to proceed to astronomy or veterinary science. Besides, the examples are of the easy kind. The matter becomes much more difficult when one asks about the religious in the strictest sense, in which the explanation cannot consist in immanently procuring the infinitizing but in becoming aware of the paradox and holding on to the paradox at every moment, and most of all fearing in particular an explanation that would remove the paradox, because the paradox is not a transient form of the relation between the religious in the strictest sense and the existing person but is essentially conditioned by his being an existing person, so that the explanation that removes the paradox also fantastically transmogrifies the existing person into a fantastical something that belongs neither to time nor to eternity, but such a something is not a human being. So we shall stop with these examples. And what then, what follows from this? Nothing, absolutely nothing. I am indeed the one who continually says that between the simple person's and the wise person's knowledge of the simple there is only the ludicrous little difference—that the simple person knows it, and the wise person knows that he knows it or knows that he does not know it. But nevertheless something else does follow: Would it not be best to hold back a little on world history if this is how it stands with one's knowledge of the simple? I say no more. Perhaps the lofty sages know enough about all this; they may even be finished once and for all with the tasks in which the point is that they should be sufficient for an entire lifetime. Oh, that these invaluable thinkers who do so much for world history would also remember us little folk, who are not altogether simple, inasmuch as we feel a need to understand but still are so limited that we feel particularly the need to understand the simple.

This is the way I have tried to understand myself, and even if the understanding is slight and its yield poor, I have in compensation resolved to act with all my passion on the basis of
VII what I have understood. Perhaps, when all is said and done, it
152 is a more healthful diet to understand little but possess this
with passion's unlimited soundness in the setting of the infi-

nite than to know much and to possess nothing because I myself have fantastically become a fantastical subjective-objective something. I have considered it demeaning if I were to be more ashamed before human beings and their judgment than before the god and his judgment, cowardly and ignobly to inquire more about what shame before human beings might tempt me to do than about what shame before the god would bid. And who are those people, anyway, the ones I am supposed to fear—a few geniuses, perhaps, some literary critics, and whoever is seen on the highways and byways? Or were there no human beings alive before 1845? Or what are those people compared with the god; what is the refreshment of their busy clangor compared with the deliciousness of that solitary wellspring that is in every human being, that wellspring in which the god resides, that wellspring in the profound silence when all is quiet! And, compared with eternity, what else than a brief moment is the hour and a half of time I have to live with human beings? Will they perhaps pursue me in all eternity? The pastor does say that we shall meet again, but does that apply to every street acquaintance? I think not. Suppose there is a wall of division,[236] and suppose I had been in the wrong—then I would no doubt be excluded from their company. Suppose I had been in the right—then I presumably would be in another class. Suppose eternity is so capacious that I could not even spot His Reverence, who was so kind as to guarantee that we would meet again! But woe unto me if the god judged me in my innermost being for mendaciously wanting to be systematic and world-historical and forgetting what it is to be a human being and thereby forgetting what it means that he is the god—woe unto me! Woe unto me in time, and even more dreadfully in eternity when he gets hold of me there! His judgment is the final one, is the only one; his co-knowledge is inescapable since it is woven into and weaves through the faintest movement of my consciousness, its most secret association with itself. His presence is an eternal contemporaneity[237]—and I should have dared to be ashamed of him!

This sounds almost like earnestness. If only I dared appeal

to visions and revelations and to my being red in the face, many people would take it to be earnestness instead of assuming it to be only congestion of blood. Just as when Socrates was living it was the demand of the times that he should blubber and whine before the tribunal, imploring for mercy[238]—in
VII which case he would have been acquitted—so it is the demand
153 of the times that one must roar world-historically and bellow systematically, proclaiming oneself to be the expected one. But I have no miracle to appeal to; ah, that was Dr. Hjortespring's happy fate! According to his own very well written report,[239] he became an adherent of Hegelian philosophy through a miracle at Hotel Streit in Hamburg on Easter morning (although none of the waiters noticed anything[240])—an adherent of the philosophy that assumes that there are no miracles.[241] Wondrous sign of the times! If this man is not the expected philosopher, who is it, then, who knows the demands of the times as he does! Wondrous sign of the times, far more magnificent and important than the conversion of Paul,[242] because Paul's conversion through a miracle to a doctrine that declares itself to be a miracle is rather straightforward, but to be converted by a miracle to the teaching that accepts no miracles is rather topsy-turvy. The miracle occurred on Easter morning. With regard to such a poetic hero and such a poetic Easter morning, the year and the date are matters of complete indifference; it may well have been the same Easter morning as in Goethe's *Faust*,[243] even though the two contemporaries, Dr. Hjortespring[244] and Faust in Goethe's *Faust*, arrived at different results! Who presumes to venture an explanation of that miracle! The whole thing remains exceedingly puzzling, even if it is assumed that Easter came very early that year, for example, on April first, [245]so that in addition to becoming a Hegelian the doctor became an April fool—[246]according to the nature of poetry, a suitable poetic recompense for romantically wanting to prink up the transition to Hegelian philosophy, the merit of which lies precisely in the method, and thus it rejects romanticism.

Obviously, I cannot be of service with a miracle or with anything exceedingly important. No, I really cannot. I must implore every sensitive fellow human being, near and far, within the city or outside, to be convinced that I would be more than willing to satisfy the demands of the times in this way, but to me the truth is most cherished, and here the truth is nothing short of a miracle, and that is why the story ought not to be a miraculous and *wunderbar* [wonderful] story about an extremely insignificant event, which therefore did not occur in that remote, unfamiliar city to the west, in the Hanseatic city of Hamburg, to which a traveler only rarely makes his way.

It is now about four[247] years since the idea came to me of VII
wanting to try my hand as an author. I remember it very 154
clearly. It was on a Sunday; yes, correct, it was a Sunday afternoon. As usual, I was sitting outside the café in Frederiksberg Gardens,[248] that wonderful garden which for the child was the enchanted land where the king lived with the queen, that lovely garden which for the youth was a pleasant diversion in the happy gaiety of the populace, that friendly garden which for the adult is so cozy in its wistful elevation above the world and what belongs to the world, that garden where even the envied glory of royalty is what it indeed is out there—a queen's[249] recollection of her late lord. There as usual I sat and smoked my cigar. Regrettably, the only similarity I have been able to detect between the beginning of my fragment of philosophic endeavor and the miraculous beginning of that poetic hero[250] is that it was in a public place. Otherwise there is no similarity at all, and although I am the author of *Fragments*, I am so insignificant that I am an outsider in literature. I have not even added to subscription literature,[251] nor can it truthfully be said that I have a significant place in it.

I had been a student for a half score of years. Although I was never lazy, all my activity was nevertheless only like a splendid inactivity, a kind of occupation I still much prefer and for which I perhaps have a little genius. I read a great deal, spent the rest of the day loafing and thinking, or thinking and loafing, but nothing came of it. The productive sprout in me went for everyday use and was consumed in its first greening. An inexplicable power of persuasion, both strong and cunning, continually constrained me, captivated by its persuasion. This power was my indolence. It is not like the vehement craving of erotic love or like the intense incitement of enthusiasm; it is instead like a woman in the house who constrains one and with whom one gets on very well—so well that one never dreams of wanting to marry. This much is certain: although I am generally not unacquainted with the comforts of life, of all comforts indolence is the most comfortable.

VII So there I sat and smoked my cigar until I drifted into
155 thought. Among other thoughts, I recall these. You are getting on in years, I said to myself, and are becoming an old man without being anything and without actually undertaking anything. On the other hand, wherever you look in literature or in life, you see the names and figures of celebrities, the prized and highly acclaimed people, prominent or much discussed, the many benefactors of the age who know how to benefit humankind by making life easier and easier, some by railroads, others by omnibuses and steamships, others by telegraph, others by easily understood surveys and brief publications about everything worth knowing, and finally the true benefactors of the age who by virtue of thought systematically make spiritual existence easier and easier and yet more and more meaningful—and what are you doing?

At this point my introspection was interrupted because my cigar was finished and a new one had to be lit. So I smoked again, and then suddenly this thought crossed my mind: You must do something, but since with your limited capabilities it will be impossible to make anything easier than it has become, you must, with the same humanitarian enthusiasm as the others have, take it upon yourself to make something more difficult. This idea pleased me enormously; it also flattered me that for this effort I would be loved and respected, as much as anyone else, by the entire community. In other words, when all join together to make everything easier in every way, there remains only one possible danger, namely, the danger that the easiness would become so great that it would become all too easy. So only one lack remains, even though not yet felt, the lack of difficulty. Out of love of humankind, out of despair over my awkward predicament of having achieved nothing and of being unable to make anything easier than it had already been made, out of genuine interest in those who make everything easy, I comprehended that it was my task: to make difficulties everywhere. It was also especially striking to me that I might actually have my indolence to thank that this task became mine. Far from having found it, like an Aladdin,[252] by a stroke of good luck, I must instead assume that my indolence, by preventing me from opportunely proceeding to make things easy, has forced me into doing the only thing that remained.

Thus I, too, am striving toward the lofty goal of being hailed with acclaim—unless I should be laughed to scorn or VII
perhaps crucified, for it is probable that everyone who shouts 156
bravo also shouts "*pereat* [let him die]," *item* [also] "crucify,"[253] and does so even without becoming untrue to his character, since on the contrary he remains essentially true to himself—*qua* shouter. But even if my endeavor fails to be appreciated, I am still aware that it is as noble as the endeavors of others. When at a banquet where the guests have already gorged themselves, someone is intent on having more courses served and someone else on having an emetic ready, it is certainly true that only the former has understood what the guests demand, but I wonder if the latter might not also claim to have considered what they might require.

From that moment I have found my entertainment [*Underholdning*] in this work. I mean that the work, this work of preparation and self-development, has been entertaining to me, because my accomplishment so far has been only the tiny fragment of *Fragments*, and I have not found my livelihood [*Underholdning*][254] in that, since I financed it myself. Yet I can hardly ask people to pay money for having something made difficult; that would indeed be augmenting a difficulty with a new difficulty, and when taking medicine one is accustomed rather to have also a *douceur* [sweetener, reward]. [255]I am so far from misunderstanding this that if I were objectively sure (which I as a *subjective* author naturally am not) of the usefulness of my medicine and that this did not depend simply and solely on the way it is used, so that the manner of use is actually the medicine, I would be the first to promise every one of my readers a *raisonnable douceur* or to open to my readers, one and all, men and women, the prospect of participating in a lottery of tasteful gifts[256] so as in this way to infuse them with the strength and courage to read my pamphlets. If those who make everything easy were ever to discern that they truly derive benefit from my fragment of difficulty, lest the easiness become like a dead calm, and if, moved and touched by thus having understood my endeavor, perhaps mediated into their own effort, they should decide to support me surreptitiously with cash donations, these will be gladly accepted, and I promise absolute secrecy, lest humankind, from whom we in coalition derive benefit and profit, find out the true connection.

VII 157 What has been presented here will presumably be found quite appropriate for a subjective author. It is more remarkable when a systematician entertains us with a report that he became an adherent of the system through a miracle, something that seems to suggest that his systematic life and career do not have this in common with the system: to begin with nothing.

[257]CHAPTER II

Subjective Truth, Inwardness; Truth Is Subjectivity

Whether truth is defined more empirically as the agreement of thinking with being or more idealistically as the agreement of being with thinking, the point in each case is to pay scrupulous attention to what is understood by being and also to pay attention to whether the knowing human spirit might not be lured out into the indefinite and fantastically become something such as no *existing* human being has ever been or can be, a phantom with which the individual busies himself on occasion, yet without ever making it explicit to himself by means of dialectical middle terms how he gets out into this fantastical realm, what meaning it has for him to be there, whether the entire endeavor out there might not dissolve into a tautology within a rash, fantastical venture.

If, in the two definitions given, being [*Væren*] is understood as empirical being, then truth itself is transformed into a *desideratum* [something wanted] and everything is placed in the process of becoming [*Vorden*], because the empirical object is not finished, and the existing knowing spirit is itself in the process of becoming. Thus truth is an approximating whose beginning cannot be established absolutely, because there is no conclusion that has retroactive power. On the other hand, every beginning, when it is *made* (if it is not arbitrariness by not being conscious of this), does not occur by virtue of immanental thinking but *is made* by virtue of a resolution, essentially by virtue of faith. That the knowing spirit is an existing spirit, and that every human being is such a spirit existing for himself,[258] I cannot repeat often enough, because the fantastical disregard of this has been the cause of much confusion. VII
May no one misunderstand me. I am indeed a poor existing 158

spirit like all other human beings, but if in a legitimate and honest way I could be assisted in becoming something extraordinary, the pure *I-I*, I would always be willing to give thanks for the gift and the good deed. If, however, it can occur only in the way mentioned earlier, by saying *eins, zwei, drei, kokolorum* or by tying a ribbon around the little finger and throwing it away in some remote place when the moon is full—then I would rather remain what I am, a poor existing individual human being.

The term "being" in those definitions must, then, be understood much more abstractly as the abstract rendition or the abstract prototype of what being *in concreto* is as empirical being. If it is understood in this way, nothing stands in the way of abstractly defining truth as something finished, because, viewed abstractly, the agreement between thinking and being is always finished, inasmuch as the beginning of the process of becoming lies precisely in the concretion that abstraction abstractly disregards.

But if being is understood in this way, the formula is a tautology; that is, thinking and being signify one and the same, and the agreement spoken of is only an abstract identity with itself. Therefore, none of the formulas says more than that truth is, if this is understood in such a way that the copula is accentuated—truth *is*—that is, truth is a redoubling [*Fordoblelse*].[259] Truth is the first, but truth's other, that it *is*, is the same as the first; this, its being, is the abstract form of truth. In this way it is expressed that truth is not something simple but in an entirely abstract sense a redoubling, which is nevertheless canceled at the very same moment.

Abstraction may go on by paraphrasing this as much as it pleases—it will never come any further. As soon as the being of truth becomes empirically concrete, truth itself is in the process of becoming and is indeed in turn, by intimation, the agreement between thinking and being, and is indeed actually that way for God, but it is not that way for any existing spirit, because this spirit, itself existing, is in the process of becoming.

For the existing spirit *qua* existing spirit, the question about

truth persists, because the abstract answer is only for that *ab-
stractum* which an existing spirit becomes by abstracting from VII
himself *qua* existing, which he can do only momentarily, al- 159
though at such moments he still pays his debt to existence by existing nevertheless. Consequently, it is an existing spirit who asks about truth, presumably because he wants to exist in it, but in any case the questioner is conscious of being an existing individual human being. In this way I believe I am able to make myself understandable to every Greek and to every rational human being. If a German philosopher follows his inclination to put on an act [*skabe sig*] and first transforms himself [*skabe sig om*] into a superrational something, just as alchemists and sorcerers bedizen themselves fantastically, in order to answer the question about truth in an extremely satisfying way, this is of no more concern to me than his satisfying answer, which no doubt is extremely satisfying—if one is fantastically dressed up. But whether a German philosopher is or is not doing this can easily be ascertained by anyone who with enthusiasm concentrates his soul on willing to allow himself to be guided by a sage of that kind, and uncritically just uses his guidance compliantly by willing to form his existence according to it. When a person as a learner enthusiastically relates in this way to such a German professor, he accomplishes the most superb epigram upon him, because a speculator of that sort is anything but served by a learner's honest and enthusiastic zeal for expressing and accomplishing, for existentially appropriating his wisdom, since this wisdom is something that the Herr Professor himself has imagined and has written books about but has never attempted himself. It has not even occurred to him that it should be done. Like the customs clerk who, in the belief that his business was merely to write, wrote what he himself could not read,[260] so there are speculative thinkers who merely write, and write that which, if it is to be read with the aid of action, if I may put it that way, proves to be nonsense, unless it is perhaps intended only for fantastical beings.

When for the existing spirit *qua* existing there is a question about truth, that abstract reduplication [*Reduplikation*] of truth

recurs; but existence itself, existence itself in the questioner, who does indeed exist, holds the two factors apart, one from the other, and reflection shows two relations. To objective reflection, truth becomes something objective, an object, and
VII 160 the point is to disregard the subject. To subjective reflection, truth becomes appropriation, inwardness, subjectivity, and the point is to immerse oneself, existing, in subjectivity.

But what then? Are we to remain in this disjunction, or does mediation offer its kind assistance here, so that truth becomes subject-object? Why not? But can mediation then help the existing person so that he himself, as long as he is existing, becomes mediation, which is, after all, *sub specie aeterni*, whereas the poor existing one is existing? It certainly does not help to make a fool of a person, to entice him with the subject-object when he himself is prevented from entering into the state in which he can relate himself to it, prevented because he himself, by virtue of existing, is in the process of becoming. Of what help is it to explain how the eternal truth is to be understood eternally when the one to use the explanation is prevented from understanding it in this way because he is existing and is merely a fantast if he fancies himself to be *sub specie aeterni*, consequently when he must avail himself precisely of the explanation of how the eternal truth is to be understood in the category of time by someone who by existing is himself in time, something the honored professor himself admits, if not always, then every three months when he draws his salary.

With the subject-object of mediation, we have merely reverted to abstraction, inasmuch as the definition of truth as subject-object is exactly the same as: the truth *is*, that is, the truth is a redoubling [*Fordoblelse*]. Consequently, the exalted wisdom has again been absentminded enough to forget that it was an existing spirit who asked about truth. Or is perhaps the existing spirit himself the subject-object? In that case, I am obliged to ask: Where is such an existing human being who is also a subject-object? Or shall we perhaps here again first transmute the existing spirit into a something in general and then explain everything except what was asked about: How an existing subject *in concreto* relates himself to the truth, or what then must be asked about: How the individual existing subject then relates himself to this something that seems to have not a little in common with a paper kite or with the lump of sugar that the Dutch used to hang from the ceiling and everyone would lick.

We return, then, to the two ways of reflection and have not forgotten that it is an existing spirit who is asking, simply an individual human being, and are not able to forget, either, that VII 161 his existing is precisely what will prevent him from going both ways at once, and his concerned questions will prevent him from light-mindedly and fantastically becoming a subject-object. Now, then, which of the ways is the way of truth for the existing spirit? Only the fantastical *I-I* is simultaneously finished with both ways or advances methodically along both ways simultaneously, which for an existing human being is such an inhuman way of walking that I dare not recommend it.

Since the questioner specifically emphasizes that he is an existing person, the way to be commended is naturally the one that especially accentuates what it means to exist.

The way of objective reflection turns the subjective individual into something accidental and thereby turns existence into an indifferent, vanishing something. The way to the objective truth goes away from the subject, and while the subject and subjectivity become indifferent [*ligegyldig*], the truth also becomes indifferent, and that is precisely its objective validity [*Gyldighed*], because the interest, just like the decision, is subjectivity. The way of objective reflection now leads to abstract thinking, to mathematics, to historical knowledge of various kinds, and always leads away from the subjective individual, whose existence or nonexistence becomes, from an objective point of view, altogether properly, infinitely indifferent, altogether properly, because, as Hamlet says, existence and nonexistence have only subjective significance.[261] At its maximum, this way will lead to a contradiction, and to the extent that the subject does not become totally indifferent to himself, this is merely an indication that his objective striving is not objective enough. At its maximum, it will lead to the contradiction that only objectivity has come about, whereas subjectivity has gone out, that is, the existing subjectivity that has made an attempt to become what in the abstract sense is called subjectivity, the abstract form of an abstract objectivity. And yet, viewed subjectively, the objectivity that has come about is at its maximum either a hypothesis or an approximation, because all eternal decision is rooted specifically in subjectivity.

But the objective way is of the opinion that it has a security that the subjective way does not have (of course, existence, what it means to exist, and objective security cannot be
VII 162 thought together). It is of the opinion that it avoids a danger that lies in wait for the subjective way, and at its maximum this danger is madness. In a solely subjective definition of truth, lunacy and truth are ultimately indistinguishable, because they may both have inwardness.* But one does not become lunatic by becoming objective. At this point I might perhaps add a little comment that does not seem superfluous in an objective age. Is the absence of inwardness also lunacy? The objective truth as such does not at all decide that the one stating it is sensible; on the contrary, it can even betray that the man is lunatic, although what he says is entirely true and especially objectively true.

I shall here allow myself to relate an incident that, without any modification whatever by me, comes directly from a madhouse. A patient in such an institution wants to run away and actually carries out his plan by jumping through a window. He now finds himself in the garden of the institution and wishes to take to the road of freedom. Then it occurs to him

* Even this is not true, however, because madness never has the inwardness of infinity. Its fixed idea is a kind of objective something, and the contradiction of madness lies in wanting to embrace it with passion. The decisive factor in madness is thus not the subjective, but the little finitude that becomes fixed, something the infinite can never become.

(shall I say that he was sagacious enough or lunatic enough to have this whimsical idea?): When you arrive in the city, you will be recognized and will very likely be taken back right away. What you need to do, then, is to convince everyone completely, by the objective truth of what you say, that all is well as far as your sanity is concerned. As he is walking along and pondering this, he sees a skittle ball lying on the ground. He picks it up and puts it in the tail of his coat. At every step he takes, this ball bumps him, if you please, on his r——, and every time it bumps him he says, "Boom! The earth is round." He arrives in the capital city and immediately visits one of his friends. He wants to convince him that he is not lunatic and therefore paces up and down the floor and continually says, "Boom! The earth is round!" But is the earth not round? Does the madhouse demand yet another sacrifice on account of this assumption, as in those days when everyone assumed it to be as flat as a pancake? Or is he lunatic, the man who hopes to prove that he is not lunatic by stating a truth universally accepted and universally regarded as objective? And yet, precisely by this it became clear to the physician that the patient VII
was not yet cured, although the cure certainly could not re- 163
volve around getting him to assume that the earth is flat. But not everyone is a physician, and the demand of the times has considerable influence on the question of lunacy. Now and then, one would indeed almost be tempted to assume that the modern age, which has modernized Christianity, has also modernized Pilate's question,[262] and that the need of the age to find something in which to repose declares itself in the question: What is lunacy? When an assistant professor, every time his coattail reminds him to say something, says *de omnibus dubitandum est* [everything must be doubted][263] and briskly writes away on a system in which there is sufficient internal evidence in every other sentence that the man has never doubted anything—he is not considered lunatic.

Don Quixote is the prototype of the subjective lunacy in which the passion of inwardness grasps a particular fixed finite idea. But when inwardness is absent, parroting lunacy sets in, which is just as comic, and it would be desirable for an imag-

inatively constructing psychologist to depict it by taking a handful of such philosophers and putting them together. When the insanity is a delirium of inwardness, the tragic and the comic are that the something that infinitely pertains to the unfortunate person is a fixed detail that pertains to no one else. But when the insanity is the absence of inwardness, the comic is that the something known by the blissful person is the truth, truth that pertains to the whole human race but does not in the least pertain to the highly honored parroter. This kind of insanity is more inhuman than the other. One shrinks from looking the first one in the eye, lest one discover the depth of his frantic state, but one does not dare to look at the other at all for fear of discovering that he does not have proper eyes but glass eyes and hair made from a floor mat, in short, that he is an artificial product. If one happens to meet a mentally deranged person of that sort, whose illness is simply that he has no mind, one listens to him in cold horror. One does not know whether one dares to believe that it is a human being with whom one is speaking, or perhaps a "walking stick,"[264] an artificial contrivance of Døbler[265] that conceals in itself a barrel organ [*Positiv*].[266] To drink *Dus* with the executioner[267] can indeed be unpleasant for a self-respecting man, but to get
VII 164 into a rational and speculative conversation with a walking stick—now that is almost enough to drive one crazy.

Subjective reflection turns inward toward subjectivity and in this inward deepening will be of the truth, and in such a way that, just as in the preceding, when objectivity was advanced, subjectivity vanished, here subjectivity as such becomes the final factor and objectivity the vanishing. Here it is not forgotten, even for a single moment, that the subject is existing, and that existing is a becoming, and that truth as the identity of thought and being is therefore a chimera of abstraction and truly only a longing of creation,[268] not because truth is not an identity, but because the knower is an existing person, and thus truth cannot be an identity for him as long as he exists. If this is not held fast, then with the aid of speculative thought we promptly enter into the fantastical *I-I* that recent speculative thought certainly has used but without explaining how a particular individual relates himself to it, and, good Lord, of course no human being is more than a particular individual.

If the existing person could actually be outside himself, the truth would be something concluded for him. But where is this point? The *I-I* is a mathematical point that does not exist at all; accordingly anyone can readily take up this standpoint—no one stands in the way of anyone else. Only momentarily can a particular individual, existing, be in a unity of the infinite and the finite that transcends existing. This instant is the moment of passion. Modern speculative thought has mustered everything to enable the individual to transcend himself objectively, but this just cannot be done. Existence exercises its constraint, and if philosophers nowadays had not become pencil-pushers serving the trifling busyness of fantastical thinking, it would have discerned that suicide is the only somewhat practical interpretation of its attempt. But pencil-pushing modern speculative thought takes a dim view of passion, and yet, for the existing person, passion is existence at its very highest—and we are, after all, existing persons. In passion, the existing subject is infinitized in the eternity of imagination and yet is also most definitely himself. The fantastical *I-I* is not infinitude and finitude in identity, since neither the one nor the other is actual; it is a fantastical union with VII 165
a cloud,[269] an unfruitful embrace, and the relation of the individual *I* to this mirage is never stated.[270]

All essential knowing pertains to existence, or only the knowing whose relation to existence is essential is essential knowing. Essentially viewed, the knowing that does not inwardly in the reflection of inwardness pertain to existence is accidental knowing, and its degree and scope, essentially viewed, are a matter of indifference. That essential knowing is essentially related to existence does not, however, signify the above-mentioned abstract identity between thinking and being, nor does it signify that the knowledge is objectively related to something existent [*Tilværende*] as its object, but it means that the knowledge is related to the knower, who is essentially an existing person [*Existerende*], and that all essential knowing is therefore essentially related to existence and to existing. Therefore, only ethical and ethical-religious knowing is essential knowing. But all ethical and all ethical-religious knowing is essentially a relating to the existing of the knower.

Mediation is a mirage, just as the *I-I* is. Viewed abstractly, everything *is* and nothing becomes. Mediation cannot possibly find its place in abstraction, since it has *movement* as its presupposition. Objective knowledge can certainly have the existent [*Tilværende*] as its object, but since the knowing subject is existing [*existerende*] and himself in the process of becoming by existing, speculative thought must first explain how a particular existing subject relates himself to the knowledge of mediation, what he is at the moment, whether, for example, he is not at that very moment rather absentminded, and where he is, whether he is not on the moon. There is this continual talk about mediation and mediation. Is mediation, then, a human being, just as Per Degn assumes *Imprimatur* to be a human being?[271] How does a human being go about becoming something of that sort? Is this dignity, this great *philosophicum*,[272] attained by studying? Or does the magistrate give it away as he gives away sexton and gravedigger positions? Just try to become involved with these and other similar simple questions raised by a simple human being, who would so very much like to be mediation if he could become that in a legitimate and honorable manner, and not either by saying *eins, zwei, drei, kokolorum* or by forgetting that he himself is an
VII 166 existing human being, for whom existing is consequently something essential, and for whom existing ethically-religiously is a suitable *quantum satis* [sufficient amount]. To a speculative thinker it may seem *abgeschmackt* [in bad taste] to ask questions in this way, but it is especially important not to polemicize in the wrong place and hence not to begin fantastically-objectively a *pro* and *contra* as to whether or not there is mediation, but firmly to maintain what it means to be a human being.

[273]In order to clarify the divergence of objective and subjective reflection, I shall now describe subjective reflection in its

search back and inward into inwardness. At its highest, inwardness in an existing subject is passion; truth as a paradox corresponds to passion, and that truth becomes a paradox is grounded precisely in its relation to an existing subject. In this way the one corresponds to the other. In forgetting that one is an existing subject, one loses passion, and in return, truth does not become a paradox; but the knowing subject shifts from being human to being a fantastical something, and truth becomes a fantastical object for its knowing.

[274]*When the question about truth is asked objectively, truth is reflected upon objectively as an object to which the knower relates himself. What is reflected upon is not the relation but that what he relates himself to is the truth, the true. If only that to which he relates himself is the truth, the true, then the subject is in the truth. When the question about truth is asked subjectively, the individual's relation is reflected upon subjectively. If only the how of this relation is in truth, the individual is in truth, even if he in this way were to relate himself to untruth.**

Let us take the knowledge of God as an example. Objectively, what is reflected upon is that this is the true God; subjectively, that the individual relates himself to a something *in such a way* that his relation is in truth a God-relation. Now, on which side is the truth? Alas, must we not at this point resort
to mediation and say: It is on neither side; it is in the media- VII 167
tion? Superbly stated, if only someone could say how an existing person goes about being in mediation, because to be in mediation is to be finished; to exist is to become. An existing person cannot be in two places at the same time, cannot be subject-object. When he is closest to being in two places at the same time, he is in passion; but passion is only momentary, and passion is the highest pitch of subjectivity.

The existing person who chooses the objective way now enters upon all approximating deliberation intended to bring forth God objectively, which is not achieved in all eternity,

* The reader will note that what is being discussed here is essential truth, or the truth that is related essentially to existence, and that it is specifically in order to clarify it as inwardness or as subjectivity that the contrast is pointed out.

because God is a subject and hence only for subjectivity in inwardness. The existing person who chooses the subjective way instantly comprehends the whole dialectical difficulty because he must use some time, perhaps a long time, to find God objectively. He comprehends this dialectical difficulty in all its pain, because he must resort to God at that very moment, because every moment in which he does not have God is wasted.* At that very moment he has God, not by virtue of any objective deliberation but by virtue of the infinite passion of inwardness. The objective person is not bothered by dialectical difficulties such as what it means to put a whole research period into finding God, since it is indeed possible that the researcher would die tomorrow, and if he goes on living, he cannot very well regard God as something to be taken along at his convenience, since God is something one takes along *à tout prix* [at any price], which, in passion's understanding, is the true relationship of inwardness with God.

It is at this point, dialectically so very difficult, that the road swings off for the person who knows what it means to think dialectically and, existing, to think dialectically, which is quite different from sitting as a fantastical being at a desk and writing about something one has never done oneself, quite different from writing *de omnibus dubitandum* and then as an existing person being just as credulous as the most sensate human
VII 168 being. It is here that the road swings off, and the change is this: whereas objective knowledge goes along leisurely on the long road of approximation, itself not actuated by passion, to subjective knowledge every delay is a deadly peril and the decision so infinitely important that it is immediately urgent, as if the opportunity had already passed by unused.

* [275]In this way God is indeed a postulate, but not in the loose sense in which it is ordinarily taken. Instead, it becomes clear that this is the only way an existing person enters into a relationship with God: when the dialectical contradiction brings passion to despair and assists him in grasping God with "the category of despair" (faith),[276] so that the postulate, far from being the arbitrary, is in fact *necessary* defense [*N ø d værge*], self-defense; in this way God is not a postulate, but the existing person's postulating of God is—a necessity [*Nødvendighed*].

Now, if the problem is to calculate where there is more truth (and, as stated, simultaneously to be on both sides equally is not granted to an existing person but is only a beatifying delusion for a deluded *I-I*), whether on the side of the person who only objectively seeks the true God and the approximating truth of the God-idea or on the side of the person who is infinitely concerned that he in truth relate himself to God with the infinite passion of need—then there can be no doubt about the answer for anyone who is not totally botched by scholarship and science. If someone who lives in the midst of Christianity enters, with knowledge of the true idea of God, the house of God, the house of the true God, and prays, but prays in untruth, and if someone lives in an idolatrous land but prays with all the passion of infinity, although his eyes are resting upon the image of an idol—where, then, is there more truth? The one prays in truth to God although he is worshiping an idol; the other prays in untruth to the true God and is therefore in truth worshiping an idol.

If someone objectively inquires into immortality, and someone else stakes the passion of the infinite on the uncertainty—where, then, is there more truth, and who has more certainty? The one has once and for all entered upon an approximation that never ends, because the certainty of immortality is rooted in subjectivity; the other is immortal and therefore struggles by contending with the uncertainty.

Let us consider Socrates. These days everyone is dabbling in a few proofs or demonstrations—one has many, another fewer. But Socrates! He poses the question objectively, problematically: if there is an immortality.[277] So, compared with one of the modern thinkers with the three demonstrations, was he a doubter? Not at all. He stakes his whole life on this "if"; he dares to die, and with the passion of the infinite he has so ordered his whole life that it might be acceptable—*if* there is an immortality. Is there any better demonstration for the immortality of the soul? But those who have the three demonstrations do not order their lives accordingly. If there is an VII
immortality, it must be nauseated by their way of living—is 169
there any better counterdemonstration to the three demon-

strations? The "fragment" of uncertainty helped Socrates, because he himself helped with the passion of infinity. The three demonstrations are of no benefit whatever to those others, because they are and remain slugs and, failing to demonstrate anything else, have demonstrated it by their three demonstrations.

In the same way a girl has perhaps possessed all the sweetness of being in love through a weak hope of being loved by the beloved, because she herself staked everything on this weak hope; [278]on the other hand, many a wedded matron, who more than once has submitted to the strongest expression of erotic love, has certainly had demonstrations and yet, strangely enough, has not possessed *quod erat demonstrandum* [that which was to be demonstrated]. The Socratic ignorance was thus the expression, firmly maintained with all the passion of inwardness, of the relation of the eternal truth to an existing person, and therefore it must remain for him a paradox as long as he exists. Yet it is possible that in the Socratic ignorance there was more truth in Socrates than in the objective truth of the entire system that flirts with the demands of the times and adapts itself to assistant professors.

[279]*Objectively the emphasis is on* ***what*** *is said; subjectively the emphasis is on* ***how*** *it is said.* This distinction applies even esthetically and is specifically expressed when we say that in the mouth of this or that person something that is truth can become untruth. Particular attention should be paid to this distinction in our day, for if one were to express in a single sentence the difference between ancient times and our time, one would no doubt have to say: In ancient times there were only a few individuals who knew the truth; now everyone knows it, but inwardness has an inverse relation to it.* Viewed esthetically, the contradiction that emerges when truth becomes untruth in this and that person's mouth is best interpreted comically. Ethically-religiously, the emphasis is again on: *how*. But this is not to be understood as manner, modulation of voice, oral delivery, etc., but it is to be understood as the

* See *Stages on Life's Way*, p. 366 fn.[280]

relation of the existing person, in his very existence, to what is said. Objectively, the question is only about categories of thought; subjectively, about inwardness. At its maximum, this "how" is the passion of the infinite, and the passion of the infinite is the very truth. But the passion of the infinite is precisely subjectivity, and thus subjectivity is truth. From the objective point of view, there is no infinite decision, and thus it VII
is objectively correct that the distinction between good and 170
evil is canceled, along with the principle of contradiction, and thereby also the infinite distinction between truth and falsehood. Only in subjectivity is there decision, whereas wanting to become objective is untruth. The passion of the infinite, not its content, is the deciding factor, for its content is precisely itself. In this way the subjective "how" and subjectivity are the truth.

[281]But precisely because the subject is existing, the "how" that is subjectively emphasized is dialectical also with regard to time. In the moment of the decision of passion, where the road swings off from objective knowledge, it looks as if the infinite decision were thereby finished. But at the same moment, the existing person is in the temporal realm, and the subjective "how" is transformed into a striving that is motivated and repeatedly refreshed by the decisive passion of the infinite, but it is nevertheless a striving.

When subjectivity is truth, the definition of truth must also contain in itself an expression of the antithesis to objectivity, a memento of that fork in the road, and this expression will at the same time indicate the resilience of the inwardness. Here is such a definition of truth: *An objective uncertainty, held fast through appropriation with the most passionate inwardness, is the truth*, the highest truth there is for an *existing* person. At the point where the road swings off (and where that is cannot be stated objectively, since it is precisely subjectivity), objective knowledge is suspended. Objectively he then has only uncertainty, but this is precisely what intensifies the infinite passion of inwardness, and truth is precisely the daring venture of choosing the objective uncertainty with the passion of the infinite. I observe nature in order to find God, and I do indeed see omnipotence and wisdom, but I also see much that troubles and disturbs. The *summa summarum* [sum total] of this is an objective uncertainty, but the inwardness is so very great, precisely because it grasps this objective uncertainty with all the passion of the infinite. In a mathematical proposition, for example, the objectivity is given, but therefore its truth is also an indifferent truth.

But the definition of truth stated above is a paraphrasing of faith. [282]Without risk, no faith. Faith is the contradiction between the infinite passion of inwardness and the objective uncertainty. If I am able to apprehend God objectively, I do not have faith; but because I cannot do this, I must have faith. If I want to keep myself in faith, I must continually see to it that I
VII hold fast the objective uncertainty, see to it that in the objec-
171 tive uncertainty I am "out on 70,000 fathoms of water" and still have faith.

[283]The thesis that subjectivity, inwardness, is truth contains the Socratic wisdom, the undying merit of which is to have paid attention to the essential meaning of existing, of the knower's being an existing person. That is why, in his ignorance, Socrates was in the truth in the highest sense within paganism. To comprehend this, that the misfortune of speculative thought is simply that it forgets again and again that the knower is an existing person, can already be rather difficult in our objective age. "But to go beyond Socrates when one has not even comprehended the Socratic—that, at least, is not Socratic." See "The Moral" in *Fragments*.[284]

Just as in *Fragments*, let us from this point try a category of thought that actually does go beyond. Whether it is true or false is of no concern to me, since I am only imaginatively constructing, but this much is required, that it be clear that the Socratic is presupposed in it, so that I at least do not end up behind Socrates again.

When subjectivity, inwardness, is truth, then truth, objectively defined, is a paradox; and that truth is objectively a paradox shows precisely that subjectivity is truth, since the objectivity does indeed thrust away, and the objectivity's repulsion, or the expression for the objectivity's repulsion, is

the resilience and dynamometer of inwardness. The paradox is the objective uncertainty that is the expression for the passion of inwardness that is truth. So much for the Socratic. The eternal, essential truth, that is, the truth that is related essentially to the existing person by pertaining essentially to what it means to exist (viewed Socratically, all other knowledge is accidental, its degree and scope indifferent), is a paradox. Nevertheless the eternal, essential truth is itself not at all a paradox, but it is a paradox by being related to an existing person. Socratic ignorance is an expression of the objective uncertainty; the inwardness of the existing person is truth. In anticipation of what will be discussed later, the following comment is made here: Socratic ignorance is an analogue to the category of the absurd, except that there is even less objective certainty in the repulsion exerted by the absurd, since there is only the certainty that it is absurd, and for that very reason there is infinitely greater resilience in the inwardness. The Socratic inwardness in existing is an analogue to faith, except that the VII 172
inwardness of faith, corresponding not to the repulsion exerted by ignorance but to the repulsion exerted by the absurd, is infinitely deeper.

Viewed Socratically, the eternal essential truth is not at all paradoxical in itself, but only by being related to an existing person. This is expressed in another Socratic thesis: that all knowing is a recollecting. This thesis is an intimation of the beginning of speculative thought, but for that very reason Socrates did not pursue it; essentially it became Platonic. This is where the road swings off,[285] and Socrates essentially emphasizes existing, whereas Plato, forgetting this, loses himself in speculative thought. Socrates' infinite merit is precisely that of being an *existing* thinker, not a speculative thinker who forgets what it means to exist. To Socrates, therefore, the thesis that all knowing is a recollecting has, at the moment of parting and as a continually annulled possibility of speculating, a double significance: (1) that the knower is essentially *integer* [uncorrupted] and that for him there is no other dubiousness with regard to knowledge of the eternal truth than this, that he exists, a dubiousness so essential and decisive to him that it signifies that existing, the inward deepening in and through existing, is truth; (2) that existence in temporality has no decisive significance, because there is continually the possibility of taking oneself back into eternity by recollecting, even though this possibility is continually annulled because the inward deepening in existing fills up time.*

* This may be the proper place to elucidate a dubiousness in the design of *Fragments*, a dubiousness that was due to my not wanting immediately to make the matter as dialectically difficult as it is, because in our day terminologies and the like are so muddled that it is almost impossible to safeguard oneself against confusion. In order, if possible, to elucidate properly the difference between the Socratic (which was supposed to be the philosophical, the pagan philosophical position) and the category of imaginatively constructed thought, which actually goes beyond the Socratic, I carried the Socratic back to the thesis that all knowing is a recollecting.[286] It is commonly accepted as such, and only for the person who with a very special interest devotes himself to the Socratic, always returning to the sources, only for him will it be important to distinguish between Socrates and Plato on this point.
VII 173 The thesis certainly belongs to both of them, but Socrates continually parts with it because he wants to exist. By holding Socrates to the thesis that all knowing is recollecting, one turns him into a speculative philosopher instead of what he was, an existing thinker who understood existing as the essential. The thesis that all knowing is recollecting belongs to speculative thought, and recollecting is immanence, and from the point of view of speculation and the eternal there is no paradox. The difficulty, however, is that no human being is speculation, but the speculating person is an existing human being, subject to the claims of existence. To forget this is no merit, but to hold this fast is indeed a merit, and that is precisely what Socrates did. To emphasize existence, which contains within it the qualification of inwardness, is the Socratic, whereas the Platonic is to pursue recollection and immanence. Basically Socrates is thereby beyond all speculation, because he does not have a fantastical beginning where the speculating person changes clothes and then goes on and on and speculates, forgetting the most important thing, to exist. But precisely because Socrates is in this way beyond speculative thought, he acquires, when rightly depicted, a certain analogous likeness to what the imaginary construction set forth as that which truly goes beyond the Socratic: the truth as paradox is an analog to the paradox *sensu eminentiori* [in the more eminent sense]; the passion of inwardness in existing is then an analog to faith *sensu eminentiori*. That the difference is infinite nevertheless, that the designations in *Fragments* of that which truly goes beyond the Socratic are unchanged, I can easily show, but I was afraid to make complications by promptly using what seem to be the same designations, at least the same words, about the different things when the imaginary construction was to be presented as different from these.

The great merit of the Socratic was precisely to emphasize that the knower is an existing person and that to exist is the essential. To go beyond Socrates by failing to understand this is nothing but a mediocre merit. This we must keep *in mente* VII
[in mind] and then see whether the formula cannot be changed 174
in such a way that one actually does go beyond the Socratic.

So, then, subjectivity, inwardness, is truth. Is there *a more inward* expression for it? Yes, if the discussion about "Subjectivity, inwardness, is truth" begins in this way: "Subjectivity is untruth." But let us not be in a hurry. Speculative thought also says that subjectivity is untruth but says it in the very opposite direction, namely, that objectivity is truth. Speculative thought defines subjectivity negatively in the direction of objectivity. The other definition, however, puts barriers in its own way at the very moment it wants to begin, which makes the inwardness so much more inward. Viewed Socratically, subjectivity is untruth if it refuses to comprehend that subjectivity is truth but wants, for example, to be objective. Here, on the other hand, in wanting to begin to become truth by becoming subjective, subjectivity is in the predicament of being untruth. Thus the work goes backward, that is, backward in inwardness. The way is so far from being in the direction of the objective that the beginning only lies even deeper in subjectivity.

But the subject cannot be untruth eternally or be presupposed to have been untruth eternally; he must have become that in time or he becomes that in time.[288] The Socratic paradox consisted in this, that the eternal truth was related to an existing person. But now existence has accentuated the existing person a second time; a change so essential has taken place in him that he in no way can take himself back into eternity by

---

Now, I think there would be no objection to speaking of the paradox in connection with Socrates and faith, since it is quite correct to do so, provided that it is understood correctly. Besides, the ancient Greeks also use the word πίστις [faith], although by no means in the sense of the imaginary construction, and use it so as to make possible some very illuminating observations bearing upon its dissimilarity to faith *sensu eminentiori*, especially with reference to one of Aristotle's works where the term is employed.[287]

Socratically recollecting. To do this is to speculate; to be able to do this but, by grasping the inward deepening in existence, to annul the possibility of doing it is the Socratic. But *now* the difficulty is that what accompanied Socrates as an annulled possibility has become an impossibility. If speculating was already of dubious merit in connection with the Socratic, it is now only confusion.

The paradox emerges when the eternal truth and existing are placed together, but each time existing is accentuated, the paradox becomes clearer and clearer. Viewed Socratically, the knower was an existing person, but now the existing person is accentuated in such a way that existence has made an essential change in him.

Let us now call the individual's untruth *sin*. Viewed eternally, he cannot be in sin or be presupposed to have been eternally in sin. Therefore, by coming into existence (for the be-
VII ginning was that subjectivity is untruth), he becomes a sinner.
175 He is not born as a sinner in the sense that he is presupposed
to be a sinner before he is born, but he is born in sin and as a sinner. Indeed, we could call this *hereditary sin*.[289] But if existence has in this way obtained power over him, he is prevented from taking himself back into eternity through recollection. If it is already paradoxical that the eternal truth is related to an existing person, now it is absolutely paradoxical that it is related to such an existing person. But the more difficult it is made for him, recollecting, to take himself out of existence, the more inward his existing can become in existence; and when it is made impossible for him, when he is lodged in existence in such a way that the back door of recollection is forever closed, then the inwardness becomes the deepest. But let us never forget that the Socratic merit was precisely to emphasize that the knower is existing, because the more difficult the matter becomes, the more one is tempted to rush along the easy road of speculative thought, away from terrors and decisions, to fame, honor, a life of ease, etc. If even Socrates comprehended the dubiousness of taking himself speculatively out of existence back into eternity, when there was no dubiousness for the existing person except that he existed and,

of course, that existing was the essential—now it is impossible. He must go forward; to go backward is impossible.

Subjectivity is truth. The paradox came into existence through the relating of the eternal, essential truth to the existing person. Let us now go further; let us assume that the eternal, essential truth is itself the paradox. How does the paradox emerge? By placing the eternal, essential truth together with existing. Consequently, if we place it together in the truth itself, the truth becomes a paradox. The eternal truth has come into existence in time. That is the paradox. If the subject just mentioned was prevented by sin from taking himself back into eternity, now he is not to concern himself with this, because now the eternal, essential truth is not behind him but has come in front of him by existing itself or by having existed, so that if the individual, existing, does not lay hold of the truth in existence, he will never have it.

Existence can never be accentuated more sharply than it has been here. The fraud of speculative thought in wanting to recollect itself out of existence has been made impossible. This is the only point to be comprehended here, and every speculation that insists on being speculation shows *eo ipso* [precisely thereby] that it has not comprehended this. The individual can thrust all this away and resort to speculation, but to accept it and then want to cancel it through speculation is impossible, VII 176
because it is specifically designed to prevent speculation.

When the eternal truth relates itself to an existing person, it becomes the paradox. Through the objective uncertainty and ignorance, the paradox thrusts away in the inwardness of the existing person. But since the paradox is not in itself the paradox, it does not thrust away intensely enough, for without risk, no faith; the more risk, the more faith; the more objective reliability, the less inwardness (since inwardness is subjectivity); the less objective reliability, the deeper is the possible inwardness. When the paradox itself is the paradox, it thrusts away by virtue of the absurd, and the corresponding passion of inwardness is faith.

But subjectivity, inwardness, is truth; if not, we have forgotten the Socratic merit. But when the retreat out of existence into eternity by way of recollection has been made impossible, then, with the truth facing one as the paradox, in the anxiety of sin and its pain, with the tremendous risk of objectivity, there is no stronger expression for inwardness than—to have faith. But without risk, no faith, not even the Socratic faith, to say nothing of the kind we are discussing here.

When Socrates believed that God is,[290] he held fast the objective uncertainty with the entire passion of inwardness, and faith is precisely in this contradiction, in this risk. Now it is otherwise. Instead of the objective uncertainty, there is here the certainty that, viewed objectively, it is the absurd, and this absurdity, held fast in the passion of inwardness, is faith. Compared with the earnestness of the absurd, the Socratic ignorance is like a witty jest, and compared with the strenuousness of faith, the Socratic existential inwardness resembles Greek nonchalance.

What, then, is the absurd? The absurd is that the eternal truth has come into existence in time, that God has come into existence, has been born, has grown up, etc., has come into existence exactly as an individual human being, indistinguishable from any other human being, inasmuch as all immediate recognizability is pre-Socratic paganism and from the Jewish point of view is idolatry.[291] Every qualification of that which actually goes beyond the Socratic must essentially have a mark of standing in relation to the god's having come into existence, because faith, *sensu strictissimo* [in the strictest sense], as explicated in *Fragments*,[292] refers to coming into existence. When Socrates believed that God is [*er til*], he no doubt per-
VII 177 ceived that where the road swings off there is a road of objective approximation, for example, the observation of nature, world history, etc. His merit was precisely to shun this road, where the quantifying siren song spellbinds and tricks the existing person. [293]In relation to the absurd, the objective approximation resembles the comedy *Misforstaaelse paa Misforstaaelse* [Misunderstanding upon Misunderstanding],[294] which ordinarily is played by assistant professors and speculative thinkers.

It is by way of the objective repulsion that the absurd is the dynamometer of faith in inwardness. So, then, there is a man who wants to have faith; well, let the comedy begin. He wants to have faith, but he wants to assure himself with the aid of objective deliberation and approximation. What happens? With the aid of approximation, the absurd becomes something else; it becomes probable, it becomes more probable, it may become to a high degree and exceedingly probable. Now he is all set to believe it, and he dares to say of himself that he does not believe as shoemakers and tailors and simple folk do, but only after long deliberation. Now he is all set to believe it, but, lo and behold, now it has indeed become impossible to believe it. The almost probable, the probable, the to-a-high-degree and exceedingly probable—that he can almost know, or as good as know, to a higher degree and exceedingly almost *know*—but *believe* it, that cannot be done, for the absurd is precisely the object of faith and only that can be believed.

Or there is a man who says he has faith, but now he wants to make his faith clear to himself; he wants to understand himself in his faith. Now the comedy begins again. The object of faith becomes almost probable, it becomes as good as probable, it becomes probable, it becomes to a high degree and exceedingly probable. He has finished; he dares to say of himself that he does not believe as shoemakers and tailors or other simple folk do but that he has also understood himself in his believing. What wondrous understanding! On the contrary, he has learned to know something different about faith than he believed and has learned to know that he no longer has faith, since he almost knows, as good as knows, to a high degree and exceedingly almost knows.

Inasmuch as the absurd contains the element of coming into existence, the road of approximation will also be that which confuses the absurd fact of coming into existence, which is the object of faith, with a simple historical fact, and then seeks historical certainty for that which is absurd precisely because it contains the contradiction that something that can become historical only in direct opposition to all human understanding has become historical. This contradiction is the absurd, VII
which can only be believed. If a historical certainty is ob- 178

tained, one obtains merely the certainty that what is certain is not what is the point in question. A witness can testify that he has believed it and then testify that, far from being a historical certainty, it is in direct opposition to his understanding, but such a witness repels in the same sense as the absurd repels, and a witness who does not repel in this way is *eo ipso* a deceiver or a man who is talking about something altogether different; and such a witness can be of no help except in obtaining certainty about something altogether different. One hundred thousand individual witnesses, who by the special nature of their testimony (that they have believed the absurd) remain individual witnesses, do not become something else *en masse* so that the absurd becomes less absurd. Why? Because one hundred thousand people individually have believed that it was absurd? Quite the contrary, those one hundred thousand witnesses repel exactly as the absurd does.

But I do not need to develop this further here. In *Fragments* (especially where the difference between the follower at first hand and the follower at second hand is annulled[295]) and in Part One of this book, I have with sufficient care shown that all approximation is futile, since the point is rather to do away with introductory observations, reliabilities, demonstrations from effects, and the whole mob of pawnbrokers and guarantors, in order to get the absurd clear—so that one can believe if one will—I merely say that this must be extremely strenuous.

If speculative thought wants to become involved in this and, as always, say: From the point of view of the eternal, the divine, the theocentric, there is no paradox—I shall not be able to decide whether the speculative thinker is right, because I am only a poor existing human being who neither eternally nor divinely nor theocentrically is able to observe the eternal but must be content with existing. This much, however, is certain, that with speculative thought everything goes backward, back past the Socratic, which at least comprehended that for an existing person existing is the essential; and much less has speculative thought taken the time to comprehend what it means to be *situated* in existence the way the existing person is in the imaginary construction.

The difference between the Socratic position and the position that goes beyond the Socratic is clear enough and is essentially the same as in *Fragments*, for in the latter nothing has changed, and in the former the matter has only been made somewhat more difficult, but nevertheless not more difficult than it is. It has also become somewhat more difficult because, whereas in *Fragments* I set forth the thought-category of the paradox only in an imaginary construction, here I have also latently made an attempt to make clear the necessity of the VII
paradox, and even though the attempt is somewhat weak, it 179
is still something different from speculatively canceling the paradox.

[296]Christianity has itself proclaimed itself to be the eternal, essential truth that has come into existence in time; it has proclaimed itself as *the paradox* and has required the inwardness of faith with regard to what is an offense to the Jews, foolishness to the Greeks[297]—and an absurdity to the understanding. It cannot be expressed more strongly that subjectivity is truth and that objectivity only thrusts away, precisely by virtue of the absurd, and it seems strange that Christianity should have come into the world in order to be explained, alas, as if it were itself puzzled about itself and therefore came into the world to seek out the wise man, the speculative thinker, who can aid with the explanation. It cannot be expressed more inwardly that subjectivity is truth than when subjectivity is at first untruth,[298] and yet subjectivity is truth.

Suppose that Christianity was and wants to be a mystery, an utter mystery, not a theatrical mystery that is revealed in the fifth act, although the clever spectator [*Tilskuer*] already sees through [*gennemskue*] it in the course of the exposition. Suppose that a revelation *sensu strictissimo* [in the strictest sense] must be a mystery and be recognizable just by its being a mystery, whereas a revelation *sensu laxiori* [in the broader sense], the withdrawing into the eternal through recollection, is a revelation in the direct sense. Suppose that the difference in intellectual endowment is the difference in being able to

state more and more clearly that it is and remains a mystery for existing human beings. Suppose that the intellectual endowment in relation to misunderstanding differs according to the individual's ability more and more deceptively to give the appearance of having understood the mystery. Suppose that it is nevertheless a blessing that, situated at the extremity of existence, one relates oneself to this mystery without understanding it, only having faith. Suppose that Christianity does not at all want to be understood; suppose that, in order to express this and to prevent anyone, misguided, from taking the road of objectivity, it has proclaimed itself to be the paradox. Suppose that it wants to be only for existing persons and essentially for persons existing in inwardness, in the inwardness of faith, which cannot be expressed more definitely than this: it is the absurd, adhered to firmly with the passion of the infinite. Suppose that it does not want to be understood and that the maximum of any eventual understanding is to understand
VII 180 that it cannot be understood. Suppose that it so decisively accentuates existing that the single individual becomes a sinner, Christianity the paradox, and existence the time of decision. Suppose that speculating is a temptation, the most precarious of all. Suppose that the speculator is not the prodigal son, for this is what the concerned God presumably would call the offended one whom he continues to love nevertheless, but the naughty child who refuses to stay where existing human beings belong, in the children's nursery and the education room of existence where one becomes adult only through inwardness in existing, but who instead wants to enter God's council, continually screaming that, from the point of view of the eternal, the divine, the theocentric, there is no paradox. Suppose that the speculative thinker is the restless resident who, although it is obvious that he is a renter, yet in view of the abstract truth that, eternally and divinely perceived, all property is in common, wants to be the owner, so that there is nothing to do except to send for a police officer, who would presumably say, just as the subpoena servers say to Gert Westphaler: We are sorry to have to come on this errand.[299]

Has being human now become something different from

what it was in the old days, is the condition not the same: to be an individual *existing* being, and is not existing the essential as long as one is in existence? "But people know so much more now." "Quite right, but suppose that Christianity is not a matter of knowing; then much knowledge is of no benefit, except to ease a person more readily into the confusion of regarding Christianity as a matter of knowledge." And if people do know more now—and we are not speaking of the knowledge of railroads, machines, and kaleidoscopes, but of knowing more of the religious—how have they come to know more? Presumably, through Christianity. So this is how Christianity is rewarded. One learns something from Christianity, misunderstands it, and in new misunderstanding uses it against Christianity.

If the terror in the old days was that one could be offended, the terror these days is that there is no terror, that one, two, three, before looking around, one becomes a speculative thinker who speculates about faith. About what faith? Is it about the faith that he has and especially about whether he does or does not have it? Alas, no, that is too little for an objective speculator. Consequently, he speculates about objective faith. What does that mean—objective faith? It means a sum of tenets. But suppose Christianity is nothing of the kind; suppose that, on the contrary, it is inwardness, and therefore the paradox, in order to thrust away objectively, so that it can VII
181 be for the existing person in the inwardness of existence by placing him decisively, more decisively than any judge can place the accused, between time and eternity in time, between heaven and hell in the time of salvation. Objective faith—it is indeed as if Christianity had also been proclaimed as a little system of sorts, although presumably not as good as the Hegelian system. It is as if Christ—it is not my fault that I say it—as if Christ had been a professor and as if the apostles had formed a little professional society of scholars. Truly, if at one time it was difficult to become a Christian, I believe now it becomes more difficult year by year, because it has now become so easy to become one; there is a bit of competition only in becoming a speculative thinker. And yet the speculator is

perhaps furthest removed from Christianity, and perhaps it is preferable by far to be someone who takes offense but still continually relates himself to Christianity, whereas the speculator has understood it. To that extent there is hope that there still remains a similarity between a Christian now and in those early days and that wanting to become a Christian will once again become foolishness. In those early days, a Christian was a fool in the eyes of the world.[300] To the pagans and Jews it was foolishness for him to want to become one. Now one is a Christian as a matter of course. If someone wants to be a Christian with infinite passion, he is a fool, just as it is always foolishness to will to exert oneself with infinite passion in order to become what one is as a matter of course, as if someone would give all his fortune to purchase a precious gem[301]—which he owned. Formerly a Christian was a fool in the eyes of the world; now all people are Christians, but he nevertheless becomes a fool—in the eyes of Christians.

Suppose that it is this way. I say merely "suppose," and more I do not say. But since we are now admittedly growing weary of speculative thinkers who examine one another in print in the systematic rigmarole, it may at least be a change to go through the question in another way.

"But from the eternal, divine, and especially theocentric point of view, there is no paradox. True speculative thought, therefore, does not stop with the paradox but goes further and explains it." "May I now ask for a little peace and request that he not begin again? After all, I did say that I cannot become involved with the supraterrestrial and the subterranean." "The beginning and the consummation of the explanation are with me, and it is for this explanation that the eternal truth has been waiting; it is quite correct that it entered into time, but the first
VII 182 edition was only an imperfect attempt. Because the eternal truth required an explanation, it entered into the world and anticipated this by occasioning a discussion. Similarly, a professor publishes the outline of a system,[302] assuming that the work, by being reviewed and debated, will come out sooner or later in a new and totally revised form. Only this second edition, when it has waited for the advice and judgment of

experts, is the truth, and thus speculative thought is the true and only satisfactory edition of the provisional truth of Christianity."

By means of a few examples, we shall now illustrate how speculative thought, for the very reason that it refuses to comprehend that subjectivity is truth, has earned the gratitude of Christianity, which once and for all is the paradox[303] and is paradoxical at every point, whereas speculative thought, remaining in immanence, which is recollection's removal of itself from existence, at every point produces a volatilization. By means of the tour de force of not thinking anything decisive about what is most decisive (which, through the decision, is specifically designed to forestall immanence) but utilizing the expression of decision as a locution, the volatilization becomes a pagan reminiscence, to which there is nothing to object if it breaks directly with Christianity but much to object if it is supposed to be Christianity.

The thesis that God has existed in human form, was born, grew up, etc. is certainly the paradox *sensu strictissimo*, the absolute paradox. But as the absolute paradox it cannot be related to a relative difference. A relative paradox is related to a relative difference between more or less sagacious people. But the absolute paradox, precisely because it is absolute, can be related only to the absolute difference by which a human being differs from God;[304] it cannot be related to relative bickering between one human being and another about whether one is a little smarter than the other. But the absolute difference between God and a human being is simply this, that a human being is an individual existing being (and this holds for the best brain just as fully as for the most obtuse), whose essential task therefore cannot be to think *sub specie aeterni*, because as long as he exists, he himself, although eternal, is essentially an existing person and the essential for him must therefore be inwardness in existence; God, however, is the infinite one, who is eternal. As soon as I make the understanding of the paradox commensurate with the difference between being more or less intellectually endowed (a difference that still does not ever transcend being human, unless someone VII 183 were to become so brilliant that he became not only a human being but also God), my discussion of understanding *eo ipso* demonstrates that what I have understood is not the absolute paradox but a relative paradox, because the only possible understanding of the absolute paradox is that it cannot be understood. "But then speculative thought cannot ever grasp it." "Entirely correct, this is just what is said by the paradox, which thrusts away only in the direction of inwardness in existence." Perhaps this is so because objectively there is no truth for existing beings, but only approximations, whereas subjectively truth for them is in inwardness, because the decision of truth is in subjectivity.

The modern mythical allegorizing trend[305] summarily declares Christianity to be a myth. Such a procedure is at least forthright behavior, and everyone can easily form a judgment about it. The friendship of speculative thought is of another kind. To be on the safe side, speculative thought opposes the ungodly mythical allegorizing trend and then goes on to say, "Speculative thought, on the other hand, accepts the paradox, but it does not stop with it." "Nor is there any need for that, because when a person in faith continues to adhere firmly to it, in his existence deepening himself in the inwardness of faith, he does not stop either." Speculative thought does not stop—what does that mean? Does it mean that Messrs. Speculators cease to be human beings, individual existing human beings, and *en famille* [as a family] become all sorts of things? If not, one is certainly obliged to stop with the paradox, since it is grounded in and is the expression for precisely this, that the eternal, essential truth relates itself to existing individuals with the summons that they go further and further in the inwardness of faith.

What on the whole does it mean to *explain* something? Does explaining mean to show that the obscure something in question is not this but something else? That would be a strange explanation. I should think that by the explanation it would become clear that the something in question is this definite something, so that the explanation would remove not the thing in question but the obscurity. Otherwise the explanation

is something other than an explanation; it is a correction. An explanation of the paradox makes clear what the paradox is and removes the obscurity; a correction removes the paradox and makes clear that there is no paradox. But the latter is certainly no explanation of the paradox but rather an explanation that there is no paradox. But if the paradox emerges from the VII 184
placing together of the eternal and an existing individual human being, does the explanation, in removing the paradox, then also remove existing from the existing person? And if on his own, or with the assistance of another, an existing person has arrived at or has been brought almost to the point where it seems to him as if he did not exist, what is he then? Then he is absentminded. Consequently, the explanation of the absolute paradox that declares there is no paradox except to a certain degree, in other words, that there are only relative paradoxes, is an explanation not for existing individuals but for the absentminded. Well, then everything is in order. The explanation is that the paradox is the paradox only to a certain degree, and it is quite in order that it, namely, the explanation, is for an existing person who is an existing person only to a certain degree, since he forgets it every other moment, and an existing person of that kind is simply absentminded.

Then when someone speaks of the absolute paradox, which is an offense to the Jews, foolishness to the Greeks, and the absurd to the understanding, and addresses his words to speculative thought, it is not so impolite as to tell him bluntly that he is a fool but rather gives an explanation that contains a correction and thus indirectly gives him to understand that he was in error. This is the way a humane, superior intellect always behaves toward the more limited. The procedure is altogether Socratic; there would be an un-Socratic element only if the one speaking is indeed closer to the truth than the speculative explanation, for then there remains the dissimilarity that Socrates politely and indirectly took the untruth away from the learner and gave him the truth, whereas speculative thought politely and indirectly takes the truth away from the learner and gives him the untruth. But politeness still remains the common denominator. And when Christianity declares itself to be the paradox, the speculative explanation is not an explanation but a correction, a polite and indirect correction, such as befits a superior intellect in relation to the more limited.

Does *explaining* the paradox mean to turn the expression "paradox" into a *rhetorical* expression, into something the honorable speculative thinker indeed says has its validity—but then in turn does not have its validity? In that case, the *summa summarum* [sum total] is indeed that there is no paradox. Honor be to the Herr Professor! I say this not to take his honor away from him, as if I, too, could cancel [*hæve*] the paradox. Not at all. But if the professor has canceled it, then it is of course canceled; in that case I daresay that it is canceled—unless the annulment [*Ophævelse*] pertains to the professor more than to the paradox, so that he, instead of canceling the para-
VII dox, himself becomes an alarming, fantastical swelling
185 [*Hævelse*].[306] In other cases, one assumes that explaining something means to have it become clear in its significance, that it is this and not something else. To explain the paradox would then be to comprehend ever more deeply what a paradox is and that the paradox is the paradox.

Thus God is a supreme conception that cannot be explained by anything else[307] but is explainable only by immersing oneself in the conception itself. The highest principles for all thinking can be demonstrated only indirectly (negatively).[308] Suppose that the paradox is the boundary for an *existing person's* relation to an eternal, essential truth—in that case the paradox will not be explainable by anything else if the explanation is supposed to be for existing persons. But understood speculatively, even the absolute paradox (because speculative thought is not afraid of using decisive terms; the only thing it fears is thinking something decisive with them) expresses only a relative difference between more and less gifted and educated people. In this way the shape of the world will gradually be changed. When Christianity entered into the world, there were no professors or assistant professors whatever—then it was a paradox for all. It can be assumed that in the present generation every tenth person is an assistant professor; consequently it is a paradox for only nine out of ten. And when the fullness of time[309] finally comes, that matchless future, when a generation of assistant professors, male and female, will live on the earth—then Christianity will have ceased to be a paradox.

On the other hand, the person who takes it upon himself to explain the paradox, on the assumption that he knows what he wants, will focus directly upon showing that it must be a paradox. To explain the unutterable joy[310]—what does that mean? Does it mean to explain that it is this and that? In that case, the predicate "unutterable" becomes just a rhetorical predicate, a strong expression, and the like. The explaining jack-of-all-trades has everything in readiness before the beginning of the performance, and now it begins. He dupes the listener; he calls the joy unutterable, and then a new surprise, a truly surprising surprise[311]—he utters it. Suppose that the unutterable joy is based upon the contradiction that an existing human being is composed of the infinite and the finite, is situated in time, so that the joy of the eternal in him becomes unutterable because he is existing; it becomes a supreme drawing of breath that cannot take shape, because the existing person is existing. In that case, the explanation would be that it is unutterable; it cannot be anything else—no nonsense. If, how- VII
ever, a profound person first condemns someone or other 186
who denies that there is an unutterable joy and then says: No, I assume that there is an unutterable joy, but I go further and utter it, then he is only making a fool of himself, and the only difference between him and the other whom he condemns is that the other is more honest and direct and says what the profound person is also saying, since they both are saying essentially the same thing.

[312]Does explaining what is decisive mean to transform the expression into a rhetorical locution, so that one does not, like the light-minded person, deny all decision, but assumes it, yet assumes it only to a certain degree? What does it mean to assert that a decision is to a certain degree? It means to deny decision. Decision is designed specifically to put an end to that perpetual prattle about "to a certain degree." So the decision

is assumed—but, lo and behold, assumed only to a certain degree. Speculative thought is not afraid to use expressions of decision; the only thing it fears is thinking something decisive with them. And when Christianity wants to be the eternal decision for the existing subject and speculative thought explains that the decision is relative, it is not explaining Christianity but correcting it. Whether speculative thought is in the right is an entirely different question; here the question is only how its explanation of Christianity is related to the Christianity that it explains.

Does explaining something mean to *annul* it? I do know that the word *aufheben* has various, indeed opposite, meanings in the German language. It has often been noted that the word can mean both *tollere* [annul, annihilate] and *conservare* [preserve].[313] I am not aware that the Danish word *ophæve* [annul] allows any such equivocation, but I do know that our German-Danish philosophers use it like the German word. Whether it is a good quality in a word to have opposite meanings, I do not know, but anyone who wants to express himself with precision usually avoids the use of such a word in decisive places. There is a simple folk saying that humorously denotes the impossible: to have one's mouth full of crackers and to whistle at the same time. Speculative thought accomplishes a tour de force somewhat like that by using a word that also denotes the very opposite. In order to denote very clearly that speculation knows nothing of any decision, it itself uses an
VII ambiguous word in order to denote the kind of understanding
187 that is speculative understanding. Upon closer inspection, the confusion becomes more evident. *Aufheben* in the sense of *tollere* means to annihilate; in the sense of *conservare*, it means to preserve [*bevare*] in altogether unaltered condition, to do nothing at all to what is being preserved. If the government dissolves [*ophæve*] a political society, it abolishes it; if a man keeps or preserves something for me, it is of particular importance to me that he make no change whatever in it. Neither of these meanings is the philosophical *aufheben*. So speculation annuls all difficulty and then leaves me with the difficulty of understanding just what it is doing with this *aufheben*. But now let

this *aufheben* mean reducing something to a relative factor, which it does mean when what is decisive, the paradox, is reduced to a relative factor,[314] which means that there is no paradox, no decision, since the paradox and the decisive are what they are just because of their unyielding resistance. Whether speculative thought is in the right is a different question, but here what is asked is only how its explanation of Christianity is related to the Christianity that it explains.

By no means does speculative thought say that Christianity is untruth; on the contrary, it specifically says that speculation comprehends the truth of Christianity. More could certainly not be asked for. Has Christianity ever asked to be more than the truth? And when speculation comprehends it, everything is as it should be. And yet, no, that is not how it is. In relation to Christianity, systematic speculation is only a bit cunning in the use of all kinds of diplomatic locutions that bedazzle the credulous. Christianity as it is understood by the speculative thinker is something different from what is presented to the simple. To them it is the paradox, but the speculative thinker knows how to cancel the paradox. Then it is not Christianity that is and was and remains the truth,[315] and the speculative thinker's understanding is not the understanding that Christianity is the truth—no, it is the speculative thinker's understanding of Christianity that is the truth of Christianity. The understanding is thus something other than the truth. It is not the case that the truth is understood only when the understanding has understood everything implied in the truth, but it is rather the case that only when that κατὰ δύναμιν [potential] truth is understood in the way a speculative thinker understands it, only then—well, then it is not speculation that VII
has become true, but it is the truth that has come into exis- 188
tence. Consequently, the truth is not a given and the understanding is not what is awaited, but what is awaited is that speculation's understanding will be finished, because only then has truth come into existence. Thus speculative knowledge is not as knowledge usually is, something indifferent in relation to what is known, so that this is not changed by being known but remains the same. No, speculative knowledge is

itself the object of knowing, so that the latter is no longer the same as it was but has come into existence simultaneously with speculation as the truth.

Whether speculative thought is in the right is a different question. What is asked here is only how its explanation of Christianity is related to the Christianity that it explains. And how should they be related? Speculative thought is objective, and objectively there is no truth for an existing individual but only an approximation, since by existing he is prevented from becoming entirely objective. Christianity, on the other hand, is subjective; the inwardness of faith in the believer is the truth's eternal decision. Objectively there is no truth; an objective knowledge about the truth or the truths of Christianity is precisely untruth. To know a creed by rote is paganism, because Christianity is inwardness.

[316]Let us take the paradox of the forgiveness of sins. Socratically, the forgiveness of sins is a paradox, inasmuch as the eternal truth relates itself to an existing person, *sensu strictiori* [in the stricter sense], because the existing person is a sinner, a qualification by which existence is accentuated a second time, because it wants to be an eternal decision in time with retroactive power to annul the past, and because it is bound up with God's having existed in time. The individual existing human being has to feel himself a sinner (not objectively, which is nonsense, but subjectively, and this is the deepest pain). With all his understanding to the very last turn (if one person has a little more understanding than the other, it makes no essential difference, and to appeal to one's great understanding is merely to betray one's deficient inwardness, or else it runs out very soon), he must want to understand the forgiveness of sins—and then despair of understanding. With the understanding in direct opposition, the inwardness of faith must grasp the paradox, and that faith battles in just this way, as the
VII Romans once did, blinded by the light of the sun, is the resil-
189 ience of inwardness.* If any other understanding ever forces

* That one can battle in this way, blinded by the sun, and yet see to battle, the Romans demonstrated at Zama. That one can battle in this way, blinded,

itself upon him, he sees that he is about to lose his faith, just as a girl, when she has become the beloved's wife, upon discovering that it is easy to understand that she became this man's chosen one, ought to see that this explanation is easily understood as an indication that she is no longer in love.

But a speculative thinker goes about it in a different way. He appears before an esteemed public and says, "Ladies and gentlemen, for that is how I must address you. To a congregation of believers, the paradox can be proclaimed only by a believer, but to an esteemed public the truth can be proclaimed by a speculative thinker. Therefore the forgiveness of sins is a paradox (general excitement). The pantheistic line is a fallacy that speculative thought opposes, but speculative thought does not stop with the paradox; it explains and annuls VII 190
it." The highly esteemed speculative thinker did not, then, stake all his understanding when he despaired; his despair was

---

and yet see to conquer, the Romans demonstrated at Zama.[317] And now the battle of faith, is that supposed to be tomfoolery, a staged swordplay of gallantry, this battle that is longer than a Thirty Years' War, because one does not fight merely to acquire but fights even more vehemently to preserve, this battle in which every day is just as hot as the day of battle at Zama! While the understanding despairs, faith presses forward victoriously in the passion of inwardness. But when the believer uses all his understanding, every last turn of despair, just to discover the difficulty of the paradox, then truly no part is left with which to explain the paradox—but for all that, there can indeed be the ample firmness of faith in the passion of inwardness. Sitting calmly on a ship in fair weather is not a metaphor for having faith; but when the ship has sprung a leak, then enthusiastically to keep the ship afloat by pumping and not to seek the harbor—that is the metaphor for having faith. Even if the image ultimately contains an impossibility, this is merely the imperfection of the image, but faith holds out. While the understanding, like a desperate passenger, stretches its arms toward land, but in vain, faith works vigorously in the depths—joyful and victorious, against the understanding it rescues the soul. To exist in faith is that kind of contradiction; to an existing person, compromise is a mirage, since it is a contradiction that an eternal spirit exists. Whether anyone has done this, whether anyone is doing it—of what concern is that to me, if this is indeed what it is to have faith? Although I am still far from having fully understood the difficulty of Christianity (and an explanation that makes the difficulty easy must be regarded as a temptation), I nevertheless perceive that the battle of faith is not a topic for vaudeville poets and its strenuousness is not a divertissement for assistant professors.

only to a certain degree, a simulated movement; he reserved part of his understanding—for the explanation. This can be called: deriving benefit from one's understanding. The believer derives no benefit whatever from his; he uses up all of it in despair. But the speculator knows how to stretch it out sufficiently; he takes one-half of it for despairing (as if it were not nonsense to despair by halves) and the other half for perceiving that there is no reason for the understanding to despair. Well, of course, then the matter becomes something different; so where is the error? In the deceitfulness of the first movement, of course, and therefore not actually in his not stopping with faith but in his never reaching it.

Now, suppose that the basis of the paradox of the forgiveness of sins is that the poor existing human being is existing, that he is half-godforsaken even when in the inwardness of faith he is victorious against the understanding. Suppose that only eternity can give an eternal certainty, whereas existence has to be satisfied with a struggling certainty, which is gained not as the battle becomes easier or more illusory but only as it becomes harder. In that case, the explanation is indeed that it is and remains a paradox, and all is lost only when one thinks that there is no paradox or only to a certain degree. But, the esteemed public may say, if the forgiveness of sins is anything like that, how, then, can one *believe* it? Answer: If it is not anything like that, how, then, can one believe it?

[318]Whether Christianity is in the right is another question. Here the question is only how the speculative explanation is related to the Christianity that it explains. But if Christianity is perhaps in the wrong, this much is certain: speculative thought is definitely in the wrong, because the only consistency outside Christianity is that of pantheism, the taking of oneself out of existence back into the eternal through recollection, whereby all existence-decisions become only shadow play compared with what is eternally decided from behind. Like all *simulated* decision, the simulated decision of speculative thought is nonsense, because decision is the eternal protest against fictions. The pantheist is eternally reassured backward; the moment that is the moment of existence in time,

the seventy years, is something vanishing. The speculative thinker, on the other hand, wants to be an existing person, but an existing person who is not subjective, not in passion, indeed, is existing *sub specie aeterni*—in short, he is absentminded. But what is explained in absentmindedness must not be trusted absolutely—such an explanation, and here I agree with speculative thought, is an explanation only to a certain degree.

If the speculative thinker explains the paradox in such a way VII
that he cancels it and now consciously knows that it is can- 191
celed, that consequently the paradox is not the essential relation of eternal essential truth to an existing person in the extremities of existence, but only an accidental relative relation to limited minds—then there is an essential difference between the speculative thinker and the simple person, whereby all existence is fundamentally confused. God is insulted by obtaining a group of hangers-on, a support staff of good minds, and humankind is vexed because there is not an equal relationship with God for all human beings. The religious formula set forth above for the difference between the simple person's knowledge and the simple wise person's knowledge of the simple, that the difference is a meaningless trifle, that the wise person knows that he knows or knows that he does not know what the simple person knows—speculative thought does not respect this formula at all. Nor does it respect the equality implicit in the difference between the wise person and the simple person—that they know the same thing. That is, the speculator and the simple person in no way know the same thing when the simple person believes the paradox and the speculator knows that it is annulled. According, however, to the formula just cited, which honors God and loves human beings, the difference will be that the wise person also knows that it must be a paradox, the paradox he himself believes. Consequently, they do indeed know essentially the same thing; the wise person does not know anything else about the paradox, but he knows that he knows this about the paradox. The simple wise person will then immerse himself in comprehending

the paradox as paradox and will not become involved in explaining the paradox by understanding that it is not a paradox.

If, for example, the simple wise person spoke with a simple person about the forgiveness of sins, the simple person would most likely say, "But I still cannot comprehend the divine mercy that can forgive sins; the more intensely I believe it, the less I am able to understand it." (Thus probability does not seem to increase as the inwardness of faith is augmented, rather the opposite.) But the simple wise person will most likely say, "It is the same with me. You know I have had the opportunity to be able to devote much time to research and reflection, and yet the *summa summarum* of all this is at most that I comprehend that it cannot be otherwise, that it must be incomprehensible. Look, this difference certainly cannot distress you or make you think wistfully about your own more laborious circumstances in life or about your perhaps more modest capabilities, as if I had some advantage over you. My advantage, when regarded as the fruit of study, is something both to laugh at and to weep over. Yet you are never to scorn
VII this study, just as I myself do not regret it, since on the con-
192 trary it pleases me most when I smile at it, and just then enthusiastically resume the effort of thinking."

Such a confession is made in all sincerity, and it is not present in the wise person merely once in a while but is essentially present in him whenever he is occupied in thinking. Once a year to consider that one ought always to thank God would hardly be a proper understanding of these words. Similarly, once in a while, on a great occasion, to consider, deeply moved, that before God all human beings are essentially equal is not truly to understand this equality, particularly if one's daily work and striving in more than one way consign it to oblivion. But to comprehend equality most earnestly just when one is most earnestly aware of what differentiates—that is the noble piety of the simple wise person.

Much that is strange has been said about Christianity, much that is lamentable, much that is outrageous, but the most obtuse thing ever said is that it is true to a certain degree. Much that is strange has been said about enthusiasm, much that is lamentable, much that is outrageous, but the most obtuse thing said about it is that it is to a certain degree. Much that is strange has been said about erotic love, much that is lamentable, much that is outrageous, but the most obtuse thing said about it is that it is to a certain degree. When a person has prostituted himself by speaking in this way about enthusiasm and love, has betrayed his obtuseness, which is not, however, a matter of the understanding, since the cause of it is just that the understanding has become too large, in the same sense as the cause of liver disease is that the liver has become too large, and therefore, as another author has remarked, "It is the dumbness the salt takes on when it loses its strength"[319]—then one phenomenon still remains, and that is Christianity. If enthusiasm's vision has been incapable of helping him break with the understanding, if love has been incapable of snatching him from bondage, let him look at Christianity. Let him be offended; even so, he is a human being. Let him despair of ever becoming a Christian himself; even so, he may be closer than he thinks. Let him to his very last drop of blood work to root out Christianity; even so, he is a human being—but if here he also has it in him to say, "It is true to a certain degree," then he is obtuse.[320]

Perhaps someone thinks that I shudder in saying this, that I
must be prepared for a terrible chastisement from the specu- VII
lative thinker. Not at all. The speculator will here again be 193
consistent and say, "What the man is saying is true to a certain degree, except that one must not stop there." It would indeed also be strange if an insignificant person like me were to succeed in what not even Christianity has succeeded—bringing the speculative thinker into passion. And if that should happen, well, then my fragment of philosophy[321] would suddenly take on a significance of which I had scarcely ever dreamed. But the person who is neither cold nor hot[322] is an abomination, and God is no more served by dud individualities than a rifleman is served by a rifle that in the moment of decision clicks instead of firing. If Pilate had not asked objectively what truth is,[323] he would never have let Christ be crucified. If he had asked the question subjectively, then the passion of in-

wardness regarding *what he in truth had to do* about the decision facing him would have prevented him from doing an injustice. In that case, not only his wife would have been troubled by her frightening dream,[324] but Pilate himself would have become sleepless. But when a person has before his eyes something as immensely big as the objective truth, he can easily cross out his fragment of subjectivity and what he as a subjective individual has to do. Then the approximation-process of the objective truth is symbolically expressed by washing one's hands,[325] because objectively there is no decision, whereas the subjective decision demonstrates that one was nevertheless in untruth by not comprehending that the decision is indeed rooted in subjectivity.

If, however, subjectivity[326] is truth and subjectivity is the existing subjectivity, then, if I may put it this way, Christianity is a perfect fit. Subjectivity culminates in passion, Christianity is paradox; paradox and passion fit each other perfectly, and paradox perfectly fits a person situated in the extremity of existence. Indeed, in the whole wide world there are not to be found two lovers who fit each other as do paradox and passion, and their quarrel is only like the lovers' quarrel when the quarrel is about whether it was he who awakened her passion or it was she who awakened his—and similarly here, the existing person has been situated in the extremity of existence by the paradox itself. And what is more glorious for lovers than to be granted a long time together without the occurrence of
VII 194 any change in the relationship except that it becomes more inward? And this is indeed granted to that very unspeculative understanding between passion and paradox, for they have been granted all of time, and not until eternity is there a change.

The speculative thinker, however, behaves differently; he believes only to a certain degree—he puts his hand to the plow and looks around[327] in order to find something to know. In a Christian sense, what he finds to know is hardly anything good. Even if it were not the case that it cannot be otherwise, something a simple wise person seeking to understand the paradox will endeavor to show, even if there were a little remnant of divine willfulness in the paradox, God, I daresay, is certainly one who is allowed to attach importance to his person, and therefore he is not constrained to reduce the price of the God-relationship because of a religious slackness (and this term is much more suitable here than when we speak of a slack grain market). And even if God were willing, the passionate one would never want it. It never occurs to a girl truly in love that she has purchased her happiness at too high a price,[328] but rather that she has not purchased it at a price high enough. And just as the passion of the infinite is itself the truth, so it is also the case with the highest that you get what you pay for, and that a low price merely signifies poor business acumen, whereas in relation to God the highest price is no merit, since the highest price is precisely to will to do everything and yet know that this is nothing (for if it is something, the price is lower) and yet to will it.

Since I am not totally unfamiliar with what has been said and written about Christianity, I could presumably say a thing or two about it. I shall, however, not do so here but merely repeat that there is one thing I shall beware of saying about it: that it is true to a certain degree. It is indeed just possible that Christianity is the truth; it is indeed just possible that someday there will be a judgment[329] in which the separation will hinge on the relation of inwardness to Christianity. Suppose that someone stepped forward who had to say, "Admittedly I have not believed, but I have so honored Christianity that I have spent every hour of my life pondering it." Or suppose that someone came forward of whom the accuser had to say, "He VII
has persecuted the Christians," and the accused one re- 195
sponded, "Yes, I acknowledge it; Christianity has so inflamed my soul that, simply because I realized its terrible power, I have wanted nothing else than to root it out of the world." Or suppose that someone came forward of whom the accuser had to say, "He has renounced Christianity," and the accused one responded, "Yes, it is true, for I perceived that Christianity was such a power that if I gave it one finger it would take all of me, and I could not belong to it completely." But suppose, now, that eventually an active assistant professor came along

at a hurried and bustling pace and said something like this, "I am not like those three;[330] I have not only believed but have even explained Christianity and have shown that what was proclaimed by the apostles and appropriated in the first centuries is true only to a certain degree. On the other hand, through speculative understanding I have shown how it is the true truth, and for that reason I must request suitable remuneration for my meritorious services to Christianity."

Of these four, which position would be the most terrible? It is indeed just possible that Christianity is the truth. Suppose that its ungrateful children want to have it declared incapable of managing its own affairs and placed under the guardianship of speculative thought. Suppose, then, that Christianity, like that Greek poet whose children also insisted that their aged father be declared incompetent but who amazed the judges and the people by writing one of his most beautiful tragedies to show that he was still competent[331]—suppose that Christianity in like manner rose rejuvenated to its feet—there would still be no one whose position would become as awkward as that of the assistant professors.

I do not deny that it is prestigious to stand so high above Christianity. I do not deny that it is comfortable to be a Christian and yet to be exempted from the martyrdom that always remains even if no external persecution is inflicted, and even if a Christian remains unnoticed as if he had never lived at all—the martyrdom of believing against the understanding, the mortal danger of lying out on 70,000 fathoms of water, and only there finding God. See, the wader feels his way with his foot, lest he go out so far that he cannot touch bottom. In the same way, with his understanding, the sensible person feels his way in probability and finds God where probability suffices and thanks him on the great festival days of probability when he has obtained a really good job and there is the probability of quick advancement to boot. And he thanks him when for a wife he finds a girl both beautiful and congenial, and even Councilor of War Marcussen says that it will be a happy marriage, that the girl has the kind of beauty that in all probability will last a long time, and that she is built in such a

way that in all probability she will bear healthy and strong children. To believe against the understanding is something else, and to believe with the understanding cannot be done at all, because the person who believes with the understanding VII 196
talks only about job and wife and fields and oxen and the like,[332] which are in no way the object of faith, since faith *always* thanks God, is *always* in mortal danger in that collision of the infinite and the finite that is precisely a mortal danger for one who is composed of both. The believer cares so little for probability that he fears it most of all, since he knows very well that with it he is beginning to lose his faith.

Faith has, namely, two tasks: to watch for and at every moment to make the discovery of improbability, the paradox, in order then to hold it fast with the passion of inwardness. The improbable, the paradox, is ordinarily conceived of as something to which faith is related only passively; one will have to be satisfied temporarily with this situation, but little by little things will improve—indeed, this is probable. What wondrous confusion-compounding in speaking about faith! One is supposed to begin to believe on the basis of a confidence that there is the probability that things will surely improve. When that is done, one still manages to smuggle in probability and to keep oneself from believing. When that is done, it is easy to understand that the fruit of having had faith for a long time is that one ceases to have faith rather than, as one might think, that the fruit would be to have faith ever more inwardly. No, faith, self-active, relates itself to the improbable and the paradox, is self-active in discovering it and in holding it fast at every moment—in order to be able to believe. It already takes all the passion of the infinite and its concentration to stop with the improbable, inasmuch as the improbable and the paradox are not to be reached by the understanding's quantifying of the more and more difficult. Where understanding despairs, faith is already present in order to make the despair properly decisive, lest the movement of faith become a transaction within the haggling territory of the understanding. But to believe against the understanding is a martyrdom; to begin to enlist the understanding a little is a temptation and retrogression. The speculative thinker is exempted from this martyrdom. That he must pursue his studies and especially that he must read many of the modern books, I am willing to admit, is onerous, but the martyrdom of faith is indeed something else.

What I recoil from, then, even more than from dying or from losing my dearest treasure, is to say of Christianity that it is true to a certain degree. Even if I live to be seventy years old, even if I from year to year shorten the night's sleep and lengthen the day's work, pondering over Christianity—what is such little study but a trifle if it is supposed to justify me in judging so superiorly of Christianity! It would be much more pardonable, much more human, for me to become so embittered toward Christianity on the basis of a superficial ac-
VII 197 quaintance with it that I would declare it to be untruth. But superiority seems to me to be the real perdition that makes every saving relationship impossible—and it is indeed just possible that Christianity is the truth.[333]

This almost seems to be earnestness. If I now dared to proclaim stridently that I had come into the world and was called to counteract speculative thought, [334]that this was my judging mission, whereas my prophetic mission[335] was to herald a matchless future, and that therefore, on the basis of my being strident and called, people could safely depend on what I said—there would presumably be many who, failing to regard the whole thing as a fantastical reminiscence in the head of a silly person, would regard it as earnestness. But I can say nothing like that about myself. [336]The resolution with which I began may rather be considered a whim. In any case, it is so far from being a call to me, even remotely so, that on the contrary the call that I did follow came not to me, if you please, but to someone else; and even for him it was very far from being anything like a call in the stricter sense. But even if a call did come to him, I am still uncalled when I follow it.

The event is quite simple. It was four years ago, on a Sunday—well, perhaps no one will believe me, because once again it is a Sunday, but it is nevertheless quite certain that it was a Sunday, about two months after the Sunday mentioned previously.[337] It was rather late, toward evening. [338]Evening's taking leave of day and of the person who has experienced the day is enigmatic speech; its warning is like the caring mother's instruction to the child to come home in good time. But its invitation, even though the leave-taking is without fault in thus being misunderstood, is an inexplicable beckoning, as if rest were to be found only if one remained out for a nocturnal rendezvous, not with a woman but, womanlike, with the infinite, persuaded by the night wind as it monotonously repeats itself, as it searches forest and field and sighs as if looking for something, persuaded by the distant echo of stillness within oneself, as if it had a presentiment of something, persuaded by the sublime tranquillity of heaven, as if it had been found, persuaded by the audible soundlessness of the dew, as if this were the explanation and the refreshment of infinitude, like the fruitfulness of the quiet night, only half-understood like the semitransparency of the nocturnal mist.

Contrary to my usual practice, I had come out to that garden called the garden of the dead, where the visitor's leave- VII
taking is again doubly difficult, since it is meaningless to say 198
"once more," because the last time is already past, and since there is no reason to cease taking leave when the beginning is made after the last time is past. Most of the visitors had already gone home. Just one person disappeared among the trees. Not caring to meet anyone, he avoided me, since he was seeking the dead, not the living. In this garden there is always the beautiful agreement among the visitors that one does not go out there in order to see and to be seen, but each visitor avoids the other. One does not need company either, least of all a talkative friend, here where everything is eloquence, where the dead person calls out the brief word placed upon his grave, not as a pastor does, who preaches widely and broadly on the word, but as a silent man does, who says only this word, but says it with a passion as if the dead might burst the grave—or is it not odd to place upon his grave "We shall meet again" and then to remain down there? And yet what inwardness there is in the words just because of the contradiction. That someone who is coming tomorrow says, "We shall meet

again," is not startling. But for someone to have everything against him, to have no direct expression for his inwardness, none, and yet to stand by his word—that is true inwardness. Inwardness is untrue in direct proportion to the ready availability of external expressions in countenance and bearing, in words and assuring protestations—not just because the expression itself is untrue, but because the untruth is that the inwardness was merely an element. The dead person remains completely quiet while time passes. The famous warrior's sword has been laid upon his grave, and shamelessness has torn down the picket fence surrounding it, but the dead one did not rise up and draw his sword to defend himself and his resting place. He does not gesticulate, he does not protest, he does not flare up in a moment of inwardness, but, silent as the grave and quiet as a dead person, he maintains his inwardness and stands by his word. Praised be the living person who externally relates himself as a dead person to his inwardness and thereby maintains it, not as the excitement of a moment and as a woman's infatuation, but as the eternal, which has been gained through death. Such a person is a man. It is not unlovely for a woman to bubble over in momentary inwardness, nor is it unlovely for her to forget it again very soon—the one corresponds to the other, and both correspond to the feminine nature and to what is ordinarily understood by inwardness.

Tired from walking, I sat down on a bench, a marveling witness of how that proud ruler who now for thousands of years has been the hero of the day and will continue to be that
VII 199 until the last day, of how the sun in its brilliant departure cast a transfiguring glow over the entire surroundings, while my eyes gazed beyond the wall enclosing the garden into that eternal symbol of eternity—the infinite horizon. What sleep is for the body, rest such as this is for the soul, so that it can exhale properly. At that very moment, I discovered to my surprise that the trees that hid me from the eyes of others had hidden others from mine, for I heard a voice just beside me. It has always wounded my modesty to witness the expression of the kind of feeling that another person surrenders himself to only when he thinks he is not being observed, because there is an

inwardness of feeling that out of decency is hidden and is manifest only to God, just as a woman's beauty will be concealed from everyone and disclosed only to the beloved—therefore I decided to move away. But the first words I heard held me captive, and since I feared that the noise of my leaving might disturb more than my staying there quietly, I chose the latter and then became a witness of a situation that, however solemn it was, suffered no infringement because of my presence.

Through the leaves I saw that there were two: an old man with chalk-white hair and a child, a boy of about ten years. Both were in mourning clothes and sat beside a freshly covered grave, from which it was easy to conclude that it was a recent loss that occupied them. The old man's august form became even more solemn in the transfiguring glow of twilight, and his voice, calm and yet fervent, rendered the words clearly and distinctly with the inwardness they had in the speaker, who paused now and then when his voice choked with weeping or his mood ended in a sigh. Mood is like the Niger River[339] in Africa; no one knows its source, no one knows its outlet—only its reach is known! From the conversation I learned that the little boy was the old man's grandson and the person whose grave they were visiting was the boy's father. Presumably all the others in the family were dead, since no one was mentioned. On a later visit I verified this by reading the name on the gravestone and the names of the many dead. [340]As they talked, the old man told the child that he no longer had a father, had no one to cling to except an old man, who was too old for him and who himself longed to leave the world, but that there was a God in heaven after whom all fatherliness in heaven and on earth is called, that there was one name in which there was salvation, the name of Jesus Christ. He paused for a moment and then said half-aloud to himself: That this consolation should become for me a terror, that he, my son, who now lies buried in the grave, could abandon it! For what purpose all my hope, for what purpose VII
all my concern, for what purpose all his wisdom, now that his 200
death in the midst of his error makes a believer's soul uncertain about his salvation, brings my gray hair in sorrow to the

grave,[341] makes a believer leave the world in apprehensiveness, makes an old man hurry like a doubter after a certainty and look back dejected for the surviving one.

Then he spoke again with the child and told him that there was a wisdom that wanted to fly past faith, that on the other side of faith there was a wide range like the blue mountains, a specious continent, which to the mortal eye looked like a certainty greater than that of faith, but the believer feared this mirage as the skipper fears a similar mirage at sea, feared that it was a sham eternity in which a mortal cannot live, but in which, if he steadily stares into it, he will lose his faith. He became silent again, and then said to himself half-aloud: That he, my unhappy son, should have allowed himself to be deceived! For what purpose, then, all his learning, so that he could not even make himself intelligible to me, so that I could not speak with him about his error because it was too elevated for me! Then he rose and led the child to the grave, and in a voice the impression of which I shall never forget he said, "Poor boy, you are just a child, and yet you will soon be alone in the world. Do you promise me by the memory of your dead father, who, if he could speak to you now, would speak in this way and now speaks with my voice; do you promise by the sight of my old age and my gray hair; do you promise by the solemnity of this hallowed place, by the God whose name I trust you have learned to call upon, by the name of Jesus Christ, in whom alone there is salvation—do you promise me that you will hold fast to this faith in life and in death, that you will not let yourself be deceived by any phantom, no matter how the shape of the world is changed—do you promise me that?" Overcome by the impression, the little one dropped to his knees, but the old man raised him up and pressed him to his breast.

I owe it to the truth to confess that this was the most heartrending scene I have ever witnessed. What may momentarily make someone or other inclined to consider the whole thing a fiction—that an old man speaks this way with a child—was precisely what shook me most: the unhappy old man who had become solitary in the world with a child and had no one with

whom to speak about his concern except a child, and had only one person to save, a child, and yet could not presuppose the maturity to understand, and yet did not dare to wait for the advent of maturity, [342]because he himself was an old man. It is beautiful to be an old person, gratifying for the old man to see the generation growing up around him, a joyous arithmetical task to add to the sum every time the number is increased. But VII 201
if it becomes his lot to have to recalculate, if the arithmetical task becomes that of having to subtract every time death takes away and takes away, until quits [*qvit*] is called and the old man is left behind to give the receipt [*qvittere*]—what then is as hard as being an old person! Just as need can bring a person to extremities, so it seems to me that the old man's suffering found its strongest expression in what poetically might be called an improbability—that an old person has his one and only confidant in a child, and that a sacred promise, an oath, is required of a child.

Although only a spectator and a witness, I was deeply affected. At one moment it seemed to me as if I myself were the young man whom the father had buried in terror. At the next moment it seemed to me as if I were the child who was bound by the sacred promise. But I felt no urge to rush forward and emotionally express my sympathy to the old man, assuring him with tears and quivering voice that I would never forget this scene, or perhaps even beseeching him to put me under oath. Only for rash [*overilede*] people, barren clouds, and bursts of passing showers [*Ilinger*] is nothing more precipitous [*ilsom*] than to take an oath, because, being unable to keep it, they must keep on taking it. In my opinion, "to want never to forget this impression" is different from saying once in a solemn moment, "I will never forget this." The former is inwardness, the latter perhaps only momentary inwardness. And if one never forgets it, the solemnity with which it was said does not seem so important, since the sustained solemnity with which one day by day keeps oneself from forgetting it is a truer solemnity. The feminine approach is always dangerous.[343] A tender handshake, a passionate embrace, a tear in the eye are still not exactly the same as the quiet dedication of

resolution. Inwardness of spirit is indeed always like a stranger and foreigner in a body—why, then, gesticulations? What Shakespeare's Brutus says when the conspirators want to bind themselves by an oath to the enterprise is so true: "No, not an oath . . . . . let priests and cowards and rogues, marrowless oldsters and crushed souls swear . . . . . but do not weaken the quiet strength of our purpose, our inner invincible fire, by thinking that our cause, our performance, needs an oath [*Eed*]."[344] The momentary outpouring of inwardness fre-
VII quently leaves behind a lethargy [*Mathed*] that is dangerous.
202 Furthermore, in yet another way a simple observation has taught me circumspection with regard to making oaths and promises, so that true inwardness is even constrained to express itself with the opposite. There is nothing that hasty and easily excited people are more inclined to do than to require sacred promises, because the inner weakness needs the powerful stimulation of the moment. Having to make a sacred promise to such a person is very dubious, and therefore it is much better to forestall this solemn scene and at the same time to bind oneself with a little *reservatio mentalis* [mental reservation], that is, if the requirement of a promise is justified at all. One thereby benefits the other person, prevents profanation of the sacred, prevents him from becoming bound by an oath—it would all end with his breaking the oath anyway. For example, if Brutus, in view of the fact that the conspirators, with hardly a single exception, were no doubt excitable fellows and therefore precipitous in making oaths and sacred promises and requesting sacred promises, had pushed them aside and had for that reason prevented the making of a promise, and if at the same time he quietly dedicated himself, since he regarded it as a just cause and their turning to him as also somewhat justified—then it appears to me that his inwardness would have been even greater. Now he is a bit bombastic, and although there is truth in what he says,[345] there is still a little untruth in his saying it to the conspirators without really making clear to himself to whom he is speaking.

Then I, too, went home. I basically understood the old man right away, because in many ways my studies had led me to notice a dubious relation between modern Christian speculative thought and Christianity, but it had not occupied me in any decisive way. Now the matter had its significance. The august old man with his faith seemed to me a totally justified individuality whom existence had wronged, inasmuch as modern speculative thought, like a monetary reform, made doubtful the property title of faith. The august old man's pain over losing his son, not only through death but, as he understood it, even more terribly through speculative thought, moved me deeply, and at the same time the contradiction in his situation, that he could not even explain how the enemy force was operating, became for me a decisive summons to find a definite clue. The whole thing appealed to me like a complicated criminal case in which the very convoluted circumstances VII 203 have made it difficult to track down the truth. This was something for me. I thought as follows: You are quite bored with life's diversions, bored with girls, whom you love only in passing; you must have something that can totally occupy your time. Here it is: find out where the misunderstanding between speculative thought and Christianity lies. This, then, was my resolution. I have not spoken about it to anyone at all, and I am sure that my landlady has detected no change in me, neither the same evening nor the next day.

"But," I said to myself, "since you are not a genius and by no means have the mission of making all humankind blissfully happy at any cost, and since you have not promised anyone anything either, you can undertake the matter entirely *con amore* [with love] and proceed altogether *methodice* [methodically], as if a poet and a dialectician kept your every step under surveillance, now that you have gained a more definite understanding of your own whimsical idea that you must try to make something difficult." My studies, which had already in a sense led me to my goal, now became more definitely organized, but the old gentleman's august figure always hovered before my thoughts every time I wanted to transform my deliberations into learned knowledge. But primarily I sought through my own reflection to pick up a clue to the ultimate misunderstanding. I need not report my many mistakes, but it finally became clear to me that the deviation of speculative thought and, based thereupon, its presumed right to reduce faith to a factor might not be something accidental, might be located far deeper in the orientation of the whole age—most likely in this, that because of much knowledge people have entirely forgotten what it means to *exist* and what *inwardness* is.

When I had comprehended this, it also became clear to me that if I wanted to communicate anything about this, the main point must be that my presentation would be made in an *indirect* form. That is, if inwardness is truth, results are nothing but junk with which we should not bother one another, and wanting to communicate results is an unnatural association of one person with another, inasmuch as every human being is spirit and truth is the self-activity of appropriation, which a result hinders. Suppose that the teacher, in regard to essential truth (for otherwise the direct relation between teacher and learner is entirely in order), has much inwardness and would like, as people say, to proclaim his teaching day in and day out. If he assumes that there is a direct relation between him and the learner, then his inwardness is not inwardness but a
VII spontaneous outpouring, because respect for the learner, that
204 he in himself is his own inwardness, is the teacher's inwardness. Suppose that a learner is enthusiastic and in the strongest terms proclaims his praise of the teacher and thus, as we say, lays bare his inwardness; his inwardness is not inwardness but a spontaneous devotedness, because the pious, silent agreement, according to which the learner personally appropriates what is taught, distancing himself from the teacher because he turns inward into himself—precisely that is inwardness. Pathos is certainly inwardness, but it is spontaneous inwardness and therefore can be expressed. But pathos in the form of contrast is inwardness; it remains with the communicator even when expressed, and it cannot be appropriated directly except through the other's *self*-activity, and the contrastive form is the dynamometer of inwardness. The more consummate the contrastive form, the greater the inwardness; and the less it is present, to the point of being direct communication, the less

the inwardness. For an enthusiastic genius who would like to make all humankind blissfully happy and lead them to the truth, it can be difficult enough to learn to constrain himself in this way and to grasp the *N.B.* [*nota bene*, note well] of reduplication, because truth is not like a circular letter on which signatures are collected, but is in the *valore intrinseco* [intrinsic worth] of inwardness. Understanding this comes more naturally to a vagabond and frivolous person. As soon as truth, the essential truth, can be assumed to be known by everyone, appropriation and inwardness must be worked for, and here can be worked for only in an indirect form. The position of the apostle[346] is something else, because he must proclaim an unknown truth, and therefore direct communication can always have its validity temporarily.

Oddly enough, although there is so much clamoring for the positive and for the direct communication of results, it does not occur to anyone to complain about God, who as the eternal spirit, as the source of derived spirits, would seem to be able in the communication of truth to relate himself directly to the derived spirit in a quite different sense than when the relation is between derived spirits who, viewed *essentially*, are equals within a common derivation from God. No anonymous author can more slyly hide himself, and no maieutic can more carefully recede from a direct relation than God can. He is in the creation, everywhere in the creation, but he is not there directly, and only when the single individual turns inward into himself (consequently only in the inwardness of self-activity) does he become aware and capable of seeing VII 205
God.

The direct relationship with God is simply paganism, and only when the break has taken place, only then can there be a true God-relationship. But this break is indeed the first act of inwardness oriented to the definition that truth is inwardness. Nature is certainly the work of God, but only the work is directly present, not God. With regard to the individual human being, is this not acting like an illusive author, who nowhere sets forth his result in block letters or provides it beforehand in a preface? And why is God illusive? Precisely because he is truth and in being illusive seeks to keep a person from untruth. The observer does not glide directly to the result but on his own must concern himself with finding it and thereby break the direct relation. But this break is the actual breakthrough of inwardness, an act of self-activity, the first designation of truth as inwardness.

Or is it not the case that God is so unnoticeable, so hidden yet present in his work, that a person might very well live on, marry, be respected and esteemed as husband, father, and captain of the popinjay shooting club,[347] without discovering God in his work, without ever receiving any impression of the infinitude of the ethical, because he managed with an analogy to the speculative confusion of the ethical and the world-historical by managing with custom and tradition in the city where he lived? Just as a mother admonishes her child who is about to attend a party, "Now, mind your manners and watch the other polite children and behave as they do," so he, too, could live on and behave as he saw others behave. He would never do anything first and would never have any opinion unless he first knew that others had it, because "the others" would be his very first. On special occasions he would act like someone who does not know how to eat a course that is served at a banquet; he would reconnoiter until he saw how the others did it etc. Such a person could perhaps know ever so much, perhaps even know the system by rote; he could perhaps live in a Christian country, know how to bow his head every time God's name was mentioned, perhaps also see God in nature if he was in the company of others who saw God; in short, well,
VII he could be a congenial partygoer—and yet he would be de-
206 ceived by the direct relation to truth, to the ethical, to God.

If one were to portray such a person in an imaginary construction, he would be a satire on what it is to be a human being. It is really the God-relationship that makes a human being a human being, but this is what he would lack. Yet no one would hesitate to consider him an actual human being (for the absence of inwardness is not seen directly), although he would be more like a puppet character that very deceptively imitates all the human externalities—would even have children with his wife. At the end of his life, one would have to say that one thing had escaped him: he had not become aware of God. If God could have permitted a direct relationship, he would certainly have become aware. If God had taken the form, for example, of a rare, enormously large green bird, with a red beak, that perched in a tree on the embankment and perhaps even whistled in an unprecedented manner—then our partygoing man would surely have had his eyes opened; for the first time in his life he would have been able to be the first.

All paganism consists in this, that God is related directly to a human being, as the remarkably striking to the amazed. But the spiritual relationship with God in truth, that is, inwardness, is first conditioned by the actual breakthrough of inward deepening that corresponds to the divine cunning that God has nothing remarkable, nothing at all remarkable, about him—indeed, he is so far from being remarkable that he is invisible, and thus one does not suspect that he is there [*er til*], although his invisibility is in turn his omnipresence. But an omnipresent being is the very one who is seen everywhere, for example, as a police officer is—how illusive, then, that an omnipresent being is cognizable precisely by his being invisible,* simply and solely by this, because his very visibility would annul his omnipresence. This relation between omnipresence and invisibility is like the relation between mystery and revelation, that the mystery expresses that the revelation VII 207
is revelation in the stricter sense, that the mystery is the one and only mark by which it can be known, since otherwise a

* In order to indicate how illusive the rhetorical can be, I shall show here how one could perhaps produce an effect upon a listener rhetorically, even though what was said would be a dialectical retrogression. Suppose a pagan religious orator says that here on earth the god's temple is actually empty, but (and here the rhetorical begins) in heaven, where everything is more perfect, where water is air, and air is ether, there are also temples and shrines for the gods, but the difference is that the gods actually dwell in these temples—that the god actually dwells in the temple is dialectical retrogression, because his not dwelling in the temple is an expression for the spiritual relation to the invisible. But rhetorically it produces the effect. —Incidentally, I had in mind VII 207
a specific passage by a Greek author,[348] but I shall not quote him.

revelation becomes something like a police officer's omnipresence.

If God [*Gud*] wants to reveal himself in human form and provide a direct relation by taking, for example, the form of a man who is twelve feet tall, then that imaginatively constructed partygoer and captain of the popinjay shooting club will surely become aware. But since God is unwilling to deceive, the spiritual relation in truth specifically requires that there be nothing at all remarkable about his form; then the partygoer must say: There is nothing to see, not the slightest. If the god [*Guden*] has nothing whatever that is remarkable about him, the partygoer is perhaps deceived in not becoming aware at all. But the god is without blame in this, and the actuality of this deception is continually also the possibility of the truth. But if the god has something remarkable about him, he deceives, inasmuch as a human being thus becomes aware of the untruth, and this awareness is also the impossibility of the truth.

In paganism, the direct relation is idolatry; in Christianity, everyone indeed knows that God cannot manifest himself in this way. But this knowledge is not inwardness at all, and in Christianity it can certainly happen with a rote knower that he becomes utterly "without God in the world,"[349] which was not the case in paganism, where there was still the untrue relation of idolatry. Idolatry is certainly a dismal substitute, but that the rubric "God" disappears completely is even more mistaken.

Accordingly, not even God relates himself directly to a derived spirit (and this is the wondrousness of creation: not to produce something that is nothing in relation to the Creator, but to produce something that is something and that in the true worship of God can use this something to become by itself nothing before God); even less can one human being relate himself in this way to another *in truth*. Nature, the totality of creation, is God's work, and yet God is not there, but within the individual human being there is a possibility (he is spirit according to his possibility) that in inwardness is awakened to a God-relationship, and then it is possible to see God every-

where. Compared with the spiritual relationship in inward- VII
ness, the sensate distinctions of the great, the amazing, the 208
most crying-to-heaven superlatives of a southern nation are a retrogression to idolatry. Is it not as if an author wrote 166 folio volumes and the reader read and read, just as when someone observes and observes nature but does not discover that the meaning of this enormous work lies in the reader himself, because amazement at the many volumes and the five hundred lines to the page, which is similar to amazement at how immense nature is and how innumerable the animal species are, is not understanding.

With regard to the essential truth, a direct relation between spirit and spirit is unthinkable. If such a relation is assumed, it actually means that one party has ceased to be spirit, something that is not borne in mind by many a genius who both assists people *en masse* into the truth and is good-natured enough to think that applause, willingness to listen, signatures, etc. mean accepting the truth. Just as important as the truth, and of the two the even more important one, is the mode in which the truth is accepted, and it is of slight help if one gets millions to accept the truth if by the very mode of their acceptance they are transposed into untruth. And therefore all good-naturedness, all persuasion, all bargaining, all direct attraction with the aid of one's own person in consideration of one's suffering so much for the cause, of one's weeping over humankind, of one's being so enthusiastic, etc.—all such things are a misunderstanding, in relation to the truth a forgery by which, according to one's ability, one helps any number of people to acquire a semblance of truth.

Socrates was a teacher of the ethical, but he was aware that there is no direct relation between the teacher and the learner, because inwardness is truth, and inwardness in the two is precisely the path away from each other. Probably because he perceived this he was so very pleased with his advantageous appearance.[350] What was it? Well, guess again! In our day, we say of a clergyman that he has a very advantageous appearance; we are pleased about this and understand that he is a handsome man, that the clerical gown is very becoming to

him, that he has a sonorous voice and a figure that every tailor—but what am I saying—that every listener must be
VII pleased with. Ah, yes, when one is so equipped by nature and
209 so dressed by the tailor, one can easily be a teacher of religion, even with success, because the conditions of teachers of religion vary greatly—indeed, more than one thinks when one hears complaints that some pastoral appointments are so opulent and others so meager. The difference is much greater—some teachers of religion are crucified—and yet the religion is fully the same! No one cares much about the reduplicated repetition of the substance of the teaching in the conception of how the teacher ought to be. Orthodoxy is set forth, and the teacher is prinked up in pagan-esthetic categories. Christ is presented in biblical expressions. That he bore the sin of the whole world[351] will not really move the congregation; yet the speaker proclaims it, and in order to make the contrast strong, he describes Christ's beauty (because the contrast between guiltlessness and sin is not strong enough), and the believing congregation is stirred by this totally pagan qualification of the god in human form: beauty.

But back to Socrates.[352] He did not have an appearance as advantageous as the one described. He was very ugly, had clumsy feet, and more than that, a number of bumps on his forehead and other places, which were bound to convince everyone that he was a depraved character. This, you see, was what Socrates understood by his advantageous appearance, and he was so pleased as Punch about it that he would have considered it chicanery on the part of the god if, in order to keep him from being a teacher of morals, he had been given the pleasing appearance of a sentimental zither player, the languishing look of a *Schäfer* [amorous swain], the small feet of a dance director in the Friendship Society,[353] and *in toto* as advantageous an appearance as a job seeker in *Adresseavisen* or a theological graduate who had set his hopes on a patronage appointment could possibly wish for himself. Now, then, why was that old teacher so pleased with his advantageous appearance, unless it was because he perceived that it might help to place the learner at a distance so that he would not be caught

in a direct relation to the teacher, perhaps would admire him,
perhaps would have his clothes made in the same way, but
might understand through the repulsion of opposition, which
in turn was his irony in a higher sphere, that the learner essentially has himself to deal with [354]and that the inwardness of
truth is not the chummy inwardness with which two bosom
friends walk arm in arm with each other but is the separation VII
in which each person for himself is existing in what is true. 210

Thus I had fully realized that every direct communication with regard to truth as inwardness is a misunderstanding, even though it can vary according to the variety of that which is responsible for it, be it a lovable predilection, a nebulous sympathy, cryptic vanity, obtuseness, brashness, and other things. But just because I had become clear about the form of communication, it did not mean that I had something to communicate, although it was nevertheless entirely in order that the form first became clear to me, because the form is indeed the inwardness.

My main thought was that, because of the copiousness of knowledge, people in our day have forgotten what it means *to exist*, and what *inwardness* is, and that the misunderstanding between speculative thought and Christianity could be explained by that. I now resolved to go back as far as possible in order not to arrive too soon at what it means to exist religiously, not to mention existing Christianly-religiously, and in that way leave dubieties behind me. If people had forgotten what it means to exist religiously, they had probably also forgotten what it means to exist humanly; therefore this would have to be brought out. [355]But this must not on any account be done didactically, because then the misunderstanding would in a new misunderstanding instantly make capital of the explanatory attempt, as if existing consisted in coming to know something about a particular point. If this is communicated as knowledge, the recipient is mistakenly induced to understand that he is gaining something to know, and then we are back in knowledge again. Only the person who has an idea of a misunderstanding's tenacity in assimilating even the most rigorous attempt at explanation and yet remaining a misunderstanding, only he will be aware of the difficulty of an authorship in which care must be taken with every word, and every word must go through the process of double-reflection. Direct communication about what it means to exist and about inwardness will only have the result that the speculative thinker will benevolently take it in hand and let one slip in along with it. The system is hospitable! Just as a bourgeois-philistine, without regard to compatibility, takes along every Tom, Dick, and Harry when he goes on an excursion to the woods, inasmuch as there is room enough in the four-seated Holstein carriage, so also is the system hospitable—there is indeed plenty of room.

I will not conceal the fact that I admire Hamann,[356] although I readily admit that, if he is supposed to have worked coherently, the elasticity of his thoughts lacks evenness and his preternatural resilience lacks self-control. But the originality of genius is there in his brief statements, and the pithiness
VII 211 of form corresponds completely to the desultory hurling forth of a thought. With heart and soul, down to his last drop of blood, he is concentrated in a single word, a highly gifted genius's passionate protest against a system of existence. But the system is hospitable. Poor Hamann, you have been reduced to a subsection by Michelet.[357] Whether your grave has ever been marked, I do not know; whether it is now trampled upon, I do not know; but I do know that by hook or by crook you have been stuck into the subsection uniform and thrust into the ranks. I do not deny that Jacobi[358] has often inspired me, although I am well aware that his dialectical skill is not in proportion to his noble enthusiasm, but he is the eloquent protest of a noble, unadulterated, lovable, highly gifted mind against the systematic crimping of existence, a triumphant consciousness of and an inspired battling for the significance of existence as something longer and deeper than the few years during which one forgets oneself in studying the system. Poor Jacobi! Whether anyone visits your grave, I do not know; but I do know that the subsection-plow plows under all your eloquence, all your inwardness, while a few paltry words are being registered about your importance in the sys-

tem. It is said of Jacobi that he represented feeling with enthusiasm; such a report ridicules both feeling and enthusiasm, which have precisely the secret that neither can be reported secondhand and therefore cannot in the form of a result conveniently make a rote parroter blissfully happy through a *satisfactio vicaria* [vicarious satisfaction].

So, then, I resolved to begin, and the first thing I wanted to do in order to start from the bottom was *to have the existence-relation between the esthetic and the ethical come into existence in an existing individuality*. The task was set, and I foresaw that the work would be copious enough, and above all that I would have to be prepared to remain still at times when the spirit would not support me with pathos. But what happened then I shall tell in an appendix to this chapter.

APPENDIX VII 212

A Glance at a Contemporary Effort in Danish Literature

What happens? As I go on in this way, *Either/Or* is published.[359] What I aimed to do had been done right here. I became very unhappy at the thought of my solemn resolution, but then I thought once again: After all, you have not promised anyone anything; as long as it is done, that is just fine. But things became worse for me, because step by step, just as I wanted to begin the task of carrying out my resolution by working, there appeared a pseudonymous book that did what I wanted to do. There was something strangely ironic about it all. It was good that I had never spoken to anyone about my resolution, that not even my landlady had detected anything from my behavior, for otherwise people would have laughed at my comic situation, because it is indeed rather droll that the cause I had resolved to take up is advancing, but not through me. And every time I read such a pseudonymous book and thereby saw more clearly what I had aimed to do, I was convinced that the cause had advanced. In this way, I became a tragic-comic interested witness of the productions of Victor Eremita and other pseudonymous authors. Whether my understanding is that of the authors, I naturally cannot know for certain, since I am only a reader. On the other hand, I am pleased that the pseudonymous authors, presumably aware of the relation of indirect communication to truth as inwardness, have themselves not said anything or misused a preface to take an official position on the production, as if in a purely legal sense an author were the best interpreter of his own words, as if it could help a reader that an author "intended this and that" when it was not carried out; or as if it were certain that it had been carried out, since the author himself says so in the preface; or as if an existence-deviation were amended by being brought to a final decision, such as insanity, suicide, and the like, which female authors in particular do, and so speedily that they almost begin with it; or as if an author were served by a reader who, precisely because of the author's bungling, knew with certainty all about the book.

Either/Or, the title of which is in itself indicative, has the existence-relation between the esthetic and the ethical materialize into existence in the existing individuality. This to me is the book's indirect polemic against speculative thought,
VII which is indifferent to existence. That there is no conclusion
213 and no final decision is an indirect expression for truth as inwardness and in this way perhaps a polemic against truth as knowledge. The preface itself says something about it, but not didactically, for in that case I could know something with certainty, but in the jovial form of jest and hypothesis. The absence of an author is a means of distancing.

The first of the diapsalmata (Part I, p. 3[360]) posits a cleft in existence as the pain of a poet-existence, such as could have persisted in a poet-existence, which B uses against A (Part II, p. 217 bottom). The last word in the whole work (Part II, p. 368) reads as follows: Only the truth that *builds up* is truth *for you*. This is an essential predicate in relation to truth as inwardness, whereby its decisive qualification as upbuilding *for you*, that is, for the subject, is its essential difference from all objective knowledge, inasmuch as the subjectivity itself becomes the sign of truth.

Part I is an existence-possibility that cannot attain existence, a depression that must be worked upon ethically. Essentially it is depression, and so deep that, although autopathetic, it deceptively occupies itself with the sufferings of others ("Silhouettes") and otherwise deceives under the guise of desire, common sense, corruption, but the deception and the disguise are simultaneously its strength and its weakness, its strength in imagination and its weakness in attaining existence. It is a fantasy-existence in esthetic passion, therefore paradoxical and running aground on time. At its maximum, it is despair. Consequently, it is not existence, but existence-possibility oriented toward existence, and brought so close that one almost feels how every moment is wasted in which a decision has not yet been reached. But the existence-possibility in the existing A does not want to be conscious of this and holds existence at bay by the most subtle of all deceptions, by thinking. He has thought everything possible, and yet he has not existed at all. The result is that only the diapsalmata are purely poetical outpourings, whereas the rest has rich intrinsic thought-content, which can easily deceive, as if having thought about something were identical with existing. If a poet had designed the work, he would hardly have thought of this and perhaps, by means of the work itself, would have promoted the old misunderstanding again. In other words, the relation must not be between immature and mature thinking, but between not ex- VII
isting and existing. Therefore, as a thinker, A is advanced; as 214
a dialectician, he is far superior to B. He possesses all the seductive gifts of understanding and intellect; it thereby becomes more clear what makes B differ from him.

Part II is an ethical individuality existing on the basis of the ethical. Part II is also that which brings out Part I, since A would in turn have conceived of being an author as a possibility, actually carry it out—and then leave it there. The ethicist *has despaired* (see Part II, pp. 163-227[361]—Part I *was* despair).

In despair, he *has chosen himself* (pp. 239ff.). Through this choice and in this choice he becomes *open* (see Part II, p. 336: "The expression that sharply emphasizes the difference between the esthetic and the ethical is: it is every human being's duty to become open"—Part I was hiddenness). He is a married man (A was acquainted with every possibility in the erotic realm and yet not even actually in love, for at that very moment he would in a way have been in the process of consolidating himself) and, in direct opposition to the hiddenness of the esthetic, focuses on marriage as the most profound form of life's disclosure, whereby *time* is turned to account for the ethically existing individual, and the possibility of *gaining a history* is continuity's ethical victory over hiddenness, depression, illusory passion, and despair. Having gone through phantasmal, nebulous images, through the distractions of a luxuriant thought-content (the development of which, if it is good for anything, is the author's chief merit), one comes to a very specific human being existing on the basis of the ethical. This is the change of scenery, or, more correctly, now the scene is there; instead of a world of possibility, animated by imagination and dialectically arranged, an individual has come into existence—and only the truth that builds up is truth for you—that is, truth is inwardness, the inwardness of existence, please note, and here in ethical definition.

So this gust was over. The merit of the book, if it has any, does not concern me. If it has any, it must essentially be that it does not provide any conclusion but in inwardness transforms everything: the fantasy-inwardness in Part I into a conjuring up of possibilities with intensified passion, the dialectic
VII into a transforming, in despair, of everything into nothing;
215 the ethical pathos [362]in Part II into an embracing, with the quiet, incorruptible,[363] and yet infinite passion of resolution, of the ethical's modest task, built up thereby, open before God and men.

There is no didacticizing, but this does not mean that there is no thought-content; to think is one thing and to exist in what has been thought is something else. Existing in relation to thinking is not something that follows by itself any more

than it is thoughtlessness. It is not even a conviction that is communicated and perhaps expounded fervently, as one says, because a conviction can also be possessed in idea, whereby it so easily becomes dialectical in the sense of being more or less true. No, here the existing is in thought, and the book or work has no finite relation to anyone. The transparency of thought in existence is inwardness. Thus, for example, if speculative thought, instead of didactically discoursing on *de omnibus dubitandum*[364] and acquiring a chorus of followers who swear to swear by *de omnibus dubitandum*, had instead made an attempt to have such a doubter come into existence in existence-inwardness so that one could see down to the slightest detail how he goes about doing it—well, if it had done this, that is, if it had started to do this, then in turn it would have abandoned it and understood with shame that the grand slogan every parroter swears he has carried out is not only an infinitely difficult task but an impossibility for an existing person. And it is indeed one of the dismaying aspects of all communication that the good communicator, sometimes in order to win people, sometimes out of vanity, sometimes in thoughtlessness, fills his mouth so full that in no time he has not only done everything that is possible for an eminent existing spirit in a long life but has done what is impossible. One forgets that existing makes the understanding of the simplest truth exceedingly difficult and strenuous for the common man in the transparency of existence. With the aid of a conclusion, one automatically and mendaciously takes credit for everything (I have heard people, so obtuse that they have nothing between the ears, say that one cannot stop with Socratic ignorance) and like all windbags finally ends up with having done even the impossible. Inwardness has become a matter of knowledge, to exist a waste of time. That is why the most mediocre person who concocts a book these days talks so one would believe he had experienced everything, and simply by paying attention to his intermediate clauses one sees VII 216
that he is a rogue. That is why a person who in our age exists with merely as much energy as that of a mediocre Greek philosopher is regarded as demonic. People can recite the rigma-

role of pain and suffering by rote, likewise the glorious law of steadfastness. Everyone recites by rote. If there exists one person who for the sake of an idea exposes himself to a little unpleasantness, he is regarded as a demon—or as obtuse. People know everything, and in order not to stop with that, they know also that they are not to do the least of what they know, because with the aid of external knowledge they are in seventh heaven, and if one must begin to do it, one will become a poor, wretched existing individual who stumbles again and again and progresses very slowly from year to year. Indeed, if one can at times recall with some relief that Caesar had the Alexandrian library burned to the ground,[365] one could, well intentioned, actually wish for humankind that this superfluity of knowledge be taken away again so that one could again come to know what it means to live as a human being.

That *Either/Or* ends precisely with the upbuilding truth (yet without so much as italicizing the words, to say nothing of didacticizing) was remarkable to me. I could wish to see it emphasized more definitely in order that each particular point on the way to existing Christianly-religiously could become clear. The Christian truth as inwardness is also upbuilding, but this by no means implies that every upbuilding truth is Christian; the upbuilding is a wider category. I now concentrated again on this point, but what happened? Just as I intended to begin, *Two Upbuilding Discourses* by Magister Kierkegaard, 1843,[366] was published. Then came three upbuilding discourses,[367] and the preface repeated that they were not sermons,[368] which I, if no one else, would indeed have unconditionally protested against, since they use only ethical categories of immanence, not the doubly reflected religious categories in the paradox. If a confusion of language is to be averted, the sermon must be reserved for religious-Christian existence. These days we do occasionally hear sermons that are anything but sermons because the categories are those of immanence. Perhaps the Magister has wanted indirectly to make this clear by seeing how far one can go, purely philosophically, in the upbuilding. Thus the upbuilding discourse
VII 217 certainly has its validity, but, by emphasizing this indirectly,

the author came to the aid of the cause that I call my own, in a ludicrous way, inasmuch as I keep on arriving too late when it comes to doing something. But oddly enough, according to what the Magister told me, it turned out that some promptly called the upbuilding discourses sermons[369]—indeed, even thought that they were honoring them with this title, as if the upbuilding discourse and the sermon were related to each other like a district judge to a justice of the supreme court and as if one honored the district judge by calling him a supreme court justice when he is only a district judge. Others, however, raised the objection to the upbuilding discourses that they were not proper sermons, which is like raising the objection to an opera that it is not a tragedy.*

The ethicist in *Either/Or* had saved himself by despairing, had terminated hiddenness in disclosure, but in my opinion there was a discrepancy here. In order to define himself in the inwardness of truth in a way different from that of speculative thought, he had used despair instead of doubt, but he nevertheless made it appear that by despairing, in the despair itself, he *uno tenore* [without interruption], as it were, found himself.
If it were to be pointed out clearly in *Either/Or* where the dis- VII
crepancy lies, the book would have needed to have a religious 218

* In making this objection, some may have been thinking not so much that the upbuilding discourses were philosophical and did not use Christian categories at all, but rather that they have incorporated an esthetic element on a scale larger than is usual in the upbuilding address. As a rule, in an upbuilding discourse one refrains from the stronger and more thorough portrayal of states of mind with a psychological play of colors and, whatever the reason may be, whether the individual speaker cannot or will not, leaves that to the poet and poetic *impetus* [transport]. This, however, can easily posit a cleft in the listener, since the upbuilding discourse leaves him wanting something that he consequently must seek elsewhere. As far as I can judge, it may be all right to include the poetic portrayal. But the decisive difference between the poet and the upbuilding speaker remains, namely, that the poet has no τέλος [end, goal] other than psychological truth and the art of presentation, whereas the speaker in addition has *principally* the aim of transposing everything into the upbuilding. The poet becomes absorbed in the portrayal of the passion, but for the upbuilding speaker this is only the beginning, and the next is crucial for him—to compel the stubborn person to disarm, to mitigate, to elucidate, in short, to cross over into the upbuilding.

instead of an ethical orientation and would already have said all at once what in my opinion should be said only successively. The discrepancy was not touched upon at all, and that was quite in accord with my design. Of course, whether this point has been clear to the author, I do not know. The discrepancy is that the ethical self is supposed to be found immanently in despair, that by enduring the despair the individual would win himself. Admittedly, he has used a qualification of freedom, to choose himself, which seems to remove the difficulty that probably has not been particularly conspicuous to many, since *philosophice* [philosophically] it goes one, two, three with doubting everything and then finding the true beginning. But that does not help. In despairing, I use myself to despair, and therefore I can indeed despair of everything by myself, but if I do this I cannot come back by myself. It is in this moment of decision that the individual needs divine assistance, although it is quite correct that one must first have understood the existence-relation between the esthetic and the ethical in order to be at this point—that is, by being there in passion and inwardness, one indeed becomes aware of the religious—and of *the leap*.

Furthermore, the definition of truth as inwardness, that it is upbuilding, must also be more explicitly understood before it is even religious, to say nothing of being Christianly religious. It holds true of everything upbuilding that it first and foremost evokes the requisite adequate terror, because otherwise the upbuilding is make-believe. With the passion of the infinite, the ethicist in the moment of despair had chosen himself out of the *terror* of having himself, his life, his actuality in esthetic dreams, in depression, in hiddenness. Consequently, there can no longer be any question of terror from this angle; the arena is the ethical inwardness in the existing individuality. The terror has to be a new qualification of inwardness, whereby the individual in a higher sphere comes back again to the point where disclosure, which is the life of the ethical, once again becomes impossible, but in such a way that the relation is reversed, so that the ethical, which previously aided disclosure (whereas the esthetic hindered it), is now the hindering element, and it is something else that helps the individual to a higher disclosure over and beyond the ethical.

For the person who with infinite passion has had the inwardness to grasp the ethical, to grasp duty and the eternal validity of the universal, no terror in heaven, on earth, and in the abyss[370] can compare with that of facing a collision in which the ethical becomes the temptation. Yet everyone faces this collision, if in no other way, then by one's being religiously VII 219 assigned to relating oneself to the religious paradigm—that is, because the religious paradigm is the irregularity and yet is supposed to be the paradigm (which is like God's omnipresence as invisibility and revelation as a mystery), or because the religious paradigm does not express the universal but the singular (the particular, for example, by appealing to visions, dreams, etc.) and yet is supposed to be the paradigm. But to be the paradigm means to be for all, but one can be the prototype for all only by being what all are or ought to be, that is, the universal, and yet the *religious paradigm* is the very opposite (the irregular and the particular), whereas the *tragic hero* expresses the regular declension of the universal for all.

[371]This had become clear to me, and I was only waiting for the spirit's help in pathos in order to present it in an existing individuality, because it should not be done didactically, since in my opinion the misfortune with our age was just that it had come to know too much and had forgotten what it means to exist and what inwardness is. Consequently, the form had to be indirect. Here I shall say the same thing in another way, as is appropriate when the discussion is about inwardness. The person who is so fortunate as to be dealing with multiplicity can easily be entertaining. When he is finished with China, he can take up Persia; when he has studied French, he can begin Italian, and then take up astronomy, veterinary science, etc., and always be sure of being regarded as a great fellow. But inwardness does not have the kind of range that arouses the amazement of the sensate. For example, inwardness in erotic love does not mean to get married seven times to Danish girls, and then to go for the French, the Italian, etc., but to love one and the same and yet be continually renewed in the same

erotic love, so that it continually flowers anew in mood and exuberance—which, when applied to communication, is the inexhaustible renewal and fertility of expression. Inwardness cannot be communicated directly, because expressing it directly is externality (oriented outwardly, not inwardly), and expressing inwardness directly is no proof at all that it is there (the direct outpouring of feeling is no proof at all that one has it, but the tension of the contrastive form is the dynamometer of inwardness), and the reception intrinsic to inwardness is not
VII a direct reproduction of what was communicated, since that is
220 an echo. But the repetition of inwardness is the resonance in which what is said disappears, as with Mary when she *hid* the words in her heart.[372] But when the relationship is between human beings, not even this is the true expression for the repetition of inwardness, because she *concealed* the words as a treasure in the beautiful setting of a good heart, but there is inwardness when what is said belongs to the recipient as if it were his own—and now it is indeed his own. To communicate in that way is the most beautiful triumph of resigned inwardness. Therefore no one is as resigned as God, because he communicates creatively in such a way that in creating he *gives* independence vis-à-vis himself.[373] The most resigned a human being can be is to acknowledge the given independence in every human being and to the best of one's ability do everything in order truly to help someone retain it. But in our age such matters are not talked about, for example, whether it is legitimate, as we say, to win a person for the truth, whether the person who has some truth to communicate, if he also has the art of persuasion, knows the human heart, has ingenuity in taking by surprise, has proficiency in capturing slowly—whether he has the right to use it to win adherents for the truth. Or should he, humble before God, loving human beings in the feeling that God does not need him* and that

* God is not like a king in a predicament, who says to the highly trusted Minister of the Interior, "You must do everything; you must create the atmosphere for our proposal and win public opinion to our side. You can do it. Use your sagacity. If I cannot depend upon you, I have no one." But in relation to God, there are no secret instructions for a human being any more than

every human being is essentially spirit, rather use all these gifts to prevent the direct relationship and, instead of comfortably having some adherents, should he dutifully put up with being accused of light-mindedness, lack of earnestness, etc., because he truly disciplines himself and saves his life from the most VII
dreadful of all untruths—an adherent. 221

As I mentioned, I had grasped that most dreadful collision of inwardness and was only waiting for the spirit to come to my assistance—what happens? Well, Magister Kierkegaard and I are certainly cutting a ridiculous figure, each in his own way, with regard to the pseudonymous books. Of course, no one knows that I am sitting here quietly, continually intending to do what the pseudonymous authors are doing. Magister Kierkegaard, however, pays for it every time such a book comes out. This much is certain—if all the many things that are said in learned tea circles and in otherwise friendly company for the ennobling and improvement of this man, if the terror of fulmination and the severe voice of accusation and the judgment of denunciation could really benefit him, then he might in short order become an unusually good man. Whereas one teacher usually has several pupils to improve, he is in the enviable situation of having a highly esteemed contemporary public of men and women, the learned and unlearned and chimney sweeps, who all take his improvement upon themselves. The only trouble is that the chastisement and everything aimed at ennobling the heart and understanding occur and are spoken in his absence, never when he is present; otherwise something would surely come of it.

What happens? A book comes out: *Fear and Trembling*.[374] The inability to become open, hiddenness, is here a terror, compared with which esthetic hiddenness is child's play.

To represent this existence-collision in an existing individ-

there are any backstairs. Even the most eminent genius who comes to give a report had best come in fear and trembling, for God is not hard-pressed for geniuses. He can, after all, create a few legions of them; and wanting to make oneself indispensable in the service of God means *eo ipso* dismissal. And every human being is created in the image of God. This is the absolute; the little he has to learn from Tom, Dick, and Harry is not of great value.

uality was impossible, since the difficulty of the collision, although *lyrically* it extorts the utmost passion, *dialectically* holds back the expression in absolute silence. Therefore Johannes de Silentio is not himself portrayed as such an existing person; he is a reflecting person who, with the tragic hero as the *terminus a quo* [point from which] and the interesting as the *confinium* [border territory] and the religious paradigmatic irregularity as the *terminus ad quem* [point to which], continually knocks the forehead, so to speak, of the understanding, [375]while the lyric springs from the recoil. This is the way Johannes has portrayed himself.[376] To call this book "*eine erhabene Lüge* [a noble lie]," as the firm [*Firma*] Kts[377] did in reminiscence of Jacobi
VII and Desdemona,[378] is in my opinion significant,[379] inasmuch
222 as the expression itself contains a contradiction. The contrast of form is altogether necessary for every production in these spheres. In the form of direct communication, in the form of bellowing, fear and trembling are insignificant, because the direct communication expressly indicates that the direction is outward, toward screaming, not inward into the abyss of inwardness, where *fear and trembling* first become terrible, which when expressed can be only in a deceptive form. Of course, I cannot know with certainty Johannes de Silentio's actual situation, since I do not know him personally, and even if I did, I am not exactly inclined to think that he would want to make a fool of himself by giving a direct communication.

The ethical is the temptation; the relationship with *God* has come into existence; the immanence of the ethical despair *has been broken; the leap has been posited; the absurd is the notification.*

Having understood this, I thought that by way of precaution it would be good to see to it that what was attained would not come to nothing through a *coup de main* [surprise stroke], so that hiddenness would come to be something that is called hiddenness, a bit of the esthetic, and faith would come to be something that is called immediacy, *vapeurs* [vagaries, hysterical feelings], for example, and the religious paradigm something that is called a prototype, a tragic hero, for example.

What happens? During that same time, I receive a book from Reitzel titled *Repetition*.[380] It is not didactic, far from it,

and it was precisely what I wished, since in my view the misfortune of the age was that it had come to know too much and had forgotten to exist and what inwardness is. In such a situation, it is desirable that the communicator know how to subtract, and for this a confusing contrastive form is particularly useful. And Constantin Constantius wrote, as he calls it, "a droll book."[381] Repetition is basically the expression for immanence; thus one finishes despairing and has oneself; one finishes doubting and has the truth. Constantin Constantius, the esthetic schemer, who ordinarily despairs of nothing, despairs of repetition, and the Young Man illustrates that if it is to come into existence it must be a new immediacy, so that it is itself a movement *by virtue of the absurd*, and the teleological
suspension *an ordeal* [*Prøvelse*].[382] Ordeal, in turn, corresponds VII
to the irregularity indigenous to the religious paradigm, be- 223
cause an ordeal, viewed ethically, is inconceivable, since the ethical is the universally valid precisely by always being valid. An ordeal is the religious paradigm's highest earnestness, but for the purely ethical an ordeal is a jest, and to *exist on trial* [*paa Prøve*][383] is by no means earnestness, but a comic motif, which incomprehensibly enough no poet has yet used to depict lack of will to an almost insane degree, as if someone wanted to marry on trial etc. But that the highest earnestness of the religious life is distinguishable by jest is like saying that the paradigm is the irregularity or the particularity, and God's omnipresence his invisibility, and revelation a mystery.

On the title page, the book *Repetition* was called "an imaginary psychological construction [*psychologisk Experiment*]."[384] That this was a doubly reflected communication form soon became clear to me. By taking place in the form of an imaginary construction, the communication creates for itself an opposition, and the imaginary construction establishes a chasmic gap between reader and author and fixes the separation of inwardness between them, so that a direct understanding is made impossible. The imaginary construction is the conscious, teasing revocation of the communication, which is always of importance to an existing person who writes for existing persons, lest the relation be changed to that of a rote reciter who writes for rote reciters. If a man were to stand on one leg or, in a droll dancing posture, swing his hat, and in this pose recite something true, his few listeners would fall into two classes, and he would not have many, since most of them would promptly abandon him. The one class would say: How can what he says be true when he gesticulates that way? The other class would say: Well, it makes no difference whether he performs an entrechat or stands on his head or turns somersaults; what he says is true, and I will appropriate it and let him go.

So it is also with the imaginary construction. If what is said is earnestness to the writer, he keeps the earnestness essentially to himself. If the recipient interprets it as earnestness, he does it essentially by himself, and precisely this is the earnestness. Even in elementary education one distinguishes between "learning by rote" and an "intellectual exercise," a distinction that is remarkably apropos with regard to systematic "learning by rote." The *being-in-between* [*Mellemværende*[385]] of the imaginary construction encourages the inwardness of the two *away from each other in inwardness*. This form won my complete approval, and I believed I had also found that in it the pseudonymous authors continually aimed at *existing* and in this way sustained an indirect polemic against speculative thought.
VII 224 If a person knows everything but knows it by rote, the form of the imaginary construction is a good exploratory means; in this form, one even tells him what he knows, but he does not recognize it. [386]Later, a new pseudonym, Frater Taciturnus, showed the place of the imaginary construction in connection with the esthetic, ethical, and religious productions. (See *Stages on Life's Way*, p. 340ff. § 3.[387])

Whether in other respects *Fear and Trembling* and *Repetition* have any worth, I shall not decide. If they do have worth, the criterion will not be didactic paragraph-pomposity. If the misfortune of the age is to have forgotten what inwardness is, then one should not write for "paragraph-gobblers," but existing individualities must be portrayed in their agony when existence is confused for them, which is something different from sitting safely in a corner by the stove and reciting *de om-*

nibus dubitandum.[388] Therefore if the production is to be meaningful, it must continually have passion.

Constantin Constantius has even used a love affair, which is always a usable theme in relation to what it means to exist, even though *philosophice*, in relation to rote reciting, it is folly. [389]He has used an engagement. I completely approve of this, and when two people are said to love each other, only veteran novel readers are accustomed to and find enjoyment in what the lowest rabble profanely understand by this expression. An engagement is a pledge, a broken engagement is a broken pledge, but there is no secret footnote that would make a woman blush. This does not necessarily mean that an engagement should have a less serious touch but that its earnestness and the terror of the break are more clear-cut. To call it a pledge, a broken pledge, when in a novel a man makes the beloved heroine pregnant and then abandons her, is thoughtless and immoral and above all frustrating to further dialectical expression. Such behavior does not allow further dialectical treatment, because good common sense readily tells one that at least four crimes have been committed here: making the girl pregnant (even if one married her later, it is still a crime), thereby making the child an illegitimate child (even if this is remedied later, it is still a crime), abandoning the mother, abandoning the child, and then the hero of the novel presumably becomes involved with a new beloved, whereby he, even if this new relationship were a proper marriage, commits adultery according to Scripture and transforms the abandoned VII 225
girl's marriage, if she enters anything of the sort, into a life of fornication, according to the teaching of Scripture.[390] To that extent, I can very well understand* why the story of an engagement was chosen, later also by Frater Taciturnus.[392]

* [391]I can also well understand why the pseudonymous author or the pseudonymous authors repeatedly bring up the topic of marriage. People ordinarily stop where the difficulties begin. According to ancient custom, poetry takes the love affair and lets the marriage be what it will. But in modern poetry (in drama and the novel) it has even gone so far that adultery as a matter of course is used as a sophisticated background for a new love affair. Innocent poetry explains nothing about marriage; guilty poetry explains it as adultery.

The more purely the broken relationship can be maintained, while terror of the finest quality grows and increases, the more the dialectic can discover. But to ponder dialectically what is most appropriately dealt with by the second protocol in the criminal court[393]—yes, even to use one's paltry fragment of dialectical ability to let the hero go scot-free—must be left to novelists. A novelist would regard an engagement as such a triviality that he simply could not become involved in interpreting a broken pledge of that kind. The pseudonymous authors expressly use dialectic to make it as terrible as possible, and the hero becomes a hero through the very passion with which he interprets the terror in himself and as decisive for his life. The purity consists in the interpretation of the broken pledge along the lines of a teleological suspension, and the hero's purity consists in his highest passion of wanting to undo it, and the hero's martyrdom consists in, among other things, his perception that his life becomes meaningless for most people, who ordinarily know just as much about the ethical and the religious as most novelists do. From the ethical and religious point of view, one does not become a hero by being a brisk fellow who is able to take everything lightly, but rather by taking life with extreme heaviness—yet, please note, not in the form of a half hour of feminine screaming, but in the form of endurance in inwardness.

VII 226 [394]Nevertheless, an ordeal (on its dialectic, see *Repetition*) is a passing through; the person tested comes back again to exist in the ethical, even though he retains an everlasting impression of the terror, a more inward impression than when the gray hairs remind the tried and tested person of the moment of horror and mortal danger when he became gray-haired. The teleological suspension of the ethical must have an even more definite religious expression. The ethical is then present at every moment with its infinite requirement, but the individual is not capable of fulfilling it. This powerlessness of the individual must not be seen as an imperfection in the continued endeavor to attain an ideal, for in that case the suspension is no more postulated than the man who administers his office in an ordinary way is suspended. The suspension consists in the individual's finding himself in a state exactly opposite to what the ethical requires. Therefore, far from being able to begin, every moment he continues in this state he is more and more prevented from being able to begin: he relates himself to actuality not as possibility but as impossibility. Thus the individual is suspended from the ethical in the most terrifying way, is in the suspension heterogeneous with the ethical, which still has the claim of the infinite upon him and at every moment requires itself of the individual, and thereby at every moment the heterogeneity is only more definitely marked as heterogeneity. In temptation (when *God* tempts a person, as is said of Abraham in Genesis[395]), Abraham was not heterogeneous with the ethical. He was well able to fulfill it but was prevented from it by something higher, which by *absolutely* accentuating itself transformed the voice of duty into a temptation. As soon as that something higher sets the tempted one free, everything is in order again, even though the terror, that this could happen even for one-tenth of a second, remains forever. How long the suspension lasts is of minor importance; that it is, is the crucial point. But people do not care about such things. The sermon presentation freely uses the category "ordeal" (where the ethical is a temptation), which absolutely confuses the ethical and, on the whole, all plain human thinking, and it all goes as if it were nothing—and it is not much more than that either.[396]

The situation is different now. Duty is the absolute, its requirement the absolute, and yet the individual is prevented from fulfilling it. Indeed, in a desperately ironic way he is as if exempted (in the same sense as Scripture speaks of being free
from God's law[397]) by becoming heterogeneous with it, and VII
the more profoundly its requirement is proclaimed to him, the 227
more clear his dreadful exemption becomes to him. The dreadful exemption from doing the ethical, the individual's heterogeneity with the ethical, this suspension from the ethical, is *sin* as a state in a human being.

[398]Sin is a crucial expression for the religious existence. As long as sin is not posited, the suspension becomes a transient factor that in turn vanishes or remains outside life as the totally

irregular. Sin, however, is the crucial point of departure for the religious existence, is not a factor within something else, within another order of things, but is itself the beginning of the religious order of things. Sin was not brought up in any of the pseudonymous books. The ethicist in *Either/Or* did indeed give a religious touch to the ethical category of choosing oneself by accompanying the act of despair with repenting oneself out of continuity with the race,[399] but this was a vitiation that no doubt had its basis in the aim of keeping the work ethical—quite as if in accordance with my wishes—namely, in order that every factor could become clear separately. The upbuilding observation at the end of *Either/Or*, "that in relation to God we are always in the wrong,"[400] is no qualification of sin as fundamental but is a misrelation between the finite and the infinite set at rest in the reconciliation of the infinite in enthusiasm. It is the last ardent cry of the finite spirit (in the sphere of freedom) to God: "I cannot understand you, but I will love you; you are always in the right. Yes, even if it seemed to me as if you did not want to love me, I will still love you." This is why the theme is worded: the upbuilding that lies in the thought etc. The upbuilding is sought not in annulling the misunderstanding but in enthusiastically willing to endure it, and in this final courage canceling it, as it were. In *Fear and Trembling*, sin was used occasionally in order to throw light on Abraham's ethical suspension,[401] but no more than that.

This is how matters stood when a book titled *The Concept of Anxiety* was published[402]—a simple, psychologically orienting deliberation on the dogmatic issue of hereditary sin. Just as *Either/Or* had ensured that the teleological suspension would not be confused with esthetic hiddenness, so now the three pseudonymous books ensured that sin, when it is
VII brought up, would not be confused with this and that, with
228 weakness and imperfection, that sorrow over it would not be confused with all sorts of things, sighing and crying as well as sniveling over ourselves and this vale of tears, that the suffering in it would not be confused with a *quodlibet* [whatever you like]. Sin is crucial for a whole existence-sphere, the religious

sphere in the strictest sense. Just because in our day people perhaps know far too much, it is very easy to confuse everything in a confusion of language, where estheticians use the most decisive Christian-religious categories in brilliant remarks, and pastors use them thoughtlessly as officialese that is indifferent to content.

But if it is the misfortune of our age that it has come to know too much, has forgotten what it means to exist and what inwardness is, then it was important that sin not be conceived in abstract categories, in which it cannot be conceived at all, that is, decisively, because it stands in an essential relation to existing. Therefore it was good that the work was a psychological inquiry, which in itself makes clear that sin cannot find a place in the system, presumably just like immortality, faith, the paradox, and other such concepts that are essentially related to existing, just what systematic thinking ignores. The expression "anxiety" does not lead one to think of paragraph-pomposity but rather of existence-inwardness. Just as "fear and trembling" is the state of the teleologically suspended person when God tempts him,[403] so also is anxiety the teleologically suspended person's state of mind in that desperate exemption from fulfilling the ethical. [404]When truth is subjectivity, the inwardness of sin as anxiety in the existing individuality is the greatest possible distance and the most painful distance from the truth.

The contents of the book I shall not treat further; I mention these books only insofar as they constitute elements in the realization of the idea I had but which in an ironical way I was exempted from realizing. When I look at them in this way, a new oddity appears, like the prophecy about the relation between Esau and Jacob, that the larger shall serve the smaller[405]—in the same way the large pseudonymous books serve my *Fragments*. But I do not want to be so presumptuous as to say this, since I prefer to say that while the books have their own significance they also have significance for my little fragment of production.

[406]*The Concept of Anxiety* differs essentially from the other VII
pseudonymous works in that its form is direct and even some- 229

what didactic [*docerende*]. Perhaps the author thought that at this point a communication of knowledge might be necessary before a transition could be made to inward deepening. The latter task pertains to someone who is presumed essentially to possess knowledge and who does not merely need to know something but rather needs to be influenced. The somewhat didactic form of the book was undoubtedly the reason it found a little favor in the eyes of the assistant professors as compared with the other pseudonymous works. I cannot deny that I regard this favor as a misunderstanding, wherefore it pleased me that a merry little book was published simultaneously by Nicolaus Notabene.[407] The pseudonymous books are generally ascribed to one writer, and now everyone who had hoped for a didactic author suddenly gave up hope upon seeing light literature from the same hand.

Finally, then, came my *Fragments*.[408] By now, existence-inwardness was defined to the extent that the Christian-religious could be brought up without being immediately confused with all sorts of things. Yet one thing more. [409]Magister Kierkegaard's upbuilding discourses had steadily kept pace with [the pseudonymous books], which to my mind was a hint that he had kept himself posted, and to me it was striking that the four most recent discourses[410] have a carefully shaded touch of the humorous. What is arrived at in immanence presumably ends in this way. Although the requirement of the ethical is affirmed, although life and existence are accentuated as a difficult course, the decision is nevertheless not placed in a paradox, and the metaphysical withdrawal [*Tilbagetagen*] through recollection into the eternal is continually possible and gives immanence a touch of humor as the infinite's revocation [*Tilbagekaldelse*] of the whole in the decisiveness of the eternity behind.* The paradoxical expression of existence (that is, ex-

* The humorous appears when one answers the question of *Fragments* (Can a historical point of departure be given for an eternal happiness?[411]) not with a yes or no of decision but with a sad smile (this is the lyrical in humor), which signifies that both the old man's seventy years and the almost stillborn infant's half hour of life are too little to become a decision for an eternity. Just as one can voluptuously pull the eiderdown quilt over one's head and let the whole

isting) as sin, the eternal truth as the paradox by having come VII
into existence in time, in short, what is decisive for the Chris- 230
tian-religious, is not found in the upbuilding discourses, which some people, according to the Magister, thought could *very well* be called sermons, whereas others raised the objection that they were not proper sermons. Humor, when it uses Christian categories, is a false rendition of the Christian truth, since humor is not essentially different from irony, but is essentially different from Christianity, and essentially is not different from Christianity otherwise than irony is. It is only

---

world go hang, so the humorist with the aid of immanence hides himself away in recollection's eternity behind and smiles sadly at temporal existence with its brief busyness and illusory decision. The humorist does not teach immorality—far from it. He honors the moral and for his part does everything
as best he can and again smiles at himself, but he is femininely infatuated with VII
immanence, and recollection is his happy marriage and recollection his happy 230
longing. It could admittedly occur to a humorist to work more zealously than anyone else and to deal with time more tight-fistedly than a dutiful laborer and actually do it. But if this work is supposed to have the slightest importance with regard to the decision of an eternal happiness, he would smile. To him, temporality is a fleeting episode and of very doubtful significance, and within time it is for him a foretaste of his happiness that through recollection out of temporality he has his eternity assured behind. From the point of view of the eternal, only an eternal happiness is thinkable. The paradox, therefore, consists in this (just as much as it consists in thinking an eternal unhappiness), that life in time is to be the point of departure, as if the existing individual had lost recollection's eternity behind, as if he would receive an eternal happiness at a definite moment in time, whereas an eternal happiness indeed eternally presupposes itself. Whether humor and speculative thought are in the right is something else, but they are never in the right in declaring themselves to be Christianity. —When eternity's essential decisiveness is to be reached backward in recollection, then quite consistently the highest spiritual relationship with God is that the god [*Guden*] dissuades, restrains, because existence in time can never become commensurate with an eternal decision. Thus Socrates' genius,[412] as is well known, was only dissuasive, and this is how the humorist, too, must understand his relationship with God. The metaphysical authority of eternal recollection to loosen and untie surpasses the disjunction, which the humorist does not reject but acknowledges, and yet, and yet despite all acknowledgment dissolves in the decisiveness of eternity behind. In the paradox, it is the reverse; there the spirit is inciting, but this in turn is the paradoxical expression for how paradoxically time and existence in time have been accentuated.

apparently different from irony by apparently having appropriated all the essentially Christian, yet without having appro-
VII priated it in a *decisive* way (but the essentially Christian con-
231 sists precisely in decision and decisiveness), whereas what is essential for irony, recollection's withdrawal from temporality into the eternal, is in turn the essential for humor. To all appearances humor gives greater significance to what it means to exist than irony does, but nevertheless immanence is *übergreifend* [encroaching], and the more or less is a vanishing quantifying compared with the qualitative decisiveness of the essentially Christian. Therefore, humor becomes the last *terminus a quo* [point from which] in defining Christianity. Humor, when it uses Christian categories (sin, forgiveness of sin, atonement, God in time, etc.), is not Christianity but a pagan speculative thought that has come *to know* all the essentially Christian. It can come deceptively close to the essentially Christian, but at the point where the decision captures [*fange*], at the point where existence captures the existing person, just as when the table captures [*Bordet fanger*][413] when a card is played, so that he must remain in existence, while the bridge of recollection and immanence behind is demolished; at the point where the decision comes in the moment and the movement is forward toward the relation to the eternal truth that came into existence in time—at that point humor is not present. Modern speculative thought deceives in the same way. Well, one cannot even say that it deceives, for soon there will be no one to deceive, and speculation will do it *bona fide* [in good faith]. Speculation performs the feat of understanding all Christianity, but, please note, it does not understand it Christianly but speculatively, which is precisely the misunderstanding, since Christianity is the very opposite of speculation.

Magister Kierkegaard most likely knew what he was doing when he called the upbuilding discourses *Upbuilding Discourses* and also knew why he refrained from using Christian-dogmatic categories, from mentioning Christ's name etc., which otherwise in our day is done freely, although the categories, thoughts, the dialectic in the presentation, etc. are only those of immanence. Just as the pseudonymous books, in addition

to what they are directly, are indirectly a polemic against speculative thought, so also are these discourses, not by not being speculative, for they are indeed speculative,* but by not being
sermons. If the author had called them sermons, he would VII
have been a rattlebrain. They are upbuilding discourses; in the 232
prefaces the author repeats word for word "that he is not a teacher" and the discourses are not "*for* upbuilding,"[417] a stipulation that already in the preface humorously revokes their teleological significance. They are "not sermons"; that is, the sermon corresponds to the essentially Christian, and a pastor corresponds to the sermon, and a pastor is essentially what he is by ordination, and ordination is a teacher's paradoxical transformation in time, by which he in time becomes something other than what would be the immanent development of genius, talent, gifts, etc. Certainly no one is ordained from eternity, nor is anyone, as soon as he is born, able to recollect himself as ordained. On the other hand, ordination is a *character indelebilis* [indelible mark]. What does this mean except that here again time becomes decisive for the eternal, whereby recollection's immanental withdrawal into the eternal is prevented. The Christian *nota bene* is in turn written alongside ordination. Whether this is right, whether speculative thought and humor are not in the right, is a totally different question; but even if speculation were ever so much in the right, it never is in the right in passing itself off as Christianity.

* So the firm Kts (in Professor Heiberg's *Intelligensblad*) was entirely right in making an exception of the one discourse, "The Lord Gave, and the Lord
Took Away; Blessed Be the Name of the Lord,"[414] and saying of the others VII
that they were too philosophical to be sermons;[415] but he was not right in 232
disregarding the author's having said the same thing himself by calling them upbuilding discourses and by specifically pointing out in the preface that they were not sermons. That speculative thought in our day is in the process of confusing the sermon presentation—of that there is no doubt. One can call attention to this directly by, for example, writing a little article in a journal, but it can also be done indirectly and then it takes much more work, as in the writing of upbuilding discourses that are philosophical and are not sermons. When people then say of them that they can very well be called sermons, this will show that the confusion is present, but it also shows that the author who does it and specifically points out the misunderstanding does not exactly need to be informed that it exists.[416]

[418]Then I came along with my *Fragments*. Whether I was successful with this little pamphlet in placing Christianity indirectly into relation to what it means to exist, in bringing it through an indirect form into relation to a knowing reader,
VII whose trouble perhaps is precisely that he is one who knows—
233 this I shall not decide. It could not be done by direct communication, since this always pertains to a recipient only in terms of knowledge, not essentially to an existing person. Perhaps a little sensation could have been made with a direct communication, but a sensation does not pertain to existing but rather to chattering. Existing in what one understands cannot be directly communicated to an existing spirit, not even by God, still less by a human being. As stated, whether the little pamphlet was successful in this, I shall not decide; neither do I want to go to the bother of reviewing it myself, which, to be consistent, would again have to be done in the indirect form of double reflection. What so rarely happens to me is here the case with me—I agree with everybody. If no one cared to review it, neither do I.* If it was successful, so much the better.

* However, come to think of it, I have just learned that it has been reviewed, and, strange to say, in a German journal, *Allgemeines Repertorium für Theologie und kirchliche Statistik*.[419] The reviewer has an excellent quality: he is brief and refrains almost entirely from what is usually found in reviews, the introductory and concluding examination-ceremony of lauding the author, of citing him for special distinction or perhaps even for special distinction and congratulation. This I appreciate all the more, since I was struck with terror by the words "*Besprechung* [review]" and "*nicht unwerth* [not unworthy]" in the reviewer's first sentence ("*Diese Schrift eines der produktivsten Schriftsteller Dänemarks ist wegen der Eigenthümlichkeit ihres Verfahrens einer kurzen Besprechung nicht unwerth* [Because of its distinctive mode of procedure this publication by one of Denmark's most productive writers is not unworthy of a review]"). The reviewer states that the substance of the book is a development of the positive-Christian presuppositions and notes that this is done in such a manner "*dasz unsere Zeit, die Alles nivellirt, neutralisirt und vermittelt, sie kaum wiedererkennen wird* [that our age, which levels, neutralizes, and mediates everything, will hardly recognize them]," and then goes on to give an account (that is, without having utilized the touch of irony contained in what he himself says about presenting the Christian presuppositions to our age in such a way that it, even though it is finished with them and goes beyond, cannot even recognize them again). His report is accurate and on the whole dialectically reliable, but now comes the hitch: although the report is accurate, anyone

If it did not succeed, well, the mishap is not too serious. I can VII 234
write such a pamphlet quickly, and if it were to become clear
to me that I cannot benefit some of my contemporaries in VII 235
some way even by making something difficult, this depressing consciousness also exempts me from the trouble of writing.

---

who reads only that will receive an utterly wrong impression of the book. This mishap, of course, is not too serious, but on the other hand this is always less desirable if a book is to be discussed expressly for its distinctive character.
The report is didactic, purely and simply didactic; consequently the reader VII 234
will receive the impression that the pamphlet is also didactic. As I see it, this is the most mistaken impression one can have of it. The contrast of form, the teasing resistance of the imaginary construction to the content, the inventive audacity (which even invents Christianity), the only attempt made to go further (that is, further than the so-called speculative constructing), the indefatigable activity of irony, the parody of speculative thought in the entire plan, the satire in making efforts as if something *ganz Auszerordentliches und zwar Neues* [altogether extraordinary, that is, new] were to come of them, whereas what always emerges is old-fashioned orthodoxy in its rightful severity—of all this the reader finds no hint in the report. And yet the book is so far from being written for nonknowers, to give them something to know, that the person I engage in conversation in this book is always knowledgeable, which seems to indicate that the book is written for people in the know, whose trouble is that they know too much. Because everyone knows the Christian truth, it has gradually become such a triviality that a primitive impression of it is acquired only with difficulty. [420]When this is the case, the art of being able to *communicate* eventually becomes the art of being able to *take away* or to trick something away from someone. This seems strange and very ironic, and yet I believe I have succeeded in expressing exactly what I mean. When a man has filled his mouth so full of food that for this reason he cannot eat and it must end with his dying of hunger, does giving food to him consist in stuffing his mouth even more or, instead, in taking a little away so that he can eat? Similarly, when a man is very knowledgeable but his knowledge is meaningless or virtually meaningless to him, does sensible communication consist in giving him more to know, even if he loudly proclaims that this is what he needs, or does it consist, instead, in taking something away from him? When a communicator takes a portion of the copious knowledge that the very knowledgeable man knows and communicates it to him in a form that makes it strange to him, the communicator is, as it were, taking away his knowledge, at least until the knower manages to assimilate the knowledge by overcoming the resistance of the form. Suppose, now, that the trouble with the very knowledgeable person is that he is accustomed to one particular form, "that he can demonstrate the mathematical theorem if the letters read ABC but not if they read ACB";[421] then the changed form would indeed take his knowl-

VII 236 I have really wondered, however, whether I am not mistaken, whether I am presupposing something in readers and am wrong in presupposing it. I want to be altogether forthright: my idea of communication through books is very different from what I generally see presented on the topic and

---

edge away from him, and yet this taking away is precisely communication. When an age in systematic, rote fashion has finished with the understanding of Christianity and all the attendant difficulties and jubilantly proclaims how easy it is to understand the difficulty, then, of course, one must harbor a sus-
VII 235 picion. In other words, it is better to understand that something is so difficult that it simply cannot be understood than to understand that a difficulty is so very easy to understand; for if it is so very easy, then perhaps there is no difficulty, since a difficulty is indeed recognizable by its being difficult to understand. When in such an order of things the communication does not aim at making the difficulty even easier, the communication becomes a taking away. The difficulty is invested with a new form and thus actually made difficult. This is communication to the person who already has found the difficulty so very easy to explain. If it so happens, as the reviewer suggests, that a reader can scarcely recognize in the presented material that with which he was finished long ago, the communication will bring him to a halt—yet not in order to communicate something new to him, which would be adding to all that knowledge, but in order to take something away from him.

[422]In other regards, there is nothing to say about the review, except that the four last lines are again a demonstration of how in our didactic age everything is conceived didactically: "*Wir enthalten uns jeder Gegenbemerkung, denn es lag uns, wie gesagt, blosz daran, das eigenthümliche Verfahren des Verfassers zur Anschauung zu bringen. Im Uebrigen stellen wir es dem Ermessen eines Jeden anheim, ob er in dieser apologetischen Dialektik Ernst oder etwa Ironie suchen will* [We refrain from offering any rejoinders, since we were concerned, as we said before, only with demonstrating the author's distinctive procedure. In other regards, we leave it to each person to consider whether he wants to look for earnestness or possibly for irony in this apologetical dialectic]." But my distinctive procedure, if there is to be any mention of it and especially of "demonstrating," consists in the contrastive form of the communication and not at all in the perhaps new dialectical combinations by which the issues become more clear. It consists primarily and decisively in the contrastive form, and if and when this is pointed out there can be, if necessary, brief mention of a fragment of didactic distinctiveness. When the reporter leaves it up to each one whether he will look for earnestness or irony in the pamphlet, this is misleading. Ordinarily one says something of the kind when one does not know anything else to say, and if the presentation in a book is unmixed, pure didactic ultra-earnestness, there can be some point in saying it, provided one says something about the book that is not in the book: the book is sheer ear-

from what is silently taken for granted. Indirect communication makes communicating an art in a sense different from what one ordinarily assumes it to be in supposing that the communicator has to present the communication to a knower, so that he can judge it, or to a nonknower, so that he can acquire something to know. But no one cares about the next thing, the very thing that makes communication so difficult dialectically: that the receiver is an existing person, and that this is the essential. To stop a man on the street and to stand still in order to speak with him is not as difficult as having to say something to a passerby in passing, without standing still oneself or delaying the other, without wanting to induce him to go the same way, but just urging him to go his own way—and such is the relation between an existing person and an existing person when the communication pertains to the truth as existence-inwardness.

With regard to my dissenting conception of what it is to communicate, I sometimes wonder whether this matter of indirect communication could not be directly communicated. For example, I see that Socrates, who ordinarily held so strictly to asking and answering (which is an indirect method), because the long speech, the didactic discourse, and reciting by rote lead only to confusion, at times himself speaks at length and then states as the reason that the person with

---

nestness. Then the reviewer says: God knows whether it is irony or earnestness, and thereby says something, says something by leaving it up to the reader *to look* or whether he *wants to look*—for something that is not directly in the book. Not so, however, when it is only a matter of *finding* what is there. But the pamphlet was far from being pure and simple earnestness—it was only the report that became sheer earnestness. In a way, the concluding comment in the report may very well have some meaning with regard to the report (for example, as a satire of it), but with regard to the book, it is foolish. Suppose that someone had been present at one of Socrates' ironic conversations; suppose that he later gives a report of it to someone but leaves out the irony and says: God knows whether talk like that is irony or earnestness—then he is satirizing himself. But the presence of irony does not necessarily mean that the earnestness is excluded. Only assistant professors assume that. That is, while they otherwise do away with the disjunctive *aut* [or] and fear neither God nor the devil, since they mediate everything—they make an exception of irony; they are unable to mediate that.

VII 236

whom he is speaking needs an elucidation before the conversation can begin. This he does in the *Gorgias*,[423] for example. But this seems to me an inconsistency, an impatience that fears it will take too long before they come to a mutual understand-
VII ing, because through the indirect method it must still be pos-
237 sible to achieve the same thing, only more slowly. But haste is utterly worthless in understanding when the inwardness is the understanding. To me it seems better truly to come to a mutual understanding separately in inwardness, even though this occurs slowly. Yes, even if it never did happen because time went by and the communicator was forgotten without ever being understood by anyone, it seems to me to be more consistent on the part of the communicator not to have made the slightest adaptation in order to have someone understand him, and first and last to watch himself lest he become important in relation to others, which, far from being inwardness, is external, noisy conduct. If he does that, he will have consolation in the judgment when the god [*Guden*] judges that he has made no concessions to himself in order to win anyone but to the utmost of his capability has worked in vain, leaving it to the god whether it should have any significance or not. And this will no doubt please the god more than if the go-getter were to say to him, "I have gained ten thousand adherents for you. Some I won by weeping over the miserableness of the world and warning of its impending destruction, others by opening bright, smiling prospects if they accepted my teaching, others in other ways, by knocking off a little, adding a little. They all became adherents, fair to middling adherents. Indeed, if while I was alive you had descended to earth to inspect, I would have enchanted your eyes with the sight of the many adherents, just as Potemkin enchanted Catherine's eyes" . . . . . yes, just as Potemkin enchanted Catherine's eyes, precisely in the same way—namely, with the help of theater sets,[424] and in the same way the ten thousand adherents of the truth would also be a theatrical entertainment.

[425]That subjectivity, inwardness, is truth was my thesis. I have tried to show how in my view the pseudonymous authors tend toward this thesis, which at its maximum is Chris-

tianity. That it is possible to exist with inwardness also outside Christianity, the Greeks among others have adequately shown, but in our day things seem actually to have gone so far that although we are all Christians and knowledgeable about Christianity, it is already a rarity to encounter a person who VII 238
has even as much existing inwardness as a pagan philosopher. No wonder that people are so quickly finished with Christianity when they begin by putting themselves in a state in which receiving an ever-so-little impression of Christianity is entirely out of the question. One becomes objective, one wants to consider objectively—that the god [*Guden*] was crucified—an event that, when it occurred, did not permit even the temple to be objective, for its curtain tore, did not even permit the dead to remain objective, for they rose up from their graves.[426] Thus what is able to make even the inanimate and the dead subjective is now considered objectively by Messrs. Objective.

One becomes objective, wants in an objective way to consider Christianity, which as a preliminary takes the liberty of making the considerer a sinner, if there is to be any question at all of getting to see something. And to be a sinner, which must be subjectivity's most dreadful suffering, one wants to be that—objectively. But then assistance is given in long, systematic introductions and world-historical surveys—in this connection, utter tomfoolery, in relation to the decision for Christianity, utter procrastination. One becomes objective and more objective, the sooner the better. One scorns being subjective, despises the category of individuality, wants to console oneself with the category of the race, but does not comprehend what cowardice and despair there are in the subject's grabbing for a glittering something and becoming nothing at all. One is a Christian as a matter of course. On solemn occasions one still considers the question that certainly was proper for the stern church fathers—whether pagans could be saved—and does not detect the satire that paganism is much closer to Christianity than an objective Christianity of the sort in which Christ has become "Yes and No," whereas in Corinth, as proclaimed by Paul, he was not "Yes and No" (II Corinthians 1:19)! To exist subjectively with passion (and it is possible to exist objectively only in absentmindedness) is on the whole an absolute condition for being able to have any opinion about Christianity. Anyone who is unwilling to do that and yet wants to have anything to do with Christianity, whoever he may be and however great he may be, is in this matter essentially a fool.

Whether my interpretation of the pseudonymous authors coincides with what they themselves intended, I am unable to decide, since I am only a reader, but that they do have a relation to my thesis is sufficiently clear. If it is not seen in any-
VII 239 thing else, it is seen in their refraining from being didactic. In my view, the true interpretation of the confusion of our age is that there must not be didactic instruction, since the confusion arises simply because of the excess of the didactic. Prominent assistant professors have made light of the pseudonymous books, also of my little pamphlet because it was not didactic. Many have straightway concluded that it was because the authors and I, too, were incapable of rising to the heights required for instructing didactically, to the objectivity that is the position of assistant professors. Perhaps so, but suppose that subjectivity is truth; then the lofty heights of the assistant professors would certainly become precarious. It has also amazed me that, although any theological graduate is assumed to be more or less able to instruct didactically, people cannot be persuaded to think that the pseudonymous authors, including myself, Johannes Climacus, could instruct didactically just about as well as many others who are didactic, but on the contrary readily assume that we all should be singled out as such complete incompetents that we were incapable of doing what nowadays, when a whole German literature has developed solely in this area, is just about as easy for a college student who wants to excerpt German books as it is nowadays to write verse, a skill that may soon be required of domestic servants. Be that as it may, it is always good to be known for something, and I ask for nothing more than to be singled out as the only person who is *unable* to instruct didactically, and thereby

also as the only person who does not understand the demands of the times.

That subjectivity, inwardness, is truth, is my thesis; that the pseudonymous authors relate themselves to it is easy enough to see, if in no other way, then in their eye for the comic. The comic is always a sign of maturity, and then the essential thing is only that a new shoot emerges in this maturity, that the *vis comica* [comic force] does not suffocate pathos but merely indicates that a new pathos is beginning. I consider the power in the comic a vitally necessary legitimation for anyone who is to be regarded as authorized in the world of spirit in our day. When an age is as thoroughly reflective as ours and as ours is said to be, then if this is true the comic must have been discovered by everyone and been discovered primitively by everyone who wants to speak. But assistant professors are so devoid of comic power that it is shocking; even Hegel, according to the assurance of a zealous Hegelian,[427] is utterly devoid of a sense for the comic. A ludicrous sullenness and paragraph-pomposity that give an assistant professor a remarkable likeness to a VII
Holberg bookkeeper[428] are called earnestness by assistant professors. 240
Anyone who does not have this appalling ceremoniousness is light-minded. Perhaps.

But what does it mean to have *actually* reflected oneself out of the immediate without having become a master in the comic—what does it mean? Well, it means that one is lying. What does it mean to give assurances that one has reflected oneself out and to communicate this in direct form as information—what does it mean? Well, it means that one is lying. In the world of spirit, the different stages are not like cities on a journey, about which it is quite all right for the traveler to say directly, for example: We left Peking and came to Canton and were in Canton on the fourteenth. A traveler like that changes place, not himself; and thus it is all right for him to mention and to *recount* the change in a direct, unchanged form. But in the world of spirit to change place is to be changed oneself, and therefore all direct assurance of having arrived here and there is an attempt à la Münchhausen. The presentation itself demonstrates that one has reached that far place in the world of spirit. If it testifies to the contrary, all the giving of assurances is just a contribution to the comic. The power in the comic is the policeman's badge, the emblem of jurisdiction that every agent who in our day actually is an agent must carry. But this comic power is not impetuous or reckless, its laughter not shrill; on the contrary, it is careful with the immediacy that it lays aside. Similarly, the reaper's scythe is equipped with wooden slats that run parallel to the sharp blade, and while the scythe cuts the grain, the grain sinks down almost voluptuously upon the supporting cradle, thereupon to be laid neatly and beautifully in a swath. So it is with the legitimized comic power in relation to matured immediacy. The task of cutting down is a solemn act; the one who cuts down is not a dreary reaper, but nevertheless it is the sharpness and the biting blade of the comic before which the immediacy sinks, not unbeautifully, supported by the cutting down even in the falling. This comic power is essentially humor. If the comic power is cold and bleak, it is a sign that there is no new immediacy sprouting; then there is no harvest, only the empty passion of a sterile wind storming over bare fields.

To be known for something can always be good; I ask for nothing better than to be known for being the only one who
VII in our *earnest* times was not earnest. Far from coveting any
241 change in this judgment, I desire only that the honored assistant professors, not just those gesticulating at the lectern but also those vociferous in tea circles, will abide by their judgment and will not suddenly have forgotten the earnest words frequently enough spouted privately against the pseudonymous authors in order, on the other hand, to be able to recollect clearly that they were the ones who wanted to make the comic into a qualification of earnestness and jest [429]into a savior from the most lamentable of all tyrannies: the tyranny of sullenness and obtuseness and rigidity. The pseudonymous authors and I along with them were all subjective. I ask for nothing better than to be known in our *objective* times as the only person who was not capable of being objective.

That subjectivity, inwardness, is truth, that existing is the decisive factor, that this was the way to take to Christianity, which is precisely inwardness, but, please note, not every inwardness, which was why the preliminary stages definitely had to be insisted upon—that was my idea. I thought that I had found a similar endeavor in the pseudonymous writings, and I have tried to make clear my interpretation of them and their relation to my *Fragments*. [430]Whether I have hit upon the authors' purpose, I cannot know for sure, but in any case I shall apologize to them here for having reviewed them after a fashion, although my discussion, simply by not becoming involved in the contents, is actually no review. It has never been puzzling to me why the pseudonyms have again and again requested that there be no reviews.[431] Since the contrastive form of presentation makes it impossible to give a report, because a report takes away precisely what is most important and falsely changes the work into a didactic discourse, the authors have a perfect right to prefer to be satisfied with a few actual readers rather than to be misunderstood by the many who pick up in a report something to talk about. This is also my opinion *qua* author, and I am reminded here of a remark by Zeno, who with reference to Theophrastus's having so many pupils,[432] said: "His is the larger chorus, mine is the more harmonious." I recently read these words again in Plutarch in a little treatise on "how one may praise oneself in a permissible way."[433]

My *Fragments* approached Christianity in a decisive way, VII
without, however, mentioning its name or Christ's name. In 242
an age of knowledge, in which all are Christians and know what Christianity is, it is only all too easy to use the holy names without meaning anything thereby, to rattle off the Christian truth without having the least impression of it. If anyone wishes to suppose that the reason the names were not mentioned was my ignorance, that I did not know that the founder of Christianity was named Christ and his teaching Christianity, he may very well suppose that. It is always good to be known for something; I on my part can ask for nothing better than to be the only one in the midst of Christianity who does not know that the founder of Christianity was Christ—to be ignorant is still always better than to be as knowledgeable about it as about a hundred other trivialities.

When my *Philosophical Fragments* had come out and I was considering a postscript to "clothe the issue in its historical costume,"[434] yet another pseudonymous book appeared: *Stages on Life's Way*, a book that has attracted the attention of only a few (as it itself predicts on pp. 309, 376[435]) perhaps also because it did not, like *Either/Or*, have "The Seducer's Diary," for quite certainly that was read most and of course contributed especially to the sensation. [436]That *Stages* has a relation to *Either/Or* is clear enough and is definitely indicated by the use in the first two sections of familiar names from that work. If the author of *Stages* had approached me, I would have advised him on esthetic grounds against calling attention to an earlier work by using familiar names.* With regard to everything that must be considered risky and that is risky because it re-
VII quires good luck, it is always precarious to prompt a recollec-
243 tion. To avoid this is easy; to do it is to risk oneself and one's luck in a daring venture, the danger of which is expressed in many places in the book.**[438]

There is a story about a sailor who fell from the top of the mast without injuring himself, got up on his feet, and said: Now copy me—but most likely he himself also refrained from doing it again. Likewise, repetition that involves good luck

* Also for another reason (assuming, as is commonly done, that the pseudonymous books are by one author[437]) I would have advised him against the strenuous work. In other words, sagacity dictates not working too zealously and too perseveringly—then obtuse people think it is slovenly work. No, great commotion and then a little piece of work—then the plebeians think it is something. Perhaps I still would not have accomplished anything, for it is not inconceivable that the author himself has perceived this, but disdained acting sagaciously, and regarded it as precarious to gain the admiration of various people.

** See p. 16:[**439] "How easy to give a banquet, and yet Constantin has maintained that he would never again risk it! How easy it is to admire, and yet Victor Eremita has maintained that he will never give expression to his admiration (namely, for Mozart), because a defeat is more terrible than becoming an invalid in war!" Judge William as an ethicist expresses the opposite with ethical passion, p. 86: "This will have to be enough on the subject of marriage. At this moment I have no more that I want to say; another time, perhaps tomorrow, I shall say more, but 'always the same and about the same thing,' for it is only gypsies and robbers and swindlers who have the motto: Never go back where you have once been."

and inspiration is always a daring venture. In other words, because of the ensuing comparison, an absolute requirement of richness of expression is made, since it is not difficult to repeat one's own words or to repeat a felicitously chosen phrase word for word. Consequently, to repeat the same also means to change under conditions made difficult by the precedent. Whereas the inquisitive reader is put off by its being the same, since the inquisitive reader demands external change in names, scenery, clothes, hair styles, etc., the attentive reader is made more rigorous in his demands because there is nothing enticing at all, nothing diverting, no embellishments, no particulars pertaining to the externalities of the unknown characters and the climatic conditions of far-off territories etc.

But the risk was taken, and the unknown author has not been ignorant of the danger, just as he was hardly ignorant of why Socrates staked his honor and pride on one thing: continually to say the same thing and about the same thing.*[440]

By taking the risk, the pseudonymous author has won an VII
indirect victory over an inquisitive public. That is, when this 244
reading public peers** into the book and sees the familiar

* An opportunity to gain a deep insight into a person—as to whether he is spiritually or merely sensately qualified—can generally be had by finding out
what he understands by an author's wealth and what by his poverty. If a pastor VII
could keep on preaching all year on the same text, continually rejuvenating 244
himself in new fertility of expression, he would in my opinion be matchless, but a sensate listener would find him boring. If Oehlenschläger, at the moment he had written his *Valborg*,[441] could have written it again, in my eyes he would have been even greater than he is. To write *Signe*[442] is already easier, because the conditions, the country where the action takes place, the surroundings, etc. are different. But to write *Valborg*, have the reader read it, and then write the same *Valborg* again, the same—that is, all the externals would be the same and familiar; only erotic love's deliciousness in the expression on Valborg's lips would be new, new as a new blossoming of flowers—well, even if ever so many would find it boring, I would presume to find it amazing. Among the things I have admired most in Shakespeare is his Falstaff, partly also because he is repeated.[443] Of course, Falstaff does not have many scenes each time, but if Shakespeare could have kept Falstaff unaltered in all five acts and then again in five acts—well, even if ever so many would find it boring, I would presume to find it divine.

** It is undoubtedly with regard to such an inquisitive reader that the first third of the book has these words by Lichtenberg as its epigraph: *Solche Werke*

names Victor Eremita, Constantin Constantius, etc.,[445] it tosses the book aside and says wearily: It is just the same as *Either/Or*.[446] So the inquisitive reader says: It is the same. And if such a reader says it aloud, the pseudonymous author may think something like this: "Would that it actually were as you say, because this judgment is a compliment, since it cannot be understood to mean that it is literally the same word for word; but I indeed feel that I do not have such a great range of this fertility of inwardness, and therefore I have ventured to repeat only in considerable abridgment and with considerable alteration in points of departure. But as an author I nevertheless have a fortunate advantage over the editor of *Either/Or*, because the interest in novelty and the large book and the seducer's diary created a stir, inasmuch as people believed that something was going on there. So the book was bought and is now even supposed to be sold out[447]—alas, a most questionable argument for the excellence of the book; one is almost
VII tempted to assume it was a New Year's gift.[448] I, however, am
245 free from being sniffed at by curiosity."

In other words, along with Tivoli's[449] attractions and New Year's literary gifts, it holds true for potboiler writers, and then for those who are captivated by them, that change is the supreme law; but with regard to truth as inwardness in existence, with regard to a more incorruptible joy in life, which has nothing in common with ennui's hankering for diversion, the opposite holds true, and the law is: the same, and yet changed, and yet the same.[450] Therefore the fanciers of Tivoli value eternity so little, since it is the nature of eternity to be always the same, and soberness of spirit is recognizable by its knowing that change in the external is diversion, but change in the same is inwardness. But on the whole the reading public is so inquisitive that an author who wishes to be rid of it needs only to drop a little hint in order to be rid of it, just a name, and then it says: It is the same. Otherwise the difference between *Stages* and *Either/Or* is conspicuous enough. In the first

sind Spiegel: wenn ein Affe hinein guckt, kann kein Apostel heraus sehen [Such works are mirrors: when an ape looks in, no apostle can look out].[444]

third (not to mention that two-thirds of *Stages* is almost as different as is categorically possible*), Victor Eremita, who previously was just the editor, is transformed into an existing individuality, Constantin and Johannes the Seducer are more distinctly defined, the Judge is preoccupied with marriage from an entirely different angle than in *Either/Or*, whereas the most attentive reader will find hardly a single phrase, a single turn of thought or language, as it was in *Either/Or*.

I have deliberately dwelt longer on this because, even though it may please an outsider author who loves this very isolation, it signifies something else to me, since it is related to what I have continually emphasized, that the age has forgotten what it means to exist and what inwardness is. It no
longer believes that inwardness enriches the apparently poor VII
contents, whereas change in the external is only the diversion 246
that world-weariness and life-emptiness clutch at. That is why existence-tasks are rejected. In passing one learns to know what faith is; then, of course, one knows it. Then one clutches at a speculative result, and thus one is again no closer. Then astronomy turns up for a day, and in this way one traipses through all the sciences and spheres and yet does not live, while the poets, merely in order to entertain their readers, ramble around in Africa, America, and, devil take them, in Trapezunt and R——,[453] so that soon a new continent must be discovered if poetry will not have to declare "I pass." Why? Because inwardness is being lost more and more.

[454]Let us, then, begin with the last two-thirds of the book, the contents of which are a *story of suffering*.[455] Now, there can be suffering everywhere in the various stages of existence, but when a book is arranged with an esthetic stage, then an ethical stage, and finally a religious stage, and only here the word "suffering" is used, this seems to indicate that the relation of

* Indeed, the book itself also predicts that the reading public will find the two-thirds boring (see pp. 268 top, 367 bottom, and 368 top[451]). A love story is a love story, says a reading public of that kind; if one is to read about it once again, the setting must be in Africa, because it is the setting that provides the change, and such a reading public needs "pageantry, localities, many characters—and then the cows."[452]

suffering to the religious is not the same as to the esthetic and the ethical. The phrase "story of suffering," therefore, seems to be used pregnantly as a category, as if suffering has a crucial meaning in relation to the religious. Thus "A Story of Suffering" as a title seems to intend something different from Goethe's title, *Leiden des jungen Werther* [The Sufferings of Young Werther], or Hoffmann's *Leiden eines armen Theaterdirectors* [The Sufferings of a Poor Theater Director]. In other words, suffering in relation to esthetic and ethical existence is accidental; it can be absent and there can still be an esthetic and ethical existence, or if it finds a deeper meaning here it is as a transient element. It is different here where suffering is posited as crucial for religious existence and specifically as characteristic of inwardness: the more that is suffered, the more religious existence, and the suffering continues. The author, then, was not at a loss for a title for his book when he chose the title "A Story of Suffering" but had something very specific in mind with it and stressed it himself (see all of § 5, pp. 353ff.,[456] especially the middle of p. 357). Whereas esthetic existence is essentially enjoyment and ethical existence is essentially struggle and victory, religious existence is suffering, and not as a transient element but as a continual accompaniment. Suffering is, to recall Frater Taciturnus's words,[457] the 70,000 fathoms of water[458] upon whose depths the religious person is
VII continually. But suffering is precisely inwardness and is sepa-
247 rated from esthetic and ethical existence-inwardness. Even in everyday conversation, when it is said of a person that he probably has suffered much, we are accustomed promptly to associate with it the notion of inwardness.

The story of suffering has the title, " 'Guilty?'/'Not Guilty?' " The question marks are obviously an allusion to legal proceedings. A novelist would very likely have conflated the two parts of the title, and a reading public that desires a conclusion would presumably have been pleased with it. Then the title would have been, for example: "Unfaithful and yet a Man of Honor," "A Broken Pledge and yet Eternal Fidelity," *ad modum* [in the manner of] "An Officer of the Hussars and yet a Good Husband," etc. On the title page, it is immediately decided which is which, and the reader is safe and secure. The reader is not made uneasy either by existence or by the dialectical accuracy of the category; the story is a charming hodgepodge of a little of the esthetic, a little of the ethical, and a little of the religious. But what really occupies a thinking person is not to come to know something afterward, but just to become contemporary with the existing person in his existence. And in the tension between the inquisitorial questions, squeezed into the penetrating examination of the questions exists Quidam of the imaginary construction. If it is the misfortune of the age to have forgotten what inwardness is and what it means to exist, it is indeed especially pertinent to come as close to existence as possible. Therefore, the imaginary construction does not take as its starting point a later moment in time and relate a remarkable conflict as something past, nor does it slacken the tension of the conflict in a reassuring conclusion, but by means of its teasing form makes the reader even more contemporary than he is able to become by way of a contemporary actuality and leaves him stuck in it by not giving a conclusion. A book without an ending has no doubt been written before; the author may have died or chose not to complete it etc. Such is not the case here; that there is no end, no conclusion, is understood, like suffering previously, as a categorical qualification with regard to religious existence. Frater Taciturnus develops this himself (see § 3, pp. 340, 343 top[459]). But the absence of a conclusion is expressly a qualification of inwardness, because a conclusion is something external, and the communication of a conclusion an external relation between a knower and a nonknower.

The "Story of Suffering" was called an imaginary construction, and Frater Taciturnus himself explains the meaning of it (§ 3[460]).

The "Story of Suffering" (see pp. 313, 339 bottom[461]) has a connection with *Repetition*. The difference is very striking,
however, if one considers the categorical qualification, which VII 248
alone can have interest for thought, whereas the difference in costumes occupies the gallery, which therefore very likely also assumes that the greatest actress is the one who can play not

only in various fantastic female costumes but even in trousers and jacket with collar attached, since the range of the artistic performance is determined by the range of costumes, and therefore the actress playing chiefly the parts in which she acts in her own clothes is considered to be the poorest actress. In *Repetition*, common sense and the higher immediacy of youth are kept separate in Constantin as the man of common sense and the Young Man as the one in love, but in *Stages* the two factors are combined in one, in Quidam of the imaginary construction, whereby the double movement becomes necessary and clear, and even *earnestness* is a compound of jest and earnestness (see p. 283[462]). It is the same person who with his understanding sees the comic and who suffers the tragic* and out of the unity of the comic and the tragic chooses the tragic (see pp. 327 and 328 top). In *Repetition*, irony and sentimentality are brought into relation to each other; in the "Story of Suffering," humor is brought forward. Constantin himself must be involved and play *partes* [roles], whereas Frater Taciturnus stands entirely outside as a "street inspector," for Quidam has understanding enough, and humor is achieved because of his being himself the various elements. If the feminine character is left out, who in the "Story of Suffering" as in *Repetition* is present only indirectly, then there are two characters in *Repetition*, in the "Story of Suffering" only one. "It becomes more and more boring; there is not even so much as a suicide or madness or covert childbirth or anything else like that. Moreover, once the author has written a love story, he has exhausted the material; then he must try his hand in a new direction—for example, the robber story."

Frater Taciturnus defines himself as lower in existence than
VII Quidam's existence, inasmuch as the latter has a new imme-
249 diacy. Even Constantin was not disinclined to define himself in relation to the Young Man but had the common sense and irony that the Young Man lacked. Ordinarily one supposes it

* A little motto[463] by Quidam promptly suggests the humorous double mood, whereas the Latin epigraph "*Periissem nisi periissem* [I would have perished had I not perished]"[464] is a suffering, humorous revocation of the whole thing.

to be otherwise, supposes that the imaginative constructor, the observer, is higher or stands higher than what he produces. This accounts for the ease in providing a conclusion. Here it is the reverse; the imaginatively constructed character discovers and makes manifest the higher—higher not in the direction of understanding and thinking but in the direction of inwardness. Quidam's inwardness is distinguishable by his having his inwardness defined by the contrast within himself, by his perceiving as comic that which nevertheless is in him with all the passion of inwardness. A feminine inwardness as devotedness is less inwardness, because the direction is obviously outward, toward, whereas the presence of the contrast specifically signifies the direction inward. Quidam himself is a unity of the comic and the tragic,[465] but he is more than this unity; after it he is in passion (the comic-tragic, see § 2 *passim*[466]). Frater Taciturnus is essentially a humorist and precisely thereby repellingly manifests the new immediacy.

Thus humor is advanced as the final *terminus a quo* in relation to the Christian-religious. In modern scholarship, humor has become the highest *after* faith. That is, faith is the immediate,[467] and through speculative thought, which goes beyond faith, humor is reached. This is a general confusion in all systematic speculative thought insofar as it wants to take Christianity under its wing. No, humor terminates immanence within immanence, still consists essentially in recollection's withdrawal out of existence into the eternal, and only then do faith and the paradoxes begin. Humor is the last stage in existence-inwardness before faith. Therefore, in my judgment, it had to be advanced so that no stage behind it would be left unnoticed, which later could give rise to confusion. This has now been done in the "Story of Suffering." Humor is not faith but is before faith, is not after faith or a development of faith. In other words, Christianly understood there is no going beyond faith, because faith is the highest—for an existing person—which has been adequately developed above. Even when humor wants to try its hand at the paradoxes, it is not faith. Humor does not take in the suffering aspect of the paradox or the ethical aspect of faith but only the amusing aspect. It is,

namely, a suffering, faith's martyrdom even in times of peace: to have the eternal happiness of one's soul related to something over which the understanding despairs. Immature humor, however, which even lags behind what I properly speaking call humor in an equilibrium between the comic and the
VII tragic—this immature humor is a kind of flippancy that has
250 skipped too soon out of reflection. Weary of time and the endless succession of time, the humorist skips away and finds a humorous alleviation in asserting the absurd, just as it can be an alleviation to parody the meaning of life by paradoxically stressing the trivial, by abandoning everything and concentrating on bowling and training horses. But this is immature humor's counterfeiting of the paradox as an incitement for the arbitrariness of a thick-blooded passion. This immature humor is so far from being religiousness that it is an esthetic subtlety that skips past the ethical.

[468]Moreover, that faith and the Christian-religious have humor preceding them also shows what an enormous existence-range is possible outside Christianity, and on the other hand what life-development is the condition for properly embracing Christianity. But in our age one does not exist at all, and thus it is quite in order that everyone is Christian as a matter of course. Even as a child one becomes a Christian, which can be very beautiful and well intentioned on the part of Christian parents but is ludicrous when the person himself thinks it is all decided. Obtuse pastors do indeed appeal very literally to a Bible verse literally understood—that no one enters the kingdom of God if he does not enter it as a little child.[469] Well, what [470]a sweet charming something Christianity can become with the help of the childishness of pastors like that! Indeed, in this way the apostles would be excluded, for I do not know that they entered as small children. To say to the most mature spirit: Well, my friend, if you will just see to it that you become a child again, then you will become a Christian—see, this is a hard saying, appropriate to the teaching that was an offense to the Jews and foolishness to the Greeks.[471] But to understand this dark saying in that way, as if all difficulty were removed by being baptized as a little child and dying the

sooner the better, is an obtusity that is diametrically opposed to the category of Christianity (which paradoxically stresses temporal existence) and has not even grasped the pagan view that has the small children weep in Elysium because they died so soon,[472] which does at least grant some importance to time. Upon its entrance into the world, Christianity was not proclaimed to children but to an outworn Jewish religiosity, a world of effete science and art. First the first, then the next. If
only this age had as much existence-inwardness as a Jew or as VII
a Greek, then there could still be a question of a relation to 251
Christianity. But if at one time it was terribly difficult to become a Christian, it surely will soon be impossible because it has all become a triviality. A Greek philosopher was truly a man who could think, and therefore it means something when Christianity defines itself as the teaching that becomes an offense to the Jews and foolishness to the Greeks, because the Jew also had enough religious inwardness to be capable of being offended. But all this has become obsolete in the sluggish generation living today, which on the average unquestionably has much more culture than was the case earlier but has the passion neither of thought nor of religiousness. It is possible both to enjoy life and to give it meaning and substance outside Christianity, just as the most renowned poets and artists, the most eminent thinkers, even pious men, have lived outside Christianity. Christianity itself has unquestionably been aware of this and yet has not considered itself justified in changing the condition, and the more spiritual maturity, the more terrible a matter the paradox becomes, that unaltered condition of Christianity, the signal for offense and foolishness. But in its old age let us not change Christianity into a seedy saloon-keeper who must think of something to draw customers, or into a carpetbagger who wants to be a big success in the world. Of course, Christianity can hardly be said to have been a big success when it originally entered the world, inasmuch as it began with crucifixion, flogging, and the like. But God knows whether it actually wants to be a big success in the world. I rather think that it is ashamed of itself, like an old man who sees himself rigged out in the latest fash-

ion. Or, more correctly, I think it focuses its wrath[473] against people when it sees this distorted figure that is supposed to be Christianity, a perfume-saturated and systematically accommodated and soirée-participating scholarliness, whose whole secret is half measures and then truth to a certain degree—when it sees a radical cure[474] (and only as such is it what it is) transmogrified nowadays into a vaccination, and a person's relation to it equivalent to having a certificate of vaccination. No, the Christian paradox is not some sort of this and that, something strange and yet not so strange; its truth is not like Salomon Goldkalb's opinion: *vieles* [much] fore *und* [and] aft,
VII 252 yes *und* no also.[475] Nor is faith something that everyone has, and something that every cultured person must go beyond. If it can be grasped and held fast by the simplest of people, it is only the more difficult for the cultured to attain. What a wondrous, inspiring, Christian humanity: the highest is common for all human beings, and the most fortunately gifted are only the ones subjected to the most rigorous discipline.

But back to *Stages*. It is markedly different from *Either/Or* by a tripartition. There are three stages, an esthetic, an ethical, a religious, yet not abstract as the immediate mediate, the unity, but concrete in the qualification of existence categories as pleasure-perdition, action-victory, suffering. But despite this tripartition, the book is nevertheless an either/or. That is, the ethical and the religious stages have an essential relation to each other. The inadequacy of *Either/Or* is simply that the work ended ethically, as has been shown. In *Stages* this has been made clear, and the religious is maintained in its place.

The esthetic and the ethical stages are presented again, in a certain sense as a recapitulation, and yet as something new. Indeed, it would be poor witness to existence-inwardness if every stage of that kind could not be rejuvenated in the presentation, even though in the attempt to reject the apparent support of externals it can be risky to emphasize the difference, such as by choosing new names and the like. The ethicist again focuses on marriage as the dialectically most composite disclosure of actuality. But he does bring out a new aspect and upholds in particular the category of time and its significance as the medium for the beauty that increases with time, whereas viewed esthetically time and existence in time are more or less retrogression.

The existence-positions among the stages are reciprocally changed by the tripartition. In *Either/Or*, the esthetic standpoint is an existence-possibility, and the ethicist is existing. Now the esthetic is existing; the ethicist is struggling, struggling *ancipiti proelio* [in a battle with uncertain outcome] against the esthetic, which in turn he easily conquers, not with seductive gifts of the intellect but with ethical passion and pathos, and against the religious. In drawing to a close, the ethicist does his utmost to guard against the decisive form of a higher standpoint. His defending himself in this way is quite
all right, since he is not, after all, a standpoint but an existing VII 253
individuality. In recent scholarship it is indeed a fundamental confusion summarily to mistake abstract contemplation of standpoints for existing, so that if someone knows about the standpoints he therefore is existing; whereas every existing individuality as existing must be more or less one-sided. Viewed abstractly, there is certainly no decisive contention between standpoints, because abstraction removes the very locus of the decision: the *existing subject*; but the immanent transition is nevertheless a chimera, a fancy, as if the one standpoint on its own necessarily determined its transition over to another, since the category of transition is itself a break in immanence, is a *leap*.

The esthete in *Either/Or* was a possibility of existence. He was a young, richly endowed, somewhat hopeful person who was experimenting with himself and with life, one "with whom one could not ever really become angry because the evil in him, like the Middle Ages' concept of it, had an additive of childishness"[476] and because he really was not an actuality but "a possibility of everything"[477]—this is how the esthete paced about, so to speak, in the Judge's living room.* In

* Even "The Seducer's Diary" was only a possibility of horror, which the esthete in his groping existence had conjured up precisely because he, without actually being anything, had to try his hand at everything as possibility.

his relationship with him, the Judge was genial, ethically assured, and essentially exhortative, just as a somewhat older and more mature person relates himself to a younger one whose talents and intellectual superiority he in a way acknowledges, although he has the upper hand over him unconditionally by virtue of his assurance, experience, and inwardness in living. In *Stages*, the esthetic comes forward in existence more definitely, and thus it is latently apparent in the presentation itself that the esthetic existence, even when a softer light falls upon it (although it is always essentially brilliant), is perdition. But it is not an alien standpoint, like the Judge's, that makes this clear as a warning to a young person whose life is not yet decided in the deepest sense. It is too late to exhort against a decidedly esthetic existence; to want to exhort Victor Eremita, Constantin Constantius, the Fashion Designer, or Jo-
VII 254 hannes the Seducer makes one ludicrous and produces an effect just as comic as a situation I once experienced. In the haste of danger, a man grabbed a toy cane from his child in order to strike a huge ruffian who had forced his way into the room. Although I shared the danger, I could not help laughing, because it looked as if he were beating clothes. The relation between the Judge and the esthete in *Either/Or* made it natural and psychologically proper for the Judge to be exhortative. But even in that work there was no decision in the final sense (the preface[478]) so the reader could say: See—now it is decided. A reader who needs the trustworthiness of a severe lecture or an unfortunate outcome (for example, madness, suicide, poverty, etc.) in order to see that a standpoint is in error still sees nothing and is merely deluding himself, and to behave that way as an author is to write effeminately for childish readers.*

* Here I wish to call to mind again something that Frater Taciturnus, among others, often stresses.[479] Hegelian philosophy culminates in the thesis that the outer is the inner and the inner is the outer.[480] With this, Hegel has finished. But this principle is essentially an esthetic-metaphysical principle, and in this way Hegelian philosophy is happily and safely finished without having anything to do with the ethical and the religious, or it finishes in a fraudulent manner by combining everything (also the ethical and the religious) in the esthetic-metaphysical. The ethical already establishes a kind of

Take a character like Johannes the Seducer. The person who VII 255 needs to have him become insane or shoot himself in order to see that his standpoint is perdition does not actually see it but deludes himself into thinking that he does. In other words, the person who comprehends it comprehends it as soon as the Seducer opens his mouth; in every word he hears the ruination and the judgment upon him. The reader who requires external punishment only makes a fool of himself, because one can take a very worthy person, have him become insane, and a reader of that sort will regard it as an unjustifiable standpoint.

The esthetic stage is represented by "*In Vino Veritas*." Those who appear here certainly are esthetes but are by no means ignorant of the ethical. Therefore they are not only presented but are presented as persons who obviously know how to give an account of their existence. In our day, it is thought that knowledge determines the issue and that if one just comes to know the truth, the more concisely and quickly the better, one is helped. But existing is something quite different from knowing.

The Young Man is closest to being only a possibility, and thus there is still hope for him. He is essentially depression of thought (the ethicist explains him on pages 87, 88 top, 89[481]).

---

contrast-relation between the outer and the inner, inasmuch as it places the outer in the sphere of indifference. The outer as material for action is a matter of indifference, because the purpose is what is ethically accentuated; the outcome as the externality of action is unimportant, because the purpose is what is ethically accentuated, and it is plainly immoral to care about the outcome. Victory in the outer demonstrates nothing at all ethically, because ethically the question is only about the inner. Punishment in the outer is negligible, and far from insisting with esthetic busyness on visible punishment, the ethical proudly says: I shall punish, all right, namely, in the inner, and it is plainly immoral to class punishment in the outer as something comparable to the inner. —The religious definitely establishes the contrast between the outer and the inner, which is defined as contrast. Suffering is therein implicit as an existence-category for the religious, but this also implies the inwardly turned inner infinity of interiority [*Indvorteshed*]. If it were not reserved for our age totally to ignore existing, it would be unthinkable that wisdom such as the VII 255 Hegelian could be considered the highest, which it presumably can be for esthetic contemplators but not for either ethically or religiously existing persons.

Constantin Constantius is callousness of the understanding (see the ethicist, page 90[482]). Constantin's conception of jealousy is found on page 99 bottom and page 100 top.[483] Victor Eremita is sympathetic irony (see the ethicist, pp. 107 and 108[484]). Victor's attack on marriage is found on p. 85.[485] The Fashion Designer is demonic despair in a state of passion. Johannes the Seducer is perdition in a state of frigidity, a "marked" and extinct individuality. They are all consistent to the point of despair.

Just as in the second part of *Either/Or* one finds answers to and a rectification of every deviation in the first part, so also one will here find the explanation in the ethicist, except that the ethicist expresses himself about the essence of the matter and nowhere directly considers what he, according to the design of the work, cannot be assumed to know. Thus it is left to the reader to put it all together by himself, if he so pleases,
VII but nothing is done for a reader's comfort. This, of course, is
256 what readers want; they want to read books in the royal manner, as a king reads a petition with marginal notes that free him from being inconvenienced by the copiousness of the petitioner. With respect to the pseudonymous authors, this is certainly a mistake on the part of the reader. According to my impression of them, I do not know that they are seeking anything whatever from the exalted majority-majesty of the reading public. Indeed, that would seem very strange to me. In other words, I have always supposed that an author is someone who knows more than the reader or knows the same thing in a different way. That is why he is an author, and otherwise he should not take it upon himself to be an author. On the other hand, I have never thought that an author is a supplicant, a beggar at the reader's door, a peddler who, with the aid of a devilishly glib tongue and a little gold decoration on the binding[486] that really catches the daughters' eyes, palms off his books on families.

Johannes the Seducer ends with the thesis that *woman is only the moment.*[487] This in its general sense is the essential esthetic thesis, that the moment is all and to that extent, in turn, essentially nothing, just as the Sophistic thesis that everything is true is that nothing is true.[488] On the whole, the conception of time is the decisive element in every standpoint up to the paradox, which paradoxically accentuates time. To the degree that time is accentuated, to the same degree there is movement from the esthetic, the metaphysical, to the ethical, the religious, and the Christian-religious.

Where Johannes the Seducer ends, the Judge begins: *Woman's beauty increases with the years.*[489] Here time is accentuated ethically, but still not in such a way that precludes the possibility of recollection's withdrawal out of existence into the eternal.

The esthetic stage is very briefly suggested, and, presumably in order to emphasize the religious properly, the author has called the first part "A Recollection" in order to bring the ethical stage and especially the religious more into the foreground by forcing back the esthetic.

I shall not deal any further with a detailed account of the contents of the book. Its significance, if it has any, will consist
in the existence-inwardness of the different stages variously VII 257
elucidated in passion, irony, pathos, humor, dialectic. Such things, of course, do not occupy assistant professors. *Am Ende* [In the end], it may not be inconceivable that an assistant professor would go so far in courtesy that he *en passant* [in passing] in a clause, in a note to a paragraph in the system, would say of the author: He represents inwardness. [490]Then the author and an ignorant reading public would have come to know everything. Passion, pathos, irony, dialectic, humor, enthusiasm, etc. are considered by assistant professors to be something subordinate that everyone possesses. Therefore, when it is said: He represents inwardness—then in these brief words, which everyone can say, everything is said, and much more than the author has said. Everyone knows what he is supposed to think about it, and every assistant professor could easily have achieved everything in this area but has left it to subjective individuals in reduced circumstances. Whether everyone actually does know more concretely what inwardness is, and whether everyone as author can achieve something in this area, I shall leave undecided. I am willing to assume this of

everyone who remains silent, but the assistant professors do not remain silent.[491]

Yet, as said previously, I have nothing to do with the contents of the book. My thesis was that subjectivity, inwardness, is truth. For me this was crucial with regard to the issue of Christianity, and out of the same regard I thought that I ought to pursue a certain endeavor in the pseudonymous writings, which to the very last have honestly refrained from didacticizing, and I thought that I ought to pay special attention to the latest one, because it came out after my *Fragments* and, freely reproducing earlier themes, calls to mind the earlier books and by means of humor as a *confinium* [border territory] defines the religious stage.

Chapter III[492]

Actual Subjectivity, Ethical Subjectivity; the Subjective Thinker

§ 1[493]

[494]*What It Means to Exist; Actuality*

In the language of abstraction, that which is the difficulty of existence and of the existing person never actually appears; even less is the difficulty explained. Precisely because abstract VII 258 thinking is *sub specie aeterni*, it disregards the concrete, the temporal, the becoming of existence, and the difficult situation of the existing person because of his being composed of the eternal and the temporal situated in existence.* If abstract thinking is assumed to be the highest, it follows that scientific scholarship and thinkers proudly abandon existence and leave the rest of us to put up with the worst. Yes, something follows from this also for the abstract thinker himself—namely, that in one way or another he must be absentminded, since he, too, is an existing person.

To ask abstractly about actuality (even though it is proper to ask about it abstractly, since the particular, the accidental, is indeed a constituent of the actual and in direct opposition to

* That Hegel in his *Logic* nevertheless continually allows an idea to come into play that is only all too informed about concretion and about the next thing that the professor, despite the necessary transition, needs every time in order to go further, is of course a mistake, which Trendlenburg has superbly pointed out.[495] To call to mind what is nearest at hand, how is the transition formed by which *die Existenz* is the existences? *Die Existenz ist die unmittelbare Einheit der Reflexion-in-sich und der Reflexion-in-Anderes. Sie ist* ***daher*** *(?) die unbestimmte Menge von Existirenden* [Existence is the immediate unity of reflection-into-self and reflection-into-another. It follows *from this* (?) that existence is the indefinite multitude of existents (*sic*)].[496] How does the purely abstract definition of existence come to split up in this way?

abstraction) and to answer abstractly is not nearly as difficult as to ask and answer what it means that this definite something is an actuality. Abstraction disregards this definite something, but the difficulty lies in joining this definite something and the ideality of thinking by willing to think it. Abstraction simply cannot concern itself with such a contradiction, since abstraction expressly prevents it.

The dubiousness of abstraction manifests itself precisely in connection with all existential questions, from which abstraction removes the difficulty by omitting it and then boasts of having explained everything. It explains immortality in general, and see, it goes splendidly, inasmuch as immortality becomes identical with eternity, with the eternity that is essentially the medium of thought. But abstraction does not care about whether a particular existing human being is immortal,
VII 259 and just that is the difficulty. It is disinterested, but the difficulty of existence is the existing person's interest, and the existing person is infinitely interested in existing. Thus abstract thinking helps me with my immortality by killing me as a particular existing individual and then making me immortal and therefore helps somewhat as in Holberg the doctor took the patient's life with his medicine—but also drove out the fever.[497] Therefore, when one considers an abstract thinker who is unwilling to make clear to himself and to admit the relation his abstract thinking has to his being an existing person, he makes a comic impression, even if he is ever so distinguished, because he is about to cease to be a human being. Whereas an actual human being, composed of the infinite and the finite and infinitely interested in existing, has his actuality precisely in holding these together, such an abstract thinker is a double creature, a fantastic creature who lives in the pure being of abstraction, and an at times pitiful professorial figure which that abstract creature sets down just as one sets down a cane. When reading the biography of such a thinker[498] (for his books may very well be excellent), one sometimes shudders at the thought of what it means to be a human being.* Even if a

* And then when one reads in his writings that thinking and being are

lacemaker made lace ever so lovely, it is still sad to think of this poor stunted creature, and thus it is comic to see a thinker who, despite all his bravura, personally exists as a fussbudget, who personally did marry but was scarcely acquainted with or moved by the power of love, whose marriage therefore was presumably as impersonal as his thinking, whose personal life was without pathos and without passionate struggles and was philistinely concerned only about which university provided the best job. One would suppose that such a misrelation would be an impossibility in thinking; one would suppose that it would belong only to the wretchedness of the external world, where one human being slaves for the other, so that one cannot admire the lace without tears if one thinks of the lacemaker. One would believe that a thinker would lead the richest human life—so it was in Greece.

It is another matter with the abstract thinker inasmuch as, VII
without having understood himself and the relation of ab- 260
stract thinking to existence, he either follows the inclination of a talent or is trained to be something of the sort. I know very well that people usually admire the artist-life of a person who follows his talent without accounting to himself for what it means to be human, so that the admirer forgets him in admiration over his work of art. But I also know that the tragedy of an existing person of that sort is that he is a variant [*Differents*] and the differential is not personally reflected in the ethical. I also know that in Greece a thinker was not a stunted existing person who produced works of art, but he himself was an existing work of art. Surely, to be a thinker should least of all mean to be a variant from being a human being. [500]If it is taken for granted that an abstract thinker lacks a sense of the comic, this is *eo ipso* proof that all his thinking is the feat of a perhaps outstanding talent but not of a human being who in an eminent sense has existed as a human being. Yet it is didactically expounded that thinking is the highest, that thinking subsumes everything under itself, and

---

one,[499] one ponders his life and biography and thinks: The being with which thinking is identical is certainly not what it means to be human.

at the same time no objection is raised that the thinker is existing not essentially *qua* human being but as a variant in talent. That the statement about thinking does not reduplicate itself in the concept of the thinker, that the thinker's own existence contradicts his thinking, shows that one is merely didacticizing. Thinking is superior to feeling and imagination—this is didactically expounded by a thinker who himself has neither pathos nor passion. It is didactically expounded that thinking is superior to irony and humor, and this is didactically expounded by a thinker who totally lacks a sense of the comic. How comic! Just as all abstract thinking in relation to Christianity and to all existence-issues is a trial in the comic, so also the so-called pure thinking is primarily a psychological oddity, an admirable kind of ingenuity in joining and constructing in a fantastic medium: pure being. Straightway to idolize this pure thinking as the highest shows that the thinker has never existed *qua* human being, that among other things he has not acted in the eminent sense—I do not mean in terms of achievement but in terms of inwardness. But to act in the eminent sense belongs essentially to existing *qua* human being. By acting, by venturing the decisive thing (which every human being is capable of doing) in utmost subjective passion and in full consciousness of an eternal responsibility, one comes to know something else, also that to be a human being is something other than year in and year out pinning something together into a system. By essentially existing *qua* hu-
VII 261 man being, one also gains a responsiveness to the comic. I am not saying that everyone who actually exists as a human being is therefore able to be a comic poet or a comic actor, but he has a responsiveness to it.

That the language of abstraction really does not allow the difficulty of existence and of the existing person to come up, I shall illustrate with regard to a crucial issue about which so much is spoken and written. As is well known, Hegelian philosophy has canceled the principle of contradiction,[501] and Hegel himself has more than once emphatically held judgment day on the kind of thinkers who remained in the sphere of understanding and reflection and who have therefore insisted that there is an either/or.[502] Since that time, it has become a popular game, so that as soon as someone hints at an *aut/aut* [either/or][503] a Hegelian comes riding trip-trap-trap on a horse (like Jens Skovfoged in *Kallundborgs-Krøniken*[504]) and wins a victory and rides home again. Among us, too, the Hegelians[505] have several times been on the move, especially against Bishop Mynster, in order to win speculative thought's brilliant victory; and Bishop Mynster has more than once become a defeated standpoint, even though for being a defeated standpoint he is holding up very well, and it is rather to be feared that the enormous exertion of the victory has been too exhausting for the undefeated victors. And yet there may be a misunderstanding at the root of the conflict and the victory. Hegel is perfectly and absolutely right in maintaining that, looked at eternally, *sub specie aeterni*, there is no *aut/aut* in the language of abstraction, in pure thought and pure being. Where the devil would it be, since abstraction, after all, simply removes the contradiction; therefore Hegel and the Hegelians should instead take the trouble to explain what is meant by the masquerade of getting contradiction, movement, transition, etc. into logic. The defenders of *aut/aut* are in the wrong if they push their way into the territory of pure thinking and want to defend their cause there. Just as the giant who wrestled with Hercules lost his strength as soon as he was lifted from the earth,[506] so the *aut/aut* of contradiction is *eo ipso* canceled when it is lifted out of existence and taken into the eternity of abstraction. On the other hand, Hegel is just as much in the wrong when he, forgetting the abstraction, plunges from it down into existence in order by hook or by crook to cancel the double *aut*. It is impossible to do this in existence, VII 262 because then he cancels existence also. If I take existence away (if I abstract), there is no *aut/aut*; if I take it away in existence, this means that I take existence away, but then I do not cancel it in existence. If it is incorrect that there is something true in theology that is not true in philosophy,[507] then it is entirely correct that there is something true for an existing person that is not true in abstraction; and it is also ethically true that the pure being is fantasy, and an existing person is debarred from wanting to forget that he is an existing person.

Therefore one must be very cautious about becoming involved with a Hegelian and above all must ascertain who it is with whom one has the honor of speaking. Is he a human being, an existing human being? Is he himself *sub specie aeterni*, also when he sleeps, eats, blows his nose, and whatever else a human being does? Is he himself the pure *I-I*—something that certainly has never occurred to any philosopher, and if he is not that, then how does he, existing, relate himself to it, to the middle term, in which the ethical responsibility in and with and by existing is duly respected? Does he exist? And if he exists, is he not then in a process of becoming? And if he is in a process of becoming, is he not then related to the future? Does he never relate himself to the future in such a way that he acts? And if he never acts, will he not then forgive an ethical individuality for saying with passion and with dramatic truth that he is an idiot? But if he acts *sensu eminenti* [in the eminent sense], does he not then relate himself to the future with infinite passion? Is there, then, not an *aut/aut*? For an existing person, is not eternity not eternity but the future, whereas eternity is eternity only for the Eternal, who is not in a process of becoming? Ask him if he can answer the following question—that is, if such a question can be put to him: Is the relinquishment of existing for the sake of being *sub specie aeterni*, insofar as that is possible, something that happens to him or something one does by virtue of a resolution; is it perhaps even something one ought to do? If I ought to do it, then *eo ipso* an *aut/aut* is established even in relation to being *sub specie aeterni*. Or was he born *sub specie aeterni* and since that time did he live *sub specie aeterni* and hence cannot even understand what I am asking about, inasmuch as he has never had anything to do
VII 263 with the future or never been aware of any decision? In that case, I perceive well enough that it is not a human being with whom I have the honor of speaking. But I am still not finished with the matter, because to me it is strange that such enigmatic beings are turning up.

Prior to the outbreak of cholera there usually appears a kind of fly not otherwise seen; in like manner might not these fabulous pure thinkers be a sign that a calamity is in store for humankind—for example, the loss of the ethical and the religious? Therefore, be cautious with an abstract thinker who not only wants to remain in abstraction's pure being but wants this to be the highest for a human being, and wants such thinking, which results in the ignoring of the ethical and a misunderstanding of the religious, to be the highest human thinking. On the other hand, do not go and say that there should be an *aut/aut sub specie aeterni*, "where everything is and nothing originates"* (the Eleatics' doctrine[509]). But where everything is in a process of becoming, where only so much of the eternal is present that it can have a constraining effect in the passionate decision, where the *eternal* relates itself as the *future* to the *person in a process of becoming*—there the absolute disjunction belongs. In other words, when I join eternity and becoming, I do not gain rest but the future. Certainly this is why Christianity has proclaimed the eternal as the future, because it was proclaimed to existing persons, and this is why it also assumes an absolute *aut/aut*.

All logical thinking is in the language of abstraction and *sub* VII
specie aeterni. To think existence in this way is to disregard the 264

* Misled by repeated talk about a continual process in which opposites combine in a higher unity and then again in a higher unity etc., people have drawn a parallel between Hegel's doctrine and that of Heraclitus: all flows and nothing abides.[508] This, however, is a misunderstanding, because everything that is said in Hegel about process and becoming is illusory. Therefore the system lacks an ethics; therefore the system knows nothing when the living generation and the living individual ask in earnest about becoming in order, namely, to act. Therefore, despite all his talking about process, Hegel does not understand world history in a becoming but by means of an illusion of the past understands it in a conclusiveness in which all becoming is excluded. Therefore a Hegelian cannot possibly understand himself with the aid of his philosophy; he can understand only what is past, is finished, but a person who is still living is not dead and gone. Presumably he consoles himself with the thought that if one can understand China and Persia and six thousand years of world history, then never mind a single individual, even if it is oneself. I see it differently, and I understand it better the other way around, that if a person cannot understand himself, his understanding of China and Persia etc. is certainly very odd.

difficulty, that is, the difficulty of thinking the eternal in a process of becoming, which one is presumably compelled to do since the thinker himself is in a process of becoming. Therefore, to think abstractly is easier than to exist, unless this is to be understood as what people usually call existing, just like being a subject of sorts. Here again is an example of how the simplest task is the most difficult. To exist, one thinks, is nothing much, even less an art. Of course, we all exist, but to think abstractly—that is something. But truly to exist, that is, to permeate one's existence with consciousness, simultaneously to be eternal, far beyond it, as it were, and nevertheless present in it and nevertheless in a process of becoming—that is truly difficult. If in our day thinking had not become something strange, something secondhand, thinkers would indeed make a totally different impression on people, as was the case in Greece, where a thinker was also an ardent existing person impassioned by his thinking, as was the case at one time in Christendom, where a thinker was a believer who ardently sought to understand himself in the existence of faith. If it were the same with thinkers in our day, pure thinking would have led to one suicide after another, because suicide is the only existence-consequence of pure thinking if, in relation to what it means to be a human being, this thinking is not to be something merely fractional and ready to make a deal with ethical and religious personal existing, but is to be everything and the highest. We do not praise suicide, but certainly the passion. Now, however, a thinker is a creature worth seeing, who at certain times of the day is singularly ingenious but otherwise has nothing in common with a human being.

To think existence *sub specie aeterni* and in abstraction is essentially to annul it, and the merit of it resembles the much-heralded merit of canceling the principle of contradiction. Existence without motion is unthinkable, and motion is unthinkable *sub specie aeterni*. To omit motion is not exactly a masterstroke, and to introduce it into logic as transition, and along with it time and space, is only new confusion. But since all thinking is eternal, the difficulty is for the existing person. Existence, like motion, is a very difficult matter to handle. If

I think it, I cancel it, and then I do not think it. It would seem correct to say that there is something that cannot be thought—namely, existing. But again there is the difficulty that existence puts it together in this way: the one who is thinking is existing.

Because Greek philosophy was not absentminded, motion VII
was a perpetual topic for its dialectical efforts. The Greek phi- 265
losopher was an existing person, and he did not forget this. Therefore he resorted to suicide or to dying in the Pythagorean sense[510] or to being dead in the Socratic sense[511] in order to be able to think. He was aware that he was a thinking being, but he was also aware that it was existence as medium that perpetually prevented him from thinking in continuity because it continually placed him in a process of becoming. Consequently, in order to be able truly to think, he did away with himself. Modern philosophy smiles superiorly at such childishness, just as if every modern thinker, as surely as he knows that thinking and being are one, did not also know that it is not worth the trouble to be what he thinks.

It is on this point of existing and on the requirement of the ethical to the existing person that resistance must be made when an abstract philosophy and pure thinking want to explain everything by explaining away the decisive factor. One has only to dare intrepidly to be a human being and to refuse to be frightened into or by embarrassment to be tricked into becoming something [512]like a phantom. It would be another matter if pure thinking would explain its relation to the ethical and to an ethically existing individuality. But this is what it never does; indeed, it does not even make a show of wanting to do it, since in that case it would also have to become involved with another kind of dialectic, the Greek or existence-dialectic. The endorsement of ethics is what every existing person has a legitimate right to demand of all that is called wisdom. If the beginning is once made, if it is an imperceptible transition that a person little by little forgets to exist in order to think *sub specie aeterni*—then the objection is of another kind. Within the realm of pure thinking many, many objections can perhaps be made against Hegelianism, but that leaves everything essentially unchanged. But willing as I am (in the capacity of a poor reader who by no means presumes to be a judge) to admire Hegel's logic, willing as I am to admit that there can be much for me to learn when I turn to it again, I shall also be just as proud, just as defiant, just as obstinately assertive, just as intrepid in my assertion that Hegelian philosophy confuses existence by not defining its relation to an existing person, by disregarding the ethical.

The most dangerous skepticism is always that which least
VII 266 appears as such, but the idea that pure thinking is supposed to be the positive truth for an existing person is skepticism, because this positivity is chimerical. To be able to explain the past, all of world history, is magnificent, but if the ability to understand only the past is supposed to be the highest for one still living,[513] then this positivity is skepticism, and a dangerous skepticism, because the enormous mass that one understands has such a deceptive appearance. Therefore something terrible can happen to Hegel's philosophy—an indirect attack can be the most dangerous. Let a doubting youth, but an existing doubter[514] with youth's lovable, boundless confidence in a hero of scientific scholarship, venture to find in Hegelian positivity the truth, the truth for existence—he will write a dreadful epigram on Hegel. Do not misunderstand me. I do not mean that every youth is capable of overcoming Hegel, far from it. If a young person is conceited and foolish enough to try that, his attack is inane. No, the youth must never think of wanting to attack him; he must rather be willing to submit unconditionally to Hegel with feminine devotedness, but nevertheless with sufficient strength also to stick to his question—then he is a satirist without suspecting it. The youth is an existing doubter; continually suspended in doubt, he grasps for the truth—so that he can exist in it. Consequently, he is negative, and Hegel's philosophy is, of course, positive—no wonder he puts his trust in it. But for an existing person pure thinking is a chimera when the truth is supposed to be the truth in which to exist. Having to exist with the help of the guidance of pure thinking is like having to travel in Denmark with a small map of Europe on which Denmark is no larger

than a steel pen-point[515]—indeed, even more impossible. The youth's admiration, his enthusiasm, and his limitless confidence in Hegel are precisely the satire on Hegel.

This would have been discerned long ago if pure thinking had not maintained itself with the aid of a reputation that impresses people, so they do not dare to say anything except that it is superb, that they have understood it—although in a certain sense that is indeed impossible, since no one can be led by this philosophy to understand himself, which is certainly an absolute condition for all other understanding. Socrates has rather ironically said that he did not know for sure whether he was a human being or something else,[516] but in the confessional a Hegelian can say with all solemnity: I do not know
whether I am a human being—but I have understood the sys- VII
tem. I prefer to say: I know that I am a human being, and I 267
know that I have not understood the system. And when I have said that very directly, I shall add that if any of our Hegelians want to take me in hand and assist me to an understanding of the system, nothing will stand in the way from my side. In order that I can learn all the more, I shall try hard to be as obtuse as possible, so as not to have, if possible, a single presupposition except my ignorance. And in order to be sure of learning something, I shall try hard to be as indifferent as possible to all charges of being unscientific and unscholarly.

Existing, if this is not to be understood as just any sort of existing, cannot be done without passion. Therefore, every Greek thinker was essentially also a passionate thinker. I have often thought about how one might bring a person into passion. So I have considered the possibility of getting him astride a horse and then frightening the horse into the wildest gallop, or even better, in order to draw out the passion properly, the possibility of getting a man who wants to go somewhere as quickly as possible (and therefore was already in something of a passion) astride a horse that can hardly walk—and yet existing is like that if one is conscious of it. Or if a Pegasus and an old nag were hitched to a carriage for a driver not usually disposed to passion and he was told: Now drive—I think it would be successful. And this is what existing is like if one is to be conscious of it. Eternity is infinitely quick like that winged steed, temporality is an old nag, and the existing person is the driver, that is, if existing is not to be what people usually call existing, because then the existing person is no driver but a drunken peasant who lies in the wagon and sleeps and lets the horses shift for themselves. Of course, he also drives, he is also a driver, and likewise there perhaps are many who—also exist.

Inasmuch as existence is motion, it holds true that there is indeed a continuity that holds the motion together, because otherwise there is no motion. Just as the statement that everything is true means that nothing is true, in the same way the statement that everything is in motion means that there is no
VII 268 motion.*[517] The motionless belongs to motion as motion's goal [*Maal*[520]], both in the sense of τέλος [end, goal] and μέτρον [measure, criterion]; otherwise the statement that everything is in motion—if one also takes away time and says that everything is always motion—is *eo ipso* stagnation. Aristotle, who in so many ways emphasizes motion, therefore says that God, himself unmoved, moves everything.[521] Now, whereas pure thinking summarily cancels all motion, or meaninglessly introduces it into logic, the difficulty for the existing person is to give existence the continuity without which everything just disappears. An abstract continuity is no continuity, and the existing of the existing person essentially prevents continuity, whereas passion is the momentary continuity that simultaneously has a constraining effect and is the impetus of motion. For an existing person, the goal of motion is decision and repetition. The eternal is the continuity of motion, but an abstract eternity is outside motion, and a concrete eternity in the existing person is the maximum of passion. That is, all idealizing** passion is an anticipation of the eternal in existence

* This was unquestionably what was meant by Heraclitus's pupil who said
VII 268 that one could not even go once through the same river.[518] Johannes de Silentio (in *Fear and Trembling*[519]) made a reference to this pupil's statement, but more with rhetorical flourish than with truth.

** Earthly passion hinders existing by changing existence into the momentary.

in order for an existing person to exist;* the eternity of abstraction is gained by disregarding existence. An existing person can have gained admission into pure thinking only by a dubious beginning, a dubiousness that indeed backlashes by making the existing person's existence trivial and his parlance somewhat demented. This is just about the case with the majority of people in our day, when one seldom or never hears a person speak as if he were conscious of his being an individual existing human being, but instead pantheistically lets himself become dizzy when *he*, too, talks about millions and the na- VII 269
tions and world-historical development. For an existing person, however, passion's anticipation of the eternal is still not an absolute continuity but the possibility of an approximation to the only true continuity there can be for an existing person. Here one is again reminded of my thesis that subjectivity is truth, because the objective truth for an existing person is like the eternity of abstraction.

Abstraction is disinterested,[524] but to exist is the highest interest for an existing person. Therefore, the existing person continually has a τέλος and it is of this τέλος that Aristotle speaks when he says (*De anima*, III, 10, 2) that νοῦς θεωρητικός [theoretical thought] is different from νοῦς πρακτικὸς τῷ τέλει [practical thought in its end].[525] But pure thinking is totally in suspension and is not like abstraction, which does indeed disregard existence but still maintains a relation to it, [526]whereas pure thinking, in mystical suspension and with no relation to an existing person, explains everything within itself but not itself, explains everything within itself, whereby the decisive explanation regarding the real question becomes impossible. When, for example, an existing person asks how pure thinking relates itself to an existing person, how he goes about being admitted into it, pure thinking gives no answer but explains existence within its pure thinking and thereby

* Poetry and art have been called an anticipation of the eternal.[522] If one wants to call them that, one must nevertheless be aware that poetry and art are not essentially related to an existing person, since the contemplation of poetry and art, "joy over the beautiful," is disinterested,[523] and the observer is contemplatively outside himself *qua* existing person.

confuses everything, because that upon which pure thinking must become stranded, existence, is in a volatilized sense assigned a place within pure thinking, whereby whatever might be said within it about existence is essentially revoked. When in pure thinking mention is made of an immediate unity of reflection-in-itself and reflection-in-the-other and of the annulment of this immediate unity, then something must indeed come between the elements of the immediate unity. What is this? Yes, it is time. But time cannot be assigned a place within pure thinking. What, then, do annulment and transition and a new unity signify? What, if anything, does it mean to think in such a way that one always merely makes a show of it because everything that is said is absolutely revoked? And what does it mean not to admit that one thinks this way but then continually to proclaim from the housetops the positive truth of this pure thinking?

Just as existence has joined thinking and existing, inasmuch as an existing person is a thinking person, so are there two
VII media: the medium of abstraction and the medium of actual-
270 ity. But pure thinking is yet a third medium, very recently invented. It begins, it is said, after the most exhaustive abstraction. Pure thinking is—what shall I say—piously or thoughtlessly unaware of the relation that abstraction still continually has to that from which it abstracts. Here in this pure thinking there is rest for every doubt; here is the eternal positive truth and whatever else one cares to say. This means that pure thinking is a phantom. And if Hegelian philosophy is free from all postulates, it has attained this with one insane postulate: the beginning of pure thinking.

For the existing person, existing is for him his highest interest, and his interestedness in existing is his actuality. What actuality is cannot be rendered in the language of abstraction. Actuality is an *inter-esse* [between-being][527] between thinking and being in the hypothetical unity of abstraction. Abstraction deals with possibility and actuality, but its conception of actuality is a false rendition, since the medium is not actuality but possibility.[528] Only by annulling actuality can abstraction grasp it, but to annul it is precisely to change it into possibil-

ity. Within abstraction, everything that is said about actuality in the language of abstraction is said within possibility. That is, in the language of actuality all abstraction is related to actuality as a possibility, not to an actuality within abstraction and possibility. Actuality, existence, is the dialectical element in a trilogy,[529] the beginning and end of which cannot be for an existing person, who *qua* existing person is in the dialectical element. Abstraction merges the trilogy. Quite right. But how does it do it? Is abstraction a something that does it, or is it not the act of the abstracter? But the abstracter is, after all, an existing person, and as an existing person is consequently in the dialectical element, which he cannot mediate or merge, least of all absolutely, as long as he is existing. If he does do it, then this must be related as a possibility to actuality, to the existence in which he himself is. He must explain how he goes about it—that is, how he as an existing person goes about it, or whether he ceases to be an existing person, and whether an VII
existing person has a right to do that. 271

As soon as we begin to ask such questions, we are asking ethically and are maintaining the claim of the ethical upon the existing person, which cannot be that he is supposed to abstract from existence, but that he is supposed to exist, which is also the existing person's highest interest.

As an existing person, he can least of all hold absolutely fast the annulment of the dialectical element (existence); for that there is required a medium other than existence, which is indeed precisely the dialectical element. If an existing person can know the annulment, he can know it only as a possibility, which cannot exercise a restraining influence when the interest is posited, and that is why he can know it only in a disinterested way, which is not entirely possible for him *qua* existing person and which he *qua* existing person has no right whatever, ethically viewed, to want to attain *approximando*, since, on the contrary, the ethical makes the interest of existence infinite for him, so infinite that the principle of contradiction has absolute validity.

Here again, as shown previously, abstraction does not become involved at all in the difficulty that is the difficulty of existence and of the existing person. To think actuality in the medium of possibility does not entail the difficulty of having to think in the medium of existence, where existence as a process of becoming will hinder the existing person from thinking, as if actuality could not be thought, although the existing person is nevertheless a thinking person. In pure thinking one is over one's ears in profundity, and yet one *mitunter* [now and then] has the impression that there is some absentmindedness in it all, because the pure thinker is not clear about what it means to be an existing human being.

All knowledge about actuality is possibility. The only actuality concerning which an existing person has more than knowledge about is his own actuality, that he exists, and this actuality is his absolute interest. The demand of abstraction upon him is that he become disinterested in order to obtain something to know; the requirement of the ethical upon him is to be infinitely interested in existing.

The only actuality there is for an existing person is his own ethical actuality; concerning all other actuality he has only knowledge about, but genuine knowledge is a translation into possibility.

The trustworthiness of sense perception is a deception. Greek skepticism has already adequately shown this, and modern idealism likewise. The trustworthiness claimed by knowledge about the historical is also only a deception insofar as it claims to be the trustworthiness of actuality, since the knower cannot know about a historical actuality until he has
VII dissolved it into possibility.[530] (More about that later.) Ab-
272 straction is possibility, either the preceding or the subsequent possibility. Pure thinking is a phantom.

The actual subjectivity is not the knowing subjectivity, because with knowledge he is in the medium of possibility, but is the ethical existing subjectivity. Surely an abstract thinker exists, but his existing is rather like a satire on him. To demonstrate his existence on the grounds that he is thinking is a strange contradiction, because to the degree that he thinks abstractly he abstracts to the same degree precisely from his existing. To that extent, his existence certainly does become clear as a presupposition from which he wants to extricate himself, but nevertheless the abstraction itself does indeed become a strange demonstration of his existence, since his existence would simply cease if he were completely successful. The Cartesian *cogito ergo sum* [I think therefore I am] has been repeated often enough. If the *I* in *cogito* is understood to be an individual human being, then the statement demonstrates nothing: I *am* thinking ergo I am, but if I *am* thinking, no wonder, then, that I am; after all, it has already been said, and the first consequently says even more than the last.[531] If, then, by the *I* in *cogito*, one understands a single individual existing human being, philosophy shouts: Foolishness, foolishness, here it is not a matter of my *I* or your *I* but of the pure *I*. But surely this pure *I* can have no other existence than thought-existence. What, then, is the concluding formula supposed to mean; indeed, there is no conclusion, for then the statement is a tautology.

If it is said that the abstract thinker, far from demonstrating by his thinking that he exists, instead makes it plain that his abstraction will not be entirely successful in demonstrating the opposite—if this is said, then on that basis to want to conclude inversely that an existing person who actually exists does not think at all is an arbitrary misunderstanding. Surely he thinks, but he thinks everything inversely in relation to himself, infinitely interested in existing. Surely Socrates was a thinking person, but he placed all other knowledge in the sphere of indifference and infinitely accentuated ethical knowledge, which relates itself to the existing subject infinitely interested in existence.

To conclude existence from thinking is, then, a contradiction, because thinking does just the opposite and takes existence away from the actual and thinks it by annulling it, by transposing it into possibility. (More about that later.) With regard to every actuality other than the individual's own, it
holds true that he can know about it only by thinking it. With VII
regard to his own actuality, it would depend upon whether his 273
thinking could be completely successful in abstracting from actuality. That is indeed what the abstract thinker wants, but

it is of no use; he still continues to exist, and this continuance of his existence, "this sometimes sad professorial figure," is an epigram on the abstract thinker, not to mention the allegation of ethics against him.

[532]In Greece, however, attention was paid to what it means to exist. The skeptical ataraxia was therefore an existence-attempt to abstract from existing. In our day one abstracts in print, just as in print one doubts everything once and for all. Among the things that have occasioned so much confusion in modern philosophizing is that the philosophers make so many brief statements about infinite tasks and mutually respect this paper money, although it almost never occurs to anyone, existing, to want to try his hand at fulfilling the task's requirement. In this way one can easily be finished with everything and manage to begin without any presuppositions. The presupposition, for example, of doubting everything would take a whole lifetime; now, however, it is done as swiftly as it is said.

§ 2[533]

Possibility Superior to Actuality; Actuality Superior to Possibility; Poetic and Intellectual Ideality; Ethical Ideality[534]

Aristotle remarks in his *Poetics* that poetry is superior to history, because history presents only what has occurred, poetry what could and ought to have occurred,[535] i.e., poetry has possibility at its disposal. Possibility, poetic and intellectual, is superior to actuality; the esthetic and the intellectual are disinterested. But there is only one interest, the interest in existing; disinterestedness is the expression for indifference to actuality. The indifference is forgotten in the Cartesian *cogito—ergo sum*, which disturbs the disinterestedness of the intellec-
VII 274 tual and offends speculative thought, as if something else
should follow from it. I think, ergo I think; whether I am or it is (in the sense of actuality, where *I* means a single existing human being and *it* means a single definite something) is infinitely unimportant. That what I am thinking *is* in the sense of

thinking does not, of course, need any demonstration, nor does it need to be demonstrated by any conclusion, since it is indeed demonstrated. But as soon as I begin to want to make my thinking teleological in relation to something else, interest enters the game. As soon as it is there, the ethical is present and exempts me from further trouble with demonstrating my existence, and since it obliges me to exist, it prevents me from making an ethically deceptive and metaphysically unclear flourish of a conclusion.

While the ethical in our day is ignored more and more, this ignoring has also had the harmful result that it has confused both poetry and speculative thought, which have relinquished the disinterested elevation of possibility in order to clutch at actuality—instead of each being given its due, a double confusion has been created. Poetry makes one attempt after the other to look like actuality, which is altogether unpoetic; within its sphere, speculative thought repeatedly wants to arrive at actuality and gives assurances that what is thought is the actual, that thinking is not only able to think but also to provide actuality,[536] which is just the opposite; and at the same time what it means to exist is more and more forgotten. The age and human beings become less and less actual—hence these surrogates that are supposed to replace what is lost. The ethical is more and more abandoned; the single individual's life becomes not only poetically but world-historically disturbed and is thereby hindered in existing ethically; thus actuality must be procured in other ways. But this misunderstood actuality is like a generation or individuals in a generation who have become prematurely old and now are obliged to procure youthfulness artificially. Existing ethically is actuality, but instead of that the age has become so predominantly an observer that not only is everyone that but observing has finally become falsified as if it were actuality. We smile at monastic life, and yet no hermit ever lived as nonactual a life as is being lived nowadays, because a hermit admittedly abstracted from the whole world, but he did not abstract from himself. We know how to describe the fantastical setting of a

monastery in an out-of-the-way place, in the solitude of the forest, in the distant blue of the horizon, but we do not think
VII 275 about the fantastical setting of pure thinking. And yet the recluse's pathos-filled lack of actuality is far preferable to the comic lack of actuality of the pure thinker, and the recluse's passionate forgetfulness that takes the whole world away is far preferable to the comic distraction of the world-historical thinker who forgets himself.

From the ethical point of view, actuality is superior to possibility. The ethical specifically wants to annihilate the disinterestedness of possibility by making existing the infinite interest. Therefore the ethical wants to prevent every attempt at confusion, such as, for example, wanting *to observe* the world and human beings ethically. That is, to observe ethically cannot be done, because there is only one ethical observing—it is self-observation. The ethical immediately embraces the single individual with its requirement that he shall exist ethically; it does not bluster about millions and generations; it does not take humankind at random, any more than the police arrest humankind in general. The ethical deals with individual human beings and, please note, with each individual. If God knows how many hairs there are on a person's head,[537] then the ethical knows how many people there are, and the ethical census is not in the interest of a total sum but in the interest of each individual. The ethical requires itself of every human being, and when it judges, it judges in turn every single individual; only a tyrant and a powerless man are satisfied with taking one out of ten. The ethical grips the single individual and requires of him that he abstain from all observing, especially of the world and humankind, because the ethical as the internal cannot be observed by anyone standing outside. The ethical can be carried out only by the individual subject, who then is able to know what lives within him—the only actuality that does not become a possibility by being known and cannot be known only by being thought, since it is his own actuality, which he knew as thought-actuality, that is, as possibility, before it became actuality; whereas with regard to another's actuality he knew nothing about it before he, by coming to know it, thought it, that is, changed it into possibility.

With regard to every actuality outside myself, it holds true that I can grasp it only in thinking. If I were actually to grasp VII 276 it, I would have to be able to make myself into the other person, the one acting, to make the actuality alien to me into my own personal actuality, which is an impossibility. [538]That is, if I make the actuality alien to me into my own actuality, it does not mean that by knowing about it I become he, but it means a new actuality that belongs to me as different from him.

When I think something I want to do but as yet have not done, then what I have thought, however precise it is, however much it may be called a *thought-actuality*, is a possibility. Conversely, when I think something that someone else has done, therefore think an actuality, then I take this given actuality out of actuality and transpose it into possibility, inasmuch as a *thought-actuality* is a possibility and in terms of thinking superior to actuality but not in terms of actuality. —This also means that ethically there is no direct relation between subject and subject. When I have understood another subject, his actuality is for me a possibility, and this thought-actuality is related to me *qua* possibility just as my own thinking of something I still have not done is related to the doing of it.

Frater Taciturnus (*Stages on Life's Way*, p. 341[539]) says: Anyone who, with regard to the same thing, does not reach the conclusion just as well *ab posse ad esse* [from possibility to actuality] as *ab esse ad posse* [from actuality to possibility] does not grasp the ideality, that is, he does not understand it, he does not think it (the reference is, namely, to understanding an alien actuality). In other words, if the thinking person with the dissolving *posse* (a thought-actuality is a possibility) encounters an *esse* he cannot dissolve, he must say: This I am unable to think. Therefore he suspends thinking. If he is going to or, rather, if he nevertheless wants to relate himself to this actuality as actuality, he does not relate himself to it in thought

but paradoxically. (Please recall the previously stated definition of faith [in the Socratic sense, *sensu laxiori* (in the wider
VII 277 sense), not *sensu strictissimo* (in the strictest sense)]): The *objective uncertainty*, namely because the dissolving *posse* has come up against an obdurate *esse, held fast in passionate inwardness.*

To ask with regard to the esthetic and the intellectual whether this or that is indeed actual, did it actually occur, is a misunderstanding that does not grasp esthetic and intellectual ideality as possibility and forgets that determining the order of rank esthetically and intellectually in this way is the same as assuming sensation to be superior to thinking. —When the question is asked: Is it actual, ethically the question is properly asked, but, please note, in such a way that the individual subject ethically asks himself about his own actuality. But for him someone else's actuality is to be conceived only by thinking it, that is, as possibility.

Scripture teaches: "Judge not, that you be not judged."[540] This is said as an admonition and warning, but it is also an impossibility. One person cannot ethically judge another, because the one can understand the other only as a possibility. Thus when someone is occupied with wanting to judge another, this is a manifestation of his weakness, that he is only judging himself.

In *Stages on Life's Way* (p. 342[541]) it says: "It is spirit to ask about two things: (1) Is what is being said possible? (2) Am I able to do it? But it is lack of spirit to ask about two things: (1) Did it actually happen? (2) Has my neighbor Christophersen done it; has he actually done it?" The question of actuality is thereby accentuated ethically. Esthetically and intellectually, it is foolish to ask about its actuality; ethically, it is foolish to ask about its actuality in terms of observation; but in asking ethically with regard to my own actuality, I am asking about
VII 278 its possibility, except that this possibility is not esthetically and intellectually disinterested but is a thought-actuality that

is related to my own personal actuality—namely, that I am able to carry it out.

The *how* of the truth is precisely the truth. Therefore it is untruth to answer a question in a medium in which the question cannot come up: for example, to explain actuality within possibility, within possibility to distinguish between possibility and actuality. By not asking esthetically and intellectually about actuality, but asking only ethically about actuality—and ethically in turn with regard to his own personal actuality—every individual is ethically set apart by himself. With regard to the observational question about ethical interiority, irony and hypocrisy as antitheses (but both expressing the contradiction that the outer is not the inner—hypocrisy by appearing good, irony by appearing bad) emphasize that actuality and deception are equally possible, that deception can reach just as far as actuality. Only the individual himself can know which is which. To ask about this ethical interiority in another individual is already unethical inasmuch as it is a diversion. But if the question is asked nevertheless, then there is the difficulty that I can grasp the other person's actuality only by thinking it, consequently by translating it into possibility, where the possibility of deception is just as thinkable. —For existing ethically, it is an advantageous preliminary study to learn that the individual human being stands alone.

To ask esthetically and intellectually about actuality is a misunderstanding; to ask ethically about another person's actuality is a misunderstanding, since one ought to ask only about one's own. Here the difference between faith (which *sensu strictissimo* [in the strictest sense] refers to something historical) and the esthetic, the intellectual, the ethical, manifests itself. To be infinitely interested and to ask about an actuality that is not one's own is to will to believe and expresses the paradoxical relation to the paradox. Esthetically it is not possible to ask in this way, except thoughtlessly, since esthetically possibility is superior to actuality. It is not possible intellectually, since intellectually possibility is superior to actuality. Nor is it

possible ethically, because ethically the individual is simply and solely interested infinitely in his own actuality. —Faith's
VII 279 analogy to the ethical is the infinite interestedness by which the believer is absolutely different from an esthete and a thinker, but in turn is different from an ethicist by being infinitely interested in the actuality of another (for example, that the god [*Guden*] actually has existed).

Esthetically and intellectually, it holds true that only when the *esse* of an actuality is dissolved into its *posse* is an actuality understood and thought. Ethically, it holds true that possibility is understood only when each *posse* is actually an *esse*. When the esthetic and the intellectual inspect, they protest every *esse* that is not a *posse*; when the ethical inspects, it condemns every *posse* that is not an *esse*, a *posse*, namely, in the individual himself, since the ethical does not deal with other individuals. —In our day everything is mixed together; one responds to the esthetic ethically, to faith intellectually, etc. One is finished with everything, and yet scant attention is given to which sphere it is in which each question finds its answer. This produces even greater confusion in the world of spirit than if in civic life the response to an ecclesiastical matter would be given by the pavement commission.

Is actuality, then, the outer?[542] By no means. Esthetically and intellectually, it is quite properly emphasized that the outer is nothing but deception for one who does not grasp the ideality. Frater Taciturnus declares (p. 341[543]) "Knowledge [of the historical] merely assists one into an illusion that is infatuated with the palpably material. What is that which I know historically? It is the palpably material. Ideality I know by myself, and if I do not know it by myself, then I do not know it at all, and all the historical knowledge does not help. Ideality is not a chattel that can be transferred from one person to another, or something thrown in to boot when the purchase is a large one. If I know that Caesar was great, then I know what the great is, and this is what I see—otherwise I do not know that Caesar was great. History's account—that reliable men assure

us of it, that there is no risk involved in accepting this opinion since it must be obvious that he was a great man, that the outcome demonstrates it—does not help at all. To believe the ideality on the word of another is like laughing at a joke not be- VII
cause one has understood it but because someone else said that 280
it was funny. In that case, the joke can really be omitted for the person who laughs on the basis of belief and respect; he is able to laugh with equal *emphasis* [significance]." —What, then, is actuality? It is ideality. But esthetically and intellectually ideality is possibility (a transfer *ab esse ad posse*). Ethically, ideality is the actuality within the individual himself. Actuality is interiority infinitely interested in existing, which the ethical individual is for himself.

When I understand a thinker, then, precisely to the same degree to which I understand him, his actuality (that he himself exists as an individual human being, that he *actually* has understood this in such a way etc. or that he himself has *actually* carried it out etc.) is a matter of complete indifference. Philosophy and esthetics are right in this, and the point is to maintain this properly. But in this there is still no defense of pure thought as a medium of communication. Just because his actuality is a matter of indifference to me, the learner, and conversely mine to him, it by no means follows that he himself dares to be indifferent to his own actuality. His communication must be marked by this, not directly, of course, for it cannot be communicated directly between man and man (since such a relation is the believer's paradoxical relation to the object of faith), and cannot be understood directly, but must be present indirectly to be understood indirectly.

If the particular spheres are not kept decisively separate from one another, everything is confused. If one is inquisitive about a thinker's actuality, finds it interesting to know something about it, etc., then one is intellectually censurable, because in the sphere of intellectuality the maximum is that the thinker's actuality is a matter of complete indifference. But by being such a blatherer in the sphere of intellectuality, one acquires a confusing similarity to a believer. A believer is infinitely interested in the actuality of another. For faith, this is decisive, and this interestedness is not just a little inquisitiveness but is absolute dependence on the object of faith.

The object of faith is the actuality of another person; its relation is an infinite interestedness. The object of faith is not a
doctrine, for then the relation is intellectual, and the point is
VII not to bungle it but to reach the maximum of the intellectual
281 relation. The object of faith is not a teacher who has a doc-
trine, for when a teacher has a doctrine, then the doctrine is *eo ipso* more important than the teacher, and the relation is intellectual, in which the point is not to bungle it but to reach the maximum of the intellectual relation. But the object of faith is the actuality of the teacher, that the teacher actually exists. Therefore faith's answer is absolutely either yes or no. Faith's answer is not in relation to a doctrine, whether it is true or not, not in relation to a teacher, whether his doctrine is true or not, but is the answer to the question about a fact: Do you accept as fact that he actually has existed? Please note that the answer is with infinite passion. In other words, in connection with a human being it is thoughtless to lay so infinitely much weight upon whether he has existed or not. Therefore, if the object of faith is a human being, the whole thing is a prank by a foolish person who has not even grasped the esthetic and the intellectual. The object of faith is therefore the god's actuality in the sense of existence. But to exist signifies first and foremost to be a particular individual, and this is why thinking must disregard existence, because the particular cannot be thought, but only the universal. The object of faith, then, is the actuality of the god in existence, that is, as a particular individual, that is, that the god has existed as an individual human being.

Christianity is not a doctrine about the unity of the divine and the human, about subject-object, not to mention the rest of the logical paraphrases of Christianity. In other words, if Christianity were a doctrine, then the relation to it would not be one of faith, since there is only an intellectual relation to a doctrine. Christianity, therefore, is not a doctrine but the fact that the god has existed.

Faith, then, is not a lesson for slow learners in the sphere of intellectuality, an asylum for dullards. But faith is a sphere of its own, and the immediate identifying mark of every misunderstanding of Christianity is that it changes it into a doctrine and draws it into the range of intellectuality. What holds as the maximum in the sphere of intellectuality, to remain completely indifferent to the actuality of the teacher, holds in just the opposite way in the sphere of faith—its maximum is the *quam maxime* [in the greatest degree possible] infinite interestedness in the actuality of the teacher.

The individual's own ethical actuality is the only actuality. — VII
That this seems strange to many does not surprise me. To me 282
it seems odd that one has finished with the system and systems without asking about the ethical. If only dialogue in the Greek style were introduced again in order to test what one knows and what one does not know—then all the artificiality and unnaturalness, all the exaggerated ingenuity, would be blown away. It is not at all my idea that Hegel should engage in conversation with a hired man and that it would prove anything if he were not understood by him, although the simple statement of Diogenes that Socrates philosophized in the workshops and in the marketplace[544] will always remain a beautiful eulogy on Socrates. Yet this is not what I mean, and my proposal is anything but a vagabond attack upon scientific scholarship. But have a Hegelian philosopher or Hegel himself converse with a mature person who is dialectically experienced by having existed, and right away at the beginning all that is affected and chimerical will be prevented. When someone goes on continuously writing or dictating sections of a work, with promises that everything will become clear at the end, it becomes more and more difficult to discover where the beginning of the confusion lies and to acquire a firm point of departure. By means of "Everything will become clear at the end" and the category "This is not the place to go into this further," the cornerstone of the system, a category often used as ludicrously as if under the rubric of printers' errors someone were to cite one and then add: "There presumably are more in the

book, but this is not the place to go into them further"—by means of these two qualifications one is continually bamboozled, since the one deceives definitively, the other temporarily. In the situation of dialogue, the whole fantasticality involving pure thinking will make a poor showing.

Instead of admitting that idealism is in the right—but, please note, in such a way that one would reject the whole question about actuality (about a self-withholding *an sich*[545]) in relation to thinking as a temptation, which like all other temptations cannot possibly be canceled by surrendering to it—instead of putting a stop to Kant's deviation, which brought actuality into relation to thinking, instead of referring actuality to the ethical, Hegel certainly went further, inas-
VII much as he became fantastical and overcame the skepticism of
283 idealism by means of pure thinking, which is a hypothesis and, although it does not proclaim itself as such, is fantastical. This triumph of pure thinking (that in it thinking and being are one) is both laughable and lamentable, because in pure thinking there can really be no question at all of the difference. —Greek philosophy assumed as a matter of course that thinking has reality [*Realitet*]. In reflecting upon it, one must come to the same result, but why is thought-reality [*Tanke-Realitet*] confused with actuality [*Virkelighed*]? Thought-reality is possibility, and thinking needs only to reject any further questioning about whether it is actual.

[546]The dubiousness of "the method" is already apparent in Hegel's relation to Kant. A skepticism that confiscates thinking itself cannot be halted by being thought through, because this must indeed be done by thinking, which is on the side of the mutineer. It must be broken off. To reply to Kant within the fantastical *Schattenspiel* [shadow play] of pure thinking is precisely not to reply to him. —The only *an sich* that cannot be thought is existing, with which thinking has nothing at all to do. But how would it be possible for pure thinking to be able to cancel this difficulty, since as pure thinking it is abstract? But from what does pure thinking abstract? From existence, consequently from what it is supposed to explain.

If existing cannot be thought, and the existing person is thinking nevertheless, what does this mean? It means that he thinks momentarily; he thinks before and he thinks afterward. His thinking cannot attain absolute continuity. Only in a fantastical way can an existing person continually be *sub specie aeterni.*

Is thinking the same as creating, giving existence? I know very well and am willing to admit the correctness of the objections made to a foolish attack on the philosophical thesis of the identity of thinking and being. It has been rightly objected VII
that the identity of thinking and being must not be understood 284
thus in relation to imperfect existences,[547] as if, for example, by thinking a rose I could produce it. (In the same sense and with a certain disrespect for the advocates of the principle of contradiction, it has been shown that this appeared most clearly in the lowest existences, in the intellectual relations between finite entities: before and behind, right and left, up and down,[548] etc.)

But then does it hold true of the more perfect existences that thinking and being are one? With regard to the ideas, for example? Well, Hegel is in the right, and yet we have not gone one step further. The good, the beautiful, the ideas are in themselves so abstract that they are indifferent to existence and indifferent to anything other than thought-existence. The reason that the identity of thinking and being holds true here is that being cannot be understood as anything but thinking. But then the answer is an answer to something that cannot be asked about in the realm where the answer belongs.

But surely an existing individual human being is not an idea; surely his existence is something other than the thought-existence of the idea? Existing (in the sense of being this individual human being) is surely an imperfection compared with the eternal life of the idea, but a perfection in relation to not being at all. Existing is a somewhat intermediate state like that, something that is suitable for an intermediate being such as a human being is. How is it, then, with the presumed identity of thinking and being in relation to the kind of existence that is the existence of an individual existing human being?

Am I the good because I think it, or am I good because I think the good? Not at all. Do I exist because I think it? The advocates of the philosophical principle of the identity of thinking and being have themselves said that it does not hold true with regard to imperfect existences, but to exist as an individual human being—is this, then, a perfect idea-existence? And this, after all, is what is being asked about. Surely the opposite holds true here—namely, that because I exist and am thinking I therefore think that I exist. Here existence separates the ideal identity of thinking and being; I must exist in order to be able to think, and I must be able to think (for example, the good) in order to exist in it.

To exist as this individual human being is not as imperfect
VII 285 an existence as, for example, to be a rose. This is indeed why we human beings say that, however unhappy one is, to exist is nevertheless always a good, and I recollect a depressed person who, at one time in the midst of his suffering when he wished himself dead, at the sight of a basket of potatoes was prompted to ask himself the question whether he still did not have more joy in existing than a potato. But to be an individual human being is not a pure idea-existence either. Only humanity in general exists in this way, that is, does not exist. Existence is always the particular; the abstract does not *exist*. To conclude from this that the abstract does not have reality [*Realitet*] is a misunderstanding, but it is also a misunderstanding to confuse the discussion by asking about existence in relation to it or about actuality in the sense of existence. If, then, an *existing person* asks about the relation between thinking and being, between thinking and existing [*existere*], and philosophy explains that this relation is one of identity, it does not answer the question, because it does not answer the questioner. Philosophy explains: Thinking and being are one—but not in relation to that which is what it is only by existing [*være til*], for example, a rose, which has no idea at all in itself, thus not in relation to that in which one most clearly sees what it means to exist [*existere*] in contrast to thinking; but thinking and being are one in relation to that whose existence is essentially a matter of indifference because it is so abstract that it

has only thought-existence. But in this way one omits an answer to what was actually asked about: existing as an individual human being. In other words, this means not to be [*være*] in the same sense as a potato is, but not in the same sense as the idea is, either. Human existence has an idea within itself but nevertheless is not an idea-existence. Plato gave the idea second place as the connecting link between God and matter,[549] and as existing the human being must indeed participate in the idea but is not himself the idea.[550]

In Greece, just as in philosophy's youth on the whole, the difficulty was to attain the abstract, to abandon existence, which continually yields the particular; now there is the opposite difficulty, to attain existence. Abstraction is easy enough, but one distances oneself more and more from existence, and pure thinking is most distant from existence.

In Greece, to philosophize was an act; therefore the one philosophizing was an existing person. He knew only a little but knew that little thoroughly, because early and late he occupied himself with the same thing. What is it to philosophize nowadays, and just what is it a philosopher is actually informed VII 286
about these days?—for I do not deny that he knows everything.

The philosophical thesis of the identity of thinking and being is just the opposite of what it seems to be; it expresses that thinking has completely abandoned existence, that it has emigrated and found a sixth continent where it is absolutely sufficient unto itself in the absolute identity of thinking and being. Abstractly, in a volatilized metaphysical sense, existing eventually becomes evil; abstractly, in a humorous sense, it becomes a very *langweilig* [boring] affair, a ludicrous delay. Yet there is still a possibility here for the ethical to exercise a restraining influence, since the ethical accentuates existing, and abstraction and humor still have a relation to existing. Pure thinking, however, has recovered from its victory[551] and has nothing, nothing, to do with existence.

If thinking could give actuality in the sense of actuality and not thought-reality [*Tanke-Realitet*] in the sense of possibility, then thinking must also be able to take away existence, to take away from the existing person the only actuality to which he relates himself as actuality, his own (to the actuality of another he relates himself, as has been shown, only as thinking); that is, in the sense of actuality he must be able to think himself away, so that he would actually cease to exist. I would like to know if anyone will accept this, which conversely would betray just as much superstitious belief in pure thinking as do the words of a lunatic (in a novel): that he is going to climb down into Dovrefjeld and blow up the whole world with a single syllogism.[552] —One can be absentminded, or one can become absentminded by perpetual association with pure thinking, but it is not completely successful, or rather it is a complete failure, and with the help of "the at times pitiful professorial figure" one becomes what the Jews feared so much: a proverb.[553]—I can abstract from myself, but my abstracting from myself also explicitly signifies that I exist.

VII 287 God does not think, he creates; God does not exist [*existere*], he is eternal. A human being thinks and exists, and existence [*Existents*] separates thinking and being, holds them apart from each other in succession.[554]

What is abstract thinking? It is thinking where there is no thinker. It ignores everything but thought, and in its own medium only thought is. Existence is not thoughtless, but in existence thought is in an alien medium. What does it mean, then, in the language of abstract thinking to ask about actuality in the sense of existence when abstraction expressly ignores it? —What is concrete thinking? It is thinking where there are a thinker and a specific something (in the sense of particularity) that is being thought, where existence gives the existing thinker thought, time, and space.

If Hegel had published his *Logic* under the title "Pure Thinking,"[555] had published it without the author's name, published it without a date, without a preface, without notes, without didactic self-contradiction, without confusing expla-

nation of what could only explain itself, had published it as a counterpart to the nature sounds on Ceylon[556]—the movements belonging to pure thought—it would have been treated in the Greek way. That is how a Greek would have done it if he had had the idea. The reduplication of the contents in the form is the artistry, and the point is especially to abstain from all expressions of the same thing in an inadequate form. Now the *Logic* with all its notes makes an odd impression, just as if a man were to exhibit a letter fallen from heaven[557] and then even left the blotting paper lying in it, which would all too clearly indicate that the letter from heaven had come into existence on earth. —In such a work to polemicize in notes against this and that person by name, to communicate instructive clues, what does that mean? It betrays that here is a thinker who thinks pure thinking, a thinker who puts in a word "within the movements belonging to thought," and presumably even speaks to another thinker with whom he VII 288
accordingly wants to become involved. But if there is a thinker who thinks pure thinking, then at that very same moment the whole Greek dialectic together with the security police of existence-dialectic seize his person and grab him by the coattails, yet not in the role of adherents, but in order to find out how he goes about relating himself to pure thinking, and at the very same moment the magic vanishes. Just try to add Socrates to this. With the aid of the notes, he soon comes to grips with Hegel. Unaccustomed to allowing himself to be put off by the assurance that everything will become clear at the end, he who did not allow even five minutes of continuous discourse, to say nothing of seventeen volumes of it, will exercise all his powers of restraint—just in order to tease Hegel.[558]

What does it mean to say that being is superior to thinking? If this statement is something to be thought, then in turn thinking is indeed *eo ipso* superior to being. If it can be thought, then the thinking is superior; if it cannot be thought, then no system of existence is possible. It is of no help whatever to be either polite or rough with being, either to let it be something

superior, which nevertheless follows from thinking and is syllogistically attained, or something so inferior that it accompanies thinking as a matter of course. When, for example, it is said: God must have all perfections, or the highest being must have all perfections, to be is also a perfection; ergo the highest being must be, or God must be[559]—the whole movement is deceptive.* That is, if in the first part of this statement God actually is not thought of as being, then the statement cannot come off at all. It will then run somewhat like this: A supreme being who, please note, does not exist, must be in possession of all perfections, among them also that of existing; ergo a supreme being who does not exist does exist. This
VII 289 would be a strange conclusion. The highest being must either not be in the beginning of the discourse in order to come into existence in the conclusion, and in that case it cannot come into existence; or the highest being was, and thus, of course, it cannot come into existence, in which case the conclusion is a fraudulent form of developing a predicate, a fraudulent paraphrase of a presupposition. In the other case, the conclusion must be kept purely hypothetical: if a supreme being is assumed to be, this being must also be assumed to be in possession of all perfections; to be is a perfection, ergo this being must be—that is, if this being is assumed to be. By concluding within a hypothesis, one can surely never conclude from the hypothesis. For example, if this or that person is a hypocrite, he will act like a hypocrite, a hypocrite will do this and that; ergo this or that person has done this and that. It is the same with the conclusion about God. When the conclusion is finished, God's being is just as hypothetical as it was, but inside it there is advanced a conclusion-relation between a supreme being and being as perfection, just as in the other case between being a hypocrite and a particular expression of it.

The confusion is the same as explaining actuality in pure thinking. The section is titled *Actuality*;[561] actuality is ex-

* Hegel, however, does not speak this way; by means of the identity of thinking and being he is elevated above a more childlike manner of philosophizing, something he himself points out, for example, in relation to Descartes.[560]

plained, but it has been forgotten that in pure thinking the whole thing is within the sphere of possibility. If someone has begun a parenthesis, but it has become so long that he himself has forgotten it, it still does not help—as soon as one reads it aloud, it becomes meaningless to have the parenthetical clause change into the principal clause.

When thinking turns toward itself in order to think about itself, there emerges, as we know, a skepticism. How can there be a halt to this skepticism of which the source is that thinking selfishly wants to think itself instead of serving by thinking something? When a horse takes the bit in its teeth and runs away, it would be all right, apart from the damage that might be done in the meantime, for one to say: Just let it run; it will surely become tired. With regard to thinking's self-reflection, this cannot be said, because it can keep on for any length of time and runs in circles. Schelling halted self-reflection and VII
understood intellectual intuition not as a discovery within self- 290
reflection that is arrived at by rushing ahead but as a new point of departure.[562] Hegel regards this as a mistake and speaks *absprechend* [deprecatingly] about intellectual intuition—then came the method.[563] Self-reflection keeps on so long until it cancels itself; thinking presses through victoriously and once again gains reality [*Realitet*]; the identity of thinking and being is won in pure thinking.*

* It is quite certain that at the bottom of all skepticism there is an abstract certainty that is the foothold of doubt and is like the line one draws as the base upon which the figure is sketched. Therefore it is quite certain that nothing is accomplished even by the most rigorous attempt of Greek skepticism to round off the hovering of skepticism by emphasizing that the statement about doubt must not be understood θητικῶς [as a position],[564] but it still does not follow that doubt overcomes itself. The basic certainty that sustains doubt can at no moment hypostatize itself as long as I am doubting, because doubt continually leaves it in order to doubt. If I want to keep on doubting, I shall never in all eternity advance any further, because doubt consists precisely in and by passing off that certainty as something else. If I hold on to the certainty as certainty for one single moment, I must also stop doubting for that moment. But then it is not doubt that cancels itself; it is I who stop doubting. Therefore a mediocre doubter will be most likely to succeed in gaining certainty, and

What does it mean to say that self-reflection keeps on so long until it cancels itself? In order to discover the dubious character of self-reflection, it does not have to keep on long, but on the other hand as long as it keeps on it is entirely the same dubiousness. What does it mean to say "so long until"? This is nothing but bedazzling talk that wants to bedazzle the reader's conception by quantifying, as if it were better to
VII 291 understand that self-reflection cancels itself if it takes a long time before it happens. This quantifying is a counterpart to the astronomers' infinitely small angles, which finally become so small (the angles) that they can be called parallel lines. The story that self-reflection keeps on "so long until" draws attention away from what is dialectically the main issue: how self-reflection is canceled. If someone is said to have kept on telling a lie in jest so long until he himself believed it was truth, then the ethical accent is upon the transition, but the mitigating, the diverting element is this "so long." One almost forgets the decisiveness of the transition because it lasts so long. In narrative and description, in the rhetorical address, the abstract "so long until" evokes a very illusory effect, whether as an optical illusion (for example, the book of Judith, chapter 10, verse 10: "And Judith went out, she and her maid with her, but the men of the city watched her *until* she had gone down the mountain and *until* she passed through the valley and they could no longer see her"; the girl sat on the seashore and followed her beloved with her eyes until she could see him no longer)—or as a fantastical vanishing of time because there is no criterion, nothing to measure with in the abstract "so long until." (Then desire conquered, and he strayed from the path of truth—*until* the bitterness of repentance halted him; great mastery in psychological depiction is required to produce by concretion such a great effect as this abstract "until," which

---

next a doubter who merely joins categories in order to see how they look the best without bothering in the least to carry out any of them. —I cannot stop returning to this point, because it is so decisive. If it is the case that doubt overcomes itself, that by doubting everything one in this very doubt wins truth without a break and an absolutely new point of departure, then not one single Christian category can be maintained, then Christianity is abolished.

evokes the imagination.) But dialectically this fantastical length is utterly meaningless. When a Greek philosopher was asked what religion is, he requested a postponement. When the deadline came, he again requested that it be extended, etc.; he wanted to suggest thereby that the question could not be answered.[565] This was Greek and beautiful and ingenious. If, however, since it had lasted so long, he would have considered that he had even in the remotest manner come closer to the answer, this would indeed have been a misunderstanding, just as when a debtor remains "in debt so long until" it is paid—through its having been so long that it had not been paid. The abstract "so long—until" has something strangely bedazzling VII
about it. 292 If one says: Self-reflection cancels itself, and then seeks to show how, hardly anyone would understand it. But if one says: Self-reflection keeps on so long until it cancels itself—then one perhaps thinks: Well, that is another matter; there is something to that. Then one becomes anxious and fearful about this length; one loses patience and thinks: All right—and then pure thinking begins. In a way, pure thinking may be right in not beginning *bittweise* [beggingly, by begging the presuppositions] as do the older mediocre philosophers, for the reader, fearing the dreadful length of "until," thanks God that it begins.

The skepticism of self-reflection is canceled, then, by the method, and the advance of the method is safeguarded in a double way. First and foremost with the marvelous phrase "so long—until." Whenever a transition must be made, the opposite continues so long until it switches over into its opposite—and then one proceeds further. Good Lord, we are all frail human beings and are very fond of change,[566] as the saying goes. Consequently, if it cannot ever be otherwise, if the opposite keeps on so long until it switches over into its opposite, this keeps on forever, which would be extremely boring—well, let it pass, that is, it is assumed. In this way the method advances—*by necessity*. But if there is an obstinate fellow, an extremely boring person, who dares to raise an objection: "Indeed, it seems as if the method were a human being one has to indulge, for whose sake one has to do something,

so that one does not methodically speculate for the sake of truth but speculates for the sake of the method, which surely must be assumed to be such an extraordinarily great good that one must not be all too scrupulous—if only one has the method and the system"—if there is an obstinate fellow like that, then woe to him. What he represents is the spurious infinity. But the method gets on both with the good and with the evil, and as for the spurious infinity, the method does not understand jest. The obstinate one is pointed out as a dunce, most likely so long—until. Good Lord, we are all weak, mortal human beings, and we all would like to be regarded as sensible by our esteemed contemporaries; so if it cannot be otherwise, then let it pass. Thus the method advances—by necessity. "What does he say—is it not by necessity?" "O you
VII 293 great Chinese god, I am saying nothing else; it is by necessity, I am willing to swear to it. If it cannot be otherwise, then it surely must be by necessity." —The spurious infinity is the hereditary enemy of the method; it is the nisse that accompanies every time there is a move[567] (a transition) and prevents the transition. The spurious infinity is infinitely stubborn; if it is to be overcome, there must be a break, a qualitative leap, and that is the end of the method, of the dexterity of immanence and the necessity of transition. This explains why the method is so strict, and this explains in turn why people are just as afraid of representing the spurious infinity as of being left holding the bag [*være Sorte-Peer*]. [568]If the system otherwise lacks an ethics, it is in return completely moral with the aid of the category of the *spurious* infinity, and so exaggeratedly moral that it uses it even in logic.

If what is thought were actuality, then what is thought out as perfectly as possible, when I as yet have not acted, would be the action. In this way there would be no action whatever, but the intellectual swallows the ethical. That I should now be of the opinion that it is the external that makes action into action is foolish; on the other hand, to want to show how ethical intellectuality is, that it even makes the thought into action, is a sophism that is guilty of a doubleness in the use of the words "to think." If there is to be a distinction at all between thinking and acting, this can be maintained only by assigning possibility, disinterestedness, and objectivity to thinking, and action to subjectivity. But now a *confinium* is readily apparent. For example, when I think that I will do this and that, this thinking is certainly not yet an act and is forevermore qualitatively different from it, but it is a possibility in which the interest of actuality and action is already reflected. Therefore, disinterestedness and objectivity are about to be disturbed, because actuality and responsibility want to have a firm grip on them. (Thus there is a sin in thought.)

The actuality is not the external action but an interiority in which the individual annuls possibility and identifies himself with what is thought in order to exist in it. This is action. Intellectuality seems so rigorous in making the thought itself into action, but this rigorousness is a false alarm, because allowing intellectuality to cancel action at all is a relaxation. Just
as in the analogies cited earlier, it holds true that to be rigorous VII
within a total relaxation is only illusion and essentially only a 294
relaxation. If someone, for example, were to call sin ignorance, and then *within* this definition rigorously interpret specific sins, this is totally illusory, since every definition stated *within* the total definition that sin is ignorance becomes essentially frivolous, because the entire definition is frivolousness.

With regard to evil, the confusion of thinking and acting deceives more easily. But if one looks more closely, it appears that the reason for it is the jealousy of the good[569] for itself, which requires itself of the individual to such a degree that it defines a thought of evil as sin. But let us take the good. To have thought something good that one wants to do, is that to have done it? Not at all, but neither is it the external that determines the outcome, because someone who does not possess a penny can be just as compassionate as the person who gives away a kingdom. When the Levite on the road from Jericho to Jerusalem passed by the unfortunate man who had been assaulted by robbers,[570] it perhaps occurred to him when he was still a little distance from the unfortunate man that it would indeed be beautiful to help a sufferer. He may even have already thought of how rewarding such a good deed is in itself; he perhaps was riding more slowly because he was immersed in thought; but as he came closer and closer, the difficulties became apparent, and he rode past. Now he probably rode fast in order to get away quickly, away from the thought of the riskiness of the road, away from the thought of the possible nearness of the robbers, and away from the thought of how easily the victim could confuse him with the robbers who had left him lying there. Consequently he did not act. But suppose that along the way repentance brought him back; suppose that he quickly turned around, fearing neither robbers nor other difficulties, fearing only to arrive too late. Suppose that he did come too late, inasmuch as the compassionate Samaritan had already had the sufferer brought to the inn—had he, then, not acted? Assuredly, and yet he did not act in the external world.

Let us take a religious action. To have faith in God—does that mean to think about how glorious it must be to have faith, to think about what peace and security faith can give? Not at all. Even to wish, where the interest, the subject's interest, is far more evident, is not to have faith, is not to act. The indi-
VII vidual's relation to the thought-action is still continually only
295 a possibility that he can give up. —It is not denied that with regard to evil there are cases in which the transition is almost undetectable, but these cases must be explained in a special way. This is due to the fact that the individual is so in the power of habit that by frequently having made the transition from thinking to acting he has finally lost the power for it in the bondage of habit, which *at his expense* makes it faster and faster.

Between the thought-action and the actual action, between possibility and actuality, there perhaps is no difference at all in content; the difference in form is always essential. Actuality is interestedness by existing in it.

It is not denied that the actuality of action is so often confused with all sorts of ideas, intentions, preliminaries to resolutions, preludes of mood, etc. that there is very seldom any action at all; on the contrary, it is assumed that this has greatly

contributed to the confusion. But take an action *sensu eminenti* [in the eminent sense]; then everything shows up clearly. The external in Luther's action was his appearing at the Diet of Worms,[571] but from the moment he with all the passionate decision of subjectivity existed in willing, when every relation of possibility to this action had to be regarded by him as temptation—then he had acted.* When Dion boarded ship to overthrow the tyrant Dionysius, he is supposed to have said that even if he died on the way he would nevertheless have done a magnificent deed[572]—that is, he had acted. That the decision in the external is supposed to be superior to the decision in the internal is the despicable talk of weak, cowardly, and sly people about the highest. To assume that the decision in the ex- VII
ternal can decide something eternally so that it can never be 296
done over again, but not the decision in the internal, is contempt for the holy.

To give thinking supremacy over everything else is gnosticism; to make the subjective individual's ethical actuality the only actuality could seem to be acosmism.[573] That it will so appear to a busy thinker who must explain everything, a hasty pate who traverses the whole world, demonstrates only that he has a very poor idea of what the ethical means for the subjective individual. If ethics deprived such a busy thinker of the whole world and let him keep his own self, he would very likely think: "Is this anything? Such a trifling thing is not

* Ordinarily the relation between thought-action and actual action (in the inner sense) is recognizable by this, that whereas any further consideration and deliberation with regard to the former must be regarded as welcome, with regard to the latter it must be regarded as temptation. If it nevertheless appears to be so meaningful that it is respected, this signifies that its path goes through repentance. When I am deliberating, the art is to think every possibility; the moment I have acted (in the inner sense), the transformation is that the task is to defend myself against further deliberation, except insofar as repentance requires something to be *done over again*. The decision in the external is jest, but the more lethargically a person lives, the more the external becomes the only decision he knows. People have no idea of the individual's eternal decision within himself, but they believe that if a decision is drawn up on stamped paper, then it is decided, not before.

worth keeping. Let it go along with all the rest"—then, then it is acosmism. But why does a busy thinker like that talk and think so disrespectfully of himself? Indeed, if the intention were that he should give up the whole world and be satisfied with another person's ethical actuality, well, then he would be in the right to make light of the exchange. But to the individual his own ethical actuality ought to mean, ethically, even more than heaven and earth and everything found therein,[574] more than world history's six thousand years, and more than astrology, veterinary science, together with everything the times demand, which esthetically and intellectually is a prodigious narrow-mindedness. If it is not so, it is worst for the individual himself, because then he has nothing at all, no actuality at all, because to everything else he has at the very most only a relation of possibility.

The transition from possibility to actuality is, as Aristotle rightly teaches, κίνησις, a movement.[575] This cannot be said in the language of abstraction at all or understood therein, because abstraction can give movement neither time nor space, which presuppose it or which it presupposes. There is a halt, a leap. When someone says that this is because I am thinking of something definite and not abstracting, since in that case I would discern that there is no break, then my repeated answer would be: Quite right; abstractly thought, there is no break,
VII but no transition either, because viewed abstractly everything
297 *is*. However, when existence gives movement time and I reproduce this, then the leap appears in just the way a leap can appear: it must come or it has been. Let us take an example from the ethical. It has been said often enough that the good has its reward in itself, and thus it is not only the most proper but also the most sagacious thing to will the good. A sagacious eudaemonist is able to perceive this very well; thinking in the form of possibility, he can come as close to the good as is possible, because in possibility as in abstraction the transition[576] is only an appearance. But when the transition is supposed to become actual, all sagacity expires in scruples. Actual time separates the good and the reward for him so

much, so eternally, that sagacity cannot join them again, and the eudaemonist declines with thanks. To will the good is indeed the most sagacious thing—yet not as understood by sagacity but as understood by the good. The transition is clear enough as a break, indeed, as a suffering. —In the sermon presentation there often appears the illusion that eudaimonistically transforms the transition to becoming a Christian into an appearance, whereby the listener is deceived and the transition prevented.

Subjectivity is truth; subjectivity is actuality.

Note. *Necessity* must be treated by itself. Placing necessity together with the interpretation of world history, as has been done by modern speculative thought, has only caused great confusion, whereby possibility, actuality, and necessity are confused. In *Philosophical Fragments*[577] I have briefly tried to point this out.[578]

§ 3[579]
The Contemporaneity of the Particular Elements of Subjectivity in the Existing Subjective Individual; Contemporaneity as the Opposite of the Speculative Process

Suppose, now, that speculative thought is in the right in mocking a trichotomy such as that a human being consists of
soul, body, and spirit;[580] suppose that the merit of speculative VII
thought is to define the human being as spirit, and within this 298
to construe the elements soul, consciousness, and spirit as stages of development in the same subject* who is developing

* What is this same subject? Certainly not an individual existing person but the abstract definition of pure humankind. Scientific scholarship cannot deal with anything else and is perfectly justified in treating this. But here, too, there is often a playing with words. It is said again and again that thinking becomes concrete. But in what way does it become concrete? Certainly not in the sense in which one speaks of a specific existing something? Consequently, *within* the qualification "abstract," thinking becomes concrete, that is, it continues to be essentially abstract, because concretion means to exist, and to exist corresponds to the particular, which the thinking ignores. It can be entirely proper for a thinker *qua* thinker to think humanity in general, but *qua* existing individual he is forbidden by ethics to forget himself, to forget

before us. It is another question whether a direct transfer of the scientific-scholarly to existence, which can happen all too easily, does not produce great confusion. In the scientific-scholarly, the movement is from the lower to the higher, and to think becomes the highest. In the interpretation of world history, the movement is from the lower to the higher; the stages of imagination and feeling are left behind, and the stage of thinking as the highest is last. Everywhere it is acknowledged as settled that thinking is the highest; scholarship more and more turns away from a primitive impression of existence; there is nothing to live through, nothing to experience, everything is finished, and the task of speculative thought is to rubricate, classify, and methodically order the various categories of thought. One does not love, does not have faith, does not act; but one knows what erotic love is, what faith is, and the question is only about their place in the system. In the same way the domino player also has the pieces lying about, and the game consists in placing them together. For six thousand years now people have loved and the poets have celebrated erotic love; therefore in the nineteenth century people certainly should know what erotic love is, and now the task is to assign it, especially marriage, a place in the system[582]—for the professor himself marries absentmindedly. Politicians have pointed out that ultimately all wars will cease, and everything will be decided in the chambers of the diplomats who sit and tally the military forces etc.—if only in life it does not so turn
VII 299 out that one ceases to live while professors and assistant professors speculatively decide the relation of the separate elements to humanity in general. To me it seems that just as there is something human even in the horrors of the bloodiest wars compared with this diplomatic silence, so in the same way there is something appalling, something bewitched in the extinction by which the actual life becomes a shadow existence.

---

that he is an existing human being. The ethical is so far removed from rejoicing over one more new thinker[581] that it makes him ethically responsible for answering whether it is legitimate to use his existence for this purpose, in the same sense as the ethical—without allowing itself to be blinded by the conspicuous—makes every other person responsible for the use of his life.

From the point of view of science and scholarship it may seem all right that thinking is the highest; likewise from the world-historical point of view it may seem all right that the earlier stages are left behind. But then in our day a generation of individuals is born who have neither imagination nor feeling—is one born to begin with § 14 in the system? Above all, let us not confuse the world-historical development of the human spirit with the particular individuals.

In the animal world, the particular animal is related directly as specimen to species, participates as a matter of course in the development of the species, if one wants to talk about such a thing. When a breed of sheep, for example, is improved, improved sheep are born because the specimen merely expresses the species. But surely it is different when an individual, who is qualified as spirit, relates himself to the generation. Or is it assumed that Christian parents give birth to Christian children as a matter of course?[583] At least Christianity does not assume it; on the contrary, it assumes that sinful children are born of Christian parents just as in paganism. Or will anyone assume that by being born of Christian parents one has come a single step closer to Christianity than the person born of pagan parents if, please note, he also is brought up in Christianity? And yet it is of this confusion that modern speculative thought is, if not directly the cause, nevertheless often enough the occasion, so that the individual is regarded as related to the development of the human spirit as a matter of course (just as the animal specimen is related to the species), as if development of spirit were something one generation could dispose of by a will in favor of another, as if the generation and not individuals were qualified as spirit, which is both a self-contradiction and an ethical abomination. Development of spirit is self-activity; the spiritually developed individual takes his spiritual development along with him in death. If a succeeding individual is to attain it, it must occur through his self-activity; therefore he must skip nothing. Now, of course it is easier and simpler and *wohlfeilere* [cheaper] to bellow about being born in the speculative nineteenth century.

If the individual were related directly to the development of

the human spirit as a matter of course, the result would be that
VII in every generation only defective specimens of human beings
300 would be born. But there surely is a difference between a generation of human beings and a shoal of herring, although it has now become very fashionable to prefer to amuse oneself with the play of colors of the shoal and to disdain individuals, who have no more value than herring. Scientifically-scholarly and world-historically, one can perhaps be indifferent to such an objection, but ethics certainly ought to have a voice in every life-view. But ethics, to repeat, has indeed been shoved out of the system and at most has been replaced with a surrogate that confuses the world-historical and the individual and confuses the bewildering, bellowing demands of the times with the eternal demands of conscience upon the individual. Ethics focuses upon the individual, and ethically understood it is every individual's task to become a whole human being, just as it is the presupposition of ethics that everyone is born in the state of being able to become that. Whether no one achieves it is irrelevant; the main thing is that the requirement is there; and if ever so many cowardly and mediocre and bedazzled individuals join forces and abandon themselves in order to become something *en masse* with the help of the generation, ethics does not haggle.

In a scientific-scholarly way it may indeed be quite proper—and perhaps so masterly that I am far from assuming to be a judge—it may be quite proper to ascend abstractly-dialectically in psychological categories from the psychical-somatic to the psychical, to the pneumatic—but this scientific-scholarly output must nevertheless not play havoc with existence. In existence, the abstract scientific-scholarly definition of being human is something that perhaps is superior to being an individual existing human being, but perhaps it is also inferior; but at least in existence there are only individual human beings. With respect to existence, therefore, it will not do to unite the differences in terms of thinking, inasmuch as the advancing method does not correspond to existing *qua* human being. In existence, the important thing is that all elements are present simultaneously. With respect to existence, thinking is

not at all superior to imagination and feeling but is coordinate. In existence, the supremacy of thinking plays havoc. When, for example, someone says: The expectancy of an eternal happiness *hereafter* is a conception based upon the finite reflection of the understanding, a conception that cannot maintain itself under the scrutiny of thinking—ergo, one may very well talk about it in popular address to simple folk who never VII
outgrow the sphere of the conceptual, but for the thinking 301
person this distinction is canceled—then one must answer: Quite right, under the scrutiny of thinking, of abstract thinking, it cannot maintain itself; but then, in turn, abstract thinking cannot maintain itself against existence. As soon as I must actually exist, the distinction is there, and the existence-consequence of canceling the distinction, as shown above, is suicide.

The absoluteness of the principle of contradiction is said to be an illusion that disappears under the scrutiny of thinking. Correct, but then in turn the abstraction of thinking is a phantom that disappears before the actuality of existence, because the annulment of the principle of contradiction, if it is going to be something and not be a literary whim in the imagination of a fanciful being, means for an existing person that he himself has ceased to exist.

It is said that faith is the immediate;*[584] thinking annuls the immediate. Looked at abstractly, this seems good enough, but I would like to know how an existing person manages to exist after canceling his whole immediacy. Not without reason does Frater Taciturnus complain that everyone writes books in which immediacy is canceled, but no one gives a hint about how one manages to exist.[585]

Scientific scholarship orders the elements of subjectivity within a knowledge about them, and this knowledge is the

* That this is some of the most confusing talk in modern speculative thought has frequently been pointed out by the pseudonymous authors. If one wants to speak of an immediacy that is canceled, this must be an esthetic-ethical immediacy, and faith itself must be the new immediacy that can never be canceled in existence, since it is the highest, and by canceling it one becomes null and *nichts*.

highest, and all knowledge is an annulment of, a removal from existence. In existence this does not hold true. If thinking makes light of imagination, then imagination in turn makes light of thinking, and the same with feeling. The task is not to elevate the one at the expense of the other, but the task is equality, contemporaneity, and the medium in which they are united is *existing*.

By the positing of the scientific-scholarly process rather than existential contemporaneity (as task), havoc is wrought
VII with life. Even with regard to the various ages in life, where
302 the successive appears so clearly, it is a matter of contemporaneity as task. One may wittily say that the world and the human race have become older, but for all that is not everyone born as a baby? And in the individual the point is to ennoble the successive in contemporaneity. To have been young, then to have grown older, and then finally to die is a mediocre existence, for the animal also has that merit. But to unite the elements of life in contemporaneity, that is precisely the task. And just as it is a mediocre existence when the adult cuts away all communication with childhood and is a fragmentary adult, so is it a poor existence when a thinker, who is indeed also an existing person, has given up imagination and feeling, which is just as lunatic as giving up the understanding.

And yet this is what people seem to want. They oust and dismiss poetry as a surmounted element because poetry corresponds most closely to imagination. In a scientific-scholarly process, it may be all right to classify it as a surmounted element, but in existence it holds true that as long as there is a human being who wants to claim a human existence, he must preserve poetry, and all his thinking must not disturb for him the enchantment of poetry but rather enhance it. It is the same with religion. Religion is not something for the childlike soul, in the sense that with the years it should be laid aside; on the other hand, wanting to do that is a childish, superstitious belief in thinking. The true is not superior to the good and the beautiful, but the true and the good and the beautiful[586] belong essentially to every human existence and are united for an existing person not in thinking them but in existing.

But just as in one era people wear round hats, in another three-cornered hats, in the same way a fashion in our generation would have a person forget the ethical requirement. I am well aware that every human being is somewhat one-sided, and I do not consider it a defect; but on the other hand it is a defect when a fashionable taste would make a one-sidedness into the whole. *Non omnes omnia possumus* [We cannot all do everything][587] holds true everywhere in life, but the task should not be forgotten on that account, and one-sidedness should on the one hand not be regarded without sadness and on the other hand should result from a strong resolution that would prefer to be something thoroughly than to dabble in everything. Every individuality of distinction always has some one-sidedness, and the one-sidedness itself can be an indirect declaration of his actual greatness, but it is not the greatness itself. VII 303 We human beings are so far from actualizing the ideal that second place, the energetic one-sidedness, is more or less the highest attained, but it still must never be forgotten that it is second place. Now, one could say: But in that case this generation, which so one-sidedly wants to be intellectual and scholarly, is indeed praiseworthy. To that I would answer: Its misfortune is not that it is one-sided but that it is abstractly many-sided. The one-sided person clearly and definitely rejects what he does not want to have, but the abstract many-sided person wants to have everything by means of the one-sidedness of thinking. A one-sided believer, for example, wants to have nothing to do with thinking; a one-sided person of action wants to have nothing to do with scientific scholarship. But the one-sidedness of thinking produces an appearance of having everything; a one-sided person of this kind has faith, has passion as surmounted elements, so he says—and nothing is easier to say.

§ 4[588]

The Subjective Thinker; His Task; His Form, That Is, His Style

If the venture in pure thinking is decisive for whether a man is to be called a thinker or not, then the subjective thinker is *eo ipso* eliminated. But inasmuch as he is eliminated, all the existence-issues also disappear, and the sad result of that sounds as a sober "Take note" in modern speculative thought's jubilation over the system.

There is an old proverb: *oratio, tentatio, meditatio faciunt theologum* [prayer, trial, meditation make a theologian].[589] Similarly, for a subjective thinker, imagination, feeling, and dialectics in impassioned existence-inwardness are required. But first and last, passion, because for an existing person it is impossible to think about existence without becoming passionate, inasmuch as existing is a prodigious contradiction from which the subjective thinker is not to abstract, for then it is easy, but in which he is to remain. In a world-historical dialectic, individuals fade away into humankind; in a dialectic such as that, it is impossible to discover you and me, an individual existing human being, even if new magnifying glasses for the concrete are invented.

VII 304 The subjective thinker is a dialectician oriented to the existential; he has the intellectual passion to hold firm the qualitative disjunction. But, on the other hand, if the qualitative disjunction is used flatly and simply, if it is applied altogether abstractly to the individual human being, then one can run the ludicrous risk of saying something infinitely decisive, and of being right in what one says, and still not say the least thing. Therefore, in the psychological sense it is really remarkable to see the absolute disjunction deceitfully used simply for evasion. When the death penalty is placed on every crime, the result is that no crimes at all are punished. It is the same with the absolute disjunction when applied flatly and simply; it is just like a silent letter—it cannot be pronounced or, if it can be pronounced, it says nothing. The subjective thinker, therefore, has with intellectual passion the absolute disjunction as belonging to existence, but he has it as the final decision that prevents everything from ending in a quantifying. Thus he has it readily available, but not in such a way that by abstractly recurring to it he just frustrates existence. The subjective thinker, therefore, has also esthetic passion and ethical passion, whereby concretion is gained. All existence-issues are passionate, because existence, if one becomes conscious of it, involves passion. To think about them so as to leave out passion is not to think about them at all, is to forget the point that one indeed is oneself an existing person. Yet the subjective thinker is not a poet even if he is also a poet, not an ethicist even if he is also an ethicist, but is also a dialectician and is himself essentially existing, whereas the poet's existence is inessential in relation to the poem, and likewise the ethicist's in relation to the teaching, and the dialectician's in relation to the thought. The subjective thinker is not a scientist-scholar; he is an artist. To exist is an art. The subjective thinker is esthetic enough for his life to have esthetic content, ethical enough to regulate it, dialectical enough in thinking to master it.

The subjective thinker's task is to *understand himself in existence*. True enough, abstract thinking does indeed speak about contradiction and about the immanental forward thrust of contradiction,[590] although by disregarding existence and existing it cancels difficulty and contradiction. But the subjective thinker is an existing person, and yet he is a thinking person. He does not abstract from existence and from the contradiction, but he is in them, and yet he is supposed to think. In all VII
his thinking, then, he has to include the thought that he himself is an existing person. 305
But then in turn he also will always have enough to think about. One is soon finished with humanity in general and also with world history, for the hungry monster—the world-historical process—swallows even such enormous portions as China and Persia etc. as if they were nothing. One is soon finished with faith viewed abstractly, but the subjective thinker, who as he thinks is also present to himself in existence, will find it inexhaustible when his faith is to be declined in the manifold *casibus* [cases] of life. It is not waggery either, because existence is the most difficult for a thinker when he must remain in it, inasmuch as the *moment* is commensurate with the highest decisions and yet in turn is a little vanishing minute in the possible seventy years. Poul Møller has correctly pointed out that a court fool uses more wit in one year than many a witty author in his whole life,[591]

and why is that if it is not because the former is an existing person who every moment of the day must have wittiness at his disposal, whereas the other is witty only momentarily.

If one is unwilling to believe that to understand oneself, thinking, in existence involves difficulties, then I am more than willing to venture a test. Let one of our systematicians take it upon himself to explain to me just one of the simplest existence-issues. I am very willing to admit that in the systematic bookkeeping I am not worthy to be counted even as zero if I am to be compared with the likes of them.[592] I am willing to admit that the tasks of systematic thinking are much greater and that such thinkers stand far above a subjective thinker; but if this is truly the case, then they must also easily be able to explain what is simpler.

Instead of having the task of understanding the concrete abstractly, as abstract thinking has, the subjective thinker has the opposite task of understanding the abstract concretely. Abstract thinking turns from concrete human beings to humankind in general; the subjective thinker understands the abstract concept to be the concrete human being, to be this individual existing human being.

To understand oneself in existence was *the Greek principle*, and however little substance a Greek philosopher's teaching
VII 306 sometimes had, the philosopher had one advantage: he was never comic. I am well aware that if anyone nowadays were to live as a Greek philosopher, that is, would existentially express what he would have to call his life-view, be existentially absorbed in it, he would be regarded as lunatic. Be that as it may. But to be ingenious and more ingenious and extremely ingenious, and so ingenious that it never occurs to the most honored philosopher, who is nevertheless speculating upon existence-issues (for example, Christianity), to whom in all the world this could pertain, least of all that it pertains to himself—this I find to be ludicrous.

All skepticism is a kind of idealism. When the skeptic Zeno, for example, made a study of skepticism by trying, as existing, to remain unaffected by everything he encountered, so that, put to shame when he once went out of the way of a mad dog, he confessed that even a skeptical philosopher is still at times a human being,[593] I find nothing ludicrous in this. There is no contradiction here, and the comic always consists in a contradiction. But if one considers the miserable, idealistic lectern witticisms, the jesting and the coquetry involved in being an idealist at the lectern, so that one was not even an actual idealist but merely played the very popular game of being an idealist, if one recollects the lectern-phrase "to doubt everything"—at the lectern—then, well, then it is impossible not to write a satire[594] if one simply relates the truth. By trying, as existing, to be an idealist, within a half year one would have come to know things altogether different from what one would by playing hide-and-seek at the lectern. To be an idealist in imagination is not at all difficult, but to have to *exist* as an idealist is an extremely rigorous life-task, because existing is precisely the objection to it. [595]To express, as existing, what one has understood about oneself, and in this way to understand oneself, is not at all comic, but to understand everything but not oneself is exceedingly comic.

In a certain sense, the subjective thinker speaks just as abstractly as the abstract thinker, because the latter speaks about humanity in general, subjectivity in general, the other about the one human being (*unum noris, omnes* [if you know one, you know all][596]). But this one human being is an existing human being, and the difficulty is not left out.

To understand oneself in existence is also *the Christian principle*, except that this *self* has received much richer and much more profound qualifications that are even more difficult to VII 307
understand together with existing. The believer is a subjective thinker, and the difference, as shown above, is only between the simple person and the simple wise person. Here again this *oneself* is not humanity in general, subjectivity in general, and other such things, whereby everything becomes easy inasmuch as the difficulty is removed and the whole matter is shifted over into the *Schattenspiel* [shadow play] of abstraction. The difficulty is greater than for the Greek, because even greater contrasts are placed together, because existence is accentuated paradoxically as sin, and eternity paradoxically as

the god [*Guden*] in time. The difficulty is to exist in them, not abstractly to think oneself out of them and abstractly to think about, for example, an eternal divine becoming[597] and other such things that appear when one removes the difficulty. Therefore, the existence of the believer is even more passionate than that of the Greek philosopher (who to a high degree needed passion even in connection with his ataraxia), because existence yields passion, but existence accentuated paradoxically yields the maximum of passion.

To abstract from existence is to remove the difficulty, but to remain in existence in such a way that one understands one thing at one moment, something else the next, is not to understand oneself. But to understand extreme opposites together and, existing, to understand oneself in them is very difficult. Just pay attention to yourself and to what people say, and you will see how seldom it succeeds.

One person is good, another is sagacious, or the same person acts as good at one time, as sagacious at another, but simultaneously to see in the same thing what is most sagacious and to see it only in order to will the good is certainly difficult. One person will laugh, another will weep, or the same person does it at different times, but simultaneously to see the comic and tragic in the same thing is difficult. To be brokenhearted over one's sin, and then in turn to be a jaunty fellow, is not difficult, but simultaneously to be brokenhearted and nonchalant is difficult. To think one thing and to have forgotten everything else is not difficult, but to think one thing and the very same moment to have the opposite within you and to unite them in existence, that is difficult. At the age of seventy to have gone through all possible moods and left one's life as a sample book that one can look through at will is not so difficult either, but to have the one mood fully and richly and
VII then to have the opposite, so that as one gives the one mood
308 words and pathos one cunningly slips in the opposite mood—
that is difficult. And so on.

Despite his effort, the subjective thinker is rewarded with only a slender yield. The more the generation-idea has taken over even in the common view, the more terrible is the tran-

sition to becoming an individual existing human being instead of being a part of the race and saying "we," "our age," "the nineteenth century." That this is extremely little is not denied; therefore it takes a great deal of resignation not to disdain it. Indeed, what is an individual existing human being? Our age knows all too well how little it is, but therein lies the specific immorality of the age. Every age has its own; the immorality of our age is perhaps not lust and pleasure and sensuality, but rather a pantheistic, debauched contempt for individual human beings. In the midst of all the jubilation over our age and the nineteenth century there sounds a secret contempt for being a human being—in the midst of the importance of the generation there is a despair over being a human being. Everything, everything must be together; people want to delude themselves world-historically in the totality; no one wants to be an individual existing human being. This may account for the many attempts to hold fast to Hegel even by people who have seen the dubiousness of his philosophy. People fear that by becoming an individual existing human being one will vanish without a trace so that not even the daily newspapers, still less the critical journals and even less the world-historical speculative thinkers, will be able to catch sight of one. People fear that by becoming an individual existing human being a person will have to live more forgotten and abandoned than a country dweller, and if an individual lets go of Hegel there will not even be the possibility of having a letter addressed to himself. And it is undeniable that if a person does not have ethical and religious enthusiasm he will despair over being
598 an individual human being—otherwise not.

When Napoleon was advancing in Africa, he reminded his soldiers that from the peaks of the pyramids the recollection of forty centuries was looking down upon them.[599] Just to read about it makes one shudder. No wonder, then, that in the moment of conjuration this must have transformed even the most cowardly soldier into a hero! But if we assume that the world has stood for six thousand years and that God has certainly existed just as long as the world, then the recollection of six thousand years looking down from heaven on the indi-

vidual existing human being must be equally inspiring! But in the midst of the courage of the generation it is easy to discover
VII 309 the individual's discouragement and cowardice. Just as in the desert individuals must travel in large caravans out of fear of robbers and wild animals, so individuals today have a horror of existence because it is godforsaken; they dare to live only in great herds and cling together *en masse* in order to be at least something.

Every human being must be assumed to possess essentially what belongs essentially to being a human being. The subjective thinker's task is to transform himself into an instrument that clearly and definitely expresses in existence the essentially human. To depend upon differences in this regard is a misunderstanding, because being a little smarter and the like amounts to nothing. That our age has taken refuge in the generation and has abandoned individuals has its basis quite correctly in an esthetic despair that has not reached the ethical. It has been discerned that to be ever so distinguished an individual human being makes no difference, because no difference makes any difference. Consequently a new difference has been selected: to be born in the nineteenth century. So everyone as quickly as possible attempts to define his little fragment of existence in relation to the generation and consoles himself. But it is of no use and is only a loftier and more glittering delusion. And just as in ancient times and ordinarily in every generation there have been fools who in their conceited imaginations have confused themselves with some great and distinguished man, have wanted to be this one or that, so the distinctiveness of our time is that the fools are not satisfied with confusing themselves with a great man but confuse themselves with the age, the century, the generation, humankind. —To will to be an individual human being (which one unquestionably is) with the help of and by virtue of one's difference is flabbiness; but to will to be an individual existing human being (which one unquestionably is) in the same sense as everyone else is capable of being—that is the ethical victory over life and over every mirage, the victory that is perhaps the most difficult of all in the theocentric nineteenth century.[600]

The subjective *thinker's form*, the form of his communication, is his *style*. His form must be just as manifold as are the opposites that he holds together. The systematic *eins, zwei, drei*[601] is an abstract form that also must inevitably run into trouble whenever it is to be applied to the concrete. To the same degree as the subjective thinker is concrete, to the same degree his form must also be concretely dialectical. But just as he himself is not a poet, not an ethicist, not a dialectician, so also his form is none of theirs directly. His form must first and last be related to existence, and in this regard he must have at
his disposal the poetic, the ethical, the dialectical, the reli- VII
gious. Compared with that of a poet, his form will be abbre- 310
viated; compared with that of an abstract dialectician, his form will be broad. That is, viewed abstractly, concretion in the existential is breadth. For example, relative to abstract thinking the humorous is breadth, but relative to concrete existence-communication it is by no means breadth, unless it is broad in itself. Relative to his thought, an abstract thinker's person is a matter of indifference, but existentially a thinker must be presented essentially as a thinking person, but in such a way that as he expresses his thought he also describes himself. Relative to abstract thinking, jest is breadth, but relative to concrete existence-communication it is not breadth if the jest itself is not broad. But because the subjective thinker is himself essentially an existing person in existence and does not have the medium of imagination for the illusion of esthetic production, he does not have the poetic repose to create in the medium of imagination and esthetically to accomplish something disinterestedly. Relative to the subjective thinker's existence-communication, poetic repose is breadth. Subordinate characters, setting, etc., which belong to the well-balanced character of the esthetic production, are in themselves breadth; the subjective thinker has only one setting—existence—and has nothing to do with localities and such things. The setting is not in the fairyland of the imagination, where poetry produces consummation, nor is the setting laid in England, and historical accuracy is not a concern. The setting is inwardness in existing as a human being; the concretion is the

relation of the existence-categories to one another. Historical accuracy and historical actuality are breadth.

But existence-actuality cannot be communicated, and the subjective thinker has his own actuality in his own ethical existence. If actuality is to be understood by a third party, it must be understood as possibility, and a communicator who is conscious of this will therefore see to it, precisely in order to be oriented to existence, that his existence-communication is in the form of possibility. A production in the form of possibility places existing in it as close to the recipient as it is possible between one human being and another. Let me elucidate this once again. One would think that, by telling a reader that this person and that person *actually* have done this and that (something great and remarkable), one would place the reader closer to wanting to do the same, to wanting to exist in the same, than by merely presenting it as possible. Apart from what was pointed out in its proper place, that the reader can understand the communication only by dissolving the *esse* of actuality into
VII *posse*, since otherwise he only *imagines* that he understands,
311 apart from this, the fact that this person and that person actually have done this and that can just as well have a delaying as a motivating effect. The reader merely transforms the person who is being discussed (aided by his being an *actual* person) into the rare exception; he admires him and says: But I am too insignificant to do anything like that.

Now, admiration can be very legitimate with regard to differences, but it is a total misunderstanding with regard to the universal. That one person can swim the channel and a second person knows twenty-four languages and a third person walks on his hands etc.—one can admire that *si placet* [if you please]. But if the person presented is supposed to be great with regard to the universal because of his virtue, his faith, his nobility, his faithfulness, his perseverance, etc., then admiration is a deceptive relation or can easily become that. What is great with regard to the universal must therefore not be presented as an object for admiration, but as a *requirement*. In the form of possibility, the presentation becomes a requirement. Instead of presenting the good in the form of actuality, as is ordinarily done, that this person and that person have actually lived and have actually done this, and thus transforming the reader into an observer, an admirer, an appraiser, it should be presented in the form of possibility. Then whether or not the reader wants to exist in it is placed as close as possible to him. Possibility operates with the ideal human being (not with regard to difference but with regard to the universal), who is related to every human being as requirement. To the same degree as one insists that it was this specific person, the exception is made easier for others.

One does not exactly need to be something of a psychologist to know that there is a deceptiveness that wants to be excluded, by the very means of admiration, from the ethical impression. The ethical and religious prototype is to turn the observer's gaze inward into himself and thrust him away by placing between the observer and the prototype the possibility common to them. Instead of this, however, the presentation in the form of actuality draws the eyes of a crowd esthetically upon itself, and whether it is "actually now" etc. is discussed and examined and turned and turned over, and that it is "actually now" etc. is admired and blathered about. To take an example, that Job believed should be presented in such a way that for me it comes to mean whether I, too, will have faith, but by no means should it mean that I am at a comedy or am a member of an esteemed public that is to examine whether it is "actually now" and applaud that it is "actually now" etc. It is a low-comedy concern that a touchy congregation and its individual members sometimes have for the appointed cler- VII 312
gyman—whether he "actually now"—and a low-comedy joy and admiration over having a clergyman about whom it is certain that he actually etc. Never in all eternity is it true that someone has been assisted in doing the good by someone else's *actually* having done it, because if he himself actually did come to do it, it would be by understanding the other's actuality as possibility. When Themistocles became sleepless over the idea of Miltiades' triumphs,[602] it was his understanding of actuality as possibility that made him sleepless. If he had busied himself about whether Miltiades "actually now" etc. and

had been satisfied that Miltiades actually had done it, he would hardly have become sleepless but would indeed have become a sleepy admirer, or *höchstens* [at most] a clanging[603] admirer, but not Miltiades the Second. Ethically understood, there is nothing on which one sleeps so soundly as on admiration over an actuality. And, ethically understood, if anything is able to stir up a person, it is possibility—when it ideally requires itself of a human being.

Chapter IV[604]

The Issue in *Fragments*: How Can an Eternal Happiness Be Built on Historical Knowledge?

DIVISION 1[605]

For Orientation in the Plan of *Fragments*

§ 1

That the Point of Departure Was Taken in Paganism, and Why

The reader of the fragment of philosophy in *Fragments* will recollect that the pamphlet was not didactic but was imaginatively constructing. It took its point of departure in paganism
in order by imaginatively constructing to discover an under- VII
standing of existence that truly could be said to go beyond 313
paganism. Modern speculative thought seems almost to have performed the feat of going *beyond* Christianity *on the other side* or of having gone so far in understanding Christianity that it has returned almost to paganism. That someone prefers paganism to Christianity is not at all confusing, but to make paganism out to be the highest within Christianity is an injustice both to Christianity, which becomes something different from what it is, and to paganism, which becomes nothing whatever, although it was indeed something. Speculative thought, which has completely understood Christianity and declares itself to be the highest development within Christianity, has remarkably enough made the discovery that there is no "beyond,"[606] that "hereafter" and "beyond" and the like are the dialectical narrow-mindedness of a finite understanding. The beyond has become a pleasantry, a claim so problematical that not only does no one honor it, but no one makes it, so

that one is merely amused to remember that there was a time when this idea transformed all existence.

It is immediately apparent what response can be expected from this angle to the issue: The issue itself is dialectical narrow-mindedness, because in the heavenly *sub specie aeterni* of pure thinking the distinction is canceled. But note, the issue is not, after all, a logical issue—indeed, what does logical thinking have in common with the most pathos-filled issue of all (the question of an eternal happiness)? And the issue is an existence-issue, but to exist does not mean to be *sub specie aeterni*. Here again one will perhaps perceive the correctness of using precautionary measures before becoming involved with such speculative thought. The first is to separate speculation and the speculative philosopher, and then, just as with enchantment, witchcraft, and demon possession, to use a powerful incantation in order to get the bewitched speculative thinker transformed or changed into his actual form, into an individual *existing* human being.

The pamphlet, in order to obtain a breathing space, did not say that what was imaginatively constructed is Christianity, lest it immediately be swept into historical, historical-dogmatic, introductory, and ecclesiastical issues about what actually is Christianity and what is not. No human being has ever been in such hot water as Christianity has been of late. At
VII 314 times Christianity is explained speculatively and the result is paganism; at times it is not even known for sure what Christianity is. We merely have to read through a catalog of new books to see the times we are living in. In daily life, when we hear shrimp hawked on the street, we almost think that it is midsummer, when wreaths of woodruff are hawked that it is spring, when mussels are hawked that it is winter. But when, as happened last winter, one hears shrimp, wreaths of woodruff, and mussels hawked on the same day, one is tempted to assume that life has become confused and that the world will not last until Easter.[607] But one receives an even more confusing impression if one pays attention for a moment to what is being offered for sale in a catalog of new books,[608] by authors as well as by publishers, who to a high degree have also gained

a voice in literature. *Summa summarum*, we are living in very turbulent times—at least, very confused.

In order to gain a day of rest, something that Christian terminology, calm, profound, and unfathomable, but in life overstrained and soon short of breath and meaningless, may need very much, and in order to avoid as much as possible getting into a scrape, I chose to suppress the name "Christianity," to abstain from the expressions that again and again are confused and tossed about in discussions. The whole Christian terminology has been confiscated by speculative thought, since speculative thought, of course, is Christianity; even the newspapers use the most sublime dogmatic expressions as brilliant ingredients, and while politicians anxiously expect a bankruptcy of nations, a far greater bankruptcy is perhaps impending in the world of the mind, because the concepts are gradually being canceled and the words are coming to mean everything, and therefore dispute sometimes becomes just as ludicrous as agreement. To dispute about loose words and to be in agreement on loose words are indeed always ludicrous, but when even the firmest words have become loose—what then? Just as an old man who has lost his teeth now munches with the help of the stumps, so the modern Christian language about Christianity has lost the power of the energetic terminology to bite—and the whole thing is toothless "maundering."

To me it is clear enough that the confusion in Christianity is due to its having been set back one whole stage in life. That we became Christians as children has promptly given rise to
the assumption that one is what has been anticipated κατὰ δύ- VII
ναμιν [potentially]. Infant Baptism can very well be defensi- 315
ble and commendable both as the Church's well-intentioned interest, a safeguard against fanatics, and as the beautiful, providential care of pious parents—the responsibility lies on the individual himself at a later stage.[609] But it is and continues to be ludicrous to see people behave *à la* Christians on solemn occasions but who are Christians simply and solely by virtue of a baptismal certificate, because the most ludicrous thing Christianity can ever become is to become what is called cus-

tom and habit in the banal sense. To become persecuted, hated, taunted, mocked, or to become blessed, praised—that is appropriate for the greatest of all powers, but to become a tame custom, *bon ton* [good style], and the like is its absolute opposite.

Let us try to picture it. It is appropriate for a king to be loved by his people, to be honored in his majesty, or, if things go badly, well, then let him be toppled from the throne in a revolt, let him fall in battle, let him languish in a prison far, far removed from everything that is reminiscent of him. But a king changed into a meddlesome part-time waiter who is extremely satisfied in his position—that is a more shocking change than murdering him.

The opposite can be ludicrous, for example, that Christians at funerals sometimes resort to pagan expressions about Elysium and the like. But it is also ludicrous that a man for whom Christianity has meant nothing at all, not even so much that he cared to give it up, dies, and then at the graveside the pastor as a matter of course ushers him into the eternal happiness as it is understood in Christian [610]terminology. Please do not remind me, however, that there must always be a distinction between the visible and the invisible Church and that no one may presume to judge hearts. Far from it, oh, far from it. But when one at a more mature age became a Christian and was baptized, then there could at least be the possibility of a kind of assurance that Christianity had some meaning for the baptized. So let it be left to God to judge hearts! But when one is baptized at the age of fourteen days, when it must be considered a convenience to continue to be a Christian *de nomine* [nominally], when it would become troublesome and inconvenient to renounce Christianity, when public opinion, to repeat, would be something like this: It is rather insipid of him to make such a commotion about it—well, then one cannot
VII 316 deny that to belong to the visible Church has become very doubtful testimony that one actually is a Christian.

The visible Church is expanding in such a way that finally the relation is reversed, and just as courage and energy of conviction were at one time required to become a Christian, so nowadays, even though the formula is not to be recommended, courage and energy will be required to give up being Christian—whereas it requires only thoughtlessness to be that now. Nevertheless it may be good to defend infant Baptism; therefore no new custom needs to be introduced. But since everything is changed, the clergy themselves must perceive that if it was once their task, when only a few were Christians, to win people for Christianity, then the task now must be to win them if possible by scaring them away—since the misfortune, of course, is that they are Christians of sorts.

When Christianity entered into the world, people were not Christians, and the difficulty was to become a Christian; nowadays the difficulty in becoming a Christian is that one must self-actively transform an initial being-Christian into a possibility in order to become Christian in truth. The difficulty is much greater because this must and should occur quietly within the individual without any decisive external action, so that it does not become an Anabaptist heresy or the like. But everyone knows that, even in the external world, to jump from the spot where one is standing and to come down again on the same spot is the most difficult of all jumps, and the jump becomes easier if there is a space between the spot where the jumper is standing and the spot where the jump is to be made. Similarly, the most difficult decision is the one in which the person deciding is not distanced from the decision (as is the non-Christian who is going to decide whether he wants to be a Christian), but the decision seems to have been made already. In this case, the difficulty of the decision is twofold: first, that the initial decision is a semblance, a possibility, and then the decision itself. If I am not a Christian, and the decision is to become a Christian, then Christianity helps me to become aware of the decision, and the distance between us helps just as the running start helps the jumper. But if the decision seems to have been made already, if I am already a Christian (that is, am baptized, which is still only a possibility), then there is nothing to help me become properly aware of the decision; but on the other hand there is something (which is the increased difficulty) that hinders me in becoming

VII 317 aware of it—namely, the semblance of a decision. In short: *it is easier to become a Christian if I am not a Christian than to become a Christian if I am one, and this decision is reserved for the person who has been baptized as an infant.*[611]

What is Baptism without appropriation? It is the possibility that the baptized child can become a Christian, neither more nor less. The parallel would be: just as one must be born, must have come into existence, in order to become a human being, inasmuch as an infant is not yet that, so one must be baptized in order to become a Christian. For the adult who was not baptized as an infant, it holds true that he becomes a Christian through Baptism because in Baptism he can have faith's appropriation. Take appropriation away from the essentially Christian, and what is Luther's merit then? But open his books. Note the strong pulse-beat of appropriation in every line; note it in the vibrant forward thrust of his whole style, which continually seems to have behind it that thunderstorm of terror that killed Alexius and created Luther.[612] Did not the papacy have objectivity and objective definitions and the objective, more of the objective, the objective in superabundance? What did it lack? Appropriation, inwardness. "*Aber unsere spitzfindigen Sophisten sagen in diesen Sacramenten nichts von dem Glauben, sondern plappern nur fleiszig von den wirklichen Kräften der Sacramente (the objective), denn sie lernen immerdar, und kommen doch nimmer zu der Erkentnisz der Wahrheit* [But in treating the sacraments our quibbling sophists say nothing at all of this faith, but only babble with all their might about the virtues of the sacraments themselves . . ., because they are always learning, and yet never arrive at a knowledge of the truth]" (*Von der babylonischen Gefangenschaft*, Gerlach's little edition,[613] IV, p. 195). But if objectivity were the truth, they would indeed have to arrive at the truth along that road.

Let it be ten times true, then, that Christianity does not consist in differences; let it be the most blessed comfort of earthly life that the sacred humaneness of Christianity is that it can be appropriated by everyone—but must and should this be understood to mean that everyone is a Christian as a matter of

course by being baptized when he was a fortnight old?*[614] To
be a Christian is not a matter of comfort. The simple as well VII
as the wise must be so obliging as to exist in it—therefore, to 318
be a Christian becomes something different from having a baptismal certificate lying in the drawer and producing it when one is to be a student or wants to have a wedding, something different from going through one's whole life with a baptismal certificate in a vest pocket. But being a Christian has gradually become something that one is as a matter of course, and as far as responsibility is concerned, it is something that pertains to one's parents rather than to oneself: that they at least have not neglected to have one baptized.

This accounts for a strange phenomenon, which, however, may not be rare in Christendom, that a man, as far as he himself was concerned, has believed that surely his parents had seen to it that he was baptized and with that has let the matter rest. Then when he himself becomes a father, he experiences quite properly the awakening of a concern to have his child baptized. In this way the concern to become Christian has passed from the individual himself to the guardian. In his capacity as guardian, the father is concerned that the child be baptized, perhaps also in view of all the inconveniences with the police and the troubles the child will become exposed to if it is not baptized.[616]

Eternity in the next world and the solemn earnestness of the judgment (in which, please note, it will be decided whether I was a Christian, not whether I in the capacity of guardian saw to it that my child was baptized) are changed into a street setting or a passport office setting, where the dead come running with their certificates—from the parish clerk.

Let it be ten times true that Baptism is a divine passport for eternity, but if light-mindedness and worldliness want to use

* In *Fragments*, I expressed the dubiousness by saying that an attempt has been made to naturalize Christianity,[615] so that in the end to be a Christian and
to be a human being are identical, and one is born a Christian just as one is VII
born a human being, or at least birth and rebirth are moved together in the 318
space of a fortnight.

it as a permit, is it then still a passport? Baptism is certainly not the piece of paper the parish clerk issues—and sometimes fills out erroneously. Baptism is certainly not merely the external fact that one was baptized at eleven o'clock on September 7. That time, that existence in time, becomes decisive for an eternal happiness is on the whole so paradoxical that paganism cannot think it, but to have the whole thing decided at the age of two weeks on September 7 in the course of five minutes still seems to be almost a little too much of a paradox. All that is lacking is that one would also be married in the cradle to someone, be registered in some occupation, etc. Then at the young age of two weeks one would have decided everything
VII 319 for one's whole life—unless the later decision were that one would do it over again, which one surely would find worth the trouble with regard to the projected marriage, but perhaps not with regard to Christianity. At one time in the world it was the case that when everything went to pieces for a person, there still remained the hope of becoming a Christian; now one is that, and is tempted in very many ways to forget—to become one.

Under such circumstances in Christendom (the dubiousness of speculative thought on the one hand and that one is Christian as a matter of course on the other), it becomes more and more difficult to find a point of departure if one wants to know what Christianity is. In other words, speculative thought makes paganism the outcome of Christianity, and to be Christian as a matter of course by being baptized changes Christendom into a baptized paganism. That is why I resorted to paganism and to Greece as representative of intellectuality and to its greatest hero, Socrates. After having made sure of paganism, I tried to find in it the most decisive heterogeneity possible. Whether what was imaginatively constructed was therefore Christianity is another question, but this much was gained by it, however, that if modern Christian speculative thought has categories essentially in common with paganism, then modern speculative thought cannot be Christianity.

§ 2
The Importance of a Preliminary Agreement about What Christianity Is Before There Can Be Any Question of a Mediation of Christianity and Speculative Thought; the Absence of an Agreement Favors Mediation, Although Its Absence Renders Mediation Illusory; the Supervention of an Agreement Prevents Mediation[617]

That an eternal happiness is decided in time by the relation to something historical was the substance of what was imaginatively constructed and what I now call the essentially Christian. Surely no one will deny that the teaching of Christianity in the New Testament is that the question of the individual's eternal happiness is decided in time and is decided by the relation to Christianity as something historical. In order not to cause unrest by prompting any thought about an eternal unhappiness, I want to point out that I am speaking only of the positive, that the believer becomes sure of his eternal happiness in time by his relation to something historical. In order VII
not to cause confusion, I do not wish to call attention to other 320
Christian qualifications; they all inhere in this one qualification and can be consistently derived from it, just as this qualification forms the sharpest contrast to paganism. I only repeat once again: whether Christianity is in the right, I do not decide. In that pamphlet, I have already said what I continually confess, that my fragment of merit, if there is to be any mention of that, is to state the issue.[618]

However, if I just name Christianity and the New Testament, an endless deliberation will very easily begin. Nothing will be easier for a speculative thinker than to find some Bible verse that he can appeal to in his *faveur* [favor]. Speculative thought has not even made clear in advance in what sense it will use the New Testament. Sometimes it is summarily stated that the New Testament is in the sphere of the conceptual, from which it seems to follow that one cannot argue from it; sometimes there is great boasting about having the authority of the Bible on its side when speculative thought finds a Bible verse it can appeal to.

A preliminary agreement about which is which, about what Christianity is before one explains it, lest instead of explaining Christianity one hits upon something oneself and explains it as Christianity—this preliminary agreement is of utmost and decisive importance.[619] This meeting of both parties before the conciliation board[620] (lest mediation itself become one party and in addition the board before whom the meeting is held) seems to be of no concern to speculative thought, which more likely wants only to have its benefit from Christianity. To take a minor example, just as there surely have been some who simply have not cared very much about understanding Hegel but have certainly cared about the benefit one has by *even going beyond* Hegel, so also it is tempting enough to go beyond in connection with something as great and meaningful as Christianity. Then one must include Christianity, not just for the sake of Christianity, but in order to be able to make a really good show of going beyond. —On the other hand, it is important that deliberation about what Christianity is does not become learned deliberation, because at that very moment, as shown in the first part of this book, we enter into an approximation that cannot be finished. Mediation between Christianity and speculation will not be possible for another reason, because deliberation cannot be finished.

The question about what Christianity is must therefore be raised, but it must not be done in a learned or partisan manner
VII 321 on the presupposition that Christianity is a philosophical theory, for in that case speculative thought is more than a party or is simultaneously party and judge. The question must therefore be raised in terms of existence, and it must be able to be answered and to be answered briefly. That is, while it may be all right for a learned theologian to spend his whole life learnedly investigating the doctrine of Scripture and the Church, it would indeed be a ludicrous contradiction if an existing person asked what Christianity is in terms of existence and then spent his whole life deliberating on that—for in that case when should he exist in it?

Therefore, the question about what Christianity is must not be confused with the objective question about the truth of Christianity, which we discussed in the first part of this book. It is certainly possible to ask objectively about what Christianity is, if the questioner wants to put this before himself objectively and for the time being let it be undecided whether it is truth or not (truth is subjectivity). Then the questioner declines all reverential busyness with demonstrating its truth, together with all speculative ambition to go beyond; he desires tranquillity, desires neither recommendations nor haste, but desires to find out what Christianity is.

Or is one unable to find out what Christianity is without becoming a Christian oneself? All analogies seem to say that one can come to know it, and Christianity itself must indeed regard as false Christians those who merely know what Christianity is. Here again the matter has been confused by the acquisition of the semblance of being a Christian through having been baptized promptly as an infant. But when Christianity came into the world or when it is introduced into a pagan country, it did not and does not cross out the contemporary generation of adults [621]and take possession of the small children. At that time the relations were in proper order—then it was difficult to become a Christian, and one did not become occupied with understanding Christianity. Now we have almost reached the parody that to become a Christian is nothing, but it is difficult and a very busy task to understand it. Everything is thereby reversed. Christianity is transformed into a kind of philosophical theory, and the difficulty quite properly consists in understanding it; but Christianity essentially relates itself to existence, and becoming a Christian is what is difficult.* This is why faith, in relation to understand- VII 322

* Understanding is the maximum with regard to a doctrine, and becoming an adherent is a cunning way by which people who do not understand something slyly pretend that they have understood. With regard to an existence-communication, existing in it is the maximum and wanting to understand it VII 322
is a cunning evasion that wants to shirk the task. To become a Hegelian is open to suspicion, to understand Hegel is the maximum; to become a Christian is the maximum, to want to understand Christianity is open to suspicion. —

ing, is dethroned instead of quite rightly being the maximum when the difficulty is to become a Christian. Let us, then, consider a pagan philosopher to whom Christianity has been proclaimed—yet surely not as one more philosophical theory he should understand but with the question whether he would be a Christian; has he not been told what Christianity is so that he could choose?

[622]That one can know what Christianity is without being a Christian must, then, be answered in the affirmative. Whether one can know what it is to be a Christian without being one is something else, and it must be answered in the negative. On the other hand, the Christian must indeed also know what Christianity is and be able to tell us—provided he himself has become one. I think that the dubiousness of becoming a Christian at the age of two weeks cannot be expressed more strongly than[*] by pointing out that by its help it is possible to find Christians—who have not yet become Christians. The transition to Christianity is made so early that it is merely a possibility of being able to make the transition. In other words, a person who actually has become a Christian must certainly have had a period when he was not a Christian; he must in turn have had a period when he found out what Christianity is; then, in turn, if he has not totally forgotten how he himself existed before he became a Christian, he must be able for his part to say what Christianity is by comparing his earlier life with his Christian life.

As soon as the transitional situation is made contemporary with the entry of Christianity into the world or with its introduction into a pagan country, everything will be clear. To become a Christian then becomes the most terrible of all decisions in a person's life, since it is a matter of winning faith through despair and offense (the Cerberus[623] pair who guard the entry to becoming a Christian). An infant two weeks old

---

This corresponds completely to what was developed in the previous chapter about possibility and actuality. The relation of possibility is the maximum with regard to a doctrine; actuality is the maximum with regard to an existence-communication; wanting to understand an existence-communication is wanting to transform one's relation to it into a relation of possibility.

cannot have passed the most terrible examination in this life, one in which eternity is the examiner, even if it has ever so many Baptism certificates from the parish clerk. But for the VII 323
baptized person there must also come a later moment that essentially corresponds to the transitional situation contemporary with Christianity's coming into the world; thus for the baptized person there must come a later moment when he, although a Christian, asks what Christianity is—in order to become a Christian. By Baptism, Christianity gives him a name, and he is a Christian *de nomine*; but in the decision he becomes a Christian and gives Christianity his name (*nomen dare alicui* [to give a name to someone]).[624]

Let us take a pagan philosopher. He surely did not become a Christian when he was two weeks old, when he did not know what he was doing (truly the strangest explanation of the most decisive step that it is made when an individual does not himself know what he is doing!). He knew very well what he was doing, that he resolved to relate himself to Christianity until the wonderful thing happened to him, that he became a Christian (if we want to express it this way), or until he chose to become that—consequently he knew what Christianity was at the time he accepted Christianity when he as yet was not a Christian.

But while everyone is busy with learnedly defining and speculatively understanding Christianity, one never sees the question "What is Christianity?" presented in such a way that one discovers that the person asking about it is asking in terms of existing and in the interest of existing. And why does no one do that? Ah, naturally because we are all Christians as a matter of course. And by means of this superb invention, being a Christian as a matter of course, things have gone so far in Christendom that one does not know for sure what Christianity is. Or by being confused with a learned and speculative explanation of Christianity, the explanation of what Christianity is becomes such a prolix affair that one is still not entirely finished but is looking forward to a new book. The person who actually became a Christian on the presupposition of the contemporaneity of the transitional situation with

Christianity's coming into the world indeed knew what Christianity is; and the person who is actually going to become a Christian must feel this need, a need that I do not think even the most doting mother will discover in her infant at the young age of two weeks. But, of course, we are all Christians. The learned Christians argue about what Christianity actually is, but it never occurs to them to think otherwise than that
VII they themselves are Christians, as if it were possible to know
324 for sure that one is something without knowing definitely what it is. The sermon addresses itself to the "Christian congregation," and yet it almost always moves *toward* the essentially Christian, recommends embracing the faith (that is, becoming a Christian), coaxes people to accept Christianity—and the people being spoken to are the Christian congregation and thus presumably Christians. If a listener who yesterday was so very gripped by the pastor's recommendation of Christianity that he thought, "It will take very little more for me to become a Christian,"[625] were to die tomorrow, he would be buried the day after tomorrow as a Christian—for he was, after all, a Christian.

Therefore what in itself seems so obvious, namely, that a Christian surely must know what Christianity is, know it with the concentration and decisiveness both presupposed and provided in having made the most decisive step, is now actually not understandable anymore. We are all Christians, of course; a speculative thinker was also baptized when he was two weeks old. Now when a speculative thinker says, "I am a Christian (*N.B.*, meaning thereby that one was baptized when one was two weeks old), and a Christian surely must know what Christianity is; true Christianity, I maintain, is the mediation of Christianity, and I vouch for the correctness of it by my being a Christian myself"—what should we then answer? The response must be: If a man says, "I am a Christian; ergo I indeed must know what Christianity is," and does not say one word more, then one must leave it at that. It would indeed be foolish to contradict him, since he says nothing. But if he begins to explain what he understands by Christianity, then, even without being a Christian, one must be able to know whether or not it is Christianity, if without being a Christian one can know what Christianity is. If, for example, what he explains to be Christianity is essentially identical with paganism, then one is justified in denying that it is Christianity.

Before there can be any question of mediation, first of all it must be decided what Christianity is. Speculative thought does not become involved in this; it does not proceed in such a way that it first sets forth what speculative thought is, then what Christianity is, in order to see whether the opposites can be mediated; it does not ascertain the attested respective identity of the opposing parties involved before proceeding to a compromise. If asked what Christianity is, it answers immediately, "the speculative conception of Christianity," without bothering itself about whether there is something in the distinction that distinguishes between something and the concep- VII
tion of something, which seems here to be important for spec- 325
ulation itself, because if Christianity itself is speculation's conception of it, then there is indeed no mediation, since in that case there are, of course, no contrasts, and a mediation between identical entities is really meaningless. But in that case it perhaps is better to ask speculation what speculation is. But then one learns that speculation is reconciliation, is mediation—is Christianity. But if speculative thought and Christianity are identical, what does it mean to mediate them? Then Christianity is essentially paganism, since speculation certainly will not deny that paganism had speculation. I readily admit that in a certain sense speculation now speaks altogether consistently, but this consistent speaking also shows that prior to the compromise no preliminary agreement took place, very likely because it was impossible to find a third position where the two opposing parties could meet.

But even if speculative thought assumes a distinction between Christianity and speculative thought, if for no other reason than merely the satisfaction of mediating, if it still does not definitely and decisively state the distinction, then one must ask: Is not *mediation* speculative thought's idea? Consequently, when the opposites are *mediated*, the opposites (speculative thought—Christianity) are not equal before the arbitrator, but Christianity is an element within speculation, and speculation acquires dominance because it had dominance, and because there was no moment of balance when the opposites were weighed against each other. When two opposites are mediated and these are mediated in a higher unity, the opposites can perhaps be *ebenbürtig* [of equal standing] because neither of them is the opposite of speculation. But when the one opposite is speculation itself, the other an opposite of speculation, and mediation occurs, and mediation is speculation's idea, then it is an illusory gesture to speak of an opposite of speculation, since the reconciling power is itself speculation (namely, its idea, which is mediation). Within speculation it is possible for whatever makes a claim of being speculation to be assigned its relative place and the opposites to be mediated—namely, the opposites that have this in common, that each is a speculative endeavor.

For example, when speculative thought mediates between the doctrine of the Eleatics and that of Heraclitus,[626] this can
VII be altogether proper, because the doctrine of the Eleatics is not
326 related as an opposite of speculation but is itself speculative, and likewise the doctrine of Heraclitus. Not so when the opposite is the opposite of speculation on the whole. If there is to be mediation here (and mediation is indeed speculation's idea), this means that speculation judges between itself and the opposite of itself and consequently is itself party and judge. Or it means that speculation assumes in advance that there can be no opposite of speculation at all, so that all opposition is only relative by being within speculation. But this is precisely what should be dealt with in the preliminary agreement. Perhaps the reason speculation is so afraid of stating clearly what Christianity is, perhaps the reason it is in such a hurry to start mediation and to recommend it, is that it would have to fear the worst if it became clear what Christianity is. Just as in a country where a mutinous cabinet has seized power the king is kept at a distance while the mutinous cabinet acts in the king's name, so is speculation's conduct in mediating Christianity.

Yet the dubiousness of the idea that Christianity is an ele-

ment within speculative thought has presumably caused speculative thought to compromise a little. Speculative thought has assumed the title "Christian," has wanted to recognize Christianity by adding this adjective, just as a hyphenated two-family name is sometimes created by a marriage involving noble families or when business firms are united in one firm that still carries the names of both. Now, if it were the case, as is so easily assumed, that to become a Christian is nothing, then Christianity must indeed be pleased as Punch over having made such a good match and having gained honor and rank almost equal to that of speculation. But if becoming a Christian is the most difficult of all tasks, then the honorable speculative thinker seems to profit instead, inasmuch as he attains being a Christian through the firm. But to become a Christian is actually the most difficult of all tasks, because the task, although the same, varies in relation to the capabilities of the respective individuals. This is not the case with tasks involving differences. With regard, for example, to comprehension, a person with high intelligence has a direct advantage over a person with limited intelligence, but this is not true with regard to having faith. That is, when faith requires that he relinquish his understanding, then to have faith becomes just as difficult for the most intelligent person as it is for the person of the most limited intelligence, or it presumably becomes even more difficult for the former. Here again one sees the dubiousness of changing Christianity into a doctrine,
where it is a matter of understanding, because in this way be- VII
coming a Christian is due to the difference. What is lacking 327
here? The preliminary agreement, where the status of each party is settled before the new firm is established.

But to go on: this Christian speculative thought, then, speculates within Christianity. But this speculative thought is not the same as that *usus instrumentalis* [instrumental use][627] of reason and not the same as the speculation that altogether consistently, since it was speculation only *within* Christianity, assumed that something is true in philosophy that is not true in theology. Understood in this way, it is quite in order to speculate within a presupposition, which that Christian speculation indeed means to suggest by the predicate "Christian." But if this speculation, which begins with a presupposition, goes further and further as speculation and finally speculates the presupposition also, that is, removes the presupposition—what then? Well, then the presupposition was masquerading. There is a story about the inhabitants of Mols,[628] that upon seeing a tree leaning out over the water and prompted by the thought that the tree was thirsty, they resolved to help it. To that end, the first Molbo grabbed the tree, the next one grabbed his legs, and in this way, with the common purpose of helping the tree, they formed a chain—all on the presupposition that the first one would hold fast, because the first one was the presupposition. But what happens? Suddenly he lets go in order to spit on his hands so he can get an even better grip—and what then? Then all the Molboer fall into the water—and why? Because the presupposition was abandoned. To speculate within a presupposition in such a way that finally one also speculates the presupposition is exactly the same feat as to think, within a hypothetical "if," something so evident that it acquires the power to transform into actuality the hypothesis within which it has its power.

In so-called Christian speculative thought, what other presupposition can there be at all than that Christianity is the very opposite of speculative thought, that it is the miraculous, the absurd, with the requirement that the individual is to exist in it and is not to waste time on speculatively understanding. If there is speculative thinking within this presupposition, then the speculative thought will instead have as its task a concen-
VII tration on the impossibility of speculatively understanding
328 Christianity, something that was described earlier as the task of the simple wise person.

But the speculative thinker may say, "If Christianity is supposed to be the very opposite of speculative thought, the absolute opposite, then I cannot begin to speculate on it at all, because all speculative thought consists in mediation and assumes that there are only relative opposites." "Perhaps it is so," I would reply, "but why do you speak this way? Is it to frighten me, so that I will be afraid of speculative thought and of the enormous prestige it enjoys in public opinion, or is it to win me over to regard speculation as the highest good?" Here the question is not whether Christianity is in the right but about what Christianity is. Speculation leaves out this preliminary agreement, and this accounts for its success with mediation. Before it mediates, it has already mediated, that is, changed Christianity into a philosophical theory. But as soon as the agreement establishes Christianity as the opposite of speculative thought, then *eo ipso* mediation is impossible, because all mediation is within speculation. If Christianity is the opposite of speculation, then it is also the opposite of mediation, since mediation is speculation's idea—what, then, does it mean to mediate it? But what is the opposite of mediation? It is the absolute paradox.

Suppose that someone who does not purport to be a Christian asks what Christianity is. This simplifies matters, and one avoids the both sad and ludicrous confusion that Tom, Dick, and Harry, who are Christian *as a matter of course*, create new confusion by busily explaining Christianity speculatively, which is almost to insult it. In other words, if Christianity were a philosophical theory, then one could honor it by saying that it is difficult to comprehend (speculatively), but if Christianity itself assumes that the difficulty is to become and to be a Christian, then it should not even be difficult to understand—namely, to understand in such a way that one can begin with the difficulty—to become a Christian and to be a Christian.

Christianity is not a doctrine,* but it expresses an existence-

* Now, if only a hasty pate does not promptly explain to a reading public
how foolish my whole book is, which is more than adequately seen in my
alleging anything such as: Christianity is not a doctrine. Let us understand
one another. Surely a philosophical theory that is to be comprehended and VII
speculatively understood is one thing, and a doctrine that is to be actualized 329
in existence is something else. If there is to be any question of understanding
with regard to this latter doctrine, then this understanding must be: to understand that it is to be existed in, to understand the difficulty of existing in it,
what a prodigious existence-task [*Existents-Opgave*] this doctrine assigns to
the learner. When with regard to a doctrine of this kind (an existence-communication [*Existents-Meddelelse*]) it at a given time becomes common to as-

contradiction and is an existence-communication. If Christi-
VII 329 anity were a doctrine, it would *eo ipso* not constitute the opposite of speculative thought but would be an element within it. Christianity pertains to existence, to existing, but existence and existing are the very opposite of speculation. The Eleatic doctrine, for example, is not related to existing but to speculation; therefore it must be assigned its place within speculation. Precisely because Christianity is not a doctrine, it holds true, as developed previously, that there is an enormous difference between knowing what Christianity is and being a Christian. With regard to a doctrine, this distinction is unthinkable, because the doctrine is not related to existing. I cannot help it that our age has reversed the relation and changed Christianity into a philosophical theory that is to be comprehended and being a Christian into something negligible. Furthermore, to say that Christianity is empty of content because
VII 330 it is not a doctrine is only chicanery. When a believer exists in faith, his existence has enormous content, but not in the sense of a yield in paragraphs.

I have tried to express the existence-contradiction of Christianity in the issue: an eternal happiness is decided here in time by a relation to something historical. If I were to say that

---

sume that to be what the doctrine enjoins is so very easy, but to understand the doctrine speculatively is very difficult, then a person can be in harmony with this doctrine (the existence-communication) when he tries to show how difficult it is, existing, to comply with the teaching. With regard to such a doctrine, however, it is a misunderstanding to want to speculate on it. Christianity is a doctrine of this kind. To want to speculate upon it is a misunderstanding, and as one goes further and further along this way one becomes guilty of a greater and greater misunderstanding. When one finally arrives at the point that one not only wants to speculate but has speculatively understood it, then one has arrived at the ultimate of misunderstanding. This point is reached in the mediation of Christianity and speculative thought, and thus modern speculation is quite correctly the ultimate misunderstanding of Christianity. When this is now the case, and when, furthermore, it is the case that the nineteenth century is so frightfully speculative, it is to be feared that the word "doctrine" is immediately understood as a philosophical theory that is to be and ought to be comprehended. To avoid this mistake, I have chosen to call Christianity an existence-communication in order to designate very definitely how it is different from speculative thought.

Christianity is a doctrine about the Incarnation, about the Atonement, etc., misunderstanding would immediately be made easy. Speculative thought takes possession of this doctrine and points out the less perfect interpretation etc. in paganism and Judaism. Christianity becomes an element, perhaps a supreme element, but essentially speculation.

§ 3
The Issue in Fragments[629] *as an Introductory Issue, Not to Christianity but to Becoming a Christian*

Since I neither presumed in *Fragments* nor presume here to explain the issue, but only to present it, my procedure is continually to approach it, to introduce it. But please note that this introducing is of a singular nature, because from the introduction there is no direct transition to becoming a Christian, but, on the contrary, this is the qualitative leap. Therefore, an introduction of this kind (because an introduction in the usual sense is a contradiction in relation to the decision of the qualitative leap) is repelling. It does not make it easy to enter into what it introduces; on the contrary, it makes it difficult. Although it may be beautiful and well intentioned, inasmuch as being a Christian is supposed to be the highest good, to want to help people to become Christians by making it easy, I venture according to my poor ability to take on the responsibility of making it difficult, as difficult as possible, yet without making it more difficult than it is—I take the responsibility upon myself. One can certainly do that, in an imaginary construction. My thinking goes something like this: if it is the highest good, then it is better that I definitely know that I do not possess it, so that I can aspire to it with all my might, than to be entranced in illusion and to imagine that I possess it and consequently do not even consider aspiring. I do not deny that I regard infant Baptism, understood in this way, not only defensible as orthodox and laudable as an expression of the piety of parents who cannot bear to be separated from their children with regard to what to them is a matter of their eternal hap- VII 331
piness, but also, in yet another sense that one may not be

aware of, to be a good—because it makes it even more difficult to become a Christian. I have already pointed this out in another place;[630] here I shall merely add something.

The fact that the decision in the external by which I become a Christian is anticipated has the effect that the decision, if it is made, becomes purely inward and its inwardness therefore even greater than when in addition the decision takes place in the external. The less externality, the more inwardness. That the most passionate decision occurs in a person in such a way that it is not outwardly detected at all is something profound and wonderful—he was a Christian, and yet he became that. Thus, if a Christian baptized as an infant truly becomes a Christian and becomes that with the same inwardness as a non-Christian who converts to Christianity, the inwardness of his transition must be the greatest precisely because there is no externality. But, on the other hand, the absence of the external is certainly a temptation and can easily become a temptation for many to put off the decision, as may best be seen in the possibility that someone or other will be taken aback by the idea that being baptized as an infant could mean that it would be more difficult to become a Christian. It is, however, the case, and all the analogies will confirm the correctness of the statement: the less externality, the more inwardness, if it is truly there; but it is also the case that the less externality, the greater the possibility that the inwardness will entirely fail to come. The externality is the watchman who awakens the sleeper; the externality is the solicitous mother who calls one; the externality is the roll call that brings the soldier to his feet; the externality is the reveille that helps one to make the great effort; but the absence of the externality can mean that the inwardness itself calls inwardly to a person—alas, but it can also mean that the inwardness will fail to come.

Yet it is not only in this way that what I must call an introduction to becoming a Christian is very different from what is usually called an introduction, but it is also very different from an introduction to Christianity that is based on the view that Christianity is a doctrine. Such introducing [*Indleden*] does not lead [*lede*] to becoming a Christian but *höchstens* [at best] to seeing, by way of a world-historical view, the superiority of Christianity to paganism, Judaism, etc.

The introducing that I take upon myself consists, by repelling, in making it difficult to become a Christian and understands Christianity not as a doctrine but as an existence-contradiction and existence-communication. Therefore, it introduces VII 332 psychologically, not world-historically, by evoking an awareness of how much must be lived and how difficult it is to become really aware of the difficulty of the decision. As I have frequently said but cannot repeat enough, both for my own sake because it concerns me so deeply, and for the sake of others lest I confuse, I repeat here: it is not the simple person for whom this introducing can make it difficult to become a Christian.[631] I certainly do believe that the utmost effort to become Christian is required also of him and that no one does him a service by making it all too easy, but every essential existence-task pertains equally to every human being and therefore makes the difficulty proportionate to the individual's endowment. For example, self-control is just as difficult for the sagacious as for the simple, perhaps even more difficult because his sagacity will help him with many cunning evasions. To understand that a human being is capable of nothing (the beautiful and profound expression for the relationship with God) is just as difficult for a remarkably endowed king as for a poor, wretched person, perhaps even more difficult, because he is so easily tempted by being capable of so much. So also with becoming and being a Christian. When culture and the like have managed to make it so very easy to be a Christian, it is certainly in order that a single individual, according to his poor abilities, seeks to make it difficult, provided, however, that he does not make it more difficult than it is. —But the more culture and knowledge, the more difficult to become a Christian.

If the dialogue *Hippias*[632] is regarded as an introduction to what the beautiful is, it can serve as a kind of analogy to the sort of introduction of which I am speaking. That is, after several attempts to explain what the beautiful is, all of which are demolished, the dialogue ends with Socrates' saying that he

has benefited from the conversation, that he has found out that it is difficult.[633] Whether Socrates is right in such a procedure, since the beautiful is an idea and is not related to existence, I shall not decide. But when in Christendom it seems that so much has been done or attempted to make one forget what Christianity is, then in my opinion it is better to regard an
VII introduction appropriate (to say nothing of being the only one
333 with regard to becoming a Christian) if instead of resembling the usual introductions—and the hired waiters whom hotels send out to meet the travelers immediately at the customhouse and to recommend their lodging and cuisine—it ends with having made becoming a Christian difficult, although the introduction has also tried to show what Christianity is. The hotel needs the travelers; with regard to Christianity, it would be even more appropriate if people grasped that they need Christianity. The distinction between knowing what Christianity is (the easier) and being a Christian (the more difficult) is not appropriate to the beautiful or to the *doctrine* about the beautiful. If the dialogue *Hippias* had clarified what the beautiful is, nothing would have been left that was made difficult, and that dialogue would have nothing that corresponds to the duplexity of our enterprise—which illuminates what Christianity is but only makes it difficult to become a Christian.

But if becoming a Christian is the difficulty, the absolute decision, then the only possible introduction is a repelling one that just by the repulsion points out that it is the absolute decision. Even with the most prolonged introduction in the direction of decision, one does not come a single step closer to the decision, because in that case the decision is not the absolute decision, the qualitative leap, and one is tricked instead of being helped. That the introduction, however, at best does not come a single step closer to what it is introducing expresses in turn that it can only be repelling. Philosophy leads directly to Christianity; the historicizing and rhetorical introduction does likewise, and it is successful—because the introductions are to a doctrine, but not to becoming a Christian.

DIVISION 2

The Issue Itself

> The individual's eternal happiness is decided in time through a relation to something historical that furthermore is historical in such a way that its composition includes that which according to its nature cannot become historical and consequently must become that by virtue of the absurd.

The issue is pathos-filled and dialectical. The pathos is in the first part, since a person's passion culminates in the pathos- VII 334
filled relation to an eternal happiness. The dialectical is in the last part, and the difficulty is precisely that the issue is composed in this way. To love is plain and simple pathos; to relate oneself to an eternal happiness is, in the sphere of reflection, plain and simple pathos. The dialectical consists in this, that the eternal happiness to which the individual is assumed to relate himself with proper pathos is itself made dialectical by additional qualifications, which in turn work as an incitement that brings passion to its extreme. When in existing a person expresses and for some time has expressed that he is giving up and has given up everything in order to relate himself to the absolute τέλος [end, goal], the presence of conditions exerts an absolute influence in raising passion as high as possible. Even in connection with relative pathos, the dialectical is like oil on the fire and extends the range of inwardness and intensively inflames the passion. But since we have forgotten what it means to exist *sensu eminenti*, since we usually trace the pathos-filled to imagination and feeling and allow the dialectical to annul it instead of uniting both in the contemporaneity of existence, the pathos-filled in our philosophical nineteenth century has fallen into discredit and the dialectical has become passionless, just as it likewise has become so easy and facile to think contradictions, because passion is the very tension in the

contradiction, and when this is taken away the passion is a pleasantry, a witty remark. An existence-issue, however, is pathos-filled and dialectical. The one set forth here requires existence-inwardness in order to grasp the pathos, passion of thought to grasp the dialectical difficulty, and concentrated passion because one is supposed to exist in it.

[634]In order to clarify the issue, I shall first of all discuss the pathos-filled and then the dialectical, but I ask the reader continually to recollect that the difficulty finally consists in combining the two, that the existing person who in absolute passion and filled with pathos expresses by his existence his pathos-filled relation to the eternal happiness—must now relate to the dialectical decision. He must Socratically fear being in error just as much as he, in pathos-filled tension, is in relation to his eternal happiness. Therefore his exertion is the greatest possible, all the more so since delusion is so very easy because there is nothing external to look at. In erotic love, the individual is still involved with another human being and can hear that person's yes or no. In every enthusiasm-inspired project, the individual still has something external, but in relation to eternal happiness the individual has only himself to deal with in inwardness. He has the phrase gratis in his mother tongue; he can soon learn to recite by rote a little of this and a little of that. Externally, the idea of an eternal happiness is of
VII 335 no advantage to a person, because it is first present when he has learned to scorn the external and has forgotten the earthly mind's interpretation of what is advantageous. Externally, the lack of this conception does not *harm* him; he can very well become "a husband, a father, and captain of the popinjay shooting club"[635] without it, and if he craves something like that, this idea will only disturb him. The essential existential pathos in relation to an eternal happiness is purchased so dearly that in a finite sense it must be plainly regarded as lunacy to purchase it, as is often enough expressed in various ways: an eternal happiness is a security whose market price is no longer quoted in the speculative nineteenth century; at best the reverend clerics can use a canceled bond of that sort to

trick the peasants. The deception is so easy that finite commonsensicality must simply be proud of not foolishly venturing to become involved in it. That is why it is so foolish, unless one's life is dialectical *à la* an apostle, to want to reassure people about their eternal happiness, because, with regard to something in which the individual person has only himself to deal with, the most one person can do for another is to unsettle him.

A
PATHOS

§ 1

The Initial Expression *of Existential Pathos, the Absolute Orientation (Respect) toward the Absolute* τέλος *Expressed through Action in the Transformation of Existence— Esthetic Pathos—the Illusiveness of Mediation— the Monastic Movement of the Middle Ages— Simultaneously to Relate Oneself Absolutely to One's Absolute* τέλος *and Relatively to Relative Ends*

In relation to an eternal happiness as the absolute good, pathos does not mean words but that this idea transforms the whole existence of the existing person. Esthetic pathos expresses itself in words and can in its truth signify that the individual abandons himself in order to lose himself in the idea, whereas existential pathos results from the transforming relation of the idea to the individual's existence. If the absolute τέλος [end, goal] does not absolutely transform the individual's existence VII 336 by relating to it, then the individual does not relate himself with existential pathos but with esthetic pathos—for example, by having a correct idea, but, please note, by which he is outside himself in the ideality of possibility with the correctness of the idea; he is not in himself in existence with the correctness of the idea in the ideality of actuality, is not himself transformed into the actuality of the idea.

For an existing person, an eternal happiness relates itself essentially to existing, to the ideality of actuality, and consequently the pathos must correspond to it. If falling in love is interpreted esthetically, it holds true that the poet's conception of falling in love is higher than anything actuality offers. The poet can have an ideality compared with which actuality is but a weak reflection; for the poet, actuality is merely an occasion that prompts him to abandon actuality in order to seek the ideality of possibility. Poetic pathos, therefore, is essentially fantasy. But if one wants ethically to establish a poetic relation to actuality, this is a misunderstanding and a retrogression. The point here as everywhere is to keep the specific spheres separated from one another, to respect the qualitative dialectic, the tug of decision that changes everything, so that what was the highest in another sphere must be absolutely rejected in this. With regard to the religious, the point is that this has passed through the ethical. A religious poet, therefore, is in an awkward position. That is, such a person wants to relate himself to the religious by way of imagination, but just by doing that he ends up relating himself esthetically to something esthetic. To *celebrate* a hero of faith is just as fully an esthetic task as to celebrate a war hero. If the religious is truly the religious, has passed through the ethical and has it in itself, then it cannot forget that religiously the pathos is not a matter of singing praises and celebrating or composing song books but of existing oneself. Thus the poet-production, if it is not totally absent, or if it is just as rich as before, is regarded by the poet himself as the accidental, which shows that he understands himself religiously, because esthetically the poet-production is the important thing, and the poet is the accidental.

Therefore a poetic nature who by way of circumstances, upbringing, and the like has taken a direction away from the theater to the Church can cause great confusion. Dazzled by the esthetic in him, people think that he is a religious individuality, alas, a *prominent* religious individuality (and to be a
VII prominent individuality is just an esthetic reminiscence, be-
337 cause, viewed religiously, there is no prominence except an apostle's paradoxical-dialectical authority, and prominence, viewed religiously according to the qualitative dialectic that

separates the spheres, is simply retrogression), although he may not be a religious individuality at all. His pathos is a poet-pathos, the pathos of possibility, with actuality as an occasion. Even if he has world-historical pathos, it is the pathos of possibility—and, viewed ethically, the pathos of immaturity, because, ethically, maturity is to comprehend one's own ethical actuality as infinitely more important* than the interpretation of the whole of world history.

The pathos that corresponds to and is adequate to an eternal happiness is the transformation by which the existing person in existing changes everything in his existence in relation to
that highest good.** In relation to possibility, words are the VII 338

* Although in the world we frequently enough see a presumptuous religious individuality who, himself so exceedingly secure in his relationship with God and jauntily sure of his eternal happiness, is self-importantly busy doubting the salvation of others and offering them his help, I believe it would be appropriate discourse for a truly religious person if he said: I do not doubt anyone's salvation; the only one I have fears about is myself; even if I see a person sink low, I still dare not despair of his salvation, but if it is myself, then I certainly would be forced to endure the terrible thought. An authentic religious individuality is always so lenient with others, so inventive in thinking up excuses; only toward himself is he cold and severe like a grand-inquisitor. With others, he is as a kindly old man usually is with a young person; only with regard to himself is he old and uncompromising.

** This is how the individual conducts himself (also) in minor matters when he plans his life. Whether he must work for a living or in this regard is privileged, whether he will marry or remain unmarried, etc. will change his existence for him at the moment of choice or at the moment of taking responsibility. But since this itself is changeable, since he can suddenly fall in love, can suddenly become poor, etc., it cannot, except unreasonably, transform his existence absolutely. Strangely enough, the worldly wisdom that pertains to this and to that is not very rare in life, and it is not at all unusual to see an existing person who existentially expresses that he relates himself to a relative goal, has built his life on this, renounces what will frustrate him in this, and hopes for what is to be gained therein. But an existing person who existentially expresses that he relates himself to the absolute good is perhaps a great rarity, an existing person who truthfully can say: I exist in such a way, in renunciation I have transformed my existence in such a way, that if I hoped for this life alone I would be the most wretched of all people[636]—that is, the
most horribly deceived, deceived by myself in not taking hold. —How VII 338
alarmed financiers become when the interest payment suddenly stops; how horrified mariners would be if the government blocked the harbors; but if

highest pathos; in relation to actuality, actions are the highest pathos. That a poet, for example, does not allow himself to be influenced by his own poet-production is esthetically quite in order or is a matter of complete indifference, because esthetically the poet-production and possibility are the highest. But ethically it is inversely of infinite importance, because ethically the poetic work is a matter of infinite indifference, but his own existence ought to be infinitely more important to the poet than all else. Esthetically, therefore, it would be the highest pathos on the part of the poet to annihilate himself, to be demoralized if this were made necessary, in order to produce poetic works of first rank. To use a strong expression to bring to mind what may be done even more often than one thinks, it is esthetically proper to sell one's soul to the devil—but then produce wonderful works. Ethically it would perhaps be the highest pathos to renounce the brilliant poet-existence without saying a word. If a so-called religious individuality deigns to depict an eternal happiness with all the allurement of the imagination, this means that he is a poet escaped from the esthetic who wants to have citizenship in the religious without even being able to understand its native language. The pathos of the ethical is to act. So when a man says, for example, that for the sake of his eternal happiness he has suffered hunger, cold, been in prison, in peril at sea, has been despised, persecuted, whipped, etc.,[637] these simple words are a testimony to ethical pathos inasmuch as they quite simply refer to what he, acting, has suffered. Wherever the ethical is present, all attention is called back to the individual himself and to acting. Thus the pathos of marriage is to act; the pathos of falling in love is poetry.

Ethically the highest pathos is the pathos of interestedness (which is expressed in this way, that I, acting, transform my whole existence in relation to the object of interest); esthetically the highest pathos is the pathos of disinterestedness. If an

---

posito, I suppose, that the eternal happiness fails to come—how many of the expectant gentlemen (and we all, of course, expect an eternal happiness) will thereby find themselves in an awkward situation?

individual throws himself away in order to grasp something VII 339 great, he is esthetically inspired; if he gives up everything in order to save himself, he is ethically inspired.

What I am writing here must be regarded as ABC reading, not in the speculative but in the simple sense. Every child knows it, even though not with quite the same experience; everyone understands it, even though not with quite the same definiteness; everyone can understand it, because the ethical is quite consistently always very easy to understand, probably in order that no time will be wasted on understanding but one will be able to begin immediately. But, in return, it is very difficult to accomplish—just the same for the sagacious as for the simple, since the difficulty does not lie in understanding, for in that case the sagacious would have a great advantage.

Existence is composed of the infinite and the finite; the existing person is infinite and finite. Now, if to him an eternal happiness is his highest good, this means that in his acting the finite elements are once and for all reduced to what must be surrendered in relation to the eternal happiness. An eternal happiness relates itself with pathos to an essentially existing person, not to a speaker who is courteous enough to include it on the list of the good things for which he supplicates. Usually people abhor denying that such a good exists; so they include it but, just by *including it*, show that they do not include it. I do not know whether one should laugh or weep on hearing the enumeration: a good job, a beautiful wife, health, the rank of a councilor of justice[638]—and in addition an eternal happiness,[639] which is the same as assuming that the kingdom of *heaven* is a kingdom along with all the other kingdoms on *earth* and that one would look for information about it in a geography book. How strange that simply by talking about a thing a person can show that he is not talking about that thing, because one would think that this could be shown only by not talking about it. If that is the case, then a great deal would indeed be said about the eternal happiness, and yet, when one talks this way, nothing is said about it or, even more definitely expressed, it is not spoken about.

Esthetically one can very well wish for wealth, good for-

tune, the most beautiful girl—in short, everything that is esthetic-dialectical; but then to *wish* for eternal happiness *in addition* is double gibberish, partly because one does it *in addition* and thereby converts an eternal happiness into a prize on a Christmas tree, and partly because one *wishes*, since an eternal happiness essentially relates itself to existing and not esthetically-dialectically to a romantic wish-maker. Eternal happiness, however, often must be content to be included among other *bon bons* [confections], and it is regarded as *très bien* [very
VII 340 good] of a person that he at least includes it; it is regarded as almost the maximum that one can do in this regard. And one goes further. Although the other good things are not assumed to come because one wishes for them, it is assumed that eternal happiness comes, all right, if one just wishes for it. The man of experience knows that the gifts of good fortune are variously distributed (because difference is the very dialectic of good fortune), but eternal happiness (which, please note, was also transformed into a gift of good fortune) is distributed equally to all wishing gentlemen. Double confusion: first that eternal happiness becomes a good of that kind (regarded as an unusually fat livelihood and other such things), and then that it is distributed *equally*, which is a contradiction when it comes to the gifts of good fortune. The esthetic and the ethical have been mixed together in comfortable balderdash—the definition of kind is taken from the esthetic and the equality in distribution from the ethical.

But one of the gentlemen wishers, a "serious man" who really wants to do something for his eternal happiness, may say, "Is it not possible to find out for certain, clearly and briefly, what an eternal happiness is? Can't you describe it to me 'while I shave,'[640] just as one describes the loveliness of a woman, the royal purple, or distant regions?" It is good that I cannot do it, good that I am not a poetic nature or a kindly clergyman, because then I would be capable of beginning to do it, and perhaps I might succeed—in once again subsuming eternal happiness under esthetic categories so that the maximum of pathos would become the marvelousness of description, even though it is a task that esthetically is enough to despair over—esthetically to have to make something out of an abstraction such as an eternal happiness. Esthetically it is altogether appropriate that I as a spectator am enchanted by the stage scenery, the theatrical moonlight, and go home after having spent a very pleasant evening, but ethically it holds true that there is no change other than my own. Ethically it is entirely consistent that the highest pathos of the essentially existing person corresponds to what esthetically is the poorest idea, and that is an eternal happiness. It has been said appropriately (esthetically understood) and wittily that the angels are the most boring of all beings, eternity the longest and most boring of all days, since even a Sunday is boring enough, an eternal happiness perpetual monotony, and that even unhappiness VII 341 is to be preferred. But ethically this is quite in order so that the existing person will not be lured into wasting time imagining and imagining—but be prompted to act.

If an existing person is to relate himself with pathos to an eternal happiness, then the point is that his existence should express the relation. As soon as one knows how an individual exists, then one also knows how he relates himself to an eternal happiness, that is, whether he does or does not; *tertium non datur* [there is no third], precisely because the absolute τέλος cannot *be included*. Yet no one knows it except the individual himself in his own consciousness, and therefore no one needs to hear another person's talk or to read another person's book or to go to the pastor, to a comedy or to the comedy at the pastor's—in order to see and hear: the theatrical moonlight in the hereafter, the murmuring of the brook in the green meadows of eternity. He needs only to attend to his own existence; then he knows it. If it does not *absolutely* transform his existence for him, then he is not relating himself to an eternal happiness; if there is something he is not willing to give up for its sake, then he is not relating himself to an eternal happiness.

Even a relative τέλος partially transforms a person's existence. But since existence in our speculative nineteenth century has unfortunately been changed into a thinking about everything possible, we even more rarely see an energetic existence oriented just to a relative τέλος. To will to amass

money energetically already transforms a human life, to say nothing of the absolute τέλος, willing in the highest sense. All relative willing is distinguished by willing something for something else, but the highest τέλος must be willed for its own sake. And this highest τέλος is not a something, because then it relatively corresponds to something else and is finite. But it is a contradiction absolutely to will something finite, since the finite [*endelig*] must indeed come to an end [*Ende*], and consequently there must come a time when it can no longer be willed. But to will absolutely is to will the infinite, and to will an eternal happiness is to will absolutely, because it must be capable of being willed at every moment. And the reason it is so abstract and, viewed esthetically, the meagerest of conceptions is that it is the absolute τέλος for a person who wills and will strive absolutely—and does not thoughtlessly imagine that he is finished and does not foolishly become involved in haggling, whereby he only loses the absolute τέλος. And the reason it is foolishness in the finite sense is precisely
VII 342 that it is the absolute τέλος in the infinite sense. The person who wills does not want to know anything about this τέλος except that it exists, because as soon as he finds out something about it, he already begins to be slowed down in his pace.

But the pathos lies in the individual's expressing this existentially in existence; the pathos lies not in testifying to an eternal happiness but in transforming one's own existence into a testimony to it. Poetic pathos is a pathos of difference, but existential pathos is the poor man's pathos, the pathos for everyone, because every human being can act within himself, and at times one finds in a maidservant the pathos sought in vain in the existence of a poet. The individual himself can then easily examine how he relates himself to an eternal happiness or whether he relates himself to it. He needs only to allow resignation to inspect his entire immediacy with all its desires etc. If he finds a single fixed point, an obduracy, he is not relating himself to an eternal happiness. Nothing is easier—that is, if it is difficult, it is just because his immediacy is unwilling to expose itself to inspection; but that, of course, is already more than sufficient evidence that the individual is not relating himself to an eternal happiness. When resignation makes a visitation to immediacy, it gives notice that the individual must not have his life in it, and resignation gives it notice of what can happen in life. But if the individual flinches at this point—whether he is so happy that he does not dare to know about anything different or, imagining himself the unhappiest of mortals, yet suspects that he could become even unhappier; whether he is shrewd and counts on probabilities or weak and relies on others—in short, if he flinches at this point, he is not relating himself to an eternal happiness. —If, however, the inspecting resignation discovers no irregularity, this shows that the individual at the time of inspection is relating himself to an eternal happiness.

But someone who is situated with a wife and children in a good living, cozily indoors, and is a councilor of justice, a "serious man" who nevertheless wants to do something for his eternal happiness, provided the duties of his office and his wife and children permit it, an enthusiast who, by Jove, is not afraid of spending ten rix-dollars on it, may say, "Well, all right, go ahead with this inspection business, but when, as quickly as possible, it is over, then we will come to mediation, won't we? Mediation, I must say, is a glorious invention; it seems to have been taken out of my own heart. It belongs entirely to the nineteenth century and thus entirely to me, for I also belong to the nineteenth century. And I greatly admire its great inventor, and everyone must admire him, everyone who is world-historically oriented, who has comprehended the rel- VII 343
ative legitimacy of all the earlier standpoints as well as the necessity of its all having to come to mediation." Oh, to be in the position of mediation: to be recognized in this way even by councilors of justice, even by a councilor of justice who contemplates world history, consequently an unusual councilor of justice, indeed—but, no, I am forgetting the time in which we live, the theocentric nineteenth century; we all contemplate world history—from God's point of view.

But let us forget the councilors of justice and world history and what the two can have to settle with each other. When a high government official or the king himself travels around to inspect the treasuries, a disloyal official may at times succeed in having the cash box in order for the inspection day, and he thinks: If I can just get through this day, then everything will be back in the old groove again. But resignation is not a king inspecting another man's cash box but is in possession of the individual's own private knowledge about himself. Neither is resignation a traveler; it takes the liberty of remaining with the person concerned in order to make every day an inspection day, unless it is thrown out, whereby everything is lost, and this certainly is not mediation. But when resignation remains there and never sleeps, when it is present at the slightest deviation and does not leave his side when he goes out, whether he undertakes something big or something small, and lives next door to his most secret thoughts—what then, where is mediation then? Outside, I think.

What, then, is mediation when it wants to force its way into the ethical and the ethical-religious? It is a wretched invention by a person who became untrue to himself and to resignation; it is indeed a forgery by sloth, which nevertheless presumptuously passes itself off also as resignation, which is the most dangerous of all, just as when a thief passes himself off as a policeman. The same thing shows up in minor matters. Someone may keep on working enthusiastically for a half year or a whole year in some undertaking without asking about wages, about whether anything is being accomplished, and about security and guarantees, because the uncertainty of enthusiasm is higher than all such things. But then he becomes weary and wants to have certainty, at least have something for his trouble. And when people became weary with regard to the eternal, became as hardheaded as a Jewish peddler, as thin-skinned as a flabby preacher, as sleepy as a foolish brides-
VII maid;[641] when they no longer had the capacity to grasp the
344 truth of existence (that is, what it means to exist) as a time of falling in love and as enthusiasm's race in the uncertain[642]—then along came mediation.

To be in love for a half year and rash enough to risk everything, that is really something; but then one must jolly well also get the girl and stretch one's weary limbs on the privileged marriage bed. [643]Mediation can still have its significance with regard to the relative τέλος [end, goal], and it must put up with being mediated, because an absolute relation to a relative τέλος would be unreasonable. But the absolute τέλος is present only when the individual relates himself absolutely to it, and they cannot, as an eternal happiness relating itself to an existing person, possibly have each other or tranquilly belong to each other in existence, that is, in temporality, in the same way as a girl and a young man can very well have each other in time because they both are existing persons. But what does it mean that they cannot have each other in time? Anyone in love knows that; it means that time here is a time for being in love. With regard to a relative τέλος, part of time is a time for being in love, and then comes the time of certainty. But since eternal happiness is higher in rank than a little miss, yes, even a queen, it is quite in order that the time for being in love becomes somewhat longer, no, not somewhat longer, because eternal happiness is not something higher in rank than a queen but is the absolute τέλος, but then it is indeed quite in order that all time, existence, is a time for being in love.

In connection with this orientation toward the absolute τέλος, every outcome, even the most magnificent that can originate in a wisher's mind and in a creative poet's imagination, is an absolute loss if it is supposed to be the reward, and the one striving is better off saying: No, thank you, may I only be allowed to relate myself to the absolute τέλος.

Who has not admired Napoleon, who has not thought, with a shiver of devotion—just as the child listens to the fairy tale and hears it once again with a reluctant but therefore more admiring shiver, because the adult usually allows the fairy tale to belong to the imagination—that here the most fantastic tale has become actuality! Thiers has taken it upon himself to tell the story about it, and behold, with the greatest calm, with a statesman's experience, as if this were entirely appropriate, he more than once says as he admiringly describes Napoleon's world plans: But, here as everywhere, everything depended on the outcome.[644] In my opinion, anyone who simultane- VII
ously pictures to himself Napoleon's greatness and recalls the 345

remark tossed out so casually, so naturally, so *geläufigt*[645] [glibly] by Thiers will have the greatest possible feeling of sadness at the thought of what constitutes human glory. If Napoleon is as great as the most reckless notion, if his whole life is like a fairy tale, then, just as in the fairy tale, there is in truth still another fanciful figure. It is a shrunken old witch, a shriveled being, a little creature, a spider on whose one feeler there are some numbers—they are the outcome. And the suprahuman hero of the fairy tale, whom nothing, nothing can withstand, is nevertheless in the power of this little creature—and if this little creature does not will it, then the whole adventure comes to naught, or it becomes the tale of a spider with an odd dot on one feeler. The poorest and most miserable person who stakes absolutely everything in order to relate himself to the absolute τέλος—yes, of course, it becomes no fairy tale, but also not a fairy tale about a little creature with a red dot on one feeler.

In the case of the most sagacious, the boldest plan to transform the whole world, it is true that it becomes great by virtue of the outcome; but in the case of a simple and guileless resolution by a poor human being, it is true that this plan is superior to any outcome; its greatness is not dependent on the outcome. And it is indeed more blessed to be there where we all are small, are nothing before God, than to be the greatest man in the world and be a slave of the outcome, whether it comes as wished or fails to come—there where the outcome is zero and infinitely less than even the least in the kingdom of heaven, whereas in the world the outcome is lord of all lords and tyrant of all tyrants.

Who has not admired Napoleon—that he could be a hero and an emperor and regarded being a poet as something secondary that he included, because his speech, his lines—indeed, no poet who would be content with being the greatest poet would be able to give him more masterly lines. Yet I believe that it once happened that he did not know what he himself was saying. It is a true story. While making the rounds at the outpost, he met a young officer who attracted his attention. He returned and the officer at that particular outpost was

awarded the order of the cross. But the officer had been re-
lieved and a new one had taken his place. No one could understand the why and wherefore of this special recognition.
The right person became aware of it and sent Napoleon a petition with the request that it be rectified. Napoleon answered:
No, I cannot use that man; he has no luck. If it is so that a
person can sense it when death walks over his grave;[646] if it is VII
so—and so it is in fairy tales, and we are indeed in a fairy tale— 346
that a person standing as large as life among others goes to
pieces at the mention of a word, turns into dust and is as if
blown away, then in the spirit of the fairy tale this ought to
have happened to Napoleon here, because the words pertained
to him more than to the officer.

In a previous section,[647] I sought to show the chimerical character of mediation when there is supposed to be a mediation between existence and thinking for an *existing person*, inasmuch as[648] everything said about mediation can be true and glorious but becomes untruth in the mouth of an existing person since he as an existing person is prevented from obtaining such a foothold outside existence that from it he can mediate that which by being in a process of becoming also precludes completion. It was also shown that with regard to an existing person all the talk about mediation is deceptive, since abstract thinking, to say nothing of pure thinking, expressly ignores existence, which from the ethical point of view is so lacking in merit that it is the opposite, is culpable. There are two ways in which an existing person can be outside existence, but in neither of these ways does he mediate. One way is by abstracting from himself, by gaining a skeptical impassivity and ataraxia, an abstract indifference (μετρίως παθεῖν), which in Greece was regarded as something very difficult. The other way in which the individual can be outside existence is by being in a state of passion, but it is in the very moment of passion that he gains the momentum to exist. To assume that an existing person succeeds in mediation little by little is the usual attempt to trick attention away from the qualitative dialectic with the aid of a fantastic vanishing of time and a specious quantification.

This is how mediation was discussed in the philosophical sense. Here we are engaged in an ethical inquiry, and hence mediation must be mediation between the separate elements of existence—if the absolute τέλος is also an element among the other elements. Now, here lies the misunderstanding, and it will readily appear that mediation as something higher than resignation is in fact retrogression. Resignation has made the
VII 347 individual face or has seen to it that he faced toward an eternal happiness as the absolute τέλος. This τέλος, then, is not an element among other elements. Thus the both-and of mediation is not much better, even though less naive, than the previously described jovial chatter that includes everything. At the moment of resignation, of collecting oneself, of choice, the individual is allowed to salute the absolute τέλος—but then, then comes the mediation. So, too, a dog can be taught to walk on two legs for a moment* but then, then comes the mediation, and the dog walks on four legs—mediation also does that. Spiritually understood, a human being's upright walk is his absolute respect for the absolute τέλος; otherwise he walks on all fours. When it is a matter of relative elements, mediation can have its significance (that they are all equal before mediation), but when it is a matter of the absolute τέλος, mediating means that the absolute τέλος is reduced to a relative τέλος. It is not true, either, that the absolute τέλος becomes concrete in the relative ends, because resignation's absolute distinction will at every moment safeguard the absolute τέλος against all fraternizing. It is true that the individual oriented toward the absolute τέλος is in the relative ends, but he is not in them in such a way that the absolute τέλος is exhausted in them. It is true that before God and before the absolute τέλος we are all equal, but it is not true that God or the absolute

* Not quite so, because the person who has ever been properly turned in the direction of the absolute τέλος can indeed degenerate, sink, sink very low, but he can never forget it entirely, which is correctly stated when one says that it requires an elevation in order to sink low. But the shrewd invention of mediation shows that the person mediating has never even stood properly positioned toward the absolute τέλος.

τέλος is equal with everything else for me or for a particular individual.

It may be very commendable for a particular individual to be a councilor of justice, a good worker in the office, no. 1 lover in the society,[649] almost a virtuoso on the flute, captain of the popinjay shooting club, superintendent of an orphanage, a noble and respected father—in short, a devil of a fellow who can *both-and* and has time for everything. But let the councilor take care that he does not become too much a devil of a fellow and proceed to do *both* all this *and* have time to VII
direct his life toward the absolute τέλος. In other words, this 348
both-and means that the absolute τέλος is on the same level with everything else. But the absolute τέλος has the remarkable quality of wanting to be the absolute τέλος at every moment. If, then, at the moment of resignation, of collecting oneself, of choice, an individual has understood this, it surely cannot mean that he is supposed to have forgotten it the next moment. Therefore, as I said before, resignation remains in the individual and the task is so far from getting the absolute τέλος mediated into all sorts of *both-and* that, on the contrary, it is to aim at the form of existence that permanently has the pathos of the great moment.

What has particularly helped mediation to grow and prosper in the ethical sphere is the deterring way in which the monastic movement of the Middle Ages has been used. People were made to believe that the existing person's absolute respect for the absolute τέλος would lead to entering the monastery. The movement itself was an enormous abstraction, monastic life a continued abstraction, so that life would be spent in praying and singing hymns—instead of playing cards at the club. If it is permissible as a matter of course to caricature the one, then it surely must also be permissible to depict the other as it has caricatured itself. In order, then, to stop the monastic movement, from which worldly wisdom has known how to derive great advantage, which even now it sometimes uses to preach indulgence from all engagement with the religious (indeed, in a Protestant country where Protestantism has prevailed for three hundred years, where anyone who

wanted to enter a monastery would get into even greater difficulties than was the worried father who wrote: Where shall I send my son to school;[650] in the nineteenth century, in which secularism is triumphant, we now and then still hear a pastor who, in a discourse urging his listeners to participate in life's innocent joys, warns against entering the monastery; one hears this and sees, behold, the pastor is so gripped by his subject that he perspires and wipes away the perspiration)—consequently, in order to stop the monastic movement people hit upon this foolish talk about mediation. Just as it is foolish talk to bring up God's name in ordinary chatter, so also is it foolish
VII to place the absolute τέλος on the same level as the rank of
349 captain of the popinjay shooting club and the like. But even if the Middle Ages erred in eccentricity, it by no means follows that mediation is commendable. The Middle Ages has a certain similarity to Greece and had what the Greeks had, passion. Thus the monastic movement is a passionate decision, as is appropriate with respect to the absolute τέλος, and to that extent is far preferable in its nobility to the wretched brokerage wisdom of mediation.

[651]Mediation wants to recognize (but deceptively, please note, nor can it be done in any other way) the pathos-filled moment of resignation, the orientation toward the absolute τέλος, but then it wants to include this τέλος among the others, and wants to profit in the finite sense from the relation to this τέλος. Let us then ask: What is the maximum a person gains by relating himself to the absolute τέλος? In the finite sense there is nothing to gain, but everything to lose. In temporality, the *expectancy* of an eternal happiness is the highest reward, because an eternal happiness is the absolute τέλος, and the specific sign that one relates oneself to the absolute is that not only is there no reward to expect but suffering to endure. As soon as the individual cannot be satisfied with that, it signifies that the individual regresses to worldly wisdom, to Jewish attachment to promises for this life, to chiliasm[652] and the like. Therein lies precisely the difficulty of the task of relating oneself absolutely to the absolute τέλος.

It happens repeatedly in human life that people seek escapes,

seek to be free from walking on tiptoe this way, free from—being satisfied with the relation to the absolute. Indeed, the pastor says that there are two paths, and it is certainly a pious wish that the pastor might say this with proper emphasis. So there are two paths, says the pastor, and when he begins this discourse we know very well what he means, but we can gladly hear it again, because this is no anecdote or witticism that can be heard only once. There are two paths: the one, smiling and carefree, easy to travel, beckoning, strewn with flowers, meanders through lovely regions, and walking on it is as light as dancing in the meadow; the other path is narrow, stony, difficult in the beginning, but little by little . . . . . It is the path of pleasure and the path of virtue. At times the pastor speaks this way, but what happens? Just as the path of virtue VII
changes little by little, so the pastor's discourse also changes,* 350
and little by little the two paths begin to resemble each other quite closely. In order to entice the listener to virtue, the description of the path of virtue becomes almost seductive. But to entice is a dangerous matter. The speaker abandons the ethical and operates in an esthetically correct way with the help of the foreshortened perspective, and what then? Well, then there actually are not two paths, or there are two paths of pleasure, one of which is a little more sagacious than the other, just as when climbing a mountain to enjoy the view it is more sagacious not to turn around too soon—in order to enjoy it all the more. Then what? Then the sensualist (the eudaemonist) is not only lunatic because he chooses the path of pleasure instead of the path of virtue, but he is a lunatic sensualist for not choosing the pleasurable path of virtue. As soon as this "little by little" on the way of virtue acquires an esthetic coloration

* I would really like to know what passage in the New Testament the pastor uses as the basis for the upbuilding discourse about "little by little." In the New Testament, it also says that there are two paths and that the path is hard and the gate is narrow that leads to salvation and those who find it are few,[653] but nothing at all is said about "little by little." But just as there is a committee in Copenhagen[654] that works to beautify the city, so there seems to be a modern pastoral wisdom at work to beautify the path of virtue with esthetic decorations.

in the pastor's mouth—then it is a lie in your throat,[655] old man! Then His Reverence deigns to forget that he is disposing of existence as no person should dare to do. He sets forth a τέλος in time, and all his teaching about virtue is a doctrine of sagacity. But if a religious person heard a sermon like that, he would say to his soul, "Do not let him disturb you; he himself may not be aware that he wants to deceive you, that he wants to make you impatient when this 'little by little' lasts for years, perhaps lasts for your whole life. No, instead let me know from the beginning that it can remain narrow, stony, and thorny until the very end, so that I may learn to hold fast to the absolute τέλος, led by this light in the night of sufferings, but not misled by probability and temporary consolation."

It is well known that over the temple at Delphi there was also the inscription: *ne quid nimis* [nothing too much].[656] This
VII motto is the *summa summarum* of all finite worldly wisdom. If
351 it is supposed to be the maximum, Christianity should immediately be revoked as a juvenile and immature whim. Just try once to apply this *ne quid nimis* to the god [*Guden*] who allows himself to be crucified, and you will immediately conjure up mockery of religion as witty as is seldom heard in this world, since mockers of religion are ordinarily hotheaded and obtuse. It would be almost the wittiest objection, tinged with humor and devoid of any attack on the historical and eternal truth of Christianity, that would simply excuse itself from relation to it with these words: "It is much too much, Your Reverence, that the god allows himself to be crucified." That maxim, *ne quid nimis*, may be valid in many life relationships, but applied to the absolute passionate relationship, to the absolute τέλος, it is nonsense. On the contrary, the point is absolutely to venture everything, absolutely to stake everything, absolutely to desire the highest τέλος, but then in turn the point is that even the absolute passion and the renunciation of everything else does not acquire the appearance of meriting, of earning an eternal happiness. The first true expression of relating oneself to the absolute τέλος is to renounce everything, but lest retrogression begin at once, one must truly under-

stand that this renunciation of everything is nothing if it is supposed to merit the highest good. The error of paganism consists in the first position: not willing to venture everything; the error of the Middle Ages consists in the second position: misunderstanding the meaning of venturing everything; the hodgepodge of our age mediates.

The dubious character of the monastic movement (apart from the error of presumed meritoriousness) was that the absolute interiority, probably in order to demonstrate very energetically that it existed, acquired its obvious expression in a distinctive separate outwardness, whereby it nevertheless, however one twists and turns, became only relatively different from all other outwardness. Mediation either allows the relation to the absolute τέλος to be mediated in relative ends, whereby it becomes relative itself, or allows the relation to the absolute τέλος as an abstract noun to exhaust itself in relative ends as predicates, whereby the majesty of the absolute relation becomes meaningless, becomes an ostentatious introduction to life that nevertheless remains outside life, is like a title page that is not included when the book is bound. But the relation to the absolute τέλος cannot be said to exhaust itself in relative ends, since the absolute relation can require renunciation of all of them. On the other hand, the person who relates himself to the absolute τέλος may very well live in the relative ends just in order to practice the absolute relation in renunciation.

Since almost everyone in our age is a tremendous fellow on VII 352
paper, one sometimes has groundless worries to deal with. An example of this is the danger in which people are today, that they finish everything so fast that they are in the awkward situation of finding something to fill their time. One writes on paper, "Doubt everything"—then one has doubted everything. If a person is only thirty years old, he is in the awkward situation of finding something to fill up his time, especially "if one has only poorly taken care of one's old age by not having learned to play cards."[657] So it is also with renouncing everything—now one is finished with it. One says: To renounce everything is an enormous abstraction—that is why one must

proceed to hold on to something. But if the task is to renounce everything, what if one began by renouncing something? Just as it must be tedious for the teacher (and just as the mediocre pupil in a school is usually recognized by his running up with his paper scarcely ten minutes after the task has been assigned and saying, "I have finished," so also in life the mediocrities promptly come running and have finished, and the greater the task the more quickly they have finished), so also it must be wearisome for the power who governs existence to have to deal with a generation like this. Holy Scripture speaks of God's patience with sinners as being incomprehensible,[658] which it is indeed, but what angelic patience it takes to deal with human beings like that—who are promptly finished.

Insofar, then, as the individual, after having become absolutely oriented toward the absolute τέλος, is not to leave the world (and to what purpose is this outwardness, but let us never forget that interiority without outwardness is the most difficult interiority, in which self-deception is easiest), what then? Well, then it is his task existentially to express that he continually has the absolute orientation toward the absolute τέλος, the absolute respect (*respicere* [to look to]). He is to express it existentially, because verbal pathos is esthetic pathos. He is to express it existentially, and yet it must not be directly expressed by any direct or distinctive outwardness, for then we have either the monastic movement or mediation. Hence he can live just like other human beings, but resignation will see to it early and late that he works to maintain the
VII 353 solemnity with which he existentially gained the orientation toward the absolute τέλος the first time. He does not and will not recognize a *both-and*; he abhors it just as he abhors taking God's name in vain, just as the lover abhors loving anyone else. And resignation, the direction chief of existence, will make an inspection. But if it discovers that he is losing elevation, that he is longing to walk on all fours, that he is associating with a suspicious character, mediation, that the latter finally carries off the victory—then resignation will stand outside this individual, will stand there, as the guardian angel of death is pictured, bending over an extinguished torch,[659]

because there the absolute τέλος vanished from the individual's dimmed vision. [660]Outwardly perhaps no change will be discernible, because the relation to the absolute τέλος did not mean entering the monastery and then, when one was tired of it, wearing secular clothes again, whereby the change becomes outwardly discernible. Nor did the relation to the absolute τέλος mean that the absolute τέλος exhausted itself in the relative, because then the change that occurred in a person would again have to be discernible outwardly.

In a certain sense it is somewhat appalling to speak this way about a person's interiority [*Indvorteshed*], that it can be there and not be there without being directly discernible outwardly. But it is also glorious to speak this way about interiority—if it is there—because this is precisely the expression for its inwardness [*Inderlighed*]. As soon as interiority is supposed to be decisively and commensurably expressed outwardly, we have the monastic movement. Mediation is not actually aware of any relation to an absolute τέλος, because mediation exhausts itself in the relative. But then what happens with the interiority? Well, this is what happens. The task is to practice the absolute relation to the absolute τέλος in such a way that the individual strives to reach this maximum: to relate himself simultaneously to his absolute τέλος and to the relative—not by mediating them but by relating himself absolutely to his absolute τέλος and relatively to the relative. The latter relation belongs to the world, the former to the individual himself, and it is difficult simultaneously to relate oneself absolutely to the absolute τέλος and then at the same moment to participate like other human beings in one thing and another. If a person is involved in some great plan, that alone makes it difficult to be like others. He is absentminded, does not care to participate in anything else, is tormented by all the commotion around him. The busyness of others is irksome; he would like a little cubbyhole to himself where he could sit and ponder his great plan—and it can be a suitable task for diplomats and police agents to acquire the art and self-control to be VII 354
able to hold fast to the great plan and simultaneously to go to dances, converse with the ladies, go bowling, and do what-

ever one likes. But the absolute τέλος is the greatest plan to which a human being can relate himself, and therefore the Middle Ages wanted a little cubbyhole in order to be able to occupy itself properly with the absolute; but it was precisely by this that the absolute lost, because it still became something outward.

When a married couple have been busy socially, perhaps for a whole week, they sometimes say that they have had no time in the past week to live for each other, and they say that even though they have been together in the same place and consequently have seen each other. They look forward to a day when they are really able to live for each other, and this can be very beautiful for married people. The person who wants to relate himself to his absolute τέλος but is continually hindered in doing it by being in existence and the multiplicity of existence seems to be in a similar situation. But then it would seem quite in order if once in a while he really lived a day for his absolute τέλος. But right here is the difficulty. That is, the husband and wife relate themselves to each other relatively, and therefore it is quite in order to have that day in which they really live for each other. But to relate oneself to one's absolute τέλος once in a while is to relate oneself relatively to one's absolute τέλος, yet to relate relatively to the absolute τέλος is to relate to a relative τέλος, because the relation is the decisive thing. Consequently, the task is to practice one's relation to one's absolute τέλος so that one continually has it within while continuing in the relative objectives of existence—and let us not forget that it was the case at least in school that the mediocre pupil was recognized by his running up with his paper ten minutes after the task was assigned and saying: I have finished.

Mediation, therefore, remains outside. I shall take falling in love as the τέλος and have an individual through a misunderstanding interpret this as the absolute τέλος. He does not want to leave the world; he wants to be like the rest of us, perhaps a councilor of justice, perhaps a merchant, etc. But just as he once understood absolutely that his falling in love was for him the absolute, so his absolute task will be contin-

ually to understand it that way, and just as it once was horrible to him that his falling in love would not be the absolute but be prattled into a both-and, so he will work with all his might so that it may never happen. What became of mediation, then? And what was the mistake? The mistake was that he interpreted falling in love as the absolute τέλος. But in relation to the absolute τέλος, the individual behaves properly in behaving in this way. In everything he undertakes, wherever he is, whatever his condition, whether the world beckons or threatens, whether he jests or is earnest, resignation sees to it first VII
and foremost that the absolute respect for the absolute τέλος 355
is maintained absolutely. But there is no mediating here, any more than there is a mediating between heaven and hell to say that there is a chasmic abyss established between them;[661] and out of respect a chasmic abyss of that sort is established between the absolute τέλος and the relative ends.

But if this is the way it is and the task is to practice the absolute relation, then existence becomes exceedingly strenuous because a double movement is continually being made. The monastic movement wants to express interiority by an outwardness that is supposed to be interiority. Herein lies the contradiction, because to be a monk is just as much something outward as being councilor of justice. Mediation abolishes the absolute τέλος. But a truly pathos-filled existing person will at every moment express for himself that the absolute τέλος is the absolute τέλος.

The profundity rests in the quiet incorruptibility of the interiority, but therein also lies the possibility of deception and the temptation to say that one has done it and is doing it. Now, if someone wants to tell a lie in this regard, that is his own affair, and I shall be delighted to believe all that he says. If it is something great, I perhaps could be helped to do the same, and whether he actually has done it does not concern me at all. I would only give him the rule of prudence that he should not add that he *also*[662] mediates, because then he informs against himself. The existing person who has his absolute orientation toward the absolute τέλος and comprehends the task of practicing the relation may be a councilor of justice, may be one of the other councilors, and yet he is not like the other councilors, but when one sees him he is exactly like the others. Perhaps he gains the whole world, but he is not like one who craves that. Perhaps he becomes king, but every time he places the crown on his head and every time he extends his scepter, resignation first inspects to see if he, existing, is expressing the absolute respect for the absolute τέλος—and the crown dwindles into insignificance, even if he wears it regally. It dwindles into insignificance as it did that time in the great moment of resignation, even though he now wears it in the third decade of his rule. It dwindles into insignificance as it will some day before the spectators' eyes and before his own dying eyes in the hour of death, but it dwindled into insignificance this way for him at the peak of his vigor. What, then, became of mediation? And yet there was indeed no one who entered the monastery.

The individual does not cease to be a human being, does not take off the multitudinously compounded suit of finitude in order to put on the abstract attire of the monastery, but he
VII does not mediate between the absolute τέλος and the finite.
356 In immediacy, the individual is firmly rooted in the finite; when resignation is convinced that the individual has the absolute orientation toward the absolute τέλος, everything is changed, the roots are cut. He lives in the finite, but he does not have his life in it. His life, like the life of another, has the diverse predicates of a human existence, but he is within them like the person who walks in a stranger's borrowed clothes. He is a stranger in the world of finitude, but he does not define his difference from *worldliness* by foreign dress (this is a contradiction, since with that he defines himself in a worldly way); he is incognito, but his incognito consists in looking just like everyone else. Just as the dentist loosens the gum tissue and cuts the nerve and lets the tooth remain, so also is his life in finitude loosened, and the task is not to have the tooth grow fast again, which would be mediation. Just as in the great moment of resignation one does not mediate but chooses, now the task is to gain proficiency in repeating the impassioned choice and, existing, to express it in existence. So the individ-

ual is certainly in the finite (and the difficulty is indeed to preserve the absolute choice in the finite), but just as he took away the vital power of the finite in the moment of resignation, so the task is to repeat this. Suppose the world offers the individual everything. Perhaps he accepts it, but he says: Oh, well, but this "Oh, well" signifies absolute respect for the absolute τέλος. Suppose the world takes everything away from him; he may wince, but he says: Oh, well—and this "Oh, well" signifies the absolute respect for the absolute τέλος. In this way, one does not exist immediately in the finite.

Whether to the Eternal, the All-Knowing, the Everywhere-Present One it is of equal importance that a human being forfeits his eternal happiness or a sparrow falls to the ground; whether it will be manifest when everything is settled in eternity that the most insignificant circumstance was absolutely important—I do not decide. I can truthfully say that *time* does not allow me to do that—simply because I am in time. In existence, it cannot possibly be this way for an existing person, since he is in a process of becoming, and for an existing person a grandiloquent mediating (which in the Greek sense is not accomplished in even an entire lifetime but in the German sense legitimatizes itself on paper) is nothing but monkey tricks! A mortal eye cannot endure and ethics forbids him to will absolutely to venture to endure the dizziness of seeing that the most insignificant thing is just as important as the absolutely decisive, and an *existing person* cannot find rest and dares not give himself rest to become extravagantly fantastical, be- VII
cause he still does not become eternal as long as he is in existence. 357
tence. In existence, the word is continually "forward,"[663] and as long as it is "forward" the point is to practice the absolute distinction, the point is to have gained a proficiency in doing it more and more readily and a good self-awareness. But once again it is not mediation when the very practiced person places confidence in the private knowledge that he is making the absolute distinction with facility and joy. When the elderly wife is happily convinced that her husband is absolutely faithful to her, of what is she convinced? Is it of his mediating and of his heart divided in mediation, or is she not convinced that se-

cretly he continually makes love's absolute distinction, only that in joyous confidence she is convinced that he is doing it with ease and reliability, and therefore she needs no external proof? But do not forget that marriage is not the absolute τέλος, and therefore what is absolutely true of the absolute is only imperfectly true of marriage.[664]

If God were directly the ideal for being a human being, it would be all right to want to express the direct likeness. If, for example, a first-rate person is to me the ideal, it is quite all right for me to want to express a direct likeness, because by being human beings we both exist within the same sphere. But between God and a human being (let speculative thought just keep *humankind* to perform tricks with) there is an absolute difference;[665] therefore a person's absolute relationship with God must specifically express the absolute difference, and the direct likeness becomes impudence, conceited pretense, presumption,* and the like. If God in his sublimity were to say to a human being, "You are no more important to me
VII 358 than a sparrow," and if a human being had it as his task to express a direct likeness to the divine sublimity, then the merit would indeed consist in replying, "Neither are you and your existence of any more importance to me than a sparrow"—whether this should be interpreted positively, because everything had become equally important for this exalted person, or negatively, because everything was of such equal importance to him that nothing was important to him. But this, of course, is surely demented blasphemy.

Precisely because there is the absolute difference between God and man, man expresses himself most perfectly when he

* It is something different when, in a very childlike era and in innocent naïveté, God becomes a venerable old man or something similar and lives on a friendly footing with the pious. For example, I recollect having read about one of the saintly characters discussed in Weil's *Biblische Legenden der Muselmänner* that God himself personally walked ahead of the coffin in the funeral procession and four angels walked behind.[666] That something like this is innocent naïveté is shown, for example, by the fact that when one reads it now
VII 358 it creates a pure and innocent humorous effect. This childlike piety does not, of course, want to offend God but on the contrary is happy to adorn him with the best it can devise.

absolutely expresses the difference. *Worship* is the maximum for a human being's relationship with God, and thereby for his likeness to God, since the qualities are absolutely different. But worship signifies that for him God is absolutely everything, and the worshiper is in turn the absolutely differentiating one. The absolutely differentiating one relates himself to his absolute τέλος, but *eo ipso* also to God. The absolute distinction is equipped to clear the way just as a policeman does in a procession; it clears away the crush, the mob of relative ends, in order that the absolutely differentiating one can relate himself to the absolute. There is no merit at all for an existing person in wanting to approach the equality that possibly exists for the eternal. For an existing person, the passionate decision is precisely the maximum. Existing is like walking. When everything *is* and is at rest, it deceptively looks as if everything is equally important, that is, if I can attain a view of it that is equally quiet. As soon as motion commences, however, and I am along in the motion, then the walking itself is a continual differentiating. But this comparison cannot state the absolute differentiating, because walking is only a finite motion.

But because the task is to practice the absolute distinction, it does not necessarily mean that the existing person becomes indifferent to the finite. That was the exaggeration of the Middle Ages; it did not have complete faith in inwardness unless it became an outwardness. But the less outwardness, the more inwardness, and inwardness expressed by its opposite (but the opposite is that the individual is entirely like everyone else, that there is nothing at all to be noted in externals) is the highest inwardness—if it is there. This must also be added continually: the less outwardness, the easier the deception. An adult VII
may very well join in children's play with total interest, may 359
be the one who really makes the game lively, but he still does not play as a child. The person who understands it as his task to practice the absolute distinction relates himself to the finite in the same way. But he does not mediate. The Middle Ages was a distrustful inwardness that therefore wanted to see it in externals. It was to that extent an unhappy inwardness that resembled a love affair in which the lovers are zealous for the

outward expression of erotic love; thus it believed that God was zealous for expression in externals. True inwardness does not demand any sign at all in externals. In the practice of the absolute distinction, the passion of the infinite is present, but it wants to be inwardness without jealousy, without envy, without mistrust. It does not want contentiously to stand out marked as something striking in existence, whereby it simply loses, just as when God's invisible image is made visible. It does not want to disturb the finite, but neither does it want to mediate. In the midst of the finite and finitude's multiple occasions for the existing person to forget the absolute distinction, it only wants to be the absolute inwardness for him, and as for the rest, he can be councilor of justice, etc. But the maximum of the task is to be able simultaneously to relate oneself absolutely to the absolute τέλος and relatively to the relative ends, or at all times to have the absolute τέλος with oneself.

If this is not possible or if one is unwilling to accept this as the task, then analogies to the monastic movement are unconditionally to be preferred, whether one likes it or not, whether one wants to laugh or to cry over this thesis in the speculative nineteenth century. In the monastic movement there was at least passion and respect for the absolute τέλος. But the monastic movement must not be made as something meritorious; on the contrary, it must be made humbly before God and not without a certain sense of shame. Just as a sick child does not regard it as meritorious to be allowed to remain at home with his parents, just as a beloved does not regard it as meritorious that she cannot at any moment do without the sight of her lover and is unable to gain the strength to have the thought of him with her as she goes about her work as usual, just as she does not regard it as meritorious to be allowed to sit with him at his place of work and to be with him continually—so must the candidate for the monastery regard his relationship with God. And if he does that, then there can be no further objection to his choice, no matter what one deigns to say in the nineteenth century.

But the sick child will soon discover the difficulty, not because the parents are not tender and loving but because the

daily association gives rise to so many little clashes. The be- VII
loved will soon discover the difficulty, not because the beloved 360
is not a good man, but because the continual sight of him day in and day out and every hour sometimes makes for a certain flatness—and the candidate for the monastery will also surely feel the same way. Here again a pastor will often fool us. On Sundays he says that it is so quiet and solemn in the church, and if we could only remain there continually we would surely become holy people, but we must go out into the confusion of the world. Shame on the pastor for wanting to make us think that the fault is in the world and not in us. Shame on him for teaching us to be haughty, as if we were choosing the most difficult task, especially if we are not supposed to have the absolute τέλος with us at every moment also out there in the world. I thought the pastor was supposed to teach us humility and therefore to say, "Now go home. May each one of you do your work as God has assigned it to you, and thank God, who knows a person's weakness, that you are not required to remain here all day long and do nothing but sing hymns and pray and praise God. In that case, you perhaps would discover spiritual trials of which God allows you to continue to remain ignorant." Going to church once a week when one otherwise is on the move in life's multiplicity easily creates an illusion by means of the foreshortened perspective of the esthetic. But for this very reason the pastor should know how to watch out and not repeatedly misuse the Middle Ages to beguile the congregation into great conceits.

In our day there actually is no great reason to warn against the monastery, and in the Middle Ages the reason perhaps was something other than what one most likely thinks. If I had lived in the Middle Ages, I could never have resolved to choose the monastery. Why not? Because the person who did so was in all earnestness regarded in the Middle Ages as a holy person. Then when I would walk down the street and a poor wretched man, who perhaps was a far better man than I,* met

* Yet this "perhaps" is not exactly hypothetical, even if I were other than I am, because the person who in earnestness and honesty regards another per-

me, he would bow before me and in all pathos and earnestness would suppose me to be a holy person. But to me this seems the most dreadful of all and to be a profanation of the holy, to be treachery to an absolute relation to an absolute τέλος. In our time, a person would be regarded as lunatic if he entered a monastery, if one were established. When nowadays one VII 361 reads a physician's prospectus for the establishment of an insane asylum, it bears a certain resemblance to a monastery prospectus. This I regard as an extraordinary bonus. To be regarded as lunatic—there's something to that—it is encouraging. It protects the quiet inwardness of an absolute relationship, but to be assumed to be holy in earnest—that is bound to worry one to death. In my opinion, making the monastery into an insane asylum comes closest to an externality that is just like everybody else's. Then the outwardness does not correspond directly to the interiority, which was the error of the Middle Ages. I think at least as follows: Let me become anything in the world; it will hardly be something great. And however lowly it is, I shall try to put up with it, but let me be exempted from one thing—to be regarded in all earnestness as a holy person. If someone in mockery were to call me a holy person, that would be *was anders* [something else]. There is something to that; it is encouraging.

But it behooves us to have respect for the monastic movement of the Middle Ages. To be sure, the pastor does say that by entering the monastery one avoided danger, and therefore it is greater to remain in life amid the dangers—but certainly not with the help of mediation? Let us at least try to understand one another and agree on what is meant by danger. The monastery candidate thought the greatest danger was not to relate oneself absolutely to the absolute τέλος at every moment. Mediation does not know this danger. By means of mediation, one avoids the absolute danger and the absolute strenuousness, avoids the solitary and silent association with the absolute, in which the least loss is an absolute loss, in which

---

son as a holy person *eo ipso* shows by this humility that he is better than the other.

the slightest regression is perdition, in which there is no distraction (none at all, but, like a sunstroke, the recollection of the ever-so-slight regression burns the unhappy one, who has no place for escape), in which every weakness, every flatness, every state of low spirits is like a mortal sin, and every such hour is like an eternity, because time does not move—one avoids this, and this is what the pastor calls avoiding danger because a person remains in the relative dangers, in the dangers of multiplicity, where the simplest experience teaches him that he never loses everything (just because there is a multiplicity) but loses in one way and gains in another, where the dangers are those of job and livelihood, of health, of being abused in the newspapers, etc.

It is really sad that the eccentricity of the Middle Ages is repeatedly misused to teach people to plume themselves on being such deucedly great fellows, and when they talk this way in our day it is just as much a parody as for a man in an old folks' home to expound that the highest courage is not to take one's own life but to refrain from doing so and thereby VII 362 to prompt all the inmates to regard themselves as the most courageous of all people—for they, after all, had had the courage to refrain! Or it is like someone's speaking to an audience of very hardened people about the greatness of bearing one's sorrows like a man and leaving out the dialectical middle term, the greatness of being able to grieve like a man. Let us go to the theater to be deceived, let the actor and spectator cooperate beautifully to fascinate and to be fascinated in illusion: it is magnificent. If worst comes to worst, let me be deceived by my servant who flatters me, by someone who wishes a favor from me, by my shoemaker because I am his best customer whom he is reluctant to lose—but why, if I am a good listener, must I be deceived and almost be afraid for myself in a church! That is, if I am a good listener, then I hear in such a way that the pastor continually seems to be preaching about me,[667] because what otherwise is vanity and perhaps very ordinary in the world is exactly what is laudable and perhaps very rare in a church. And why do I become almost afraid for myself? Is it because the pastor describes us human beings (that is, me, if I am a good listener who assumes that it is I about whom he is preaching) as so corrupted that I shudder at being someone like that, that I grow pale and in horror but also with indignation say, "No, I am not that bad?" Alas, no. His Reverence describes us human beings (that is, me, if I am a good listener who assumes that it is I about whom he is preaching) so gloriously, as so much superior to those quiet inhabitants of the monastery, that I (who assume, after all, that it is I of whom he speaks) become utterly ashamed and embarrassed and red in the face and am obliged to say in embarrassment: No, Your Reverence is really much too polite—and look up inquiringly to see if it is a pastor who is speaking or a New Year's congratulator.*[668]

* It appears that the pastor's sermon today is somewhat different from his sermon last Sunday, in which he encouraged the *Christian* congregation to whom he preaches to accept the *Christian* faith and to become Christians (see the previous division). This is entirely in order when Baptism is supposed to make us Christians as a matter of course by being baptized as infants; the dubiousness, as was pointed out, consists only in simultaneously regarding infant Baptism as decisive with regard to becoming a Christian. It is different when the preacher as a matter of course makes all his listeners into great heroes. The religious address deals essentially with individuals and essentially functions as an intermediary between the individual and the ideal, and at its
VII maximum it helps the individual to express the ideal. It essentially assumes
363 that all the people it addresses are in error; it is informed about every wrong path of error, every one of its hiding places, about the condition of everyone straying on the path of error. But such preaching is rarely heard in our objective era. There is preaching about faith and the exploits of faith—and one is either esthetically indifferent as to whether all of us who listen are believers or one is esthetically polite enough to assume that we are. In this way faith becomes a kind of allegorical figure and the pastor a troubadour of sorts, and the sermon about faith becomes analogous to something like Saint George's battle with the dragon. The setting is in the air, and faith conquers all difficulties. The same with hope and love.[669] The ecclesiastical address becomes a counterpart to the first medieval venture into drama (the so-called mysteries), when religious subjects were treated dramatically and, strangely enough, comedies were played on Sunday of all days, and in churches of all places.[670] Because faith, hope, and love, because God and Jesus Christ are talked about in church in a solemn voice (whether this is the more or less artistic or the inartistic deep bass voice of a revivalist), it still by no means follows that this is a godly address. The decisive point is how the speaker and the listeners relate themselves to the discourse or are presumed to relate themselves to it.

No, it behooves us to have respect for the monastic move- VII
ment of the Middle Ages. Mediation, on the other hand, is a 363
revolt of the relative ends against the majesty of the absolute, VII
which is to be drawn down to the level of everything else, and 364
against the dignity of the human being, who is to be made a servant solely of the relative ends. Insofar as it wants to be higher than the absolute disjunction, mediation is a fantastic invention.

Mediation looks fairly good on paper. First one assumes the finite, then the infinite, and then one says on paper: This must be mediated. An existing person has unquestionably found there the secure foothold outside existence where he can mediate—on paper. The Archimedean point has been found, but one does not notice that it has succeeded in moving the whole world. When, however, the setting is not on paper but in ex-

---

The speaker must not relate himself to his subject only through the imagination but must himself be that of which he speaks or, striving toward it, must have the "how" of his own experience or the "how" of continuing experience. The listeners must be enlightened by the discourse and be encouraged to become that of which it speaks (in the main this is the same whether a direct or indirect relation is assumed between the speaker and the listener; if an indirect relation is assumed as the true relation, the discourse will become a monologue, but, please note, about the speaker's personally experienced "how," and in this "how" and by talking about himself he will indirectly speak about the listener). In the godly discourse about faith, the main point is that it informs us how you and I (that is, single individuals) become believers and that the speaker helps tear us out of all illusions and knows about the long and laborious way and about relapse etc. If becoming a believer is made an easy matter (for example, by being baptized as an infant) and if the discourse is only about faith, the whole relationship is only esthetic and we are indeed attending a comedy—in the church. For a bagatelle, we gain admission to the pastor's dramatic performances, where we sit and observe what faith is capable of doing—not as believers, but as spectators of the achievements of faith,
just as in our day we do not have speculative thinkers but spectators of the VII
achievements of *speculative thought*. But for a theocentric, speculative, and ob- 364
jective age it is, of course, most likely far too little—to become involved in the ultimate difficulties, where the question ultimately becomes as sharp, as penetrating, as disturbing, as uncompromising as possible about whether the individual, you and I, is a believer and about how we relate ourselves to faith from day to day.

istence, because the person mediating is an existing person (and thereby prevented from being a mediating person), he will then, if he becomes aware of what it means to exist (that is, that *he* exists), at that very same moment become the one who absolutely differentiates, not between the finite and the infinite, but between existing finitely and existing infinitely. The infinite and the finite are joined together in existing and in the existing person, who does not need to bother with creating existence, or with thinking about reproducing existence, but all the more with existing. With the help of mediation, even existence is produced on paper.[671] In existence, where the existing person finds himself, the task is simpler: whether he will be so kind as to exist. As an existing person, then, he need not form existence out of the finite and the infinite, but, composed of the finite and the infinite, he, existing, is supposed to *become* one of the parts, and one does not *become* both parts simultaneously, because one *is* that by *being* an existing person, for this is exactly the difference between being and becoming, and the chimerical proficiency of mediation, if it be-
VII longs anywhere at all, is an expression—for the beginning. In
365 several regards, this is what has happened in the most recent philosophy—namely, having had the task of combating a mistaken reflection and having finished that, it confuses the end of this work with the end of everything, but instead the end of this work is *höchstens* [at best] the beginning of the real task.

A person can *be both* good and evil, just as it is quite simply said that a human being has a disposition to both good and evil, but one cannot *simultaneously become* good and evil. Esthetically, the poet has been required not to depict these abstract models of virtue or diabolical characters but to do as Goethe does, whose characters are both good and evil. And why is this a legitimate requirement? Because we want the poet to depict human beings as they *are*, and every human being *is* both good and evil, and because the poet's medium is the medium of imagination, is being but not becoming, at most is becoming in a very foreshortened perspective. But take the individual out of this medium of imagination, out of this being, and place him in existence—then ethics immediately confronts him with its requirement, whether he now deigns to become, and then he becomes—either good or evil. In the earnest moment of self-contemplation, in the sacred moment of confession, the individual removes himself from the process of becoming and in the realm of being inspects how he is. Alas, the result unfortunately is that he *is both* good *and* evil, but as soon as he is again in the process of becoming, he becomes either good or evil. This *summa summarum*, that all human beings *are* both good and evil, is of no concern at all to ethics, which does not have the medium of *being* but of *becoming* and therefore denounces every explanation of becoming that deceitfully wants to explain becoming within being, whereby the absolute decision of becoming is essentially revoked and all talk about it is essentially a false alarm.

Ethics, therefore, must also denounce all the jubilation heard in our day over having surmounted reflection. Who is it who is supposed to have surmounted reflection? An existing person. But existence itself is the sphere of reflection, and an existing person is in existence and therefore in reflection—how, then, does he go about surmounting it? It is not difficult to perceive that in a certain sense the principle of identity is higher, is the basis of the principle of contradiction. But the principle of identity is only the boundary; it is like the blue mountains, like the line the artist calls the base line—the drawing is the main thing. Therefore, identity is a lower view than
contradiction, which is more concrete. Identity is the *terminus* VII
a quo [point from which] but not *ad quem* [to which] for exis- 366
tence. An existing person can *maxime* arrive at and continually arrive at identity by abstracting from existence. But since ethics regards every existing person as its bond servant, it absolutely forbids him to commence this abstracting at any moment. Instead of saying that the principle of identity annuls contradiction, it is contradiction that annuls identity or, as Hegel so often says, lets it "go to the ground."[672]

Mediation wants to make existence easier for the existing

person by omitting an absolute relation to an absolute τέλος. The practice of the absolute distinction makes life absolutely strenuous, especially when one must also remain in the finite and simultaneously relate oneself absolutely to the absolute τέλος and relatively to relative ends. But there is nevertheless a tranquillity and a restfulness in all this strenuousness, because it is no contradiction to relate oneself absolutely to the absolute τέλος, that is, with all one's might and in renunciation of everything else, but it is the absolute reciprocity in like for like. In other words, the agonizing self-contradiction of worldly passion results from the individual's relating himself *absolutely* to a relative τέλος. Thus vanity, avarice, envy, etc. are essentially lunacy, because the most common expression of lunacy is just this—to relate oneself absolutely to the relative—and esthetically it is to be interpreted comically, since the comic always lies in contradiction. It is demented (viewed esthetically, it is comic) for a being who is eternally structured to apply all his power to grasp the perishable, to hold fast to the changeable, and to believe that he has won everything when he has won this nothing—and is duped—to believe he has lost everything when he has lost this nothing—and is no longer duped. The perishable is nothing when it is past, and its essence is to be past, as swiftly as the moment of sensual pleasure, which is the furthest distance from the eternal—a moment in time filled with emptiness.[673]

But someone, "a serious man," may say, "But is it certain and definite that there is such a good, is it certain and definite that there is an eternal happiness in store?—because in that case I surely would aspire to it; otherwise, I would be lunatic to risk everything for it." This or a similar locution frequently appears in the pastoral discourse and forms the transition to that part of the discourse in which, to the consolation and relief of the congregation, it is demonstrated that there is an
VII eternal happiness in store—so that the congregation may as-
367 pire to it all the more zealously. Such a demonstration is like milk to the cat and goes down as God's Word with the student—"the practical exercises are as usual deferred." It is good

that I am not a serious man, an asseverating philosopher, or a surety-guaranteeing clergyman, since otherwise I, too, might be obliged to demonstrate. Fortunately my levity releases me from demonstrating, and in the capacity of a man of levity I venture to have the opinion that if a person, trusting in the asseverations of all the philosophers and the security-guarantee of the entire clergy, decides to aspire to an eternal happiness, he still does not aspire to it, and his *trust* in the asseverations of all the philosophers and the security-guarantee of the entire clergy is precisely what hinders him (the pastor, of course, believes that it is a lack of trust) and prompts him to want to be jolly well *included*, to want to make an intellectual transaction, a profitable stock-exchange speculation, instead of a daring venture, prompts him to make a simulated movement, a simulated pass at the absolute, although he remains completely within the relative, a simulated transition such as that from eudaemonism to the ethical within eudaemonism. On the whole, it is incredible how cunning and inventive people are in avoiding the final decision, and anyone who has witnessed the strange behavior of a number of rural militiamen[674] when they are ordered into the water will find plenty of analogies to that in the world of spirit.

The point is this: the individual first becomes infinitized by the daring venture; it is not the same individual and the daring venture is not one among several undertakings, one more predicate about the one and the same individual—no, through the daring venture he himself becomes someone else. Before he has made the venture, he can understand it only as lunacy (and this is far preferable to being a thoughtless blatherpate who sits and fancies that he understands it as wisdom—and yet desists from doing it, whereby he directly denounces himself as lunatic, whereas the person who regards it as lunacy still comes off as sagacious by leaving it alone), and when he has ventured it, he is no longer the same person. Thus the *discrimen* [distinctive mark] of the transition gains suitable room, an intervening chasmic abyss,[675] a suitable setting for the passion of the infinite, a chasm that the understanding cannot cross over, neither forth nor back.

But since I have in no way involved myself in demonstrating that there is an eternal happiness (partly because it is not my business, but *höchstens* [at best] that of Christianity, which proclaims it, partly because it would not exist at all if it could be demonstrated, since the existence of the absolute ethical
VII good can be demonstrated only by the individual who, him-
368 self existing [*existerende*], expresses that it exists [*er til*]), I shall for a moment consider more closely the words of that serious man; they are surely worthy of attention. So, then, he demands that it be certain and definite that there is such a good in store. But it is actually too much to demand that something that is in store shall be definite and certain, because the future and the present do have a little moment between them, which makes it possible to expect the future but impossible *in praesenti* to have certainty and definiteness. The present situation is one of certainty and definiteness, but a present relation to a future is *eo ipso* one of uncertainty and therefore quite correctly a relation of expectancy. Speculatively, it holds true that I, recollecting backward, am able to reach the eternal; it holds true that the eternal relates itself directly to the eternal, but an existing person can relate himself forward to the eternal only as the future.

The serious man continues: If he can have certainty that such a good is in store, he will venture everything for it; otherwise it would indeed be lunacy to venture everything. The serious man speaks almost like a jester. It is quite clear that he wants to poke fun at us, just like the militiaman when he makes a run in order to leap and does indeed make the run—but says goodbye to the leap. If it is certain, then he will venture everything. But what is it to venture? To venture is the correlative of uncertainty; as soon as there is certainty, venturing stops. If, then, he gains certainty and definiteness, he cannot possibly venture everything, because then he ventures nothing even if he gives up everything—and if he cannot find certainty, well, then, so says the serious man in dead earnest-

ness, well, then he will not venture everything—indeed, that would be lunacy. In this way the serious man's venturing becomes a false alarm. If that of which I am to gain possession by venturing is certain, then I am not venturing, then I am *trading*. Thus I do not venture by giving an apple for a pear if I am holding the pear in my hand as I make the trade. Shysters and rogues know all about this. They do not trust one another and therefore want to have in their hands what they are to acquire by trading. Indeed, they have such a narrow concept of venturing that they even regard it as risky if the other person turns around and spits, lest he do some kind of hocus-pocus. It is not venturing for me to give away all my possessions for a pearl[676] if in the moment of trading I hold the pearl
in my hand. If it is perhaps an imitation pearl, I have been VII 369
tricked and thus have made a bad trade, but I have not ventured anything. But if that pearl is perhaps far away in Africa in a secret place difficult to reach, if I have never had the pearl in my hand, and I then leave house and home, give up everything, make that long and arduous journey without certainty that my undertaking will succeed—well, then I am venturing*—and then some evening at the club one will hear what

* I shall with pleasure illustrate the same with a more elevated example. The lover can "venture" everything for his love, for the possession of his beloved; but the married man, who is in possission of his beloved, ventures nothing for her, even if with her he endures everything, even when he submits to everything for her sake, and therefore the married man insults his wife if he uses the expression that is the lover's loftiest enthusiasm. The married man has possession of his beloved, and if eternal happiness could be present with a person in the same way, then he would not be venturing, either. But the trouble is that it cannot be totally present in this way even for the existing person who has ventured everything—as long as he is existing—and therefore one more little *N.B.*, namely, that he must have ventured everything, since he did not receive certainty in advance and in hand from an asseverating philosopher or a surety-guaranteeing pastor. Strangely enough, although eternal happiness is the highest good and is far greater than landed property and kingdoms, it is nevertheless absolutely the good when the one who gives it away does not ask at all about the other man's surety and when the one who is to receive it is not helped at all by having all people as guarantors, but the matter is decided simply and solely between the one who gives it and the respective recip-

the serious man said: that it is lunacy. But whatever strange events that adventurer may experience on the long and dangerous journey to Africa, I still do not think that anything more strange can happen to him than what happens to the serious man's words, since the only true words that remain in all his seriousness are these: it is lunacy.* It certainly is lunacy.
VII 370 It is always lunacy to venture, but to venture everything for an expected eternal happiness is general lunacy. But the question about certainty and definiteness is sagacity, because it is a subterfuge in order to avoid the strenuousness of action and venturing and shades the issue into knowledge and nonsensical talk. No, if I, acting, am truly to venture and truly to aspire to the highest good, then there must be uncertainty and, if I may put it this way, I must have room to move. But the greatest space in which I can move, where there is space enough for the most rigorous gesture of infinite passion, is uncertainty of knowledge with regard to an eternal happiness, or that choosing it is lunacy in the finite sense—see, now there is room, now you can venture!

Therefore eternal happiness, as the absolute good, has the

---

ient—almost as great a lunacy, I was about to say, on the part of the one who gives it away for not looking better after his own advantage and security as on the part of the recipient for not becoming mistrustful and suspecting mischief as he in solitude loses sight of all guarantors.

* All worldly wisdom is indeed abstraction, and only the most mediocre eudaemonism has no abstraction whatever but is the enjoyment of the moment. To the same degree that eudaemonism is sagacious, it has abstraction; the more sagacity, the more abstraction. Eudaemonism thereby acquires a
VII 370 fleeting resemblance to the ethical and the ethical-religious, and momentarily it can seem as if they could walk together. And yet it is not so, because the first step of the ethical is infinite abstraction, and what happens? The step becomes too great for eudaemonism, and although some abstraction is sagacity, infinite abstraction, understood eudaemonistically, is lunacy. —A philosopher will perhaps say that I move only in the sphere of the conceptual.[677] Yes, it certainly is easier to join things on paper; there one ventures everything and at the same moment has everything. But if in existence I am supposed to venture everything, that is already a lifetime task, and if I am supposed to remain in existence with my venturesome deed, then I must continually keep on venturing. The esteemed philosopher, as usual, moves the setting from existence to paper.

remarkable quality that *it can be defined only by the mode in which it is acquired*, whereas other goods, just because the mode of acquisition is accidental or at any rate relatively dialectical, must be defined by the good itself. Money, for example, can be acquired by work and can also be obtained without work, and in turn both are different in many ways, but money still remains the same good. Knowledge, for example, is acquired differently according to talent and outward circumstances and therefore cannot be defined by the mode of acquisition. But nothing else can be said of eternal happiness than that it is the good that is attained by absolutely venturing everything. Any description of the gloriousness of this good is already an at- VII 371
tempt, as it were, to make various modes of acquisition possible—an easier way, for example, and a harder way, which shows that the description is not describing the absolute good but only fancies doing it and essentially is talking about relative goods. The reason that in a certain sense it is so easy to talk about this good is that it is certain—when everything is made uncertain—and that the speaker will never be in a predicament, as is the case with relative goods when it is manifest that what helps one person does not help another. And the discourse about this good is so short because there is nothing else to say than: Venture everything. There are no anecdotes to tell about how Peter became rich by working, and Paul by playing the lottery, and Hans by inheritance, and Matthew by monetary reform,[678] and Christopher by purchasing a piece of furniture from a secondhand dealer, etc. But in another sense the discourse is long, indeed, the longest of all discourses, because to venture everything demands a transparency[679] of consciousness that is acquired only very slowly.

Right here is the task of the religious discourse. If it is supposed to say only the brief word, "Venture everything," no more than one speaker would be needed in the whole kingdom; on the other hand, the longest discourse must never forget the daring venture. The religious address can deal with everything, but it must continually bring everything into relation to the absolute category of religiousness. It must walk along every path, must know the habitat of every error, where

moods have their hiding places, how passions regard themselves in solitude (and every human being who has passion is always somewhat solitary; it is only drivelers who are swallowed up in social life), know where illusions tempt, where the paths swing off, etc.—in order to bring everything continually into relation with the absolute category of religiousness. If one human being can do something for another in this regard, then he must not go to the trouble of switching over to China and Persia, because just as religious discourse is higher than all other discourse, so all truly religious discourse knows nothing on the other side of the absolute good, an eternal happiness, [680]since it knows that the task is not to move from the individual to the race but from the individual through the race
VII (the universal) to reach the individual. The religious discourse
372 is the path to the good, that is, it copies* the path, which is just as long as life; it copies the path that the religious person describes, not in the sense in which the planet describes its course or the mathematician describes a circle.

But there is no shortcut to the absolute good, and since it is defined only by the mode of acquisition, the absolute difficulty of this is the only sign that one is relating oneself to the absolute good. To chance upon it in an easier way (by being born in especially propitious years, for example, in the nineteenth century, by being very intelligent, by being born in the same town as a great man or being related by marriage to an apostle), to be a favorite of fortune, is merely evidence that one is duped, because Messrs. Favorites of Fortune do not belong in the religious sphere. [681]The merit of the religious discourse is in making the way difficult, because the way is the decisive thing—otherwise we have esthetics. But Christianity has made the way most difficult, and it is only an illusion, which has snared many, that Christianity has made the way

* Here again we see why the religious speaker must not use the foreshortened perspective. In other words, from the esthetic point of view there is no path, because the esthetic is related to immediacy, and the expression for that is the foreshortened perspective. Ethically and ethically-religiously, however, it is precisely the path that is reflected upon, and therefore what esthetically is truth is ethically and ethically-religiously a deception.

easy, since it helps people precisely and only by making the beginning such that everything becomes much more difficult than ever.

If a pagan has caught just a glimpse of the absolute good, then Christianity has helped—by the absurd. If this is left out, then everything has indeed become much easier than in paganism; but if this is held fast, then everything is much more difficult, because it is easier to maintain a weak hope by one's *own powers* than to gain certitude by virtue of the absurd. If an esthetic sufferer winces and seeks consolation in the ethical, this does indeed have comfort—*aber* [but] first it makes the esthetic sufferer suffer even more than before. If this is left out, the ethical certainly makes everything all too easy and comfortable, but then one is also taking the ethical in vain. An esthetic sufferer, even if he winces ever so much, can most likely come to suffer even more, and then when he sends for the ethical—well, it first helps him out of the frying pan into VII 373
the fire so that he really has something to scream about—and only then does it help him.

It is the same with Christianity. Christianity requires that the individual, existing, venture everything (the pathos-filled). A pagan can also do that, for example, venture everything upon the "if" of immortality. But then it requires that the individual also risk his thought, venture to believe against understanding (the dialectical). Whereas that serious man never came to the point of venturing at all because he wanted to have certainty, it is certain that there is one certainty, namely, that this is the absolute daring venture. To struggle through life, existing, on the basis of the "if" of immortality might seem arduous enough, and to obtain a demonstration of a resurrection an enormous relief—if the demonstration itself were not the most difficult of all. To gain everything with the help of an intermediary does seem easy enough in comparison with paganism, where the wise by his greatest efforts achieved only a little, but suppose that the most difficult of all is that there is an intermediary! To obtain everything with the help of a gospel does seem easy enough—if the greatest difficulty of all were not that there is a gospel. To be capable of doing everything through God is easy enough—if the greatest difficulty of all were not that one is capable of doing nothing oneself, so difficult that probably there are few in any generation who can truthfully say that day in and day out they are even moderately aware that a human being is capable of doing nothing at all.

But if the dialectical is skipped, what then? Then it becomes woman-chatter and old wives' blather, for, as is known, Jews and women blather in one minute what a man is unable to do in a lifetime. If the dialectical is skipped, then the demonstration of the resurrection, ironically enough, becomes too much of a demonstration, and the certainty of immortality becomes less than in paganism. Then the intermediary becomes a dubious character, an esthetically ostentatious person with a halo and a wishing cap; then the gospel becomes a rumor, a bit of town gossip; then the person who through God is capable of everything becomes one who by himself is able to do a little and is polite enough to pretend as if it were through God, becomes one who is far behind the person who, existing, even moderately practices the strenuous consciousness that he is capable of nothing. If the dialectical is skipped, then the whole of Christianity becomes an easy notion, becomes nothing but superstition. Indeed, it is the most dangerous kind of superstition, because it is a superstitious belief in the truth, if Christianity is the truth. Superstitious belief in untruth includes the possibility that the truth can come and awaken it, but when the truth is and superstition by relating to it transforms it into untruth, then no deliverance is possible. No, the easiness of
VII Christianity is distinguished by one thing only: by the diffi-
374 culty. Thus its yoke is easy and its burden light[682]—for the person who has cast off all his burdens, all of them, the burdens of hope and of fear and of despondency and of despair—but it is very difficult. And in turn the difficulty is absolute, not comparative dialectical (easier for one person than for another), because the difficulty pertains absolutely to each individual in particular and absolutely requires his absolute effort, but no more, because in the sphere of the religious there are

no unjustly treated individualities, just as there are no favorites of fortune or lottery drawings.

§ 2

The Essential *Expression of Existential Pathos:* Suffering—*Fortune and Misfortune as an Esthetic Life-View in Contrast to Suffering as a Religious Life-View (Illustrated by the Religious Address)—the Actuality of Suffering (Humor)—the Actuality of Suffering in the Latter State as a Sign That an Existing Individual Relates Himself to an Eternal Happiness—the Illusion of Religiousness—Spiritual Trial—*[683]*the Basis and Meaning of Suffering in the Former State: Dying to Immediacy and Yet Remaining in the Finite—an Upbuilding Diversion—Humor as the Incognito of Religiousness*

From the preceding portion it must be recalled that existential pathos is action or the transformation of existence. The appointed task is simultaneously to relate oneself absolutely to the absolute τέλος [end, goal] and relatively to relative ends. But this task must now be understood more specifically in its concrete difficulty, lest the existential pathos be revoked within esthetic pathos, as if it were existential pathos to *say* this once and for all, or once a month, with the unchanged passion of immediacy. If everything were decided on paper, one would start on the ideal task at once; but in existence the beginning must be made by practicing the relation to the absolute τέλος and taking power away from immediacy. On paper, the individual is a third party, a rapid something that is promptly "at your service." The actual individual is, after all, in immediacy and to that extent is actually in the relative ends
absolutely. Now the individual begins, not, please note, by VII
simultaneously relating himself absolutely to the absolute τέ- 375
λος and relatively to the relative ends, because by being in immediacy he is exactly reversed, but he begins by practicing the absolute relation through renunciation. The task is ideal and perhaps is never accomplished by anyone; it is only on paper that one begins summarily and is promptly finished. In order

to relate himself absolutely to the absolute τέλος, the individual must have practiced renunciation of the relative ends, and only then can there be any question of the ideal task: simultaneously to relate oneself absolutely to the absolute and relatively to the relative. Not prior to this, because before this has been done the individual is continually more or less immediate and to that extent relates himself absolutely to relative ends. And even when he has surmounted immediacy, with his victory he is nevertheless again in existence and thereby again hindered from absolutely expressing the absolute relation to the absolute τέλος. The esthetic pathos distances itself from existence or is present in it through an illusion, whereas the existential pathos immerses itself in existing, pierces all illusions with the consciousness of existing, and becomes more and more concrete by acting to transform existence.

Now, to act might seem the very opposite of to suffer, and thus it might seem strange to say that the essential expression of existential pathos (which is acting) is suffering. But this is only apparently the case, and again the sign of the religious sphere is manifest here—that the positive is distinguished by the negative* (in contrast to the directness** of immediacy and the relative directness of reflection)—that to act religiously is marked by suffering. The ambiguity consists in this, that act-
VII ing can also mean acting in the external, which can be alto-
376 gether true but can also mean and suggest that the discourse is not in the sphere of the religious but in another sphere. Action in the external does transform existence (as when an emperor conquers the whole world and makes the people slaves), but not the individual's own existence; and action in the external

* The reader will recall that revelation is marked by mystery, eternal happiness [*Salighed*] by suffering, the certitude of faith by uncertainty, easiness by difficulty, truth by absurdity; if this is not maintained, then the esthetic and the religious merge in common confusion.

** The existence-sphere of paganism is essentially the esthetic, and therefore it is quite in order that this is reflected in the conception of God, according to which he himself, unchanged, changes all.[684] This is the expression for acting in the external. The religious lies in the dialectic of inward deepening, and therefore, with regard to the conception of God, this means that he himself is moved, is changed.[685]

does transform the individual's existence (as when a lieutenant becomes emperor[686] or a street peddler becomes a millionaire,[687] or whatever else of that sort can come about), but it does not transform the individual's inner existence. Therefore, all such action is only esthetic pathos, and its law is the law for the esthetic relation: the nondialectical individual changes the world but remains himself unchanged, because the esthetic individual never has the dialectical within himself but outside himself, or the individual is changed in the external but inwardly remains himself unchanged. The setting, then, is in the external world, and therefore even the introducing of Christianity into a country can be an esthetic matter, unless it is an apostle who does it, inasmuch as his existence is paradoxically dialectical. Otherwise, if the individual is not changed and continually changed within himself, the introducing of Christianity into a country is no more a religious action than the conquering of countries. But the essential existential pathos relates itself to existing essentially, and existing essentially is inwardness, and the action of inwardness is suffering, because the individual is unable to transform himself [*skabe sig selv om*]. It becomes, as it were, a feigning [*Skaberi*] of self-transformation, and that is why the highest action in the inner world is to suffer. How difficult this feat is will be understood even by someone who has only a small part of the impatience of immediacy, who is oriented outward and not inward, not to mention someone who is almost totally turned outward—provided he does not in that way remain altogether ignorant of the existence of inwardness.

Immediacy is good fortune, because in immediacy there is no contradiction; the immediate person, viewed essentially, is fortunate, and *the life-view of immediacy is good fortune*. If one were to ask from whence he has this life-view, this essential relation to good fortune, he might naively answer: I do not understand it myself. The contradiction comes from outside and is misfortune. If it does not come from outside, the immediate person remains ignorant of its existence. When it does come, he *feels* the misfortune, but he does not *comprehend* [*fatte*] the suffering. The immediate person never comes to an

understanding with misfortune—that is, he does not become dialectical within himself. And if he does not escape from it, in the end it becomes evident that he lacks *self-composure* [*Fat-*
VII 377 *ning*]—that is, he despairs because he does not comprehend it. Misfortune is like a narrow pass on the way of immediacy. Now he is in it, but essentially his life-view must continually imagine that it will in turn end because it is something alien. If it does not end, he despairs, whereby immediacy ends, and the transition to another understanding of misfortune is made possible, that is, to comprehending suffering, an understanding that does not merely comprehend this or that misfortune but essentially comprehends suffering.

Fortune, misfortune, fate, immediate enthusiasm, despair—these are what the esthetic life-view has at its disposal. Misfortune is an occurrence in relation to immediacy (fate). Viewed ideally (with regard to immediacy's life-view), it is not there or it must be removed. The poet expresses this by lifting immediacy up into an ideality, which is the good fortune of immediacy as it was not found in the finite world. Here the poet uses good fortune. On the other hand, the poet (who must always operate only within the compass of immediacy) leads the individual to succumb to the misfortune. This is the commonly understood meaning of the hero's or heroine's death. But to comprehend the misfortune, to come to an understanding with it, to reverse everything and obtain suffering as the point of departure for a life-view—the poet is unable to do that; the poet must not embark on that, for then he dabbles.

Inwardness (the ethical and ethical-religious individual), however, comprehends suffering as essential. Whereas the immediate person involuntarily looks away from misfortune, does not know that it exists as soon as it is not present externally, the religious person continually has suffering with him,
VII 378 wants suffering* in the same sense as the immediate person

* Thus it is an altogether proper religious collision, but also a not unremarkable esthetic misunderstanding of the religious, when (for example, in the Weil edition of Mohammedan biblical legends[688]) the religious man prays to God that he may become tried in such great sufferings as Abraham or an-

wants good fortune, and wants and has suffering even if the misfortune is not present externally, because it is not misfortune he wants, since then the relation would still be esthetic and he would be essentially undialectical within himself.

A religiously proper address that is clear about what categories it should use and how it should use them is perhaps more rarely seen or heard than a consummate poetic work. But just as in a poetic work we sometimes find lines put into a particular character's mouth that are so reflective that they reflect the character right out of the whole compass of poetry, so also the religious address is often enough a sad conglomeration of bits from every sphere. But, of course, to become a poet requires a call; to become a religious speaker requires only three examinations[689]—then one is sure to receive a call.[690]

Of course, the religious address does not always have to speak about suffering, but in whatever it says, however it skips around, whatever road it takes in order to catch people,[691] however much it witnesses in monologue to the speaker's own existence, it must always have its totality-category present as a criterion, so that the experienced person promptly perceives the total orientation in the life-view of the address. Therefore, the religious address can speak about everything if only it directly or indirectly has its absolute criterion continually present. Just as it is confusing* to learn geography from nothing but special maps and never see on a global map the

---

other chosen one was. A prayer about that is a frothing of religiousness in the same sense as an Aladdin's enthusiasm and a young girl's happiness are the frothing of immediacy. The misunderstanding is that the religious person nevertheless comprehends the suffering as coming from outside, therefore
esthetically. In those narratives, the outcome is usually that the religious per- VII
son proves to be too weak to endure the suffering. But this explains nothing, 378
and the issue in turn rests in a not unremarkable *confinium* [border territory] between the esthetic and the religious.

* But if it is assumed, something I willingly admit with regard to various religious addresses, that it is more difficult to be a listener to a discourse like that than to be the speaker, then in an ironical way the religious address is indeed made superfluous and serves only as a purgatory where the individual disciplines himself so as to be built up by everything in God's house.

relation of the countries to one another, that is, when it deceptively looks as if Denmark, for example, is just as large as Germany, the particular details of a religious address likewise dis-
VII turb if the totality-category does not provide orientation
379 throughout, even if indirectly.

Essentially, the religious address has [the task] of *uplifting through suffering*. Just as the faith of immediacy is in fortune, so the faith of the religious is in this, that life lies precisely in suffering. Therefore, it must go resolutely and mightily out upon the deep. As soon as the religious address casts a sidelong glance at fortune, comforts with probability, strengthens temporarily, it is a false teaching, is a regression into the esthetic and therefore is dabbling. For immediacy, poetry is the transfiguration of life; but for religiousness, poetry is a beautiful and amiable jest, whose consolation religiousness nevertheless rejects, because it is precisely in suffering that the religious breathes. Immediacy expires in misfortune; in suffering the religious begins to breathe. The point is continually to keep the spheres sharply separate from each other by means of the qualitative dialectic, lest everything become one; but the poet certainly becomes a bungler when he wants to dabble in a little of the religious, and the religious speaker becomes a deceiver who delays the listeners by wanting to dabble in the esthetic. As soon as a religious address divides people into the fortunate and the unfortunate, it is *eo ipso* dabbling, because from the religious point of view all human beings are suffering, and the point is to enter into the suffering (not by plunging into it but by discovering that one is in it) and not to escape the misfortune. Viewed religiously, the fortunate person, whom the whole world favors, is just as much a suffering person, if he is religious, as the person to whom misfortune comes from outside. Viewed religiously, the distinction "fortune/misfortune" may be used, but only jestingly and ironically to encourage with it in order to get the individual into the suffering and from it to define the religious.

But the religious address heard these days[692] is rarely correct in its categories. The highly honored speaker forgets that religiousness is inwardness, that inwardness is the individual's

relation to himself before God, its reflection within himself, and that it is precisely from this that the suffering comes, but its essential belonging is also rooted in this, so that its absence signifies the absence of religiousness. The speaker perceives the individual as relating himself only to a world, a small or a great surrounding world, and now he serves up something about fortune and misfortune, that the unfortunate person must not lose courage, for there are many who are even more unfortunate. Moreover, there is, after all, the probability that
"with the help of God things will surely get better,"* and fi- VII
nally one becomes something through adversities—indeed, 380
would Councilor of Justice Madsen have become a councilor if he had not etc. etc.! See, people really like to listen to this, because it is religious to preach indulgent exemption from the religious—from the enthusiasm of religiousness in suffering. When the religious speaker forgets that his setting is inwardness and the individual's relation to himself, he then has essentially the same task as the poet and should keep his mouth shut, because the poet can do it better. When the religious speaker speaks about misfortune in the way mentioned, then, viewed religiously, it is not only scandalous (namely, because he passes himself off as a religious speaker), but he also brings down upon himself the satirizing nemesis that the conclusion is drawn from this address that there are favorites of fortune who do not suffer at all—which from a religious point of view is most dubious.

The invitation to a religious address is quite simply this: Come here, all you who labor and are burdened[693]—and the address presupposes that all are sufferers—indeed, that they all should be. The speaker is not to go down among the listeners and single out one, if there is such a one, and say, "No, you are much too happy to need my discourse," because if this is heard from the lips of a religious speaker, it must sound like

* Many people assume as a matter of course that if God's name is mentioned the discourse is godly. In that way cursing, if one uses God's name, is VII
also godly discourse. No, an esthetic life-view, even if larded with the names 380
of God and Christ, is still an esthetic life-view, and if it is delivered in an address, it is an esthetic address, not a religious one.

the most scathing irony. The distinction between fortunate and unfortunate is only jest, and therefore the speaker ought to say, "We are all sufferers, but joyful in our suffering—this is what we strive for. There he sits, the fortunate one whom everything, everything, everything favors as in a fairy tale, but woe to him if he is not a sufferer." But the religious address is rarely designed that way. At best, the religious observation proper comes in part three, that is, after every possible subterfuge has been used in the first two-thirds in order to escape from the religious, and the religious listener is left wondering whether he was at a dance with the poet or at a devotional service with the pastor. To speak in this way easily makes it look as if the religious, instead of being equally for all people and being so through the equal suffering, which is the victory of the religious over the jest about fortune and misfortune, is
VII only for the exceedingly unfortunate—a magnificent honor
381 for the religious to be included in a paltry subdivision of a section of the esthetic. To be sure, the religious is the ultimate comfort, but there is a wretchedness even greater than being the most unfortunate in the poetic sense, and that is to be so matchlessly fortunate that one has no understanding whatever of the suffering that is the life element of the religious.

Presumably the pastor usually thinks that such matchlessly fortunate ones appear only in fairy tales, but in life misfortune catches most people on the hip and the pastor then gets them for further treatment. That may be, but the pastor should have such trust in the religious that he does not foist it upon people in that way. He should nonchalantly jest about a man's becoming just as fortunate as someone in a fairy tale and yet be of the opinion that suffering belongs to the true life. He should come down hard on everyone who wants only to grieve over his misfortune and wants only to hear the consolation that in turn his misfortune will surely pass, because such a person actually wants to evade the religious. Just as Lafontaine sat weeping and made his heroes unhappy in three volumes[694] (quite properly a poetic task), so the religious speaker, if I may say so, should have his fun in making his heroes just as fortunate as they want to be, turn them into kings and emperors and millionaires and happy lovers who win the girl and so on—but he must also see to procuring suffering for them in their inner beings. The more good fortune and favor in the external world, when there nevertheless is suffering, the more clear it is that this is in the inner world, precisely in the inner world, and the more clear it becomes that in the *prima* quality the religious is different from the pastor's mixture.

When the religious life-view is upheld according to its category, the religious speaker should have the religious loftiness to make comic use of the whole range of poetry. Take an individuality who wishes for something. If he goes to the poet, the latter promptly sees that he is usable in two ways, either along the line of fortune by means of the magic of the wish or along the line of misfortune to the point of despair. Poetically, the task is the enlargement of the imagination, whether he becomes fortunate or unfortunate, and the point is—no dabbling. But have the same individuality go to the pastor, who in religious loftiness is to change the whole thing into a jest for him. In a religious, enthusiastic conviction of the meaning
of suffering for the highest life, the pastor is to teach him to VII 382
rise above the hankering of the wish and teach him to elevate himself above the pain of the denied wish—by proclaiming greater sufferings. In a tough spot, when the carriage is stuck in the impassable or it is tipping in the sinkhole, the driver uses the whip, not out of cruelty but in the conviction that it will help, and only mollycoddlers dare not strike. But no dabbling. The religious address maintains the respectful freedom to include quite directly what it means to be a human being, much the way death does, which also directly includes being a human being, whether these persons are emperors, councilors, or day laborers, whether they are extremely fortunate and graded by fortune with a first-rate plus or their position is very unfortunate and graded third-rate minus. If the pastor is unable to make a religious person out of the wisher or, rather, if this is not what the pastor wants to do, then the pastor is only a poet-quack—then one should let the poet prevail and either become fortunate or despair. The relation

should be such that if the poet's discourse is so enrapturing that it makes young people blush with enthusiasm, then the enthusiasm of the religious discourse should be such that it makes the poet pale with envy that there is such an enthusiasm in which becoming fortunate is not the point, nor abandoning oneself to the recklessness of despair—no, in which suffering inspires. But the secular mentality will say that poetry is a maiden's over-excitement, religiousness a man's frenzy. That is why the religious speaker does not need to use powerful address, since he most surely demonstrates his loftiness by the very invincibility with which he keeps himself within the impregnable position of the religious, since the religious does not contend with the esthetic as with an equal—it does not contend with it but has conquered it as a jest.

Just as the poet ought to be distinguishable by his knowing how to handle with pathos the imagination-passion of the infinite in fortune and despair, also by his comically and hilariously taking all finite passions and philistinism by the nose—just so the religious speaker ought to be distinguishable by his knowing how to manage with pathos the enthusiasm of suffering and jestingly to peek into the imagination-passion of the infinite. And just as the poet should be a benevolent spirit who is promptly ready to serve the fortunate people in the enchanted land of illusion or a spirit of sympathy who is promptly ready to serve the unfortunate, also by benevolently being a loud voice for the person in despair, so with regard to the imagination-passion of the infinite the religious speaker
VII should either be just as morose and oppressed and slow as the
383 day is in the living room and the night by the sick bed and the week in worry about livelihood—so that it will not seem to be easier in the church than in the living room—or he should be even swifter than the poet in making everyone as fortunate as he desires, but, please note, ironically, in order to show that all this fortune is extraneous, and the misfortune likewise; but suffering belongs essentially to the highest life.

When Juliet swoons because she lost Romeo, when immediacy has expired in her breast and she has lost Romeo in such a way that even Romeo could no longer give comfort because the possession itself would only become a sorrowful daily recollection, and when the last friend, the last friend of all unhappy lovers, the poet, falls silent, the religious speaker should nevertheless dare to break the silence. Perhaps to present a little assortment of excellent grounds of comfort? In that case, the offended Juliet would surely turn to the poet, and he, with his esthetically triumphant authority, by assigning His Reverence a place in the farcical parts* of the tragedy, would defend what in all eternity belongs by right to the poet: the lovable, the despairing Juliet. No, the religious speaker should dare to proclaim new suffering, even more terrible suffering, and this will bring Juliet to stand up again.

Or when a despairing person, just as he is approached by someone, with a haughty glance promptly passes judgment on him as a traitor, namely, one who wants to bring comfort, when the wrath in his face sentences to death the person who
dares to want to comfort, so all the comforters and the VII
grounds of comfort coagulate in farcical terror, just as milk 384
curdles in a thunderstorm—then the religious speaker will know how to make himself heard—by speaking of more terrible suffering and danger.

Above all, the religious address must never use the foreshortened perspective, which as a simulated ethical movement corresponds to the esthetic. Esthetically, this perspective is the

* As soon as a pastor is unsure of his religious category and confuses himself with poetic *Anklänge* [undertones] bound up with life experiences, then the poet is naturally far superior to him. The person who understands how to reckon the relation of the categories to each other will readily perceive that such a spiritual adviser would come rather close to being one of the most common motifs for a comic character in a tragedy. An ordinary person who represented the same rubbish, of which the secret is that it has missed even the poetic point, a barber's apprentice, for example, or an undertaker, would naturally be comic, but not as basically comic as the spiritual adviser, whose name and black gown lay claim to the highest pathos. To use, with pathos, a spiritual adviser in a tragedy is a misunderstanding, because if he essentially represents what he essentially is, the whole tragedy breaks down, and if he does not represent it essentially he is *eo ipso* to be interpreted as comic. We frequently enough see hypocritical and sinister monks in tragedies; I believe that a clerical-secular rattlebrain in full canonicals would come closer to the situation in our day.

magic of illusion and the only thing to do, because poetry is related to an observer. But the religious address ought to relate itself to an acting person, who when he comes home must work at doing accordingly. If, then, the religious address uses that perspective, the result is the baleful confusion that the task appears much easier in church than at home in the living room, and then one has only harm from going to church. Therefore the speaker ought to reject the foreshortened perspective as a mirage of youth—lest the one tested in his living room be constrained to reject the speaker's address as immaturity. When a poet uses it, and the observer sits still, absorbed in his role of spectator, it is glorious, fascinating; but when the religious speaker uses it, and the one listening is a person in motion, acting, he merely helps him to bump his nose against the living room door. The religious speaker operates in the opposite way with the lack of an end, the absence of a result, precisely because suffering belongs essentially to the religious life.

Although people often enough are foolishly occupied with whether the pastor himself actually does what he says, I am of the opinion that any presumptuous criticism of that kind should be renounced and constrained. But one thing may and must be required of the speaker, that his address be such that it *can* be acted upon, lest a fool be made of the true listener—just when he wants to do what the pastor says—because preacher-talk is vapor off in the blue, whether the pastor is busily engaged with vast world-historical visions and matchless hawk-eye views that are impossible to act upon, or he esthetically talks a lot of obscure nonsense that is also impossible to act upon, or he describes imaginary states of mind for which the acting person vainly seeks in actuality, or consoles with illusions that the acting person does not find in actuality, or conjures up passions as they at most seem only to one who does not have them, or conquers dangers that are not there and leaves the actual ones unmentioned, conquers them by theatrical dynamics that are not found in life and leaves the dynamics of actuality unutilized—in short, he plays trump esthetically, speculatively, world-historically and declares "I pass" in the religious.

But suffering as the essential expression of existential pathos means that there is actual suffering or that the actuality of the suffering is the existential pathos, and by *the actuality of the suffering is understood its continuance as essential for the pathos-filled relation to an eternal happiness*, so that the suffering is not deceitfully revoked and the individual does not advance beyond it, which is a regression, accomplished by somehow shifting the setting from existence into an imaginary medium. Just as resignation saw to it that the individual had the absolute orientation toward the absolute τέλος, the continuance of suffering is the guarantee that the individual is in position and keeps himself in position. The immediate person cannot comprehend misfortune; he only feels it. Thus the misfortune is stronger than he, and this relation of the imagination-passion to immediacy is despair. By means of the foreshortened perspective the poet quite rightly depicts this in the medium of the imagination as if it were all over. This manifests itself differently in existence, and here the immediate person frequently becomes ludicrous by momentary feminine squealing that is forgotten the next moment. When immediacy in the existing individual has received a little injury, a little knock—then a solution must be found, since the setting is not in the medium of the imagination. Then the whole crowd of experienced and commonsensical people, of tinkers and patchers, shows up and with the help of probability and grounds of comfort rivets the scraps or holds the rags together. Life goes on; advice is sought from the sagacious men of ecclesiastic or secular rank, and it all becomes a muddle—one relinquishes the poetic and does not grasp the religious. VII 385

Viewed religiously, the point, as mentioned above, is to comprehend the suffering and remain in it in such a way that reflection is *on* the suffering and not *away from* the suffering. Although poetic production is in the medium of imagination, a poet-existence may at times provide a *confinium* [border territory] to the religious, although qualitatively different from it. A poet often suffers in existence, but what is reflected upon

is the poetic work produced in the process. The existing poet who suffers in existence does not, however, comprehend the suffering in this way. He does not concentrate upon it but in the suffering seeks to escape the suffering and to find alleviation in the poetic production, in the poetic anticipation of a more perfect (a happier) order of things. An actor, especially
VII a comic actor, may likewise at times be suffering in existence,
386 but he does not concentrate on the suffering; he seeks to escape from it and finds alleviation in the confusion that his art encourages. But the poet and actor return from the fascination of the poetic work and imagination's wished-for order of things, from the confusion with the poetic character, to the suffering of actuality that they cannot comprehend because they have their existence in the esthetic dialectic between fortune and misfortune. The poet can explain (transfigure) all existence, but he cannot explain himself, because he does not want to become religious and comprehend the secret of suffering as the form of the highest life, higher than all good fortune and different from all misfortune. The rigor of the religious is that it begins with making everything more rigorous, and its relation to poetry is not as a new wishing device, not as a totally new subterfuge that poetry has not dreamed of, but as a difficulty that creates men just as war creates heroes.

The actuality of the suffering is therefore not identical with the truth of the expression, although a person who is actually suffering will always express himself truly; but here the issue is not about the expression, because the discourse itself is always somewhat foreshortened, inasmuch as words are a more abstract medium than existing. For example, if I were to imagine a poet-existence suffering physically and psychically in his last agony and that among the posthumous papers was found the following outburst: "Just as the sick person longs to cast off the bandages, so my healthy spirit longs to throw off this physical exhaustion, the suffocating poultice that is the body and the exhaustion of the body. Just as the conquering general shouts as his horse is shot from under him: A new horse—oh, would that the victorious healthiness of my spirit might shout: A new body, for only the body is worn out. Just as the person whose life is in danger at sea shoves away with the strength of despair when another drowning person wants to clutch him, so my body hangs like a heavy weight on my spirit so it becomes the downfall of death.[695] Like a steamship in a storm, with machinery too large in proportion to the structure of the hull, so do I suffer."[696] In that case, one cannot deny the truth of the expression, nor the dreadfulness of the suffering, but surely can deny the pathos-filled actuality of the suffering. How can that be, someone asks—is this not the actuality of suffering, this horror? No, because the existing person nevertheless understands the suffering as accidental. Just as he abstractly wants to discard the body, so he likewise wants to discard the suffering as accidental, and the point is that the actuality of the suffering, as it is for the religious person, would be a hard teaching.

The actuality of the suffering means its essential continu- VII
ance and is its essential relation to the religious life. Estheti- 387
cally, suffering is related to existence as something accidental. Therefore this accidental suffering can continue, but a continuance of what is accidental is no essential continuance. As soon, therefore, as the religious speaker uses the foreshortened perspective, whether he concentrates all suffering in one moment or he opens up a pleasant prospect of better times, he returns to the esthetic, and his conception of suffering becomes a simulated religious movement. When Scripture says that God dwells in a broken and a contrite heart,[697] this is not an expression for an accidental, transitory, momentary condition (in that case the word "dwells" would be very unsuitable) but rather for the essential meaning of suffering for the relationship with God. If, however, the religious speaker is not at home and experienced in the sphere of the religious, he understands the words this way: misfortune comes from outside and crushes a man's heart; then the relationship with God begins, and then, yes, then little by little the religious person becomes happy again—wait a minute, does he become happy through the relationship with God? In that case, he also remains in suffering. Or does he perhaps become happy by coming into some money from a rich uncle, or by acquiring a

new sweetheart, or by means of the appeal His Reverence kindly initiated in *Adresseavisen*? In that case, the discourse regresses,* although at times it is in this last part that His Rev-
VII erence the pastor becomes most eloquent and gesticulates most
388 vigorously, presumably because the religious category will not taste right, but it goes more easily by dabbling a bit in being a poet. By dabbling—indeed, by dabbling—because the worldly wisdom that such a spiritual adviser adds to the poetic is a direct offense to poetry; it is a disgusting and defamatory attempt to treat Juliet as being only apparently dead. Someone who, after being dead, awakens to the same life was only apparently dead, and Catherine (her name is not Juliet; as we say to children, a peasant girl has replaced poetry's well-beloved)

* The religious discourse also regresses when a man says, for example, "After many errors, I finally learned to cling to God in earnest, and since that time he has not left me. My business flourishes, my projects prosper, I am now happily married and my children are healthy, etc." The religious man has again returned to the esthetic dialectic, for even if he deigns to say that he thanks God for all these blessings, the question still is how he thanks him, whether he does it directly or first makes the movement of uncertainty that is the mark of the relationship with God. In other words, just as a person experiencing misfortune does not have the right to say to God directly that it is misfortune, since he must suspend his judgment in the movement of uncertainty, so also he may not appropriate all these good things as a sign of the
VII relationship with God. The direct relationship is esthetic and indicates that
388 the man giving thanks does not relate himself to God but to his own idea of fortune and misfortune. That is, if a person cannot know with certainty whether the misfortune is an evil (the uncertainty of the relationship with God as the form for always thanking God), then neither can he know with certainty whether the good fortune is a good. The relationship with God has only one evidence, the relationship with God itself; everything else is equivocal. With regard to the dialectic of the external, it holds true religiously for every human being, even if he became ever so old: we were born yesterday and know nothing.[698] When, for example, the great actor Seydelmann (as I read in Rötscher's biography of him), on the night he was crowned with a wreath in the opera house "to applause that lasted several minutes,"[699] then went home and very fervently thanked God for it—the very fervency of his giving thanks shows that he did not thank God. With the same passion with which he gave thanks, he would have revolted against God if he had been booed. If he had given thanks religiously and therefore thanked God, then the Berlin public and the laurel wreath and the applause lasting several minutes would have become equivocal in the dialectical uncertainty of the religious.

will prove it by finding a new husband for herself. But someone dead who awakens to life in a new sphere was and is and remains truly dead. No, then it is magnificent of poetry to have Juliet die, but that life-wisdom, which is an insult to poetry, is to religiousness an abomination. The religious address honors Juliet as dead and for that very reason will work to the border of miracle by bidding Juliet to awaken to a new life in a new sphere. And the religious is a new life, whereas that preacher-prattle had neither the esthetic magnanimity to slay Juliet* nor the enthusiasm of suffering to believe in a new VII
life. 389

Consequently, the actuality of suffering means its essential continuance as essential for the religious life, whereas, viewed esthetically, suffering stands in an accidental relation to existence, may be, but may end; viewed religiously, however, with the end of the suffering, the religious life ends. Since an existing humorist is the closest approximation to the religious person, he also has an essential conception of the suffering in which he is, because he does not understand existing as one thing and fortune and misfortune as something that happens to the existing person, but he exists in such a way that suffering stands in relation to existing. But it is then that the humorist makes the deceptive turn and revokes the suffering in the form of jest. He comprehends the meaning of suffering in relation to existing, but he does not comprehend the meaning of suffering. He comprehends that it belongs together with existing, but he does not comprehend its meaning otherwise than that suffering belongs together with it. The first is the pain in the humorous; the second is the jest—and this is why one both weeps and laughs when he speaks. He touches the secret of existence in the pain, but then he goes home again.

The profundity is that he comprehends suffering together

* When it was stated previously that the religious address smites whereas the esthetic mitigates, and it is now stated that poetry has the courage to kill Juliet, this also strikes home without involving our presentation in any self-contradiction. To have Juliet die is the tender sympathy of the esthetic, but to proclaim new suffering and consequently to smite is the rigorous sympathy of the religious.

with existing and that therefore all human beings suffer as long as they exist. By suffering, the humorist does not understand misfortunes, as if an existing person would be happy if these specified misfortunes were not there. The humorist understands this very well, and thus it can occur to him at times to mention an altogether incidental little annoyance that no one would call a misfortune and say that if it were not present he would then be happy. For example, when a humorist says, "If I could live to see the day when my landlord had a new bell pull installed in the courtyard of the place where I live so that one could clearly and swiftly know for whom the bell is being rung in the evening, then I would consider myself extremely fortunate." Upon hearing something like this, anyone who understands rejoinders promptly understands that the speaker has canceled the distinction between fortune and misfortune
VII in a higher lunacy—because all are suffering. The humorist
390 comprehends the profundity, but at the same time it occurs to
him that it most likely is not worth the trouble to become involved in explaining it. This revocation is the jest. Therefore, when an existing humorist converses with an immediate person, for example with an unfortunate person who has his life in the distinction between fortune and misfortune, he again gives the situation a humorous twist. The expression for suffering that the humorist has at his disposal* satisfies the unfortunate one, but then profundity comes and removes the distinction in which the unfortunate one has his life, and then comes the jest. If, for example, the unfortunate one were to say, "It is all over for me, all is lost," the humorist would perhaps continue, "Yes, what poor wretches we human beings

* In contradistinction, irony would promptly be distinguishable by its not expressing the pain but teasingly replying with the aid of the abstract dialectic, which protests the excessiveness that is in the unfortunate person's cry of pain. The humorist is more inclined to think that it is too little, and the humorist's indirect expression for suffering is also much stronger than any direct expression. The ironist levels everything on the basis of abstract humanity; the humorist on the basis of the abstract relationship with God, inasmuch as he does not enter into the relationship with God. It is precisely there that he parries with a jest.

are in the various miseries of this life; we are all sufferers; if I could only live to see the day when my landlord had a new bell pull installed . . . . . I would consider myself extremely happy." And the humorist in no way says this to affront the unfortunate one. But the misunderstanding is that when all is said and done the unfortunate one believes in fortune (immediacy cannot comprehend suffering), which is why the misfortune for him is a specific something on which he focuses all his attention in the thought that if it were not there, then he would be happy. The humorist, on the other hand, has comprehended suffering in such a way that he finds all documentation superfluous and expresses this by mentioning the first thing at hand.

The Latinist says: *Respicere finem* [Look to the end][700] and employs this expression in earnest; but the phrase itself contains a kind of contradiction inasmuch as *finis* as the end has not arrived yet and consequently lies ahead of one, whereas *respicere* means to look back—the humorous explanation of existence is actually a similar contradiction. It assumes that if
existing is like walking along a road, then the oddity of exis- VII
tence is that the goal lies behind—and yet one is compelled to 391
continue walking ahead, because walking ahead is indeed the metaphor for existing. The humorist comprehends the meaning of suffering as inherent in existing, but then he revokes it all, because the explanation lies behind.

As a humorist exists, so also does he express himself. In life one sometimes hears a humorist speak; in books his lines are usually affected. Have a humorist speak, and he will say, for example, something like this: "What is the meaning of life? Yes, tell me. How should I know? We were born yesterday and know nothing. But this I do know, that the greatest pleasure is to trudge through life unknown, unknown to His Majesty the King, to Her Majesty the Queen, to Her Majesty the Queen Dowager, to His Royal Highness Prince Ferdinand,[701] because such aristocratic acquaintanceship only makes life burdensome and awkward, just as it must be for a prince living in poverty in a rural village to be known by his royal family. Similarly, it also seems to me that to be known *in time by*

God makes life enormously strenuous. Wherever he is present, every half hour is of infinite importance. But to live in that way cannot be endured for sixty years; one can hardly endure three years of strenuous study for an examination, which still is not as strenuous as a half hour like that. Everything disintegrates in contradiction. At times we are preached at and told that we must live with the full passion of the infinite and purchase the eternal. So one commences, puts forward the best foot of the infinite, and plunges in with the most precipitous speed of passion. No man in the bombing attack[702] could hurry faster; the Jew who fell down from the gallery could not fall headlong more precipitously.[703] What happens? Then we hear: The auction is postponed; there will be no stroke of the hammer today, but perhaps in sixty years. So one packs up and starts to go—what happens? At the very same moment the speaker comes rushing after one and says: But it is still possible, perhaps this very moment, that all will be decided by the judgment-day stroke of death.

"What does this mean? Everyone advances equally far *am Ende* [in the end]. With existence, things go just as they did with me and my physician. I complained about not feeling well. He answered: No doubt you are drinking too much coffee and don't walk enough. Three weeks later I speak with him again and say: I really do not feel well, but now it cannot be from drinking coffee, because I do not touch coffee, nor can it be from lack of exercise, because I walk all day long. He
VII answers: Well, then the reason must be that you do not drink
392 coffee and that you walk too much. So it was: my not feeling well was and remained the same, but when I drink coffee, it comes from my drinking coffee, and when I do not drink coffee, it comes from my not drinking coffee.

"And so it is with us human beings. Our entire earthly existence is a kind of ill health. If someone asks the reason, he is first asked how he has organized his life; as soon as he has answered that, he is told: There it is—that is the reason. If someone else asks the reason, one goes about it in the same way, and if he answers the opposite, he is told: There it is—that is the reason. Then the adviser leaves with the superior air of one who has explained everything—until he has turned the corner, and then he sticks his tail between his legs and sneaks away. Even if someone gave me ten rix-dollars, I would not take it upon myself to explain the riddle of existence. Indeed, why should I? If life is a riddle, in the end presumably the one who has proposed the riddle will himself explain it. I have not invented temporality, but I have noticed that in *Den Frisindede*,[704] *Freischütz*,[705] and other papers that offer riddles the explanation follows in the next issue. Now, of course, it usually happens that an old maid or pensioner is mentioned and congratulated for having guessed the riddle—consequently knew the solution one day in advance—the difference is not so great."

[706]In our day, people have frequently enough been inclined to mistake the humorous for the religious, even for the Christian-religious, and that is why I try to return to it everywhere. There actually is nothing far-fetched in this, because the humorous, precisely as the *confinium* [border territory] of the religious, is very comprehensive. It can assume, especially in a wistful tone, a deceptive likeness to the religious in the wider sense, but nevertheless deceptive only for one who is not accustomed to looking for the totality-category. No one can know this better than I, who am myself essentially a humorist and, having my life in immanence, am seeking the Christian-religious.

In order to illustrate the actuality of suffering in its essential
continuance, I shall now again emphasize a final dialectical attempt to revoke it, to transform it into a continually annulled
element. Viewed esthetically, misfortune is related as the accidental to existence; viewed esthetically, reflection is not on
the suffering but away from the suffering. Esthetically maun- VII 393
dering, worldly wisdom or worldly sagacity wants to let suffering have its significance in a finite teleology; through adversities a human being is trained to become something in the
finite. Humor comprehends suffering together with existence
but revokes the essential meaning of suffering for the existing
person. Let us now see if it is possible to revoke suffering by
means of an infinite teleology. Suffering itself does indeed

have meaning for a person's eternal happiness—ergo, I must indeed be glad for suffering. Therefore, can an existing person at the same time as he by his suffering expresses his relation to an eternal happiness as the absolute τέλος, can he at the same time, by knowing about the relation, be beyond suffering, since in that case the expression for the essential relation to an eternal happiness is not suffering but joy—not, of course, the direct joy the religious address sometimes wants to make us believe it is and thus to lead us back to a little esthetic, free-and-easy, old-fashioned waltz—no, joy in the consciousness that the suffering signifies the relation.

Now, let us not proceed to set down on paper: Which is higher?—and, having established that the latter is the higher, perhaps even be finished with it. Instead, let us impress upon ourselves that the question is not asked *in abstracto*, "Which of these two relations is the higher?" but "Which of them is possible for an existing person?" To be in existence is always somewhat troublesome, and the question is whether this is not another one of its pressures—namely, that the existing person cannot make the dialectical transaction by which suffering is converted into joy. There is no suffering in the eternal happiness, but when an existing person relates himself to it, the relation is quite properly expressed by suffering. If, through his knowing that this suffering indicates the relation, an existing person were able to lift himself above the suffering, he would then also be able to transform himself from an existing into an eternal person, but that he will no doubt leave alone. But if he is unable to do this, he is again in the position of suffering, so that this knowledge must be held fast in the existence-medium. At the same moment, the perfection of joy is frustrated, as it always must be when it must be possessed in an imperfect form. The pain over this is again the essential expression for the relation.

But one does indeed read in the New Testament that the apostles when they were flogged went away joyful, thanking God that it was granted them to suffer something for the sake
VII of Christ.[707] Entirely correct, and I do not doubt that the apos-
394 tles had the power of faith to be joyful even in physical pain

and to thank God, just as even among pagans we find examples of fortitude, like Scaevola,[708] for instance, who were joyful even in the moment of physical pain. But the suffering spoken of in that passage is not religious suffering, of which there is on the whole very little mention in the New Testament, and if a so-called religious address wants to make us think that everything an apostle suffers is *eo ipso* religious suffering, this shows only how unclear such an address is about the categories, because this is a counterpart to the assumption that every address in which God's name appears is a godly address. No, when the individual is secure in his relationship with God and suffers only in the external, this is not religious suffering. That kind of suffering is esthetic-dialectical, similar to misfortune in connection with the immediate—it can come and it can be absent—but no one has a right to deny that a person is religious because he has experienced no misfortune in his life. But being without this kind of misfortune does not mean that he is without suffering if he is indeed religious, because suffering is the expression for the relationship with God, that is, the religious suffering that is the sign of the relationship with God, and of his not having become happy by being exempted from the relation to an absolute τέλος.

Thus at the same time as the martyr (I shall not say more about an apostle at this point, since his life is paradoxically dialectical, and his situation qualitatively different from that of others,[709] and his existence justified when it is as no one else's can possibly be) is being martyred, in his joy he may well be beyond the physical suffering. But at the same time as the individual is suffering religiously, he, in his joy over the significance of this suffering as relationship, cannot be beyond the suffering, because the suffering pertains specifically to his being separated from the joy, but it also indicates the relationship, so that to be without suffering indicates that one is not religious. The immediate person is not an essentially existing person, because as immediate he is the happy unity of the finite and the infinite, to which correspond, as was shown, fortune and misfortune as coming from outside. The religious person is turned inward and is aware that he, existing, is in the

process of becoming but still relates himself to an eternal happiness. As soon as the suffering terminates and the individual
VII 395 gains security so that he, just like the immediate consciousness, is related only to fortune and misfortune, this is a sign that he is an esthetic individuality who has strayed into the religious sphere, and to confuse the spheres is always easier than to keep them separate. A straying esthete of that kind may be a revivalist or a speculative thinker. A revivalist is absolutely secure in his relationship with God (poor fellow, this security is unfortunately the only sure sign that an existing human being does not relate himself to God) and busies himself only with treating [*tractere*] the rest of the world in and with tracts [*Tractater*]; a speculative thinker has finished on paper and mistakes this for existence.

The Apostle Paul somewhere mentions religious suffering, and there one will also find that the suffering is a sign of blessedness. I refer, of course, to the passage in Corinthians about the thorn in the flesh.[710] He tells that it happened to him once; he does not know whether it was in or out of the body that he was caught up into the third heaven.[711] Let us once and for all recollect that it is an apostle who is speaking and then talk simply and directly about it. So it happened to him once, only once. Now, of course it surely cannot happen to an existing person every day; he is prevented from that just by existing, yes, prevented to the extent that only an apostle, as the exception, experiences such a thing once. He does not know whether he was in or out of the body, but this surely cannot happen to an existing person every day, just because he is a particular existing human being; indeed, we learn from the apostle that it happens so rarely that it happened to the apostle, the exceptional individual, only once. And what then? What sign did the apostle have that this had happened to him? A thorn in the flesh—that is, a suffering.

The rest of us human beings are satisfied with less, but the situation remains exactly the same. The religious person is not transported into the third heaven, but neither does he comprehend the suffering that is the thorn in the flesh. The religious person relates himself to an eternal happiness, and the relationship is distinguishable by suffering, and suffering is the essential expression of the relationship—for an existing person.

Just as for an existing person the highest principles of thinking can be demonstrated only negatively, and to want to demonstrate them positively promptly betrays that the demonstrator, insofar as he is indeed an existing person, is on the
point of becoming fantastical—so also for an existing person VII
the existence-relation to the absolute good can be defined only 396
by the negative—the relation to an eternal happiness by suffering, just as the certitude of faith that relates itself to an eternal happiness is defined by uncertainty. If I remove the uncertainty in order to obtain an even higher certainty, then I do not have a believer in humility, in fear and trembling, but an esthetic coxcomb, a devil of a fellow who, figuratively speaking, wants to fraternize with God but, strictly speaking, does not relate himself to God at all. Uncertainty is the sign, and certainty without it is the sign that one does not relate oneself to God. Similarly, in the period of courtship, to be absolutely certain that one is loved is a sure sign that one is not in love.* But, despite that, no one can make a person in love think that it is not blissful to be in love.

It is the same also with the uncertainty of faith; but, despite that, no one can make a believer imagine that it might not be blessed to believe. But just as a little miss is related to a hero, so a lover is related to a believer, and why? Because the lover is related to a woman, but a believer to God—[712]and the Latin phrase *interest inter et inter* [there is a difference between the one and the other] absolutely applies to this. This is also why the lover is only relatively in the right but the believer absolutely in the right in refusing to hear anything about any other kind of certainty. To love—yes, that is beautiful, enchanting. Oh, would that I were a poet who could really proclaim the

* Since erotic love is not the absolute τέλος, the comparison must be taken *cum grano salis* [with a grain of salt], all the more so because, in the sphere of the esthetic, to be in love is outright bliss.

praise of erotic love and explain its magnificence. Would that I might at least deserve to sit on the bench and listen when the poet does it, but it is still only jest, and I do not mean this contemptuously, as if erotic love were a fleeting feeling. No, but it is still only jest even when the happiest erotic love finds its most lasting expression in the happiest marriage—indeed, it is magnificent to be wedded [*viet*] and dedicated [*indviet*] to this blissful pastime, all its adversities and toil notwithstanding.

Would that I were an orator who could really eulogize marriage so that the unhappy one who remains outside, sad, would not dare to hear me, and the presumptuous one who
VII 397 stands outside, mocking, would by hearing discover in horror what he had forfeited—but it is still only a jest. I see this when I put marriage together with the absolute τέλος, with an eternal happiness, and in order to be certain that it is the absolute τέλος of which I speak, let death as the arbitrator judge between the two—then I dare to say with truth: It is a matter of indifference whether one has been married or not, just as it is a matter of indifference whether one is Jew or Greek, free or slave.[713] Marriage is still a jest, a jest that must be treated with all earnestness, except that the earnestness does not therefore inhere in marriage itself but is a reflection of the earnestness of the relationship with God, a reflection of the husband's absolute relation to his absolute τέλος and of the wife's absolute relation to her absolute τέλος.

But back to suffering as a sign of eternal happiness. If, because only a revivalist succeeds in avoiding suffering and a speculative thinker in revoking (*revocare*) it and making eternal happiness itself a sign of happiness (just as all immanent speculative thought is essentially a revocation of existence, which eternity certainly is, but the speculator is certainly not in eternity), thus, if, because an *existing person* cannot succeed in revoking suffering and making eternal happiness itself a sign of eternal happiness, which would mean that the existing person died and entered eternal life, one wanted to call religiousness an illusion—well, then, please recollect that it is an illusion that comes after understanding.[714]

Poetry is illusion before understanding, religiousness illusion after understanding. Between poetry and religiousness, worldly wisdom about life performs its vaudeville. Every individual who does not live either poetically or religiously is obtuse. Why obtuse? Those sagacious and experienced people who know everything, who have a remedy for everything and advice for everyone—[715]are they obtuse? And wherein lies their obtusity? Their obtusity is that, after they have lost the poetic illusion, they do not have enough imagination and imagination-passion to penetrate the mirage of probability and the reliability of a finite teleology, all of which breaks up as soon as the infinite stirs. If religiousness is an illusion, then there are three kinds of illusion: the illusion of poetry, the beautiful illusion of immediacy (the happiness is in the illusion, and then with actuality suffering comes afterward); the comic illusion of obtusity; and the happy illusion of religiousness (the pain is in the illusion, and the happiness comes afterward). Obtusity's illusion is, of course, the only intrinsically VII
comic one.[716] 398

Although a whole trend in French poetry has been rather active in presenting the esthetic illusion comically,[717] which is an insult to the esthetic and by no means a merit in the eyes of the religious person (namely, that a poet will do it), it would be more useful if poetry would properly concern itself with the worldly wisdom about life, which is—and this is the very sign of how comic it is—equally comic whether it calculates correctly* or calculates incorrectly, because all its calculating

* And perhaps most comic when it calculates correctly, because, when it calculates incorrectly, one has a little sympathy for the poor fellow. Thus, for example, when a man calculates on making a rich match through his various and sundry connections and with the aid of his knowledge of the world and it comes true and he wins the girl and she has money—then the comic is jubilant, because now he has become frightfully obtuse. Suppose he won the girl, but, lo, she did not have money; there would still be a little sympathy involved in it. But ordinarily most people recognize the comic through something else, in the unhappy outcome (which nevertheless is not the comic but the pitiable), just as they recognize the pathos-filled through something else, in the happy outcome (which nevertheless is not the pathos-filled but the accidental). For example, it is not as comic, either, if a lunatic with his fixed

is a delusion, a busyness within the chimerical notion that there is something certain in the world of the finite.

But was Socrates, then, not wise about life? Indeed, but I have explained several times that in a worldly sense his first thesis is still a lunatic's talk just because it makes the movement of infinity. No, poetry is youth, and worldly wisdom comes with the years, and religiousness is the relation to the eternal; but the years make a person only more and more obtuse if he has lost his youth and has not won the relation to the eternal. [718]The serious man we talked about before, the man who wanted to know that an eternal happiness is certain and definite in order then to venture everything, because otherwise it is indeed lunacy—I wonder if he would not find it to
VII 399 be general lunacy to venture everything when suffering becomes the certainty—the correct expression for the uncertainty.

Within religious suffering lies the category of spiritual trial [*Anfægtelse*],[719] and only there can it be defined. [720]Although I ordinarily concern myself with religious address only insofar as this is the organ of the religious life-view, I can in passing still consider its factual nature in our day (and in turn illuminate here the religiousness of our day, which pretends to have advanced beyond the religiousness of the Middle Ages), and by trying to assign spiritual trial its place call to mind that nowadays one almost never hears spiritual trial mentioned or, if it is mentioned at all, hears it summarily lumped together with temptations [*Fristelse*], indeed, even with adversities. As soon as the relation to an absolute τέλος is omitted and allowed to exhaust itself into relative ends, spiritual trial ceases. In the sphere of the relationship with God, it is what temptation is in the sphere of the ethical relation. When the individual's maximum is the ethical relation to actuality, temptation is his highest danger. It is, therefore, entirely in order to omit spiritual trial, and to use it as identical with temptation is only

idea brings himself and others into confusion, involving loss and injury, as it is when existence conforms to his fixed idea. In other words, it is not comic that existence allows one to discover that a lunatic is lunatic, but it is comic that it hides this.

additional negligence. But not only does spiritual trial differ from temptation in this way; the individual's position is also different. In temptation, it is the lower that tempts; in spiritual trial it is the higher. In temptation, it is the lower that wants to lure the individual; in spiritual trial, it is the higher that, seemingly envious of the individual, wants to frighten him back.

Therefore, spiritual trial begins only in the sphere of the religious proper, and there only in the final course, and quite rightly increases in proportion to the religiousness, because the individual has discovered the boundary, and the spiritual trial expresses the response of the boundary against the finite individual. Thus it is a false alarm, as indicated earlier, when the pastor declares on Sunday that it is so good to be in church and that, if we dared to stay there, no doubt we would become holy, but we must go out into the world again.[721] In other words, if a person were permitted to remain there, he would discover spiritual trial, and very likely he would come off so badly from this activity that he would not exactly want to thank the pastor for it. The moment the individual succeeds in practicing the absolute relation through the renunciation of relative ends (and it can indeed be this way at particular moments, although later the individual is again drawn into this conflict) and now is to relate himself absolutely to the absolute, he then discovers the boundary, spiritual trial then be- VII
comes the expression for the boundary. The individual is cer- 400
tainly innocent in spiritual trial (whereas he is not innocent in temptation), but nevertheless the suffering is probably terrible. [I say "probably"], for I know nothing about that, and if anyone seeks ambiguous comfort, I will readily inform him that anyone who is not very religious will not be exposed to spiritual trials either, because spiritual trial is the response to the absolute expression of the absolute relation. Temptation attacks the individual in his weak moments; spiritual trial is a nemesis upon the intense moments in the absolute relation. Therefore, temptation has a connection with the individual's ethical constitution, whereas spiritual trial is without continuity and is the absolute's own resistance.

That there is spiritual trial cannot be denied, however, and for that very reason there could be in our time a not unremarkable psychological occurrence. Suppose that a person with a deeply religious need continually heard only the kind of pious address in which everything is rounded off by having the absolute τέλος exhaust itself in relative ends—what then? He would sink into the deepest despair, since he in himself experienced something else and yet never heard the pastor talk about this, about suffering in one's inner being, about the suffering of the God-relationship. Out of respect for the pastor and the pastor's rank, he perhaps would be led to interpret this suffering as a misunderstanding, or as something that other people presumably also experienced but found so easy to overcome that it is not even mentioned—until, with the same horror as the first time it happened, he discovered the category of spiritual trial. Let him suddenly come upon one of the old devotional books[722] and there quite rightly find spiritual trial described—indeed, he would very likely be as happy as Robinson Crusoe was to meet Friday;[723] but what, I wonder, would he think of the Christian-religious address he was accustomed to hearing? The religious address should really be such that by hearing it one would gain the most accurate insight into the religious delusions of his era and into himself as belonging to the era. But what am I saying? This insight may be gained also by listening to a religious address that does not even hint at spiritual trials. One gains the insight, of course, but only indirectly by way of the address.

This, then, is the essential continuance of the suffering, its actuality, whereby it continues even in the most developed re-
VII ligious person, even if it is certain that the religious person had
401 fought his way through the suffering of dying to immediacy. Consequently, suffering remains as long as the individual lives, but lest we be in too great a hurry to return to the last suffering, we shall stop the individuals in the first, because its struggle is so prolonged and regression to it so frequent that an individual very rarely succeeds in making his way through it or in having overcome it for a long time.

The basis of this suffering is that in his immediacy the in-

dividual actually is absolutely within relative en
ing is the turning around of the relation, dying
or existentially expressing that the individual
doing nothing himself but is nothing before
here again the relationship with God is distinguishable by the negative, and self-annihilation is the essential form for the relationship with God. This must not be expressed in the external realm, because then we have the monastic movement and the relationship is indeed secularized; and the individual must not imagine that it can be done all at once, because this is esthetics. And even if it could be done all at once, the individual, since he is an existing person, would experience suffering again in the repetition. In immediacy, the wish is to be capable of everything, and immediacy's faith, ideally, is in being capable of everything; and the incapability of immediacy is rooted in a hindering something that comes from outside, which it therefore disregards in the same sense as it disregards misfortune, because immediacy is not intrinsically dialectical. Religiously, the task is to comprehend that a person is nothing at all before God [724]or to be nothing at all and thereby to be before God, and he continually insists upon having this incapability before him, and its disappearance is the disappearance of religiousness. The youthful capability of immediacy can become comic to a third party, whereas the incapability of religiousness can never become comic to a third party, because there is no trace of any contradiction.* The religious person

* There is no contradiction in a person's being capable of nothing at all before God except that he becomes aware of this, since this is only another expression for the absoluteness of God, and that a person would not even κατὰ δύναμιν [potentially] be capable of this would be an expression for his not existing at all.[725] There is no contradiction, and therefore it is not comic
either. On the other hand, it is comic, for example, that going about on one's VII
knees should mean anything before God, just as the comic on the whole is 402
most clearly manifest in idol worship, in superstition, and the like. But still one must never forget to pay attention to the childlikeness that can be the basis of the error and make it more sad than comic. Just as a child who wishes to make an old man really happy can hit upon the strangest things, but nevertheless does it all with the pious intention of pleasing the old fellow, so the religious person can also make a sad impression if in pious zeal there is noth-

cannot become comic in this way, but on the other hand the
402 comic can be manifest to him, that is, when to all appearances in the external world it seems that he was capable of a great deal. But if this jest is to be a holy jest and continue, it must at no moment disturb for him the earnestness that before God he is nothing and is capable of nothing, and the work of holding this fast, and the suffering of expressing it existentially. If, for example, Napoleon had been a genuinely religious individuality, he would have had a rare opportunity for the most divine amusement, because seemingly to be capable of everything and then divinely to understand this as an illusion—indeed, that is jest in earnest!

On the whole, the comic is present everywhere, and every existence can at once be defined and assigned to its particular sphere by knowing how it is related to the comic. The religious person is one who has discovered the comic on the greatest scale and yet he does not consider the comic as the highest, because the religious is the purest pathos. But if he looks upon the comic as the highest, then his comic is *eo ipso* lower, because the comic is always based on a contradiction, and if the comic itself is the highest, it lacks the contradiction in which the comic exists and in which it makes a showing. That is why it holds true without exception that the more competently a person exists, the more he will discover the comic.*

Even the person who has only conceived a great plan with the aim of achieving something in the world will discover it. In other words, let him have his resolution within himself and live solely and entirely for it, and then let him go out and be-

---

ing he would not do to please God and finally hits upon something utterly unreasonable.

* But the comic at its highest, just like the pathos-filled at its highest, seldom draws people's attention and cannot even be presented by the poet, because it does not *make a showing*, as one says, whereas the lower pathos and the lower comic do make a showing by being known through a third something. The highest does not make a showing [*tage ud*], because it belongs to the final sphere of inwardness and in a sacred sense is taken up [*indtaget*] with itself.

come involved with people—then the comic will appear—if VII
he remains silent. Most people do not have great plans and 403
most often speak in terms of finite common sense or out of sheer immediacy. If he just remains silent, then almost every other word that is said will touch his great resolution comically. But if he abandons his great resolution and his intense inward existence in relation to it, the comic vanishes. If he cannot keep silent about his great plan but has to babble about it immaturely, he himself becomes comic. But the resolution of the religious person is the highest of all, infinitely higher than all plans to transform the world and to create systems and works of art—therefore of all people the religious person must discover the comic, if he actually is religious, because otherwise he himself becomes comic. (But more on that later.)

Suffering as dying to immediacy is, therefore, not flagellation and other such things; it is not *self-torment*. In other words, the self-tormentor by no means expresses that he is capable of nothing before God, because he considers self-torment to be indeed something. But still the suffering is present and can continue as long as a person exists, because just as easy as it is to state that a human being is nothing before God, so is it difficult to express this in existence. But to describe and depict this in more detail is in turn difficult, because speech is surely a more abstract medium than existence, and in relation to the ethical all speech involves a little deception, because speech, despite the most subtle and skilled precautionary measures, always still has an appearance of the foreshortened perspective. Therefore, even if the discourse makes the most enthusiastic and most desperate effort to show how difficult it is, or makes an extreme effort in an indirect form, it still always remains more difficult to do than it appears in the discourse.

But whether existentially expressing this dying to [immediacy] is spoken of or not, it nevertheless must be done; and religiousness is not thoughtlessness, a matter of saying the highest occasionally and then, mediating, letting things take their course. The religious person does not preach indulgence but proclaims that the greatest effort is nothing—but also re-

quires it. Here again the negative is the sign, because the greatest effort is distinguishable by one's becoming nothing through it; if one becomes something, the effort is *eo ipso* less. However ironic this seems, it is nevertheless the case in lesser situations, in a lower sphere. With half application and a little dabbling, a person will begin to fancy that he understands many various sciences, and he will make a hit in the world and be widely read; with total application and absolute honesty, he will have difficulty understanding even a tiny little frag-
VII ment of what everyone understands, and he will be considered
404 a boring loiterer. But what holds true only relatively in this lower sphere holds true absolutely in the religious sphere, and the ultimate spiritual trial cited by tried and tested religious persons is always that the utmost effort wants to delude one with the notion of importance, that it is something.

Since I am now forced into the sorry admission that I am unable to speak about China, Persia, the system, astrology, or veterinary science, I have (in order to come up with at least something in my predicament) trained my pen, in proportion to the capabilities granted me, to be able to copy and describe as concretely as possible everyday life, which quite often is different from Sunday life. If anyone finds this kind of presentation or my presentation boring, then let him. I am not writing for any prize medal and shall gladly admit, if this is required of me, that it is much more difficult and involves much more commotion and an entirely different kind of responsibility to kill a rich uncle in a novel in order to get money into the story (or to skip ten years, let time go by in which the most important thing happened, and then begin with its having happened), and that it takes a totally different pithy brevity to describe the victory of faith in a half hour—than to describe that with which an ordinary person fills up a day in the living room. It does indeed take speed to write a narrative of thirty pages in which the action takes place over a hundred years, or a drama in which the action takes place within three hours, but so much takes place and events precipitate in such a way that their like could not happen to a human being in a whole lifetime!

But what does it take to describe a person in everyday life, provided one does not become hard pressed by the inadequacy of language, because, compared with existing in actuality, language is very abstract. But the religious speaker should indeed prevail upon himself to do it, since he is involved precisely with the living room. The religious speaker who does not know how the task appears in everyday life and in the living room could just as well keep quiet, because Sunday vistas into eternity are so much air. Of course, the religious speaker should not remain in the living room; he must know how to hold fast the totality-category of his sphere, but he also must know how to begin everywhere. It is in the living room that the battle must be fought, lest the skirmishes of religiousness become a changing-of-the-guard parade one day a week. It is in the living room that the battle must be fought, not imaginatively in church, with the pastor shadowboxing and the listeners VII 405 looking on. It is in the living room that the battle must be fought, because the victory must be that the home becomes a shrine. Let the work be done directly in the church by holding inspection of the contending forces—under whose banner the battle will be fought, in whose name the victory will be won—by describing the position of the enemy, by imitating the attack, by praising the omnipotent ally and strengthening trust by arousing mistrust, trust in him through mistrust of oneself. Let the work be done indirectly by the ironic but yet most tender sympathy of secret concern. But the main point still is that the single individual will go home from church willing wholeheartedly and eagerly to battle in the living room. If the pastor's activity in the church is merely a once-a-week attempt to tow the congregation's cargo ship a little closer to eternity, the whole thing comes to nothing, because a human life, unlike a cargo ship, cannot lie in the same place until the next Sunday. Therefore, the church is the very place where the difficulty must be presented, and it is better to go from the church discouraged and to find the task easier than one thought than to go from church overly confident and to become discouraged in the living room.

In order not to deceive himself and others, the religious

speaker will, then, even guard against concentrating his intense moments in a discourse or having his most intense moment in a discourse. He will rather be like one who certainly could speak in a higher key but does not dare to do so, lest "the secret of faith" be defrauded and debased by far too much publicity instead of "being held" (I Timothy 3:9) in such a way that it is even greater and more powerful within himself than it seems to be in his discourse. Since it is the speaker's main task, as well as everyone else's, to express in existence what he proclaims and not to electrify the congregation once a week and galvanically make them twitch,[726] he will be careful that he himself does not experience the disgust of having what looked so magnificent in the grandiloquent address turn out to be entirely different for daily use. But not for anything in the world may he give in, reduce the price, or haggle. Even when he seems furthest away from the absolute requirement of religiousness, it must be present, must determine the price and the judgment. Even when he becomes involved with the most wretched fractions of everyday life, this absolute common denominator must always be there, even if concealed, ready at any second to posit the absolute requirement.

What does the task look like in everyday life, for I continually have my favorite theme *in mente* [in mind]: whether everything is indeed all right with the craving in our theocentric nineteenth century to go beyond Christianity, the craving
VII 406 to speculate, the craving for continued development, the craving for a new religion or for the abolition of Christianity. As for my own insignificant person, the reader will please recall that I am the one who finds the issue and the task so very difficult, which seems to suggest that I have not carried it out, I, who do not even pretend to be a Christian, yet, please note, not in the sense that I have ceased to be a Christian by going beyond it. But it is always something to point out that it is difficult, even if it is done, as it is here, only in an upbuilding divertissement, which is carried out essentially with the aid of a spy whom I have go out among people on weekdays, and with the support of a few dilettantes who against their will come to join in the game.

Last Sunday, the pastor said, "You must not put your trust in the world, and not in people, and not in yourself, but only in God, because a human being is himself capable of nothing." And we all understood it, myself included, because the ethical and the ethical-religious are so very easy to understand but on the other hand so very difficult. A child can understand it; the simplest person can understand, just as it is stated, that we are capable of nothing at all, that we should give up everything, renounce everything. On Sundays it is understood terribly easily (yes, terribly, because this easiness often enough goes the same way as good intentions) *in abstracto*, and on Mondays it is so very difficult to understand that it is this little and specific thing within the relative and concrete existence in which the individual has his daily life, in which the powerful one is tempted to forget humility and the lowly one to mistake relative modesty toward people of status for humility before God, and yet a little bit is indeed something very specific, a mere trifle in comparison with everything. Yes, even when the pastor complains that no one acts according to his admonition, this is terribly easy to understand, but the next day it is very difficult to understand that by means of this simple thing, this little trifle, one makes one's contribution, merits one's share of the blame. —Then the pastor added, "We should always keep this in mind." And we all understood it, because "always" is a magnificent word. It says everything at once and is so very easy to understand, but on the other hand always to do something is the most difficult thing of all, and it is extremely difficult on Monday afternoon at four o'clock to understand this "always" as applying to a mere half hour. Even in the pastor's discourse there was a touch of something that indirectly made one aware of this difficulty, because there were some figures of speech so formulated that they seemed to suggest that he did not do it quite always, indeed, that he scarcely had done it in any of the few moments in which he VII 407
meditated on his sermon—indeed, he scarcely did it in any part of the short period of the discourse.

Today it is Monday, and the spy has much good time to become involved with people, because the pastor speaks before people but the spy speaks with them. So, then, he engages in conversation with someone, and the conversation eventually focuses on what the spy wants to talk about. He says, "That is true enough, but there is still something you are not capable of doing; you are not able to build a palace with four wings and marble floors." The person addressed answers, "No, you are right in that. How should I be able to do that? I more or less make a living, lay by a little each year, but certainly have no funds to build palaces, and, furthermore, I know nothing about building anyway." Consequently, he is not capable of doing it. The spy leaves him and now has the honor of meeting a man of great power. He flatters his vanity, and finally the conversation turns to the palace. "But a palace with four wings and marble floors perhaps exceeds Your Lordship's powers." "How so?" answers the person addressed. "You seem to forget that I have already done it; my big palace on Palace Square is precisely the building you are describing." Consequently, he is capable of doing it, and the spy congratulates the powerful man and bows himself out. As he walks along, he meets a third man and tells him the conversation he has had with the two men, and the third man exclaims, "Yes, a human being's lot in the world is strange; human capabilities are very different. One person is capable of so much, and another of so very little; and yet every human being is supposed to be capable of something, provided he learns from experience and worldly knowledge to stay within his limits." Consequently, the diversity is remarkable, but is it not even more remarkable that three different speakers about diversity say one and the same thing, say that all human beings are equal in capability? Man no. 1 is unable to do this and that because he has no money; that is, viewed essentially, he is capable. Man no. 2 is able to do it; he is essentially capable, and the fact that he is able to do it is demonstrated incidentally by his having money. By sagacity, man no. 3 is even able to do without some of the conditions and yet be capable; what a capable man he would be if he had the conditions!

But Sunday, that was yesterday, the pastor declared that a human being is capable of nothing at all, and we all under-

stood it. When the pastor says it in church, we all understand it, and if someone wanted to try to express it existentially in the six days of the week and showed signs of it, all of us would VII 408
be close to thinking: he is lunatic. Even the most God-fearing person will have scores of opportunities every day to catch himself in the delusion that he is still capable of something. But when the pastor says that a human being is capable of nothing at all, we all understand it terribly easily; and a speculative philosopher, in turn, understands this easiness in such a way that by it he demonstrates the necessity of going further, to go over to what is more difficult to understand: China, Persia, the system, because the philosopher speculatively disdains the paltry *Witz* [witticism] about the living room, because, instead of going home to himself from church and Sunday's abstract concept of the human being, he goes from church directly to China and Persia, astronomy—yes, to astronomy. That old master Socrates did the opposite; he gave up astronomy and chose the higher and more difficult thing: before the god to understand himself.

But the speculative philosopher demonstrates this necessity of going further with such necessity that even a pastor loses his balance and in the pulpit has the *ex-cathedra* opinion that the understanding with which the single individual apprehends that he is capable of nothing at all is only for simple and lowly folk. He even warns them *ex cathedra*—I mean from the pulpit—to be satisfied with this poor task and not to become impatient because it is denied them to elevate themselves to understand China and Persia. And the pastor is right in this, that the task is for the simple; but its secret is that it is just as difficult for the most eminent intellect, since the task is indeed not comparative—for a simple person in comparison with a distinguished intellect, but for a distinguished intellect in comparison with himself before God. And the philosopher is right in this, that understanding China and Persia is always somewhat more than the abstract Sunday-understanding of the abstract Sunday-man; that is, China and Persia are somewhat more concrete. But more concrete than any other understanding, the one and only absolutely concrete understanding, is the one with which the single individual understands himself in comparison with himself before God; and it is the most difficult understanding, because here the difficulty may not serve as an excuse.

And so it goes, for six days of the week we are all capable of something. The king is capable of more than the prime minister. The witty journalist says: I will show so-and-so what I am capable of doing—namely, make him look ridicu-
VII lous. The policeman says to the man dressed in a jacket: You
409 very likely do not know what I am capable of doing—namely, arrest him. The cook says to the poor woman who comes on Saturdays: You apparently have forgotten what I am capable of doing—namely, of prevailing upon the master and mistress so that the poor woman no longer receives the leftovers of the week. We are all capable of something, and the king smiles at the prime minister's capability, and the prime minister laughs at the journalist's, and the journalist at the policeman's, and the policeman at the blue collar worker's, and the blue collar worker at the Saturday-woman's—and on Sunday we all go to church (except the cook, who never has time, because on Sunday there is always a dinner party at the councilor's house) and hear the pastor declare that a human being is capable of nothing at all—that is, if by good fortune we have not gone to a speculative pastor's church.

But wait a minute. We have entered the church; with the help of a very capable sexton (for the sexton is especially capable on Sundays and with a silent glance indicates to so-and-so what he is capable of doing), each of us takes a place in relation to one's specific capability in society. Then the pastor enters the pulpit—but at the last moment there is a very capable man who has come late, and the sexton must demonstrate his capability. Then the pastor begins, and now all of us, from our respective different seats and points of view, understand what the pastor is saying from his elevated standpoint: that a human being is capable of nothing at all. Amen. On Monday, the pastor is a very capable man; we must all attest to the truth of that, with the exception of those who are more capable. —But one of the two must be a jest: either what the pastor says is a jest, a kind of parlor game one plays at times and bears in mind that a human being is capable of nothing, or the pastor must indeed be right when he says that a person must always bear this in mind—and the rest of us, the pastor, and I, too, are wrong in that we exegete the word "always" so poorly, even though a person is granted thirty, forty, or fifty years for perfecting himself, even if this makes each day a day of preparation and a day of testing.

Now it is Tuesday, and the spy is on a visit to a man who is having a huge building erected outside the city. He again directs the conversation to a human being's capability and to the esteemed host's capability. But now this man says, not without a certain solemnity, "A human being is capable of nothing; it is by God's help I have been able to amass this great wealth, and it is by God's help that I . . . . . ." Here the solemn quiet of the conversation is broken because a noise outside is heard. The man excuses himself and rushes out. He
leaves the doors half-open after him, and our spy, who has VII
long ears, now to his great amazement hears blow upon blow 410
with these words: "I'll show you what I am capable of doing." The spy can hardly keep from laughing—well, the spy is, after all, also a human being who at any moment can be tempted by the delusion that he is capable of something, as is the case, for example—that it was he who had caught the capable man in his ridiculousness.

But if a person, existing, is supposed to bear in mind every day and hold fast to what the pastor says on Sundays and comprehend this as the earnestness of life, and thereby in turn comprehend all his capability and incapability as jest—does this mean that he will not undertake anything at all because all is vanity and futility? Oh no, in that case he will not have the opportunity to understand the jest, since there is no contradiction in putting it together with life's earnestness, no contradiction that everything is vanity in the eyes of a vain person. Laziness, inactivity, snobbishness about the finite are a poor jest or, more correctly, are no jest at all. But to shorten the night's sleep and buy the day's hours and not spare oneself, and then to understand that it is all a jest: yes, that is earnestness. Viewed religiously, the positive is always distinguishable by the negative—earnestness by the jest—that it is religious earnestness, not direct earnestness, a councilor's obtuse official self-importance, a journalist's obtuse self-importance for contemporaries, a revivalist's obtuse self-importance before God, as if God could not create millions of geniuses if he were in any kind of predicament. To have the fate of many people in one's hand, to transform the world, and then continually to understand that this is jest—yes, that is earnestness! But in order to be capable of this, all the passions of finitude must be dead, all selfishness rooted out, the selfishness that wants to have everything and the selfishness that proudly turns away from everything. But that is just the trouble, and here is the suffering in dying to oneself, and although the distinguishing feature of the ethical is that it is so easy to understand in its abstract expression, it is so difficult to understand *in concreto*.

We ought always keep in mind that a human being is capable of nothing, says the pastor. Consequently, also when a man wants to go out to Deer Park, he is supposed to keep this in mind, for example, that he is incapable of enjoying himself; in addition, that the illusion that he is easily capable of enjoying himself in Deer Park, since he has a great desire to go out there, is a temptation of immediacy; furthermore, that the illusion that he is easily capable of going out there since he has the means to do it is a temptation of immediacy. Now, today is Wednesday, and a Wednesday in the amusement-park season;[727] so let us once again send out our spy.

VII 411 Some religious people may be of the opinion that it is not seemly of him to go out to the amusement park. If that is the case, I must, by virtue of the qualitative dialectic, request respect for the monastery, because dabbling leads to nothing. If the religious person is in any way to be conspicuous in his outward appearance, then the monastery is the only powerful expression for that—the other is nothing but dabbling. But our era, of course, has gone further than the Middle Ages in religiousness; what, then, did the religiousness of the Middle Ages express? That in the finite world there is something that cannot be thought together with or, in existing, held together with the thought of God. The passionate expression for that was to break with the finite. If the religiousness of our time has gone further, then as a result it is, in existing, capable of holding the thought of God together with the flimsiest expression of the finite, for example, with amusement in the amusement park, unless the religiousness of our age has advanced so far that it has come back to childish forms of religiousness, compared with which the youthful enthusiasm of the Middle Ages is something magnificent.

It is a childish form of religiousness, for example, to receive permission once a week from God, as it were, to make merry all next week, and then in turn on the following Sunday request permission for the next week by going to church and hearing the pastor say: We must always keep in mind that a human being is capable of nothing at all. The child has no reflection and therefore has no urge to think dissimilarities together. For the child, the earnest moment is when it must ask permission from the parents; if I just have permission, thinks the child, I surely will have fun, all right. And when he has seen his father at the office and received permission, he comes out jubilant and trusts that he will easily receive permission from his mother. He already is enjoying a foretaste of the pleasure, and with regard to that earnest moment at the office, he thinks something like this: Thank God, now that is over and done with. I think that the child thinks this, because the child actually does not think. If the same relation is repeated in an adult's life in relationship with God, it is childishness, which, like the child's talking, is distinguishable by a predilection for abstract terms: "always," "never," "just this once," etc.

The Middle Ages made a powerful attempt to think God and the finite together in existence but came to the conclusion that it could not be done, and the expression for that conclusion is the monastery. The religiousness of our age goes further. But if the relationship with God and the finite down to its most minor aspects (where the difficulty becomes greatest) are, in existing, to be held together, then the accord must find its expression even in the sphere of religiousness and be of such a nature that the individual cannot go over from the re-

VII 412 lationship with God to existing entirely in other categories. Forms lower than the monastic movement of the Middle Ages will be directly distinguishable by this split, whereby the relationship with God becomes something separate and the rest of existence something else. Thus there are three lower forms: (1) when the individual returns home from the Sunday relationship with God to exist purely immediately in the dialectic of the pleasant and the unpleasant; (2) when the individual returns home from the Sunday relationship with God to exist in a finite ethic and is not aware of the persistent claim of the relationship with God while he does his job, earns money, etc.; (3) when the individual returns home from the Sunday relationship with God to have his life in a speculative-ethical view that as a matter of course lets the relationship with God exhaust itself in relative ends, a life-view with this formula: competence in one's occupation as king, as cabinetmaker, as a tightrope walker, etc. is the highest expression of the relationship with God, and thus one does not actually need to go to church. In other words, by going to church once a week, all such religiousness emancipates itself from having the relationship with God present every day in everything. On Sunday, it obtains permission—not quite like the child, to make merry all week long—but permission not to think anymore about God all week long.

Thus the religiousness that goes further than the Middle Ages must in its godly reflection find it expressed that the religious person on Monday is supposed to exist in the same reflection, and on Monday he must exist in the same categories. What was venerable about the Middle Ages was that it was concerned about this in earnest, but then it came to the conclusion that this could be done only in the monastery. The religiousness of our era goes further. On Sunday, the pastor says that we must always keep in mind that we are capable of nothing; in other respects, we are to be just like other people. We must not enter the monastery; we may go out to the amusement park—but, please note, we certainly must first keep in mind the relationship with God by way of the religious middle term, that a human being is capable of nothing at all.

This is what makes life so extremely strenuous; and this is what makes it possible that perhaps all human beings may in truth be truly religious, because hidden inwardness is true religiousness, the hidden inwardness in the religious person who even uses all his skill in order that no one will detect anything in him. True religiousness, just as God's omnipresence is distinguishable by invisibility, is distinguishable by invisibility, that is, is not to be seen. The god to whom one can point is an idol, and the religiousness to which one can point is an imperfect kind of religiousness.

But what strenuousness! A singer cannot incessantly sing VII
vibrato; once in a while a note is tremolo. But the religious 413
person whose religiousness is hidden inwardness strikes the vibrato, if I may so speak, of the relationship with God in everything, and what is the most difficult of all, even when a special time is designated for it, he does it so easily he does it in no time. Thus the wittiness comes exactly at the right place, although he first of all gently makes the God-movement privately; then when invited he arrives right on time with the desirable cheerfulness, although he first makes the God-movement. Alas, ordinarily if a person has just a little external strain, it disturbs him while dressing for a party and he arrives late, and it shows on him. But the most strenuous of all thoughts, compared with which even the earnest thought about death is lighter—the thought of God—can move the religious person with the same ease as you and I and Peter and Paul and Councilor Madsen, for it is quite certain there is no one who detects anything on us.

Now the spy goes out. He may meet a person who is incapable of going out to the amusement park because he has no money, that is, one who is capable of doing it. If the spy were to give him money and say, "You are still incapable of doing it," the man would most likely consider him lunatic or assume that there must be a catch, that it perhaps was counterfeit money, or that the gates of the city and the customhouses[728] would perhaps be closed—in short, out of courtesy to the spy and in order not to reward his kindness by promptly declaring him lunatic, the man would probably attempt some keen guesses, and when all these failed because the spy denied that there was anything like that in the way, he would regard him as lunatic, thank him for the gift—and thereupon go out to the amusement park! And the same man would understand the pastor very well next Sunday when he preaches that a human being is capable of nothing at all, and that we should always keep this in mind. The amusing aspect is precisely this—that he can understand the pastor very well, because if there were one single person so simple that he could not understand the task the pastor essentially has to set forth, who then could endure life!

Then the spy meets another man, who says, "To go out to
VII the amusement park—if one can afford it, if one's business
414 affairs allow it, if one takes along wife and children, yes, and the servants, and comes home at a decent time—is an innocent joy, and one ought to participate in the innocent joys, but one ought not cravenly enter the monastery, which is an evasion of the danger." The spy answers, "But at the beginning of our conversation did you not say that you heard the pastor say on Sunday that a human being is capable of nothing at all and that we ought always to keep this in mind, and did you not say that you understood it?" "Yes." "Then you surely are forgetting what the discussion is about. When you say that it is an innocent pleasure, this is the opposite of a guilty pleasure, but this contrast belongs to morals or ethics. The pastor, however, was speaking about your relationship with God. Because it is ethically permissible to go to the amusement park, it is not thereby stated that it is religiously permissible, and in any case, according to the pastor, this is the very thing that you must demonstrate by placing it together with the thought of God, not, please note, in general terms, because you are certainly not a pastor who is supposed to preach on this theme, although in daily life you and many others seem to confuse yourselves with such a person, so that one sees it must not be the most difficult thing even to be the pastor. A pastor speaks in general terms about the innocent pleasures, but you, existing, are supposed to express what the pastor says.

"Today, then, on the occasion of your going out to the

amusement park, you are not to present a little discourse on the innocent pleasures of life; that is the speaker's affair. But on the occasion of your going out to the amusement park today, Wednesday the fourth of July, together with wife, children, and servants, you must keep in mind what the pastor said on Sunday—that a human being is capable of nothing at all, and that he must always keep this in mind. It was about your procedure in this regard that I desired information from you, because if I had desired a kind of discourse, I would have gone to the pastor." "How unreasonable," the man replies, "to expect more from me than from the pastor. I find it entirely in order that the pastor preaches this way. After all, he is paid for it by the state, and as for my spiritual guide, Pastor Mikkelsen, I shall always be willing to testify that he preaches the true evangelical doctrine, and that is why I go to his church. I am no heretic who wants to have the faith changed. Even if, according to what you say, it can be judged doubtful to what extent I actually am a believer, it is certain that I am an orthodox who abhors the Baptists. On the other hand, it never occurs to me to bring such trifles as going out to the amusement park into connection with the thought of God—indeed, to me it seems to be an insult to God, and I know that it does not occur to a single one of the many people I know, either." VII 415

"So you think it is fine, just as you think it is all right that the pastor preaches this way and all right that the pastor preaches about the fact that no one does as he says." "Unreasonable talk!" replies the man. "Of course I think it is all right for such a man of God to speak this way on Sundays and at funerals and weddings. Indeed, not more than two weeks ago I thanked him in *Adresseavisen* for the magnificent talk he gave on his own initiative and which I shall *never* forget." "Say, instead, which you will *always* remember, because this expression better calls to mind the subject of our conversation, that we must *always* keep in mind that a human being is capable of nothing at all. But let us break off this conversation, because we do not understand each other at all, and I am not receiving from you the information I was seeking, about how you go about doing what the pastor says, although I willingly concede to you an unmistakable talent for becoming a pastor. But you can do me this favor, if you will: give me in writing your assurance and, if you can, similar testimonies from the many you know, that it never occurs to you and to them to bring the thought of God together with anything such as going out to the amusement park."

We shall now dismiss the spy, but, just to put him out on thin ice, we shall ask him how he plans to use these testimonies and what he actually has up his sleeve. He speaks as follows: "Why do I want these testimonies? Well, I shall tell you. According to what I have heard, the clergy are holding some conventions where the reverend brothers raise and answer the question: What do the times demand—in the religious sense, of course, for otherwise such a convention would resemble a city council meeting. They say that now the convention is supposed to have come to the conclusion that this time it is a new hymnbook that the times demand.[729] That the times demand it is, of course, very possible, but this still does not mean that they need it. Why should that which is the case with
VII other moral characters not be the case with the times, as a
416 moral character, although not exactly because the times are
moral—namely, that they demand what they do not need, that all their many demands, even if they obtained them, would not satisfy their craving, because this is: to demand, to make claims. The times may soon demand that the pastor have a new gown[730] in order to be able to edify all the more. It is not impossible that the times actually could demand this, and with regard to such a demand, I would not be disinclined to assume that the times actually would feel a craving for it. My intention now is to collect some written assurances concerning the way people understand the pastor's Sunday sermon on Mondays and the other weekdays, so that, if possible, I might contribute to answering the question: What is it that the times demand? Or, as I would prefer to express myself: What do the times need? Then the question would not read: What does the religiousness of our times lack?—because it is always misleading to include the answer in the question—but this way: What do our times lack? Religiousness.

"Everyone is busy with what the times demand; no one seems to care about what the individual needs. Maybe there is no need for a new hymnbook at all. Why does no one think up a proposal that seems so obvious, more obvious than many believe: make a provisional attempt by having the old hymnbook rebound in a new way to see if the new binding would do it, especially if the bookbinder were allowed to place on the spine: The New Hymnbook.[731] To be sure, some may object that, because of the good old binding, it would be a shame to do this since, strangely enough, the congregation's copies of the old hymnbook are said to be in especially good condition, probably because the book is used so little, and the new binding would be a totally superfluous expense. But this objection must be answered in a deep voice, please note, in a deep voice: Every earnest man in our seriously troubled times perceives that something must be done—then every objection vanishes as nothing. Then it would not be such a serious matter that a few private little congregations[732] and dogmatic isolationists actually felt the need for a new hymnbook in order to have their watchwords heard in the vaulted church from the sounding board of the awakening. But when the whole age in unison and polyphonically demands a new hymnbook, indeed, perhaps several new hymnbooks, then something must be done. The situation cannot continue as it is now, or it will become the downfall of religiousness.

"Why, indeed, is church attendance as relatively sparse as it VII
is in the capital city? Well, naturally and obviously it is the 417
fault of the old hymnbook. Why is it that those who go to church arrive irregularly just when the pastor is entering the pulpit or a bit later? Well, naturally and obviously it is because of their disgust with the old hymnbook. What was it that destroyed the Assyrian Empire? Dissension, Madam.[733] Why do people indecorously run out of the church promptly as soon as the pastor says amen? Well, naturally and obviously, because of their disgust with the old hymnbook. Why are home devotions so rare, even though one could freely choose to use other hymnbooks there? Well, naturally and obviously, their disgust with the old hymnbook is so great that one is disin-

clined as long as it exists; its mere existence quenches all devotion. Why is it that the congregation unfortunately acts so little upon what it sings about on Sundays? Well, naturally and obviously, because the old hymnbook is so bad that it even hinders one in doing according to what is said in it. And why does it happen that unfortunately all this was the case long before the need for a new hymnbook was mentioned? Well, naturally and obviously it was the congregation's deep need, the deep need that as yet had not itself become clear—since there was no convention.

"But for that very reason it seems to me that we should hesitate to abolish the old hymnbook lest we be in the considerable embarrassment of having to explain the same phenomena when the new one is introduced. If the old hymnbook was of no benefit before, it is now; by means of it everything can be explained, everything that otherwise would be inexplicable if one keeps in mind that the times are so seriously troubled, and the clergy likewise, not only each one for his own little congregation and the individuals in it, but for the whole age. On the other hand, just suppose something else happened before the new hymnbook was ready; suppose the single individual decided to place the accent of guilt somewhere else and sadly sought reconciliation with the hymnbook and the confirmation day it calls to mind. Suppose the single individual solicitously went to church, arrived on time, sang the hymns, listened to the sermon, observed decorum, retained the impression on Monday, went further, retained it on Tuesday, yes, even on Saturday—then the demand for a new hymnbook might decrease. But, on the other hand, since the individuals had gradually learned to help themselves, the clergy would have the time and leisure to devote themselves entirely to sitting in conventions, where the reverend brothers raise
VII and answer the question: what is it the times demand—in the
418 religious sense, of course, for otherwise such a convention would resemble a city council meeting."

So much for the spy, who now must look after himself, and then back to what the pastor says, that a human being is capable of nothing at all and that we must always keep this in mind—therefore even when we go to the amusement park. Probably many have been bored for some time with this concrete example that never comes to an end and yet says nothing compared with the statement that we are capable of nothing at all and that we must always keep this in mind. But that is the way it is—in abstract generality, the ethical and the ethical-religious are so quickly said and so terribly easy to understand, whereas in the concretion of daily life speaking about it is so slow and practicing it so very difficult. Nowadays a pastor hardly dares to speak in church about going to the amusement park or even mention the word—so difficult is it even in a godly discourse to join an amusement park and the thought of God.

But, on the other hand, we all are capable of doing it. Where, then, are the difficult tasks? In the living room and on the coastal road to the amusement park. Nowadays the religious address, although it preaches against the monastery, observes the most strict monastic propriety and distances itself from actuality just as much as the monastery and thereby indirectly betrays quite adequately that everyday existence is actually in other categories, or that the religious does not assimilate daily life. In this way one goes further than the Middle Ages. But in that case the religious, by virtue of the qualitative dialectic, must call for the monastery. If this is not supposed to be preached and religiousness is still supposed to be ahead of the Middle Ages, then let the pastor be so good as to speak of the most simple things and abstain from the eternal truths *in abstracto*. Certainly nobody is going to lead me to think that it is very easy to keep the conception of God together with the most trivial of trivialities.

But this does not mean, either, that the pastor is supposed to sit in the living room like a watering-place guest [*Kildehans*] and talk about going to the woods, because that is really easy enough unless his own dignity would make it a little difficult for him. No, it means to speak devoutly about it and with the divine authority of the religious to transform even speaking about this into an upbuilding discourse. If he is unable to do that, if he thinks it cannot be done, he must warn against it—

and then judge the Middle Ages respectfully. But if the religious address indirectly strengthens one in the delusion that religiousness consists in having a fantastical-decorous notion about oneself once a week, in hearing some eternal truths delivered *in abstracto* and an attack on those who do not go to church, and in then otherwise living in different categories—
VII is it any wonder then that the confusion of wanting to go fur-
419 ther increasingly gains the upper hand? A competent clergy ought to be the moderator of the age, and if it is a pastor's task to comfort, then he also ought to know how, when necessary, to make the religious so difficult that it brings every insubordinate to his knees. Just as the gods piled mountains upon the heaven-defying Titans in order to constrain them,[734] the pastor should also lay the hundredweight of the religious task upon every mutineer (by laying it, of course, upon himself), lest anyone fancy that the religious is something to gad about with, a prank, or at most something for simple and obtuse people, or fancy that the religious is relatively and comparatively dialectical and identical with the conventional drill-training of the finite, or that the religious should be made difficult by world-historical surveys and systematic results, by which it only becomes even easier.

Thus when the religious speaker, as he explains that a human being is capable of nothing at all, joins something altogether specific to it, he prompts the listener to look deeply into his own inner being, helps him to disperse illusions and delusions, to set aside at least for a moment the bourgeois-citified sugar coating in which he otherwise finds himself. Ultimately, the religious speaker really works with the absolute relation that a human being is capable of nothing at all, but he makes the transposition by means of the specifics he brings together with it. If he limits himself merely to saying, "nothing," "always," "never," "everything," it could easily happen that it all would amount to nothing.* But if he forgets himself

* Therefore the religious address may very well be a little teasing, just as existence is, because the basis of the teasing is that we human beings have our heads full of great ideas, and then existence comes along and offers us the everyday.

and the foundational absolute "nothing," "always," "never," "everything," then he is transforming the temple, if not into a robber's den,[735] then at least into a stock exchange.

If no one else wants to try to present the absoluteness of the religious placed together with the specific, a combination that in existence is the very basis and meaning of suffering, then I will do it, I who am neither a religious speaker nor a religious person, but just a humorous, imaginatively constructing psychologist. If anyone wants to laugh at this, let him do so, but VII
I would still like to see the esthetician or the dialectician who 420
is able to show the slightest trace of the comic in the suffering of religiousness. If there is anything I have studied thoroughly, from A to Z, it is the comic. It is just for this reason that I know that the comic is excluded in religious suffering, that it is inaccessible to the comic, because suffering is precisely the consciousness of contradiction, which therefore is tragically assimilated with pathos into the religious person's consciousness, and thereby the comic is excluded.

The effect that a person's conception of God or of his eternal happiness should have is that it transforms his entire existence in relation to it, a transformation that is a dying to immediacy. This takes place slowly, but then finally* he will feel absolutely captive in the absolute conception of God, because the absolute conception of God is not to have the absolute conception *en passant* but is to have the absolute conception at every moment. This is the cessation of immediacy and the death warrant of annihilation. Just like the bird that flutters about carefreely when it is captive, just like the fish (which undauntedly cuts through the water and unerringly steers between the enchanted regions in the shoals) when it is lying on the ground outside its element, so, too, the religious person is captive, because absoluteness is not directly the element of a finite existence. Just like someone who is sick and cannot move because it pains all over, and just like someone who is

* Here I am using an imaginative form in connection with the vanishing of time: "slowly—but then finally." Since the concern of my task has not as yet commenced, this is quite all right.

sick but cannot keep from moving as long as there is life, even though it pains all over, so, too, the religious person, in his human lowliness, is bound in the finite with the consciousness of the absolute conception of God. But the bird in the cage, the fish on the beach, the invalid on his sickbed, and the prisoner in the narrowest prison cell are not as captive as the person who is captive in his conception of God, because, just as God is, the captivating conception is everywhere present and at every moment. Indeed, just as it is supposed to be terrible for a person who is thought to be dead if he is still alive, has the power of his senses, can hear what those present are saying about him but can in no way express that he is still alive, so also is the suffering of annihilation for the religious person when he in his nothingness has the absolute conception but no reciprocity. If it is supposed to have happened and to be poet-
VII 421 ical truth that merely a great and comprehensive plan, when it should be implanted and held fast in a person's mind, has shattered the fragile vessel; if it is supposed to have happened that a girl by being loved by the one she admired is annihilated in the suffering of happiness—no wonder then that the Jew assumed that the sight of God was death[736] and the pagans that the God-relationship was the harbinger of madness! Even though the conception of God is the absolute help, it is also the one and only help that is absolutely able to show a person his own helplessness. The religious person lies in the finite as a helpless infant; he wants to hold on to the conception absolutely, and this is what annihilates him; he wills to do everything, and while he is willing it, the powerlessness begins, because for a finite being there is indeed a meanwhile. He wills to do everything; he wants to express this relation absolutely, but he cannot make the finite commensurate with it.

Is there anyone who wants to laugh? If the position of the stars in the heavens has ever indicated something terrible, so, too, the position of the categories here does not indicate laughter and joking. To this now try to add going out to the amusement park. You will shudder; you will seek evasions; you will think that there are higher ends for which one can live. Yes, of course. And then you will turn away. But there is indeed a meanwhile—and meanwhile the powerlessness returns. You will say: Little by little. But that is just where the terror is, there where for the first time the first beginning of this little by little manifests itself as the transition from the absolute combined with this. Novelistically to allow a year's time to intervene is, of course, only a way of religiously ridiculing myself and the religious person.

The religious person has lost the relativity of immediacy, its diversion, its whiling away of time—precisely its whiling away of time. The absolute conception of God consumes him like the fire of the summer sun when it refuses to set, like the fire of the summer sun when it refuses to cease. But in that case he is ill; a refreshing sleep will strengthen him—and sleeping is an innocent pastime. Indeed, the person who has never had any other association than with bedfellows, let him find it sleepily quite in order that he should go to bed. But even for the person who has merely entertained a great plan, for him the watchman's call was certainly a sad memento, and
the suggestion of sleep more wretched than the coming of VII
death, because the sleep of death is but a moment and a mo- 422
ment's pause, but sleep is a protracted delay.

But in that case he must start on something. Perhaps the first thing that comes along? No, let a handy shop-clerk of the finite always have something at hand to diddle with. The person who had a relationship with the beloved only in the thought of love knows something else—when willing to do everything still does not seem enough, and the effort of willing everything creates powerlessness, and he once again stands at the beginning. But in that case he must come to himself, understand himself. Perhaps say the words? If the person who believes that to speak means to be talkative can pride himself on never having been at a loss for words, never having hunted in vain for words—even the person who just fell silent in admiration of human greatness surely learned that at least in that moment he needed no warning to keep his tongue under control. And the person who never went to bed weeping, weeping not because he could not sleep but because he dared not stay awake any longer, and the person who never suffered through the powerlessness of the beginning, and the person who never fell silent—he should at least never engage in talking about the sphere of religiousness but remain where he belongs: in the bedroom, in the shop, in street gossip. But how relative that can be which allows a person to experience something of this sort, how relative in comparison with the religious person's absolute relation to the absolute!

A human being is capable of nothing at all; this he must always keep in mind. The religious person is in this state—consequently he is not capable of going out to the amusement park either. And why not? Because in his own eyes he is better than other people? *Absit* [far from it], this is the exclusiveness of the monastic movement. No, because he actually is a religious person, not a fantastical pastor who speaks about "always" or a fantastical listener who understands "always—and nothing"; no, because hour after hour he understands that he is capable of nothing. In the state of illness, the religious person is not capable of joining the God-conception together with an incidental finitude such as going out to the amusement park. He comprehends the pain, and it is indeed a deeper expression of his powerlessness that he understands it in relation to something as trivial as this rather than to the grandiloquent expression "nothing," which easily becomes meaningless if nothing more is said. The difficulty is not that he is
VII 423 not capable of it (humanly speaking), but the difficulty is to understand first and foremost that he is not capable of it and to cancel the illusion (since he must indeed always keep in mind that he is not capable of anything at all)—he is past this difficulty, and thus the difficulty is: with God to be capable of it.

The more decisive an undertaking, a resolution, an event is, the easier it is (just because it is more direct) to join the God-conception together with it—the easier it is, that is, it is easier because one can be very easily tricked by oneself into an illusion. In the great crises in novels and short stories, one not infrequently sees either the fictional characters kneeling in prayer in a pictorial group or the main character kneeling in prayer in a secluded spot. But the esteemed authors and authoresses are naive enough to betray indirectly through the content of the prayer, its form, and the attitude of those praying that their heroes and heroines have not prayed many times before in their lives, even though the scene takes place in the year 1844, in a Christian country, and the acting characters are Christians, and the novel, as well as the short story, has the task of portraying people as they actually are, even a little better. With great inwardness the fictional protagonist joins the God-conception with the highly important event—but viewed religiously, the inwardness of the prayer is definitely not its vehemence at the moment but its continuance. But the more unimportant something is, the more difficult it is to join the God-conception together with it. And yet it is right here that the relationship with God will be known. In the making of a great resolution, in the publication of a work that presumably will transform the whole world, in an earthquake, in golden wedding celebrations, in peril at sea, and at clandestine births, God's name is perhaps used just as often interjectionally as it is used religiously. Therefore one should not be fooled when a pastor omits the minor events of life and concentrates his eloquence and mimic art on great episodes, and at most half-ashamedly, for the sake of decency, adds at the end that also in the everyday life one ought to show the same faith, the same hope, and the same courage (a religious discourse should rather be designed in the opposite way and speak about minor events, everyday life, and then at most add a few words of admonition against the illusion that can so easily be the basis for the religiousness that is perceptible only on leap year days*) because this is esthetic, and, viewed estheti- VII 424

* On the whole, there is nothing as protectively escorted by the comic as the religious, and its nemesis is nowhere so promptly at hand as in the sphere of the religious. When one hears an estheticizing religious discourse in a VII 424
church, it is, of course, one's duty to be edified, even if His Reverence blathers ever so madly. But if one comes back to it some other time, the comic effect is not without interest, and the law for it is that where the speaker hoists all sails in order to express the highest, he satirizes without knowing it. "The person kneeling in prayer stands up so strengthened, ah, so strengthened, so extraordinarily strengthened." But from a religious point of view, the true strength is that which is prepared for the struggle that can begin again, per-

cally, the calling upon God is neither more nor less than the most vociferous interjection, and God's revelation in the events is a theatrical tableau.

We left the religious person in the crisis of sickness; but this sickness is not unto death.[738] We shall now let him be strengthened by the very same conception that destroyed him, by the conception of God. [739]Once again I use a foreshortened perspective, because the interest of my task is still not here, and do not dwell on how the ethical (which nevertheless is always somewhat distanced from the absolute God-relationship) must intervene regulatively and take command. I shall, however, interrupt the reader with a few comments. First and foremost, in each generation there certainly are not many who suffer through even the beginning of the absolute religious relationship; and next, that a beginning in the existence-medium is anything but something that is decided once and for all, because it is only on paper that one is finished with the first phase and then has nothing more to do with it. The ab-
VII solute decision in the existence-medium still is and remains
425 only an approximation (but this is not to be understood comparatively in relation to the more and less of others, for then the individual has lost his ideality), because the eternal aims from above at the existing person, who by existing is in motion and thus at the moment the eternal touches is already a little moment away from there.[740] The beginning of the absolute decision in the existence-medium is least of all once and for all, something accomplished, because the existing person

---

haps the very next moment. "The individual attaches himself to God by a pledge, by a holy pledge, that he forever and always etc., and then he feels so reassured, ah, so reassured." But from a religious point of view, one is circumspect about making pledges (see Ecclesiastes[737]), and the inwardness of the pledge, viewed religiously, is distinguishable by the brevity of the fixed term and by the mistrust of oneself. No, the inwardness of the whole soul and the assent of the heart cleansed of double-mindedness in the pledge for the day today, or for this morning—viewed religiously, such a pledge has much more inwardness than that estheticizing hobnobbing with our Lord. The one suggests that the one making the pledge has his everyday life in the religious sphere; the other quite satirically betrays that the one praying is a visiting member introduced by a pastor.

is not an abstract X who accomplishes something and then goes further, goes through life, if I may put it this way, undigested; but the existing person becomes concrete in what has been experienced, and as he proceeds he has it with him and can lose it at any moment. [741]He has it with him, not the way one has something in a pocket, but through this, this specific thing, he is what he is more specifically defined and loses his own more specific definition by losing it. Through the decision in existence, an existing person, more specifically defined, has become what he is. If he sets it aside, it is not he who has lost something, so that he does not have himself and has lost something, but then he has lost himself and must start from the beginning.

The religious person has, then, recovered from his sickness (tomorrow there may be a relapse due to a little injudiciousness). He perhaps fortifies himself with the upbuilding reflection that God, who created man, certainly knows best all the numerous things that to a human being appear to be incapable of being joined together with the thought of God—all the earthly desires, all the confusion in which he can be trapped, and the necessity of diversion, of rest, as well as a night's sleep. It is obvious that the discussion here is not about the indulgence that is preached in the world, where one human being consoles himself through another, consoles himself reciprocally and leaves God out. Every human being is gloriously structured, but what destroys so many is, for example, this confounded talkativeness between man and man about what must be suffered but also be matured in silence, this confession before human beings instead of before God, this candid communication to this one and that one of what ought to be a secret and be before God in secret, this impatient hankering for makeshift consolation. No, in the pain of annihilation, the religious person has learned that human indulgence is of no benefit; therefore he listens to nothing from that corner, but he is before God and suffers through what it means to be a human being and then to be before God. Therefore he cannot be comforted by what the human crowd mutually knows, people who have a market-town idea of what it means

to be a human being, and a fluent, talkative idea at seventeenth hand of what it means to be before God. From God he must
VII 426 draw his comfort, lest his entire religiousness become a rumor. This does not at all mean that he is supposed to discover new truths etc. No, he is only to keep watch on himself lest, by being muddled up in talkativeness and a lust for preaching, he be hindered in experiencing within himself what thousands and thousands before him have experienced. If it is true even of falling in love that a love becomes ennobling only when it teaches a person to make a secret of his feelings, how much more true it is of the religious!

Let us consider what paganism poetized about, that a god fell in love with a mortal woman. If she continued to be unaware that he was a god, this relationship would be the worst possible misery, because, under the impression that the same standard was to apply to both of them, she would despair through demanding conformity from herself. But if she found out that he was a god, she would at first be almost annihilated in all her lowliness, so that she would hardly dare to admit her lowliness. She would make one desperate attempt after the other to elevate herself to him. She would be alarmed every time her lowliness made it necessary that they be parted; she would be thoroughly alarmed by the torment that it was lack of will or lack of ability.[742]

Let us now make the application to the religious. Where, then, is the boundary for the single individual in his concrete existence between what is lack of will and what is lack of ability; what is indolence and earthly selfishness and what is the limitation of finitude? For an existing person, when is the period of preparation over, when this question will not rise again in all its initial, troubled severity; when is the time in existence that is indeed a preparation? Let all the dialecticians convene—they will not be able to decide this for a particular individual *in concreto*. Dialectic in its truth is a kindly disposed, ministering power that discovers and helps to find where the absolute object of faith and worship is, where the absolute is—namely, there where in unknowing the difference between knowledge and nonknowledge collapses in absolute worship, there where

the objective uncertainty resists in order to force out the passionate certitude of faith, there where in absolute subjection the conflict about right and wrong collapses in absolute worship. Dialectic itself does not see the absolute, but it leads, as it were, the individual to it and says: Here it must be, that I can vouch for; if you worship here, you worship God. But VII 427
worship itself is not dialectic. A dialectic that mediates is a miscarried genius.

Consequently, the mortal woman who was loved by the god would at first be annihilated in her lowliness, but then she presumably would be raised up by the idea that he surely must know all this better than she. She would be annihilated by thinking divinely about him, but in turn would be raised up by the thought that he thought humanly about her. Indeed, if a girl of low estate was married even to a king of a foreign nation—how would she suffer in order to find bold confidence with regard to everything that called to mind her lowliness in such a way that it seemed bound to disturb the relationship, in order to find peace in the border war between being accommodating to herself and demanding too much of herself?

[743]But it is also part and parcel of this human being's lowliness that he is temporal and in temporality cannot endure to lead uninterruptedly the life of eternity. And if his life is in temporality, it is *eo ipso* piecemeal; if it is piecemeal, it is, of course, mixed with diversion, and in diversion he is absent from his relationship with God or he is not present as he is in the intense moment. If people say it is hard for lovers to be separated, should this not then be hard for the religious person, and is it less hard that it is a diversion and not a difficulty that separates when the necessity of the diversion is precisely that which manifests his lowliness most strongly? Our religious person is not in a position such that the pastor must admonish him to desire to seek God; rather the opposite, he is gripped in such a way that there must be diversion lest he perish. Here the monastic movement is tempting. Would it not be possible by suprahuman effort to come closer to God, to maintain the relationship without interruption, without sleep, if possible!

It is commonly said that love is able to make the two equal. Yes, that is correct if one is speaking about the relationship of two human beings, because essentially they stand on the same level, and the difference is accidental. But since there is an absolute difference between God and man, this direct equality is a presumptuous, giddying thought, but that this is so is no comparative human release from the utmost effort. But since there is this absolute difference between God and man, how does love's equality express itself? By the absolute difference. And what is the form of the absolute difference? Humility. What kind of humility? The humility that entirely acknowledges its human lowliness with humble bold confidence before God as the one who certainly knows this better than the person himself. The monastic movement is an attempt at
VII wanting to be more than a human being, an enthusiastic, per-
428 haps pious attempt to be like God. But right there is the deep suffering of true religiousness, the deepest imaginable: to relate oneself to God absolutely decisively and to be unable to have any decisive outward expression for it (happy erotic love expresses itself outwardly in the joining of the lovers), because the most decisive outward expression is only relative, is both too much and too little, too much because it implies arrogance with regard to others, and too little because it still is a worldly expression.

So, then, there are two ways for consideration: the way of humble diversion and the way of desperate effort, the way to the amusement park and the way to the monastery. To the amusement park? Well, let us just mention it; I could just as well mention many other things under the same rubric. A fool will probably laugh at this thought, a dignified religious person will feel insulted, and both will demonstrate its correctness. But why mention such a word as the amusement park? It is indeed much more respectable on Sunday to speak in very indefinite and ambiguous, general, Sunday-proper expressions about these innocent joys and then on weekdays to speak about them in everyday language. Yes, it is surely more respectable, and in this connection I have an inkling of what indignation the term "amusement park" will arouse in a respectable man, because in this connection it perhaps indirectly calls to mind the sense in which the religiousness of our age is further ahead than the Middle Ages, and because it is unpleasant to have a word like that bring the religious so close to one's own life, instead of viewing it at a distance by saying "nothing," "everything," "always," "never," "daily vigilance," etc.

Our religious person chooses the way to the amusement park, and why? Because he does not dare to choose the way to the monastery. And why does he not dare to do that? Because it is too exclusive. So he goes out there. "But he does not enjoy himself," someone may say. Yes, he does indeed. And why does he enjoy himself? Because the humblest expression for the relationship with God is to acknowledge one's humanness, and it is human to enjoy oneself. If a woman can succeed in totally changing herself just to please her husband, why should the religious person in his relationship with God not succeed in enjoying himself if this is the humblest expression for the relationship with God?

If a poor common laborer were to fall in love with a princess and believed he was loved by her, what would be the humblest way to maintain the relationship? I wonder if it would not be this, to be just like the other laborers, to go to work as usual, to participate with the others, and then, when during work he indulges in thinking about the relationship, to exhort himself
with the idea that humility would be more pleasing to the VII
princess than anything else if he still thought about her contin- 429
ually in his secret heart and was more than ready to express the relationship in a stronger way if he dared. It could never occur to the humble laborer that the princess was so foolish and so foolishly worldly-minded that she would enjoy having the world become aware through the laborer's odd gestures that she was loved by a common laborer.

But there is a certain kind of religiousness, presumably because the initial beginning of the annihilation was not complete and is not thoroughly inward, that has the conception of God as a jealous despot of limited understanding who is consumed with a vehement desire to have the world informed by a particular person's odd gestures that God was loved by a particular person. As if God desired any distinction, or as if this were an appropriate distinction for God, since everyone can perceive that even for a princess it is no distinction to be loved by a common laborer! A religiousness like that is itself sickly and ailing, and therefore it also makes God sickly. That it can occur to a domineering [*herskesyg*, sick for power] person to insist that it really become clear to the world, through the conspicuous submissiveness of others, how much power he has over them certainly does not demonstrate anything with regard to God. Or would the religious person consider doing all that if it could occur to him to think this way about God, namely, that God actually was in need—of the world's wonder and the revivalist's odd gestures that would elicit the world's wonder and thereby would draw the world's highest attention to the existence of God—the poor God who, in his awkward position of being invisible and yet so eager to have public attention drawn to him, is sitting and waiting for someone to do it for him.

But I have kept this rather abstract and now will have it take place as if it were today, because today it is indeed a Wednesday in the amusement park season, and our religious person is going out to the forest, as I, imaginatively constructing, attend to the psychological states. To speak about it is easy enough; to do it is something else. But to speak about it is in a certain sense perhaps not so easy; I am well aware of the risk I am taking, that I am staking my fragment of renown as an author, since everyone will find this extremely boring. It is still the same Wednesday in the amusement park season; the whole thing revolves around going out to the amusement park, and yet so many pages have already been used that a novelist would be in a position to have narrated the most interesting events of ten years, including great scenes and excit-
VII 430 ing situations and secret trysts and clandestine births. Indeed, so many pages have been used that with half as many a pastor could have finished with time and eternity and death and resurrection, with "everything" and "always" and "never" and "nothing," and finished in such a way that a person could have enough from the one sermon for a whole lifetime.

So it is a Wednesday in the amusement park season. The religious person has come to agree with the common view of the significance of necessary diversion, but it by no means follows that it is necessary on this very day. Right here is where the difficulty of the concretion lies, which continues as long as the religious person is in existence if he is to join this view with the particular moment on the particular day, with this and that particular state of mind, with this and that particular circumstance. If life is understood in this way, the vain quantitative differences vanish, because the "how" of inwardness determines the meaning, not the quantitative "what."

Our religious person is an independent and prosperous man who himself owns a horse and carriage. For that matter, he has both the time and the means to go out to the amusement park every day if he so pleases. The matter is best presented this way, because, as stated above, the religious address must be sufficiently ironic to make people exceedingly happy in external regards simply in order that the religious can appear more clearly. A man who has only one Wednesday free during the amusement park season may not have very many difficulties in taking off, but this ease and the difficulty of not being able to take off on the other days also make it possible that the religious does not become the determining factor. It is the same here as with earnestness. Many a man believes he is earnest because he has a wife and children and burdensome business affairs. But this does not necessarily mean that he has religious earnestness; his earnestness might also be perverseness and ill humor. When religious earnestness is to be portrayed, it shows up to best advantage in favorable external conditions, because in that case it cannot so easily be identified with something else.

He will, then, first ascertain that it is not a momentary inclination, a fancy of immediacy, that determines him. He wants to be sure that he needs the diversion and trusts that God also must surely know it. This is not a revivalist's impertinent self-assurance in relation to God, as is generally the case when an esthetic, jaunty fellow like that is distinguishable by having received his permanent letter of credit from God.

VII But although he knows this for sure and that he is not seeking
431 diversion out of an inclination of immediacy, because he would more than willingly dispense with it, the concern will still arouse distrust of himself and make him wonder if he could not dispense with it a little longer. But here, too, he knows for sure that already last Sunday he felt the need for diversion without yielding to it in order to test from which corner the impulse came. Where the boundary is so difficult to find between what is apathy and what is the limitation of finitude, he is convinced that God will not leave him in the lurch but will help him find what is the right thing. But at the same moment that he in his concern would, if possible, dispense with the diversion in order to hold out one more day, almost at the same moment there awakens the human irritability that really feels the sting of being dependent in this way, of always having to understand that one is capable of nothing at all. And this irritability is defiant and impatient; it almost wants to be united with the concern in a dubious conspiracy, because the concern would relinquish the diversion out of enthusiasm, but the defiance would relinquish it out of pride. And this irritability is sophistical. It wants to make him think that the relationship with God is warped by being brought into connection with such trifles and that it manifests itself in its truth only in the greater decisions. And this irritability is proud, because, although the religious person has more than once assured himself that to yield to the necessary diversion is the humblest expression for the relationship with God, in the intense moment of enthusiasm when the work is going smoothly it is always enticing to understand what one perhaps is not to carry out at the same moment, enticing in comparison with understanding it precisely when it must be carried out as something very specific.

But in turn this temptation vanishes, because the religious person is silent, and the person who is silent before God[744] learns to give way, to be sure, but he also learns that this is blessed. If our religious person had had a talkative friend at hand, he would easily have arrived at the amusement park, because it is a small matter when one has a horse and carriage,

plenty of money, and is talkative—but then he would not have
been our religious person, and our religious person also arrives at the amusement park. Now it is decided to seek diversion; at the very same moment the task is changed. If a little
later the thought goes through his soul that it was after all a
mistake, then he simply sets an ethical consideration in opposition to it, because in the face of a decision made after honest VII
deliberation, a fleeting thought must not play lord and master. 432
He disarms this thought ethically in order not to arrive again
at the highest relationship, whereby the meaning of the diversion decided upon would be destroyed. Consequently the direction is not toward the relationship with God, as when the
pastor preaches, but it is the relationship with God that itself
bids the religious person to seek elsewhere for a moment, as
if it were an agreement between God's solicitude and the person's self-defense. The ethical consideration is quite simply
this, that when worst comes to worst it is worse to become
maundering than with decisiveness to carry out what has been
decided, which perhaps was less properly considered, because
maundering is the absolute downfall of every spiritual relationship.

We all, of course, are waiting for a great event so that we can have an opportunity to show in action what fine fellows we are. When a crown prince takes over the government in the mightiest kingdom in Europe, assumes responsibility for the fate of millions, there is an opportunity to make a decision and to act *sensu eminenti* [in the eminent sense]. Undeniably! But this is the profundity and likewise the irony of existence, that the acting can be done *sensu eminenti* fully as well when the person acting is a very simple person and the feat is to go out to the amusement park. The highest His Imperial Highness is able to do, however, is to make his decision before God. The accent is upon this: "before God"; the many millions are only an illusion. But the lowliest human being can also make his decision before God, and he who actually was a religious person of such a kind that he could decide before God to go out to the amusement park will not be put to shame alongside any imperial highness.

So much for religious suffering, which is dying to immediacy. Let this be enough on that subject. I myself well know how poor it looks to carry out an investigation of such everyday matters about which everybody down to the simplest maidservant and soldier is informed, how uncircumspect it is to acknowledge the difficulty of it and thereby perhaps betray an inability to rise even a little bit above the horizon of the lowest class, how close to satire it is that one has spent time and energy for a number of years and ends up with nothing more than what the most obtuse person knows—rather than, alas, during the same time and with the same energy, possibly having accomplished something pertaining to China, Persia, even astronomy. There perhaps are not ten people who can bear to read what is presented here, and scarcely one person in the kingdom who would take the trouble to concoct some-
VII thing like this; but I am consoled in a way by the latter, be-
433 cause even if everybody can do it, if the production is actually only copyist work, then it is indeed to my credit that I have done what everyone is able to do (this is what is so discouraging to the weak human heart) but what no one else cares to do. So no one cares to present it—but, existing, to express it, to do it? Well, of course the deed always has the advantage over presentation; what takes a long time in presentation can be done very quickly—if one is able to do it. But now before one has advanced to the point of being able, what inconvenience before one is able to do it? Well, I merely say that I am unable to do it, but since the secret rests precisely in the hidden inwardness of religiousness, then perhaps everyone is able to do it—at least one does not notice anything on them.

If, on the other hand, someone flinches from the enormous strenuousness that living in this way must be—and how strenuous it is, I am adequately aware, since I, who merely sit and do an imaginary construction of it and thus keep myself essentially detached, feel the strenuousness of even this work—well, I prefer saying nothing else, although I admire the inner achievement of religiousness, admire it as the greatest marvel, but also frankly admit that I do not succeed in being able, from and with the highest conception of God and his eternal happiness, to enjoy myself in the amusement park. As I see it, it is marvelous, and I certainly do not speak of it with the intention, if it were up to me, of making the life of poor people even more difficult (ah, far from it!), since it is difficult enough, or to torment anyone by making life more difficult for him (God forbid!), since it is difficult enough. On the contrary, I hope to do the cultured a service either by eulogizing the hidden inwardness of their religiousness (because the secret entails that no one must notice anything, and there certainly is no one who notices anything) or, if possible, by making the matter so difficult that it could satisfy the demands of the cultured, since in their going further they, of course, already have so very many difficulties behind them. If someone flinches from the enormous strenuousness of living in this way, I find it still more appalling that they even go further, and, on top of that, go further by embracing speculative thought and world history—I find that still more appalling. But what am I saying—everything that goes further is, after all, distinguishable by its being not *merely* this but *also* something more; therefore I find this more appalling—and also something more: appallingly obtuse.

The meaning of the religious suffering is dying to immedi- VII
acy; its actuality is its essential continuance, but it belongs to 434
inwardness and must not express itself externally (the monastic movement). When we take a religious person, the knight of hidden inwardness, and place him in the existence-medium, a contradiction will appear as he relates himself to the world around him, and he himself must become aware of this. The contradiction does not consist in his being different from everyone else (this self-contradiction is precisely the law for the nemesis the comic brings upon the monastic movement), but the contradiction is that he, with all this inwardness hidden within him, with this pregnancy of suffering and benediction in his inner being, looks just like all the others—and inwardness is indeed hidden simply by his looking exactly like others.* There is something comic here, because here is a con-

* Another author has correctly traced (in *Either/Or*) the ethical to the qual-

tradiction, and where there is a contradiction the comic is also present. This comic aspect, however, is not for others, who know nothing about it, but is for the religious person himself when humor is his incognito, as Frater Taciturnus says (see *Stages on Life's Way*[746]). This is worth understanding more precisely, because next to the confusion in recent speculative thought that faith is immediacy, perhaps the most confusing confusion is that humor is the highest, because humor is still not religiousness, but its *confinium* [border territory]. There
VII are already some comments about this above, which I must
435 ask the reader to recall.

But is humor the incognito of the religious person? Is not his incognito this, that there is nothing whatever to be noticed, nothing at all that could arouse suspicion of the hidden inwardness, not even so much as the humoristic? At its very maximum, if this could be reached in existence, this would no doubt be so;* yet as long as the struggle and the suffering in

ification that it is every human being's duty to become *open*[745]—thus to *disclosure*. Religiousness, on the other hand, is hidden inwardness, but, please note, not the immediacy that is supposed to become open, not the untransformed inwardness, but the inwardness whose transformed qualification is to be hidden. —Incidentally, it hardly needs to be recalled that when I say the religious person's incognito is to look exactly like all the others, this does not mean that his incognito is the actuality of a robber, a thief, a murderer, because the world certainly has not sunk so deep that an open breach of legality can be regarded as the universally human. No, the expression "to look exactly like all other human beings" naturally makes sure of legality, but this may very well also be without there being any religiousness in a person.

* In *Fear and Trembling*, a "knight of faith" such as this was portrayed.[747] But this portrayal was only a rash anticipation, and the illusion was gained by depicting him in a state of completeness, and hence in a false medium, instead of in the existence-medium, and the beginning was made by ignoring the contradiction—how an observer could become at all *aware* of him in such a way that he could place himself, admiring, outside and admire that there is nothing, nothing whatever, to *notice*, unless Johannes de Silentio would say that the knight of faith is his own poetic production. But then the contradiction is there again, implicit in the duplexity that as poet and observer he simultaneously relates himself to the same thing, consequently as poet creates a character in the medium of imagination (for this, of course, is the poet-medium) and as observer observes the same poetic figure in the existence-medium. —Frater Taciturnus seems already to have been aware of this dialec-

inwardness continue he will not succeed in hiding his inwardness completely, but he will not express it directly, and he will hinder it negatively with the aid of the humorous. An observer who mingled with people in order to find the religious person would therefore follow the principle that everyone in whom he discovered the humorous would be made the object of his attention. But if he has made the relation of inwardness clear to himself, he will also know that he can be fooled, because the religious person is not a humorist, but in his outer appearance he is a humorist. Thus an observer who is looking for the religious person and intends to recognize him by the humorous would be fooled if he met me. He would find the humorous, but would be fooled if he drew any conclusion from it, because I am not a religious person but simply and solely a humorist. Perhaps someone thinks that it is frightful VII 436
arrogation to attribute the designation of "humorist" to myself, and furthermore thinks that if I actually were a humorist he would surely show me respect and honor. I shall not take exception to or dwell upon this, because the person who makes this objection obviously assumes humor to be the highest. I, on the contrary, declare that the religious person *stricte sic dictus* [in the strict sense of the word] is infinitely higher than the humorist and qualitatively different from the humorist. Moreover, concerning his unwillingness to regard me as humorist, well, I am willing to transfer the role of observer from me to the one who is making the objection; let the observer become aware of him: the result will be the same—the observer is fooled.

There are three existence-spheres: the esthetic, the ethical, the religious. To these there is a respectively corresponding *confinium* [border territory]: irony is the *confinium* between the

tical difficulty, for he has avoided this irregularity by means of the form of an imaginary construction. He is not in an observational relation to Quidam of the imaginary construction[748] but transforms his observation into a psychological-poetic production and then draws this as close as possible to actuality by using the form of the imaginary construction and the proportions of actuality rather than the foreshortened perspective.

esthetic and the ethical; humor is the *confinium* between the ethical and the religious.

Let us take irony. As soon as an observer discovers an ironist, he will be attentive, because it is possible that the ironist is an ethicist. But he can also be fooled, because it is not certain that the ironist is an ethicist. The immediate person is distinguishable at once, and as soon as he is recognized it is a certainty that he is not an ethicist, because he has not made the movement of infinity. The ironical rejoinder, if it is correct (and the observer is assumed to be a tried and tested man who knows all about tricking and unsettling the speaker in order to see if what he says is something learned by rote or has a bountifully ironic value such as an existing ironist will always have), betrays that the speaker has made the movement of infinity, but no more. The irony emerges by continually joining the particulars of the finite with the ethical infinite requirement and allowing the contradiction to come into existence. The one who can do it with proficiency and not let himself be caught in any relativity, in which his proficiency becomes diffident, must have made a movement of infinity, and to that extent it is possible that he is an ethicist.* Therefore the ob-
VII 437 server will not even be able to catch him in his inability to perceive himself ironically, because he is also able to talk about himself as about a third person, to join himself as a vanishing

* If the observer is able to catch him in a relativity that he does not have the strength to comprehend ironically, then he is not really an ironist. In other
VII 437 words, if irony is not taken in the decisive sense, every human being is basically ironical. As soon as a person who has his life in a certain relativity (and this definitely shows that he is not ironical) is placed outside it in a relativity that he considers to be lower (a nobleman, for example, in a group of peasants, a professor in the company of parish clerks, a city millionaire together with beggars, a royal coachman in a room with peat cutters, a cook at a manor house together with women who do weeding, etc.), then he is ironical—that is, he is not ironical, since his irony is only the illusory superiority of relativity, but the symptoms and the rejoinders will have a certain similarity. But the whole thing is only a game within a certain presupposition, and the inhumanity is distinguishable in the inability of the person concerned to perceive himself ironically, and the inauthenticity is distinguishable by the same person's obsequiousness when a relativity shows up that is higher than his. This, alas, is what the world calls modesty—the ironist, he is proud!

particular together with the absolute requirement—indeed, to *join* them *together*.[749] How strange that an expression that signifies the final difficulty of existence, which is to join together the absolutely different (such as the conception of God with going out to the amusement park), that the same expression in our language also signifies teasing! But although this is certain, it is still not certain that he is an ethicist. He is an ethicist only by relating himself within himself to the absolute requirement. Such an ethicist uses irony as his incognito. In this sense Socrates was an ethicist, but, please note, bordering on the religious, which is why the analogy to faith in his life was pointed out earlier (Section II, Chapter II).

What, then, is irony, if one wants to call Socrates an ironist and does not, like Magister Kierkegaard, consciously or unconsciously want [750]to bring out only the one side?[751] Irony is the unity of ethical passion, which in inwardness infinitely accentuates one's own *I* in relation to the ethical requirement—and culture, which in externality infinitely abstracts from the personal *I* as a finitude included among all other finitudes and particulars. An effect of this abstraction is that no one notices the first, and this is precisely the art, and through it the true infinitizing of the first is conditioned.* Most people live in the VII 438
opposite way. They are busy with being something when someone is watching them. If possible, they are something in their own eyes as soon as others are watching them, but inwardly, where the absolute requirement is watching them, they have no taste for accentuating the personal *I*.

Irony is an existence-qualification, and thus nothing is more

* The desperate attempt of the miscarried Hegelian ethics to make the state into the court of last resort of ethics[752] is a highly unethical attempt to finitize individuals, an unethical flight from the category of individuality to the category of the race (see Section II, Chapter I). The ethicist in *Either/Or* has already protested against this directly and indirectly, indirectly at the end of the essay on the balance between the esthetic and the ethical in the personality, where he himself must make a concession with regard to the religious, and again at the end of the article on marriage (in *Stages*), where, even on the basis of the ethics he champions, which is diametrically opposite to Hegelian ethics, he certainly jacks up the price of the religious as high as possible but still makes room for it.

ludicrous than regarding it as a style of speaking or an author's counting himself lucky to express himself ironically once in a while. The person who has essential irony has it all day long and is not bound to any style, because it is the infinite within him.

Irony is the cultivation of the spirit and therefore follows next after immediacy; then comes the ethicist, then the humorist, then the religious person.

But why does the ethicist use irony as his incognito? Because he comprehends the contradiction between the mode in which he exists in his inner being and his not expressing it in his outer appearance. The ethicist certainly becomes open insofar as he exhausts himself in the tasks of factual actuality, but the immediate person also does this, and what makes the ethicist an ethicist is the movement* by which he inwardly
VII 439 joins his outward life together with the infinite requirement of the ethical, and this is not directly apparent. In order not to be disturbed by the finite, by all the relativities in the world, the ethicist places the comic between himself and the world and thereby makes sure that he himself does not become comic through a naive misunderstanding of his ethical passion. An immediate enthusiast bawls out in the world early and late; always in his swagger-boots, he pesters people with his enthusiasm and does not perceive at all that it does not make them enthusiastic, except when they beat him. No doubt he is well informed, and the order calls for a complete transformation—of the whole world. Indeed, it is here that he has heard

* When Socrates related himself negatively to the actuality of the state, this was consistent in part with his discovering of the ethical, in part with his dialectical position as an exception and *extraordinarius*, and finally with his being an ethicist bordering on the religious. Just as an analogy to faith is to be found in him, so an analogy to hidden inwardness can also be found, except that externally he expressed this only by negative action, by abstaining, and thus contributed to drawing the attention of others to it. The hidden inwardness of religiousness in the incognito of humor avoids attention by being like the others, except that there is a background tone of the humorous in the simple rejoinder and a flourish of it in the everyday way of life, but one must indeed be an observer to become aware of this. Everyone was bound to notice Socrates' reserve.

wrongly, because the order calls for a complete transformation of oneself. If such an enthusiast is contemporary with an ironist, the latter naturally makes comic capital of him. The ethicist, however, is sufficiently ironical to be well aware that what engages him absolutely does not engage the others absolutely. He himself grasps this misrelation and places the comic in between in order to be able more inwardly to hold fast the ethical within himself. Now the comedy starts, because people's opinion of a person like that will always be: for him nothing is important. And why not? Because for him the ethical is absolutely important; in this he is different from the generality of people, for whom so many things are important, indeed, almost everything is important—but nothing is absolutely important. —Yet, as mentioned, an observer can be fooled if he assumes an ironist to be an ethicist, since irony is only a possibility.

So it is also with the humorist and the religious person, since according to the above the special dialectic of the religious does not allow direct expression, does not allow recognizable difference, protests against the commensurability of the outer, and yet esteems, if worst comes to worst, the monastic movement far above mediation. The humorist continually (not in the sense of the pastor's "always" but at every time of day, wherever he is and whatever he thinks or undertakes) joins the conception of God together with something else and brings out the contradiction—but he does not relate himself to God in religious passion (*stricte sic dictus* [in the strict sense of the word]). He changes himself into a jesting and yet profound transition area for all these transactions, but he does not relate himself to God.[753]

The religious person does the same, joins the conception of
God together with everything and sees the contradiction, but VII
in his innermost being he relates himself to God, whereas im- 440
mediate religiousness rests in the pious superstition of seeing
God directly in everything, and the revivalist impertinently
employs God to be present where he is, so that if one only
sees him one can be sure that God is there, since the revivalist
has him in his pocket. Therefore, religiousness with humor as

the incognito is the unity of absolute religious passion (inwardly deepened dialectically) and spiritual maturity, which calls religiousness back from all outwardness into inwardness and therein it is again indeed the absolute religious passion. The religious person discovers that what engages him absolutely seems to engage others very little, but he draws no conclusions, partly because he has no time for that and partly because he cannot know for sure whether all these people are not knights of hidden inwardness. He lets himself be constrained by his surroundings to do what the dialectical inward deepening requires of him—to place a veil between people and himself in order to guard and protect the inwardness of his suffering and his relationship with God. This does not mean that such a religious person becomes inactive; on the contrary, he does not leave the world but remains in it, because precisely this is his incognito. But before God he inwardly deepens his outward activity by acknowledging that he is capable of nothing, by cutting off every teleological relation to what is directed outward, all income from it in finitude, even though he still works to the utmost of his ability—and precisely this is enthusiasm. A revivalist always adds God's name outwardly;* the certitude of his faith is sufficiently sure. But the certitude of faith is indeed distinguishable by uncertainty, and just as its certitude is the highest of all, so this same certitude is the most ironic of all, otherwise it is not the certitude of faith. It is certain that everything that pleases God will succeed for the pious—it is certain, oh, so certain; indeed, nothing is as certain as this.

But now to the next point, and please note that the investigation is not on paper but in existence, and the believer is a particular existing person in the concretion of existence. So this is the eternal certainty, that what pleases God will succeed for the pious. But now to the next point—what is it that pleases God? Is it this or that, is it this lifetime occupation he

* Please recall that an apostle's life is paradoxically dialectical; therefore he turns outward. Everyone who is not an apostle thereby becomes only an esthetician gone astray.

is to choose, this girl he is to marry, this work he is to begin,
this project he is to give up? Well, perhaps, and perhaps not. VII
Is this not really ironic? And yet it is eternally certain and there 441
is nothing as certain as this, that what pleases God will succeed for the pious. Yes, but for that very reason the religious person is not to be much concerned about externals but is to desire the highest goods, peace of soul, his soul's salvation—this always pleases God. And it is certain, as certain as God lives, that what pleases God will succeed for the pious. So it pleases God that he will do this, but when will he be successful? Right away, or in a year, or perhaps not until the end of mortal life—may not the strife and the ordeal last that long? Perhaps, perhaps not. Is this not really ironic? And yet it is certain, so certain, that what pleases God succeeds for the pious. If this certainty fails, faith fails, but if the uncertainty that is its mark and its form ceases, then we have not advanced in religiousness but have relapsed to childish forms. As soon as uncertainty is not the form of certitude, as soon as uncertainty does not continually keep the religious person hovering in order continually to grasp certitude, as soon as certainty seals with lead, as it were, the religious person—well, then he is naturally about to become part of the mass.

But hidden inwardness with humor as its incognito seems to imply that the religious person is safeguarded against becoming a martyr, which the enthusiast would be most pleased to become. Yes, indeed, the knight of hidden inwardness is safeguarded. He is a foster child compared with the revivalist, who walks boldly toward martyrdom—unless martyrdom means the suffering of annihilation, which dying to immediacy is, means the divine opposition itself to an existing person who is kept from relating himself absolutely, and finally means life in the world with this inwardness without having an expression for it. Psychologically, the law very simply holds true that a power capable of doing this and that when directed externally needs an even greater power to keep that power from reaching out externally. Power directed externally and opposition from the outside—then the opposition is to be estimated as only half opposition; half is support. Hid-

den inwardness has its martyrdom within itself. But then is it possible that every other person is such a knight of hidden inwardness? Well, why not? Whom can it harm? Perhaps someone who does indeed have some religiousness and finds it indefensible that this is not properly appreciated, hence someone who would be incapable of bearing to see the most passionate inwardness deceptively resembling its opposite in the external world. But why does such a religious person not
VII choose the monastery, where there is even advancement and
442 promotion, an order of rank for the religious persons? This cannot disturb the true knight of hidden inwardness; he is solely occupied with being that, less with appearing (to that extent he must use some effort to prevent it), not at all concerned whether everyone else is regarded as being religious.

But let us leave this hypothetical glimpse and go back to the observer. He can be fooled if he as a matter of course assumes a humorist to be a religious person. In his innermost being, the religious person is anything but a humorist; on the contrary, he is absolutely engaged in his relationship with God. Neither does he place the comic between himself and the others in order to make them ludicrous or to laugh at them (such an outward orientation is away from religiousness), but since he, by virtue of true religiousness as hidden inwardness, does not dare to express it in the outer world, because it is thereby secularized, he must continually discover the contradiction. Just because he still has not been entirely successful in calling back the inwardness, humor becomes his incognito and an *indicium* [indicator]. He does not hide his inwardness in order to perceive others as comic; no, just the opposite—in order that the inwardness within him can truly be, he hides it, and he thereby discovers the comic, but he does not take the time to comprehend it. Neither does he feel himself to be better than others, because such comparative religiousness is outwardness and thus not religiousness. Nor does he think that what to him is all-important is regarded by anyone as nonsense; even if someone says that, he has no time to listen but knows that the absolute passion is the boundary for mutual understanding.

Absolute passion cannot be understood by a third party; this holds for the relation of others to him and for his to others. In absolute passion, the passionate person is at the peak of his concrete subjectivity by having reflected himself out of every external relativity, but a third party is definitely a relativity. Someone absolutely in love already knows about this. Someone absolutely in love does not know whether he is more in love or less in love than others, because anyone who knows that is definitely not absolutely in love. Neither does he know that he is the only person who has truly been in love, because if he knew that, he definitely would not be absolutely in love—and yet he knows that a third party cannot understand him, because a third party will understand him generally in relation to an object of passion but not in relation to the absoluteness of passion. If anyone thinks that this is because the object of erotic love has an element of the accidental by being this particular individual and then objects that God, after all, is not some particular entity and that consequently one reli- VII 443
gious person must understand another in the absolute passion, the answer must be that all understanding between individuals must always be in some third, something more abstract, which neither of them is. But in absolute passion, which is subjectivity's extremity, and in the intense "how" of this passion, the individual is definitely most removed from this third. But erotic love is dialectically altogether different from religiousness, because erotic love can be expressed in the external realm and religiousness cannot, that is, if true religiousness is hidden inwardness and even the monastic movement is a mistake.

If anyone says that this hidden inwardness with humor as its incognito is pride, he only divulges that he himself is not a religious person, since otherwise he would be in the very same circumstances as the other, be absolutely turned inward. What the objector actually intends with his objection is to have the religious person swept into a relativity wrangle about which of the two is more religious and thereby manage so that neither of them becomes that. On the whole, a great number of objections are nothing more than self-denunciations, and in thinking about them I am often reminded of the story about a lieutenant and a Jew who met on the street. The lieutenant became angry because the Jew was looking at him, and he exclaimed: "What are you staring at, Jew!" The Jew, with ironical propriety, answered: "How do you know, Mr. Lieutenant, that I am looking at you?" No, if anything is pride and arrogation, without therefore aiming at anyone, still less implying that he was conscious of this himself—then every direct expression for the relationship with God is that, every direct expression whereby the religious person wants to make himself distinguishable.

If the relationship with God is a person's highest distinction (even though this distinction is available to everyone), then direct expression is arrogation, yes, even the direct expression for being what is called an outcast, yes, even the changing of the world's mockery of oneself into a direct expression of one's being religious is arrogation, because the direct expression indirectly charges everyone else with not being religious. The human is hidden inwardness in absolute passion; here again is the implication that everyone else must be equally able to approach God, because the person who in absolute inwardness wants to be conscious of being a chosen one *eo ipso* lacks inwardness, since his life is comparative. It is this comparing and relativizing that, often unconsciously, deceptively seeks an alleviating indulgence in the form of mutual heartfelt effusions. Someone who is absolutely in love has nothing to do
VII with any third party; he willingly assumes that everyone else
444 is just as much in love. He considers no person ludicrous in the role of a lover, but he does consider it ludicrous that he in the role of a lover is supposed to relate himself to a third party, just as, conversely, every lover is bound to consider him ludicrous if he wanted to be a third party.

In the religiousness of hidden inwardness, a person does not consider himself better than anyone else, does not consider himself distinguished by the relationship with God in a way that is not possible for everyone. The person who humbles himself before the ideal scarcely considers himself good, still less better than others, but he also knows that if a third party is present as witness (with his knowledge, otherwise it is indeed the same as if there were no one) to the fact that he humbles himself before God, then he is not humbling himself before God. From this it follows quite consistently that he will definitely participate in the outward divine worship, partly because his desire to be there will be like everyone else's, partly because his abstaining would be a worldly attempt to call attention to himself negatively, and, finally, because no third party is *there*, at least not to the knowledge of the religious person. He naturally assumes that everyone who is present is there for his own sake, not to observe others, which is not even the case with the person who, according to the word of an aristocratic landed proprietor, goes to church for the sake of his servants in order to set them a good example—of how not to go to church.

The comic emerges through the relation of hidden inwardness to the surrounding world as the religious person hears and sees what produces a comic effect when it is joined together with his inward passion. Therefore, even if two religious persons speak with each other, the one would produce a comic effect upon the other, because each of them would continually have his inwardness *in mente* [in mind] and now hear, together with this, what the other said and hear it as comic, because neither of them would dare to express directly the hidden inwardness. At most they would suspect each other because of the consonance of the humorous.

Whether there actually is now or has been such a religious person, whether all are that or no one, I do not decide and I cannot possibly decide. Even if I actually were an observer, with regard to such a religious person, I would still never go any further than to begin to suspect him on the basis of the humorous—and as far as I myself am concerned, I know all too well that I am not a religious person. Well, but nevertheless I presumably will be granted the pleasure of sitting here and imaginatively constructing how a religious person of that sort would be in life without speculatively becoming guilty of VII 445
the paralogism of inferring from the hypothetical to being, contrary to the old principle: *conditio non ponit in esse* [an as-

sumption does not bring into being], still less from my hypothetical thinking to the conclusion that it is myself, by virtue of the identity of thinking and being. My imaginary construction is as innocent and as far removed from offending anyone as possible, because it does not come too close [*for nær*] to anyone by saying of him that he is the religious person and does not offend [*fornærme*] anyone by denying that he is. It opens the possibility that no one is that and everyone is that—with the exception of those whom it cannot offend, since they themselves say that they are not religious in this way, either say it directly, as I do, or indirectly by having gone further. Included here must also be this or that revivalist, who would be offended if it were said of him that he was a religious person of that kind—and my imaginary construction must not offend anyone. It willingly admits that an enthusiast such as that is not the knight of hidden inwardness; that is obvious enough, because the enthusiast is obvious enough. Just as there is an ungodliness that makes itself conspicuous and wants to be conspicuous, so there is also a similar godliness, even though one ought to pay attention to the extent to which the basis of this distinguishability is that the revivalist, overwhelmed by the religious, is sick, and therefore the distinguishability is a helplessness under which he himself suffers, until the religiousness within him more healthily concentrates itself inwardly. But the situation is different where godliness wants to be known. It is a pious and in the strictest sense godly expression for the relationship with God to confess oneself to be a sinner; there is an ungodliness that wants to be known by the defiance that loudly denies it. But now the other side of distinguishability. If three revivalists have a dispute of honor with one another about which one of them is the greatest sinner, a rough-and-tumble fight over this rank—then, of course, this godly expression has become for them a worldly title.

In the previous century, a thesis propounded by Lord Sheftesbury that makes laughter the test of truth engendered sev-
VII 446 eral little research projects to find out whether it is so.[754] In our day, Hegelian philosophy has wanted to give predominance to the comic,[755] which might seem especially odd on the

part of Hegelian philosophy, which of all philosophies was least able to stand a blow from that corner. In everyday life, we laugh when something is made ludicrous, and after laughing one sometimes says: But it is indefensible to make something like that ludicrous. But if it is made really ludicrous, one cannot keep from spreading the story—naturally, with the edifying primary clause following the laughter: It is indefensible to make something like that ludicrous. It goes unnoticed how ludicrous it is that the contradiction rests in the feigned attempt to act ethically by way of an edifying subordinate clause rather than by abandoning the antecedent. When things are as they are now, when the universalizing and advance of culture and polish and the refinement of life contribute to developing the sense of the comic so that a preponderant predilection for the comic is characteristic of our time, which in both the right and wrong senses seems to rejoice in the Aristotelian viewpoint that elevates the sense of the comic as the distinguishing mark of human nature[756]—then the religious address must have been aware for a long time how the comic is related to the religious. The religious does not dare to ignore what occupies people's lives so very much, what continually comes up again every day in conversations, in social intercourse, in books, in the modification of the entire life-view, unless the Sunday performances in church are supposed to be a kind of indulgence in which with morose devoutness for one hour a person buys permission to laugh freely all week long. The question of the legitimacy of the comic, of its relation to the religious, whether it itself has legitimate significance in the religious address, this question is of essential importance for a religious existence in our time, in which the comic runs off with the victory everywhere. To cry "alas and woe" over this manifestation merely shows how little the defenders respect the religious that they are defending, since it shows far greater respect for the religious to demand that it be installed in its rights in everyday life rather than affectedly to hold it off at a Sunday distance.

The matter is very simple. The comic is present in every VII
stage of life (*except that the position is different*), because where 447

there is life there is contradiction, and wherever there is contradiction, the comic is present. The tragic and the comic are the same inasmuch as both are contradiction, but *the tragic is suffering contradiction, and the comic is painless contradiction.** It makes no difference that something that the comic interpre-

* The Aristotelian definition (*Poetics*, V): τὸ γὰρ γελοῖόν ἐστιν ἁμάρτημά τι καὶ αἶσχος ἀνώδυνον [καὶ] οὐ φθαρτικόν [the ludicrous may be defined as a mistake or deformity not productive of pain or harm to others][757] is not of such a nature that it does not allow whole families of the comic to be secure in their ludicrousness, and it does indeed become doubtful to what extent the definition, even in relation to the comic it embraces, does not bring us into collision with the ethical. His example: that one laughs at an ugly and distorted face if, please note, this does not cause pain to the one who has the face, is neither entirely correct nor so aptly chosen that with one stroke, as it were, it explains the secret of the comic. The example lacks reflection, because, even if the distorted face does not cause pain, it is indeed still painful to be so fated as to prompt laughter merely by showing one's face. It is right and beautiful of Aristotle to want to separate from the ludicrous that which prompts sympathy, to which the pitiful and the pitiable also belong. Even in otherwise first-rate comic poets there are examples of the use of a mixed form of the ludicrous with an addition of the pitiful (for example, in several scenes Trop is more pitiful than ludicrous.[758] The busy trifler,[759] on the other hand, is unqualifiedly ludicrous simply because he possesses all the conditions required for living happily and painlessly). In this sense, the Aristotelian example lacks reflection, but the definition lacks it inasmuch as it perceives the ludicrous as a something instead of perceiving that the comic is a relation, the misrelation of contradiction, but painless.

I shall here throw out at random a few examples to show that the comic is present wherever there is contradiction and where one justifiably disregards the pain because it is nonessential.

Hamlet swears by the fire tongs;[760] the comic is in the contradiction between the solemnity of the oath and the reference that annuls the oath, no matter what the object is.

VII 448 If someone were to say, "I venture to stake my life on there being at least four and a half shillings' worth of gold in the binding of this book,"[761] that would be comic. The contradiction is between the highest pathos (to stake his life) and the object; it is teasingly intensified by the phrase "at least," which holds out the prospect of four and a half shillings' worth, as if that were less contradictory.

Holophernes is said to be fourteen and one-fourth feet tall.[762] The contradiction is essentially in the latter part. The fourteen feet is fantastic, but the fantastic does not as a rule speak of fourths; the fraction "one-fourth" calls actuality to mind. The person who laughs at the fourteen feet does not laugh

tation sees as comic can cause the comic figure imaginary suf- VII 448
fering. If it did, it would be wrong, for example, to perceive
the busy trifler as comic. Satire also causes pain, but this pain VII 449
is teleologically dialectical and oriented toward healing. The
difference between the tragic and the comic consists in the re- VII 450

---

appropriately, but the person who laughs at fourteen and one-fourth feet knows what he is laughing at.

When the pastor gesticulates most vehemently where the category is from a lower sphere, it is comic. It is as if someone, calm and indifferent, were to say "I would give my life for my fatherland," and then with highest pathos, with gestures and facial expression, were to add, "Indeed, I would do it for ten rix-dollars." But when this happens in church, I must not laugh at it, because I am not an esthetic spectator but a religious listener, whatever the pastor is.

It is genuinely comic when Pryssing says "he" to Trop.[763] Why? Because the Maecenas-relativity Pryssing wants to claim with Trop by this address contradicts the total ludicrousness within which Pryssing and Trop are equals on an equal basis. [764]When a child four years old turns to a child of three and a half years and says solicitously, "Come, now, my little lamb," this is comic, even though one smiles rather than laughs (and does not smile without some emotion), because in themselves neither of the children is ludicrous. But the comic is in the relativity the little one wants to claim in relation to the other little one. The emotion lies in the childlike manner in which it is done.

When a man applies for a permit to go into business as an innkeeper and the application is turned down, this is not comic. But if it is turned down because there are so few innkeepers, it is comic, because the reason for the application is used as the reason against it. For example, there is a story about a baker who said to a poor woman, "No, mother, she does not get anything; there was another one recently who didn't get anything, either. We can't give to everybody." The comic is in his seemingly arriving at the sum total "everybody" by subtracting.

When a girl applies for a permit to go into business as a public prostitute
and the application is turned down, this is comic. One correctly considers that
it is difficult to become something respectable (for example, when someone
applies to become Master of the Royal Hunt and is turned down, this is not VII 449
comic), but the turning down of an application to become something con-
temptible is a contradiction. Of course, if she receives a permit, that also is comic, but the contradiction is a different one, that the legal authority shows its powerlessness simply in showing its power, its power by granting the permit, its powerlessness by being unable to make it permissible.

Mistakes are comic and are all to be explained by contradiction, however complicated the combinations become. When something intrinsically comic has become customary and belongs to the order of the day, one does not take

lation of the contradiction to the idea. The comic interpreta-
VII 451 tion produces the contradiction or allows it to become apparent by having *in mente* [in mind] the way out; therefore the
contradiction is painless. The tragic interpretation sees the
VII 452 contradiction and despairs over[775] the way out. It follows that

---

exception to it and does not laugh at it until it manifests itself raised to the second power. If one knows that a man is absentminded, one becomes used to it and does not reflect upon the contradiction until it occasionally doubles, and the contradiction is that what is supposed to serve to conceal the first absentmindedness reveals it even more. For example, an absentminded person reaches his hand into a spinach casserole, becomes aware of his absentmindedness, and in order to conceal it says, "Oh, I thought it was caviar"—for one does not take caviar with the fingers either.

A gap in speaking can have a comic effect because the contradiction is the gap and the rational conception of speaking, that this is indeed coherent. If the speaker is an insane person, one does not laugh at it. When a peasant knocks on the door of a man who is German and talks with him to find out whether there is a man living in the house whose name the peasant has forgotten but who has ordered a load of peat, and the German, impatient at being unable to understand what the peasant is saying, bursts out, "*Das ist doch wunderlich* [That is strange]," to the immense joy of the peasant, who says, "That's right! The man's name is Wunderlich"—then the contradiction is that the German and the peasant are unable to speak together because the language is a hindrance, and that the peasant nevertheless obtains the information by means of the language.

[765]Something that is not intrinsically ludicrous can by way of contradiction evoke laughter. Thus if a man ordinarily goes around oddly dressed and then finally shows up properly dressed for once, we laugh at this because we recollect the other.

When a soldier stands in the street staring at the glorious window display in a fancy gift shop and comes closer in order to see better, when with his face really aglow and his eyes fixed on the finery in the window he does not notice that the basement entrance extends out inordinately far so that he vanishes into the basement just when he is about to have a proper look—then the contradiction is in the movement, the upward direction of the head and gaze and the underground direction down into the basement. If he had not been gazing upward, it would not have been so ludicrous. Thus it is more comic if a man who is walking and gazing at the stars falls into a hole[766] than if it happens
VII 450 to someone who is not as elevated above the earthly.

A drunken man can have such a comic effect because he expresses a contradiction of motion. The eye insists upon evenness in walking; the more there is some reason to insist upon it, the more comic is the effect of the contradiction (thus a stone-drunk person is less comic). If a superior, for example,

this must be understood in such a way that the different nuances in turn obey the qualitative dialectic of the spheres, which denounces subjective arbitrariness. If someone, for example, wanted to make everything comic without any basis, one would see at once that his comic effect is irrelevant, be- VII 453

---

comes along and the drunken man, aware of him, wants to pull himself together and walk straight, the comic becomes more obvious because the contradiction becomes more obvious. He succeeds for a few steps, until the spirit of contradiction once again carries him away. If he succeeds completely while passing by his superior, the contradiction becomes a different one, that we know he is drunk and yet this is not visible. In the one case, we laugh at him when he staggers because the eye insists upon evenness; in the other case, we laugh at him because he is holding himself straight when our knowing that he is drunk insists upon seeing him stagger. In the same way there is also a comic effect when we see a sober man in hearty and intimate conversation with a man he does not know is drunk but the onlooker knows it. The contradiction is in the reciprocity of the two men conversing—namely, that it does not exist and the sober man has not detected this.

It is comic when in everyday conversation a man uses the sermonic rhetorical question form (which does not require an answer but merely forms the transition for answering it oneself). It is comic when the person with whom he is speaking misunderstands it and chimes in with the answer. The comic is in the contradiction between wanting to be an orator and a converser at the same time, or wanting to be an orator in a conversation. The other person's mistake makes it apparent and is a just nemesis, because the person who talks in such forms with another person is indirectly saying: We two are not speaking together, but I am the one who is speaking.

Caricature is comic. By what means? By means of the contradiction between likeness and unlikeness. The caricature must resemble a person, indeed, an actual, specific person. If it resembles no one at all, it is not comic but a direct attempt at meaningless fantasy. The shadow of a man on a wall while you are sitting and talking with him can have a comic effect because it is the shadow of the man with whom one is speaking (the contradiction: that one at the same time sees that it is not he). If one sees the same shadow on the wall but there is no man or if one sees the shadow and does not see the man, that is not comic. The more the man's actuality is accentuated, the more comic the shadow becomes. For example, if one is fascinated by the facial expression, by the melodiousness of the voice, or by the appropriate comments—and at the same moment sees there the grimacing shadow—the comic effect is greatest, unless it wounds. If it is a blatherpate with whom one is speaking, the shadow does not have a comic effect as much as it rather convinces one that the shadow somehow resembles him perfectly. VII 451

Contrast produces a comic effect through contradiction, whether the rela-

cause it lacks a basis in any sphere, and the inventor himself would be made comic from the viewpoint of the ethical sphere, because he himself as an existing person must have his basis in existence in one way or another.

If someone would say: Repentance is a contradiction, ergo

---

tion is that the in-itself nonludicrous is used to make the ludicrous ludicrous, or that the ludicrous makes the in-itself nonludicrous ludicrous, or that the ludicrous and the ludicrous reciprocally make each other ludicrous, or that the in-itself nonludicrous and the in-itself nonludicrous become ludicrous through the relation. When a German-Danish pastor declares in the pulpit, "The Word became pork (*Fleisch*),"[767] this is comic. The comic is not just the ordinary contradiction that arises when someone speaks a foreign language he does not know and evokes by the words an effect totally different from the one he wants. But because he is a pastor and he is preaching the contradiction is sharpened, since in a pastor's discourse speaking is used only in a more special sense, and the least that is assumed as a given is that he can speak the language. Moreover, the contradiction also strays into ethical territory: a person may innocently make himself guilty of blasphemy.

[768]When, out in the cemetery, one reads on a gravestone the effusions in verse of a man who, mourning in three lines the loss of his little son, at the end bursts forth in the line, "Take comfort, reason, he lives!" and this effusion is signed: Hilarius, Executioner—this certainly will produce a comic effect on everyone. First, the name itself (Hilarius) in this connection produces a comic effect; one involuntarily thinks: Well, if a man is called Hilarius,[769] no wonder he knows how to comfort himself! Then comes his position as executioner. It is true that every human being can have feelings, but there still are certain occupations that cannot be perceived as standing in a close relation to feeling. Finally the outburst, "Take comfort, reason!" It is thinkable that it could occur to a philosophy professor to confuse himself with reason, but an executioner will be less successful in this. If someone says that the executioner is not addressing himself (Take comfort, you reasonable man!) but reason, then the contradiction becomes even more comic, because, say what you will about reason in our day, it is still somewhat risky to assume that it is on the road to despair at the thought that Hilarius has lost his son.

Let these examples suffice, and everyone whom this footnote disturbs may leave it unread. It is easy to see that the examples are not carefully scraped together, but also that they are not flotsam from estheticians. Certainly there
VII is enough of the comic everywhere and at any time if only one has an eye for
452 it. One might go on as long as necessary if one, clear about where one is to laugh, did not also know where one is not to laugh. Only let the comic be included; it is no more immoral to laugh than it is immoral to weep. [770]But just as it is immoral to go around sniveling all the time, so it is immoral to abandon oneself to the titillation of indefiniteness that is implicit in laughing

it is comic—one would promptly see that this is nonsense. Repentance is in the ethical-religious sphere and thus is qualified in such a way that it has only one higher sphere, namely, the religious in the strictest sense. But this, of course, would not be what one would use in order to make repentance ludicrous. Ergo, one would use something lower, and in that case the comic is illegitimate or is something chimerically higher (abstraction), and in that case the person easily provoked to laughter is himself comic, just as I have frequently pointed out above with regard to speculative philosophers—namely, that by becoming fantastical and by having arrived at the highest along that road they have become comic. The lower can never make the higher comic, that is, cannot legitimately interpret

---

when one does not quite know whether one ought to laugh or not, so that one does not have joy out of the laughter, and that makes it impossible to regret if one has laughed in the wrong place. The reason the comic has become tempting in our day is that the comic itself almost seems to desire the appearance of illicitness in order to have the fascination of the forbidden, and in turn, as the forbidden, intimate that laughter can consume everything.[771] Although I *qua* author do not have much to be proud of, I still am proud in the consciousness that I have scarcely misused my pen along the lines of the comic, have never allowed it to be in the service of the moment, have never applied the comic interpretation to anything or anyone without first seeing, by comparing the categories, from which sphere the comic came and how it was related to the same thing or to the same person interpreted with pathos. It is also satisfying to analyze properly the source of the laughter, and many a person would perhaps lose laughter by understanding it; but a person like that has never really had a sense of the comic, and yet people who dabble in the comic actually count on the laughter of such people. [772]Perhaps there is also someone who can be comically productive only in flippancy and excessive mirth, who, if it was said to him, "Remember that you are ethically responsible for your use of the comic," could lose his *vis comica* [comic power] if he took the time to heed the warning.[773] Yet when it comes to the comic, it is the very opposition that gives it its pith and prevents it from capsizing. [774]Flippancy and wantonness as productive powers result in the shrill laughter of indefiniteness and sense-titillation, which is exceedingly different from the laughter that accompanies the quiet transparency of the comic. If one wishes to go through good training, one should for a time renounce laughing at what prompts antipathetic passion, in which dark forces can so easily carry one away, and practice seeing the comic in this or that thing that one cares about, in which sympathy and interest, indeed, partiality, form an improving opposition to wantonness.

the higher as comic and does not have the power to make it comic. It is quite another matter that the lower, by being joined to the higher, can make the relation ludicrous. Thus a horse can be the occasion for a man to look ludicrous, but the horse does not have the power to make him ludicrous.

The different existence-stages rank according to their relation to the comic in proportion to their having the comic inside or outside themselves, yet not in the sense that the comic should be the highest. Immediacy has the comic outside itself, because wherever there is life there is contradiction, but the contradiction is not in the immediacy and therefore comes from the outside. Finite common sense wants to interpret immediacy as comic but in doing that becomes comic itself, because what presumably is supposed to justify its comic effect is that it easily knows the way out, but the way out that it knows is even more comic. This is an illegitimate comic effect. Whenever there is a contradiction and one does not know the way out, does not know the contradiction to be canceled and set right in a higher stage, the contradiction is not painless,* and where the legitimacy is a chimerical something higher (from the frying pan into the fire), this is even more comic because the contradiction is greater. For example, in the
VII 454 relation between immediacy and finite common sense. The comic effect of despair is also illegitimate, because despair knows no way out, does not know the contradiction canceled, and therefore ought to interpret the contradiction as tragic—which is precisely the way to its healing.

That whereby humor is legitimized is its tragic side, that it reconciles itself with the pain from which despair wants to withdraw, although it knows no way out. Irony is legitimized in connection with immediacy, because the balance, not as abstraction but as an existence-art, is higher than immediacy.

* Yet this must be understood in such a way that one does not forget that not to know the way out can be interpreted as comic. Thus the busy trifler[776] is comic, because it is comic that an intelligent person, a prosperous man, does not know the way out of all this bookkeeping rubbish, the way out that quite simply consists not in engaging yet another pair of pen-pushers with whom to confer, but in sending them all packing.

Therefore only an existing ironist is legitimized in connection with immediacy. Like all abstraction, total irony once and for all, like a cheap, fanciful idea on paper, is unauthorized in connection with every existence-sphere. In other words, irony certainly is abstraction and the abstract compounding of things, but the legitimacy of the existing ironist is that he himself, existing, expresses it, that he keeps his life in it and does not dally with the grandness of irony and have his own life in philistinism, because then his comic is illegitimate.

Immediacy has the comic outside itself; irony has it *within* itself.* The ethicist who has irony as his incognito is able in turn to see the comic in irony, but he has legitimation to see it only by continually keeping himself in the ethical and thus sees it only as constantly disappearing.

Humor has the comic *within itself,* is legitimate in the exist- VII 455
ing humorist (for humor *in abstracto* is, like everything abstract, once and for all illegitimate; the humorist gains legitimation by having his life in it). It is legitimate except in relation to the religious, but it is legitimate with regard to everything that pretends religiousness. The religiousness that has humor as its incognito is able in turn to see the humorous as comic, but it has legitimation to see it only by continually keeping itself in religious passion oriented to the relationship

* Aristotle makes the comment (*Rhetoric* 3, 18): ἔστι δ' ἡ εἰρωνεία τῆς βωμολοχίας ἐλευθεριώτερον. ὁ μὲν γὰρ αὑτοῦ ἕνεκα ποιεῖ τὸ γελοῖον, ὁ δὲ βωμολόχος ἑτέρου [Irony better befits a gentleman than buffoonery; the ironical man jokes to amuse himself, the buffoon to amuse other people].[777] The ironist himself enjoys the comic, in contrast to the joker, who is at the service of others in making something ludicrous. Therefore, an ironist who needs the help of relatives and friends and claqueurs in order to enjoy the comic is *eo ipso* a second-class ironist and on the way to becoming a *scurra* [professional joker]. But in yet another sense the ironist has the comic within himself and by becoming conscious of it has protected himself against having it outside himself. As soon as an existing ironist slips out of his irony, he becomes comic, just as Socrates, for example, would have been if he had become pathos-filled on his day of judgment. Here is the legitimizing when irony is not an impertinent fanciful idea but an existence-art, because then an ironist works out greater tasks than a tragic hero precisely through his ironic control of himself.

with God, and thus perceives it only as continually disappearing.

Now we are standing at the boundary. The religiousness that is hidden inwardness is *eo ipso* inaccessible for comic interpretation. It cannot have the comic outside itself because it is *hidden* inwardness and consequently cannot come into contradiction with anything. It has itself brought into consciousness the contradiction that humor dominates, the highest range of the comic, and has it within itself as something lower. In this way it is absolutely armed against the comic or is protected by the comic against the comic.

When at times religiousness in Church and state has wanted legislation and police as an aid in protecting itself against the comic, this may be very well intentioned; but the question is to what extent the ultimate determining factor is religious, and it does the comic an injustice to regard it as an enemy of the religious. The comic is no more an enemy of the religious—which, on the contrary, everything serves and obeys—than the dialectical. But the religiousness that essentially lays claim to outwardness, essentially makes outwardness commensurable, certainly must watch its step and fear more for itself (that it does not become esthetic) than fear the comic, which could legitimately help it to open its eyes. There is much in Catholicism that can serve as examples of this. With regard to the individual, it is true that the religious person who wants all to be serious, presumably even just as serious as he is, because he is obtusely serious, is in a contradiction. The religious person who could not bear, if it so happened, that everyone laughed at what absolutely occupies him lacks inwardness and therefore wants to be consoled by illusion, that many people are of the same opinion, indeed, with the same facial expression, as he has, and wants to be built up by adding the world-historical to his little fragment of actuality, "since now a new life is indeed beginning to stir everywhere, the heralded new year with vision and heart for the cause."[778]

VII Hidden inwardness is inaccessible to the comic. This would
456 also be illustrated if a religious person of that kind could be stirred suddenly to assert his religiousness in the external

world, if, for example, he forgot himself and came into conflict with a comparable religious person and again forgot himself and the absolute requirement of inwardness by wanting comparatively to be more religious than the other—in that case he is comic, and the contradiction is: simultaneously wanting to be visible and invisible. Against arrogating forms of the religious, humor legitimately uses the comic because a religious person surely must himself know the way out if he only is willing. If this may not be presupposed, then such an interpretation becomes dubious in the same sense as a comic interpretation of the busy trifler would be if it was the case that he actually was mentally deranged.

The law for the comic is very simple: the comic is wherever there is contradiction and where the contradiction is painless by being regarded as canceled, since the comic certainly does not cancel the contradiction (on the contrary, it makes it apparent). But the legitimate comic is able to do it; otherwise it is not legitimate. The talent is to be able to depict it *in concreto*. The test of the comic is to examine what relation between the spheres the comic statement contains. If the relation is not right, the comic is illegitimate, and the comic that belongs nowhere is *eo ipso* illegitimate. Thus the sophistical in connection with the comic has its basis in nothing, in pure abstraction, and is expressed by Gorgias[779] in the abstraction: to annihilate earnestness by means of the comic and the comic by means of earnestness (see Aristotle, *Rhetoric*, 3, 18). The quittance with which everything ends here is rubbish, and the irregularity that an existing person has changed himself into a fantastical X is easily discovered, because it must still be an existing person who wants to use this procedure, which only makes him ludicrous if one applies to him the formula of exorcism used against speculative thinkers in the foregoing: May I have the honor of asking with whom I have the honor of speaking, whether it is a human being, etc.? In other words, Gorgias, along with his discovery, ends up in the fantastic fringe of pure being, because, if he annihilates the one by means of the other, nothing remains. But Gorgias no doubt merely wanted to describe the ingenuity of a shyster lawyer, who wins by chang-

VII 457 ing his weapon in relation to his opponent's weapon. But a shyster lawyer is no legitimate court of appeals with regard to the comic; he will have to whistle for legitimation—and be satisfied with the profit, which everyone knows has always been the Sophists' pet conclusion—money, money, money, or whatever is on the same level as money.

In the religious sphere, when this is kept pure in inwardness, the comic is auxiliary. It might be said that repentance, for example, is a contradiction, *ergo* is something comic, certainly not to the esthetic or to finite common sense, which are lower, or to the ethical, which has its power in this passion, or to abstraction, which is fantastic and thereby lower (it wanted to interpret as comic from this standpoint what was rejected as nonsense in the foregoing), but to the religious itself, which knows a remedy for it, a way out. But this is not the case; the religious knows of no remedy for repentance that disregards repentance. On the contrary, the religious continually uses the negative as the essential form.* Thus the consciousness of sin definitely belongs to the consciousness of the forgiveness of sin. The negative is not once and for all and then the positive, but the positive is continually in the negative, and the negative is the distinctive mark. Therefore, the regulating principle *ne quid nimis* [nothing too much] cannot be applied here. When the religious is interpreted esthetically, when indulgence for four shillings is preached in the Middle Ages and this is assumed to settle the matter, if one wants to cling to this fiction—then repentance is to be interpreted as comic, then the person broken in repentance is comic just like the busy trifler, provided he has the four shillings, because the way out is indeed so easy, and in this fiction it is indeed assumed that it is the way out. But all this balderdash is the result of having made the religious a farce. But in the same degree as the neg-

* This is also why the religious, even when it interprets the esthetic suffering with a certain touch of the comic, nevertheless does it gently, because it is recognized that this suffering will have its day. Repentance, however, viewed religiously, will not have its day and then be over; the uncertainty of faith will not have its day and then be over; the consciousness of sin will not have its day and then be over—in that case we return to the esthetic.

ative is abolished in the religious sphere, or is allowed to be once and for all and thereby sufficient, in the same degree the comic will assert itself against the religious, and rightfully VII 458
so—because the religious has become esthetics and still wants to be the religious.

There are examples enough of a mistaken effort to assert the pathos-filled and earnestness in a ludicrous, superstitious sense as a beatifying universal balm, as if earnestness in itself were a good or something to be taken without prescription; then everything would be good just as long as one is earnest, even if it so oddly happened that one was never earnest in the right place. No, everything has its dialectic—not, please note, a dialectic by which it is made sophistically relative (this is mediation), but by which the absolute becomes distinguishable as the absolute by means of the dialectical. Therefore, it is just as questionable, precisely just as questionable, to be pathos-filled and earnest in the wrong place as it is to laugh in the wrong place. We one-sidedly say that a fool always laughs, one-sidedly, because it is true that it is foolishness always to laugh; but it is one-sided to label only the misuse of laughter as foolishness, since foolishness is just as great and just as corruptive when it expresses itself by always being equally earnest-obtuse.

§ 3

The Decisive *Expression of Existential Pathos Is* Guilt—*That the Inquiry Goes Backward Rather Than Forward—the Eternal Recollection of Guilt Is the Highest Expression of the Relation of the Guilt-Consciousness to an Eternal Happiness—Lower Expressions of the Guilt-Consciousness and Corresponding Forms of Satisfaction—Penance of One's Own Making—Humor—the Religiousness of Hidden Inwardness*

The dialectical reader will readily see that this investigation is going backward instead of forward. In § 1 the task was assigned: simultaneously to relate oneself absolutely to the absolute τέλος [end, goal] and relatively to relative ends. Just as

a beginning was to be made on this, it appeared that first of all immediacy had to be surmounted or the individual had to die to it before there could be any question of carrying out the task in § 1. § 2 made suffering the essential expression of the existential pathos, suffering as dying to immediacy, suffering as the distinctive mark of an existing person's relation to the absolute τέλος. In § 3, guilt is made the decisive expression for the existential pathos, and the distance from the task in § 1 is even greater, yet not in such a way that the task is forgotten
VII but in such a way that the examination, with an eye on the
459 task and immersing itself in existence, goes backward. That is, this is what happens in existence, and the examination seeks to reproduce it. *In abstracto* and on paper, it goes more easily. There one sets forth the task, has the individual be an abstract something that in every way is "at your service" just as soon as the task is set forth—and then one is finished.

In existence, the individual is a concretion, time is concrete, and even while the individual deliberates he is ethically responsible for the use of time. Existence is not an abstract rush job but a striving and an unremitting "in the meantime." Even at the moment the task is assigned, something is already wasted, because there is an "in the meantime" and the beginning is not promptly made. This is how it goes backward: the task is given to the individual in existence, and just as he wants to plunge in straightway (which can be done only *in abstracto* and on paper, because the garb of the abstracter, the big spender's trousers, is very different from the existing person's straitjacket of existence), and wants to begin, another beginning is discovered to be necessary, the beginning of the enormous detour that is dying to immediacy. And just as the beginning is about to be made here, it is discovered that, since meanwhile time has been passing, a bad beginning has been made and that the beginning must be made by becoming guilty, and from that moment the total guilt, which is decisive, practices usury with new guilt. The task looked so grand, and one thought "like for like"; as the task is, so must the person be who is supposed to carry it out. But then along came existence with one *aber* [but] after another; then came suffering as a more definite qualification, and one thought: Well, a poor existing person must put up with it since he is in existence. But then came guilt as the decisive qualification—now the existing person is really in agony—that is, now he is in the existence-medium.

This backward movement is nevertheless a forward movement inasmuch as immersing oneself in something means to go forward. The deception *in abstracto* and on paper is that the individual, like Icarus,[780] is supposed to be up and off in the ideal task. But this progress, as chimerical, is sheer retrogression, and every time an existing person begins anything like that, the inspector of existence (the ethical) notices him, notices that he is making himself guilty, even if he does not notice it. But the more the individual with the task immerses
himself in existence, the more he goes forward, although the VII 460
expression, if you please, goes backward. But just as all more profound deliberation is a return to the ground,[781] so the task's recall to the more concrete is an immersion in existence. Compared with the totality of the task, to carry out a little of it is a retrogression, and yet it is an advance when compared with the whole task and carrying out none of it at all. Somewhere I read a summary of an Indian drama[782]—the drama itself I have not read. Two armies stand facing each other. Just as the battle is about to begin, the commander becomes lost in thought. With that begins the drama that contains his thoughts. This is the way the task looks to an existing person. For a moment it deceives, as if this sight were the whole thing, as if he were now finished (for the beginning always has a certain resemblance to the end), but then existence intervenes, and the more he, acting, striving, immerses himself in existence (this is the essential distinguishing feature of the existence-medium—a thinker more or less withdraws from existence), the further he in the task is from the task.

But how can the consciousness of guilt become the decisive expression for an existing person's pathos-filled relation to an eternal happiness, and in such a way that every existing person who does not have this consciousness is *eo ipso* not relating himself to his eternal happiness? Indeed, one would think that

this consciousness expresses that one is not relating oneself to it, decisively expresses that it is lost and the relation abandoned. The answer is not difficult. Because it is an existing person who is supposed to relate himself to it, but guilt is the most concrete expression of existence, the consciousness of guilt is the expression for the relation. The more abstract the individual is, the less he relates himself to an eternal happiness and the more he distances himself from guilt, because abstraction places existence in the sphere of indifference; but guilt is the expression for the strongest self-assertion of existence, and it is, after all, an *existing person* who is supposed to relate himself to an eternal happiness. The difficulty, however, is certainly something else, because, inasmuch as the guilt is explained by existing, the existing person seems to be made guiltless; it seems that he must be able to shove the guilt onto
VII 461 the one who placed him in existence or onto existence itself. In that case, the guilt-consciousness is only a new expression for suffering in existence, and the investigation has come no further than § 2, and therefore § 3 certainly ought to be dropped or treated as an appendix to § 2.

So, then, the existing person would be able to shove the guilt away from himself onto existence, or onto the one who placed him in existence, and thus be without guilt. Without any ethical thunder, let us very simply and dialectically look where we are going. The proposed procedure contains a contradiction. It can never occur to someone who is essentially guiltless to shove guilt away from himself, because the guiltless person has nothing at all to do with the category of guilt. Therefore, when in a particular case someone shoves the guilt away from himself and considers himself without guilt, at that very same moment he makes a concession, that on the whole he is one who is essentially guilty, except that in this particular case he possibly is not guilty. But here it is not a question of a particular instance, in which someone, informing on himself as essentially guilty precisely through his exoneration, shoves the guilt away from himself, but of an existing person's essential relation in existence. But to want essentially to shove guilt away from oneself, that is, the total qualification of guilt, in

order to become guiltless, is a contradiction, since this behavior is expressly a self-denunciation. If it is true of any category, it is true of *guilt*: it traps [*fange*].[783] Its dialectic is so cunning that the person who totally exonerates himself simply denounces himself, and the person who partially exonerates himself denounces himself totally. Yet this does not mean the same as that old adage: *Qui s'excuse s'accuse* [Whoever excuses himself accuses himself]. The proverb means that the person who defends or excuses himself with regard to something can do it in such a way that he accuses himself of the same thing, so that the excusing and the accusing pertain to the same thing. This is not the meaning here. No, if someone actually exonerates himself in the particular, he denounces himself totally. Anyone who is not living merely comparatively will readily be aware of this. In everyday affairs, total guilt, as a universally given, gradually becomes so taken for granted that it is forgotten. And yet it is this totality of guilt that ultimately makes it possible for someone to be guilty or not guilty in the particular. The person who is totally or essentially guiltless cannot be guilty in the particular either, but the person who is totally guilty may very well be guiltless in a particular. Therefore, not only by being guilty in the particular does the single VII 462
individual denounce himself as being essentially guilty (*totum est partibus suis prius* [the whole is prior to its parts[784]]), but also by being guiltless in this particular (*totum est partibus suis prius*).

The priority of the total guilt is no empirical qualification, is no *summa summarum* [sum total], because a totality-qualification is never produced numerically. The totality of guilt comes into existence for the individual by joining his guilt, be it just one, be it utterly trivial, together with the relation to an eternal happiness. That was why we began by saying that the consciousness of guilt is the decisive expression for the relation to an eternal happiness. The person who does not relate himself to this never comes to comprehend himself as totally or essentially guilty. The slightest guilt, even if the individual henceforth were an angel, when joined together with the relation to an eternal happiness is sufficient, because the joining together yields the qualitative category. Moreover, all immersion in existence consists in *joining together*. Comparatively, relatively, before a human court, perceived in memory (instead of in the recollection of eternity), *one* guilt (collectively understood) is not at all adequate for this; neither is the sum of all of them. The snag, however, is that it is simply unethical to have one's life in the comparative, the relative, in the external, and to have the police court, the conciliation court, a newspaper, or some of Copenhagen's dignitaries, or the urban rabble, be the highest court with regard to oneself.

In the books of older orthodox theologians, when they defend eternal punishment in hell, one reads the analysis that the magnitude of sin requires such a punishment and the magnitude of sin is in turn defined by being sin against God.[785] The naïveté and externality of this is that it does take on the appearance of being a court, a tribunal, a third party, which hears and votes in the case between God and man. There is always some naïveté and externality as soon as a third party talks about that which essentially pertains to the individual specifically in his isolation before God. The naïveté and externality vanish completely when it is the individual himself who joins the conception of God together with the conception of his guilt, whether it is ever so little—no, wait a minute, the individual does not know this, because this, after all, is the comparative that leads astray. When the conception of God is included, the category of guilt changes to a category of quality. Joined together with the comparative as the criterion, guilt
VII becomes quantitative; directly face-to-face with the absolute
463 quality, guilt becomes dialectical as quality.*

* In the religious discourse there sometimes are instances of the opposite tactic. The religious speaker, thundering guilt upon the individual's head, wants to force the individual comparatively into the totality of the guilt-consciousness. That just cannot be done; the more he thunders, the more he makes the individual feel more loathsome *than* others, and the less it is accomplished, and when he gesticulates most vehemently, he is furthest from it, to say nothing of the ironic insight it gives into the state of His Reverence's soul. Another way is better, when the religious speaker, "humble before God, submissive to the royal majesty of the ethical," himself in fear and trembling for his own person, joins the guilt together with the conception of an eternal happiness. Then the listener is not incited but is influenced indirectly, since it

Childishness and the comparative guilt-consciousness are distinguished by not having a comprehension of the requirement of existence: *to join together*. Childishness with regard to thinking is distinguished by thinking only occasionally, in connection with this and that, and then in turn about something else, is distinguished by really having not one thought but many thoughts. With regard to guilt-consciousness, childishness assumes that today, for example, he is guilty in this and that, then for eight days he is guiltless, but then on the ninth day everything goes wrong again. The comparative guilt-consciousness is distinguished by having its criterion outside itself, and when the pastor on Sunday uses a very high criterion (without, however, using eternity's criterion), the person doing the comparing thinks that what he has been responsible for is terrible. When he is in good company on Monday, it does not seem so bad to him, and in this way the external context determines an utterly different interpretation, which despite its variations still always misses out on one thing: the essence-qualification [*Væsens-Bestemmelse*] of eternity.

Thus the essential consciousness of guilt is the greatest pos- VII
sible immersion in existence, and it also expresses that an ex- 464
isting person relates himself to an eternal happiness (the childish and comparative guilt-consciousness relates itself to itself and to the comparative), expresses the relation by expressing the misrelation.* Yet even though the consciousness is ever so

---

seems to him as if the pastor were speaking only about himself. On the platform it is a superb gesture to point accusingly at Cataline as he sits there, but in the pulpit it is better to beat one's own breast, especially when the discourse is about the totality of guilt, because if the pastor beats his own breast, he hinders any comparison; if he points to himself, then we have the comparative again.

* That is: within the totality-category in which we now find ourselves. The reader will recall (from Section II, Chapter II, in connection with the discussion of *Fragments*[786]) that the *paradoxical* accentuating of existence immerses itself paradoxically in existence. This is the specifically Christian and will come up again in *B*.[787] The spheres are related as follows: immediacy, finite common sense; irony, ethics with irony as its incognito; humor; religiousness with humor as its incognito—and then, finally, the essentially Christian, dis-

decisive, it still is always the relation that carries the misrelation, except that the existing person cannot get a firm hold of the relation because the misrelation continually places itself in between as the expression for the relation. But on the other hand, they still do not repel each other (the eternal happiness and the existing person) so that a break establishes itself as such; on the contrary, it is only by being held together that the misrelation repeats itself as the decisive consciousness of essential guilt, not of this or that guilt.

In other words, the guilt-consciousness that still lies essentially in immanence is different from the consciousness of sin.* In guilt-consciousness, it is the same subject, who by holding the guilt together with the relation to an eternal happiness becomes essentially guilty, but the identity of the subject is such that the guilt does not make the subject into someone else, which is the expression for a break. But a break, in which the paradoxical accentuation of existence consists, cannot intervene in the relation between an existing person and the eternal, because the eternal embraces the existing person everywhere, and therefore the misrelation remains within immanence. If a break is to establish itself, the eternal itself must
VII 465 define itself as a temporality, as in time, as historical, whereby the existing person and the eternal in time have eternity between them. This is the paradox (concerning which reference is made to the foregoing in Section II, Chapter II, and to what follows in *B*).

In the religious sphere, the positive is distinguished by the negative; the relation to an eternal happiness is distinguished by suffering (§ 2). Now the negative expression is decidedly stronger: the relation is distinguished by the totality of guilt-

---

tinguished by the paradoxical accentuation of existence, by the paradox, by the break with immanence, and by the absurd. Therefore, religiousness with humor as its incognito is still not Christian religiousness. Even though this also is hidden inwardness, it relates itself to the paradox. Certainly humor is also involved in paradoxes, but it still continually constricts itself within immanence, and it continually seems to be aware of something else—hence the jest.

* On this point, see Appendix to *B*.[788]

consciousness. With regard to guilt-consciousness as a mark, suffering might seem to be a direct relation (of course, not an esthetically direct relation: happiness distinguished by happiness). If one says that, then guilt-consciousness is a repelling relation. It is more correct, however, to say that suffering is the direct reaction of a repelling relation; the guilt-consciousness is the repelling reaction of a repelling relation, yet, please note, still continually within immanence, even though an existing person is continually hindered from having his life in this, or from being *sub specie aeterni* [under the aspect of eternity], but has it only in an annulled possibility, not as one annuls the concrete in order to find the abstract but as one annuls the abstract by being in the concrete.

Guilt-consciousness is the decisive expression for the existential pathos in relation to an eternal happiness. As soon as the eternal happiness is removed, guilt-consciousness also essentially drops out, or it remains in childish categories that are on a level with the grades on a child's report card, or it becomes civil self-defense. Thus the decisive expression of guilt-consciousness is in turn the essential continuance of this consciousness or the eternal recollecting of guilt, because it is continually joined together with the relation to an eternal happiness. Therefore this is not a childish matter of beginning all over again, of being a good child again, but neither is it a matter of universal indulgence, that all people are like that. As I have said, just one guilt—then with this the existing person who relates himself to an eternal happiness is forever imprisoned; human justice sentences to life imprisonment only for the third offense,[789] but eternity sentences forever the very first time. He is forever imprisoned, buckled in the harness of guilt, and never gets out of the harness, unlike a beast of burden, from which at least at times the working harness is removed, unlike the day laborer, who at least occasionally has time off; not even at night is he essentially out of the harness. Call this recollecting of guilt a chain and say that it is never removed from the prisoner, and you will describe only one side of the matter, because a chain is most closely connected only with the idea of the loss of freedom, but the eternal rec-

ollecting of guilt is also a burden that must be dragged along
VII from place to place in time. Therefore, rather call this eternal
466 recollecting of guilt a harness and say of the prisoner: He will never be unharnessed. His consciousness is that he is decisively changed, although the subject's identity is still that it is he himself who becomes conscious of guilt by joining the guilt together with the relation to an eternal happiness.* But he still relates himself to an eternal happiness, and guilt-consciousness is a higher expression than suffering. Moreover, in the suffering of guilt-consciousness, the guilt at one and the same time alleviates and festers, alleviates because it is an expression of freedom, as this can be in the ethical-religious sphere, where the positive is distinguished by the negative, freedom by guilt, and not distinguished esthetically directly: freedom distinguished by freedom.

So, then, it goes backward. To suffer as guilty is a lower expression than to suffer as guiltless, and yet it is a higher expression, since the negative is a mark of a higher positive. An existing person who suffers only as guiltless does not *eo ipso* relate himself to an eternal happiness, unless the existing person is himself the paradox, and with this definition we are in another sphere. It holds true of every plain and ordinary existing person that if he is suffering only as guiltless (totally understood, of course, not in the sense that he suffers as guiltless in this and that instance, or in many instances), he is not relating himself to an eternal happiness and has avoided guilt-consciousness by existing abstractly. This must be firmly maintained lest the spheres be confused and we suddenly slide back into categories that are far lower than the religiousness of hidden inwardness. Only in the paradoxical religiousness, Christian religiousness, can it hold true, and of the paradox, that to suffer as guiltless is a higher expression than to suffer as guilty. In order to rank the spherical totalities, one quite simply uses humor as the terminus for defining the religious-

* The consciousness of sin is the paradox, and about this the paradox is again very consistent, that the existing person does not discover it by himself but gets to know it from outside. The identity is thereby broken.

ness of hidden inwardness and uses this religiousness as the terminus for defining the essentially Christian. The essentially Christian is also distinguished by its category, and wherever this is not present or is used maunderingly the essentially Christian is not present, unless it is assumed that mentioning Christ's name, even taking Christ's name in vain, is Christianity.

The eternal recollecting of guilt-consciousness is its decisive expression, but the strongest expression of despair in the moment is not existential pathos. To relate oneself existentially with pathos to an eternal happiness is never a matter of occa- VII 467
sionally making a huge effort but is constancy in the relation, the constancy with which it is joined together with everything. The whole existence-art consists in this, and in this, perhaps most of all, human beings fall short. What sacred pledges a person knows how to make in a moment of mortal danger,[790] but when it is over—well, then it is all very quickly and entirely forgotten, and why? Because he does not know how to join together. When the mortal danger does not come from outside, he cannot by himself join it together with his striving. When the earth shakes with the eruption of the volcano or when the plague sweeps across the land, how swiftly and how radically even the dullest, even the drowsiest, understand the uncertainty of everything! But when it is all over, well, then he is unable to join together. And yet it was precisely then that he should be using himself for that, because when existence does the joining together for him, when the raging of the elements preaches to him with more than Sunday eloquence—then the understanding comes close almost by itself, indeed, so readily that the task is rather one of preventing despair by having understood the same thing earlier.

In the eternal recollecting of guilt-consciousness, the existing person relates himself to an eternal happiness, but not in such a way that he now has come closer to it directly; on the contrary, he is now distanced from it as much as possible, but he still relates himself to it. The dialectical that is present here, still within immanence, creates a resistance that intensifies the pathos. In the relation that is the basis of the misrelation, in the intimated immanence that is the basis of the dialectic's separation, he is closely bound up with happiness, by the finest thread, as it were, by the help of a possibility that continually perishes—for this very reason the pathos, if it is there, is so much the stronger.

The guilt-consciousness is what is decisive, and one guilt joined together with the relation to an eternal happiness is sufficient, and yet it is true of guilt, more than of anything else, that it sows itself. But the total guilt is what is decisive; compared with it, making oneself guilty fourteen times is child's play—this is also why childishness always keeps to the numerical. When, however, the consciousness of the new guilt is in turn referred to the absolute consciousness of guilt, the eternal recollecting of guilt is thereby preserved, in case the existing person should be on the point of forgetting.

If someone says that no human being can endure such an eternal recollecting of guilt, that it is bound to lead to insanity or to death, then please note who it is who is speaking, because finite common sense frequently speaks that way in order
VII to preach indulgence. And this way of speaking rarely fails,
468 provided that three or four people are gathered together. I
doubt that anyone in solitude has been able to deceive himself with this talk, but when a number of people are together and one hears that the others are behaving in this way, one is less embarrassed—how inhuman, also, to want to be better than others! Once again a mask; the person who is alone with the ideal has no knowledge at all about whether he is better or worse than others. So it is possible that this eternal recollecting can lead to madness or death. Well, now, a human being cannot endure very long on water and bread, but then a physician can discern how to organize things for the single individual, not in such a way, please note, that he ends up living like the rich man but that the starvation diet is so carefully calculated for him that he can just stay alive. Just because the existential pathos is not the pathos of the moment but the pathos of continuance, the existing person himself, who in pathos is indeed inspired and is not, spoiled by habit, peeking around for subterfuges, will seek to find the minimum of for-

getfulness needed for enduring, since he himself is aware, of course, that the momentary is a misunderstanding. But since it is impossible to find an absolute certainty in this dialecticizing, he will, despite all his exertion, have a guilt-consciousness, once again totally defined by his never having dared to say that, in his relation to an eternal happiness, he had done everything he was able to do in order to hold fast to the recollecting of guilt.

The concept of guilt as a totality-category belongs essentially in the religious sphere. As soon as the esthetic wants to have something to do with it, this concept becomes dialectical like fortune and misfortune, whereby everything is confused. Esthetically, the dialectic of guilt is this: the individual is without guilt, then guilt and guiltlessness come along as alternating categories in life; at times the individual is guilty of this or that and at times is not guilty. If this or that had not been, the individual would not have become guilty; in other circumstances, one who is now considered as being without guilt would have become guilty. This *pro et contra* as the *summa summarum* (therefore not a particular instance of guilt or guiltlessness within the guilt of the totality-category) is the object of the attention of the courts, of the novelists' interest, of town gossip and the meditations of a few pastors. The esthetic categories are obvious, and one can, of course, very well use God's name, duty, guilt, etc. without speaking ethically or religiously. The basis of the esthetic is that the individual is in himself ultimately undialectical. He lives for sixty years, is convicted three times and placed under police surveillance; he lives for sixty years and is never convicted of anything, but there are various ugly rumors about him; he lives for sixty VII
years, a really fine man. So what? Have we learned anything? 469
No, on the contrary, we have gained an idea of how one human life after the other can pass off in gossip when the existing person does not have within himself the inwardness that is the native land and the home of all totality-categories.

The religious address deals essentially with the totality-category. It can use a crime, it can use a weakness, it can use a negligence, in short, any particular whatever; but what sets the religious address apart as such is that it moves from this particular to the totality-category by joining this particular together with a relation to an eternal happiness. The religious address always deals with the totality-category, not scientifically (then the particular is disregarded) but existentially, and therefore is involved in bringing the single individual, in one way or another, directly or indirectly, within the totality, not so he disappears in it but in order to join him together with it. If the religious address expatiates only in particulars, if it serves up praise at one time and censure the next time, if it bestows high honors on a few *encomio publico ornatus* [honored with public praise][791] and flunks others, then it mistakes itself for a ceremonious graduation examination of adults, only without mentioning names. If the intent of the religious address is to help the police by being able to thunder against people who evade the power of the police, it again holds true that if the religious speaker does not thunder by virtue of the totality-category—and this in itself is so earnest that it does not need much gesticulating vehemence—then His Reverence mistakes himself for a kind of police sergeant, and he more suitably ought to walk around with a policeman's club and be paid by the municipality. In everyday life, in the marketplace, in social life, one person is guilty of this, another of that, and there is nothing more to be said; but the religious address deals with inwardness, in which the totality-category seizes a person. The totality-category is the religious; everything else that lacks this is, viewed essentially, illusion, whereby even the greatest criminal is basically guiltless and a good-natured person is a saint.

Recollection's eternal storing up of guilt is the expression for existential pathos, the highest expression, even higher than
VII the most inspired penance that wants to make up for the
470 guilt.* This storing up of guilt cannot find its expression in

* Recall that the forgiveness of sin is the paradoxical satisfaction by virtue of the absurd. In order merely to become aware of how paradoxical it is, the eternal recollecting of guilt as the highest expression must come between, lest the spheres be confused and the essentially Christian be chattered into childish

any externality, whereby it is made finite; it belongs, therefore, to hidden inwardness. Here, as everywhere, the presentation affronts no one, does not affront anyone by saying of him that he is religious, by betraying what he is hiding; it does not affront anyone by denying that he is religious, because the nub of the issue is that it is hidden—and there is no one who notices anything.

I shall now briefly touch on the conceptions of guilt and the corresponding conceptions of satisfaction, which are lower than the eternal recollecting of guilt in hidden inwardness. Since I have been so detailed in the preceding §, I can be all the more brief here, because what was shown in the preceding § as lower must appear again here. Here, as everywhere, only the category is respected, and therefore I include conceptions that, although frequently called Christian, when traced back to the category often prove not to be that. That a pastor, even a silken-clad bishop, that a titled baptized Christian taking rank with real Christians puts something together cannot make this something into Christianity, any more than it follows directly, because a doctor scribbles something on a prescription pad, that this something is medicine—it may indeed be trash. There is nothing so new in Christianity that it may not appear to have been in the world before,* and yet every-

---

categories of the forgiveness of sin, which belong where the ethical has not emerged, even less the religious, and still less the Christian.

* In that case, Christianity would be directly distinguishable esthetically: newness upon newness—and everything would again be confused. Obvious newness can be the mark, for example, of a mechanical discovery, and this newness is accidentally dialectical, but this newness cannot cause offense. Offense ultimately is occasional for an individual in relation to the essential when someone wants to make new for him what he essentially believes he already has. One who has no religiousness at all certainly cannot be offended at Christianity, and the reason the Jews were closest of all to offense was that they were closest of all to it. If Christianity had only added something new to the old, it would have been able to cause offense only relatively, but just because it wanted to take all the old and make it new, offense was close at hand. If the VII 471 newness of Christianity had never arisen in a human being's heart in the sense that he previously had never had anything in its place that he considered to be the highest, it could never cause offense. Precisely because its newness is not direct but first of all must cancel an illusion, offense is possible. Thus the

VII thing is new. Now, if someone uses the name of Christianity
471 and Christ's name, but the categories (despite the terms) are anything but Christian, is this, then, Christianity? Or if someone (see Section I, Chapter II) propounds that a person must not have any followers and someone else sets himself up as an adherent of this doctrine, is there not a misunderstanding between them, despite all the adherent's assurances of admiration and of how totally he has appropriated—the misunderstanding? The mark of Christianity is the paradox, the absolute paradox. As soon as a so-called Christian speculative thought cancels the paradox and makes this qualification into an element, all the spheres are confused.

Thus every conception of guilt is lower that does not through an eternal recollecting join guilt together with the relation to an eternal happiness but through memory joins it together with something lower, something comparative (his own accidentality or others'), and allows forgetfulness to come between the particularities of guilt. This makes life free and easy, as a child's life is, because a child has much memory (oriented outward) but no recollection, at most the inwardness of the moment. There is always a question as to how many people there are who in the last analysis relate themselves absolutely in the qualification of spirit. It remains a question—I say no more, because it is of course possible that we all do it, inasmuch as hidden inwardness is precisely the hidden. Only this much is certain, that the question is not at all the same as the question of capacities, levels, proficiency, knowledge, etc. The most inferior person can relate himself absolutely in the qualification of spirit fully as well as the gifted person, because endowments, proficiency, and knowledge are a "what," but the absoluteness of the relation of spirit is a "how" with regard to what one is, be it much or little.

Every conception of guilt is lower that wants to join guilt

---

newness of Christianity has behind it, as the terminus, the eternal religiousness of hidden inwardness, because in relation to the eternal a newness is certainly a paradox. Lumped together with other newnesses, or canceled out by an assurance that among all newnesses it is the most remarkable, it is merely esthetics.

together with the idea of an eternal happiness momentarily—on Sunday, for example, on New Year's morning at matins VII
on an empty stomach, and then be free all week or all year 472
long.

Every mediation is a lower conception of guilt, because mediation continually releases from the absolute relation to the absolute and lets this exhaust itself in fractional designations, in the same sense as a hundred-dollar bill is only so many ones. But the absolute relationship is the absolute specifically by one's having one's own for oneself, by relating oneself to the absolute, a treasure that can be possessed only as a whole and cannot be exchanged. Mediation releases a person from immersing himself in the totality-category and makes him busy externally, makes his guilt external, his suffering of punishment external, because the watchword of mediation and its indulgence are that the outer is the inner and the inner is the outer,[792] whereby the individual's absolute relation to the absolute is abolished.

To every lower conception of guilt there corresponds a satisfaction that is lower than that highest conception, which is eternal recollecting, which therefore accepts no satisfaction, although the underlying immanence, within which the dialectical is, is an intimated possibility.

The civil concept of punishment is a lower satisfaction. This concept corresponds to this or that guilt and therefore is altogether outside the totality-category.

The esthetic-metaphysical concept of Nemesis[793] is a lower satisfaction. Nemesis is externally dialectical, is the consistency of externality or natural justice. The esthetic is unopened inwardness; therefore that which is or is to be inwardness must manifest itself externally. It is similar to a tragedy in which the hero from the past appears as a spirit to the sleeper—the spectator must see the spirit, although its appearing is the sleeper's inwardness. So also with the consciousness of guilt: the inwardness becomes outwardness. Therefore the Furies[794] were visible, but their very visibility made the inwardness less terrible and because of their visibility a boundary was established for them: the Furies did not dare to enter

the temple. If, however, one takes the consciousness of guilt simply as remorse over a specific guilt, this hiddenness is precisely what is terrible, because no one can see remorse, and remorse accompanies one across every threshold. But the visibility of the Furies symbolically expresses the commensura-
VII 473 bility between the outer and the inner, whereby the guilt-consciousness is finitized, and satisfaction consists in the suffering of punishment in time, and the reconciliation consists in death, and everything ends in the sad exaltation that is death's mitigation, that it is all over now and there was no eternal guilt.

All self-inflicted penance is a lower satisfaction, not only because it is self-inflicted, but because even the most enthusiastic penance makes guilt finite by making it commensurable, whereas its merit is inwardly to discover guilt that evades the attention not only of the police but even of Nemesis. What was said previously about the monastic movement of the Middle Ages holds true again here: respect for the penance of the Middle Ages. It is still a childlike and enthusiastic venture in greatness, and anyone who is unable to enter into the outlook of the Middle Ages and can actually prize forgetfulness and thoughtlessness and "look at my neighbor" as something more true must have lost all imagination and with his considerable common sense must have become just about totally obtuse. If the penance of the Middle Ages was untrue, then it was a stirring and enthusiastic untruth, and even if forgetfulness and thoughtlessness are not guilty of the false idea about God that he would take pleasure in a person's scourging himself, it surely is an even more dreadful untruth to leave God, if I dare to put it this way, continually out of the picture and thus to take comfort because one has not been sentenced for anything, and one is even dance manager at the club. The Middle Ages, on the other hand, allowed God to be in the picture, so to speak; of course, the concepts are rather childlike, but God is still included absolutely.

Let us try an imaginary construction in thought. Imagine a person who joins his guilt together with the idea of an eternal happiness and who thereby becomes alone with himself, with

his guilt, and with God (herein is what is true, in contrast to all comparative hustle and bustle and carefreeness in the shoal of herring). Imagine his desperate brooding over whether there might not still be something he could hit upon as satisfaction for the guilt. Imagine the agony of the ingenuity, whether it would not be possible to hit upon something that could make it up with God. Laugh, if you can, at the sufferer who hits upon penance, provided one assumes—which one may always do in an imaginary construction—that in all honesty his intention and his desire are that God might be moved and mollified by all this suffering. Admittedly, there is something comic in this, because this interpretation makes God into a fabulous character, a Holophernes,[795] a pasha with three horsetails,[796] whom such things could please. But is it better to abolish God in such a way that he becomes a titular deity or VII 474
a fussbudget who sits in heaven and cannot do anything, so no one notices him because his effect touches the single individual only through the solid bulk of intermediary causes, and the thrust therefore becomes an indetectable touch! Is it better to abolish God by having him decoyed into natural law and the necessary development of immanence! No, all respect for the penance of the Middle Ages and for what outside of Christianity is analogous to it, in which there is always the truth that the individual does not relate himself to the ideal through the generation or the state or the century or the market price of human beings in the city where he lives—that is, by these things he is prevented from relating himself to the ideal—but relates himself to it even though he errs in his understanding of it.

What will a girl not hit upon in order to make it up with her beloved if she believes him to be angry; even if she hits upon something ludicrous, does erotic love within her not sanctify the ludicrousness? And is it not the truth in her that she relates herself ideally to her love in the amorous originality of the idea and therefore does not seek the company of any gossipy Gertie who can tell her how other girls handle their beloveds? Anyone who has an eye for the categories readily perceives that the first girl is comic only to a purer interpretation, which therefore sympathetically smiles a little at her in order to help her to something better, but always with respect for her passion; on the other hand, he also perceives that a gossipy Gertie, a gadabout, who knows something at third hand, is unconditionally comic in the role of a girl in love, in which secondary pursuits of that sort are a mark of dabbling in feelings, which, worse than unfaithfulness, proves that she has nothing about which to be faithful.

It is the same with the religious person who goes astray in originality; the passion of originality throws a benevolent light upon him, in contrast to the religious person who knows—from the street, the newspaper, and the club—how to deal with God and how other Christians know how to deal with God. Because of the jumbling together with the idea of the state, of sociality, of community, and of society, God can no longer catch hold of the single individual. Even if God's wrath were ever so great, the punishment that is to fall upon the guilty one must make its way through all the courts of objectivity—in this way, with the most affable and most appreciative philosophical terminology, people have managed to smuggle God away. They are busy obtaining a truer and truer conception of God but seem to forget the first basic principle: that one ought to fear God.[797] An objective religious person in the objective human mass does not fear God; he does not hear
VII him in the thunder, because that is a law of nature, and per-
475 haps he is right. He does not see him in events, because they
are the immanental necessity of cause and effect, and perhaps he is right. But what about the inwardness of being alone before God? Well, that is too little for him; he is not familiar with it, he who is on the way to accomplish the objective.

Whether our age is more immoral than other ages, I shall not decide, but just as a degenerated penance was the specific immorality in a period of the Middle Ages, so the immorality of our age could very easily become a fantastical-ethical debilitation, the disintegration of a sensual, soft despair, in which individuals grope as in a dream for a concept of God without feeling any terror in so doing but on the contrary boasting of this superiority, which in its dizziness of thought and with the vagueness of impersonality has an intimation, as it were, of God in the indefinite, and in imagination meets him whose existence remains more or less like that of the mermaids.[798] And the same thing could easily repeat itself in the individual's relation to himself—namely, that the ethical and the responsibility and the power to act and the strong-nerved sorting out by repentance evaporate in a brilliance of disintegration, in which the individual dreams about himself metaphysically or lets all existence dream about itself and confuses himself with Greece, Rome, China, world-history, our age, and the century. The individual immanently comprehends the necessity of his own development, and then in turn objectively lets his own *I* become moldy like a fluff on the whole,[799] forgetting that even though death changes a person's body to dust and mixes it with the elements, it is terrible in living life to become mold[800] on the immanental development of the infinite. Then instead let us sin, sin outright, seduce girls, murder men, rob on the highway—that at least can be repented, and God can at least catch hold of such a criminal.

But it is difficult to repent of this superiority that has reached such heights; it has an appearance of the profundity that deceives. Then instead let us mock God outright, as has been done before in the world; this is always preferable to the debilitating importance with which one wants to demonstrate the existence of God. To demonstrate the existence [*Tilvær*] of someone who exists [*er til*] is the most shameless assault, since it is an attempt to make him ludicrous, but the trouble is that one does not even suspect this, that in dead seriousness one regards it as a godly undertaking. How could it occur to anyone to demonstrate that he exists unless one has allowed oneself to ignore him; and now one does it in an even more lunatic way by demonstrating his existence right in front of his nose.[801]

A king's existence [*Tilværelse*] or presence [*Tilstedeværelse*] VII 476
ordinarily has its own expression of subjection and submissiveness. What if one in his most majestic presence wanted to demonstrate that he exists? Does one demonstrate it, then? No, one makes a fool of him, because one demonstrates his

presence by the expression of submissiveness, which may differ widely according to the customs of the country. And thus one also demonstrates the existence of God by worship—not by demonstrations. A poor author whom a later research scholar drags out of the darkness of oblivion must surely be pleased as Punch that the research scholar succeeds in demonstrating his existence, but an omnipresent one can be brought into this ludicrous predicament only by a thinker's pious bungling.

But if this can happen, or if it is the case in an age, how does it happen except by simply leaving out the guilt-consciousness? Just as paper money can be an important means of exchange among people but in itself is a chimerical entity if in the last resort there is no hard currency, in the same way the comparative, conventional, external, bourgeois conception of the ethical is useful enough in ordinary dealings. But if it is forgotten that the hard currency of the ethical must be present in the inwardness of the individual, if it is to be anywhere at all, if a whole generation could forget this, then that generation—even if it were assumed that not one single criminal existed but only utterly decent folk (which, by the way, enlightenment and culture cannot unconditionally be said to bring about)—is nevertheless essentially poverty-stricken ethically and is essentially a bankrupt generation. In associations with people it is quite proper to judge every third party as a third party, but if this proficiency in associations also leads each individual in his inwardness before God to judge himself as a third party, that is, only outwardly, then the ethical is lost, inwardness perishes, the thought of God becomes meaningless, and ideality disappears, because one whose inwardness does not reflect the ideal has no ideality. In relation to the crowd of people (that is, when the individual looks at others, but this, of course, goes full circle,[802] since each of the others is in turn the single individual), it is suitable to use a comparative criterion; but if this use of the comparative criterion gains the upper hand in such a way that in his innermost being the individual uses it for himself, the ethical drops out, and the cast-off ethical could properly take its place in a commercial newspaper under the rubric: average price and average quality.

The respectable aspect of the penance of the Middle Ages VII
was that the individual applied the absolute criterion to him- 477
self. If one knows nothing higher than the comparative, the political, the commercial, the sectarian-revivalist, the adjusted criterion—then one must not smile at the Middle Ages. Everyone agrees that bourgeois-philistinism is comic. But what is bourgeois-philistinism? Can one not be a bourgeois-philistine in a large city? Why not? Bourgeois-philistinism always has its roots in the use of the relative as the absolute in relation to the essential. That many a person does not notice it when it is a manifest relativity that is being used only shows one's limitation in connection with the comic. It is the same with the conception of bourgeois-philistinism as with irony. Everyone, way down to the lowliest person, dabbles in being ironical, but there where irony actually begins, they all fall away, and this crowd, each one relatively ironic on a descending scale, turns embittered against the genuine ironist. In Copenhagen, people laugh at being the best man in Køge, but to be that in Copenhagen is just as ludicrous, because the ethical and the ethical-religious have nothing at all to do with the comparative. Every comparative criterion, be it that of Køge or Copenhagen or of our age or of this century, if it is supposed to be the absolute, is bourgeois-philistinism.

As soon, however, as the individual turns to himself with the absolute requirement, analogies to self-inflicted penance will also appear, even if these do not express themselves as naively, and above all are maintained in the shelter of inwardness and kept from the manifest externality that so easily becomes an invitation to misunderstanding equally harmful to the individual and to others. All comparison delays, and that is why mediocrity likes it so much and, if possible, traps everyone in it by its despicable friendship, whether the captive even becomes admired as something outstanding—among mediocrities—or is tenderly embraced by equals. It is altogether and entirely in order that every human being, even the most excellent, as a third party in relation to another human being, whether he is motivated by sympathy or whatever, applies a lesser criterion than the one every human being should and can have within himself through the silent relation to the ideal. Therefore, a person who blames others, that they have corrupted him, is talking nonsense and only informs against himself, that he has sneaked away from something and now wants to sneak back to something. Why did he not prevent it, VII 478 and why is he continuing instead of making up, if possible, for what has been wasted, by seeking in silence the criterion that is in his innermost being?

It is quite certain that a person can require of himself efforts that his most well-intentioned friend, if he were aware of it, would advise against, but let no one blame the friend; let him blame himself for having sought this relief by haggling. Everyone who in truth has ventured his life has had the criterion of silence. A friend can and should never recommend it, quite simply for the reason that the person who, if he is going to venture his life, needs a confidant with whom he will deliberate about it—is not fit for it. But when things begin to be hot, and the final effort is required—then he jumps away, then he seeks relief from a confidant and receives the well-intentioned advice: Be careful of yourself. Then time passes, and the need vanishes. Then when he is visited later by a recollection, he blames people—new proof that he has lost himself and has his ideality among lost property. But the person who is silent blames no one but himself and affronts no one by his effort, because it is his triumphant conviction that there is and can and shall be in every human being this co-knowledge with the ideal, which requires everything and comforts only in annihilation before God. Let anyone who wants to be the spokesman of mediocrity grumble or rant about him; if it is permissible to defend oneself against a highway robber, then there is also a permissible, above all, a God-pleasing self-defense against the persecutions of mediocrity—it is silence.

In the relation of silence to the ideal, a judgment is passed upon a person. Woe to him who as a third party would dare to judge a person in this way. There is no appeal from this judgment to anything higher, because this is absolutely the

highest. But there is a way out, and then one receives an indescribably more lenient judgment. If a person then visualizes his past life, he is appalled and blames people—new proof that one's case is still continually in abeyance in the forum of mediocrity. In the relation of silence to the ideal, there is a criterion that changes even the greatest effort into a trifle, changes the year-after-year continued striving into a chicken step—but in talkativeness a giant step is made without effort. Thus when despondency has gained the upper hand in a person, when he has found it cruel of the lofty aim that all his effort devoted to it vanished as nothing, when he could not bear it that impassability is the path and the criterion of the ideal—then he sought relief and found it. Perhaps he found it with someone,
perhaps in all honesty well intentioned, who did what one can VII
and should request of a third party. And he thanked him for it 479
until like a fool he ended up with blaming people because he himself on the easily passable path of mediocrity made no progress. In the agreement of silence with the ideal, a word is lacking that is not missed, because what it designates does not exist, either—it is the word "excuse." In the vociferousness outside, in the whispered agreement among neighbors, this word is the root word and its derivatives are countless. —Let this be said to the honor of the ideality of silence. He who lives in this way cannot, of course, say so, because he is silent. Well, then I shall say it and thus need not add that I do not pass myself off as doing it.

The person who turns toward himself with the absolute criterion will of course not be able to go on living in the bliss that if he keeps the commandments and has received no sentence for anything and is regarded by the clique of revivalists as a really sincere person he then is a good fellow, who, if he does not die soon, will in a short time become all too perfect for this world. He will, on the contrary, again and again discover guilt and in turn discover it within the totality-category: guilt. But it is deeply rooted in human nature that guilt requires punishment. How natural, then, to think up something by oneself, a toilsome task, perhaps, even if it is dialectical in such a way that it can possibly benefit others, charity to the needy, denying oneself a wish, etc. Is this so ludicrous? I find it childlike and beautiful. Yet this is indeed analogous to self-inflicted penance, but, however well intentioned it is, it still makes guilt finite. There is in it a childlike hope and a childlike wish that everything could be all right again, a childlikeness in comparison with which the eternal recollecting of guilt in hidden inwardness is terrible earnestness.

What is it that makes the child's life so easy? It is that so often "quits" can be called and a new beginning is so frequently made. The childlikeness of self-inflicted penance is that the individual still wants piously to persuade himself that the punishment is worse than the recollecting of the guilt. No, the most rigorous punishment is the recollecting itself. Punishment is most rigorous for the child because the child has no recollection and thinks as follows: If I could only escape the punishment, I would be happy and contented. But what is inwardness? It is recollection. The thoughtlessness of the commonplace comparative people, who are just like everyone else here in the city and resemble one another like tin soldiers
VII in a box, is that all their comparing lacks a true *tertium compa-*
480 *rationis* [third element in a comparison, a standard]. The childlike inwardness in the adult is attentiveness to oneself, but the deceitfulness is calling "quits." But earnestness is an eternal recollecting and is not simply to be confused with the earnestness of getting married, having children, having gout, taking the final examination for a degree in theology, being a member of the provincial consultative assembly or even an executioner.

Humor as the *confinium* [border territory] of the religiousness of hidden inwardness comprehends the totality of the guilt-consciousness. Therefore, the humorist seldom speaks of this or that guilt, because he comprehends the total, or he incidentally stresses this or that particular guilt because the totality is thereby indirectly expressed. The humorous emerges by allowing the childlike to reflect itself in the total consciousness. The cultivation of spirit in the relation of absoluteness and childlikeness joined together yields humor. Often enough one meets full-grown, confirmed, "hearty" people who, although older in years, do everything as a child would and even at forty would doubtlessly be regarded as promising children if it were customary for people to become 250 years old. But childishness and impudence are very different from humor. The humorist possesses the childlike but is not possessed by it, continually keeps it from expressing itself directly but allows it only to shine through a consummate culture. If, therefore, a fully cultured person is placed together with a child, they always jointly discover the humorous: the child says it and does not know it; the humorist knows that it was said. However, a relative culture placed together with a child discovers nothing, because it pays no attention to the child and its foolishness.

I recall a remark made in a specific situation that I shall now relate. It was in one of those transitory little groups formed in the context of a larger social gathering. A young married woman, prompted by an unhappy event that was being discussed, not inappropriately expressed her pain over life, that it keeps so very little of what it promises—"No, a happy childhood or, rather, the happiness of a child!" She fell silent, bent down to a child fondly clinging to her, and patted the little one's cheek. One of the group, whose emotion was clearly in sympathy with the young woman, continued, "Yes, and above all the happiness of childhood to be spanked,"* and VII 481

* [803]When the remark was made, people laughed at it. This was a sheer misunderstanding. People regarded the remark as irony, which was not at all the case. If the retort was intended as irony,[804] the speaker would have been a mediocre ironist, because there was in the remark a tone of pain, which from the point of view of irony is entirely incorrect. The remark was humorous and therefore made the situation ironic through the misunderstanding. This in turn is quite all right, because an ironic remark cannot make the situation ironic; at most it can create an awareness that the situation is ironic, whereas a humorous remark can make the situation ironic. The ironist asserts himself and prevents the situation, but the humorist's hidden pain contains a sympathy whereby he himself cooperates in shaping the situation and thus makes an ironic situation possible. But very frequently what is said ironically is confused with that which, when said, can have an ironic effect in the situation. In this case, the ironic effect was created by people's laughing and taking the remark as teasing, without discerning that the remark contained much more sadness with regard to the happiness of childhood than did the young married

thereupon turned away and spoke to the hostess, who was just walking by.

VII 482 For the very reason that the jest in humor lies in the revocation (an incipient profundity that is revoked), it naturally often regresses to childhood. If a man like Kant, standing on the pinnacle of scientific scholarship, were to say in reference to demonstrations of the existence of God: Well, I do not

---

woman's remark. The sad interpretation of childhood has a rank proportional to the contrast from which the nostalgic view is taken. But the greatest contrast is the eternal recollecting of guilt, and the saddest longing is quite properly expressed by the longing to be spanked. When the young married woman spoke, people were stirred a little; they were almost offended at the humorist's remark, although they laughed, and yet he said something far more profound. To long for the happiness of childhood away from all the stuff and nonsense in life, from vexation of spirit and sore travail,[805] yes, from the morose earnestness of financial difficulties, yes, even from the daily pain of an unhappy marriage, is still not nearly as sad as to long for it away from the eternal recollecting of guilt. This was what the humorist was sadly reflecting upon, because away from the totality of guilt-consciousness to long for an illusory conception of the pure guiltlessness of the child is actually tomfoolery, although it is often touchingly used—by superficial people. The remark was not rude teasing; on the contrary, it was sympathetic.

It is told of Socrates that a man came to him and complained that people were slandering him in his absence. Socrates replied: "Is that anything to care about? It makes so little difference to me what people do with me in my absence that they are even quite welcome to beat me in my absence."[806] This remark is proper irony; it is devoid of the sympathy with which Socrates
VII 482 could create a mutual situation with another (and the law for teasing irony is quite simply this: the ironist's cunning prevents the conversation from being a conversation, although in every way it looks like a conversation, perhaps even a sincere conversation). It is ironically teasing, even if it is oriented toward the ethical in order to arouse the man to gain self-assertiveness. Therefore Socrates quite properly says less than the man says, since slander is indeed something, but to beat someone in his absence is meaningless. A humorous retort, on the other hand, must always have something profound, although hidden in the jest, and must therefore say more. When, for example, a man turns to an ironist to confide a secret to him under the pledge of silence and the latter answers, "You may absolutely rely on me; one can unconditionally confide a secret to me, because I forget it the moment it is said," the confidence is here quite properly annihilated by means of the abstract dialectic. If the other one actually does confide his secret to him, they are indeed talking together, but if it is supposed to be a confidential conversation, it is a misunderstanding. If, however, the man persecuted by slander had said, for exam-

know anything more about that than that my father told me it was so—this is humorous and actually says more than a whole book about demonstrations, if the book forgets this. But just because there is always a hidden pain in humor, there is also a sympathy. In irony there is no sympathy; it is self-assertion, and its sympathy is therefore an altogether indirect sympathizing, not with any one person, but with the idea of self-assertion as every human being's possibility. Therefore, one often finds humor in women, but never irony. Any attempt at it on her part is unbecoming, and a purely feminine nature will consider irony to be a kind of cruelty.

Humor reflects upon the consciousness of guilt totally and therefore is truer than all comparative measuring and rejecting. But the profundity is revoked in the jest, just as before in VII 483
the interpretation of suffering. Humor comprehends the total, but just when it is to explain, it becomes impatient, revokes everything: "It would very likely become too prolix and too profound; therefore I revoke everything and give back the money." "We are all guilty," a humorist would say; "we fall many times and into many pieces, all of us who belong to the animal species called human, which Buffon[807] describes as follows . . . . . ." Thereupon a definition entirely along the lines of natural history could follow. The contrast here has reached its highest: between an individual who in eternal recollecting has the totality of guilt-consciousness and a specimen of an animal species. Thus there is no analogy to a human being's metamorphosis of development insofar as he undergoes the highest development: to subject himself to the absolute qualification of spirit. The plant as a seedling is essentially what it becomes as a developed plant, and so it is also with an animal, but not with a child, which is why there certainly are many in every generation who never come absolutely under the quali-

---

ple, to a young girl what he said to Socrates, had complained about this person and that person that he spoke ill of him in his absence, and the young girl answered, "Then I must count myself lucky, because he has completely forgotten me," this retort has a ring of humor, although it is not humorous insofar as it does not reflect upon any totality-category, the specific contrast of which constitutes the humorous.

fication of spirit.* Moreover, the humorous swing away from the individual to the species is a retrogression to esthetic qualifications, and the profundity in humor does not consist in this at all. The totality of guilt-consciousness in the single individual before God in relation to an eternal happiness is the religious. Humor reflects upon that but in turn revokes it. In other words, viewed religiously, the species is a lower category than the individual, and to shove oneself under the species is equivocation.**

Humor joins the eternal recollecting of guilt together with everything but in this recollecting does not relate itself to an
VII 484 eternal happiness. Now we have come to hidden inwardness. The eternal recollecting of guilt cannot be expressed in the external realm, which is incommensurate with it, since every expression in the external makes the guilt finite. But the eternal recollecting of guilt in hidden inwardness is not despair either, because despair is always the infinite, the eternal, the total in the moment of impatience, and all despair is a kind of ill temper. No, the eternal recollecting is a mark of the relation to an eternal happiness, as far removed as possible from being a direct mark, but nevertheless always sufficient to prevent the shifting of despair.

Humor discovers the comic by joining the total guilt together with all the relativity between individuals. The basis of the comic is the underlying total guilt that sustains this whole comedy. In other words, if essential guiltlessness or goodness underlies the relative, it is not comic, because it is not comic that one stipulates more or less within the positive qualifica-

* Please recall that here it is not a matter of differences in talent but that there is the possibility of this for every human being, whereas the metamorphosis is such a qualitative change that it cannot be explained by the little-by-little of a direct development, even though the eternal consciousness, since it is posited, eternally presupposes itself.

** Only in the final qualification of the religious, the paradoxical-religious, does the race become higher, but then only by virtue of the paradox; and in order to become aware of the paradox one must have the qualification of the religious in between, that the individual is higher than the species, lest the differences of the spheres coalesce and one speak esthetically about the paradoxical-religious.

tion. But if the relativity is based upon the total guilt, then the more or less is based upon that which is less than nothing, and this is the contradiction that the comic discovers. Insofar as money is a something, the relativity between richer and poorer is not comic, but if it is token money, it is comic that it is a relativity.[808] [809]If the reason for people's hustle-bustle is a possibility of avoiding danger, the busyness is not comic; but if, for example, it is on a ship that is sinking, there is something comic in all this running around, because the contradiction is that despite all this movement they are not moving away from the site of their downfall.

Hidden inwardness must also discover the comic, which is present not because the religious person is different from others but because, although most heavily burdened by sustaining an eternal recollecting of guilt, he is just like everyone else. He discovers the comic, but since in eternal recollecting he is continually relating himself to an eternal happiness, the comic is a continually vanishing element.

THE INTERMEDIATE CLAUSE [*MELLEMSÆTNING*] BETWEEN A AND B

The issue set forth (see Section II, Chapter IV) was an existence-issue and as such pathos-filled and dialectical. The first subdivision (A), the pathos-filled part, the relation to an eternal happiness, has been discussed. Now we shall proceed to VII 485
the dialectical subdivision (B), which is the decisive part for the issue. The religiousness that has been discussed up until now and that for the sake of brevity will from now on be termed Religiousness *A* is not the specifically Christian religiousness. On the other hand, the dialectical is decisive only insofar as it is joined together with the pathos-filled and gives rise to a new pathos.

Ordinarily one is not simultaneously aware of both parts. The religious address will represent the pathos-filled and cross out the dialectical, and therefore—however well intentioned, at times a jumbled, noisy pathos of all sorts, esthetics, ethics, Religiousness *A*, and Christianity—it is therefore at times self-contradictory; "but there are lovely passages in it," especially lovely for the person who is supposed to act and exist according to it. The dialectical has its revenge by covertly and ironically mocking the gestures and big words, and above all by its ironic critique of a religious address—that it can very well be heard, but it cannot be done.

Scientific scholarship wants to take charge of the dialectical and to that end bring it over into the medium of abstraction, whereby the issue is again mistreated, since it is an existence-issue, and the actual dialectical difficulty disappears by being explained in the medium of abstraction, which ignores existence. If the turbulent religious address is for sentimental people who are quick to sweat and to be sweated out, then the speculative interpretation is for pure thinkers; but neither of the two is for acting and, by virtue of acting, for existing human beings.

The distinction between the pathos-filled and the dialectical must, however, be qualified more specifically, because Religiousness *A* is by no means undialectical, but it is not paradoxically dialectical. Religiousness *A* is the dialectic of inward deepening; it is the relation to an eternal happiness that is not conditioned by a something but is the dialectical inward deepening of the relation, consequently conditioned only by the inward deepening, which is dialectical. On the other hand, Religiousness *B*, as it will be called from now on, or paradoxical religiousness, as it has been called, or the religiousness that has the dialectical in second place,[810] makes conditions in such a way that the conditions are not the dialectical concentrations of inward deepening but a definite something that qualifies the eternal happiness more specifically (whereas in *A* the more specific qualification of inward deepening is the only more specific qualification), not by qualifying more specifically the individual's appropriation of it but by qualifying more specifically the eternal happiness, yet not as a task for thinking but as paradoxically repelling and giving rise to new pathos.

VII Religiousness *A* must first be present in the individual be-
486 fore there can be any consideration of becoming aware of the
dialectical *B*. When the individual in the most decisive expres-

sion of existential pathos relates himself to an eternal happiness, then there can be consideration of becoming aware of how the dialectical in second place (*secundo loco*) thrusts him down into the pathos of the absurd. Thus it is evident how foolish it is if a person without pathos wants to relate himself to the essentially Christian, because before there can be any question at all of simply being in the situation of becoming aware of it one must first of all exist in Religiousness *A*. But often enough the mistake has been made of making capital, as a matter of course, of Christ and Christianity and the paradoxical and the absurd, that is, all the essentially Christian, in esthetic gibberish. This is just as if Christianity were a tidbit for dunces because it cannot be thought, and just as if the very qualification that it cannot be thought is not the most difficult of all to hold fast when one is to exist in it—the most difficult to hold fast, especially for brainy people.

Religiousness *A* can be present in paganism, and in Christianity it can be the religiousness of everyone who is not decisively Christian, whether baptized or not. Of course, to become a *wohlfeil* [cheap] edition of a Christian in all comfort is much easier, and just as good as the highest—after all, he is baptized, has received a copy of the Bible and a hymnbook as a gift; is he not, then, a Christian, an Evangelical Lutheran Christian? But that remains the business of the person involved. In my opinion, Religiousness *A* (within the boundaries of which I have my existence) is so strenuous for a human being that there is always a sufficient task in it.

My intention is to make it difficult to become a Christian, yet not more difficult than it is, and not difficult for the obtuse and easy for the brainy, but qualitatively and essentially difficult for every human being, because, viewed essentially, it is equally difficult for every human being to relinquish his understanding and his thinking and to concentrate his soul on the absurd; and it is comparatively most difficult for the person who has much understanding, if one recalls that not everyone who has not lost his understanding over Christianity thereby demonstrates that he has it. That is my aim, that is, to the extent that an imaginative constructor, who does every-

thing for his own sake, can have an intention. Every human being, the wisest and the simplest, can just as essentially (the comparative makes for the misunderstanding, as when a brainy person compares himself with a simpleminded person,
VII instead of understanding that the same task is for each one and
487 not for the two in comparison) draw the distinction qualitatively between what he understands and what he does not understand (of course, it will be the fruit of his highest effort, this strenuous concentration, and two thousand years lie between Socrates and Hamann, the two proponents of this distinction[811]), can discover that there is something that is, despite its being against his understanding and thinking. If he stakes his whole life on this absurd, then his movement is by virtue of the absurd, and he is essentially deceived if the absurd he has chosen turns out not to be the absurd. If this absurd is Christianity, then he is a believing* Christian. But if he understands that it is not the absurd, then he is *eo ipso* no longer a believing Christian (no matter if he is baptized, confirmed, possessor of the Bible and hymnbook, even if it is the awaited new hymnbook), until once again he wipes out the understanding as an illusion and a misunderstanding and relates himself to the Christian absurd. In other words, if Religiousness *A* does not enter in as the *terminus a quo* [point from which] for the paradoxical religiousness, then Religiousness *A* is higher than *B*, because in that case the paradox, the absurd, etc. are not to be understood *sensu eminenti* [in the eminent sense] (that they absolutely cannot be understood either by the wise or by the obtuse) but are employed esthetically with regard to the marvelous among many other things, the marvel-

* The definition of faith was given in Section II, Chapter II, and in Chapter III, on ideality and reality. If the argument goes like this: One cannot stop with not understanding the paradox because it is too small and too easy or too soft a task—then the reply must be: No, on the contrary, it is just the opposite; it is the most difficult of all to relate oneself day in and day out to something upon which one bases one's eternal happiness, while maintaining the passion with which one understands that one cannot understand, especially since it is very easy to slip into the illusion that now one has understood it.

ous that certainly is marvelous but that one nevertheless can comprehend. Speculative thought (insofar as it does not want to abolish all religiousness in order to introduce us *en masse* into the promised land of pure being) must consistently be of the opinion that Religiousness *A* is higher than *B*, since it is the religiousness of immanence, but why, then, call it Christian? Christianity will not be content to be an evolution within the total category of human nature; an engagement such as that is too little to offer to the god.[812] Neither does it even want to be the paradox for the believer, and then surreptitiously, little by little, provide him with understanding, be- VII
cause the martyrdom of faith (to crucify one's understanding) 488
is not a martyrdom of the moment, but the martyrdom of continuance.

A person existing religiously can express his relation to an eternal happiness (immortality, eternal life) outside Christianity, and it certainly has also been done, since it must be said of Religiousness *A* that even if it had not been present in paganism it could have been, because it has only universal human nature as its presupposition, whereas the religiousness with the dialectical in second place cannot have been prior to itself, and after having come it cannot be said to be able to have been where it has not been. The specific for Christianity is the dialectical in second place, except, please note, that this is not a task for thinking (as if Christianity were a doctrine, not an existence-communication; see Section II, Chapter II; Section II, Chapter IV, Division 1, § 2) but is a relating to the pathos-filled as an impetus for new pathos. In Religiousness *A*, an eternal happiness is a particular, and the pathos-filled becomes the dialectical in the dialectic of inward deepening; in Religiousness *B*, the dialectical becomes dialectical in second place, since the communication is oriented toward existence, is pathos-filled in inward deepening.

Accordingly as the individual in his existing expresses the existential pathos (resignation—suffering—the totality of guilt-consciousness), in like degree his pathos-filled relation to an eternal happiness increases. Then when the eternal happiness, because it is the absolute τέλος [end, goal], has become for him absolutely the only comfort, and when in existential immersion the relation to it is reduced to its minimum, since the guilt-consciousness is the repelling relation and continually wants to take it away from him, and yet this minimum and this possibility are absolutely more to him than everything else—then is the appropriate time to begin the dialectical. It will, when he is in this state, give rise to a pathos that is even higher. But one does not prepare oneself to become aware of Christianity by reading books or by world-historical surveys, but by immersing oneself in existing. Any other preliminary study is bound *eo ipso* to end in a misunderstanding, because Christianity is an existence-communication. It declines the understanding (see Section II, Chapter II). The difficulty is not to understand what Christianity is but to become and to be a Christian (see Section II, Chapter IV, Division 1, § 2).

Note. Insofar as the upbuilding is the essential predicate of all religiousness, Religiousness *A* also has its upbuilding. Wherever the relationship with God is found by the existing person in the inwardness of subjectivity, there is the upbuilding, which belongs to subjectivity, whereas by becoming objective
VII one relinquishes that which, although belonging to subjectivity, is neverthe-
489 less no more arbitrariness than erotic love and being in love, which indeed one also relinquishes by becoming objective. The totality of guilt-consciousness is the most upbuilding element in Religiousness *A*.* The upbuilding element in the sphere of Religiousness *A* is that of immanence, is the annihilation in which the individual sets himself aside in order to find God, since it is the individual himself who is the hindrance.** Here the upbuilding is quite properly distinguishable by the negative, by the self-annihilation that finds the relationship with God within itself, that suffering-through sinks into the relationship with God, finds its ground in it, because God is in the ground only

* The reader will please recall that the direct relationship with God is esthetics and is actually no relationship with God, any more than a direct relation to the absolute is an absolute relation, since the separation of the absolute has not commenced. In the religious sphere, the positive is distinguishable by the negative. The highest well-being of a happy immediacy, which jubilates joy over God and all existence, is very endearing but not upbuilding and essentially not any relationship with God.

** The esthetic always consists in the individual's fancying that he has been busy reaching for God and taking hold of him, consequently in the illusion that the undialectical individual is really clever if he can take hold of God as something external.

when everything that is in the way is cleared out, every finitude, and first and foremost the individual himself in his finitude, in his cavilling against God. Esthetically, the sacred resting place of the upbuilding is outside the individual; he seeks that place. In the ethical-religious sphere, the individual himself is the place, if the individual has annihilated himself.

This is the upbuilding in the sphere of Religiousness *A*. If one does not pay attention to this and to having this qualification of the upbuilding in between, everything is confused again as one defines the paradoxical upbuilding, which then is mistakenly identified with an external esthetic relation. In Religiousness *B*, the upbuilding is something outside the individual; the individual does not find the upbuilding by finding the relationship with God within himself but relates himself to something outside himself in order to find the upbuilding. The paradox is that this apparently esthetic relationship, that the individual relates himself to something outside himself, nevertheless is to be the absolute relationship with God, because in immanence God is neither a something, but everything, and is infinitely everything, nor outside the individual, because the upbuilding consists in his being within the individual. The paradoxical upbuilding therefore corresponds to the category of God in time as an individual human being, because, if that is the case, the individual relates himself to something outside himself. That this cannot be thought is precisely the paradox. Whether the individual is not thrust back from this[813] is another matter—that remains his affair. But if the paradox is not held fast in this way, then Religiousness *A* is higher, and all Christianity is pushed back into esthetic categories, despite Christianity's insistence that the paradox it speaks VII
about cannot be thought, is thus different from a relative paradox, which 490
höchstens [at best] can be thought with difficulty. It must be conceded to speculative thought that it holds to immanence, even though it must be understood as different than Hegel's pure thinking, but speculative thought must not call itself Christian. That is why I have never called Religiousness *A* Christian or Christianity.

B
THE DIALECTICAL

This is essentially what *Fragments* has dealt with; therefore I may continually refer to it and can be briefer. The difficulty is only to hold fast to the qualitative dialectic of the absolute paradox and to keep the illusions at bay. What can and shall and will be the absolute paradox, the absurd, the incomprehensible, depends on the passion in dialectically holding fast the distinction of incomprehensibility. Just as in connection with something that can be understood it is ludicrous to hear superstitious and fanatical, abstruse talk about its incomprehensibility, so its opposite is equally ludicrous—to see, in connection with the essentially paradoxical, attempts at wanting to understand it, as if this were the task and not the qualitatively opposite: to maintain that it cannot be understood, lest understanding, that is, misunderstanding, end up by also confusing all the other spheres. If the paradoxical-religious address does not pay attention to this, it abandons itself to the mercy of a legitimate ironic interpretation, whether the address peers behind the curtain with a revivalist's muzziness and spiritual intoxication, reads the obscure runes, catches a glimpse of the explanation, and now sermonizes it in a singing tone that is the echo of the seer's unnatural association with the marvelous, since the absolute paradox expressly declines all explanation—or the paradoxical-religious address modestly forgoes an understanding, yet willingly acknowledges that it is something far higher—or it makes a preliminary run toward an understanding and only then concedes the incomprehensibility—or it parallels the incomprehensibility of the paradox with something else etc.

The basis of all this, which irony must nose out and bring to the light of day, is that the qualitative dialectic of the spheres is not respected—that what is meritorious in connection with
VII 491 the incomprehensible that nevertheless is essentially comprehensible is, namely, to understand it—that this is far from being meritorious in connection with the essentially incomprehensible. The basis of the misunderstanding is that, despite the use of Christ's name etc., Christianity has been shoved back into the esthetic (something the superorthodox unwittingly are especially successful in doing), where the incomprehensible is the relatively incomprehensible (relative either with regard to its not yet having been understood or to the need for a seer with an eagle eye to understand it), which in time has its explanation in something higher behind itself, rather than in Christianity's being an existence-communication that makes existing paradoxical, which is why it remains the paradox as long as there is existing and only eternity has the explanation. But therefore it is not meritorious, as long as one is in time, to want to dabble in explanation, that is, to

fancy that one is in eternity. As long as one is in time, the qualitative dialectic charges every attempt of that sort with being illegitimate dabbling. The qualitative dialectic continually enjoins that one is not to flirt *in abstracto* with that which is the highest and then want to dabble in it, but one is to comprehend one's essential task *in concreto* and essentially express it.

But there are certain things that enter into some people's heads with more difficulty, and among these is the passionate qualification of the incomprehensible. The address perhaps begins altogether properly, but, presto, nature exceeds discipline, and His Reverence cannot resist the fancy that to catch a glimpse is something higher, and then the comedy begins. Even with regard to many a relative issue, people frequently enough can make themselves ludicrous by their busy officiousness in explaining with a profound hint. But with regard to the absolute paradox, this glimpsing and squinting with the eyes, this listening silence of the congregation of revivalists that is broken only as one after the other stands up and in a tense posture tries to catch a glimpse of what His Reverence glimpses, while the women remove their hats[814] in order to catch every prophetic word—all this excitement about what His Reverence glimpses is very ludicrous. And most ludicrous of all is the notion that this glimpsing is supposed to be something higher than the passion of faith. If it is to be anything, it must rather be tolerated as a weakness in a weaker believer who does not have the strength passionately to accentuate incomprehensibility and therefore has to glimpse a little, because all glimpsing is impatience. Ordinarily, the inclination to glimpse and to point fingers is tempting only to a certain class of limited and fanciful people. Every more competent VII
and more earnest person strives to know which is which, 492
whether it is something that can and should be understood, and then he will not glimpse, or something that cannot and should not be understood, and then he will glimpse [*skimte*] just as little or, what in this case is the same thing, will jest [*skjemte*], because, despite the earnest facial expressions and the raised eyebrows, this glimpsing is nothing but skylarking,

even if Mr. Knud, who does it, believes that this is sheer, pure earnestness.

All this glimpsing and everything associated with it—which, to be sure, whatever the reason is, seldom appears in our time—is neither more nor less than pious flirting. A Christian clergyman who does not know how, with humility and the passion of existence-effort, to keep himself and his congregation in check by proclaiming that the paradox cannot and should not be understood, who does not set forth the task as being precisely to maintain this and to endure this crucifixion of the understanding but speculatively has understood everything—he is comic. But the more a person stresses the incomprehensible, if he ends up with glimpsing, the more corruptive is his flirtation, because it all becomes a compliment to himself. Whereas difficulty and incomprehensibility are an obstacle to "the dull," he is brilliant enough—to catch a glimpse into the dark saying. Christianity is an existence-communication that makes existing paradoxical, makes it more difficult than it has ever been and can ever be outside it, but it is no shortcut to becoming matchlessly brilliant. Perhaps the phenomenon appears especially in the revivalists among the students that when one is unable to make any progress on the hard road[815] of scientific scholarship and knowledge and thinking, one leaps aside and becomes absolutely revived—and matchlessly brilliant. Better, in that case, speculative thought's misunderstanding, in which, apart from this, there is an abundance both to learn and to admire in the men who combine the power of genius with the endurance of iron; better speculative thought's misunderstanding—that it can explain everything.

The same thing happens with faith's crucifixion of the understanding as with many ethical qualifications. A person renounces vanity—but he wants to be admired because he does it. A person relinquishes, as he says, the understanding in order to believe—but then he acquires a higher understanding, an understanding so high that by virtue of it he carries on as a matchlessly brilliant seer etc. But it is always dubious to want to have benefit or receive conspicuous benefit from one's reli-

giousness. Because an individual in faith relinquishes the understanding and believes against the understanding, he should not for that reason think poorly of the understanding or suddenly ascribe falsely to himself a splendid distinction within VII
the total range of the understanding; a higher understanding 493
is still, of course, also an understanding. Right there is the arrogation of the revivalist, but just as one should be deferential in dealing with a Christian, and just as one should be gentle with the sickliness that sometimes can disturb and have a disturbing effect in a period of transition, so one should calmly hand an arrogating revivalist over to the treatment of irony.

If the inhabitant of the monastery in the degenerated period of the Middle Ages wanted to benefit from his life by becoming honored as a holy person, it is just as reprehensible and only a little more ludicrous to want to become matchlessly brilliant by means of one's religiousness. And if it is a sorry error literally to want to be like God[816] through virtue and holiness instead of becoming more and more humble, then it is all the more ludicrous to want to be that in consideration of one's being an unusually brilliant mind, because virtue and purity are indeed essentially related to the nature of God, but the second stipulation makes God himself ridiculous as the *tertium comparationis* [third element in a comparison, a standard]. The person who has truly relinquished his understanding and believes against his understanding will always preserve a sympathetic respect for the capacity whose power he knows best by having it against himself. Moreover, in his daily efforts to keep himself in the passion of faith, which presses its way forward against the understanding (which is like rolling a weight up a mountain), in this effort he will be prevented from playing the genius on the score of his religiousness. The contradiction in the arrogating revivalist is that he, after having through faith entered into the innermost sanctum of inwardness against his understanding, also wants to be out on the street and be matchlessly brilliant. In its progress, the farce or benefit performance becomes equally ludicrous, whether he makes capital of the world's admiration when it seems to be profitable (a new inconsistency: that someone who has a higher understanding will allow himself to be admired by the world, which, after all, has only a lower understanding, and whose admiration therefore is nonsense) or whether he thunderingly denounces the world's lack of spirit when it will not admire (a curious ceremony, since he himself of course knows that the world has only a lower understanding) and complains that he is being misunderstood, which, however, is just as it should be, and the complaint about it is only a misunderstanding that betrays the secret connection he maintains with what is worldly.

The misunderstanding continually consists in the delusion that the incomprehensibility of the paradox is supposed to be connected with the difference of greater and lesser understanding, with the comparison between good and poor
VII minds. The paradox is connected essentially with being a hu-
494 man being, and qualitatively with each human being in particular, whether he has much or little understanding. Thus the most intelligent person can very well believe (against the understanding) and is hindered in believing by his considerable understanding only by having also the advantage of really experiencing what it is to believe against the understanding. Socrates, whose ignorance was shown above (Section II, Chapter II) to be a kind of analogy to faith (keeping continually in mind, however, that there are no analogies to the paradoxical-religious in its entirety), was no fool because he did not want to dally with glimpsing and knowing this and that but wanted to be absolutely ignorant. But, on the other hand, neither did it ever occur to Socrates, after having disparaged ordinary human knowledge, to want to be admired for a higher understanding or to want to involve himself directly with any human being, since he in his ignorance had essentially destroyed communication with all of them.

The revivalists have frequently enough busied themselves with the ungodly world, which mocks them, something they themselves in another sense desire in order to be really sure that they are revived—since they are mocked—and then in turn to have the advantage of being able to complain about the world's ungodliness. But it is always a dubious demonstration of the world's ungodliness that it laughs at an enthusiast—especially when he begins to glimpse, because then he is actually ludicrous. In our era, whose tolerance or indifference is so great, it certainly would not be at all impossible for an actual Christian—who, rigorous with himself, does not engage in judging others—to be able to be allowed to live on in peace. But, of course, he would still have within himself the martyrdom: to believe against understanding. But everything that is arrogating, if in addition it is self-contradictory, is comic.

Let us take a few examples from minor situations in life, but in the application continually bear in mind the absolute difference that there is no analogy to the sphere of the paradoxically religious, and thus the application, when it is understood, is a revocation. A man arranges his life in a special way, a way that according to his knowledge of himself, his capabilities, faults, etc. is both the most serviceable to him and to that extent also the most comfortable. Therefore, it may very well be that this mode of life, and especially the consistency in carrying it out, may at first glance, or from many another view of life that has a different slant, appear to be ludicrous. If he is an arrogating person, his strange mode of life will naturally be hailed as a higher understanding etc. If, however, he is an earnest person, VII
he will calmly listen to another person's view. 495
In the way in which he engages in conversation about it, he will show that he himself perceives very well the comic aspect it can have for a third party—and thereupon he will very calmly go home and follow his own mode of life conceived according to his knowledge of himself.

[817]It is the same also with the person who is truly a Christian—if we bear in mind that there is no analogy. He may very well have understanding (indeed, he must have it in order to believe against the understanding). He can use it in all other circumstances, use it in his association with others (since, of course, it is an inconsistency to want to converse with someone who does not have a higher understanding if one wants to

use a higher understanding oneself, because conversation is the expression for the universal, and the relation between one who has a higher understanding and an ordinary person will be that of an apostle or of an absolute teacher, but not of a fellow human being). He will be very capable of understanding every objection, even of advancing them himself as well as anybody, because in any other case a higher understanding will in a dubious way become an ambiguous furtherance of stuff and nonsense. It is easy enough to shift away from the laborious task of developing and sharpening one's understanding and then gain for oneself a higher hop-dance [*Hopsasa*] and defend oneself against every charge with the observation that it is a higher understanding.* Consequently the believing Christian both has and uses his understanding, respects the universally human, does not explain someone's not becoming a Christian as a lack of understanding, but believes Christianity against the understanding and here uses the understanding[818]—in order to see to it that he believes against the understanding. Therefore he cannot believe nonsense against the understanding, which one might fear, because the understanding will penetratingly perceive that it is nonsense and hinder him in believing it, but he uses the understanding so much that through it he becomes aware of the incomprehensible, and now, believing, he relates himself to it against the understanding.

An enthusiastic ethical individuality uses the understanding to discover what is most sagacious in order not to do it, because what we as a rule call the most sagacious is rarely the noble. But even this conduct (a kind of analogy to the be-
VII 496 liever's, except that an understanding of the application is a revocation) is rarely understood. When one sees a person enthusiastically sacrificing himself, enthusiastically choosing strenuousness instead of comfort, indeed, a strenuousness that

* That is why it was stated above that it is always a precarious business to pass off as the absurd, the incomprehensible, something that someone else can declare is easy to understand.

is rewarded only with ingratitude and loss, instead of a comfortableness that would be rewarded with admiration and advantage—then many a person thinks that this is a kind of shallowness, smiles at him, and perhaps, in a fit of kindness, even goes so far as to help the poor fellow to see what is the most sagacious thing to do—although he helps the poor simpleton only to have an ironic little glimpse into the counselor's soul. Such counsel is a misunderstanding that is rooted not so much in a lack of understanding as in a lack of enthusiasm. Therefore the enthusiastic ethicist will take no exception whatever to the objection or to the mockery. Long before it happens to him, he would have become aware that it would probably happen to him. He will be better able than anyone else to interpret his effort as comic and then, very calmly resolved, use the understanding to see what is the most sagacious in order not to do it. The analogy is not direct, because for such an enthusiast there is no suffering in this relation against the understanding. His enthusiastic action is still an understanding of the infinite, and he breaks only with the sagacious paltriness. In him there is no break, and no suffering of a break. But a believer who believes, that is, believes against the understanding,* takes the secret of faith in earnest and does not dally with understanding but is aware that curiosity about glimpsing is unfaithfulness and betrays the task.

The dialectical aspect of the issue requires thought-passion—not to want to understand it but to understand what it means to break in this way with the understanding and thinking and immanence, in order then to lose the last foothold of immanence, the eternity behind, and to exist, situated at the edge of existence, by virtue of the absurd.

As said previously, it was particularly this dialectic that *Fragments* discussed. I shall be briefer and, referring to those

* Faith belongs essentially in the sphere of the paradoxical-religious, as has been continually emphasized (see among other places Section II, Chapters II and III). All other faith is only an analogy that is no [analogy],[819] an analogy that can serve to make aware, but no more, the understanding of which is therefore a revocation.

fragments, shall only try as far as possible to summarize it even more clearly.

VII § 1

497 *The Dialectical Contradiction That Constitutes the Break: to Expect an Eternal Happiness in Time through a Relation to Something Else in Time*

In this contradiction, existence is paradoxically accentuated, and the distinction *here* and *hereafter* is absolutely defined by the paradoxical accentuation of existence because the eternal itself has come into existence at a moment of time. Please keep in mind continually that I am not taking it upon myself to explain the issue, but only to present it.

The interpretation of the distinction "here and hereafter" is decisive for every existence-communication. *Speculative thought* annuls it absolutely (it is an expression for the principle of contradiction) in pure being; this annulment in turn expresses that speculative thought is no existence-communication, which makes speculation dubious insofar as it wants to explain existence. *Religiousness A*, which is not speculation but nevertheless is speculative, reflects upon this distinction by reflecting upon existing, but even the decisive category of guilt-consciousness is still within immanence. *The paradoxical-religious* defines the distinction absolutely by paradoxically accentuating existing. In other words, because the eternal has come into existence at a moment of time, the existing individual in time does not come to relate himself to the eternal or to collect himself in his relation (this is *A*) but *in time* comes to relate himself to the eternal *in time*. Consequently, the relation is within time, a relation that runs directly counter to all thinking, whether one reflects upon the individual or upon the god [*Guden*].

The interpretation of the distinction "here and hereafter" is fundamentally the interpretation of *existing*, and around this in turn the distinctions gather, if one takes care to note that Christianity is not a doctrine but an existence-communication. *Speculative thought* ignores existence; for speculation, "to exist" becomes "to have existed" (the past); existence is a vanishing and annulled element in the pure being of the eternal. Speculation as abstraction can never become contemporary with existence and therefore cannot comprehend existence as existence, but only afterward. This is what explains why speculation wisely abstains from ethics and why it becomes ludicrous when it sets about it. *Religiousness A* accentuates existing as actuality, and eternity, which in the underlying immanence still sustains the whole, vanishes in such a way that the positive becomes distinguishable by the negative. For speculation, existence has vanished and only pure being is; for Religiousness VII 498 *A*, only the actuality of existence is, and yet the eternal is continually hidden by it and in hiddenness is present. *The paradoxical-religious* establishes absolutely the contradiction between existence and the eternal, because this, that the eternal is present at a specific moment of time, expresses that existence is abandoned by the hidden immanence of the eternal. In Religiousness *A*, the eternal is *ubique et nusquam* [everywhere and nowhere] but hidden by the actuality of existence; in the paradoxical-religious, the eternal is present at a specific point, and this is the break with immanence.

In Section II, Chapter II, it was stated that what our age has forgotten, which accounts for speculative thought's misunderstanding of Christianity, is: what it means to exist and what inwardness is. It is entirely correct that the religious is the existing inwardness, and religiousness heightens in accord with the deepening in this qualification, and the paradoxical-religious becomes the last.

All interpretations of existence take their rank in relation to the qualification of the individual's dialectical inward deepening. Presupposing what has been developed on this subject in this book, I shall now only recapitulate and point out that of course speculative thought plays no role, since, as objective and abstract, it is indifferent to the category of the existing subjective individual and at most deals only with pure humanity. Existence-communication, however, understands something different by *unum* [one] in the saying *unum noris, omnes* [if you know one, you know all], understands something different by "yourself" in the phrase "know yourself,"[820] understands thereby an actual human being and indicates thereby that the existence-communication does not occupy itself with the anecdotal differences between Tom, Dick, and Harry.

If in himself the individual is undialectical and has his dialectic outside himself, then we have the *esthetic interpretations*. If the individual is dialectically turned inward in self-assertion in such a way that the ultimate foundation does not in itself become dialectical, since the underlying self is used to surmount and assert itself, then we have the *ethical interpretation*. If the individual is defined as dialectically turned inward in self-annihilation before God, then we have *Religiousness A*. If the individual is paradoxical-dialectical, every remnant of original immanence annihilated, and all connection cut away, and the individual situated at the edge of existence, then we have the *paradoxical-religious*. This paradoxical inwardness is
VII the greatest possible, because even the most dialectical quali-
499 fication, if it is still within immanence, has, as it were, a possibility of an escape, of a shifting away, of a withdrawal into the eternal behind it; it is as if everything were not actually at stake. But the break makes the inwardness the greatest possible.*

The various existence-communications in turn take their rank in relation to the interpretation of existing. (As abstract and objective, speculative thought completely disregards existing and inwardness and, since Christianity indeed paradoxically accentuates existing, is the greatest possible misunderstanding of Christianity.) *Immediacy, the esthetic*, finds no contradiction in existing; to exist is one thing, contradiction is something else that comes from without. *The ethical* finds contradiction but within self-assertion. *Religiousness A* comprehends contradiction as suffering in self-annihilation, yet within immanence; but, ethically accentuating existing, it

* According to this plan, one will be able to orient oneself and, without being disturbed by anyone's use of Christ's name and the whole Christian terminology in an esthetic discourse, will be able to look only at the categories.

hinders the existing person in abstractly remaining in immanence or in becoming abstract by wanting to remain in immanence. The *paradoxical-religious* breaks with immanence and makes existing the absolute contradiction—not within immanence but in opposition to immanence. There is no immanental underlying kinship between the temporal and the eternal, because the eternal itself has entered into time and wants to establish kinship there.

Note. Please compare this with the first two chapters of *Fragments* about learning the truth, the moment, the god in time as teacher. In the *esthetic interpretation*, the one is the teacher, the other the learner; then he in turn is teacher, etc.—in short, the relation is one of relativity. *Religiously*, there is no pupil and no teacher ("the teacher is only the occasion," see *Fragments*); every individual is essentially structured equally eternally and essentially related to the eternal; the human teacher is a vanishing transition. *Paradoxically-religiously*, the teacher is the god [*Guden*] in time, the pupil is a new creation ("The god as teacher in time provides the condition," see *Fragments*). Within the paradoxical-religious, Religiousness *A* holds true between persons. Thus when a Christian (who paradoxically is a follower of the god in time in the sense of being a new creation) within Christianity becomes in turn a follower of this one and that one, this arouses an indirect suspicion that all his Christianity is very likely a bit of esthetic nonsense.

The issue continually dealt with here was: how can a historical point of VII
departure be given etc. In Religiousness *A* there is no historical point of de- 500
parture. Only in the realm of time does the individual discover that he must presuppose himself to be eternal. The moment in time is therefore *eo ipso* swallowed by the eternal. In time, the individual reflects upon his being eternal. This contradiction is only within immanence. It is different when the historical is outside and remains outside, and the individual, who was not eternal, now becomes eternal, and therefore does not reflect on what he is but becomes what he was not, and, please note, becomes something that has the dialectic that as soon as it is it must have been, because this is the dialectic of the eternal. —What is inaccessible to all thinking is: that one can become eternal although one was not eternal.

In *A*, existing, my existence, is an element within my eternal consciousness (please note, the element that is, not the element that is past, because the latter is a volatilizing by speculative thought), consequently a lesser thing that hinders me in being the infinitely higher that I am. Conversely, in *B*, existing, although even lower by being paradoxically accentuated, is nevertheless so much higher that I first become eternal in existence, and as a result existing gives rise by itself to a qualification that is infinitely higher than existing.

§ 2
The Dialectical Contradiction That an Eternal Happiness Is Based on the Relation to Something Historical

For thinking it holds true that the eternal is higher than everything historical, since it is the basis. In the religiousness of immanence, therefore, the individual does not base his relation to the eternal on his existing in time; but in the dialectic of inward deepening the individual's relation to the eternal stipulates that he transform his existence according to the relation, express the relation by the transformation.

Here, as everywhere, the confusion of speculative thought is that it loses itself in pure being. Irreligious and immoral life-views make existing into a zero, nonsense. Religiousness *A* makes existing as strenuous as possible (outside the sphere of the paradoxically-religious); yet it does not base the relation to an eternal happiness upon one's existing but has the relation to an eternal happiness as the basis for the transformation of existence. The "how" of the individual's existence is the result of the relation to the eternal, not the converse, and that is why infinitely more comes out than was put in.

VII 501 Here, however, the dialectical contradiction is essentially that the historical is in second place. In other words, it holds true of all historical learning and knowledge that even at its maximum it is only an approximation. The contradiction is to base one's eternal happiness on an approximation, which can be done only if one has no eternal qualification in oneself (which in turn cannot be thought any more than how one then comes to think of it; therefore the god must provide the condition), which is why this in turn is coherent with the paradoxical accentuation of existence.

In regard to the historical, all learning about it and all knowledge of it is at its maximum an approximation, even in regard to the individual's own knowledge of his own historical externality. The reason is partly the impossibility of being able to identify oneself absolutely with the objective, and partly that everything historical, inasmuch as it must be known, is *eo ipso* past and has the ideality of recollection. In

Section II, Chapter 3, the thesis is propounded that the individual's own ethical actuality is the only actuality,[821] but the ethical actuality is not the individual's historical externality. That my intention was this and that, I can in all eternity know absolutely, because this is an expression of the eternal within me, is myself, but the historical externality in the next moment can be reached only *approximando* [by approximation].

The historian seeks to reach the greatest possible certainty, and the historian is not in any contradiction, because he is not in passion; at most he has the research scholar's objective passion, but he is not in subjective passion. As a research scholar, he belongs to a major endeavor from generation to generation; it is at all times objectively and scientifically important for him to come as close to certainty as possible, but it is not subjectively important to him. If, for example, it suddenly became a matter of purely personal honor (which, then, is a defect in a research scholar) for a research scholar to obtain absolute certainty about this and that, he, having become liable to a righteous nemesis, would discover that all historical knowledge is only an approximation. This is no minimizing of historical research, but it illustrates the contradiction in bringing the most extreme passion of subjectivity into relation with something historical, which is the dialectical contradiction in the issue, which is not a question of some illegitimate passion but of the deepest passion of all. —The philosopher seeks to penetrate historical actuality with thought; he is objectively occupied with this work, and the more he succeeds the less important the historical detail becomes to him. Here, again, there is no contradiction.

The contradiction first appears when the subjective individual at the peak of his subjective passion (in his concern for an
eternal happiness) is to base this on historical knowledge, of VII
which the maximum remains an approximation. The research 502
scholar calmly goes on living. That which occupies him objectively and scientifically makes no difference one way or the other in his subjective being and existing. If it is assumed that someone is in subjective passion in some way and then the task is to relinquish this, the contradiction will also disappear. But

to require the greatest possible subjective passion, to the point of hating father and mother,[822] and then join this together with historical knowledge that at its maximum can become only an approximation—this is the contradiction. And the contradiction is in turn a new expression for the paradoxical accentuation of existing, because, if there is any remnant of immanence, any eternal qualification remaining in the existing person, then it cannot be done. The existing person must have lost continuity with himself, must have become someone else (not different from himself within himself), and now, by receiving the condition from the god, becomes a new creation.[823] The contradiction is that becoming a Christian begins with the miracle of creation, and that this happens to someone who is created, and that Christianity is proclaimed to all people, whom Christianity must regard as not existing, since the miracle through which they would come into existence must come between as actual or as an expression of the break with immanence and opposition, which absolutely makes the passion of faith paradoxical as long as there is existing in faith, that is, for a whole lifetime, because one does indeed continually have one's eternal happiness based upon something historical.

To the person who is in the greatest possible passion, in anguish, about his eternal happiness, it is or ought to be of interest that such and such has existed; he must be interested in the slightest detail; and yet he cannot reach more than an approximation and is absolutely in contradiction. Granted that the historicity of Christianity is true—if all the historiographers of the world united to do research and to establish certainty, it would still be impossible to establish more than an approximation. Thus, historically, there are no objections to make, but the difficulty lies elsewhere. It arises when the subjective passion is to be joined together with something historical, and the task is not to relinquish the subjective passion. If a woman in love received at second hand positive knowledge that her beloved, who was dead and from whose mouth she had never heard the declaration, had declared that he loved
VII 503 her—let the witness or witnesses be the most trustworthy per-

sons, let the matter be in such shape that a historian and a hair-splitting and doubting lawyer will say: It is certain—the woman in love will soon discover the dubiousness, and it is simply not a compliment to the lover who does not do it, because objectivity is not a lover's crown of honor. If someone by way of historical documents found absolute certainty as to whether he was a legitimate or illegitimate child, and all his passion was attached to this matter of personal honor, and the circumstances were such that there was no court of law or any other appropriate legal authority that could finally decide the case, so that he could possibly find peace—I wonder if he would be able to find the certainty that would be sufficient for his passion, even if the certainty were found that satisfied the most hair-splitting lawyer and an objective person. Yet the woman in love and the man concerned for his honor would surely strive to relinquish this passion, finding comfort in the eternal, which is more blessed than the most legitimate birth and is the special happiness of being in love, whether she was loved or was not loved. But concern for an eternal happiness cannot be relinquished, because with regard to it he has nothing else that is eternal with which to comfort himself, and yet he must base his eternal happiness on something historical, of which the knowledge, at its maximum, is an approximation.

Note. Please see *Fragments*, Chapters III, IV, V *passim*. —The objective interpretation of Christianity is responsible for the error and aberrancy that by coming to know objectively what Christianity is (in the same way as a research scholar, a learned person, finds it out by way of investigation, information, instruction) one becomes a Christian (who bases his happiness on the relation to this historical knowledge). The very difficulty is left out, or one assumes, as the Bible theory and Church theory basically assume, that in a way we are all what in a way one calls Christians. And now (for at the time we became Christians, it was not so necessary),[824] we must afterward learn objectively what Christianity really is (presumably in order to cease to be Christians, which one indeed became so easily that one did not even need to know what Christianity is—that is, in order to stop being Christians and to become research scholars). The difficulty (which, please note, is essentially the same in every generation; thus now and in the year 1700 etc. it is just as difficult to become a Christian as in the first generation, and as in every generation when Christianity was introduced into a country) consists in subjectively coveting information about the historical in the interest of one's eternal happiness, and the person who does not have this highest subjective passion is not a Christian, because, as was stated someplace earlier,[825] an objective Christian is a pagan.

With regard to Religiousness *A*, the following applies: let the world's six thousand years of history be true or let it not be true—in the matter of his happiness it makes no difference one way or the other to the existing person, because he rests ultimately in the consciousness of eternity.

VII 504 Objectively, it is not at all more difficult to find out what Christianity is than to find out what Mohammedanism and anything else historical are, except insofar as Christianity is not something merely historical; but the difficulty is to become Christian, because every Christian is Christian only by being nailed to the paradox of having based his eternal happiness on the relation to something historical. Speculatively to transform Christianity into an eternal history, the god-in-time into an eternal becoming-of-the-deity, etc., is nothing but evasion and playing with words. To repeat: the difficulty is that I cannot come to know anything historical in such a way that I (who objectively can indeed be very well satisfied with information) subjectively can base on it an eternal happiness, not someone else's, but my own—that is, that I can think it. If I do that, I break with all thinking and then should not be foolish enough to want to understand later, since I, if I am to understand, can neither before nor afterward come to understand anything else except that it goes against all thinking.

§ 3
The Dialectical Contradiction That the Historical under Consideration Here Is Not Something Historical in the Ordinary Sense But Consists of That Which Can Become Historical Only against Its Nature, Consequently by Virtue of the Absurd

The historical is that the god [*Guden*], the eternal, has come into existence at a specific moment in time as an individual human being. The special nature of the historical in this case, that it is not something historical in the ordinary sense but the historical that has been able to become historical only against its nature, has helped speculative thought into a pleasant illusion. Something historical like that, something eternal-historical, as they say—yes, one can easily understand that, indeed, even understand it eternally. Thanks for the climax; it has the oddity that it goes backward, because to understand it eternally is the easier way, provided that one does not let oneself be embarrassed by its being a misunderstanding. If the contradiction is to base an eternal happiness on the relation to something historical, then surely this contradiction is not canceled because the historical of which we are speaking is formed by a contradiction, if it is still held fast that it is something historical. And if this is not to be held fast, then the eternal has indeed not become historical, and even if it were not to be held fast, the climax always becomes ludicrous, since, if it were to be formed, it would have to be formed conversely.[826]

Something eternal-historical is a playing with words and is a changing of the historical into myth, even if in the same paragraph one combats the mythologizing endeavor. Instead of being aware that there are two dialectical contradictions—first, basing one's eternal happiness on the relation to some- VII
thing historical, and then that this historical is constituted con- 505
trary to all thinking—one omits the former and volatilizes the latter. A human being according to his possibility is eternal and becomes conscious of this in time: this is the contradiction within immanence. But that the by-nature eternal comes into existence in time, is born, grows up, and dies is a break with all thinking. If, however, the coming into existence of the eternal in time is supposed to be an eternal coming into existence, then Religiousness *B* is abolished, "all theology is anthropology,"[827] Christianity is changed from an existence-communication into an ingenious metaphysical doctrine addressed to professors, and Religiousness *A* is prinked up with an esthetic-metaphysical ornamentation that in categorical respects neither adds nor detracts.

Please compare this with *Fragments*, Chapters IV and V, where the distinctive dialectic of the paradoxical-historical is emphasized. The reason the difference between the follower at first hand and the follower at second hand is also canceled is that in relation to the paradox and the absurd we are all equally close. See in this book Section II, Chapter II.

Note. This is the paradoxical-religious, the sphere of faith. All of it can be believed—against the understanding. If anyone fancies that he understands this, he can be sure that he misunderstands it. The person who understands it directly (in contrast to understanding that it cannot be understood) will confuse Christianity with one or another analogy of paganism (delusion's analogy to factual actuality), or he will confuse it with the underlying possibility

of all the illusory analogies of paganism (which do not have God's essential invisibility as a higher dialectical middle term, but are deceived by esthetic-direct recognizability; see Section II, Chapter II, Appendix). Or he will confuse Christianity with something that has arisen in man's, that is, humanity's, heart,[828] confuse it with the idea of human nature and forget the qualitative difference that accentuates the absolutely different point of departure: what comes from God and what comes from man. Instead of using the analogy in order by it to define the paradox (the newness of Christianity is not a direct newness and for this very reason is the paradox; see above), he conversely will mistakenly revoke the paradox by means of the analogy, which still is only an analogy of deception, the use of which is therefore the revocation of the analogy, not of the paradox. He will, misunderstanding, understand Christianity as a possibility and forget that what is possible in the fantasy-medium of possibility, possible in illusion, or what is possible in the fantastic medium of pure thinking (and basic to all speculative talk about an eternal becoming-of-
VII the-deity is this shifting of the setting into the medium of possibility) must,
506 in the medium of actuality, become the absolute paradox. He will, misunderstanding, forget that understanding holds only for something of which the possibility is higher than its actuality; whereas here, just the opposite, actuality is the higher, is the paradox, because Christianity as a proposal is not difficult to understand—the difficulty and the paradox are that it is actual. Therefore it was shown in Section II, Chapter III, that faith is a totally unique sphere, which, paradoxically from the esthetic and the metaphysical points of view, accentuates actuality and, paradoxically from the ethical point of view, accentuates the actuality of another person, not one's own. The reason a religious poet is a dubious category in relation to the paradoxical-religious is that, esthetically, possibility is higher than actuality, and the poetic consists in the ideality of imaginative intuition. This is why we not infrequently see hymns that, although stirring and childlike and poetic through a tinge of imagination verging on the fantastic, are not, viewed categorically, Christian. These hymns, through what is so lovely viewed poetically—sky blue, the ding-dong sound of bells—promote the mythical far better than any atheist, because the atheist declares that Christianity is a myth; the naive orthodox poet loathes this and affirms the historical actuality of Christianity—in fanciful verse. The person who understands the paradox (in the sense of understanding it directly) will, misunderstanding, forget that what he at one time in the decisive passion of faith grasped as the absolute paradox (not as a relative paradox, because then the appropriation would not be faith), that is, as that which absolutely was not his own thoughts, can never become his thoughts (in the direct sense) without changing faith to an illusion. If he does so, he will later come to see that his absolutely believing that it was not his own thoughts was an illusion. In faith, however, he can very well continue to preserve his relation to the absolute paradox. But within the sphere of faith there can never be the circumstance that he understands the paradox (in the direct sense), because, if that happens, then the whole sphere of faith drops out as a misun-

derstanding. Actuality, that is, that such and such actually has happened, is the object of faith, and yet is surely not any human being's or humanity's own thoughts, because then thought is at best possibility, but possibility as understanding is the very understanding by which the retrogression is made—that faith ceases. The person who understands the paradox will, misunderstanding, forget that Christianity is the absolute paradox (just as its newness is the paradoxical newness) precisely because it annihilates a possibility (the analogies of paganism, an eternal becoming-of-the-deity) as an illusion and turns it into actuality. And just this is the paradox—not the strange, the unusual in a direct (esthetic) sense, but the apparently familiar, and yet the absolutely strange, which as actuality turns the apparent into a deception. The person who understands the paradox will forget that by understanding (possibility) he has gone back to the old and lost Christianity. In the fantasy-medium of possibility, God can very well coalesce with humankind in the imagination, but to coalesce in actuality with the individual human being is precisely the paradox.

But to confound and go further by going backward or to pronounce judg- VII
ment and roar in defense of Christianity when one oneself noisily and self- 507
importantly uses the categories of misunderstanding is considerably easier than to hold to the strict dialectical diet, and ordinarily it is better rewarded—if one considers it a reward (and not an alarming *nota bene* [note well]) to acquire adherents, if one considers it a reward (and not an alarming *nota bene*) to have satisfied the demands of the times.[829]

APPENDIX TO *B*

The Retroactive Effect of the Dialectical on Pathos Leading to a Sharpened Pathos, and the Contemporaneous Elements of This Pathos

The religiousness that does not have something dialectical in second place, namely *A*, which is the individual's own pathos-filled transformation of existence (not the paradoxical transformation of existence by faith through the relation to something historical), is oriented toward the purely human in such a way that it must be assumed that every human being, viewed essentially, participates in this eternal happiness and finally becomes eternally happy. The difference between the religious person and the person who does not religiously transform his existence becomes a humorous difference: that whereas the religious person utilizes his entire life in becoming aware of the relation to an eternal happiness and the other does not concern himself with it (but note that the religious person has the satisfaction within himself and, turned inward, is not busily engaged in meaningless complaints that others easily attain what he seeks with difficulty and with most extreme effort), they both, viewed eternally, go equally far. Herein lies the sympathetic humor, and the earnestness is that the religious person does not allow himself to be disturbed by comparison with others. Thus in Religiousness *A* there is the continual possibility of taking existence back into the eternity lying behind.

Religiousness *B* is isolating, separating, is polemical. Only on this condition do I become blessed, and as I absolutely bind myself to it, I thereby exclude everyone else. This is the impetus of particularism in the ordinary pathos. Every Christian has pathos as in Religiousness *A*, and then this pathos of separation. This separation gives the Christian a certain likeness to a person who is happy by way of preferential treatment, and if a Christian selfishly perceives it as this, we have the desperate arrogation of predestination.[830] The happy person cannot
VII 508 essentially sympathize with others who do not have or are unable to have preferential treatment. Therefore the happy person either must continue to be ignorant that others exist or himself become unhappy because of this awareness. Having his eternal happiness based on something historical means that the Christian's good fortune is distinguished by suffering, just as the religious category of being God's elect is as paradoxically opposite to being a favorite of fortune as possible, because the elect is not the unhappy person; but neither is he, directly understood, the happy person—no, this is so difficult to understand that for anyone else but the elect it must be something to despair over. That is why the conception of being the elect that esthetically wishes to be, for example, in an apostle's place is so repulsive. The happiness linked to a historical condition excludes all who are outside the condition, and among those are the countless ones who are ex-

cluded through no fault of their own but by the accidental circumstance that Christianity has not yet been proclaimed to them.

The sharpened pathos, more closely defined, is:

a. *The consciousness of sin.** This consciousness is the expression for the paradoxical transformation of existence. Sin is the new existence-medium. "To exist [*existere*]" generally signifies only that by having come into existence the individual does exist [*er til*] and is becoming; now it signifies that by having come into existence he has become a sinner. "To exist" generally is not a more sharply defining predicate but is the form of all more sharply defining predicates; one does not become something [qualitative] by coming into existence, but now to come into existence is to become a sinner. In the totality of guilt-consciousness, existence asserts itself as strongly as possible within immanence, but the consciousness of sin is the break. By coming into existence the individual becomes another person, or in the instant he is to come into existence he becomes another person by coming into existence, because otherwise the category of sin is placed within immanence. The individual is not a sinner from eternity. When the being intended for eternity, who in birth comes into existence, becomes a sinner in birth or is born as a sinner—then it is existence that wraps itself around him in such a way that every communication of immanence by way of recollection through regression into the eternal is broken, and the predicate "sinner," which first, but also immediately, appears through the coming into existence, gains such a paradoxically overwhelming VII 509 power that the coming into existence makes him into another person. This is the consequence of the appearance of the god [*Guden*] in time, which prevents the individual from relating himself backward to the eternal, since he now moves

* Compare this with what was said about the consciousness of guilt in *A*, § 3. See also Section II, Chapter II.

forward in order to become eternal in time through the relation to the god in time.

The individual is therefore unable to gain the consciousness of sin by himself, which is the case with guilt-consciousness, because in guilt-consciousness the subject's self-identity is preserved, and guilt-consciousness is a change of the subject within the subject himself. The consciousness of sin, however, is a change of the subject himself, which shows that outside the individual there must be the power that makes clear to him that he has become a person other than he was by coming into existence, that he has become a sinner. This power is the god in time. (Compare this with *Fragments*, Chapter I, on the moment.[831])

In the consciousness of sin, the individual becomes aware of himself in his difference from the universally human, which in itself is only an awareness of what it means to exist *qua* human being. Since the relation to that historical event (the god in time) conditions the consciousness of sin, there could not have been the consciousness of sin during all the time before this historical event occurred. But inasmuch as the believer in his consciousness of sin will also become aware of the sin of the whole race, another isolation[832] appears. The believer expands the consciousness of sin to the whole race and at the same time does not know the whole race to be saved, inasmuch as the single individual's salvation indeed depends on his being brought into relation to that historical event, which precisely because it is historical cannot be everywhere at once but uses time in order to become known to human beings, during which time one generation after the other dies. In Religiousness *A*, the sympathy is with all humankind, because it is related to the eternal, a relation of which every human being is assumed to be essentially capable, and because the eternal is everywhere, so that no time is spent in waiting or in sending a messenger for that which by being historical is prevented from being everywhere at once, and about whose having existed countless generations through no fault of their own could continue to be unaware.

To have one's existence qualified in this way is sharpened

pathos, both because it cannot be thought and because it is isolating. In other words, sin is no teaching or doctrine for thinkers; then it all becomes nothing. It is an existence-category and simply cannot be thought.

b. *The possibility of offense* or the autopathetic collision. In Re- VII
ligiousness *A*, offense is not at all possible, because even the 510
most decisive qualification is within immanence. But the paradox, which requires faith against the understanding, promptly makes offense manifest, whether this is, more closely defined, the offense that suffers or the offense that derides the paradox as foolishness. Thus as soon as the person who has had the passion of faith loses it, he is *eo ipso* offended.

But this in turn is the sharpened pathos—namely, continually to have a possibility that, if it is actualized, is a fall as much deeper as faith is higher than all the religiousness of immanence.

In our day, Christianity has become so naturalized and domesticated in such a way that no one dreams of offense. Well, it is quite in order, because one is not offended by a triviality, and that is what Christianity is on the point of becoming. Otherwise it is surely the only power that truly can cause offense, and the narrow gate to the hard way[833] of faith is offense, and the terrible resistance against the beginning of faith is offense; and if becoming a Christian proceeds properly, offense is bound to take its share in every generation as it did in the first. Christianity is the only power that truly can cause offense, because hysterical and sentimental spasms of offense over this and that can simply be rejected and explained as a lack of ethical earnestness that is coquettishly busy accusing the whole world instead of itself. For the believer, offense comes at the beginning, and the possibility of it is the continual fear and trembling in his existence.

c. *The pain of sympathy*, because the believer does not, as in Religiousness *A*, latently sympathize and cannot sympathize with every human being *qua* human being, but essentially only with Christians. The person who with the passion of his

whole soul bases his happiness on one condition, which is the relation to something historical, obviously cannot at the same time regard this condition as nonsense. Such a thing can be done only by a modern dogmatician, who has no difficulty doing the latter, since he lacks pathos for the first. For the believer it holds true that outside this condition there is no eternal happiness, and for him it holds true, or it can come to hold true for him, that he must hate father and mother.[834] Is it not the same as hating them if his eternal happiness is bound to a condition that he knows they do not accept? And is that not a terrible sharpening of pathos with regard to an eternal happiness? And suppose this father or this mother or this beloved
VII were dead without having his or her eternal happiness based
511 upon this condition! Or if they were alive but he could not win them! He can be willing to do his utmost for them, to fulfill all the duties of a faithful son and a faithful lover with the greatest enthusiasm—in this way Christianity does not enjoin hating—and yet, if this condition separates them, separates them forever, is it not as if he hated them?

Such things have been experienced in the world. Nowadays they are not experienced; of course, we all are Christians. But what, I wonder, have we all become because of this, and what, I wonder, has Christianity become because we all are Christians of sorts as a matter of course?

Chapter V

Conclusion

The present work has made it difficult to become a Christian, so difficult that the number of Christians among the cultured in Christendom will perhaps not even be very great—perhaps, because I cannot know something like that. Whether this demeanor is Christian, I do not decide. But to go further than Christianity and then to grope in categories familiar to the pagans, to go further and then to be a long way from being able to compare favorably with pagans in existential competency—this at least is not Christian. But the difficulty is not made (in the imaginary construction, since the book has no τέλος [end, goal]) in order to make it difficult for lay people to become Christians. First of all, everyone can indeed become a Christian, and, second, it is assumed that everyone who says he is a Christian and that he has done the highest is a Christian and has done the highest, if by thrusting himself ahead in importance he has not given someone occasion to take a closer look purely psychologically and to learn something for himself. Woe to him who wants to judge hearts. But when a whole generation, although in various ways, seems to want to unite in going further *en masse*; when a whole generation, although with various understandings, covets becoming objective as the highest, whereby one ceases to be Christian if one was—this surely can give a person occasion to become aware of the difficulties. But it must not give him occasion VII 512 for new confusion by wanting, through a presentation of the difficulties, to have importance for any other person, to say nothing of the generation, because then he, too, begins to become objective.

In times when an individual in adulthood, perhaps tossed about and experienced in life, perhaps with the pain of having to break the tenderest relationships with parents and relatives, perhaps with his dearest, decided to become a Christian—he scarcely felt any need to go further, because he understood what effort it took every day to keep himself in this passion, understood in what terrors he had his life. In our day, however, when it looks as if one is actually a Christian even as a week-old child, whereby in turn Christ has been changed from the sign of offense into a friend of children *à la* Uncle Frank, Goodman,[835] or a teacher at a charity school: one thinks that, after all, as a man one ought to do something, and so one must go further. The only trouble is that one does not go further by actually becoming a Christian but by speculative thought, and the world-historical only regresses to lower and in part fanciful conceptions of existence. Since we are accustomed to being Christians and being called Christians as a matter of course, the dubious situation has also developed in which life-views that are far lower than Christianity are introduced within Christianity and have pleased people (the Christians) more, which is natural, since Christianity is the most difficult, and then they are praised as higher discoveries that transcend plain and simple Christianity.

It would undoubtedly be preferable to the indifferent maintenance of the name, would be a sign of life, if a number of people in our day would simply confess to themselves that they could wish that Christianity had never entered the world or that they themselves had never become Christians. But let the confession be without scorn and mockery and wrath; to what purpose? One can very well have respect for what one cannot force oneself into. Christ himself says that he was taken with the young man who could not resolve to give all his possessions to the poor.[836] The young man did not become a Christian, and yet Christ was taken with him. So, then, honesty rather than half measures. Christianity is a glorious life-view in which to die, the only true comfort, and the moment of death is Christianity's situation. Perhaps that is why even
VII the indifferent are not willing to give it up, but just as one
513 makes a deposit in a burial society in order to be able in due
time to defray the expenses, so one keeps Christianity in store

until the very end—one is a Christian and yet becomes one only at the moment of death.

There may be someone who, if he understood himself in all honesty, would rather confess that he wished that he had never been brought up in Christianity instead of disregarding it in indifference. Honesty is preferable to half measures. But let the confession be without wrath, without defiance, with a quiet respect for the power that, as he sees it, has disturbed him, perhaps his life, for the power that certainly could have shown him the way but has not helped him. If it happened that a father, even the most loving and solicitous father, at the very moment he wanted to do the best for his child, did the worst, did the worst that may have disturbed the child's entire life—should the son, if he remembers the circumstances, therefore drown his piety in the oblivion of indifference or change it into wrath? Well, let shabby souls who are able to love God and people only when everything goes their way, let them hate and defy in ill temper—a faithful son loves, unchanged. It is always a sign of a mediocre person if he, when he is convinced that the one who made him unhappy did it for the purpose of doing the best for him, can be separated from him in wrath and bitterness. A rigorous upbringing in Christianity may have made a person's life too difficult, without having in turn helped him. He may secretly harbor a wish, as did those inhabitants who begged Christ to leave their region because he terrified them.[837] But the son whom the father made unhappy, if he has magnanimity, will continue to love his father. And when he suffers the consequences, he will at times probably sigh despondently: Would that it had never happened to me! But he will never surrender to despair; he will work against the suffering by working through it. And as he works, his sorrow will be mitigated; he will soon feel more sorry for his father than for himself; he will forget his own pain in his deep, sympathetic sorrow over how grievous it must be for his father if he understood it. So he will exert himself more and more vigorously; his salvation will be important to him for his own sake and now almost be more precious for his father's sake—so he will work and will no doubt be successful.

And if he is successful, then he will, so to speak, lose his mind
VII in his enthusiastic rejoicing, for what father has done so much
514 for his son, what son can come to owe his father so much!

It is the same also with Christianity. Although it has made him unhappy, he does not therefore give it up, because it never occurs to him that Christianity would have entered the world in order to harm human beings; he continually retains respect for it. He does not abandon it, and even if he sighs despondently, "Would that I had never been brought up in this doctrine," he does not abandon it. And the despondency becomes sadness, that it must indeed be almost grievous for Christianity that such a thing could happen—but he does not abandon it. In the end, Christianity must certainly make it up to him. In the end, indeed, it is not little by little; it is much less and yet infinitely much more. But only slovenly souls abandon what once made an absolute impression upon them, and only contemptible souls despicably exploit their own suffering by making from it the wretched profit of being able to disturb others, of becoming self-important by the most dastardly of all arrogation: wanting to bar others from finding comfort because one has not found it oneself. If there is anyone in our day whom Christianity disturbs, which I do not doubt and which can be demonstrated factually, one thing can be demanded of him—that he keep silent, because, viewed ethically, his discourse is a robber assault and in its consequences is even worse, since it ends up with both having nothing, both the robber and the victim.

Christianity in its decisive form is not suitable for every age in life any more than Christianity entered into the world in the childhood of humankind but in the fullness of time.[838] There are times in life that demand something that Christianity seemingly wants to omit altogether, something that to a person at a certain age appears to be the absolute, although in later life the same person sees its vanity. Christianity cannot be poured into a child, because it always holds true that every human being grasps only what he has use for, and the child has no decisive use for Christianity. As Christianity's entrance into the world indicates by what preceded it, the law is continually this: *No one begins with being Christian; each one becomes that in the fullness of time—if one becomes that.* A strict Christian upbringing in Christianity's decisive categories is a very venturesome undertaking, because Christianity makes men whose strength is in their weakness; but if a child is cowed into Christianity in its totally earnest form, it ordinarily makes a very unhappy youth. The rare exception is a stroke of luck.

The Christianity that is recited to a child or, rather, the VII
Christianity the child himself puts together if no pressure is 515
used to drive it existentially into decisive Christian categories, is actually not Christianity but idyllic mythology. [839]It is the idea of childlikeness raised to the second power, and the relation is sometimes turned around so that it is the parents who learn from the child rather than the child who learns from the parents. It is turned around so that the child's lovable misunderstanding of the essentially Christian transfigures father love and mother love into a piety that nevertheless is not actually Christianity. There is no lack of examples of people who themselves have not previously been religiously moved but are now so moved by a child. But this piety is not the religiousness that should essentially belong to an adult, and the parents' religiousness should no more find its decisive expression in this piety than the mother herself is nourished by the milk that nature provides the child. Father love and mother love are so deeply attached to the child, surround it so tenderly, that the piety itself discovers, so to speak, what is indeed taught: that there must be a God who makes little children his own. But if this mood is the parents' entire religiousness, then they lack authentic religiousness and find their refreshment only in a sadness that indirectly sympathizes with being a child. This parental piety and the child's teachability and ease of understanding this blessedness are lovely and lovable, but it is not really Christianity. It is Christianity in the medium of fantasy-perception; it is a Christianity from which the terror has been removed: the *innocent* child is led to God or Christ. Is this Christianity, the point of which is that it is the sinner who takes refuge in the paradox? It is beautiful and moving, and as it ought to be, that an old person feels his guilt

upon seeing a child and sadly comprehends the child's innocence, but this mood is not decisively Christian. The sentimental view of the child's innocence forgets that Christianity does not acknowledge anything like that in fallen humankind, and that the qualitative dialectic defines the consciousness of sin as more explicit than all innocence. The rigorously Christian conception of the child as sinner cannot provide the period of childhood with any advantage, because the child has no consciousness of sin and therefore is a sinner without the consciousness of sin.

But there is indeed a Bible passage to cite, and at times it is understood, perhaps unconsciously, in such a way that the understanding contains the most profound satire upon all Christianity and makes Christianity into the most comfortless view
VII of life, since it makes it indescribably easy for a child to enter
516 into the kingdom of heaven, impossible for an adult, and the conclusion is that the best and only proper wish would be to wish death for the child, the sooner the better.

The passage is in the nineteenth chapter of Matthew, where Christ says, "Leave the small children alone and do not forbid them to come to me, for to such belongs the kingdom of heaven."[840] The whole chapter speaks of the difficulty of entering the kingdom of heaven, and the expressions are as strong as possible. Verse 12: "There are eunuchs who have castrated themselves for the sake of the kingdom of heaven." Verse 24: "It is easier for a camel to go through the eye of a needle than for a rich man to enter the kingdom of God." The disciples become so terrified that they say (verse 25): "Who then can be saved?" After Christ has answered this, there is in turn mention in verse 29 of the reward for those who have left houses and brothers or sisters or father or mother or wife or children or lands for the sake of Christ's name—all of them terrible expressions of the collisions in which a Christian can be tested. Consequently, the entrance into the kingdom of heaven is made as difficult as possible, so difficult that even teleological suspensions of the ethical[841] are mentioned.

In the same chapter there is the very brief account of the little event, that small children were brought to Christ and he said those words to them—yet, please note, there is an intermediate clause and intermediate event in between—that the disciples rebuked the children or, more correctly, rebuked those who carried the children (see Mark 10:13). Now, if Christ's words about being a child are to be understood literally, then the confusion arises that whereas it is made as difficult as possible for the adult to enter into the kingdom of heaven, the only difficulty for a child is that the mother carries it to Christ and that the child is carried there—and then we quickly have the climax of despair: best to die as a child. But in Matthew the meaning is not difficult. Christ says the words to the disciples who rebuked the children—and the disciples, after all, were not small children. In Matthew 18:2, it is told that Jesus called a child to himself, placed him among the disciples, and said: Truly, I say to you, unless you turn and become like children, you will certainly not enter the kingdom of heaven. He does not become involved with the child, but he uses the child against the disciples. If, however, the meaning is supposed to be simply about the loveliness of being a little child, a proper little angel (and Christianity does not seem to have a preference even for angels, since it pertains to sinners)—then it is cruel to say these words in the presence of the apostles, who in that case would indeed be in the sad situation of being grown men; then with this one explanation all VII
Christianity is explained away. Why, I wonder, did Christ 517
want to have disciples who were adults before they became disciples? Why did he not say: Go out and baptize small children?

If it is sad to see an arrogating speculative thought that wants to understand everything, then it is always just as sad that someone under the guise of orthodoxy wants to make Christianity into moonlight and charity-school sentimentality. But to say to men—at the very moment when they perhaps became too obtrusive [*nærgaaende*] with Christ and wanted to demand finite reward for the close [*nær*] relation-

ship or at least to emphasize in a worldly way the close relationship—that to such* (namely, small children) belongs the kingdom of heaven, in this way to place a little distance between himself and the disciples by means of a paradox—that is indeed a dark saying. Humanly speaking, it is still possible to castrate oneself and leave father and children and wife, but to become a little child when one has become an adult is to protect oneself against all obtrusiveness by means of the distance of the paradox. The apostles rebuke the small children, but Christ does not rebuke in turn. He does not even reprimand the apostles; he turns to the small children, but he is speaking to the apostles. And just like that look he gave to Peter,[842] this turning to the children is understood as addressing the apostles, the judgment pronounced upon them, and in the nineteenth chapter of Matthew, which otherwise deals with the difficulty of entering the kingdom of heaven, as the most powerful expression of the difficulty. The paradoxical lies in making a child the paradigm, *partly* because, humanly speaking, a child simply cannot be that at all, since it is immediate and explains nothing (this is why a genius cannot be a paradigm, either—the sadness in the distinction of being a
VII genius), not even to other children, because every child is itself
518 only in an immediate way, and *partly* because it is made a paradigm for an adult, who in the humility of guilt-consciousness is supposed to resemble the humility of innocence.

But enough about that. A childish view of Christianity such as that only makes it ludicrous. If the assertion about being a child must be understood literally, then it is nonsense to preach Christianity to adults. Yet this is the way Christianity

* τοιοῦτοι; precisely this word adequately shows that Christ is not speaking about children or literally to children but that he is speaking to the disciples. Literally understood, a child is not τοιοῦτος; τοιοῦτος implies a comparison, which presupposes a difference. Therefore, this does not say anything about children literally, does not say that a little child (literally understood) has free admission, but it says that only the person who is like a child can enter into the kingdom of heaven. But just as for the adult it is of all things most impossible to become a little child (literally understood), so for a little child it is of all things most impossible to be *like* a child, simply because it is a child.

is defended by orthodox fencers. But, of course, if anyone wants something to laugh at, there is scarcely any more abundant material than the way in which Christianity is defended and attacked these days. An orthodox thunders against the egotism of atheists, "who do not want to enter into God's kingdom as little children but want to be something." Here the category is correct, but now he is going to make his discourse weightier and appeals to that Bible passage, literally understood, about being a little child (literally understood). Can one blame the atheist for assuming His Reverence to be a bit lunatic, quite literally understood? The difficult discourse with which the orthodox began has become balderdash, because for a little child it is not at all difficult, and for an adult it is impossible. In a certain sense, to be something and to want to be something is the condition (the negative condition) for entering the kingdom of heaven as a little child—if it is supposed to be difficult—otherwise it is no wonder that one remains outside when one has become forty years old. So, then, the atheist perhaps wants to mock Christianity, and yet there is no one who makes it as ludicrous as the orthodox.

From the psychological viewpoint, this misunderstanding fits the cozy security with which people have managed to make being a Christian and being a human being synonymous, fits the light-minded and melancholy abhorrence of decisions, which pushes aside and pushes aside, and thus manages to get becoming a Christian pushed so far back that it is decided before one knows about it. The Sacrament of Baptism is orthodoxly stressed to such an extreme that one quite properly becomes heterodox in the dogma of rebirth and forgets Nicodemus's objection and the answer to him,[843] because hyperorthodoxly a little child is regarded as actually having become a Christian by being baptized.

[844]Childlike Christianity, which in a little child is lovable, in
an adult is the childish orthodoxy that, beatified in the fanciful, has managed to draw Christ's name into it. An orthodoxy VII
such as that confuses everything. [845]If it notices that the cate- 519
gory "faith" has begun to sink in price, that all want to go
further and let faith be something for obtuse people, then it is

about to jack up the price. What happens? Faith becomes something very extraordinary and rare, "not for just everybody"—in short, faith becomes a genius-differential. If that is the case, then with this one stipulation all Christianity is revoked—by an orthodox. The orthodox is quite right in wanting to jack up the price, but the valuation-differential confuses everything, because the genius-differential is not difficult for the genius and is impossible for others. Faith is properly made the most difficult of all, but qualitatively-dialectically, that is, equally difficult for all. It is the ethical qualification in faith that helps here, because this quite simply bars the one believer from being inquisitive and comparative; it forbids all comparison between individuals, and thus it becomes equally difficult for all.

A childish orthodoxy such as this has also managed to draw decisive attention to the fact that Christ at his birth was wrapped in rags and laid in a manger[846]—in short, on the humiliation of his coming in the humble form of a servant,[847] and believes that this is the paradox in contrast to coming in glory. Confusion. The paradox is primarily that God, the eternal, has entered into time as an individual human being. Whether this individual human being is a servant or an emperor makes no difference. It is not more adequate for God to be a king than to be a beggar; it is not more humiliating for God to become a beggar than to become an emperor. The childlike is immediately recognizable. Simply because the child has no developed conception or actual conception of God (but only fantasy-inwardness), it cannot become aware of the absolute paradox but has a touching understanding of the humorous: that the mightiest of all, the Almighty (yet without any decisive thought-category, and therefore with only a fairy-tale difference from what is on the same level, to be king and emperor) at his birth was laid in a crib and wrapped in rags. If, however, childish orthodoxy insists upon this humiliation as the paradox, then it shows *eo ipso* that it is not aware of the paradox. Of what use, then, is all its defending! If it is given and assumed that it is easy to understand that God becomes a particular human being, [848]then the difficulty is only in the next—that he becomes a lowly and despised human being—then in *summa summarum* Christianity is humor. Humor diverts a little of the attention away from the first, the qualification "God," and now stresses that the greatest, the most powerful one, who is greater than all kings and emperors, that VII 520 he became the lowliest of all. But the qualification "the greatest, the most powerful one, who is greater than all kings and emperors," is a very vague qualification, is fantasy, is not a qualitative qualification like that of being God. On the whole, it is remarkable how orthodoxy, when it is in a fix, uses fantasy—and so produces the greatest effect. But to repeat, the greatest, the most powerful one, who is greater than all kings and emperors, is not therefore God. If someone wants to talk about God, then let him say: God. That is the quality. If the pastor wants to talk about eternity, then let him say: eternity. And yet at times, when he really [849]wants to say something, he says: The eternity of eternities, world without end. But if Christianity is humor, then everything is confused; then it ends with my becoming the best of Christians, because regarded as a humorist I am not bad, but yet bad enough to regard this as humorous as possible in comparison with being a Christian, which I am not.

A childish orthodoxy misleadingly emphasizes Christ's suffering. In the most fanciful categories, which are by no means suitable for calling human understanding to silence, since it easily perceives this to be balderdash, the frightfulness of the suffering is emphasized, Christ's sensitive body that suffers so enormously, or it is quantitatively and comparatively stressed that he, who was so holy, the purest and the most guiltless of all, that he had to suffer. The paradox is that Christ entered into the world *in order to suffer*. If this is taken away, then a militia force of analogies summarily captures the impregnable fortress of the paradox. The fact that the innocent may suffer in this world (heroes in the realms of the intellect and art, martyrs for the truth, the silent martyrs of womanhood, etc.) is by no means absolutely paradoxical, but humorous. But the martyrs' destiny when they came into the world was not to suffer; their destiny was this and that, and in order to accom-

plish this they had to suffer, to endure suffering, to face death. But the suffering is not the τέλος. Religiousness comprehends suffering, defines it teleologically for the sufferer, but suffering is not the τέλος. Therefore, just as the suffering of the ordinary martyrs is not any analogy to Christ's, so also the believer's suffering is not, and the absolute paradox is indeed distinguishable in such a way that every analogy is a deception. [850]It might instead seem to be an analogy if, according to a fantastical life-view (transmigration of souls) one were to assume that a human being, who at one time had existed, returned to the world *in order to suffer*. But since the analogy belongs to a fantastical view, it is *eo ipso* a deception, and, quite apart from that, the "in order to" of the suffering is just the opposite: a guilty person returns to the world *in order to*
VII 521 suffer his punishment. It seems as if a fate hovers over childish orthodoxy. It is often well intentioned, but since it lacks orientation, it is frequently prompted to exaggerate.

Therefore, when an orthodox continually talks about childhood faith, what is learned as a child, a womanly heart, etc., he may only be a somewhat humorous character (as a humorist I nevertheless protest against all association with him, since his emphasis is wrong) who has managed to mix up Christianity with the childlike (literally understood) and who now longs for childhood, and whose longing is therefore especially distinguishable by a longing for the loving tenderness of the pious mother. He may also be a deceitful fellow who is seeking to avoid the terrors when truly becoming a child as an adult is to be taken in earnest and not as a humorous joining of the childlike with the adult. This much is certain—if a little child (literally understood) is to provide the definition of what Christianity is, then there is no terror; it is not that fact which was an offense to the Jews and foolishness to the Greeks.[851]

When a child is told about Christianity and the child is not violently mistreated in a figurative sense, it appropriates all that is gentle, childlike, endearing, and heavenly. It lives together with the little Jesus-child, with the angels, and with the three kings; it sees the star in the dark night, journeys the long road, and now is in the stable, wonder upon wonder, and al-

ways sees the heavens open; with all the inwardness of the imagination he longs for these pictures. And now let us not forget the peppernuts and all the other magnificent things that come out on that occasion. Above all, let us not become jolly old louts who lie [*lyve*] about childhood, who falsely attribute [*tillyve*] its exaggerated enthusiasm to themselves and cheat [*fralyve*] childhood of its reality. He would truly have to be a good-for-nothing fellow who does not find childlikeness touching, lovely, and blissful. Neither, presumably, should one want to suspect a humorist, that unhappy-happy lover of the recollections, of failure to appreciate the reality of childhood. But, on the other hand, surely the person is a blind leader[852] who in any way whatever claims that this is the decisive conception of Christianity, which became an offense to the Jews and foolishness to the Greeks. Christ becomes the divine child, or for the somewhat older child the friendly figure with the kindly face (the mythical commensurability), not the paradox in whom no one could detect anything (literally understood), not even John the Baptizer (see John 1:31,33),
not even the disciples before they had been made aware (John VII
1:36,42), [853]what Isaiah had prophesied (53:2,3,4, especially 522
verse 4). The child-conception of Christ is essentially a fantasy-perception, and fantasy-perception's idea is commensurability, and commensurability is essentially paganism, whether it is power, glory, beauty, or is within a little humorous contradiction that is still not an actual concealment but an incognito easily seen through. Commensurability is direct recognizability. The form of a servant is the incognito,[854] but the kindly face is the direct recognizability.

Here as everywhere, there is a certain orthodoxy that, when it wants to make a big splash on the great festival days and decisive occasions, *bona fide* [in good faith] makes use of a little paganism—and then it succeeds best of all. A pastor perhaps ordinarily stays more or less within the strict and proper orthodox categories, but what happens—one Sunday he must make a special effort. In order to show how vividly Christ stands before him, he will give us a glimpse into his soul. Now this is quite proper. Christ is the object of faith, but faith is anything but a fantasy-perception, and a fantasy-perception is simply not something higher than faith. Now it begins: the gentle countenance, the friendly form, the sorrowful gaze etc. There is nothing at all comic in a man's teaching paganism instead of Christianity, but there is something comic when an orthodox pulls out all the stops on the great festival days and mistakenly, without knowing it, pulls out the stop of paganism. If the organist ordinarily played a waltz, he certainly would be dismissed; but if an organist, who otherwise played the hymn tunes quite properly, on the great and solemn occasions and since he is accompanied by trumpets, were to play a waltz—in order to make the day really festive—this would certainly be comic. Yet a little of this sentimental and mawkish paganism is found among the orthodox, not ordinarily, but particularly on the great festival days, when they really open their hearts, and especially toward the end of the discourse.

Direct recognizability is paganism; all solemn assurances that this is indeed Christ and that he is the true God are futile as soon as it ends with direct recognizability. A mythological figure is directly distinguishable. If one charges an orthodox
VII with this, he becomes furious and flares up: Yes, but Christ is
523 indeed the true God and therefore is certainly no mythological figure . . . . . one can see that in his gentle countenance. But if one can see it in him, then he is *eo ipso* a mythological figure. It is easy to see that a place remains for faith; take away direct recognizability, and faith is in the right place. The crucifixion of the understanding and of fantasy-perception, which cannot have direct recognizability—that is the sign. But it is easier to sneak away from the terror and sneak into a little paganism, which is made unrecognizable by the curious connection that it serves as the final and highest explanation in an address that perhaps began in perfectly correct orthodox categories. If in a confidential moment an orthodox were to confide to someone that he actually did not have faith, well, there would be nothing ludicrous in that; but when an orthodox in blissful enthusiasm, himself almost amazed at his lofty rhetoric, completely opens himself to someone in confidence and is so unfortunate

as to take the wrong direction so that he *ascends* from the higher to the lower, then it is rather difficult not to smile.

With regard to becoming a Christian, then, childhood (literally understood) is not the true age. On the contrary, adulthood, maturity, is the time when it is to be decided whether a person will be a Christian or not. The religiousness of childhood is the universal, abstract, and yet imaginative-inward basis for all later religiousness; to become a Christian is a decision that belongs to a much later age. The child's receptivity is so entirely without decision that it is no wonder people say: A child can be made to believe anything. Of course, the adult bears the responsibility for what he allows himself to make the child believe, but it is certain and true. That the child is baptized can neither make the child older in understanding nor mature it for decision. A Jewish child, a pagan child, brought up from the beginning by tender Christian foster parents who treat the child just as lovingly as parents treat their own child, will appropriate the same Christianity as the baptized child.

However, if a child is not allowed, as it ought to be, to play innocently with the most holy, if in its existence it is rigorously coerced into decisively Christian qualifications, such a child will suffer a great deal. Such an upbringing will either plunge immediacy into despondency and anxiety or incite lust and the anxiety of lust on a scale unknown even in paganism.

It is beautiful and lovable—the opposite indefensible—that VII
Christian parents, just as they otherwise take care of the child, 524
so also nourish the child with the childlike ideas of the religious. As frequently said above, infant Baptism is in every way defensible as the anticipation of possibility, as hindering the terrible rending torment of the parents' having their eternal happiness bound up with something and the children not with the same. But an obtuse, sentimental, and loutish misunderstanding, not so much of infant Baptism as of childhood, is reprehensible, but then sectarian externality also is just as reprehensible, since the decision belongs best to inwardness. Be it ever so well intentioned, it is rape to coerce the child's existence into the decisive Christian categories, but it is immense obtuseness to say that childhood (literally under-

stood) is the time for really deciding to become a Christian. Just as some have deceitfully wanted to form a transition from eudaemonism to the ethical through sagacity, so it is also a deceitful device to want to identify becoming a Christian as closely as possible with becoming a human being and to want to make someone believe that one becomes that decisively in childhood. And insofar as this urge and inclination to push becoming a Christian back into childhood becomes common, this in itself will be a demonstration that Christianity is on the way to dying out, because what one wants is to try to change being a Christian into a beautiful recollection, whereas, on the contrary, to become a Christian is most decisive in a person's becoming. The aim is fancifully to prink up the lovable innocence of childhood with the further qualification that this innocence is what it means to be a Christian, and then one will let sadness substitute for decision. The sadness in legitimate humor consists in its reflecting purely humanly, honestly and without deception, on what it is to be a child (literally understood), and it then becomes forever certain and true that this cannot be done over again—childhood, when it is over, becomes only a recollection. But humor (in its truth) does not have anything to do with the decisive Christian category of becoming a Christian and does not identify becoming a Christian with being a child, literally understood, because in that case being a Christian becomes a recollection in altogether the same sense. Here it becomes very apparent how wrong it is to make humor the highest within Christianity, since humor or the humorist, provided he is within Christianity, does not have anything to do with the decisive Christian category of becoming a Christian. Humor is always a revocation (of exis-
VII tence into the eternal by recollection backward, of adulthood
525 to childhood, etc., see above), is the backward perspective: Christianity is the direction forward to becoming a Christian and becoming that by continuing to be that. Without standing still there is no humor; the humorist always has ample time, because he has eternity's amplitude of time behind him. Christianity has no room for sadness: salvation or perdition—salvation ahead of it, perdition behind for everyone who turns

around, whatever he sees. Lot's wife turned to stone when she looked back, because she saw the abomination of desolation,[855] but, Christianly understood, to look back, even if it is to gaze at the lovely, enchanting landscape of childhood, is perdition.

If a single concession is made to speculative thought with regard to beginning with the pure being, all is lost, and it is impossible to halt the confusion, since it must be halted within pure being. If a single concession is made to a childish orthodoxy concerning the specific superiority of childhood in becoming a Christian, then all is confused.[856]

But now to that Bible passage; it is indeed in the Bible! I have already made myself ludicrous enough in the foregoing by having to deal with the pusillanimous and timid biblical interpretation; I shall not try my hand at it further. If a childish orthodoxy has cast a comic light on Christianity, so also has the kind of biblical interpretation that in its timid obsequiousness, without being conscious of it, reverses the relation and is not so much concerned about understanding the Bible as about being understood by it, is not so much concerned about understanding the Bible passage as about having a Bible passage to quote—a contradiction, just as when someone in business wants to ask the advice of a person (this, of course, is a relation of dependence) but asks his advice in such a way that he requires him to answer this and that and takes every liberty to get him to answer in exactly this way.

Submission to the authority of the adviser becomes a cunning way to derive advantage from the authority. But is that consulting? Is this submitting to what is called the divine authority of the Bible? It is, after all, a cowardly attempt to push away all responsibility by never acting on one's own—just as if one had no responsibility for the manner in which one finds
a Bible passage on one's side. Psychologically, it is very re- VII
markable how clever, how ingenious, how subtle, how per- 526
severing in erudite research certain people can be, just to have a Bible passage to quote. They seem totally unaware, however, that this is simply making a fool of God, treating him like a poor fish who has been so foolish as to put something

in writing and now has to put up with what the lawyers want to make of it. This is the way a tricky little child behaves toward a strict father who has not known how to win the child's love. The child thinks something like this: If I can only get his permission, then it is all right even if I have to use a little cunning. But a relation such as that is not a tender, close relation between father and son. In the same way, it is not a close relation between God and a human being if they are so distant from each other that there is place and use for all this worried subtlety and pondering of a despondent submissiveness.

Examples of such conduct are most likely to be found among genuinely gifted people whose enthusiasm is not proportionate to their intellectuality. Whereas limited and busy people fancy that they are acting and acting and acting, the distinctive mark of a certain kind of intellectual is the virtuosity with which they know how to avoid acting. It is shocking that Cromwell, who certainly was an experienced reader of the Bible, had sufficient subtlety to find Bible passages on his side or at least to have in a *vox populi* [voice of the people] a *vox dei* [voice of God] that said it was an act, a decree of providence that he became Protector of England, not an action by him, because the people had indeed chosen him. Just as one rarely sees a downright hypocrite, so likewise rarely a downright unscrupulous person; but a subtle conscience is not rare, whether it is in the agonizing self-contradiction of simultaneously having to explain away a responsibility and remaining unaware of doing it, or it is a morbidness in a perhaps well-intentioned person, a morbidness that is bound up with great sufferings and makes the unhappy man's breathing even tighter and more painful than that of the most burdened conscience once it is able to exhale in honesty.

A childish orthodoxy, a pusillanimous Bible interpretation, a foolish and un-Christian defense of Christianity, and the defenders' bad conscience about their own relation to it are among the things that in our time contribute their part to
VII prompting passionate and demented attacks upon Christian-
527 ity. There must be no bargaining, no wanting to change Christianity; there must neither be any going out of bounds

by exercising a restraining influence at the wrong place, but only a watchfulness so that it remains what it was, an offense to the Jews and a foolishness to the Greeks, and not some fatuous something that offends neither Greeks nor Jews—they smile at it instead, and defense of it only incites them.

But very little is heard about the work of inwardness in becoming and continuing to be a Christian. Yet it is just this that especially must be experienced and must be developed through experience after Christianity is introduced into countries and in the Christian countries where individual Christians are not supposed to go out in the world as missionaries to spread Christianity. In the early periods it was different. The apostles became Christians as adults, therefore after having spent a good part of their lives in other categories (as a result, Scripture contains nothing about the collisions that can arise by being brought up from childhood in Christianity). They became Christians through a miracle* (here there is no analogy to ordinary people), or at least so speedily that no more detailed explanation of it is given. Thereupon they turn their attention outward to converting others, but here again
there is a lack of an analogy to a poor individual human being, VII
who has only the task of existing as a Christian. 528

* In the foregoing, it has often been stated that an apostle's existence is paradoxical-dialectical. I shall now show how. An apostle's *direct* relation to God is paradoxical-dialectical, for a direct relation is lower (the middle term is the religiousness of immanence, Religiousness *A*) than the indirect relation of the congregation, since the indirect relation is between spirit and spirit and the direct relation is esthetic—and yet the direct relation is higher. Thus the apostle's relation is not straightforwardly higher than that of the congregation, as a talkative pastor leads a yawning congregation to think, whereby the whole matter recedes into the esthetic. —The apostle's *direct* relation to other people is paradoxical-dialectical, because this relation of the apostle's life, turned outward and occupied with spreading Christianity in kingdoms and countries, is lower than the lay person's indirect relation to others, which is based on his essentially having to deal with himself. The direct relation is an esthetic relation (oriented outward), and to that extent lower, and yet as exceptional it is higher for the apostle—this is the paradoxical-dialectical. It is not straightforwardly higher, because in that case we have all the world-historical hustle and bustle of each and every one. The paradox is that the direct relation is higher for an apostle, but this is not the case for others.

If one is unaware of the work of inwardness, then the urge to go further is easily explained. One lives in Christendom; one is a Christian—at least just like the others. Since Christianity has lasted for so many centuries and has pervaded all relations, it is easy to become a Christian. One does not have a missionary's task. Well, then the task now is to go further and to speculate about Christianity. But to speculate about Christianity is not the work of inwardness. Consequently one disdains the daily tasks of practicing the faith, the task of sustaining oneself in its paradoxical passion and of vanquishing all illusions.

One turns the matter around and forgets that, as understanding and culture and education increase, it becomes more and more difficult to sustain the passion of faith. Indeed, if Christianity were a subtle doctrine (directly understood), culture could be a direct help; but in connection with an existence-communication, which paradoxically accentuates existing, culture helps only by—making the difficulties greater. Thus cultured people have only a very ironic advantage over simple folk with regard to becoming and continuing to be Christians: the advantage that it is more difficult.

But here again people have forgotten the qualitative dialectic and have wanted to form comparatively and quantitatively a direct transition from culture to Christianity. Therefore the work of inwardness will increase with the years and will give the Christian who is not a missionary plenty to do, not in speculating but in continuing to be a Christian. It has not become easier to become a Christian in the nineteenth century than in the first period. On the contrary, it has become more difficult, particularly for the cultured, and will become more difficult year by year. The preponderance of the understanding in the cultured person, the orientation toward the objective, will continually create in this person an opposition to becoming a Christian, and the opposition is the sin of the understanding: half measures.

If Christianity once changed the shape of the world by vanquishing the raw passions of immediacy and ennobling nations, it will find equally dangerous opposition in culture. But

if the battle is to be fought here, then it of course must be waged within the keenest qualifications of reflection. The absolute paradox will certainly hold its own, because with regard to the absolute more understanding goes no further than less understanding. On the contrary, they go equally far, the exceptionally gifted person slowly, the simple person swiftly. Let others praise culture directly—yes, let it be praised, but I prefer to praise it because it makes it so difficult to become a Christian. I am a friend of difficulties, especially of those that VII 529
have the humorous quality, so that the most cultured person, after having gone through the most enormous effort, essentially has come no further than the simplest human being can come.

The simplest human being can certainly become a Christian and continue to be one, but partly because he does not have understanding on any great scale, and partly because the simple person's condition in life turns his attention outward; he is exempted from the laboriousness with which the cultured person sustains his faith, struggling even more strenuously as his culture increases. Since the highest is to become and to continue to be a Christian, the task cannot be to reflect on Christianity but can only be to intensify by means of reflection the pathos with which one continues to be a Christian.

That is what this whole book has been about; the first part dealt with the objective interpretation of becoming or being a Christian, the latter part with the subjective.

Becoming or Being a Christian Is Defined Objectively in the Following Way:

1. A Christian is one who accepts Christianity's doctrine. But if the "what" of this doctrine is to decide ultimately whether one is a Christian, then attention is immediately turned outward in order to find out what Christianity's doctrine is, down to the slightest detail, because this "what" is not to decide what Christianity is but whether I am a Christian. —At that very moment begins the learned, the uneasy, the timorous contradiction of approximating. The approximation can

go on as long as it wants to, and because of it the decision by which the individual becomes a Christian is eventually forgotten completely.

This dubious situation has been remedied by the presupposition that everyone in Christendom is a Christian; we are all as such what people call Christians. The objective theories fare better with this presupposition. We are all Christians. The Bible theory now must examine with proper objectivity what Christianity indeed is (and yet, of course, we are Christians, and it is assumed that the objective knowledge will make us Christians, the objective knowledge that we will really come to have only now, we who are Christians—because if we are not Christians, the road taken here is the very one that will never lead to becoming Christians). The Church theory assumes that we are Christians, but now we must in a purely objective way have it made sure what the essentially Christian
VII is in order to defend ourselves against the Turk and the Rus-
530 sian and the Roman yoke, and valiantly battle Christianity forward by having our age form a bridge, as it were, to a matchless future, which is already glimpsed.[857] This is sheer estheticism. Christianity is an existence-communication. The task is to become a Christian or to continue to be a Christian, and the most dangerous illusion of all is to become so sure of being one that all Christendom must be defended against the Turk—instead of defending the faith within oneself against the illusion about the Turk.

2. No, it is said, not every acceptance of the Christian doctrine makes one a Christian. What it especially depends upon is appropriation, that one appropriates and holds fast this doctrine in a way entirely different from the way one holds anything else, that one will live and die in it, risk one's life for it, etc.

It seems as if this were something. The category "altogether different" is, however, a rather mediocre category, and the whole formula, which attempts to define being Christian somewhat more subjectively, is neither one thing nor the other, and in a way avoids the difficulty with the distraction and deceit of approximation but lacks the categorical qualification. The pathos of appropriation of which it speaks is the pathos of immediacy. One can just as well say that a rapturous lover relates himself to his erotic love in this way: he will hold it fast and appropriate it in a way entirely different from the way he holds anything else, will live in it and die in it, risk everything for it. So far there is no essential difference in inwardness between a lover and a Christian, and one is again obliged to return to the "what" that is the doctrine, and thus we again come under no. 1.

In other words, it is a matter of defining the pathos of appropriation itself within the believer in such a way that it cannot be confused with any other pathos. On this, the more subjective conception is right in saying that it is the appropriation that determines the issue, but it is wrong in its definition of the appropriation, which has no specific difference from any other immediate pathos.

Neither does this happen if one defines the appropriation as faith but promptly gives faith momentum and orientation toward understanding, so that faith becomes a temporary function whereby one temporarily adheres to something that is to become an object for understanding, a temporary function VII
with which poor folk and obtuse people must be satisfied, 531
whereas assistant professors and brainy pates go further. The mark of being a Christian (faith) is the appropriation, but in such a way that it is not specifically different from some other intellectual appropriation in which a preliminary acceptance is a temporary function in relation to understanding. Faith does not become the specific for the relation to Christianity, and it will again be the "what" that is believed that decides whether someone is Christian or not. But that takes the issue back under no. 1 again.

In other words, the appropriation by which a Christian is Christian must be so specific that it cannot be confused with anything else.

3. Becoming and being a Christian are defined neither objectively by the "what" of the doctrine nor subjectively by the appropriation, not by what has taken place within the individ-

ual but by what has taken place *with* the individual: that the individual is baptized. Insofar as acceptance of the Creed is added to Baptism, nothing decisive is gained thereby, but the definition will vacillate between accentuating the "what" (the way of approximation) and talking vaguely about acceptance and acceptance and appropriation etc., without any specific qualification.

If being baptized is supposed to be the qualification, attention will immediately turn outward in deliberation on whether I actually have been baptized. Then begins the approximation with regard to a historical fact.

If, on the other hand, someone says that he did indeed receive the spirit in Baptism and by its witness with his spirit knows that he has been baptized, the conclusion is directly reversed—from the witness of the spirit within him[858] he draws the conclusion that he must have been baptized; he does not draw the conclusion that he has spirit from his having been baptized. But if the conclusion is drawn in this way, the mark of being a Christian is quite rightly not Baptism but inwardness, and thus once again it is necessary to have a specific qualification of inwardness and appropriation, whereby the witness of the spirit in a Christian is different from all other spiritual activity (more generally defined) in a human being.

Incidentally, it is remarkable that orthodoxy, which in particular has made Baptism decisive, continually complains that there are so few Christians among the baptized, that with the exception of a little immortal flock almost all are spiritless and baptized pagans, which seems to suggest that Baptism cannot be the decisive factor in becoming a Christian, not even ac-
VII 532 cording to the subsequent view of those who first insist upon it as decisive with regard to becoming a Christian.

Being a Christian Is Defined Subjectively in this Way:

The decision rests in the subject; the appropriation is the paradoxical inwardness that is specifically different from all other inwardness. Being a Christian is defined not by the "what" of Christianity but by the "how" of the Christian. This "how" can fit only one thing, the absolute paradox. Therefore there is no vague talk that being a Christian means to accept and accept, and accept altogether differently, to appropriate, to have faith, to appropriate in faith altogether differently (nothing but rhetorical and sham definitions); but *to have faith* is specifically qualified differently from all other appropriation and inwardness. Faith is the objective uncertainty with the repulsion of the absurd, held fast in the passion of inwardness, which is the relation of inwardness intensified to its highest. This formula fits only the one who has faith, no one else, not even a lover, or an enthusiast, or a thinker, but solely and only the one who has faith, who relates himself to the absolute paradox.

Faith, therefore, cannot be some temporary function. Someone who within a higher knowledge wants to understand his faith as an annulled element has *eo ipso* ceased to believe. Faith *must not be satisfied* with incomprehensibility, because the very relation to or the repulsion from the incomprehensible, the absurd, is the expression for the passion of faith.

This definition of being a Christian hinders the learned or uneasy deliberation of approximation from luring the individual astray so that he becomes learned instead of becoming a Christian, and in most cases half-learned instead of becoming a Christian, because the decision rests in subjectivity. But inwardness has again found its specific mark, whereby it is different from all other inwardness, and is not brushed aside with the talkative category "altogether different," because that fits every passion in the moment of passion.

Psychologically, it is ordinarily a sure sign that a person is beginning to relinquish his passion if he wants to treat the object of his passion objectively. It is ordinarily the case that passion and reflection exclude each other. To become objective in this way is always a retrogression, because a person's perdition consists in passion, but also his elevation. If the dialectical and reflection are not utilized to intensify passion, it is a retrogression to become objective, and even the person who loses him- VII 533 self in passion has not lost as much as the person who lost passion, because the former has possibility.

This is the way people in our day have wanted to be objective with regard to Christianity: the passion with which everybody is a Christian has become too small for them, and by becoming objective we all have prospects of becoming—assistant professors.

But the present order of things has in turn made the dispute in Christendom comic, because in many ways the dispute is merely a matter of switching weapons, and because the dispute about Christianity is carried on in Christendom by Christians or among Christians, all of whom, by wanting to be objective and to go further, are on the point of relinquishing being Christians. At the time when the Danish government transferred the English three percent loan from Wilson to Rothschild,[859] there was a great hue and cry in the newspapers. A general meeting was held of people who did not own bonds but had borrowed one in order to meet as bearer-bond holders. There was discussion, and it was decided that they should protest the government's decision by refusing to accept the new bonds. The general meeting was made up of people who did not own bonds and who therefore would hardly come into the dubious situation of the government's proposing that they accept the new bonds. Being Christian is on the way to losing the interest of passion, and yet a *pro* and *con* battle is going on. One argues on the basis of oneself: If this is not Christianity, then I am no Christian, which, however, I certainly am. The matter has been turned in such a way that one takes an interest in being a Christian in order to be able to decide what Christianity is, and not in what Christianity is in order to be a Christian. The name "Christian" is used in the same way those people borrowed bonds—in order to attend the general meeting where the fate of the Christians is decided by Christians who for their own sakes do not care about being Christians. —For whose sake, then, is all this being done?

Because people in our day and in the Christendom of our day do not seem to be adequately aware of the dialectic of inward deepening or aware that the individual's "how" is an

equally exact and a more decisive expression for what he has than the "what" to which he appeals, there arise these days the strangest and, if one is in the mood and has time for it, the VII
most ludicrous confusions,[860] which can be demonstrated to 534
be even more comic than the confusion of paganism, because there was not so much at stake in the latter and the contrasts were not jacked up so high. But one good turn deserves another, and one must go on being an optimist. The person who imaginatively constructs in the domain of passion shuts himself out from all bright and smiling prospects of becoming an assistant professor and of what that yields. He ought to have at least a little humorous compensation because he takes to heart something that others, aiming at something much higher, consider a bagatelle: the little humorous compensation that his passion sharpens his sense for the comic. The person who, although he loves people, exposes himself to becoming loathed as an egotist, who does not objectively concern himself with Christianity for the sake of others, in his role of a friend of laughter should have a little indemnity. It really is not right to have the disgrace of being an egotist and have no profit from it—in that case one is indeed not an egotist.

An orthodox defends Christianity with the most terrible passion; with perspiring face and the most worried gestures, he maintains that he accepts Christianity pure and unadulterated; he will live and die in it—and he forgets that an acceptance of that kind is a much too ordinary expression for relating oneself to Christianity. He does everything in the name of Jesus and uses Christ's name on every occasion as a sure sign that he is a Christian and is called to defend Christendom in our day—and he has no intimation of the little ironic secret that a person, just by describing the "how" of his inwardness, can indirectly indicate that he is a Christian without mentioning Christ's name.*

* With regard to loving (to illustrate the same thing again), it holds true that a person cannot say what or whom he loves by defining his "how." All lovers have the "how" of erotic love in common, and now the particular individual must add the name of his beloved. But with regard to having faith (*sensu strictissimo* [in the strictest sense]), it holds true that this "how" fits only

A man becomes revived on New Year's Eve at precisely six o'clock. Now he is ready. Fantastically bedizened with the fact
VII of that revival, he must now run around and proclaim Chris-
535 tianity—in a Christian country. Of course, even if we are all baptized, each one perhaps needs to become a Christian in another sense. But here is the difference: in a Christian country it is not information that is lacking; something else is lacking, and one human being cannot directly communicate this something else to another. And in such fantastic categories a revivalist wants to work for Christianity, and yet he demonstrates—the busier he is propagating and propagating—that he himself is not Christian. Being a Christian is something so thoroughly reflected that it does not allow the esthetic dialectic that teleologically permits one person to be for another what he is not for himself. —On the other hand, a scoffer attacks Christianity and at the same time expounds it so creditably that it is a delight to read him, and the person who is really having a hard time getting it definitely presented almost has to resort to him.[862]

All ironic observing is a matter of continually paying attention to "how," whereas the honorable gentleman with whom the ironist has the honor of dealing pays attention only to the "what." A man declares loudly and solemnly: This is my opinion. He does not, however, limit himself to enunciating literally the brief formula; he explains himself in greater detail. He ventures to vary the expressions—indeed, to make variations is not such an easy matter as people think, and more than one student would have received *laudabilis* [praiseworthy] in composition if he had not made variations. And a great many people have that talent for varying which Socrates so much admired in Polus: they never say the same—about the same.[863] The ironist, then, is alert. Of course, he does not pay so much attention to what is written in large letters or to what betrays

---

one object. If anyone says, "Yes, but then one can in turn learn the 'how' of faith by rote and recite it," the answer to that must be: That cannot be done, [861]because the person who states it directly contradicts himself, because the substance of the statement must be continually reduplicated in the form, and the isolation in the definition must reduplicate itself in the form.

itself in the speaker's diction as being formula (the honorable gentleman's "what"), but he pays attention to a little subordinate clause that has evaded the grand attention of the honorable gentleman, a hinting little predicate etc., and now to his amazement, and pleased with the variation (*in variatione voluptas* [the enjoyment is in the variation]), he sees that the honorable gentleman does not *have* this opinion, not because he is a hypocrite (God forbid, that is too earnest a matter for an ironist) but because the good man has concentrated on bellowing it out, less on having it within. The honorable gentleman may be right about having this opinion to the extent that he makes himself believe it with all his might and main. He can do everything for it in his role as an errand boy; he can VII 536
risk his life for it; in very confused times he can even go so far as to lose his life[864] for this opinion*—now I am jolly well sure that the man must have had the opinion. Yet there may have lived at the same time an ironist who, even in the hour when the poor honorable man is executed, cannot keep from laughing, because on the basis of his circumstantial evidence he knows that the man has never been clear about himself. Ludicrous it is, but it does not make one disheartened about life that such things can happen, because the god [*Guden*] rescues from delusion the person who in quiet inwardness and honest before God is concerned for himself; even though he is ever so simple, the god leads him in the suffering of inwardness to the truth. But officiousness and noisiness are the mark of delusions, the sign of an abnormal state, like being flatulent, and to be executed by chance in a tumultuous change is not the kind of suffering that is essentially the suffering of inwardness.

It is supposed to have happened in England that a man was assaulted on the highway by a robber disguised with a large wig. He rushes at the traveler, grabs him by the throat, and shouts: Your wallet. He takes the wallet, which he keeps, but

* [865]In tumultuous times, when a government must defend its survival by means of the death sentence, it would not be at all inconceivable that a man could be executed for an opinion that he presumably had in the legal and civil sense but less in the intellectual sense.[866]

he throws away the wig. A poor man comes down the same road, finds the wig, puts it on, and arrives in the next town, where the traveler has already given the alarm. He is recognized, arrested, and identified by the traveler, who swears that he is the man. By chance, the robber is present in the courtroom, sees the mistake, turns to the judge and says, "It seems to me that the traveler is looking more at the wig than at the man" and asks permission to make an experiment. He puts on the wig, grabs the traveler by the throat, and says: Your wallet—and the traveler recognizes the robber and offers to swear to it—but the trouble is that he already has sworn an oath. So it goes with everyone who in one way or another has a "what" and pays no attention to "how"; he swears, he takes an oath, he runs errands, he risks his life and blood, he is executed—all for the wig.

VII 537 If my memory does not fail me, I have already told this story once before in this book;[867] yet I wish to end the whole book with it. I do not think that anyone will in truth be able to accuse me ironically of having varied it in such a way that it has not remained the same.

APPENDIX

An Understanding with the Reader[868]

The undersigned, Johannes Climacus, who has written this book, does not make out that he is a Christian; for he is, to be sure, completely preoccupied with how difficult it must be to become one; but even less is he one who, after having been a Christian, ceases to be that by going further. He is a humorist; satisfied with his circumstances at the moment, hoping that something better will befall his lot, he feels especially happy, if worst comes to worst, to be born in this speculative, theocentric century. Yes, our age is an age for speculative thinkers and great men with matchless discoveries, and yet I think that none of those honorable gentlemen can be as well off as a private humorist is in secret, whether, isolated, he beats his breast[869] or laughs quite heartily. Therefore he can very well be an author, if only he sees to it that it is for his own enjoyment, that he remains in isolation, that he does not take up with the crowd, does not become lost in the importance of the age, as an inquisitive spectator at a fire be assigned to pump, or merely be disconcerted by the thought that he might stand in the way of any of the various distinguished people who have and ought to have and must have and insist upon having importance.

[870]In the isolation of the imaginary construction, the whole book is about myself, simply and solely about myself. "I, Johannes Climacus, now thirty years old, born in Copenhagen, a plain, ordinary human being like most people, have heard it said that there is a highest good in store that is called an eternal happiness, and that Christianity conditions this upon a person's relation to it. I now ask: How do I become a Christian?" VII
(see Introduction). I ask solely for my own sake. Indeed, that 538
is certainly what I am doing or, rather, I have asked about it,

for that is indeed the content of the book. Therefore let no one take the trouble to say that the book is completely superfluous and totally irrelevant to the times, unless he must by all means say something, because in that case it is the desired judgment, which has, after all, already been pronounced by its author. He understands very well how inane it is, if anyone should become aware of the book, to write such a thing in our age. Therefore as soon as just one person—but what am I saying—how you do carry me away, vain heart!—no, no, it is not good to be led into temptation. All the same, I wanted to say that as soon as just one person could inform me where and to whom one applies for permission to dare to write as a solitary person or to set oneself up as an author in the name of humanity, of the century, of our age, of the public, of the many, of the majority, or what must be regarded as an even rarer favor, to dare as a solitary human being to write against the public in the name of the many, against the majority in the name of another majority concerning the same matter, to dare, when he himself owns up to belonging to the minority, to write in the name of the many, and then as a solitary person simultaneously to have polemical elasticity by being in the minority and recognition in the eyes of the world by being in the majority—if anyone could inform me about what expenses are connected with the granting of such an application, since even if the costs are not paid in money they could very well still be exorbitant—then, on the presupposition that the costs will not exceed my means, I would very likely be unable to resist the temptation to write as soon as possible an exceedingly important book that speaks in the name of millions and millions and millions and billions. Until that time, no one, in consistency with his point of view, and from my point of view the reproach is something else, can reproach the book for being superfluous if he cannot explain what is asked about.

[871]Consequently, the book is superfluous. Therefore, let no one bother to appeal to it, because one who appeals to it has *eo ipso* misunderstood it. To be an authority is much too burdensome an existence for a humorist, who regards it specifically as one of life's comforts that there are such great men

who are able and willing to be the authority, from whom one has the benefit of accepting their opinion as a matter of course, unless one is foolish enough to pull the great men down, since that is something from which no one benefits. [872]Above all, may heaven spare the book and me from any approving vehemence, so that a vociferous party-liner cites it approvingly VII
and enrolls me in the census. If it escapes him that no party 539
can be served by an imaginatively constructing humorist, then the latter can all the better perceive his unfitness for what he in every way should seek to escape. I have no qualification for being a party-liner, because I have no opinion except that it must be the most difficult of all to become a Christian. As an opinion, it is no opinion, and neither does it have any of the qualities that ordinarily characterize an "opinion." It does not flatter me, since I do not make out that I am Christian; it does not insult the Christian, since he of course can have nothing against my regarding what he has done and is doing as the most difficult of all; it does not insult the attacker of Christianity, since his triumph becomes all the greater, since he goes further—than that which is the most difficult of all. I consistently desire no proof from actuality that I actually do have an opinion (an adherent, cheers, execution, etc.), because I have no opinion, wish to have none, and am satisfied and pleased with that.

Just as in Catholic books, especially from former times, one finds a note at the back of the book that notifies the reader that everything is to be understood in accordance with the teaching of the holy universal mother Church, so also what I write contains the notice that everything is to be understood in such a way that it is revoked, that the book has not only an end but has a revocation to boot. One can ask for no more than that, either before or afterward.

To write and publish a book when one does not even have a publisher,[873] who could fall into financial difficulty in case it does not sell, is indeed an innocent pastime and amusement, a permissible private enterprise in a well-ordered state that tolerates luxury and where everyone is allowed to spend his time and his money as he pleases, whether for building houses,

buying horses, going to plays, or writing superfluous books and having them printed. But if it may be regarded in this way, may it not rather in turn be considered one of life's innocent and permissible quiet joys, which neither disturbs the Sunday-observance law nor any other precepts of duty and propriety, to imagine a reader with whom one now and then becomes involved in the book, if one does not, please note, in
VII the remotest manner make an attempt or a gesture of wanting
540 to oblige one single actual person to be [874]the reader. "Only the positive is an intervention in another person's personal freedom"[875] (see Preface); the negative is the courtesy that cannot even here be said to cost money, since only the publication does that, and even if one were so discourteous as to want to foist the book on people, it still would not be said that anyone bought it. In a well-ordered state it is, of course, permissible to be secretly in love, and the more profoundly secret the love is, the more permissible it is. It is not permissible, however, for a man to accost all the girls and assure each one separately that she is the genuinely beloved. And the one who has an actual beloved is prohibited by faithfulness and propriety from indulging in an imaginary love affair, even if he does it ever so secretly. But the person who has none—well, he has permission to do it—and the author who has no actual reader has permission to have an imagined reader; he even has permission to admit it, because there is of course no one whom he affronts.

Praise be to the well-ordered state! Enviable happiness be to him who understands how to esteem it! How can anyone be so busy wanting to reform the state and have the form of government changed! Of all forms of government, the monarchical is the best. More than any other form of government, it encourages and protects the secret fancies and the innocent follies of private persons. Only democracy, the most tyrannical form of government, obligates everyone to positive participation, about which the societies and general assemblies of our day are already reminding us often enough.[876] Is it tyranny that one person wants to rule and then lets all the rest of us be free? No, but it is tyranny that all want to rule, and on top of that want to obligate everyone to participate in the government, even the person who most urgently declines to take part in the government.

[877]Now, for an author to have an imagined reader as a secret fiction and altogether private enjoyment is of no concern to any third party. Let this be said as a civic apology and defense for something that needs no defense, since by its secrecy it avoids attack—the innocent and permissible, but nevertheless perhaps both disdained and misunderstood, pleasure of having an imagined reader, an infinite delight, the purest expression of freedom of thought, simply because it renounces freedom of speech. To the honor and praise of such a reader, I feel incapable of speaking worthily. Anyone who has had any association with him certainly will not deny that he is absolutely the most pleasant of all readers. He understands one promptly and bit by bit. He has the patience not to leap over the subordinate clauses and hurry from the woof of the episode to the warp of the table of contents. He can stick it out just as long
as the author. He can understand that the understanding is a VII
revocation—the understanding with him as the sole reader is 541
indeed the revocation of the book. He can understand that to write a book and to revoke it is not the same as refraining from writing it, that to write a book that does not demand to be important for anyone is still not the same as letting it be unwritten. Although he always yields and never goes against one, a person may still have more respect for him than for the noisy contradictions of an entire lecture hall. But then he can also speak with him in complete confidence.

My dear reader, if I may say so myself, [878]I am anything but a devil of a fellow in philosophy, called to create a new trend. I am a poor individual existing human being with sound natural capacities, not without a certain dialectical competence and not entirely devoid of study either. But I am tried and tested in the *casibus* [cases] of life and trustingly appeal to my sufferings, not in the apostolic sense[879] as a matter of honor, because all too often they have been self-incurred punishments, but still I appeal to them as my teachers, and with more pathos than Stygotius appeals to all the universities at

which he has studied and debated.[880] I stress a certain honesty that forbids me to parrot what I am unable to understand and bids me—something that in connection with Hegel has long caused me pain in my forsakenness—to renounce appealing to him except in particular cases, which is the same as having to relinquish the recognition one gains by the affiliation, while I remain what I myself admit is infinitely little, a vanishing, unrecognizable atom, just like every single human being. I stress an honesty that in turn comforts me and arms me with a more than ordinary sense of the comic and a certain capacity for making ludicrous what is ludicrous. Strangely enough, I am unable to make ludicrous what is not ludicrous—that presumably requires other capacities. As I see myself, I have developed so much just by my independent thinking, have been educated so much by reading, internally oriented so much by existing that I am in a position to be an apprentice, a learner, which is already a task. I do not pretend to be more than capable of beginning to learn in a higher sense. [881]If only the
VII teacher were to be found among us! I am not speaking of the
542 teacher of classical learning, because we do have such a person,[882] and if this were what I am supposed to learn, I would be helped as soon as I had gained the prerequisite knowledge to be able to begin. I am not speaking of the teacher of historical philosophy, in which I certainly lack the prerequisites, if only we had the teacher. I am not speaking of the teacher of the difficult art of religious address, because we do have such a distinguished person,[883] and I know I have tried my best to make use of his earnest guidance; that I do know, if not from the benefit of appropriation, lest I cunningly ascribe something to myself falsely or measure his importance by my accidental circumstance, then from the respect I have maintained for His Reverence. I am not speaking of the teacher of the beautiful art of poetry and its secrets of language and taste, because such an initiate we do have,[884] that I know, and I hope I shall forget neither him nor what I owe to him. No, the teacher of whom I speak and in a different way, ambiguously and doubtfully, is the teacher of the ambiguous art of thinking about existence and existing. So if he could be found, I dare

to guarantee that something would jolly well come of it if he in print would attend to my instruction and to that end proceed slowly and piece by piece, allowing me to ask questions, as good instruction should, and to delay going on from anything before I have completely understood it. In other words, what I cannot accept is that such a teacher would think he has nothing else to do than what a mediocre teacher of religion does in school: assign to me each day a certain section that I should be able to recite by rote the next day.

But since no such teacher, one who offers just what I am seeking, has yet come to my notice (be this a joyful or a sorrowful sign), my pursuit is *eo ipso* unimportant and only for my own enjoyment, as it indeed must be when a learner in existing, who then cannot want to teach others (and far be it from me, the vain and empty thought of wanting to be such a teacher), presents something that can be expected of a learner who essentially knows neither more nor less than what just about everyone knows, except that he knows something VII 543 about it more definitely and, on the other hand, with regard to much that everyone knows or thinks he knows, definitely knows that he does not know it. In this regard, I perhaps would not even be believed if I were to say this to anyone else but you, my dear reader. When someone these days says, "I know everything," he is believed. But the person who says, "There is much that I do not know,"[885] is suspected of a tendency to lie. You recall that in one of Scribe's plays a man experienced in loose love affairs relates that he uses the following procedure when he is tired of a girl. He writes to her: I know everything[886]—and, he adds, this method has never failed yet. Nor do I think that in our age any speculative thinker has failed who says: I know everything. Ah, but the impious and mendacious people who say that there is much that they do not know—they get what is coming to them in this the best [*bedste*] world,[887] well, the best world to all those who are pulling its leg [*have den til Bedste*] by knowing everything, or by knowing nothing at all.

J. C.

[1]A FIRST AND LAST EXPLANATION VII [545]

For the sake of form and order, I hereby acknowledge, something that really can scarcely be of interest to anyone to *know*, that I am, as is said, the author of *Either/Or* (Victor Eremita), Copenhagen, February 1843; *Fear and Trembling* (Johannes de Silentio), 1843; *Repetition* (Constantin Constantius), 1843; *The Concept of Anxiety* (Vigilius Haufniensis), 1844; *Prefaces* (Nicolaus Notabene), 1844; *Philosophical Fragments* (Johannes Climacus), 1844; *Stages on Life's Way* (Hilarius Bookbinder—William Afham, the Judge, Frater Taciturnus), 1845; *Concluding Postscript to* Philosophical Fragments (Johannes Climacus), 1846; an article in *Fædrelandet*, no. 1168, 1843 (Victor Eremita);[2] two articles in *Fædrelandet*, January 1846 (Frater Taciturnus).[3]

My pseudonymity or polyonymity has not had an *accidental* basis in my *person* (certainly not from a fear of penalty under the law, in regard to which I am not aware of any offense, and simultaneously with the publication of a book the printer and the censor *qua* public official have always been officially informed who the author was) but an *essential* basis in the *production* itself, which, for the sake of the lines and of the psychologically varied differences of the individualities, poetically required an indiscriminateness with regard to good and evil, brokenheartedness and gaiety, despair and overconfidence, suffering and elation, etc., which is ideally limited only by psychological consistency, which no factually actual person dares to allow himself or can want to allow himself in the moral limitations of actuality. What has been written, then, is mine, but only insofar as I, by means of audible lines, have placed the life-view of the creat*ing*, poetically actual individuality in his mouth, for my relation is even more remote VII
than that of a poet, who *poetizes* characters and yet in the pref- [546]
ace is *himself* the *author*. That is, I am impersonally or personally in the third person a *souffleur* [prompter] who has poeti-

cally produced the *authors*, whose *prefaces* in turn are [4]their productions, as their *names* are also. Thus in the pseudonymous books there is not a single word by me. I have no opinion about them except as a third party, no knowledge of their meaning except as a reader, not the remotest private relation to them, since it is impossible to have that to a doubly reflected communication. A single word by me personally in my own name would be an arrogating self-forgetfulness that, regarded dialectically, would be guilty of having essentially annihilated the pseudonymous authors by this one word.[5] In *Either/Or*, I am just as little, precisely just as little, the editor Victor Eremita as I am the Seducer or the Judge. He is a poetically actual subjective thinker who is found again in "*In Vino Veritas*."[6] In *Fear and Trembling*, I am just as little, precisely just as little, Johannes de Silentio as the knight of faith he depicts, and in turn just as little the author of the preface to the book, which is the individuality-lines of a poetically actual subjective thinker. In the story of suffering (" 'Guilty?'/'Not Guilty?' "),[7] I am just as remote from being Quidam of the imaginary construction as from being the imaginative constructor, just as remote, since the imaginative constructor is a poetically actual subjective thinker and what is imaginatively constructed is his psychologically consistent production. Thus I am the indifferent, that is, what and how I am are matters of indifference, precisely because in turn the question, whether in my innermost being it is also a matter of indifference to me what and how I am, is absolutely irrelevant to this production. Therefore, in many an enterprise that is not dialectically reduplicated, that which can otherwise have its fortunate importance in beautiful agreement with the distinguished person's enterprise would here have only a disturbing effect in connection with the altogether indifferent foster father of a perhaps not undistinguished production. [8]My facsimile, my picture, etc., like the question whether I wear a hat or a cap, could become an object of attention only for those to whom the indifferent has become important—perhaps in compensation because the important has become a matter of indifference to them.

In a legal and in a literary sense, the responsibility is mine,* but, easily understood dialectically, it is I who have *occasioned* the audibility of the production in the world of actuality, which of course cannot become involved with poetically actual authors and therefore altogether consistently and with absolute legal and literary right looks to me. Legal and literary, because all poetic creation would *eo ipso* be made impossible
or meaningless and intolerable if the lines were supposed to be VII
the producer's own words (literally understood). Therefore, [547]
if it should occur to anyone to want to quote a particular passage from the books, it is my wish, my prayer, that he will do me the kindness of citing the respective pseudonymous author's name, not mine—that is, of separating us in such a way that the passage femininely belongs to the pseudonymous author, the responsibility civilly to me. From the beginning, I have been well aware and am aware that my personal actuality is a constraint that the pseudonymous authors in pathos-filled willfulness might wish removed, the sooner the better, or made as insignificant as possible, and yet in turn, ironically attentive, might wish to have present as the repelling opposition.

My role is the joint role of being the secretary and, quite ironically, the dialectically reduplicated author of the author or the authors. Therefore, although probably everyone who has been concerned at all about such things has until now *summarily* regarded me as the author of the pseudonymous books even before the explanation was at hand, the explanation will perhaps at first prompt the odd impression that I, who indeed ought to know it best, am the only one who only very doubtfully and equivocally regards me as the author, because I am the author in the figurative sense; but on the other hand I am very literally and directly the author of, for example, the upbuilding discourses and of every word in them. The poetized author has his definite life-view, and the lines, which under-

* For this reason my name as editor was first placed on the title page of *Fragments* (1844), because the absolute significance of the subject required in actuality the expression of dutiful attention, that there was a named person responsible for taking upon himself what actuality might offer.

stood in this way could possibly be meaningful, witty, stimulating, would perhaps sound strange, ludicrous, disgusting in the mouth of a particular factual person. If anyone unfamiliar with cultivated association with a distancing ideality, through a mistaken obtrusiveness upon my actual personality, has distorted for himself the impression of the pseudonymous books, has fooled himself, *actually* has fooled himself, by being encumbered with my personal actuality instead of having the light, doubly reflected ideality of a poetically actual author to dance with; [9]if with paralogistic obtrusiveness anyone has deceived himself by meaninglessly drawing my private particularity out of the evasive dialectical duplexity of the qualitative contrasts—this cannot be truly charged to me, who, properly and in the interest of the purity of the relation, have from my side done everything, as well as I could, to prevent what an inquisitive part of the reading public has from the very beginning done everything to achieve—in whose interest, God knows.

The opportunity seems to invite an open and direct explanation, yes, almost to demand it even from one who is reluctant—so, then, I shall use it for that purpose, not as an author, because I am indeed not an author in the usual sense, but as one who has coöperated so that the pseudonyms could become authors.[10] First of all, I want to give thanks to Governance, who in such multitudinous ways has encouraged my
VII endeavor, has encouraged it over four and one-quarter years
[548] without perhaps a single day's interruption of effort, has granted me much more than I had ever expected, even though I can truly testify that I staked my life to the utmost of my capacity, more than I at least had expected, even if to others the accomplishment seems to be a complicated triviality. So, with fervent thanks to Governance, I do not find it unsettling that I cannot quite be said to have achieved anything or, what is of less importance, attained anything in the outer world. I find it ironically in order that the honorarium, at least, in virtue of the production and of my equivocal authorship, has been rather Socratic.

Next, after properly having asked for pardon and forgiveness if it appears inappropriate that I speak in this way, although he himself would perhaps find omission of it inappropriate, I want to call to mind, in recollecting gratitude, my deceased father, the man to whom I owe most of all, also with regard to my work.

With this I take leave of the pseudonymous authors with doubtful good wishes for their future fate, that this, if it is propitious for them, will be just as they might wish. Of course, I know them from intimate association; I know they could not expect or desire many readers—would that they might happily find the few desirable readers.

Of my reader, if I dare to speak of such a one, I would in passing request for myself a forgetful remembrance, a sign that it is of me that he is reminded, because he remembers me as irrelevant to the books, as the relationship requires, just as the appreciation for it is sincerely offered here in the moment of farewell, when I also cordially thank everyone who has kept silent and with profound veneration thank the firm Kts—that it has spoken.

Insofar as the pseudonymous authors might have affronted any respectable person in any way whatever, or perhaps even any man I admire, insofar as the pseudonymous authors in any way whatever might have disturbed or made ambiguous any actual good in the established order—then there is no one more willing to make an apology than I, who bear the responsibility for the use of the guided pen. [11]What I in one way or another know about the pseudonymous authors of course does not entitle me to any opinion, but not to any doubt, either, of their assent, since their importance (whatever that may become *actually*) unconditionally does not consist in making any new proposal, some unheard-of discovery, or in founding a new party and wanting to go further, but precisely in the opposite, in wanting to have no importance, in wanting, at a remove that is the distance of double-reflection, once again to read through solo, if possible in a more inward way,

the original text of individual human existence-relationships,
VII the old familiar text handed down from the fathers.[12]

[549] Oh, would that no ordinary seaman[13] will lay a dialectical hand on this work but let it stand as it now stands.

Copenhagen, February 1846

S. Kierkegaard.